Clued in
to Politics

Clued in to Politics

A Critical Thinking Reader in American Government

Christine Barbour
Indiana University

Matthew J. Streb
Loyola Marymount University

Houghton Mifflin Company
Boston • New York

Editor-in-chief: Jean L. Woy
Sponsoring Editor: Katherine Meisenheimer
Development Editor: Ann Kirby-Payne
Senior Project Editor: Bob Greiner
Editorial Assistants: Wendy Thayer and Trinity Peacock-Broyles
Assistant Production/Design Coordinator: Bethany Schlegel
Manufacturing Manager: Florence Cadran
Senior Marketing Manager: Nicola Poser

Printed in the U.S.A.

Library of Congress Catalog Number: 202116632

ISBN: 0-618-37309-8

3 4 5 6 7 8 9-QF-08 07 06 05 04

Contents

Topic Correlation Chart

Chapters in this reader correspond with the chapters of a typical introductory American politics text for easy incorporation into class syllabi. However, many readings address more than one issue, and can be easily integrated into other chapters. The following chart offers instructors and students an alphabetical listing of topics, and indicates specific readings related to each topic.

2002 Midterm Elections 6.3; 13.1; 13.2

Affirmative Action 2.4; 2.5; 6.1; 16.1

The Bureaucracy .Chapter 8

Campaign Finance 6.3; 11.4; 12.2; 12.3; 13.4

Citizenship and Immigration 2.1; 5.1; 12.1

Citizenship and Civic Duty . . . . .Chapter 1; 2.1; 5.1; 9.1

Civil Liberties . . . . .Chapter 4; 2.1; 3.3; 14.1; 14.2; 14.5; 15.1

Civil Rights . . . . .Chapter 5; 2.1; 2.4; 2.5; 6.1; 11.2; 12.1; 12.2

Congress . . . . .Chapter 6; 3.4; 3.5; 3.6; 7.3; 7.4; 8.2;
11.2; 12.2; 12.3; 12.4; 13.1

The Constitution and Federalism . . . . .Chapter 3; 4.1; 4.5; 6.3; 7.3; 7.5; 9.2; 9.4;
9.5; 12.5

The Courts . . . . .Chapter 9; 3.3; 3.4; 3.6; 4.1; 4.2; 7.5

Domestic Policy .Chapter 15; 4.3; 4.4; 6.2; 7.4; 12.3; 12.4

Election 2000 . . . . .2.2; 9.4; 13.3; 13.5

Foreign Policy . . . . .Chapter 16; 4.3; 7.3; 10.3; 14.2

Interest Groups .Chapter 12; 6.2; 13.2; 13.5; 15.4

Introduction to Politics . . . . .Chapter 1; 10.1; 10.2; 10.5; 13.4

Media . . . . .Chapter 14; 10.2

Participation 1.1; 10.2; 11.3; 11.4; 12.1; 13.3

Policymaking 6.1; 7.3; 7.4; 8.2; 8.4; 12.3; 12.4

Political Culture .Chapter 2; 1.3; 5.1; 5.2; 5.4; 6.4; 6.5;
10.1; 10.2; 16.2

Political Parties . . . . .Chapter 11; 6.1; 6.4; 7.4; 12.3; 12.5

The President . . . . .Chapter 7; 3.4; 3.5; 3.6; 4.3; 8.4; 8.5; 9.3; 9.4;
10.4; 13.2; 13.5; 14.2; 15.2; 15.3; 15.5; 16.1

Public Opinion . . . . .Chapter 10; 1.1; 1.2; 13.3; 13.4

September 11 and the War on Terror 1.2; 2.2; 4.3; 4.4; 8.3; 8.4; 12.4; 14.1; 14.2;
16.2; 16.3

Social Movements 5.4; 12.1

Voting and Elections . . . . .Chapter 13; 1.1; 2.2; 6.3; 11.2; 11.3; 11.4; 12.2

War with Iraq 7.3; 7.4; 10.3; 16.1; 16.4

Worldview of U.S. 2.3; 2.4; 16.2

Young Americans . . . . .Chapter 1; 5.3; 10.1; 12.1; 13.4

Preface to the Instructor

Sometimes in our efforts to get students to think critically about the texts they read we resemble nothing so much as tourists in a foreign land, convinced that if we only make our requests louder and more insistent, we will suddenly be understood by uncomprehending native shopkeepers. "NO, NO," we say loudly. "Don't just report what the author is saying. ANALYZE it." If repeating the word ANALYZE in stentorian tones were enough to do the trick, all our students would have been ace critical thinkers long ago. It isn't enough.

The reason it's not enough is that many, if not most, of our students don't really understand what it means to analyze, or to evaluate, or to assess, in short, to think critically. It isn't something that comes naturally, and we have learned the hard way that if we don't model it for them, they will be stuck at a level of descriptive understanding.

In this book we present a tool for prodding students out of the descriptive rut that we call the CLUES model. CLUES is an acronym for the five essential steps of critical thinking that we find students need to internalize in order to get the hang of thinking critically in their academic and everyday lives. We use these steps to help students work through readings together in class, and eventually at home on their own.

In this reader we teach students to think critically about important substantive areas of American politics by means of the following features:

- Engaging, contemporary articles from a variety of sources—newspapers, magazines, radio, T.V., and the Internet—illustrate American government at all levels.
- Call-out style text notes within the readings draw students' attention to key passages and help to show them what kinds of things critical thinkers ask themselves as they read.
- Consistent end-of-reading questions walk students through the CLUES method of critical thinking, helping to model the process for them so they can learn to do it automatically.
- Selections focusing on personal experiences with government open each chapter to pique student interest and show the relevance of the political process to individual lives.
- Classic readings, such as John F. Kennedy's inaugural address and *Federalist* No. 51, close each chapter to help students understand and observe the changes or constants in key political arguments over time.
- Readings are balanced between objective and opinion-based points of view and vary in length and format to provide instructors with maximum flexibility.
- Chapters correspond with the chapters of a typical introductory American politics text for easy incorporation into class syllabi.

Acknowledgments

Several people have helped us with this project, and we are grateful for their assistance. In particular, we would like to thank Gerald Wright, of Indiana University, Michael Genovese and Evan Gerstmann of Loyola Marymount University, David Kessler of the Bancroft Library at UC-Berkeley, and Carol Briley of the Harry Truman Library. We are also indebted to LMU research assistants Caroline Guidi and Jennie Haubenschild for their good work on this project, and to Linda Streb for helping us understand the mysteries of the tax code.

We would also like to thank David Pace and Joan Middendorf of the Freshman Learning Project at Indiana University for reminding us that students cannot learn to think like we do unless we model it for them. The FLP experience and particularly David's own work with modeling critical thinking for students has been invaluable in the conception of this book.

Houghton Mifflin has assembled a terrific panel of reviewers and their help has been invaluable as well. We would like to thank:

Thomas J. Barth, University of North Carolina, Wilmington

Renée A. Cramer, California State University, Long Beach

Debra L. Delaet, Drake University

Richard N. Engstrom, University of Wyoming

Andrew Rudalevige, Dickenson College

Willoughby Jarrell, Kennesaw State University

Kelechi A. Kalu, University of Northern Colorado

Edward C. Olson, Angelo State University

Donald Robinson, Casper College

Joseph Romance, Drew University

Gene T. Straughan, Lewis and Clark State College

Andrew J. Taylor, North Carolina State University

Robert Weissberg, University of Illinois, Urbana–Champaign

Michael Wolf, Indiana University–Purdue University Fort Wayne

David E. Woodard, Concordia University–St. Paul

And finally, the folks at Houghton Mifflin themselves have made this project possible with their usual skill and expertise. We want to thank Terri Wise for her assistance with the *Instructor's Resource Manual*. In addition, we are particularly grateful to Jean Woy and Katherine Meisenheimer for encouraging us to put our ideas about the "ideal reader" to the test in the first place, to Ann Kirby-Payne for her able direction and creative advice, and to Bob Greiner, for helping to pull it all together.

Preface to the Student

This is a book of readings about politics. Although politics has its tedious moments, it also has an exhilarating side. It can be exciting, challenging, and even inspiring. It touches all of our lives much more often and more deeply than we may think. While they will inevitably cover some heavy ground, the readings in this book are chosen to showcase the dramatic, fun, quirky, personal side of politics.

This is also a book about critical thinking. There's just no point reading about politics if we aren't going to do it with a laserlike vision that cuts through the fog and sees the light, as it were—that separates myth from reality, lies from truth, stupidity from intelligence. If we don't think critically we risk becoming the dupes of politicians and the system. Where's the fun in that?

So this book has two goals: first to assemble readings on American politics that capture the excitement, drama, and interest of the political world, and second, to model the kind of critical thinking about that world that will give you the tools to deal with it.

What Kind of Readings Are We Using?

In our search for selections for this book we have combed a variety of news sources, from mainstream newspapers and news magazines, to opinion journals, to radio and TV shows, to the Internet. It is both our good fortune and our curse to be living in an age when so much information about politics is available to us: our good fortune because it truly is possible for us to become informed on most matters today, and our curse because there is so much more work to be done in sorting the trustworthy from the unreliable, the true from the fraudulent, the reality from the spin. Long gone are the days when the words from a single trusted news source like Walter Cronkite could sway or soothe a nation. Today we have to dig deeper, ask tougher questions, and raise a more skeptical eyebrow in order to understand our world.

The news items we have selected show many faces of politics: quirky, personal, amusing, as well as serious, weighty and consequential. They show the good that government can do as well as the darker side. Our goal is to shake the image you may have of politics as totally irrelevant, hopelessly corrupt, or just deadly dull, and give you a healthy appreciation for what it is: a vibrant and important activity that reflects all sides of human nature, and that affects our lives in many ways.

Why Bother with Critical Thinking When It's So Much Easier Not To?

Critical thinking sounds like work and it sounds like faultfinding—two potentially unpleasant activities. While it may be hard work at first (what skill worth having isn't difficult to begin with?) in fact, what we mean by critical thinking has nothing to do with faultfinding or being negative. Critical in this case means careful evaluation, vigilant judgment. It means being wary of the surface appearance of what we hear and read, and digging deeper, looking for the subtext—what a person means and intends, whether that person has evidence for his or her conclusions, what the political implications of those conclusions really are.

Becoming adept at critical thinking has a number of benefits.

- **We become much better students.** The skills of the critical thinker are not just the skills of the good citizen; they are the skills of the scholar. When we read we figure out what is important quickly and easily, we know what questions to ask to tease out more meaning, we can decide whether what we are reading is worth our time, we know what to take with us and what to discard.

- **We are better able to hold our own in political (or other) arguments**—we think more logically and clearly, we are more persuasive, and we impress people with our grasp of reason and fact. There is not a career in the world that is not enhanced by critical thinking skills.

- **We learn to be good democratic citizens.** Critical thinking helps us sort through the barrage of information that regularly assails us and teaches us to process this information thoughtfully. Critical awareness of what our leaders are doing and the ability to understand and evaluate what they tell us is the lifeblood of democratic government.

Although it sounds like a dull and dusty activity, critical thinking can be vital and enjoyable. When we are good at it it empowers and liberates us. We are not at the mercy of others' conclusions and decisions, we can evaluate facts and arguments for ourselves, turning conventional wisdom upside down and exploring the world of ideas with confidence.

How Does One Learn to Think Critically?

The trick to learning how to think critically is to do it. It helps to have a model to follow however, and in this book we provide one. The focus of critical thinking here is understanding political argument. "Argument" in this case doesn't refer to a confrontation or a fight, but rather to a political contention, based on a set of assumptions, supported by evidence, leading to a clear, well-developed conclusion with consequences for how we understand the world.

Critical thinking involves constantly asking questions about the arguments we read about: who has created it, what is the basic case and what values underlie it, what evidence is used to back up it up, what conclusions are drawn, and what difference does the whole thing make. On the assumption that it will be easier to remember the questions one should ask with a little help, we have used a mnemonic device that creates an acronym from the five major steps of critical thinking. Eventually asking these questions will become second nature, but in the meantime, thinking of them as CLUES to critical thinking about American politics will help you to keep them in mind as you read.

This is what CLUES stands for:

> **C**onsider the source and the audience
>
> **L**ay out the argument, the values, and the assumptions
>
> **U**ncover the evidence
>
> **E**valuate the conclusion
>
> **S**ort out the political implications

We'll investigate each of these steps in a little more depth.

Consider the source and the audience

Who is writing the news item? Where did the item appear? Why was it written? What audience is it directed toward? What do the author or publisher need to do to attract and keep the audience? How might that affect content?

Knowing the source and the audience will go a long way to helping you understand where the author is coming from, what his or her intentions are. If the person is a mainstream journalist, he or she probably has a reputation as an objective reporter to preserve, and will at least make an honest attempt to provide unbiased information. Even so, knowing the actual news source will help you nail that down. Even in a reputable national paper like the *New York Times* or the *Wall Street Journal,* if the item comes from the editorial pages, you can count on it having an ideological point of view—usually (but not exclusively) liberal in the case of the *Times,* conservative in the case of the *Wall Street Journal.* Opinion magazines will have even more blatant points of view. Readers go to those sources looking for a particular perspective, and that may affect the reliability of the information you find.

Lay out the argument and the underlying values and assumptions

What is the basic argument the author wants to make? What assumptions about the world does he or she make? What values does the author hold about what is important and what government should do? Are all the important terms clearly defined?

If these things aren't clear, the author may be unclear. There is a lot of substandard thinking out there, and being able to identify it and discard it is very valuable. Often we are intimidated by a smart sounding argument, only to discover on closer examination that it is just a piece of fuzzy thinking. A more insidious case occurs when the author is trying to obscure the point in order to get you to sign on to something you might not otherwise accept. If the argument, values, and assumptions are not perfectly clear and up front, there may be a hidden agenda you should know about. You don't want to be persuaded by someone who claims to be an advocate for democracy, only to find out that he or she means something completely different by democracy than you do.

Uncover the evidence

Has the author done basic research to back up his or her argument with facts and evidence?

Good arguments cannot be based on gut feelings, rumor, or wishful thinking. They should be based on hard evidence, either empirical, verifiable observations about the world or solid, logical reasoning. If the argument is worth being held, it should be able to stand up to rigorous examination and the author should be able to defend it on these grounds. If the evidence or logic is missing, the argument can usually be dismissed.

Evaluate the conclusion

Is the argument successful? Does it convince you? Why or why not? Does it change your mind about any beliefs you held previously? Does accepting this argument require you to rethink any of your other beliefs?

Conclusions should follow logically from the assumptions and values of an argument, if solid evidence and reasoning supports it. What is the conclusion here? What is the author asking you to accept as the product of his or her argument? Does it make sense to you? Do you "buy it"? If you do, does it fit with your other ideas or do you need to refine what you previously thought? Have you learned from this argument, or have you merely had your own beliefs reinforced?

Sort out the political implications

What is the political significance of this argument? What difference does this argument make to your understanding of the way the political world works? How does it affect who gets what scarce resources, and how they get them? How does it affect who wins in the political process and who loses?

Political news is valuable if it means something. If it doesn't, it may entertain you, but essentially it wastes your time if it claims to be something more than entertainment. Make the information you get prove its importance, and if it doesn't, find a different news source to rely on.

So, How Does This Book Work?

Each chapter of this book focuses on one of the main subject areas of the introductory course in American politics. In each chapter we provide a selection of articles, transcripts, and other forms of political information. The first selection will generally take a personal (although still political) perspective, allowing you to reflect on how the subject under discussion touches individual lives. The selections build until they deal with politics at a more institutional, systemic level. Although our goal is to provide new and current information, the final selection in each chapter will be much older, presenting a classic perspective on the subject. These classics can be as vitally relevant as the daily news, and it is crucial that we be able to bring the same critical thinking skills to bear on them.

Sometimes the best way to learn how to do something is to watch someone else do it. While that might be easy when it comes to tying a knot, or chopping an onion, it is difficult when it comes to thinking. In order to show you what goes on as we read political information critically and actively, each article or item will be annotated with call-out style text notes that show you what kinds of things would be going through the mind of an experienced critical thinker as he or she reads.

Finally, to model the way the CLUES steps work, we will conclude each article with a CLUES box that sets out several questions you should be asking yourself in order to take each step. Don't just gloss over the questions, but think about them and answer each of them carefully. As you do, your understanding of the article will deepen, you will see more clearly what its strengths and weaknesses are, and you will be able to evaluate it more thoroughly. Eventually you will figure out what questions you should be asking on your own. When you get to that point, feel free to leave the CLUES boxes behind. You will be well on your way to being a critical thinker in your own right—an effective citizen and a promising scholar.

Clued in
to Politics

CHAPTER 1

Introduction to American Politics

I t's a riddle fit for a sphinx:

What is both an inspiring pursuit and a mind-numbing turnoff? A noble calling to serve an interest greater than oneself and a degrading scramble for personal advantage? A spellbinding spectacle of the human passion for excellence and a tedious litany of scandal and corruption?

The newest reality show on TV? Hardly. It's *politics* . . . the oldest reality show on earth.

How can politics embody so many contradictions? Politics is a reflection of human nature, itself a strange brew of opposites and incongruities. After all, politics is the process by which we distribute scarce resources like power and influence. Everybody wants them; not everybody can have them. The stakes are high and the methods are often cutthroat. But politics is also the means by which we come together to do what we cannot do alone—to build governments, construct highway systems, feed the poor, work for peace, and explore the skies. The same process of politics exploits our worst nature, and embraces our best nature.

As such, politics is a distinctively human activity, and in many ways, it is our saving grace. Watch the family dogs when they want the same bone—they bite and snarl and pull each other away by the throat. Not once do they stop, call a meeting, attempt to reason or compromise or share. The strongest wins by violence and intimidation—every time. Human beings sometimes resort to the same tactics, but politics offers us an alternative—a way to resolve disputes without fighting and without coercion. Politics is the process of making decisions about who should get what valued resources, through discussion and debate, compromise and cooperation, bargaining, tradeoffs, even bribery and graft sometimes, but always through human interaction that offers the possibility of a peaceful resolution.

American Government: The Democratic Experiment

In the United States we are fortunate to be living in the midst of a grand democratic experiment. In democracies, the people who are governed have rights that government cannot infringe upon, and what's more, they have a voice in the way they are governed. To the extent that they make their voice heard through the political process, their rights are expanded and protected. To the extent that they keep silent, they are often ignored by the system. Their rights can shrink, or be trumped by the demands and concerns of more vocal citizens.

The United States is the first case of democracy being practiced for such a long time, on such a large scale. We call it an experiment because, as with all experiments, we really do not know how it will turn out, although we have hopes and expectations. It is tempting to think that it will last for all time—that human beings, in America anyway, have solved the myriad problems that have afflicted societies through the ages and discovered the key to living in freedom and peace forever. But that is not likely. The founders themselves warned that they had put together a system requiring careful maintenance. As Benjamin Franklin adjured a woman outside Constitution Hall, they had created a republic, "if you can keep it."

Democracies take time and effort, and lots of it, if they are to survive. They require that those who live in them be vigilant and careful, know something about how the system works, keep an eye on their leaders, and be jealous of their rights and conscious of their obligations—in short, that they be good citizens. Political philosopher Benjamin Barber notes that "the price of liberty is citizenship," and that "free societies are sustained only by hard work."[1]

A Civic Crisis?

And yet, many observers of American politics today believe that we are in a crisis of citizenship—a civic crisis that is manifested by vast public ignorance about the political system and something worse, an indifference and cynicism that leaves citizens cold, untouched, and uninterested in learning who their leaders are and how they lead. In an important book about this problem, *Why Americans Hate Politics*, Washington Post columnist E. J. Dionne warns: "A nation that hates politics will not long survive as a democracy."[2]

In the days after September 11, 2001, Americans wore their patriotism on their sleeves. Levels of trust in government shot skyward, as did the approval ratings of Congress and President Bush. But while love of country filled our hearts, knowledge about how that country works did not fill our brains; we were as ignorant of, and in many ways as indifferent to, the democratic process itself as we had been before we launched the War on Terrorism. Patriotism did not translate into good citizenship.

Political apathy and low levels of political knowledge are not spread equally throughout the population—there are decided generational effects. Those raised during the Depression and World War II are far more likely to see government in a positive light, and far more likely to vote for the things they want. Those baby boomers raised in the '50s, '60s, and '70s may have lived through the disillusionment of Watergate, but they also had the positive political experiences of working

---

[1] Benjamin R. Barber, "Foreword," in Grant Reeher and Joseph Cammarano, eds., *Education for Citizenship.* Lanham, MD: Rowman & Littlefield, 1997, p. ix.

[2] E. J. Dionne, Jr., *Why Americans Hate Politics.* New York: Touchstone Books, 1991, p. 355.

for civil rights, protesting the Vietnam War, and supporting early environmental efforts in this country. They, too, vote in fairly large numbers. As baby boomers get ready to retire, they are lobbying government to protect their social security, to build up Medicare, to look after the interests of an aging but politically active cohort.

It is today's generation of young Americans that is most truly lost politically. Generation X, Generation Y, Generation Next—poll after poll of individuals from their thirties to their teens tells us that most young people see government as irrelevant to their lives, unresponsive to their concerns, not worth their time and trouble. Although this same generation volunteers in churches, neighborhoods, and schools in record numbers, its interest in community life does not extend to government life. And in a giant self-fulfilling prophecy, the politicians continue to respond to the issues of the middle-aged and elderly people who vote, and young people see politics as more disconnected from their lives than ever.

The Readings in This Chapter

Many different roads can bring you to the introductory week in an introductory class on American politics. Perhaps you are a politics buff, addicted to C-SPAN and up on every move our leaders make. Perhaps you've always had a suspicion that you'd enjoy politics, if you ever had the time to figure out what was going on, and you've seized on this course to give you the background you need. Perhaps you have concerns about how the world works and think that you had best arm yourself with the knowledge to make the system work for you. Or, perhaps the course is a required one for you, and your college or university stubbornly refuses to give you a degree until you take it. It is the job of this first chapter to touch base with all the readers of this book—the avid, the cynical, and the captive audience—and to cover the basics of politics while connecting with the reality that is many people's political experience.

We present three articles in this chapter that introduce you to some fundamental concepts of politics. They range from articles specifically focused on the political experience of younger people in their late teens, twenties, and early thirties, as they struggle to find some relevance in political life, to a classic statement of political engagement and committed citizenship. We picked these articles not only because they illustrate some of the basic ideas in political analysis—power, authority, democracy, and citizenship—but also because they build a case for a particular vision of citizenship that goes beyond self-interest to public service.

1.1 Election Season? Whatever: Most Twenty-Somethings Apathetic; Politicians Pay Little Attention to Group

Nahal Toosi, *Milwaukee Journal Sentinel,* 19 August 2002

This article appeared in the *Milwaukee Journal Sentinel* in August 2002. Although it concerns the 2002 election season in Wisconsin, its themes are national: the political consequences for young people of their disengagement from politics. It shows that politics is about power, and that those in a democratic system who opt out of politics render themselves powerless in very real ways. Where does power come from in a democracy? How do your own views about politics compare to those of the young people cited in this article?

They are the future, after all.

They're paying for Social Security, even though it may be extinct when they need it. They'll see property taxes that will make today's bills look like spare change. They're used to soaring tuition, but imagine what it'll cost to send their kids to college.

So you would think that the election of government leaders, including the next governor of Wisconsin, who tackle these and other issues would spur interest among the younger generation. But the future doesn't seem to care very much right now.

"It just doesn't interest me," said Megan Schulte, 21, an art student at the University of Wisconsin-Milwaukee, when asked about the governor's race. "I feel very separate from what goes on, anyway, as far as it changing."

Sure, even among young adults, a small group—the Young Republicans and the like—is actively involved in politics. But, if a series of interviews with voters under 30 is any indication, the majority are barely aware that it's election season.

So does the young adult vote matter in elections? Very rarely, political experts say.

If politicians suddenly started talking about things young people cared about, would the young people pay attention?

"Their voter turnouts are so low that I think from a candidate's point of view, it's not very cost-effective, time-effective to pay much attention to them," said Rodd Freitag, associate professor of political science at the University of Wisconsin-Eau Claire.

Whatever, some retort

"If they started to talk about things we care about, maybe we'd pay more attention," said Tammy Cantillon, 20, of Milwaukee.

Just days ago, Cantillon, a UW-Milwaukee sophomore and an aspiring writer, put in her first financial aid application, thanks to an 8% UW System tuition increase that few gubernatorial candidates have discussed—much less railed against. She wishes tuition were a hotter topic in the gubernatorial race.

"There's a circular problem in which parties don't chase young people and which they don't respond to the parties," said Kathleen Dolan, associate professor of political science at UWM.

"They don't swing elections"

It's not that candidates should ignore young people or go out of their way to offend them. It doesn't hurt to take on issues many youth hold dear, such as the environment or tuition. But generally, young people "don't matter as voters," Dolan said. "They don't swing elections."

Several of the young adults interviewed said they didn't have time to think about politics. Some were busy with school, others were busy working.

Not a lot of research exists on the voting patterns of young people, even less that's state-based. It's important to note that there can be differences in results based on what is defined as young. Of the people interviewed, those 25 or over seemed more aware of election issues than those 18 to 24, perhaps because they had recently bought a house or started a family.

Here's some of what's known:

- Wisconsin has 691,205 people ages 20 to 29, based on U.S. Census figures.
- During the 2000 presidential election, 18- to 29-year-olds made up 19% of those who voted in Wisconsin, according to a statewide exit poll conducted by the Voter News Service. The poll indicated that of that group's votes, Al Gore got 45%, George W. Bush got 45% and Ralph Nader got 9%. (Gore won Wisconsin, beating Bush 47.8% to 47.6%.)
- Between 1972 and 1996, people ages 18 to 24 were far less likely to vote in federal elections than other age groups, according to the Federal Election Commission. During the 1996 elections, 33% of 21- to 24-year-olds in the voting age population cast ballots; 64% of those ages 45 to 64 voted. That same year, voters ages 18 to 24 made up 7.6% of the U.S. vote; those ages 45 to 64 made up 33%.

When asked whether they think they matter as voters, few were willing to say yes without a few caveats.

Mark Benishek, 20, a UWM student from Cedarburg, said no. Young people just "don't pay as much attention" to politics, Benishek said while resting on a couch at Mayfair Mall. But he said the scope of an election matters: A presidential race is more likely to get attention from a twenty-something than a governor's race.

Candidates' thoughts

Of course, candidates for governor would never say young people don't matter. Spokesmen for the Kathleen Falk, Tom Barrett, Jim Doyle and Ed Thompson campaigns all insisted that young people are important.

The candidates have hired several young people to work on their campaigns. They've visited college campuses. Students have formed organizations dedicated to the candidates.

The candidates say that they support financial aid for students and that the UW System is important. Ed Thompson, the Libertarian candidate, supports lowering the drinking age to 18. Gov. Scott McCallum's campaign didn't return calls.

Why do older people get "more political lovin'"? Why do they vote more regularly than younger people?

But when it comes to the issues that get the most attention, the older you are, the more political lovin' you get. Think about how often gubernatorial candidates talk about prescription drug benefits for seniors vs. easing the tuition burden on students.

What does it take for a candidate to capture the imagination of a young person? "They'd have to make appearances at rock concerts," half-quipped Scott Butz, 26, a network administrator from Milwaukee.

Besides, age is ephemeral. Young people get old. Issues have staying power. A 21-year-old who buys a house may be just as concerned about property taxes as a 60-year-old homeowner. A 43-year-old sending her son to college could get just as upset at increasing tuition as her kid.

Young people interviewed mentioned a variety of topics that concerned them. Not all were age-related.

Becky Wallus, 28, is a reading teacher for Milwaukee Public Schools. "Obviously, education is the primary priority," Wallus said. She'd like to see more money for teacher training.

Jon Krueger, 23, is a registered nurse. During his workout at the downtown YMCA, he said he'd be interested in what candidates had to say about domestic partner registries.

And for the dozens of young people who don't pay much attention to politics, a few pay a lot.

Anne Bowman looks like a drastic stereotype of a politically uninvolved young adult—black-dyed hair, a colorful vocabulary, a nose ring and tattoos. But Bowman, 20, is passionate about politics and policy. She doesn't like school choice and supports more financial aid for students.

Bowman, who's studying history and creative writing at UWM, worked on the Barrett campaign but didn't have a good experience and won't vote for him. She's not sure who will get her vote, but she will cast a ballot, even if it's for

Mickey Mouse. "I could never not vote," Bowman said. "I'm from a very voting family."

Young vote has had impact

The young vote can have a varying rate of influence based on the context of an election.

"There have been some occasions where they have made a difference," Freitag said. He mentioned how Minnesota Gov. Jesse Ventura, a former pro wrestler, brought out a lot of first-time voters, including young adults.

In Wisconsin, Tammy Baldwin's runs for U.S. Congress have focused heavily on college-age voters, to the point where she organized the dorms.

As far as governor's races go, Lee S. Dreyfus thinks youths can make a difference. The former chancellor ran for governor partly because of student pressure, and he believes the young vote was a crucial factor in his victory. Some say, and Dreyfus agrees, that his campaign was the last time Wisconsin's young people got excited about a gubernatorial race.

"Students do not have money, but they have foot power," Dreyfus said. "Without them, there's no way I'd have taken that primary. Most of the students came out of blue-collar families and they brought their families with them into the primary. It was one hell of a lot of fun."

When November rolls around, will droves of young people head to the polls to select the next governor? Will the twenty-something vote make a difference? If history is any guide, it's not likely—even if the candidates show up at a few rock concerts.

> If young people can have an impact in some races, what does it take to get them excited? Issues? Candidates? Ideas?

Consider the source and the audience.
- This is a Wisconsin paper. Is the topic relevant to the rest of the nation, or is it too localized?

Lay out the argument, the values, and the assumptions.
- Why do the political scientists Toosi cites imply that young people don't matter, in the sense that they don't "swing" elections? What behavior is key here?
- Why do the young people in the article say they don't care about politics?

Uncover the evidence.

- To support the claim that young people don't vote, Toosi cites statistics gathered by the Voter News Service (a consortium of ABC, NBC, CBS, CNN, Fox, and the Associated Press that conducts exit polls, asking people whom they voted for as they leave their polling place), as well as by the federal government (*www.fec.gov*). Should we believe these polls? Why or why not?
- Other evidence comes from interviews with experts (political scientists), politicians, and young people themselves. How reliable is that? Which of these people's views would support broad conclusions?

Evaluate the conclusion.

- Toosi seems pessimistic about the odds that many young people would turn out in the Wisconsin gubernatorial election. By the time you read this, that election will be over and you can check the voting turnout to see if the conclusion is right. How about the more general, if unwritten, conclusion that Toosi seems to draw?

Sort out the political implications.

- If most politicians don't focus on issues that young people care about because young people don't vote, and most young people don't vote because politicians don't focus on issues they care about, then what's to be done? Whose job is it to break this cycle?
- What are the consequences for young people if the cycle stays unbroken? For the rest of the country?

1.2 Paths to Patriotism: Since September 11, Many Young Americans Have Wrestled with an Odd New Feeling

Mark Sappenfield, *Christian Science Monitor*, 3 July 2002

Paths to Patriotism is another article about youthful indifference to politics, but the focus this time is on the ways that it has been transformed by emerging feelings of patriotism since September 11, 2001. In particular, the article distinguishes between love of country, or patriotism, and good citizenship. We selected it because the issue of citizenship is central in democratic governments. Can post-9/11 patriotism rescue us from our civic crisis?

B ronwyn Burnett doesn't fit the usual image of an American patriot.

Ask the student of fine arts if she'd be willing to serve in the armed forces, and she politely declines, explaining, "I would really not be able to be myself if I were in any kind of military."

Ask her if recent events have kindled an interest in the actions of her government, and the 20-something responds, "A lot of the politics out there isn't something that interests me."

Ask her how she feels about the war on terrorism, and she struggles to find the words: "I don't know that I can judge that," she says. "The whole situation is out of my hands, is what I feel like."

She is, in many respects, a spokeswoman for her generation. Long derided as individualistic, even apathetic, young Americans today seem not to have been changed much by the world-altering attacks of Sept. 11. While 8 in 10 Americans support the war on terrorism, only 57 percent of college students approve. Following Sept. 11, military records show, the enlistment rate hardly budged.

A second Pearl Harbor this was not, it seems.

But this July 4, don't tell Ms. Burnett that she and her generation don't love their country—and haven't been touched by Sept. 11.

For most, it has nothing to do with the daily routine. True, some have been moved to actions that echo the "greatest generation"—such as offering even their joint and sinew to the cause of freedom by enrolling in the military. But more are like Burnett, who sits outside the library at Portland State University in Oregon with no stars-and-stripes pin on her clothes and no thought of how she'll spend Independence Day.

Among these young Americans, children of unprecedented peace and prosperity, the change is something unrelated to festivals and fireworks. After years of being left to themselves to navigate through video games and parental divorce, political correctness and personal computers, they are now confronted with images and emotions they have never seen or felt. Sept. 11 might not have turned them into patriots in the mold of those who stormed the beaches of Normandy, but it is stirring unfamiliar—and as yet unresolved—feelings of conflict, as many young adults struggle to reconsider America and their place in it.

> How might the experience of growing up in a time of peace and national prosperity have shaped the current generation of twenty-something Americans? How would that be different from, say, growing up during World War II?

"It is a disturbance at a deep level," says Todd Gitlin, a sociologist at New York University. "It's not actionable—it's not working on [young] people in a direct way. It's underneath."

Never have these young Americans been called on to sacrifice anything for a greater national cause. Indeed, many have been taught mainly to question their country and its symbols—from McDonald's impact on the Brazilian rain forests to America's interventions in Central America and the Middle East.

Outwardly, as 20-somethings themselves acknowledge, the cynicism and skepticism that have come to define this group seem to be intact. Nearly three-quarters of college students say they think the patriotism and unity sparked by Sept. 11 will fade, according to a poll by the Panetta Institute at California State University in Monterey Bay.

That's not surprising, say sociologists. Today's 20-somethings have been shaped by the experiences of their youth, just as the GI generation's self-sacrifice grew from the hardships of the Great Depression, and the baby boomers' antiestablishment ideals were forged amid the tumult of Vietnam. Generations X and Y, for their part, are latchkey kids or children of divorce—experiences that taught them independence. The advent of cable TV has catered to their every entertainment need and acquainted them with every political scandal. The might of money in politics has told them that only the wealthiest have a say.

The result, say observers, is a generation of survivors who rely on themselves. When it comes to politics, they have concluded that people can make a difference only when they act locally. In turn, their sense of patriotism is narrower than anything that has come before.

Burnett says she sees America not in the flag or the military, but in a yellow school bus that reminds her of her youth. Fellow student Lisa Tengo says being a good citizen means concentrating on "things that are more localized."

"I don't think being a good citizen means you can or can't burn the flag or anything great or ideal," she says. "I think it just means to be a good person."

This mentality has taken its toll on the tradition of service to the country. Ms. Tengo, for one, has never voted and vows that she never will. "It's one of those 'What's the point?' kind of things," she quips. "I feel like my life would be the same no matter who's in office, so I don't really care."

What view of citizenship are these young people articulating? Does it include rights? Duties? What is the relationship of citizenship to patriotism?

Her words may be extreme, but they are poignant. Surveys repeatedly show that many young Americans have little interest in their government—and Sept. 11 didn't change that. The Panetta poll shows that only 34 percent of college students are interested in running for elected office, and when asked how they could effectively bring change, more respondents chose volunteering than voting in a presidential election.

"There is a gap developing where young people really do not sense a duty to participate in the process," says Leon Panetta, head of the institute and former White House chief of staff under President Clinton. "They clearly care about issues, but the disconnect is that they don't see Washington as relevant to what they believe in."

Equating that with the death of patriotism, though, would not be correct.

Observers note that today's young people, since 9/11, haven't been asked to do anything except go out and spend money. In the absence of a draft or a call for volunteers, they say, it's impossible to know how they would act if they were truly called upon.

One survey found that 37 percent of college students today said they would avoid a draft, but some critics retorted that a similar survey during Vietnam might have yielded a far larger number.

"These young people are pretty strong patriots, but not necessarily in the American Legion style," says A.J. Shragge, a lecturer at the University of California in San Diego. He says that his students contributed generously to a Girl Scout campaign that sent boxes of cookies to troops in Afghanistan. "Here was some little thing they could do."

"There are not a lot of obvious outlets for patriotism," he adds. "'Get on with life' was the only message."

As their lives go on, though, it's evident that Sept. 11 is forcing many young Americans to rethink their detachment from their country. To them, American government does not evoke images of President Franklin Roosevelt fighting the Nazi empire or Lyndon Johnson battling the scourge of racism. Instead, it is sketched entirely in the colors of President Clinton and his moral foibles, Congress in its vindictiveness, and the divisiveness of an unresolved election two years ago. Now, called on to celebrate the institutions many have always ridiculed, the transition is not an easy one.

"There's a lot of confusion now about what to do," says Daryl Maas, a young lieutenant in the Air Force. "We're not really sure how to feel."

For him, patriotism has always meant a clear-cut love of country. Blond and trim, the Air Force Academy grad enlisted right after high school, but he says he feels even stronger now about the need to serve his country. But it's not something he sees in many of his peers.

"Our country is so big and powerful, we're used to protesting against it," says Lieutenant Maas, who has spent time in Japan, Colombia, Spain, and the Czech Republic since joining the Air Force. "Our generation has looked down on blind patriotism, and . . . some people have never had to decide where they stand. Before, we had the luxury of criticizing from a distance."

Since Sept. 11, the choice of cherishing or criticizing has been made—if anything—more urgent and complex.

Portland State student Burnett, who grew up with an artist father in the eclectic seaside town of Carmel, Calif., where Tudor-style British pubs mix with Gucci bags and groves of cypress trees, says the idea of war and violence is repulsive. She feels bad that America bombed Afghanistan: "I could never hurt anyone or be involved in that."

How might national leaders have called on young Americans after 9/11 in a way that would have led them to a stronger sense of citizenship and national service?

But the images of Sept. 11 evoked something unexpected in her, and she can't bring herself to condemn America's response. "I can't even describe all my emotions," she says as she twists a wire sculpture. "You can't just watch something like that and not cry—and not hurt for your own country."

What happens from here may depend in large part on what happens next in the war on terrorism. After all, Pearl Harbor became a transcendent event because it was the start of something greater—a war that has since been cast as a victory over evil.

So it may be with Sept. 11 and the nascent stirrings of a new—but different—patriotism among young adults. "If the United States is able to contain terrorism," says Gary Alan Fine, a sociologist at Northwestern University in Evanston, Ill., "then it will contribute . . . to greater patriotism."

Consider the source and the audience.

- This article comes from the *Christian Science Monitor*, a strong national newspaper with a religious heritage that does not noticeably slant the coverage but occasionally influences the stories it chooses to cover. How might this story reflect that tendency?

Lay out the argument, the values, and the assumptions.

- What argument is being made by the sociologists and other observers Sappenfield cites? Why do today's twenty-somethings feel dissociated from their government? What impact did the September 11 terror attacks have on them?
- What is the implicit concept of citizenship against which the article measures young people? What do they think citizenship means?

Uncover the evidence.

- Sappenfield's evidence comes partly in the form of testimony by experts. What kind of evidence do these experts offer? Are the claims based on this evidence reliable?
- His other evidence comes from young people he interviews. How broadly can he generalize from this?

Evaluate the conclusion.

- What does Sappenfield speculate about the possible long-term effects of September 11 on this young generation. What might a "new patriotism" look like?

Sort out the political implications.

- Do democracies require that their citizens be patriotic? What kind of citizens do they need to be to keep democracy alive? If Sappenfield is right, will today's young people do the job?

1.3 Inaugural Address

John F. Kennedy, delivered 20 January 1961

John F. Kennedy's Inaugural Address, now more than forty years old, calls on Americans facing a long battle to preserve their ideals and their way of life to exhibit a selfless citizenship and devotion to country. His words to a nation challenged by the Cold War are poignant today, when the same nation is struggling with war of a different but equally destructive kind. One definition of an effective leader may be that a leader holds up a mirror before a nation's citizens and helps them see themselves as a people bound by values and heritage, willing to sacrifice for worthy common goals. How does Kennedy take the opportunity presented by this speech to establish himself as a national leader?

W e observe today not a victory of party but a celebration of freedom—symbolizing an end as well as a beginning—signifying renewal as well as change. For I have sworn before you and Almighty God the same solemn oath our forebears prescribed nearly a century and three-quarters ago.

The world is very different now. For man holds in his mortal hands the power to abolish all forms of human poverty and all forms of human life. And yet the same revolutionary beliefs for which our forebears fought are still at issue around the globe—the belief that the rights of man come not from the generosity of the state but from the hand of God.

We dare not forget today that we are the heirs of that first revolution. Let the word go forth from this time and place, to friend and foe alike, that the torch has been passed to a new generation of Americans—born in this century, tempered by war, disciplined by a hard and bitter peace, proud of our ancient heritage—and unwilling to witness or permit the slow undoing of those human rights to which this nation has always been committed, and to which we are committed today at home and around the world.

Let every nation know, whether it wishes us well or ill, that we shall pay any price, bear any burden, meet any hardship, support any friend, oppose any foe to assure the survival and the success of liberty.

This much we pledge—and more.

To those old allies whose cultural and spiritual origins we share, we pledge the loyalty of faithful friends. United, there is little we cannot do in a host of cooperative ventures. Divided, there is little we can do—for we dare not meet a powerful challenge at odds and split asunder.

To those new states whom we welcome to the ranks of the free, we pledge our word that one form of colonial control shall not have passed away merely to be replaced by a far more iron tyranny. We shall not always expect to find them supporting our view. But we shall always hope to find them strongly supporting their own freedom—and to remember that, in the past, those who foolishly sought power by riding the back of the tiger ended up inside.

To those people in the huts and villages of half the globe struggling to break the bonds of mass misery, we pledge our best efforts to help them help themselves, for whatever period is required—not because the Communists may be doing it, not because we seek their votes, but because it is right. If a free society cannot help the many who are poor, it cannot save the few who are rich.

> *What are the essential differences between a capitalist democracy and a communist totalitarian state? What are the divisions that tear the world apart today, when there is only one Superpower left?*

To our sister republics south of the border, we offer a special pledge—to convert our good words into good deeds—in a new alliance for progress—to assist free men and free governments in casting off the chains of poverty. But this peaceful revolution of hope cannot become the prey of hostile powers. Let all our neighbors know that we shall join with them to oppose aggression or subversion anywhere in the Americas. And let every other power know that this hemisphere intends to remain the master of its own house.

To that world assembly of sovereign states, the United Nations, our last best hope in an age where the instruments of war have far outpaced the instruments of peace, we renew our pledge of support—to prevent it from becoming merely a forum for invective—to strengthen its shield of the new and the weak—and to enlarge the area in which its writ may run.

Finally, to those nations who would make themselves our adversary, we offer not a pledge but a request: that both sides begin anew the quest for peace, before the dark powers of destruction unleashed by science engulf all humanity in planned or accidental self-destruction.

We dare not tempt them with weakness. For only when our arms are sufficient beyond doubt can we be certain beyond doubt that they will never be employed.

But neither can two great and powerful groups of nations take comfort from our present course—both sides overburdened by the cost of modern weapons, both rightly alarmed by the steady spread of the deadly atom, yet both racing to alter that uncertain balance of terror that stays the hand of mankind's final war.

So let us begin anew—remembering on both sides that civility is not a sign of weakness, and sincerity is always subject to proof. Let us never negotiate out of fear. But let us never fear to negotiate.

Let both sides explore what problems unite us instead of belaboring those problems which divide us.

Let both sides, for the first time, formulate serious and precise proposals for the inspection and control of arms—and bring the absolute power to destroy other nations under the absolute control of all nations.

Let both sides seek to invoke the wonders of science instead of its terrors. Together let us explore the stars, conquer the deserts, eradicate disease, tap the ocean depths, and encourage the arts and commerce.

Let both sides unite to heed in all corners of the earth the command of Isaiah—to "undo the heavy burdens . . . [and] let the oppressed go free."

And if a beachhead of co-operation may push back the jungle of suspicion, let both sides join in creating a new endeavor, not a new balance of power, but a new world of law, where the strong are just and the weak secure and the peace preserved.

All this will not be finished in the first one hundred days. Nor will it be finished in the first one thousand days, nor in the life of this administration, nor even perhaps in our lifetime on this planet. But let us begin.

In your hands, my fellow citizens, more than mine, will rest the final success or failure of our course. Since this country was founded, each generation of Americans has been summoned to give testimony to its national loyalty. The graves of young Americans who answered the call to service surround the globe.

Now the trumpet summons us again—not as a call to bear arms, though arms we need—not as a call to battle, though embattled we are—but a call to bear the burden of a long twilight struggle, year in and year out, "rejoicing in hope, patient in tribulation"— a struggle against the common enemies of man: tyranny, poverty, disease, and war itself.

Can we forge against these enemies a grand and global alliance, North and South, East and West, that can assure a more fruitful life for all mankind? Will you join in that historic effort?

> JFK refers several times to the experiences of a new generation in American politics. How is that generation's experience different from the one that today's youth are undergoing?

In the long history of the world, only a few generations have been granted the role of defending freedom in its hour of maximum danger. I do not shrink from this responsibility—I welcome it. I do not believe that any of us would exchange places with any other people or any other generation. The energy, the faith, the devotion which we bring to this endeavor will light our country and all who serve it—and the glow from that fire can truly light the world.

And so, my fellow Americans: ask not what your country can do for you—ask what you can do for your country.

What view of citizenship does Kennedy advocate here? What is the role of sacrifice?

My fellow citizens of the world: ask not what America will do for you, but what together we can do for the freedom of man.

Finally, whether you are citizens of America or citizens of the world, ask of us here the same high standards of strength and sacrifice which we ask of you. With a good conscience our only sure reward, with history the final judge of our deeds, let us go forth to lead the land we love, asking His blessing and His help, but knowing that here on earth God's work must truly be our own.

Consider the source and the audience.
- Here you are reading a president's inaugural address. What are the goals of such a speech? Is it addressed only to Americans?

Lay out the argument, the values, and the assumptions.
- Is Kennedy making an argument in this speech? How might the claims made in an inaugural address differ from those in a more traditional argument?
- What is Kennedy's major point? Who are the new generation of Americans the torch is being passed to? How does their political experience make them different?
- What is Kennedy's view of a good government? What is his view of how the world should be ordered? What values are worth fighting for? What is his view of national service?

Uncover the evidence.
- What kind of evidence is Kennedy obliged to provide in support of the claims he makes here? When can ideals, convictions, and historical tradition substitute for factual evidence?

Evaluate the conclusion.
- What does Kennedy see as the fundamental tasks to be done?
- Were there other visions of America and its role in the world that he might have offered then? What values might this role have been based on?

Sort out the political implications.
- How effective do you imagine this speech was as a political call to arms and a call "to bear the burden"? How might it have shaped the generations to whom it was addressed?
- How might such a speech be received today?

CHAPTER 2

Political Culture

H ow do we recognize "people like us"—the people we grow up with, go to school with, attend church with, hang out with? The people who live in our neighborhoods, our towns, our cities, and our states? How do we differentiate Americans from all the other people in the world? That odd, intangible thing that separates "us" from "them"—that answers the question "Who are we?"—is called political culture, the set of ideas, beliefs, and values about who we are as a nation, what we believe in, what kind of government we should have, and what our relationship to that government should be.

Political culture can be a hard concept to grasp because it is abstract. We can't see it or touch it, and, in fact, it is very difficult to be aware of our own political culture when we are immersed in it. Like kids looking through play glasses with tinted lenses, we see everything colored by the lens of our culture. We think we are seeing truth—the way things really are—but really we see just our version of reality, shaped by our cultural preferences and values. Other people observing us from other cultures can often see more easily what our own familiarity with our values and beliefs hides from us. Sometimes we ourselves see the differences most clearly when we are traveling in another country among people who are not "like us."

Understanding political culture is important because the way we think about ourselves politically and the values we share help to shape our political systems and the way politics takes place within them. Today our political culture is based on a commitment to individual freedom from extensive government action; on the value of equality, defined as equal opportunity rather than equality of results; and on the principle that decisions should be made through a representative democracy, heeding the voices of individuals and organized interests in the formation of public policy. All these values together go into the ideal of the "American dream"—the promise that all citizens have the opportunity to live prosperous lives, that they are entitled to "life, liberty, and the pursuit of happiness."

But there is no consensus in the United States on exactly what the content of the American dream should be. Political culture can be thought of as the ideas that bring us together, that unite us as a people. It does not mean that we never disagree. Within the broad confines of our culture we disagree on all kinds of things. The ideas that divide us—the different views of the American dream, and the political views that we do not share universally—are called ideologies, subcultures of values and beliefs that may share some common foundations but diverge radically on many details.

The principal ideologies in American politics are called conservatism and liberalism. Although there are different ways of understanding these two ideologies, most people would agree that *conservatism* emphasizes traditional values and social roles, more limited government, and economic freedom whereas *liberalism* focuses on social change and diversity and a government role for buffering the effects on individuals of the economic market. In recent years, conservatives have tended to live in rural areas and in the Midwest and southern states. Liberals tend to live in urban areas and on the east and west coasts of the country.

We have chosen the selections in this chapter to showcase both the ideas that unite us as Americans (political culture) and the ideas that divide us (political ideologies). The first article, from the *Houston Chronicle*, tells the rags to riches story of a child of Mexican immigrants who makes his fortune and goes on to own a share of a Texas football team. The second article, from the *Atlantic Monthly*, is about the ideologies that seem to divide us into two Americas. The author explores those differences and considers whether they are so great that we can no longer be considered a single culture. The third article looks at the same topic, but from abroad. On the principle that we can more easily understand ourselves if we see ourselves as others do, we have chosen this article from a British newspaper, the *London Times*, to get a very different idea of the two Americas, and why our allies overseas seem to like one of us but not the other. The fourth selection was also written from the vantage point of the foreign press—in this case, the British *Guardian*. It examines the core American issues of equality and race and explores the question of whether we are divided into social classes that determine people's chances in life. Finally, a selection that touches on the concerns in all these pieces is Martin Luther King, Jr.'s, classic "I Have a Dream" speech. Here King looks at the whole culture that ties Americans together, especially its commitment to freedom and equality, and demands access to that culture for African Americans.

2.1 Self-Made Texan

Energetic Trader Loya Personifies American Dream

Dale Robertson, *Houston Chronicle*, 9 May 2002

In the 1800s, Horatio Alger, Jr., wrote over one hundred stories about boys who rose from rags to riches, primarily by demonstrating the solid virtues of hard work, courage, generosity, and moral goodness. These success stories have become so identified with the traditional view of the American dream that we often refer to the sagas of self-made Americans as Horatio Alger stories.

In this article from the sports pages of the *Houston Chronicle*, Horatio Alger appears in modern guise as a thirty-something Latino born of illegal immigrants who went on to play college football in the Ivy League, launch an oil business, and amass a fortune that enabled him to buy into the NFL expansion team, the Houston Texans. Is the Horatio Alger version of the American dream founded on blood, sweat, and tears still an inspiring and motivating vision for young Americans?

Javier Loya, the second-youngest of seven children whose mother and father first entered the United States illegally from Mexico, grew up dreaming the American dream with all the energy a kid could muster.

He played football and worshipped the Dallas Cowboys, but realized early on that, even in a land of such great opportunity, not every goal is achievable. Hope and hard work weren't enough to gain Javier a spot on the Cowboys' roster.

So he adjusted his sights. Instead, he got an Ivy League education (Columbia, class of '91), founded a spectacularly successful oil-and-gas brokerage firm, made millions and, at the age of 33, bought himself a piece of the Texans from Bob McNair, whose father never had earned more than subsistence wages.

Yes, it is a great country. Only in America. . . .

The Javier Alger story should be a reminder to those who think closing our borders tight is a solution to our problems. In the crude, cruel idiom of the day, Miguel and Ana Loya were "wetbacks." Yet people like them, people who took the risk of sneaking across the Rio Grande—or crowding into rusty trans-Atlantic steamships—while asking only for a chance to better their lot, are America's spine.

The families of Loya's parents had been displaced during the Mexican Revolution and became impoverished. But although neither Miguel, who rose from loading trucks to being a plant supervisor at the Farah Manufacturing Co. in El Paso, nor Ana went to high school, they were adamant their children put education first.

What does the author intend to convey by referring to Loya as "Javier Alger" in connection with a modern story about illegal immigrants?

"That's all we ever heard at the dinner table," Javier says.

The Loya brood listened carefully, too. The oldest, Mike, has an MBA from Harvard and owns Vitol, a London-based oil-and-gas trading company that's among the world's largest. Fernando, who won the Mexican equivalent of the Heisman Trophy as a ballhawking free safety for the University of Nuevo Leon, is a dentist in Austin. Anna is a teacher in El Paso. Irma, a Notre Dame graduate, was recently honored as the small-business person of the year in Alabama, where she founded an energy consulting firm.

Raul, who has a Rice degree and played football for the Owls in the mid-'80s, is an attorney in Dallas. And Mario, who was Javier's All-Ivy League teammate at Columbia, is a financial analyst for a pension fund in Connecticut.

When the family reunites every Easter, it's a veritable best-and-brightest convention. You play one-upmanship games in Miguel Loya's home at your peril. But Javier might have finally trumped them all when he sold McNair on including him in the Texans' partnership.

"Don't they say NFL owners make up one of the world's most exclusive clubs?" he said, feigning smugness.

It hadn't occurred to Loya to seek a small piece of the Texans until a year ago, when he read a story about how McNair wanted his group to represent a cross-section of the Houston community. Scanning the list of names—Dynegy chairman Chuck Watson, the Rev. Kirbyjon Caldwell, restaurant magnate Tillman Fertitta and former Oiler Ray Childress among them—Loya immediately noticed a conspicuous omission.

"No Hispanics," he said.

Loya dashed off a letter to McNair expressing interest. Intrigued, Bob arranged a meeting. It didn't take him long to appreciate Javier for what he had accomplished despite his humble roots. They were kindred spirits with strikingly similar stories—two self-made men of different backgrounds, generations and ethnicities who shared the common bond of having achieved financial success beyond all reasonable expectations.

They also shared the same passion for football. An invitation to invest was soon extended to Loya and, after he checked out OK with the NFL's gumshoes, the deal was done. McNair has opted not to reveal how the partnership breaks down percentage-wise—except to say he kept more than 70 percent—but remember, even 1 percent of the $800-plus million package would exceed $8 million.

How did Loya accumulate so much so quickly? He has a broker's mentality. As he tells it, when he was a senior, one of his brother Mike's associates picked him up at Columbia in a stretch limo and they went clubbing. Javier has been married for three years, but back then, as Joe College he prided himself on being a bit of a ladies' man. He chatted up every woman he met—undeterred by the fact his advances kept being rebuffed.

"My brother's friend told me that night I could make it as a trader," Loya said, laughing, "because I handled rejection so well."

It was during the Gulf War and the oil markets were, he recalls, "going crazy. The guy offered me $45,000 if I'd quit school

> *Loya makes a joke of his ability to handle rejection, suiting him for a career as a trader. What does this light-hearted story tell us about the qualities that led to his success?*

and start immediately. I couldn't do that because of my parents, but I told him I'd find a way to work a couple days a week.

"I loved the business right away. It gives you the same adrenal rush you get from sports. I haven't taken more than a week's vacation since I started."

Loya and the chap who mentored him started their own company, CHOICE! Energy, and moved it to Houston. Later, when his partner wanted to enter the dot-com/Internet wars, Javier bought him out.

But now, even as he runs an office with 30 employees, he hasn't lost his taste for the action. He remains an active trader, riveted to his computer screen every day until the market closes. He eats lunch at his desk, same as his underlings.

Loya's Texans investment represents the tangible fruits of his labors and, yes, it is a real investment, one on which he expects to make money. But he had purchased his Reliant Stadium PSLs before contacting McNair, and he admits, as a fan, he can hardly stand the wait for the season to start.

On the evening of Sept. 8, Javier's life will have, in effect, come full circle. That night, the poor immigrant's son turned wealthy entrepreneur and emergent community leader—he'll host an Hispanic forum in conjunction with next week's NFL meetings here—will cheer his fool head off for the Texans, his team, to beat the bejeebers out of the Dallas Cowboys.

His former team.

Consider the source and the audience.

- This story appears on the sports page of a Houston paper, based in the hometown for the new NFL team that Loya owns a part of. How does sports reporting differ from straight news coverage? How might the hometown twist affect the objectivity of the coverage?

Lay out the argument, the values, and the assumptions.

- What is the author's view of the American dream? What would he consider the central ingredients of "success"? What role does immigration play?
- What are the central values that Loya's parents brought him up to respect? How did these values affect Loya's achievement of the American dream?

Uncover the evidence.

- Is Loya's story good evidence for why we should keep our borders open? What negative effects of immigration might the author have considered to provide a more balanced argument?
- Is one person's or one family's experience sufficient to provide a causal link between a particular set of values and a successful result? Does this kind of story require that the author provide anything other than anecdotal evidence?

Evaluate the conclusion.

- Does the author succeed in making a case that America benefits from keeping our borders open? What, besides open borders, is needed to foster the American dream? Why don't more people reach Loya's levels of achievement?

Sort out the political implications.
- What kind of immigration policy would the author's views lead to?
- If education is so central to individual success, what changes in education policy would this argue for?

2.2 One Nation, Slightly Divisible

David Brooks, *Atlantic Monthly,* December 2001

In the closely divided 2000 presidential election in which Al Gore won the popular vote and George W. Bush the electoral college vote, the nation was split into two groups of states—what journalists took to calling, after the colored maps they used on election night, Red America (Bush Country) and Blue America (the states that went for Gore). Red America is the land between the two coasts—the midwestern and southern states, largely rural and spread out. Despite the fact that the nation is fairly evenly divided, Red America appears to be taking over the country because population is so dispersed in many Red states. Blue America, on the other hand, is highly concentrated in urban areas, especially in the east and the west. Dense Blue states line the coasts of the nation. Since the election, there has been a good deal of speculation about the cultural differences between these two "Americas," and here David Brooks in the *Atlantic Monthly* joins in. Are they different parts of the same whole, or alien territories between which the gulf gets ever wider? Is there a single American political culture?

Sixty-five miles from where I am writing this sentence is a place with no Starbucks, no Pottery Barn, no Borders or Barnes & Noble. No blue *New York Times* delivery bags dot the driveways on Sunday mornings. In this place people don't complain that Woody Allen isn't as funny as he used to be, because they never thought he was funny. In this place you can go to a year's worth of dinner parties without hearing anyone quote an aperçu he first heard on *Charlie Rose.* The people here don't buy those little rear-window stickers when they go to a summer-vacation spot so that they can drive around with "MV" decals the rest of the year; for the most part they don't even go to Martha's Vineyard.

The place I'm talking about goes by different names. Some call it America. Others call it Middle America. It has also come to be known as Red America, in reference to the maps that were produced on the night of the 2000 presidential election. People in Blue America, which is my part of America, tend to live around big cities on the coasts. People in Red America tend to live on farms or in small towns or small cities far away from the coasts. Things are different there.

Everything that people in my neighborhood do without motors, the people in Red America do with motors. We sail; they powerboat. We cross-country ski; they snowmobile. We hike; they drive ATVs. We have vineyard tours; they have tractor pulls. When it comes to yard work, they have rider mowers; we have illegal aliens.

Different sorts of institutions dominate life in these two places. In Red America churches are everywhere. In Blue America Thai restaurants are everywhere. In Red America they have QVC, the Pro Bowlers Tour, and hunting. In Blue America we have NPR, Doris Kearns Goodwin, and socially conscious investing. In Red America the Wal-Marts are massive, with parking lots the size of state parks. In Blue America the stores are small but the markups are big. You'll rarely see a Christmas store in Blue America, but in Red America, even in July, you'll come upon stores selling fake Christmas trees, wreath-decorated napkins, Rudolph the Red-Nosed Reindeer collectible thimbles and spoons, and little snow-covered villages.

We in the coastal metro Blue areas read more books and attend more plays than the people in the Red heartland. We're more sophisticated and cosmopolitan—just ask us about our alumni trips to China or Provence, or our interest in Buddhism. But don't ask us, please, what life in Red America is like. We don't know. We don't know who Tim LaHaye and Jerry B. Jenkins are, even though the novels they have co-written have sold about 40 million copies over the past few years. We don't know what James Dobson says on his radio program, which is listened to by millions. We don't know about Reba or Travis. We don't know what happens in mega-churches on Wednesday evenings, and some of us couldn't tell you the difference between a fundamentalist and an evangelical, let alone describe what it means to be a Pentecostal. Very few of us know what goes on in Branson, Missouri, even though it has seven million visitors a year, or could name even five NASCAR drivers, although stock-car races are the best-attended sporting events in the country. We don't know how to shoot or clean a rifle. We can't tell a military officer's rank by looking at his insignia. We don't know what soy beans look like when they're growing in a field.

All we know, or all we think we know, about Red America is that millions and millions of its people live quietly underneath flight patterns, many of them are racist and homophobic, and when you see them at highway rest stops, they're often really fat and their clothes are too tight.

And apparently we don't want to know any more than that. One can barely find any books at Amazon.com about what it is like to live in small-town America—or, at least, any books written by normal people who grew up in small towns, liked them, and stayed there. The few books that do exist were written either by people who left the heartland because they hated it (Bill Bryson's *The Lost Continent,* for example) or by urbanites who moved to Red America as part of some life-simplification plan (*Moving to a Small Town: A Guidebook for Moving from Urban to Rural America;* National Geographic's *Guide to Small Town Escapes*). Apparently no publishers or members of the Blue book-buying public are curious about Red America as seen through Red America's eyes.

> Is Brooks serious? What kind of tone is he adopting here? What's his point?

Crossing the Meatloaf Line

Over the past several months, my interest piqued by those stark blocks of color on the election-night maps, I have every now and then left my home in Montgomery County, Maryland, and driven sixty-five miles northwest to Franklin County, in south-central Pennsylvania. Montgomery County is one of the steaming-hot centers of the great espresso machine that is Blue America. It is just over the border from northwestern Washington, D.C., and it is full of upper-middle-class towns inhabited by lawyers, doctors, stockbrokers, and establishment journalists like me—towns like Chevy Chase, Potomac, and Bethesda (where I live). Its central artery is a burgeoning high-tech corridor with a multitude of sparkling new office parks housing technology companies such as United Information Systems and Sybase, and pioneering biotech firms such as Celera Genomics and Human Genome Sciences. When I drive to Franklin County, I take Route 270. After about forty-five minutes I pass a Cracker Barrel—Red America condensed into chain-restaurant form. I've crossed the Meatloaf Line; from here on there will be a lot fewer sun-dried-tomato concoctions on restaurant menus and a lot more meatloaf platters.

Franklin County is Red America. It's a rural county, about twenty-five miles west of Gettysburg, and it includes the towns of Waynesboro, Chambersburg, and Mercersburg. It was originally settled by the Scotch-Irish, and has plenty of Brethren and Mennonites along with a fast-growing population of evangelicals. The joke that Pennsylvanians tell about their state is that it has Philadelphia on one end, Pittsburgh on the other, and Alabama in the middle. Franklin County is in the Alabama part. It strikes me as I drive there that even though I am going north across the Mason-Dixon line, I feel as if I were going south. The local culture owes more to Nashville, Houston, and Daytona than to Washington, Philadelphia, or New York.

I shuttled back and forth between Franklin and Montgomery Counties because the cultural differences between the two places are great, though the geographic distance is small. The two places are not perfect microcosms of Red and Blue America. The part of Montgomery County I am here describing is largely the Caucasian part. Moreover, Franklin County is in a Red part of a Blue state: overall, Pennsylvania went for Gore. And I went to Franklin County aware that there are tremendous differences within Red America, just as there are within Blue. Franklin County is quite different from, say, Scottsdale, Arizona, just as Bethesda is quite different from Oakland, California.

Nonetheless, the contrasts between the two counties leap out, and they are broadly suggestive of the sorts of contrasts that can be seen nationwide. When Blue America talks about social changes that convulsed society, it tends to mean the 1960s rise of the counterculture and feminism. When Red America talks about changes that convulsed society, it tends to mean World War II, which shook up old town establishments and led to a great surge of industry.

Red America makes social distinctions that Blue America doesn't. For example, in Franklin County there seems to be a distinction between those fiercely independent people who live in the hills and people who live in the valleys. I got a hint of the distinct and, to me, exotic hill culture when a hill dweller asked me why I thought hunting for squirrel and rabbit had gone out of fashion. I thought maybe it was just more fun to hunt something bigger. But he said, "McDonald's. It's cheaper to get a hamburger at McDonald's than to go out and get it yourself."

There also seems to be an important distinction between men who work outdoors and men who work indoors. The outdoor guys wear faded black T-shirts they once picked up at a Lynyrd Skynyrd concert and wrecked jeans that appear to be washed faithfully at least once a year. They've got wraparound NASCAR sunglasses, maybe a NAPA auto parts cap, and hair cut in a short wedge up front but flowing down over their shoulders in the back—a cut that is known as a mullet, which is sort of a cross between Van Halen's style and Kenny Rogers's, and is the ugliest hairdo since every hairdo in the seventies. The outdoor guys are heavily accessorized, and their accessories are meant to show how hard they work, so they will often have a gigantic wad of keys hanging from a belt loop, a tape measure strapped to the belt, a pocket knife on a string tucked into the front pants pocket, and a pager or a cell phone affixed to the hip, presumably in case some power lines go down somewhere and need emergency repair. Outdoor guys have a thing against sleeves. They work so hard that they've got to keep their arm muscles unencumbered and their armpit hair fully ventilated, so they either buy their shirts sleeveless or rip the sleeves off their T-shirts first thing, leaving bits of fringe hanging over their BAD TO THE BONE tattoos.

The guys who work indoors can't project this rugged proletarian image. It's simply not that romantic to be a bank-loan officer or a shift manager at the local distribution center. So the indoor guys adopt a look that a smart-ass, sneering Blue American might call Bible-academy casual—maybe Haggar slacks, which they bought at a dry-goods store best known for its appliance department, and a short-sleeved white Van Heusen shirt from the Bon-Ton. Their image projects not "I work hard" but "I'm a devoted family man." A lot of indoor guys have a sensitive New Age demeanor. When they talk about the days their kids were born, their eyes take on a soft Garth Brooks expression, and they tear up. They exaggerate how sinful they were before they were born again. On Saturdays they are patio masters, barbecuing on their gas grills in full Father's Day–apron regalia.

At first I thought the indoor guys were the faithful, reliable ones: the ones who did well in school, whereas the outdoor guys were druggies. But after talking with several preachers in Franklin County, I learned that it's not that simple. Sometimes the guys who look like bikers are the most devoted community-service volunteers and church attendees.

The kinds of distinctions we make in Blue America are different. In my world the easiest way to categorize people is by headroom needs. People who went to business school or law school like a lot of headroom. They buy humongous sport-utility vehicles that practically have cathedral ceilings over the front seats. They live in homes the size of country clubs, with soaring entry atriums so high that they could practically fly a kite when they come through the front door. These big-headroom people tend to be predators: their jobs have them negotiating and competing all day. They spend small fortunes on dry cleaning. They grow animated when talking about how much they love their blackberries. They fill their enormous wall space with huge professional family portraits—Mom and Dad with their perfect kids (dressed in light-blue oxford shirts) laughing happily in an orchard somewhere.

Small-headroom people tend to have been liberal-arts majors, and they have liberal-arts jobs. They get passive-aggressive pleasure from demonstrating how modest and environmentally sensitive their living containers are. They hate people with SUVs, and feel virtuous driving around in their low-ceilinged little Hondas, which often display a RANDOM ACTS OF KINDNESS bumper sticker or one bearing an image of a fish with legs, along with the word "Darwin," just to show how intellectually superior to fundamentalist Christians they are.

Some of the biggest differences between Red and Blue America show up on statistical tables. Ethnic diversity is one. In Montgomery County 60 percent of the population is white, 15 percent is black, 12 percent is Hispanic, and 11 percent is Asian. In Franklin County 95 percent of the population is white. White people work the gas-station pumps and the 7-Eleven counters. (This is something one doesn't often see in my part of the country.) Although the nation is growing more diverse, it's doing so only in certain spots. According to an analysis of the 2000 census by Bill Frey, a demographer at the Milken Institute, well over half the counties in America are still at least 85 percent white.

Another big thing is that, according to 1990 census data, in Franklin County only 12 percent of the adults have college degrees and only 69 percent have high school diplomas. In Montgomery County 50 percent of the adults have college degrees and 91 percent have high school diplomas. The education gap extends to the children. At Walt Whitman High School, a public school in Bethesda, the average SAT scores are 601 verbal and 622 math, whereas the national average is 506 verbal and 514 math. In Franklin County, where people are quite proud of their schools, the average SAT scores at, for example, the Waynesboro area high school are 495 verbal and 480 math. More and more kids in Franklin County are going on to college, but it is hard to believe that their prospects will be as bright as those of the kids in Montgomery County and the rest of upscale Blue America.

Because the information age rewards education with money, it's not surprising that Montgomery County is much richer than Franklin County. According to some estimates, in Montgomery County 51 percent of households have annual incomes above $75,000, and the average household income is $100,365. In

Franklin County only 16 percent of households have incomes above $75,000, and the average is $51,872.

A major employer in Montgomery County is the National Institutes of Health, which grows like a scientific boomtown in Bethesda. A major economic engine in Franklin County is the interstate highway Route 81. Trucking companies have gotten sick of fighting the congestion on Route 95, which runs up the Blue corridor along the northeast coast, so they move their stuff along 81, farther inland. Several new distribution centers have been built along 81 in Franklin County, and some of the workers who were laid off when their factories closed, several years ago, are now settling for $8.00 or $9.00 an hour loading boxes.

The two counties vote differently, of course—the differences, on a nationwide scale, were what led to those red- and-blue maps. Like upscale areas everywhere, from Silicon Valley to Chicago's North Shore to suburban Connecticut, Montgomery County supported the Democratic ticket in last year's presidential election, by a margin of 63 percent to 34 percent. Meanwhile, like almost all of rural America, Franklin County went Republican, by 67 percent to 30 percent.

However, other voting patterns sometimes obscure the Red-Blue cultural divide. For example, minority voters all over the country overwhelmingly supported the Democratic ticket last November. But—in many respects, at least—blacks and Hispanics in Red America are more traditionalist than blacks and Hispanics in Blue America, just as their white counterparts are. For example, the Pew Research Center for the People and the Press, in Washington, D.C., recently found that 45 percent of minority members in Red states agree with the statement "AIDS might be God's punishment for immoral sexual behavior," but only 31 percent of minority members in Blue states do. Similarly, 40 percent of minorities in Red states believe that school boards should have the right to fire homosexual teachers, but only 21 percent of minorities in Blue states do.

From Cracks to a Chasm?

These differences are so many and so stark that they lead to some pretty troubling questions: Are Americans any longer a common people? Do we have one national conversation and one national culture? Are we loyal to the same institutions and the same values? How do people on one side of the divide regard those on the other?

I went to Franklin County because I wanted to get a sense of how deep the divide really is, to see how people there live, and to gauge how different their lives are from those in my part of America. I spoke with ministers, journalists, teachers, community leaders, and pretty much anyone I ran across. I consulted with pollsters, demographers, and market-research firms.

Toward the end of my project the World Trade Center and the Pentagon were attacked. This put a new slant on my little investigation. In the days immediately following September 11 the evidence seemed clear that despite our differences,

What was the effect of September 11 on the American political cultural divide? Why were firemen hailed as heroes more often than the doctors and scientists who came to help, or the stockbrokers and financial analysts who died?

we are still a united people. American flags flew everywhere in Franklin County and in Montgomery County. Patriotism surged. Pollsters started to measure Americans' reactions to the events. Whatever questions they asked, the replies were near unanimous. Do you support a military response against terror? More than four fifths of Americans said yes. Do you support a military response even if it means thousands of U.S. casualties? More than three fifths said yes. There were no significant variations across geographic or demographic lines.

A sweeping feeling of solidarity was noticeable in every neighborhood, school, and workplace. Headlines blared, "A NATION UNITED" and "UNITED STATE." An attack had been made on the very epicenter of Blue America—downtown Manhattan. And in a flash all the jokes about and seeming hostility toward New Yorkers vanished, to be replaced by an outpouring of respect, support, and love. The old hostility came to seem merely a sort of sibling rivalry, which means nothing when the family itself is under threat.

But very soon there were hints that the solidarity was fraying. A few stray notes of dissent were sounded in the organs of Blue America. Susan Sontag wrote a sour piece in *The New Yorker* about how depressing it was to see what she considered to be a simplistically pro-American reaction to the attacks. At rallies on college campuses across the country speakers pointed out that America had been bombing other countries for years, and turnabout was fair play. On one NPR talk show I heard numerous callers express unease about what they saw as a crude us-versus-them mentality behind President Bush's rhetoric. Katha Pollitt wrote in *The Nation* that she would not permit her daughter to hang the American flag from the living-room window, because, she felt, it "stands for jingoism and vengeance and war." And there was evidence that among those with less-strident voices, too, differences were beginning to show. Polls revealed that people without a college education were far more confident than people with a college education that the military could defeat the terrorists. People in the South were far more eager than people in the rest of the country for an American counterattack to begin.

It started to seem likely that these cracks would widen once the American response got under way, when the focus would be not on firemen and rescue workers but on the Marines, the CIA, and the special-operations forces. If the war was protracted, the cracks could widen into a chasm, as they did during Vietnam. Red America, the home of patriotism and military service (there's a big military-recruitment center in downtown Chambersburg), would undoubtedly support the war effort, but would Blue America (there's a big gourmet dog bakery in downtown Bethesda) decide that a crude military response would only deepen animosities and make things worse?

So toward the end of my project I investigated Franklin County with a heightened sense of gravity and with much more urgency. If America was not firmly united in the early days of the conflict, we would certainly not be united later, when the going got tough.

"The People Versus the Powerful"

There are a couple of long-standing theories about why America is divided. One of the main ones holds that the division is along class lines, between the haves and the have-nots. This theory is popular chiefly on the left, and can be found in the pages of *The American Prospect* and other liberal magazines; in news reports by liberal journalists such as Donald L. Barlett and James B. Steele, of *Time;* and in books such as *Middle Class Dreams* (1995), by the Clinton and Gore pollster Stanley Greenberg, and *America's Forgotten Majority: Why the White Working Class Still Matters* (2000), by the demographer Ruy Teixeira and the social scientist Joel Rogers.

According to this theory, during most of the twentieth century gaps in income between the rich and the poor in America gradually shrank. Then came the information age. The rich started getting spectacularly richer, the poor started getting poorer, and wages for the middle class stagnated, at best. Over the previous decade, these writers emphasized, remuneration for top-level executives had skyrocketed: now the average CEO made 116 times as much as the average rank-and-file worker. Assembly-line workers found themselves competing for jobs against Third World workers who earned less than a dollar an hour. Those who had once labored at well-paying blue-collar jobs were forced to settle for poorly paying service-economy jobs without benefits.

People with graduate degrees have done well over the past couple of decades: their real hourly wages climbed by 13 percent from 1979 to 1997, according to Teixeira and Rogers. But those with only some college education saw their wages fall by nine percent, while those with only high school diplomas saw their wages fall by 12 percent, and high school dropouts saw a stunning 26 percent decline in their pay.

Such trends have created a new working class, these writers argue—not a traditional factory-and-mill working class but a suburban and small-town working class, made up largely of service workers and low-level white-collar employees. Teixeira and Rogers estimate that the average household income for this group, which accounts for about 55 percent of American adults, is roughly $42,000. "It is not hard to imagine how [recent economic trends] must have felt to the forgotten majority man," they write.

As at least part of America was becoming ever more affluent, an affluence that was well covered on television and in the evening news, he did not seem to be making much progress. What could he be doing wrong to be faring so poorly? Why couldn't he afford what others could? And why were they moving ahead while he was standing still?

Stanley Greenberg tailored Al Gore's presidential campaign to appeal to such voters. Gore's most significant slogan was "The People Versus the Powerful," which was meant to rally members of the middle class who felt threatened by "powerful forces" beyond their control, such as HMOs, tobacco companies, big corporations, and globalization, and to channel their resentment against the upper class. Gore dressed down throughout his campaign in the hope that these middle-class workers would identify with him.

Driving from Bethesda to Franklin County, one can see that the theory of a divide between the classes has a certain plausibility. In Montgomery County we have Saks Fifth Avenue, Cartier, Anthropologie, Brooks Brothers. In Franklin County they have Dollar General and Value City, along with a plethora of secondhand stores. It's as if Franklin County has only forty-five coffee tables, which are sold again and again.

When the locals are asked about their economy, they tell a story very similar to the one that Greenberg, Teixeira, Rogers, and the rest of the wage-stagnation liberals recount. There used to be plenty of good factory jobs in Franklin County, and people could work at those factories for life. But some of the businesses, including the textile company J. Schoeneman, once Franklin County's largest manufacturer, have closed. Others have moved offshore. The remaining manufacturers, such as Grove Worldwide and JLG Industries, which both make cranes and aerial platforms, have laid off workers. The local Army depot, Letterkenny, has radically shrunk its work force. The new jobs are in distribution centers or nursing homes. People tend to repeat the same phrase: "We've taken some hits."

And yet when they are asked about the broader theory, whether there is class conflict between the educated affluents and the stagnant middles, they stare blankly as if suddenly the interview were being conducted in Aramaic. I kept asking, Do you feel that the highly educated people around, say, New York and Washington are getting all the goodies? Do you think there is resentment toward all the latte sippers who shop at Nieman Marcus? Do you see a gulf between high-income people in the big cities and middle-income people here? I got only polite, fumbling answers as people tried to figure out what the hell I was talking about.

When I rephrased the question in more-general terms, as Do you believe the country is divided between the haves and the have-nots?, everyone responded decisively: yes. But as the conversation continued, it became clear that the people saying yes did not consider themselves to be among the have-nots. Even people with incomes well below the median thought of themselves as haves.

What I found was entirely consistent with the election returns from November of last year. Gore's pitch failed miserably among the voters it was intended to target: nationally he lost among non-college-educated white voters by 17 points and among non-college-educated white men by 29 points. But it worked beautifully on the affluent, educated class: for example, Gore won among women with graduate degrees by 22 points. The lesson seems to be that if you run a campaign under the slogan "The People Versus the Powerful," you will not do well in the places where "the people" live, but you will do fantastically well in the places where "the powerful" live. This phenomenon mirrors, on a larger scale, one I noted a couple of years ago, when I traveled the country for a year talking about *Bobos in Paradise*, a book I had written on upscale America. The richer the community, the more likely I was to be asked about wage inequality. In middle-class communities the subject almost never came up.

Why does the theme of class divisions and power inequality appeal so much more to people in Blue America?

Hanging around Franklin County, one begins to understand some of the reasons that people there don't spend much time worrying about economic class lines. The first and most obvious one is that although the incomes in Franklin County are lower than those in Montgomery County, living expenses are also lower—very much so. Driving from Montgomery County to Franklin County is like driving through an invisible deflation machine. Gas is thirty, forty, or even fifty cents a gallon cheaper in Franklin County. I parked at meters that accepted only pennies and nickels. When I got a parking ticket in Chambersburg, the fine was $3.00. At the department store in Greencastle there were racks and racks of blouses for $9.99.

The biggest difference is in real-estate prices. In Franklin County one can buy a nice four-bedroom split-level house with about 2,200 square feet of living space for $150,000 to $180,000. In Bethesda that same house would cost about $450,000. (According to the Coldwell Banker Real Estate Corporation, that house would sell for $784,000 in Greenwich, Connecticut; for $812,000 in Manhattan Beach, California; and for about $1.23 million in Palo Alto, California.)

Some of the people I met in Franklin County were just getting by. Some were in debt and couldn't afford to buy their kids the Christmas presents they wanted to. But I didn't find many who assessed their own place in society according to their income. Rather, the people I met commonly told me that although those in affluent places like Manhattan and Bethesda might make more money and have more-exciting jobs, they are the unlucky ones, because they don't get to live in Franklin County. They don't get to enjoy the beautiful green hillsides, the friendly people, the wonderful church groups and volunteer organizations. They may be nice people and all, but they are certainly not as happy as we are.

Another thing I found is that most people don't think sociologically. They don't compare themselves with faraway millionaires who appear on their TV screens. They compare themselves with their neighbors. "One of the challenges we face is that it is hard to get people to look beyond the four-state region," Lynne Woehrle, a sociologist at Wilson College, in Chambersburg, told me, referring to the cultural zone composed of the nearby rural areas in Pennsylvania, West Virginia, Maryland, and Virginia. Many of the people in Franklin County view the lifestyles of the upper class in California or Seattle much the way we in Blue America might view the lifestyle of someone in Eritrea or Mongolia—or, for that matter, Butte, Montana. Such ways of life are distant and basically irrelevant, except as a source of academic interest or titillation. One man in Mercersburg, Pennsylvania, told me about a friend who had recently bought a car. "He paid twenty-five thousand dollars for that car!" he exclaimed, his eyes wide with amazement. "He got it fully loaded." I didn't tell him that in Bethesda almost no one but a college kid pays as little as $25,000 for a car.

Franklin County is a world in which there is little obvious inequality, and the standard of living is reasonably comfortable. Youth-soccer teams are able to raise money for a summer trip to England; the Lowe's hardware superstore carries Laura Ashley carpets; many people have pools, although they are almost always above ground; the planning commission has to cope with an increasing number of cars in the county every year, even though the population is growing only gradually. But the sort of high-end experiences that are everywhere in Montgomery County are entirely missing here.

On my journeys to Franklin County, I set a goal: I was going to spend $20 on a restaurant meal. But although I ordered the most expensive thing on the menu—steak au jus, "slippery beef pot pie," or whatever—I always failed. I began asking people to direct me to the most-expensive places in town. They would send me to Red Lobster or Applebee's. I'd go into a restaurant that looked from the outside as if it had some pretensions—maybe a "Les Desserts" glass cooler for the key-lime pie and the tapioca pudding. I'd scan the menu and realize that I'd been beaten once again. I went through great vats of chipped beef and "seafood delight" trying to drop twenty dollars. I waded through enough surf-and-turfs and enough creamed corn to last a lifetime. I could not do it.

No wonder people in Franklin County have no class resentment or class consciousness; where they live, they can afford just about anything that is for sale. (In Montgomery County, however—and this is one of the most striking contrasts between the two counties—almost nobody can say that. In Blue America, unless you are very, very rich, there is always, all around you, stuff for sale that you cannot afford.) And if they sought to improve their situation, they would look only to themselves. If a person wants to make more money, the feeling goes, he or she had better work hard and think like an entrepreneur.

I could barely get fifteen minutes into an interview before the local work ethic came up. Karen Jewell, who helps to oversee the continuing-education program for the local Penn State branch campus, told me, "People are very vested in what they do. There's an awareness of where they fit in the organization. They feel empowered to be agents of change."

People do work extremely hard in Franklin County—even people in supposedly dead-end jobs. You can see it in little things, such as drugstore shelves. The drugstores in Bethesda look the way Rome must have looked after a visit from the Visigoths. But in Franklin County the boxes are in perfect little rows. Shelves are fully stocked, and cans are evenly spaced. The floors are less dusty than those in a microchip-processing plant. The nail clippers on a rack by the cash register are arranged with a precision that would put the Swiss to shame.

There are few unions in Franklin County. People abhor the thought of depending on welfare; they consider themselves masters of their own economic fate. "People are really into the free market here," Bill Pukmel, formerly the editor of the weekly paper in Chambersburg, told me.

In sum, I found absolutely no evidence that a Stanley Greenberg–prompted Democratic Party (or a Pat Buchanan–led Republican Party) could mobilize white middle-class Americans on the basis of class consciousness. I found no evidence that economic differences explain much of anything about the divide between Red and Blue America.

Ted Hale, a Presbyterian minister in the western part of the county, spoke of the matter this way: "There's nowhere near as much resentment as you would expect. People have come to understand that they will struggle financially. It's part of their identity. But the economy is not their god. That's the thing some others don't understand. People value a sense of community far more than they do their portfolio." Hale, who worked at a church in East Hampton, New York, before coming to Franklin County, said that he saw a lot more economic resentment in New York.

Hale's observations are supported by nationwide polling data. Pew has conducted a broad survey of the differences between Red and Blue states. The survey found that views on economic issues do not explain the different voting habits in the two regions. There simply isn't much of the sort of economic dissatisfaction that could drive a class-based political movement. Eighty-five percent of Americans with an annual household income between $30,000 and $50,000 are satisfied with their housing. Nearly 70 percent are satisfied with the kind of car they can afford. Roughly two thirds are satisfied with their furniture and their ability to afford a night out. These levels of satisfaction are not very different from those found in upper-middle-class America.

The Pew researchers found this sort of trend in question after question. Part of the draft of their report is titled "Economic Divide Dissolves."

A Lot of Religion but Few Crusaders

This leaves us with the second major hypothesis about the nature of the divide between Red and Blue America, which comes mainly from conservatives: America is divided between two moral systems. Red America is traditional, religious, self-disciplined, and patriotic. Blue America is modern, secular, self-expressive, and discomfited by blatant displays of patriotism. Proponents of this hypothesis in its most radical form contend that America is in the midst of a culture war, with two opposing armies fighting on behalf of their views. The historian Gertrude

Himmelfarb offered a more moderate picture in *One Nation, Two Cultures* (1999), in which she argued that although America is not fatally split, it is deeply divided, between a heartland conservative population that adheres to a strict morality and a liberal population that lives by a loose one. The political journalist Michael Barone put it this way in a recent essay in *National Journal:* "The two Americas apparent in the 48 percent to 48 percent 2000 election are two nations of different faiths. One is observant, tradition-minded, moralistic. The other is unobservant, liberation-minded, relativistic."

> What does it mean to say that Red America is "observant, tradition-minded, moralistic," while Blue America is "unobservant, liberation-minded, relativistic"? Why is the first more drawn to the Republican Party and the second to the Democrats?

The values-divide school has a fair bit of statistical evidence on its side. Whereas income is a poor predictor of voting patterns, church attendance—as Barone points out—is a pretty good one. Of those who attend religious services weekly (42 percent of the electorate), 59 percent voted for Bush, 39 percent for Gore. Of those who seldom or never attend religious services (another 42 percent), 56 percent voted for Gore, 39 percent for Bush.

The Pew data reveal significant divides on at least a few values issues. Take, for example, the statement "We will all be called before God on Judgment Day to answer for our sins." In Red states 70 percent of the people believe that statement. In Blue states only 50 percent do.

One can feel the religiosity in Franklin County after a single day's visit. It's on the bumper stickers: WARNING: IN CASE OF RAPTURE THIS VEHICLE WILL BE UNMANNED. REAL TRUCKERS TALK ABOUT JESUS ON CHANNEL 10. It's on the radio. The airwaves are filled not with the usual mixture of hit tunes but with evangelicals preaching the gospel. The book section of Wal-Mart features titles such as *The Beginner's Guide to Fasting, Deepen Your Conversation with God,* and *Are We Living in the End Times?* Some general stores carry the "Heroes of the Faith" series, which consists of small biographies of William Carey, George Müller, and other notable missionaries, ministers, and theologians—notable in Red America, that is, but largely unknown where I live.

Chambersburg and its vicinity have eighty-five churches and one synagogue. The Bethesda–Chevy Chase area, which has a vastly greater population, has forty-five churches and five synagogues. Professors at the local college in Chambersburg have learned not to schedule public lectures on Wednesday nights, because everybody is at prayer meetings.

Events that are part of daily life in Franklin County are unheard of in most of Blue America. One United Brethren minister told me that he is asked to talk about morals in the public school as part of the health and sex-education curriculum, and nobody raises a fuss. A number of schools have a "Bible release program," whereby elementary school students are allowed to leave school for an hour a week to attend Bible-study meetings. At an elementary school in Waynesboro the Gideons used to distribute Bibles to any students who wanted them. (That ended after the village agnostic threatened to simultaneously distribute a booklet called *God Is Just Pretend*.)

There are healing ministries all throughout Franklin County, and even mainstream denominations have healing teams on hand after Sunday services. As in most places where evangelism is strong, the locals are fervently pro-Israel. Almost every minister I visited has mementos in his study from visits to Jerusalem. A few had lived in Israel for extended periods and spoke Hebrew. One delivered a tirade against CNN for its bias against the Jewish state. One or two pointed out (without quite bragging) that whereas some Jewish groups had canceled trips to Israel since the upsurge in intifada violence, evangelical groups were still going.

David Rawley, a United Brethren minister in Greencastle, spoke for many of the social conservatives I met when he said that looking at the mainstream Hollywood culture made him feel that he was "walking against the current." "The tremendous force of culture means we can either float or fight," Rawley said. "Should you drift or stand on a rock? I tell people there is a rock we can hang on—the word of God. That rock will never give way. That rock's never going to move." When I asked Rawley what he thought of big-city culture, he said, "The individual is swallowed up by the largeness of the city. I see a world that doesn't want to take responsibility for itself. They have the babies but they decide they're not going to be the daddies. I'd really have to cling to the rock if I lived there."

I met with Rawley at the height of the scandal involving Representative Gary Condit and the missing intern Chandra Levy. Levy's mother was quoted in *The Washington Times* as calling herself a "Heinz 57 mutt" when it came to religion. "All religions tie to similar beliefs," she said. "I believe in spirituality and God. I'm Jewish. I think we have a wonderful religion. I'm also Christian. I do believe in Jesus, too." The contrast between her New Age approach to spirituality and Rawley's Red America one could not have been greater.

Life is complicated, however. Yes, there are a lot of churches in Franklin County; there are also a lot of tattoo parlors. And despite all the churches and bumper stickers, Franklin County doesn't seem much different from anywhere else. People go to a few local bars to hang out after softball games. Teenagers drive recklessly along fast-food strips. Young women in halter tops sometimes prowl in the pool halls. The local college has a gay-and-lesbian group. One conservative clergyman I spoke with estimated that 10 percent of his congregants are gay. He believes that church is the place where one should be able to leave the controversy surrounding this sort of issue behind. Another described how his congregation united behind a young man who was dying of AIDS.

Sex seems to be on people's minds almost as much as it is anywhere else.

Conservative evangelical circles have their own sex manuals (Tim LaHaye wrote one of them before he moved on to the "Left Behind" series), which appear to have had some effect: according to a 1994 study conducted by researchers at the University of Chicago, conservative Protestant women have more orgasms than any other group.

Franklin County is probably a bit more wholesome than most suburbs in Blue America. (The notion that deviance and corruption lie underneath the seeming conformism of suburban middle-class life, popular in Hollywood and in creative-writing workshops, is largely nonsense.) But it has most of the problems that afflict other parts of the country: heroin addiction, teen pregnancy, and so on. Nobody I spoke to felt part of a pristine culture that is exempt from the problems of the big cities. There are even enough spectacular crimes in Franklin County to make a devoted *New York Post* reader happy. During one of my visits the front pages of the local papers were ablaze with the tale of a young woman arrested for assault and homicide after shooting her way through a Veterans of the Vietnam War post. It was reported that she had intended to rob the post for money to run away with her lesbian girlfriend.

If the problems are the same as in the rest of America, so are many of the solutions. Franklin County residents who find themselves in trouble go to their clergy first, but they are often referred to psychologists and therapists as part of their recovery process. Prozac is a part of life.

Almost nobody I spoke with understood, let alone embraced, the concept of a culture war. Few could see themselves as fighting such a war, in part because few have any idea where the boundary between the two sides lies. People in Franklin County may have a clear sense of what constitutes good or evil (many people in Blue America have trouble with the very concept of evil), but they will say that good and evil are in all neighborhoods, as they are in all of us. People take the Scriptures seriously but have no interest in imposing them on others. One finds little crusader zeal in Franklin County. For one thing, people in small towns don't want to offend people whom they'll be encountering on the street for the next fifty years. Potentially controversial subjects are often played down. "We would never take a stance on gun control or abortion," Sue Hadden, the editor of the Waynesboro paper, told me. Whenever I asked what the local view of abortion was, I got the same response: "We don't talk about it much," or "We try to avoid that subject." Bill Pukmel, the former Chambersburg newspaper editor, says, "A majority would be opposed to abortion around here but it wouldn't be a big majority." It would simply be uncivil to thrust such a raw disagreement in people's faces.

William Harter, a Presbyterian minister in Chambersburg, spans the divide between Red and Blue America. Harter was raised on a farm near Buffalo. He went to the prestigious Deerfield Academy, in Massachusetts, before getting a bachelor's degree in history from Williams College, a master's in education from Harvard, and, after serving for a while in the military, a Ph.D. in Judaism and Christian origins from the Union Theological Seminary, in Manhattan. He has lived in Chambersburg for the past twenty-four years, and he says that the range of opinion in Franklin County is much wider than it was in Cambridge or New York. "We're more authentically pluralistic here," he told me.

I found Harter and the other preachers in Franklin County especially interesting to talk with. That was in part because the ones I met were fiercely intelligent and extremely well read, but also because I could see them wrestling with the problem of how to live according to the Scriptures while being inclusive and respectful of others' freedoms. For example, many of them struggle over whether it is right to marry a couple who are already living together. This would not be a consideration in most of Blue America.

"Some of the evangelicals won't marry [such couples]," Harter told me. "Others will insist that they live apart for six months before they'll marry them. But that's not the real world. These couples often don't understand the theological basis for not living together. Even if you don't condone their situations, you have to start where they are—help them have loyal marriages."

Divorce is tolerated much more than it used to be. And none of the ministers I spoke with said that they would condemn a parishioner who was having an affair. They would confront the parishioner, but with the goal of gently bringing that person back to Jesus Christ. "How could I love that person if I didn't?" Patrick Jones, of the United Brethren's King Street Church, in Chambersburg, asked. People in Franklin County are contemptuous of Bill Clinton and his serial infidelities, but they are not necessarily fans of Kenneth Starr—at least not the Kenneth Starr the media portrayed. They don't like public scolds.

Roger Murray, a Pentecostal minister in Mercersburg, whose father was also a Pentecostal minister, exemplifies the way in which many church authorities are torn by the sometimes conflicting desires to uphold authority and respect personal freedom. "My father would preach about what you could do and what you couldn't do," Murray recalls. "He would preach about smoking, about TV, about ladies who dress provocatively, against divorce." As a boy, Murray used to go visit his uncle, and he would sit in another room when his uncle's family watched television. "I was sure they were going to hell," he told me. But now he would never dream of telling people how to live. For one thing, his congregants wouldn't defer. And he is in no rush to condemn others. "I don't think preaching against homosexuality is what you should do," he told me. "A positive message works better."

Like most of the people I met in Franklin County, Murray regards such culture warriors as Jerry Falwell and Pat Robertson as loose cannons, and televangelists as being far too interested in raising money. "I get pretty disgusted with Christian TV," he said. And that was before Falwell and Robertson made their notorious comments about the attacks of September 11 being a judgment from God. When I asked locals about those remarks, they answered with words like "disgusting," "horrendous," and "horrible." Almost no one in the county voted for Pat Buchanan; he was simply too contentious.

Certainly Red and Blue America disagree strongly on some issues, such as homosexuality and abortion. But for the most part the disagreements are not large.

For example, the Pew researchers asked Americans to respond to the statement "There are clear guidelines about what's good or evil that apply to everyone regardless of their situation." Forty-three percent of people in Blue states and 49 percent of people in Red states agreed. Forty-seven percent of Blue America and 55 percent of Red America agreed with the statement "I have old-fashioned values about family and marriage." Seventy percent of the people in Blue states and 77 percent of the people in Red states agreed that "too many children are being raised in day-care centers these days." These are small gaps. And, the Pew researchers found, there is no culture gap at all among suburban voters. In a Red state like Arizona suburban voters' opinions are not much different from those in a Blue state like Connecticut. The starkest differences that exist are between people in cities and people in rural areas, especially rural areas in the South.

The conservatism I found in Franklin County is not an ideological or a reactionary conservatism. It is a temperamental conservatism. People place tremendous value on being agreeable, civil, and kind. They are happy to sit quietly with one another. They are hesitant to stir one another's passions. They appreciate what they have. They value continuity and revere the past. They work hard to reinforce community bonds. Their newspapers are filled with items about fundraising drives, car washes, bake sales, penny-collection efforts, and auxiliary thrift shops. Their streets are lined with lodges: VFW, Rotarians, Elks, Moose. Luncheons go on everywhere. Retired federal employees will be holding their weekly luncheon at one restaurant, Harley riders at another. I became fascinated by a group called the Tuscarora Longbeards, a local chapter of something called the National Wild Turkey Federation. The Longbeards go around to schools distributing Wild About Turkey Education boxes, which contain posters, lesson plans, and CD-ROMs on turkey preservation.

These are the sorts of things that really mobilize people in Franklin County. Building community and preserving local ways are far more important to them than any culture war.

The Ego Curtain

The best explanation of the differences between people in Montgomery and Franklin Counties has to do with sensibility, not class or culture. If I had to describe the differences between the two sensibilities in a single phrase, it would be conception of the self. In Red America the self is small. People declare in a million ways, "I am normal. Nobody is better, nobody is worse. I am humble before God." In Blue America the self is more commonly large. People say in a million ways, "I am special. I have carved out my own unique way of life. I am independent. I make up my own mind."

In Red America there is very little one-upmanship. Nobody tries to be avant-garde in choosing a wardrobe. The chocolate-brown suits and baggy denim dresses hanging in local department stores aren't there by accident; people conspicuously want to be seen as not trying to dress to impress.

For a person in Blue America the blandness in Red America can be a little oppressive. But it's hard not to be struck by the enormous social pressure not to put on airs. If a Franklin County resident drove up to church one day in a shiny new Lexus, he would face huge waves of disapproval. If one hired a nanny, people would wonder who died and made her queen.

In Franklin County people don't go looking for obscure beers to demonstrate their connoisseurship. They wear T-shirts and caps with big-brand names on them—Coke, McDonald's, Chevrolet. In Bethesda people prefer cognoscenti brands—the Black Dog restaurant, or the independent bookstore Politics and Prose. In Franklin County it would be an affront to the egalitarian ethos to put a Princeton sticker on the rear window of one's car. In Montgomery County some proud parents can barely see through their back windows for all the Ivy League stickers. People in Franklin County say they felt comfortable voting for Bush, because if he came to town he wouldn't act superior to anybody else; he could settle into a barber's chair and fit right in. They couldn't stand Al Gore, because they thought he'd always be trying to awe everyone with his accomplishments. People in Montgomery County tended to admire Gore's accomplishments. They were leery of Bush, because for most of his life he seemed not to have achieved anything.

I sometimes think that Franklin County takes its unpretentiousness a little too far. I wouldn't care to live there, because I'd find it too unchanging. I prefer the subtle and not-so-subtle status climbing on my side of the Ego Curtain—it's more entertaining. Still, I can't help respecting the genuine modesty of Franklin County people. It shows up strikingly in data collected by Mediamark Research. In survey after survey, residents of conservative Red America come across as humbler than residents of liberal Blue America. About half of those who describe themselves as "very conservative" agree with the statement "I have more ability than most people," but nearly two thirds of those who describe themselves as "very liberal" agree. Only 53 percent of conservatives agree with the statement "I consider myself an intellectual," but 75 percent of liberals do. Only 23 percent of conservatives agree with the statement "I must admit that I like to show off," whereas 43 percent of liberals do.

A Cafeteria Nation

These differences in sensibility don't in themselves mean that America has become a fundamentally divided nation. As the sociologist Seymour Martin Lipset pointed out in *The First New Nation* (1963), achievement and equality are the two rival themes running throughout American history. Most people, most places, and most epochs have tried to intertwine them in some way.

Moreover, after bouncing between Montgomery and Franklin Counties, I became convinced that a lot of our fear that America is split into rival camps arises from mistaken notions of how society is shaped. Some of us still carry the old Marxist categories in our heads. We think that society is like a layer cake, with the upper class on top. And, like Marx, we tend to assume that wherever there is class division there is conflict. Or else we have a sort of *Crossfire* model in our heads: where would people we meet sit if they were guests on that show?

But traveling back and forth between the two counties was not like crossing from one rival camp to another. It was like crossing a high school cafeteria. Remember high school? There were nerds, jocks, punks, bikers, techies, druggies, God Squadders, drama geeks, poets, and Dungeons & Dragons weirdoes. All these cliques were part of the same school: they had different sensibilities; sometimes they knew very little about the people in the other cliques; but the jocks knew there would always be nerds, and the nerds knew there would always be jocks. That's just the way life is.

And that's the way America is. We are not a divided nation. We are a cafeteria nation. We form cliques (call them communities, or market segments, or whatever), and when they get too big, we form subcliques. Some people even get together in churches that are "nondenominational" or in political groups that are "independent." These are cliques built around the supposed rejection of cliques.

We live our lives by migrating through the many different cliques associated with the activities we enjoy and the goals we have set for ourselves. Our freedom comes in the interstices; we can choose which set of standards to live by, and when.

We should remember that there is generally some distance between cliques—a buffer zone that separates one set of aspirations from another. People who are happy within their cliques feel no great compulsion to go out and reform other cliques. The jocks don't try to change the nerds. David Rawley, the Greencastle minister who felt he was clinging to a rock, has been to New York City only once in his life. "I was happy to get back home," he told me. "It's a planet I'm a little scared of. I have no desire to go back."

What unites the two Americas, then, is our mutual commitment to this way of life—to the idea that a person is not bound by his class, or by the religion of his fathers, but is free to build a plurality of connections for himself. We are participants in the same striving process, the same experimental journey.

Never has this been more apparent than in the weeks following the September 11 attacks. Before then Montgomery County people and Franklin County people gave little thought to one another: an attitude of benign neglect toward other parts of the country generally prevailed. But the events of that day generated what one of my lunch mates in Franklin County called a primal response. Our homeland was under attack. Suddenly there was a positive sense that we Americans are all bound together—a sense that, despite some little fissures here and there, has endured.

On September 11 people in Franklin County flocked to the institutions that are so strong there—the churches and the American Legion and the VFW posts. Houses of worship held spontaneous prayer services and large ecumenical services. In the weeks since, firemen, veterans, and Scouts have held rallies. There have been blood drives. Just about every service organization in the county—and there are apparently thousands—has mobilized to raise funds or ship teddy bears. The rescue squad and the Salvation Army branch went to New York to help.

Early every morning Ted Hale, the Presbyterian minister who once worked in East Hampton, goes to one of the local restaurants and sits as the regulars cycle through. One of the things that has struck him since the attacks is how little partisan feeling is left. "I expected to hear a certain amount of Clinton bashing, for creating the mess in which this could take place," he told me in October. "But there's been absolutely none of that." Instead Hale has been deluged with questions—about Islam, about why God restrains himself in the face of evil, about how people could commit such acts.

The area's churches have not been monolithic in their responses. Many of the most conservative churches—the Mennonites and the Brethren, for example—have pacifist traditions. Bill Harter, in contrast, told his congregation during a recent sermon that the pacifist course is not the right one. "We must face the fact that there is a power of evil loose in the universe, which is dedicated to attacking all that is good, all that comes from God," he said. This evil, Harter continued, has cloaked itself in a perverted form of one of the world's major faiths. Citing the Protestant theologian Reinhold Niebuhr, he reminded his congregants that there is no sinless way to defend ourselves against this hostile ideology. But defend we must. "We must humbly make our choice while recognizing that we must constantly turn to God for forgiveness," he told them.

The churches and synagogues in Bethesda, too, have been struggling. Over the Jewish High Holy Days, I heard of three synagogues in which the sermon was interrupted by a member of the congregation. In one instance the rabbi had said that it is always impossible to know where good and evil lie. A man rose up angrily to declare that in this case that sentiment was nonsense.

Most people in my part of Blue America know few who will be called on to fight in the war. In Franklin County military service is common. Many families have an enlisted son or daughter, and many more have a relative in the reserves or the National Guard. Franklin County is engaged in an urgent discussion, largely absent where I live, about how to fill in for the reservists called up for active duty.

Still, there's an attitude of determination in both places. If I had to boil down all the conversations I have had in Franklin and Montgomery Counties since September 11, the essence would be this: A horrible thing happened. We're going to deal with it. We're going to restore order. We got through Pearl Harbor. We're going to get through this. "There is no flaccidity," Harter observed, in words that apply to both communities.

If the September 11 attacks rallied people in both Red and Blue America, they also neutralized the political and cultural leaders who tend to exploit the differences between the two. Americans are in no mood for a class struggle or a culture war. The aftermath of the attacks has been a bit like a national Sabbath, taking us out of our usual pleasures and distractions and reminding us what is really important Over time the shock will dissipate. But in important ways the psychological effects will linger, just as the effects of John F. Kennedy's assassination have lingered. The early evidence still holds: although there are some real differences between Red and Blue America, there is no fundamental conflict. There may be cracks, but there is no chasm. Rather, there is a common love for this nation—one nation in the end.

Consider the source and the audience.

- Brooks is writing in the *Atlantic Monthly,* a magazine that appeals to intellectuals. Who is his audience? Who is he trying to explain to whom? How might that effort affect how he frames the story and builds his argument?

Lay out the argument, the values, and the assumptions.

- Brooks himself is a member of Blue America. What are his values likely to be?
- How does he describe the characteristics of each culture? What are the main dimensions (e.g., ethnicity, education) he looks at? Can he give a fair description of Red America? Is he fair to his own part of the country?
- What are the two major hypotheses that Brooks considers in his effort to answer the question of whether we are a common people and what kinds of differences divide us?
- What is his final answer to this question? What accounts for the differences? Are we one nation or two?

Uncover the evidence.

- Brooks uses several kinds of evidence to draw his portraits of Red and Blue American culture. Does the generality of the demographic statistics and public opinion data he cites offset the limitations of using anecdotal evidence from one "Red county" in a Blue state? Could he have written this article with just one type of evidence or the other?
- What kinds of evidence does he use to support his claim that there is an "ego curtain" between the two cultures? On what basis does he ground his claim that we are a "cafeteria nation"?

Evaluate the conclusion.

- Does people's sense of "ego" play as large a role as Brooks says? How is this issue related to his "headroom" argument about what divides people in Blue America from each other?
- Does the existence of so many wealthy educated Republicans and so many poor uneducated Democrats weaken his theory, or can he account for them?
- What are the differences between being a divided nation and being a "cafeteria nation?"

Sort out the political implications.

- Brooks explains why he thought Bush appealed to Red America and Gore to Blue America. If you were a consultant for a Democratic candidate, what advice would you give him or her to do well in the Red states? How did Clinton manage it? What would you tell a Republican to do to succeed in the Blue states?

2.3 Life, Liberty and the Pursuit of Division

Anatole Kaletsky, *London Times,* 4 July 2002

David Brooks' analysis of Red and Blue America in the previous article concluded that there are deep divisions in American culture, but none so serious that they can't be bridged by a stroll across the cafeteria to visit the clique at the other table. Writing in the *London Times,* Anatole Kaletsky takes a more serious view of the cultural split in America. Asking a different question, why it is that Europe has such a love-hate relationship with the United States, he sees this cultural split as the result of an enduring division between two Americas—one lovable, one not. Why does he come to such different conclusions than Brooks? What are the advantages and disadvantages of seeing ourselves as others see us?

Today America marks its first Independence Day since September 11. Americans will celebrate their new-found sense of national unity and purpose. Yet beneath the patriotic pride, there will be a sense of unease and foreboding—and not just about the risk of another terrorist attack, or the slump on Wall Street, or the chances of another Enron or WorldCom.

To judge from my recent visits there, many Americans will be asking themselves why the world seems to dislike their country. The easiest way to answer this question is simply to point out how much the world loves America—how many people want to live there, to buy American goods, to watch American films and so on. But this doesn't deal with the problem of anti-Americanism, which has always been in essence a love-hate relationship.

How, then, can one account for the world's love-hate relationship with America? Obviously there are economic forces—envy and admiration—tugging in opposite directions. There are also genuine differences in the perception of national interest. American politicians and the vast majority of voters seem to believe that they must support the Israeli Government, come hell or high water, regardless of how irresponsibly it behaves. The rest of the world takes a very different view.

But there is another less familiar explanation for the love-hate relationship with America, especially in Europe. It is becoming more relevant by the day, as the gulf between the United States and Europe keeps widening. The European (and in this I include the British) attitude to America may be less contradictory than it seems. It is possible to admire America and simultaneously to hate it, without any contradiction. For America is now split so deeply and irreconcilably over almost every key issue of politics, lifestyle and culture that it is sometimes better to think of it as two distinct nations, rather than one.

The America that is feared, distrusted and increasingly disliked in the rest of the world, and especially in Europe, is the conservative country that constitutes George Bush's political heartland in Texas and the South—the America of

Kaletsky appears to see the choice in America as one between believing that one knows the absolute truth and believing that there are no such truths. Is there a position in between?

self-righteous Christian fundamentalists, of military machismo, of gun shops, lethal injections, anti-abortion zealots and gas-guzzling pickup trucks spewing out greenhouse gases. The America that Europeans find fascinating and beguiling, albeit a bit frightening because of its shifting moral compass, is the liberal US of Bill Clinton, centered on Hollywood, Manhattan and Silicon Valley.

Despite the appearance of unity after September 11, the gulf between the two Americas has never been deeper than it is today. This is shown by opinion polls on many divisive social issues, the almost unprecedented partisan discipline in Washington and the nervousness in the White House about November's congressional elections, which could well turn Mr. Bush, for all his apparent popularity, into a lame duck.

The origins of the great political divide seem to go back to the unresolved battles over culture and lifestyles that have obsessed Americans since the 1960s. William Schneider, a political analyst at the American Enterprise Institute, described this dichotomy in a brilliant article, "Politics Remains Stalemated," for the *Los Angeles Times:* "Europeans are often perplexed by the failure of Americans to get over the Sixties. After all, they too, were convulsed by great cultural changes during that decade. But only the US experienced a ferocious backlash against those changes, partly based on America's religious culture."

Bill Clinton was the first President to represent and embrace the counter-culture of the 1960s. That is why he was so deeply hated by the many Americans for whom this convulsive decade symbolised the start of a near-fatal national decadence, which Ronald Reagan managed to arrest in the nick of time. As Mr Schneider notes: "Conservatives never accepted Clinton as legitimate. To them, Clinton was the draft-dodger, the war protester, the womaniser, the truth-shader, the gun hater, the gay-protector, the non-inhaling drug fiend."

What exactly are the two visions of the American dream that Kaletsky sees? He describes them each in negative terms; how can they be framed more positively?

For these Clinton-hating Americans, George W. Bush represented a return to America's heyday in the 1950s. Having ousted the Democrat usurpers from the White House, the one thing they needed to complete the counter-revolution was some international challenge comparable to Eisenhower's Cold War.

The closeness of that election was one of the main reasons why America is becoming an even more divided country despite the unifying effect of September 11. The fact is that there is an almost perfect balance between the two opposing visions of the American dream. In terms of population, the two sides are equal, as demonstrated in the 2000 election and, despite the patriotic support for President Bush since September 11, the same split has persisted throughout this year in polling for November's congressional contests.

Thus it has been impossible for Americans to settle their ideological quarrels through the normal democratic process. Yet there is an ideological chasm between these apparently balanced sides: the big cities vote for the Democrats by a 70–30 margin and urban social attitudes are at least as liberal as they are in Europe, the suburbs and rural areas are as strongly Republican and conservative.

Slicing the country another way, the eastern and western seaboards are overwhelmingly liberal, while the interior of the US is more conservative than ever. This was why the election was so virulently adversarial, and simultaneously so inconclusive.

But the deepest and most worrying faultline across America is not connected with geography, domestic lifestyle or even social class. It is the religious split. Religion has become a crucial element in all American political battles, not only over abortion and sexual mores, but over such secular issues as taxation, foreign policy and global warming. And polling statistics show that the most important dividing lines are not between Protestants and Catholics or Christians and Jews. They are between religious Americans of all faiths and those who do not believe.

While the Republican Party had long been the political bastion of white Protestants, it now attracts a clear majority of the "more observant" voters from all religions, including Orthodox Jews. In the last election, the vote among "more observant" Catholics, defined as people who say they go to church once a week or more, went 57–43 per cent for Bush. Less observant Catholics voted 41–59 the other way. Among evangelic Protestants, the more observant supported Bush by an 84–16 margin, while the less observant were more evenly split at 55–45. The minority of Americans who describe themselves as "secular" voted for Gore by 65–35 per cent.

To put it another way, 54 per cent of Bush's voters were "more observant" Protestants or Catholics, while only 15 per cent were blacks, Hispanics or non-Christians. Gore's support had exactly the opposite composition: 51 per cent were black, Hispanic or non-Christian, while only 20 per cent were observant Protestants or Catholics.

The issues on which observant and non-observant Americans are most divided have nothing to do with economics or foreign policy. They are abortion, the environment and

> What's the connection here? Why would people who are more religious be against not only abortion but also environmental regulation, and gun control?

gun control. Yet the intense political allegiances and animosities created by these issues now dominate mainstream politics and determine America's stance on the worldliest of issues. Cutting taxation appeals to relatively rich Protestants. Steel tariffs appeal to observant Catholic trade unionists. Unstinting support for Israel appeals not only to orthodox Jews, but also to fundamentalist Christians.

I have heard Christian preachers on American radio saying that Israel was clearly in the right because God promised the whole of Palestine to the Jews and that fulfilment of the promise might bring forward the Second Coming of Christ.

Secular Europeans, whose pragmatic skepticism has been tempered in the furnaces of Hitler's and Stalin's dogmas, feel a certain chill when they see the poison of religious certainty seeping into the mainstream democratic politics of the world's sole nuclear superpower. And who can blame them, when the US President had the moral certitude to make the following statement at the West Point academy last month: "The 20th century ended with a single surviving model of human progress"? Maybe, but which America did he mean?

Consider the source and the audience.
- Kaletsky is writing for a British audience in the conservative *London Times.* He is trying to address the American question "Why do they hate us," but he is also speaking to Europeans who find themselves simultaneously admiring and fearing the United States. Does his perspective help or hinder his ability to understand the American character and the American dream?

Lay out the argument, the values, and the assumptions.
- Kaletsky sees the difference between what Brooks calls Red and Blue America as one between moral certainty and moral diversity. How does the European experience with people like Hitler and Stalin, who believed that they had a lock on the truth, affect the way they view those taking the moral absolutist position in America?
- According to Kaletsky, why were the 1960s so divisive in the United States? Why were they less critical in Europe?
- Does Kaletsky seem to believe that there is a single unifying American dream?

Uncover the evidence.
- Kaletsky makes some fairly broad and sweeping statements. How does he know they are true? What kind of evidence does he offer to convince his readers?
- Would Kaletsky's European audience be harder or easier to convince than an American audience? What cultural assumptions might Europeans bring to this article?

Evaluate the conclusion.
- Many people (including Brooks in the previous article) have documented the differences between the two Americas Kaletsky writes about. Is he correct in attributing Europe's ambivalence about America to that cultural divide? Can an American audience evaluate this conclusion? Why or why not?

Sort out the political implications.
- If Kaletsky's thesis is valid, is there a way for Europe and the United States to get along?
- How did the debates over the war on Iraq support or conflict with his thesis?

2.4 America Is a Class Act

The U.S. Regards Itself as the Ultimate Meritocracy, But Social Mobility Is as Feeble as Europe's—and Declining

Gary Younge, *Guardian,* 27 January 2003

Equality is an important component of the American dream. But equality can be defined in lots of ways, and Americans have always been more partial to the idea that we should provide citizens with equality of opportunity than that we should end up equal in any substantive sense. A commitment to equality of treatment usually prevails over the idea of equality of outcome. It is not surprising, then, that as a society we have so thoroughly rejected the idea of social class. Along with our founders we believe that people should get ahead on the strength of their own abilities and talents, not on the basis of who they know or who their parents are.

Writing in the British newspaper, the *Guardian,* Gary Younge claims that class plays a larger role in the United States than we think, and that we do not really have true equality of opportunity. As controversial as affirmative action is in American society, Younge implies that it will not rid us of the most insidious kind of inequality. Why would people reject a society where privilege and position are inherited by children from their parents? Why does such a society seem so incompatible with American ideals?

When Republican Senator Frank Murkowski was elected governor of Alaska in November it was his task to select his replacement in the US Senate. He scoured the state, and produced a list of 26 names, including the son of Alaska's other senator, Ted Stevens. In December, after careful consideration, he decided the best person for the job was . . . his daughter. "I felt the person I appoint should be someone who shares my basic philosophy, my values," said Murkowski as he named Lisa Murkowski as his successor. "Your mother and I are very proud."

Frank Murkowski is a principled opponent of affirmative action, with a voting record to prove it. Like most Republicans, he believes there is no need to address inequities based on race and ethnicity. Like most right-minded people, he believes the best person should get the job. In the case of Alaska's seat in the US Senate, that person just happened to be his own daughter.

With the supreme court hearing on the University of Michigan's admissions policies about to begin, the US right once again hopes to eliminate affirmative action from the political landscape. The contentious nature of their efforts can be gauged by the fact that an administration which has maintained public unity on everything from lifting taxes on the rich to dropping bombs on the poor, has been openly split on this issue.

Last week the White House filed papers with the supreme court urging the judges to find against the university, which awards extra points to black, Hispanic and Native American applicants in its scoring system for entry.

Bush spoke out against college admissions policies that "unfairly reward or penalise prospective students based solely on their race." His national security adviser, Condoleezza Rice, backed him, but went on to insist that race should be taken into consideration. And then secretary of state Colin Powell completely disagreed.

Despite the confusion coming from Washington, the case for affirmative action on racial grounds in the US is not difficult to grasp. Just start at the point where settlers stole the entire country from Native Americans, then work your way up through slavery to the end of segregation, less than 40 years ago. Then ask yourself whether that was wrong, what must be done to make it right and whether, having suffered the last few centuries, people should have to wait a few more for the wrongs to be righted.

The narratives for affirmative action based on gender and ethnicity are all different, but the plot endings are the same—redressing historical imbalances. Bitter experience shows us that time and tide will not do it alone. The number of women in the UK parliament shot up by 172% in 1997 thanks to women-only shortlists in the Labour party. It virtually stalled in 2001 after those shortlists were outlawed. Similarly, California banned affirmative action in 1996. By 2001, black undergraduate enrolment had dropped by 33%. Concerns that the best people should get the job are valid. But they make the case for affirmative action, not against it—unless, that is, you believe that the best people these last few centuries have consistently been wealthy, white men. It is not, as the plaintiffs in the Michigan case claim, about "reverse discrimination," but reversing discrimination.

Why is it that without policies of affirmative action, white males are the ones who tend to be most successful in American society? Are they naturally better qualified?

But while the debate has focused around race, at its heart lies the very concept on which the American dream was built—meritocracy. And underlying that stands the very issue in which American political culture remains in denial—class.

"Class," claims African-American intellectual Bell Hooks, "is the elephant in the room . . . as a nation we are afraid to have a dialogue about class."

There is a good reason for this. America prides itself on being a country where anyone who works hard enough can make it—a nation of taut bootstraps and rugged individualism.

Reality in the last half century has been quite different. America has a better attitude towards class than Britain. But that's not saying much. Britain is the home of genetic privilege, where the head of state—the Queen—simply inherits the job. Nor is class as socially and culturally constructed here as it is in Britain, where everything from accents to dress codes mark out status and a peevish resentment attaches itself to anyone regarded as too openly ambitious.

But that doesn't mean that class does not exist. No one here would deny that there is inequality. How could they in a country where one child in six is officially poor, and 1% of the country owns one-third of the national net worth?

But that inequality of wealth is justified on the grounds that there is equality of opportunity. Were that true, it would be debatable. The fact that it is patently not true makes it deplorable.

A recent study here showed that social mobility in America is actually decreasing. Comparing the incomes and occupations of 2,749 fathers and sons from the 1970s to the 1990s, it was found that mobility had decreased. "In the last 25 years, a large segment of American society has become more vulnerable," says Professor Robert Perrucci of Purdue University.

> What does Younge mean here when he says that social mobility is decreasing? Are new generations of Americans today not doing better than their parents?

"The cumulative evidence since the second world war is that measured mobility in the US is little different from Europe's, despite all the propaganda," writes Will Hutton in *The World We're In.*

The problem with affirmative action as currently applied, is not that it applies to race, but that it does not also apply more comprehensively to class as well. For it is in addressing the plight of the poor, white or black, that America can honestly examine its own self-image. So long as those who wish to have an honest debate about equal opportunities confine themselves to race, they will only understand inequality as an aberration in the normal order of things. Only once they wed it to class does it become a systemic flaw which underpins the order of things.

If the poor have serious problems progressing, the rich seem to have none in storming ahead. According to *Fortune* magazine, the average real annual compensation for the top 100 CEOs in America went from Dollars 1.3m in 1970—40 times the average worker's salary—to Dollars 37.5m, or more than 1,000 times, by 1998. "By the beginning of the century," writes Kevin Phillips in *Wealth and Democracy,* the US "had become the west's citadel of inherited wealth. . . . Aristocracy was a cultural and economic fact."

Class here may not have as strong a social dimension as in Britain, but there is no mistaking its political expression. Lisa Murkowski is but the most flagrant example of political power being bequeathed down the generations. Teamsters union leader Jimmy Hoffa, Chicago mayor Richard Daley, Southern Christian Leadership Conference head Martin Luther King all carry the names and the job titles their fathers did.

Which brings us to that other elephant in the room—the Republican C-grade student who made it into Yale because his father had been there and thus received preferential treatment. The man who made it to the highest office in the land purely on intelligence, who now leads the charge for meritocracy. The best man for the job—George W. Bush.

Younge is very sarcastic about the qualifications of U.S. President George W. Bush. What's his point?

Consider the source and the audience.

- Younge is writing for a liberal newspaper in England, a nation with a long history of aristocratic privilege and a persistent social class system. How might these factors affect his interpretation of American culture? Is there anything an American audience can learn from him?

Lay out the argument, the values, and the assumptions.

- How does Younge feel about affirmative action? What does he think its main goal is—to increase social diversity today or to redress past injustice?
- What does he mean when he says that the American dream is founded on the concept of meritocracy?
- What does he mean when he cites Bell Hooks as saying that "class is the elephant in the room"? Why does affirmative action focused on race miss the point? Where should it focus instead?

Uncover the evidence.

- What is Younge's evidence for the claim that there are economic classes in America? Are his references to economic inequality and declining social mobility sufficient to make his point?
- Why does he offer anecdotal evidence such as Frank Murkowski's appointment of his daughter to his Senate seat and George W. Bush's probable advantages as the son of a rich Yale alumnus? What effect is he after? Does it work?

Evaluate the conclusion.

- Is the American dream a realistic possibility for most Americans?
- Has Younge convinced you that if Americans want true equality of opportunity in this country they must eliminate the broad gaps of wealth and privilege that give some people a giant head start over others? Why or why not?

Sort out the political implications.

- How would affirmative action based on social class work? What goals would it try to achieve? How would these differ from the goals of affirmative action based on race and gender?

2.5 I Have a Dream

Martin Luther King, Jr., 28 August 1963

In this chapter we have seen several pieces that attempt to define the American dream, including some that look specifically at the place of race in that dream. While we will deal with the civil rights movement in a later chapter, we cannot separate the pervasive issue of race from fundamental questions about American political culture, particularly when we attempt to understand the central American ideal of equality.

This famous speech by Martin Luther King, Jr., given at a Washington, D.C., civil rights rally in August 1963, is a classic statement about the meaning of equality in the American dream. In this speech, King outlines the many ways that the United States had failed African Americans in the middle of the twentieth century, and he describes his hopes for an America in which the equality promised in the Declaration of Independence becomes a reality for all Americans, black and white. How does King define "equality"? How does it compare with other definitions we have seen in this chapter? How does his dream compare with the American dream implicit in the visions of Red and Blue America we have read about?

I am happy to join with you today in what will go down in history as the greatest demonstration for freedom in the history of our nation.

Five score years ago, a great American, in whose symbolic shadow we stand today, signed the Emancipation Proclamation. This momentous decree came as a great beacon light of hope to millions of Negro slaves who had been seared in the flames of withering injustice. It came as a joyous daybreak to end the long night of their captivity.

But 100 years later, the Negro still is not free. One hundred years later, the life of the Negro is still sadly crippled by the manacles of segregation and the chains of discrimination. One hundred years later, the Negro lives on a lonely island of poverty in the midst of a vast ocean of material prosperity. One hundred years later, the Negro is still languished in the corners of American society and finds himself an exile in his own land. And so we've come here today to dramatize a shameful condition.

In a sense we've come to our nation's capital to cash a check. When the architects of our republic wrote the magnificent words of the Constitution and the Declaration of Independence, they were signing a promissory note to which every American was to fall heir. This note was a promise that all men—yes, black men as well as white men—would be guaranteed the unalienable rights of life, liberty, and the pursuit of happiness.

> Did the Declaration of Independence make a promise to black men as well as white men that all would be guaranteed unalienable rights? How about women? What did the founders think about these groups?

It is obvious today that America has defaulted on this promissory note insofar as her citizens of color are concerned. Instead of honoring this sacred obligation, America has given the Negro people a bad check, a check that has come back marked "insufficient funds."

But we refuse to believe that the bank of justice is bankrupt. We refuse to believe that there are insufficient funds in the great vaults of opportunity of this nation. And so we've come to cash this check, a check that will give us upon demand the riches of freedom and security of justice. We have also come to his hallowed spot to remind America of the fierce urgency of now. This is no time to engage in the luxury of cooling off or to take the tranquilizing drug of gradualism. Now is the time to make real the promises of democracy. Now is the time to rise from the dark and desolate valley of segregation to the sunlit path of racial justice. Now is the time to lift our nation from the quicksands of racial injustice to the solid rock of brotherhood. Now is the time to make justice a reality for all of God's children.

It would be fatal for the nation to overlook the urgency of the moment. This sweltering summer of the Negro's legitimate discontent will not pass until there is an invigorating autumn of freedom and equality. Nineteen sixty-three is not an end but a beginning. Those who hoped that the Negro needed to blow off steam and will now be content will have a rude awakening if the nation returns to business as usual. There will be neither rest nor tranquility in America until the Negro is granted his citizenship rights. The whirlwinds of revolt will continue to shake the foundations of our nation until the bright day of justice emerges.

But there is something that I must say to my people who stand on the warm threshold which leads into the palace of justice. In the process of gaining our rightful place we must not be guilty of wrongful deeds. Let us not seek to satisfy our thirst for freedom by drinking from the cup of bitterness and hatred. We must forever conduct our struggle on the high plane of dignity and discipline. We must not allow our creative protest to degenerate into physical violence. Again and again we must rise to the majestic heights of meeting physical force with soul force. The marvelous new militancy which has engulfed the Negro community must not lead us to a distrust of all white people, for many of our white brothers, as evidenced by their presence here today, have come to realize that their destiny is tied up with our destiny. And they have come to realize that their freedom is inextricably bound to our freedom. We cannot walk alone.

And as we walk, we must make the pledge that we shall always march ahead. We cannot turn back. There are those who are asking the devotees of civil rights, "When will you be satisfied?" We can never be satisfied as long as the Negro is the victim of the unspeakable horrors of police brutality. We can never be satisfied as long as our bodies, heavy with the fatigue of travel, cannot gain lodging in the motels of the highways and the hotels of the cities. We cannot be satisfied as long as the Negro's basic mobility is from a smaller ghetto to a larger one. We can never be satisfied as long as our children are stripped of their selfhood and robbed of their dignity by signs stating "for whites only." We cannot be satisfied as long as a Negro in Mississippi cannot vote and a Negro in New York believes he has nothing for which to vote. No, no we are not satisfied and we will not be satisfied until justice rolls down like waters and righteousness like a mighty stream.

I am not unmindful that some of you have come here out of great trials and tribulations. Some of you have come fresh from narrow jail cells. Some of you have come from areas where your quest for freedom left you battered by storms of persecution and staggered by the winds of police brutality. You have been the veterans of creative suffering. Continue to work with the faith that unearned suffering is redemptive.

Go back to Mississippi, go back to Alabama, go back to South Carolina, go back to Georgia, go back to Louisiana, go back to the slums and ghettos of our northern cities, knowing that somehow this situation can and will be changed.

Let us not wallow in the valley of despair. I say to you today my friends—so even though we face the difficulties of today and tomorrow, I still have a dream. It is a dream deeply rooted in the American dream.

I have a dream that one day this nation will rise up and live out the true meaning of its creed: "We hold these truths to be self-evident, that all men are created equal."

> How did King's famous stance of nonviolence help make his dream more convincing?

I have a dream that one day on the red hills of Georgia the sons of former slaves and the sons of former slave owners will be able to sit down together at the table of brotherhood.

I have a dream that one day even the state of Mississippi, a state sweltering with the heat of injustice, sweltering with the heat of oppression, will be transformed into an oasis of freedom and justice.

I have a dream that my four little children will one day live in a nation where they will not be judged by the color of their skin but by the content of their character.

I have a dream today.

I have a dream that one day down in Alabama, with its vicious racists, with its governor having his lips dripping with the words of interposition and nullification—one day right there in Alabama little black boys and black girls will be able to join hands with little white boys and white girls as sisters and brothers.

I have a dream today.

I have a dream that one day every valley shall be exalted, and every hill and mountain shall be made low, the rough places will be made plain, and the crooked places will be made straight, and the glory of the Lord shall be revealed and all flesh shall see it together.

This is our hope. This is the faith that I go back to the South with. With this faith we will be able to hew out of the mountain of despair a stone of hope. With this faith we will be able to transform the jangling discords of our nation into a beautiful symphony of brotherhood. With this faith we will be able to work together, to pray together, to struggle together, to go to jail together, to stand up for freedom together, knowing that we will be free one day.

This will be the day, this will be the day when all of God's children will be able to sing with new meaning "My country 'tis of thee, sweet land of liberty, of thee I sing. Land where my father's died, land of the Pilgrim's pride, from every mountainside, let freedom ring!"

And if America is to be a great nation, this must become true. And so let freedom ring from the prodigious hilltops of New Hampshire. Let freedom ring from the mighty mountains of New York. Let freedom ring from the heightening Alleghenies of Pennsylvania.

Let freedom ring from the snow-capped Rockies of Colorado. Let freedom ring from the curvaceous slopes of California.

But not only that; let freedom ring from Stone Mountain of Georgia.

Let freedom ring from Lookout Mountain of Tennessee.

Let freedom ring from every hill and molehill of Mississippi—from every mountainside.

Let freedom ring. And when this happens, and when we allow freedom to ring—when we let it ring from every village and every hamlet, from every state and every city, we will be able to speed up that day when all of God's children—black men and white men, Jews and Gentiles, Protestants and Catholics—will be able to join hands and sing in the words of the old Negro spiritual: "Free at last! Free at last! Thank God Almighty, we are free at last!"

Consider the source and the audience.
- King is gaining access to a real national audience for the first time in this speech. How does he use symbols, language, and history to appeal to that audience?

Lay out the argument, the values, and the assumptions.
- How would King define the basic values of equality and freedom he talks about? What is his dream?
- What political tactics does he think will make his dream reality?

Uncover the evidence.
- Does King offer evidence to make his case? What kind?
- What rhetorical tactics does he use to support his case? What is the purpose of laying claim to important symbols like the Declaration of Independence, the American dream, and "My Country 'Tis of Thee"?

Evaluate the conclusion.
- Is King successful in claiming for black Americans the fundamental American rights and dreams that white people take for granted? What kind of case would his opponents have to make to argue against him?

Sort out the political implications.
- What stategies does King use to make his declaration and his intentions nonthreatening to whites? How did his strategy advance the civil rights movement in the 1960s?

CHAPTER · **3**

Federalism and the Constitution

B
y most estimations (though some of the writers you are about to read will disagree), the U.S. Constitution is a marvel. It provides a stable and flexible political structure that guarantees us unprecedented individual freedom, and yet most of the time we are barely aware that it is there. In normal times we take it for granted, but when times turn tough—when a president is impeached, an election is contested, the nation is attacked, or the country launches a war—we are sharply aware of the value of what the founders wrought. In the last five years, Americans have had more cause than usual to appreciate the brilliance of Madison and his colleagues, as events that might have blown another nation off its course have ultimately been no more than choppy seas for the American ship of state.

In this chapter we explore three of the central principles that make our Constitution work: federalism, separation of powers, and checks and balances. Some American government texts cover these subjects in one chapter; others divide them between a chapter on federalism and one on the founding. Because we make this chapter do the work of two, there are more readings here than in the other chapters.

Federalism is the concept of dividing power between the national government and its regional governments (in our case, the states). The founders had tried a system where the power is grounded in the states with the Articles of Confederation, but most of them rejected it because the absence of a strong center led to political and economic instability. The alternative, a unitary system where all the power is centralized, was unacceptable to men who feared a strong government on the English model. A federal system, where states possessed some constitutional power, but where the national government was supreme, was a compromise that has proved to be flexible enough to weather many constitutional storms. Indeed, the balance of power has shifted back and forth between nation and states throughout our history, driven by historical events and judicial interpretation.

Separation of powers and checks and balances are principles that hold that liberty is best preserved and power limited when it is divided up between three branches of government that are mostly separate, but each of which is given a little power over the others to keep an eye on them. The founders believed that by dividing power between the two federal levels, and then among three branches at each level, they were providing the best security for the new republic.

The readings in this chapter give you a variety of different perspectives on the Constitution and the principles on which it is based. The opening piece, on the idiosyncratic time zones in Vevay, Indiana, shows just how flexible federalism can be, and how important it is in terms of preserving local tradition and control. Although the particular example of time zones may seem frivolous, it raises important questions about where decisionmaking power should be located—in the cities and towns, at the state level, or in Washington? The article by Michael Greve argues that federalism is not just about protecting states' rights but also about maintaining a fundamental relationship between states, and limiting government power at all levels. Linda Greenhouse discusses ways that the War on Terrorism is likely to curtail federalism in both of the forms Greve discusses. Sanford Levinson thinks the Constitution is rife with outmoded mechanisms that don't work, and he proposes a new constitutional convention to get it fixed. Bruce Fein would reject the idea that there is anything wrong with the Constitution as written. He argues that the success of our Constitution has come from strictly adhering to the principle of checks and balances, and that the strong Bush presidency threatens to upset it. He harkens back to arguments made in that classic on checks and balances, Madison's *Federalist* No. 51, our final selection.

3.1 Indiana, Split by Time, Struggles Anew

Pam Belluck, *New York Times,* 31 January 2001

Vevay, Indiana, is clearly an unusual little town, with an inclination to have its own way about the things it values, even if they may seem pretty, well, odd to the rest of the country. One of the beauties of federalism is that Vevay can be Vevay, and there isn't much the national government or even the state of Indiana can do to stop it. The preservation of local values and differences can be an advantage of federalism, but it also has its drawbacks. What are some of the more sinister consequences of allowing local practices to thrive? When, in our history, have local customs and laws been overruled by the national government?*

It might be 3 o'clock at the tiny Vevay Post Office, but across the street at Danner's Hardware it will only be 2 o'clock.

If it is 8 P.M. in Lonna Dilts's living room, it will already be 9 P.M. in her bedroom. And at Tina and Jerry Girton's house, when the clock on his side of the bed reads 6 A.M., it will only be 5 A.M. on her side of the bed.

"Here," says Mike Danner, the hardware store owner, with a wink, "we don't ever know what time it really is."

---

* Note: The article about Indiana's reluctance to adopt daylight saving time referred incorrectly to the counties that go on Eastern Daylight. Three of them border Kentucky, not all five; two border Ohio.

The source of all this anachronism is that man-made, time-taming device: daylight saving time, a practice in which the vast majority of the country turns its clocks ahead an hour each spring and back an hour in the fall. Not Indiana, where a traditional agricultural economy and a stubborn independence streak have kept daylight saving time at bay for decades.

But now that may be changing, with farmers and other traditional daylight saving opponents losing ground to the avatars of the high-tech economy.

Leaders of technology companies and others say they are tired of outsiders being thrown into chronic confusion over where the little hand is on an Indiana clock. And places like Vevay (pronounced vee-vee), just over the border from daylight savers Kentucky and Ohio, are in a special time warp. Folks working in Kentucky factories or ordering supplies from Cincinnati find it easier to switch to daylight saving time, known here as "fast time." People whose schedules are Indiana-centric, like children going to school or employees at local bank branches, keep their clocks the same, on "slow time."

Many families keep time both ways, unable to synchronize their watches.

Now, the Indiana Legislature is considering a bill that would adopt daylight saving time statewide. Previous proposals have failed, but this time a well-financed coalition headed by Indiana's blooming high-tech community is leading the charge.

The Hoosier Daylight Coalition says the state's economy is suffering because befuddled Wall Street and Silicon Valley investors never know what time it is. Missed meetings, conference calls and flights to the coasts make the whole state look bush league, they say.

How is the market principle of competition being used by advocates of the time change?

"It's a major impediment," said Scott A. Jones, chief executive officer of Escient Technologies, a technology management company, and founder of the coalition. "A number of companies have chosen not to locate here because of it."

John Gibbs, executive vice president of Interactive Intelligence, a software company, said confusion over time caused investment bankers from Merrill Lynch and elsewhere to miss an important conference call concerning plans to take his company public.

They say politics makes strange bedfellows. Why are the teachers, the police, and the golf course operators working together on this one? Later on, why do the farmers, the restaurateurs, and the movie theater operators get together?

"It was inconvenient, it was embarrassing, it was cumbersome," Mr. Gibbs said. "It's like, gosh, what time's Indiana on?"

The coalition also includes parents, teachers and the police, who believe more evening daylight reduces crime, and park and golf course operators, anticipating extra evening leisure time. The group has raised $200,000 and is running radio advertisements: "Sometimes, we could use a little more sunshine in our lives."

Gov. Frank L. O'Bannon, a Democrat, surprised everyone this month by endorsing this political hot potato with a split-second mention in his State of the State address.

But since most polls show about half of Indianans like the status quo, this is no easy sell.

"Just leave the clocks where they're at," said Richard Mangus, a Republican state representative, who has bottled up daylight saving bills before. In 1995, he gummed things up with a joke amendment, proposing Indiana set its clocks half an hour ahead.

This year, Mr. Mangus said, he will propose amendments to "let each county council decide what time they want" and another to restrict daylight saving time to the Indianapolis area.

"The best way to hurt bills is to introduce something obnoxious," he said.

The legislation's opponents include farmers, who like daylight early so it can dry the fields, and who worry that working until sunset will make them miss evening community activities, said Bob Kraft, a lobbyist for the Indiana Farm Bureau. Owners of movie theaters and some restaurants also object, saying darkness helps business.

And then there's the iconoclast lobby, the people who say: "'We're different from the rest of the world. Everybody else is out of step,'" Mr. Kraft said.

Morton Marcus, an Indiana University economist, dismisses "the idea that people in New York can't tell what time it is and can't seem to organize their lives," adding, "What's the matter with their Palm Pilots?"

Mr. Marcus said he thought the daylight saving time push was "largely driven by the desire to play golf at night."

> Why didn't the federal government just impose daylight saving time on everyone?

When Congress imposed daylight saving time nationally in 1966, states were given the chance to exempt themselves. Only Indiana, Arizona and Hawaii opted out, but Indiana has engendered the most confusion because it essentially has three time zones. Seventy-seven of its 92 counties stay on Eastern standard time year round. Ten counties in the northwest and southwest corners of the state are on Central time, which the Indiana Legislature would be powerless to change (those counties observe daylight saving time like the rest of the Midwest). Five counties bordering Ohio follow Eastern states by setting their clocks ahead in April and back in October.

That is what happens in Rising Sun, Ind. Almost. Everyone adopts fast time except the schools, sometimes playing havoc with basketball or band schedules.

In the town of Patriot, the Patriot Pizza Parlor used to set its clocks ahead, but will not this year because its customers (mostly slow timers) would come for dinner at the restaurant's 8 P.M. closing time, thinking it was still 7 P.M.

In East Enterprise, a single building houses a fast-time post office and a slow-time bank.

And in Vevay, one can schedule a 9 A.M. dental check-up with Dr. Robert Findley and still be early for a 9 A.M. appointment with the optometrist, Dr. John Sieglitz. The Swiss immigrants who settled this inviting town of antebellum homes, county seat of Switzerland County, apparently did not import their country's exacting sense of time.

As for the daylight saving time bill, people in Vevay are, naturally, of two minds.

After all, peaceful coexistence seems rooted in the Ohio River soil. The headquarters of the Democratic and Republican Parties are right next to each other, and the Republican Party chairman owns the Democratic Party's building.

And the newspaper publishes two editions that are exactly identical except for their names—and the fact that one (the *Switzerland Democrat*) is read by Democrats and the other (the *Vevay Reveille-Enterprise*) is read by Republicans.

The editor, Patrick Lanman, says that subscribers to the *Reveille-Enterprise* actually call to complain if they get a *Democrat* by mistake, and if the drugstore is out of *Democrat*s, people will go to another store, rather than simply picking up a *Reveille-Enterprise*.

As if in deference to the two time zones, the clock on the old courthouse was stopped for many years, frozen at 9:36 A.M.

Dr. Fidelia Valenzuela, a semiretired family practitioner, would like the clocks to be consistent. When she had a full-time practice with her husband, they set their clocks on slow time in the morning and fast time in the afternoon, "so we could get home earlier," she said.

Since the television stations come from Cincinnati, the television schedule is on fast time, and they miss favorite programs until they adjust.

But Janna Pavy is happy the way things are, even though her kitchen clock stays on slow time; her husband, Gary, who works for a subsidiary of an Ohio plastics factory, sets the bedroom clock on fast time; and "we fight over the clock in the living room."

Ms. Pavy, a dental technician for the slow time dentist, Dr. Findley, said patients on fast time schedule 5:30 P.M. appointments, "and it's only 4:30 P.M. here, so we can get in quite a few people that way. I kind of want it to stay."

And Ann Mulligan, executive director of the welcome center, is appropriately ambivalent.

"I have mixed emotions about switching because it's kind of quirky, and in tourism that's good because people laugh and talk about it," she said. "Although they're always here at the wrong time, and it drives tour groups to distraction, I'm somewhat reluctant to admit it, but in a way I'd miss it like this."

Consider the source and the audience.
- The *New York Times* is a major national newspaper. Why is it covering Vevay, Indiana? What tone does the author adopt?

Lay out the argument, the values, and the assumptions.
- The article itself doesn't make an argument here, but it reports two different sides of the time change debate in Indiana. What do the pro–time change people argue? What do the anti–time changers reply? What kinds of values motivate them?
- What are the strengths and weaknesses of imposing national uniformity in a case like this? Should the state of Indiana be able to impose its will on all the counties?

Uncover the evidence.
- Do the people on either side offer compelling evidence that they are right? Do they have to?

Evaluate the conclusion.
- Does the author of the article draw any conclusions here? Do the various combatants? Does anyone persuade you? What do *you* conclude? How should the time change issue be decided, and by whom?

Sort out the political implications.
- If Indiana moves to daylight saving time at some point in the future, should Vevay have to switch? Who wins and who loses under the possible outcomes?
- How far should the national government's power extend over the states? What about when the issue goes beyond daylight saving time to recognition of gay unions? Legalized prostitution? The right to die?

3.2 A Federalism Worth Fighting For: Conservatives Should Stop Getting Bogged Down in "States' Rights"

Michael S. Greve, *Weekly Standard,* 29 January 2001

The *Weekly Standard* is a conservative opinion journal. Here Greve, himself a conservative, rejects the conservative idea that federalism is all about states' rights and state sovereignty for their own sake. Those who make this argument often get bogged down in debating the southern states' rights to engage in slavery and segregation, which puts them in an indefensible position. Furthermore, states' rights arguments can lead to big state governments, which Greve also rejects. Rather, he says, states' rights should be valued for the good results they produce. What does he mean?

Greve's article is intriguing because he shows us that conservative thought is not a uniform ideology but, rather, a complex network of multiple, even competing, ideas. He is making a difficult and sophisticated argument here. He also takes on some formidable opponents. Notice his views on unfunded mandates (federal programs that states must implement at their own expense) and block grants (federal funds given to states to fulfill a broad purpose, but with no specific restrictions). Conservatives are usually against the former and for the latter, but Greve says both are bad ideas, and wants to do away with cooperative federalism (a vision of federalism whereby the national government and the states work together). Why? What does he have in mind? What vision of federalism does he offer instead?

B ush cabinet nominees Gale Norton and John Ashcroft are running a humiliating gauntlet, forced to explain that their support for federalism in no way implies an endorsement of slavery or Jim Crow. The demagogic nature of the allegations against two honorable officials, however, should not blind conservatives to the fact that something is fundamentally wrong with their accustomed states' rights defense of federalism.

This problem demands attention. In the coming years, federalism will be the subtext of important political battles over judicial nominations, federal land use policy, education, and quite possibly abortion. A firm defense of a federalism based on competition between states and citizen choice could help conservatives win many of those battles and, moreover, might allow them to discipline a bloated, irresponsible government (at all levels). Conservatives will squander those opportunities, though, with a "states' rights" stance that forces them, time and again, to apologize for the sins of the Confederacy.

It is futile to argue that states' rights are good as a general principle (even if slavery and segregation obviously were not). As Bob Dole learned in his 1996 presidential campaign, nobody mans the political ramparts or even casts a ballot for the Tenth Amendment in the abstract. This attests not to Americans' lamentable ignorance about the Bill of Rights but to their good sense. An abstract principle is worthless (or worse) unless it produces sensible results.

States' rights sentimentality notwithstanding, federalism is *not* about protecting local affections and attachments (which, as France shows, can survive even under a completely nationalized government) or about "devolving" federal administration to supposedly more competent states. Empowered state governments, on top of an effectively omnipotent federal government, are the last thing we need. Rather, the virtues that commend federalism are, first, the virtues of markets—diversity, citizen choice, and state competition; and, second, political transparency, discipline, and responsibility.

What does Greve find valuable about the idea of federalism? Why would a conservative find the "virtues of markets" attractive?

Diversity among states enables us to manage our differences—on economic and especially on social issues—in a sensible manner. The regulatory packages offered by Maryland and Virginia differ a great deal, as do those offered by New York and New Jersey. Those differences matter both to citizens and to businesses, which will sort themselves into jurisdictions to their liking.

Competition for productive citizens will discipline state governments just as market competition disciplines private producers. State governments will be more responsible and responsive to citizens' preferences not because they are "closer to the people" (they are as interest-group ridden as the federal government, maybe more so), but because there are 50 of them. Unlike the monopolistic federal government, states will respond to the threat of losing their residents. If you doubt it, imagine how high state sales and income taxes would be if citizens couldn't choose to shop and work elsewhere.

A competitive federalism means, first, that conservatives must stop worrying about "states' rights" and instead start worrying about the federal government's power. So long as that power is taken to be unlimited, Washington will remain free to wipe out diversity and competition among the states, and the Tenth Amendment—which merely reserves to the states or the people all powers not granted to the federal government—will remain empty.

Second, conservatives must stop obsessing over the states' complaints about federal "unfunded mandates" and instead focus on the far larger problem of oppressive federal-state cooperation. State and local governments rarely cooperate with the federal government because they are compelled to do so; far more often, they sell their regulatory autonomy, in areas ranging from education to the environment to, more recently, crime control, for a handful of federal dollars. As the Supreme Court has observed on numerous occasions, federal-state cooperation obscures political accountability and responsibility, thus encouraging policy disasters. When things go awry, state and local officials blame federal regulators and a "lack of adequate funding"; federal regulators and legislators blame irresponsible state officials. In a world flattened by cooperative policies, citizens can neither identify the culprits, nor throw them out of office, nor even escape to more hospitable states.

> What's wrong with cooperative federalism? How does it reduce political accountability—the ability to figure out which individuals are responsible for what government does and to hold them responsible?

More federal money and less federal regulation—"block grants" and "devolution," in political parlance—provide no cure. Just as much as an unfunded mandate, a funded non-mandate (that is, a block grant) divides responsibility and obscures accountability. The incoming administration has promised to increase federal education funding by some $25 billion and to "block grant" existing and new programs. While that may be a necessary price to pay for the soccer mom vote, a system in which local, state, and federal officials are responsible for everything and nothing will easily absorb a few billion dollars to no net educational effect. Federal reform should disentangle the system—for instance, by sending federal dollars to parents rather than bureaucrats.

Third, conservatives must become attuned to federalism's horizontal, state-to-state dimension. Left to their own devices, the states will attempt to beggar their neighbors—for instance, by seeking to impose tax collection obligations on e-commerce sellers in other states, or by robbing out-of-state corporations in billion-dollar product liability lawsuits brought on behalf of (some) in-state plaintiffs. Given half a chance, the states will attempt to form policy cartels to suppress interstate competition, either with the help of Congress or on their own; witness the multi-state tobacco agreement, which amounts to a $250 billion tax hike that no legislator, state or federal, ever voted on. Regulatory aggression and policy cartels, however, aren't federalism but its antithesis. Conservatives should not be abashed about urging Congress to curb such practices; that is what congressional authority is for.

Fourth, conservatives have to stop looking to state and local officials and their Washington lobbying organizations as federalism's principal defenders. States consistently oppose interstate competition for the same reasons that private corporations seek monopolistic access to customers. "States' rights" rhetoric typically goes hand in hand with calls for federal "cooperation" that crowds out state competition, thus allowing state officials to do a lot of stuff, on behalf of special interests, that would otherwise drive productive citizens and businesses into other states.

Why are states not the best defenders of federalism?

Gale Norton's record as Colorado's attorney general, and John Ashcroft's record as a state attorney general, governor, and senator, indicate that both nominees understand federalism's logic and attractions; their federalism problem, grossly inflated by their enemies' distortions, lies in using a familiar but unfortunate rhetoric. Among current state leaders, one can find one attorney general (Alabama's Bill Pryor), two governors (Oklahoma's Frank Keating and Virginia's James Gilmore), and perhaps a few others who favor state competition. As for the vast majority, their idea of federalism is "send us more money, and leave us alone." That, in a nutshell, is the federalism agenda of the National Governors' Association.

Some states will be on the right side of *some* federalism issues, and there is considerable mileage in exploiting divisions among the competitive states and their no-good, cartelizing, "fund-me" cousins. But federalism is too important to be left to the states. Conservatives must identify, issue by issue, the *political* constituencies that have a stake in a more competitive and diverse politics—school choice advocates and home schoolers on education; gun owners and civil libertarians on crime control; segments of the business community on Internet privacy and e-commerce; property rights advocates and, again, sectors of the business community on environmental and land use issues.

For historical and substantive reasons, it will prove difficult to extricate federalism altogether from the states' rights legacy. But the task is not hopeless. Most citizens believe, correctly, that Washington does not care about their vote; most yawn, justifiably, when Beltway campaign-finance reformers promise to put citizens ahead of PACs. Increasingly mobile and educated citizens will care, however, about a government that responds when they vote with their feet—and about a federalism agenda that protects and enhances their right so to vote. Citizens have figured out that markets work, while Washington doesn't. They will go with what works—if they are offered a federalism of competition and choice, not a states' rights echo.

Consider the source and the audience.

- Greve is a conservative writing for other conservatives. What is his motivation, and how does this shape his message and its presentation? How might his message be different if he were writing for liberals, or for some other general audience?

Lay out the argument, the values, and the assumptions.

- Sum up Greve's reasons for not liking the current way that federalism is practiced. What does he prefer to put in its place? Why?
- What vision of "good government" underlies Greve's argument? How about "bad government"? Does he make any attempt to disguise his conservative values?
- What does Greve assume about the way markets work? How does he think that can be translated into politics?
- Why would this be a conservative argument? Might others hold it as well?

Uncover the evidence.

- Greve offers many examples of federalism gone wrong. Does he offer any empirical evidence that his ideas will work? On what does his argument rely?

Evaluate the conclusion.

- Would competition among states bring about all the good that Greve believes? Might it have negative consequences as well?
- What is the proper political role for ordinary citizens, in Greve's opinion? Do you agree?

Sort out the political implications.

- What if states want to "compete" with their neighbors not only to attract "good" citizens but also to eliminate less desirable ones? For example, what are the consequences if they compete for lower welfare benefits, in order to drive poor people out of their jurisdictions—a practice liberal critics call "the race to the bottom"?
- Why does Greve title his article "A Federalism Worth Fighting For"? In what way is it a call to action? How will it help the conservative cause?

3.3 Will the Court Reassert National Authority?

Linda Greenhouse, *New York Times,* 30 September 2001

Linda Greenhouse covers the Supreme Court for the *New York Times*. Here, in the immediate aftermath of September 11, 2001, she asks what the terror attacks and the nation's entry into war are likely to mean (1) for the Court's "federalism revolution" (the majority's commitment to greater devolution or the returning of more power to the states) and (2) for its protection of civil liberties against the power of the national government. Both the liberal and conservative scholars she cites make the same argument about the prospects of federalism. (Note: Here the word is used to mean more state power rather than a balance of power that can shift either to the states or to the national government.) Why is such federalism a "luxury of peaceful times"?

T he Supreme Court's federalism revolution has been overtaken by events.
For the last decade, the court, under Chief Justice William H. Rehnquist, has engaged in a far-reaching reappraisal of the scope of Congressional authority and the balance of powers between the national government and the states. In case after case, the court, which begins its new term tomorrow, invoked broad theories of the sovereignty of the individual states and a limited view of Congress's authority—creating a new federalism jurisprudence that has become the hallmark of the Rehnquist court. Not since the Supreme Court's resistance to the New Deal crumpled in the late 1930's has the court been so hostile to the exercise of federal power.

It is no coincidence that this federalism revival flourished in a post–cold-war atmosphere of tranquility, when it was easy to regard the federal government as superfluous at best. To many, it seemed a blundering and costly intruder into matters properly rooted at the state and local level. That attitude vanished three weeks ago, as suddenly and completely as the twin towers.

Why can devolution flourish in times of peace?

"Federalism was a luxury of peaceful times," said Walter E. Dellinger, who as the Clinton administration's acting solicitor general in 1997 fought a losing battle at the Supreme Court to preserve the Brady gun control law. The court ruled 5 to 4 that Congress had violated core principles of state sovereignty by requiring local law enforcement officials to conduct background checks of prospective gun purchasers.

To pick up that opinion today, a paean to the states as "independent and autonomous," in the words of Justice Antonin Scalia, is like unearthing an artifact from a bygone era. The majority opinion in *Printz v. United States* speaks from a consciousness far removed from a world in which a Republican president now proposes to give a new Homeland Security Agency authority over state and local as well as federal agencies engaged in domestic defense.

Reflecting on the Brady Act case, Mr. Dellinger said, "One of the things I thought then was that we wouldn't be so casually discarding the authority of the national government in this way if the cold war was still going on." He added he had the same reaction to another defeat that year, the court's rejection of presidential immunity in the Paula Corbin Jones case.

The Supreme Court's attachment to federalism and disaffection from it has often tracked changes in the nation's mood and circumstances. "Whenever you see a national emergency, federalism disappears," explained Robert C. Post, a law professor at the University of California at Berkeley who has examined the rise of nationalism during World War I. "In a national emergency, you give the national government the power to get done what needs to get done," he said.

Professor Post said the court has a "dialectical relationship with the mood of the country"—at different times playing the role of leader, consolidator or follower. "But when something intense, momentary and vivid sweeps the country in the middle of responding to a crisis, it takes a very strong-willed court to buck that."

Another scholar of the court, Prof. Sanford Levinson of the University of Texas Law School, said when the public turned to the federal government for solutions, federalism lost its "motive force," which was "a fundamental mistrust, a disdain for a national government that is seen as distant, probably corrupt and in any event as not reflecting the 'real America.'" Now, by contrast, "suddenly it becomes very, very important to trust national leadership," he added.

Why does federalism lose its "motive force" in times of national crisis?

While both professors are critics of the court's federalism rulings, even strong supporters offer, if regretfully, a similar analysis. The events of Sept. 11 "struck at the heart of the federalism revival," said John O. McGinnis, a professor at the Benjamin N. Cardozo School of Law at Yeshiva University. "We all experience it as Americans," he continued. "It brings the country together, and federalism, whatever its intellectual claims, doesn't speak to that."

The court responds not only to the domestic mood but to the justices' perception of what message the court needs to send to the wider world, according to Mary L. Dudziak, a legal historian at the University of Southern California, who has proposed a foreign-policy-based explanation for the Supreme Court's shift on racial equality at the height of the cold war. In her book, *Cold War Civil Rights: Race and the Image of American Democracy,* she asserts that the court's landmark desegregation decision, *Brown v. Board of Education,* can be seen as a reflection of the justices' belief that official racism at home was damaging the image of the United States and giving the Soviet Union ammunition in the worldwide struggle for dominance, an argument the federal government made in its brief to the court.

"As the ground shifts under us now, the justices can't take themselves out of their cultural moment," Professor Dudziak said. "Federalism jurisprudence might have felt anachronistic and quaint in an era of globalization, but after Sept. 11 it feels dangerous."

While there are cases on the court's docket for the new term that raise tangential federalism questions, none appear to provide raw material for a basic reappraisal. And, certainly, the justices are unlikely to repudiate what they have accomplished so far, said Michael S. Greve, director of the federalism project at the American Enterprise Institute, a conservative public policy organization. "It will be more subtle and nuanced, hard to trace," Mr. Greve said, predicting that the court will sidestep occasions to apply and extend the recent precedents. "It's too big not to have an effect," he said. "To sustain ancient constitutional doctrines at a time like this becomes impossible."

The end of the federalism revolution raises another question: Will the court follow another of its historical patterns and overcompensate in favor of the federal government, accepting the government's claims about the need to restrict individual liberties for the sake of national security?

In 1987, one of the court's great civil libertarians, Justice William J. Brennan Jr., offered a sober warning on this point that now sounds particularly timely. Brennan said America's record in protecting civil liberties in times of war was "shabby," in part because the country had so little experience with threats to its security that it was not sufficiently practiced at sorting out real security risks and needs from exaggerated claims.

> What did Justice William Brennan think would make the Supreme Court better at protecting the rights of individuals during crises?

"The episodic nature of our security crises" left the country and its judges vulnerable to being "swept away by irrational passion" when the unaccustomed threat arrived, Brennan said. "A jurisprudence capable of braving the overblown claims of national security must be forged in times of crisis by the sort of intimate familiarity with national security threats that tests their bases in fact, explores their relation to the exercise of civil freedom, and probes the limits of their compass."

It is a hard proposition: that only prolonged and intimate exposure to danger can develop the necessary wisdom to deal with it. By Brennan's measure, both the court and country are seriously out of practice. Both are now confronted by the end of a peaceful period that appeared, just days ago, to have no end in sight.

So often in recent years, this court has seemed to have its eye on the past. Now, with the nation, it has been abruptly propelled into an unappealing future where the search for the right balance between order and liberty may well present the Rehnquist court with its greatest test.

Consider the source and the audience.

- How does the *New York Times'* broad national audience affect Greenhouse's choice of sources for her story? Note that she cites both Michael S. Greve, the conservative author of our previous selection on federalism, and Sanford Levinson (the author of our next selection), who takes a more critical view of the trend toward increased state power.

Lay out the argument, the values, and the assumptions.

- What is the essential argument made by all the sources Greenhouse cites?
- What values do most of these sources indicate will override the usual values of liberalism and conservatism in times of external threat to the nation?

Uncover the evidence.

- Since the scholars in this article are speculating about the future, most of their evidence comes from the past. What are the strengths of relying on historical evidence? The weaknesses?

Evaluate the conclusion.

- What relatively easy way is there to evaluate predictions of the future based on past behavior? What actions has the federal government taken in the wake of the terror attacks that would signal greater national power over the states? Over individual lives? Has the Supreme Court behaved as predicted? Where does Greve, in this article, suggest we should look for evidence of the impact of September 11 on the Court?

Sort out the political implications.

- What are the political benefits of more national power? The political costs? How might more national power acquired by the government in the name of national security be used for other purposes?

3.4 | Dissent! The Constitution Got Us Into This Mess

Sanford Levinson, *Washington Post,* 17 December 2000

In the immediate wake of the 2000 presidential election, University of Texas Law Professor Sanford Levinson pulls no punches. Writing an opinion piece in the *Washington Post,* he clearly feels that there are some elements of the U.S. Constitution that need correction. He is the co-editor of a book called *Constitutional Stupidities, Constitutional Tragedies,* and he doesn't confine himself to critiquing the way we handle presidential elections through the electoral college. Indeed, he also takes on the House of Representatives' role in contested elections, lifetime tenure for Supreme Court justices, and the amendment process—all constitutional "stupidities" that he thinks should be addressed.

Are you a fan of the U.S. Constitution? Before you get offended by Professor Levinson's critique, read his argument very carefully. If the constitutional provisions he isolates don't qualify as "stupidities," they are certainly oddities, and we should understand exactly how they work and what they mean for American politics. What are the implications of the idea that we should adapt the Constitution today to contemporary needs and events and not be limited to the document as the founders wrote it in 1787?

We have crossed the constitutional bridge into the 21st century and discovered that it is rickety, maybe even falling down. An electoral system that might have made sense when devised in the late 18th and early 19th centuries has turned out to be shockingly problematic in this new millennium.

This should come as no surprise. So often, we almost literally idolize the United States Constitution, treating it with the reverence due a sacred text. But the Constitution is a most-human product, and therefore an imperfect document, with flaws and weaknesses that can threaten our stability at any time. The kind of tottering we've witnessed over the past few weeks was thoroughly predictable. But warnings that we were heading for a wreck have generally been either dismissed with a round of constitutional cheerleading, or met with denial. "It happened before, but it can't happen again," we say, when reminded of earlier crises. (Remember early 1998, when no one believed we'd see another impeachment?) Or we take refuge in the delusory belief that God has the United States in his special care.

Both responses are equally foolish, as we have seen in the post-election crisis. Our task now is to figure out how much repair is necessary to prevent a future systemic collapse. In just this past month, several of the Constitution's "stupidities" have been revealed. Chief among these is the electoral college. Not only does this feature make it possible to deny the presidency to the candidate who wins the popular vote, it also gives a significant advantage to small states, each of which is guaranteed at least three electoral votes. This means that a candidate gets significantly more benefit from carrying, say, Wyoming and the two Dakotas, with a total of nine electoral votes, than New Mexico, which has roughly the same total population as the three states combined but only five electoral votes.

The electoral college, and the disproportionate power it gives to small states, has rightly been put under the microscope. But a number of other flawed constitutional features also deserve closer scrutiny and discussion:

How the House would pick a president

This is my choice for the most dubious feature of the Constitution. It provides that deadlocks over the choice of president in the electoral college be broken by the U.S. House of Representatives on a one-state, one-vote basis. Although this hasn't happened since 1824, when the House picked John Quincy Adams as president over Andrew Jackson, it loomed as a possibility in 1948 and 1968, when third-party presidential candidates in those years each won more than 20 votes. Even if you believe that the electoral college is a good idea, and that the advantage held there by small states is defensible, there is no defense, in 2000, for allowing Vermont's single representative to offset the entire 30-member congressional delegation of my home state of Texas in the instance of a House vote for president.

> Do we really give so much power to smaller states in the electoral college and at the times when the House chooses a president in a contested election? Why did the founders choose these rules?

If the House ever has to select the president—provided we retain the electoral college and accept its risk of deadlocks—then it should do so on a one-member, one-vote basis, the theory of representation that the Supreme Court has endorsed now for almost 40 years. As it happens, if this year's election had come down to the House's choosing, it probably would not have mattered which rule we had, since the Republicans both hold a majority of individual seats and control 29 of the state delegations. Consider the situation, though, if only half a dozen congressional districts had gone Democrat instead of Republican, giving the Democrats control of the House. In that case, if the election had come to the House, Gore—the choice of the people as well of a majority of the people's representatives—could have been deprived of the presidency due to the happenstance that the Republicans control most state delegations.

Life tenure on the Supreme Court

The Supreme Court's role in the just-ended campaign highlighted the questionable wisdom of lifetime appointments for Supreme Court justices. One unfortunate consequence of lifetime tenure is revealed in a recent article in the *Wall Street Journal*, which suggested that Chief Justice William Rehnquist and Associate Justice Sandra Day O'Connor have put off resigning from the court so that their replacements could be named by a Republican president. There is every reason to believe that former justice Byron White waited, for the same purpose, until a Democratic president took office before retiring in 1993. If the United States followed the practice of many other countries—and many of the states—in im-

> What are some of the benefits of lifetime tenure for Supreme Court justices that Levinson doesn't mention?

posing term limits on the justices, then the opportunity for such partisan behavior would be limited. Moreover, as Emory University professor David Garrow writes in an article in the current *University of Chicago Law Review,* over the years, several justices, including some in the recent past, have remained on the bench far too long, even after mental debilities made it impossible for them to serve the nation well. There is no reason to believe this is true of any current members of the court, but we should not continue to rely on the judges to have the self-discipline to set their own retirement dates.

Article V

The clause for enacting amendments is one of the Constitution's most dubious features, because, as a practical matter, it makes formal constitutional change exceedingly difficult. The problems posed by Article V are a primary reason why obvious defects in the constitutional structure, like those discussed above, have not been addressed, and why more train wrecks like this year's are possible in the future. Article V provides that two-thirds of each house of Congress must first agree to propose an amendment, which then must be ratified by three-fourths of the states. Winning the "amendment game" and changing the status quo thus requires triumphing first in both Houses of Congress and then in at least 75 state legislative chambers (for example, bicameral legislatures in 37 states plus the unicameral legislature in Nebraska). Winning the game on defense—that is, preventing formal change—requires only one-third plus one of the votes in either the House of Representatives (146 votes) or the U.S. Senate (34 votes), or prevailing in at least one house of 13 state legislatures.

> What would happen if it were a lot easier to amend the Constitution?

Having been forewarned by last month's events, responsible political leaders have a duty to promote a serious analysis of the quality of our political infrastructure and to suggest necessary changes that will either prevent, or at least lower the cost of, future problems.

There is an alternative to constitutional amendments. It is drawn from Article V itself: Two-thirds of the states can petition Congress to call a constitutional convention, a gathering of elected state delegates to reflect on the adequacy of our present institutional structure. The current problems posed by the way we elect our presidents would certainly justify extended discussion by a cross-section of American leaders empowered to propose constitutional amendments for consideration by state conventions (as allowed by Article V) elected by the people of the states.

It would be foolish to deny that an Article V convention would raise many problems of its own. Like much of the Constitution, Article V is poorly drafted, and it provides no clue as to how, precisely, a convention would be organized. For example, would votes be cast on a one-member, one-vote basis, as in the

House, or on the basis of equal votes for each state, as in the Senate? (Obviously, I favor the former.) Other problems will occur to readers. But a constitutional convention is, for better or worse, the best procedure given us, by the Constitution itself, to respond to what are the decided imperfections of the document we were handed in 1787.

To reject even thinking about the possibility of changing aspects of our governmental structure is to say, in effect, that we really shouldn't worry, that the last month has been perfectly all right and that it speaks only to the strengths, and not at all to the weaknesses, of our constitutional order. One might be touched by such displays of faith, but this is no time for constitutional cheerleading. Even the Framers recognized the possibilities of imperfections, the frailties of humans, and the importance of learning from experience.

Consider the source and the audience.
- The *Washington Post* is a major national newspaper, and one that is particularly popular with Washington insiders. Moreover, Levinson is a professor at the flagship law school of the state of Texas, critiquing the constitutional arrangements that gave the presidency to Texas Governor George W. Bush. Why would the *Post* print such a provocative piece?

Lay out the argument, the values, and the assumptions.
- This is clearly an abbreviated version of an argument that appears in Levinson's book. What are the argument's essential elements?
- Is the argument driven by Levinson's scholarly views or his political values? Can we tell? Does it matter?
- If Levinson doesn't place his faith in the U.S. Constitution, who is he counting on to get it right? Is that confidence warranted?

Uncover the evidence.
- What evidence does Levinson provide to support his argument that the Constitution is flawed?
- What other kinds of evidence might be convincing here?

Evaluate the conclusion.
- Can the "totteriness" of the Constitution and Levinson's critique support any conclusions other than the one that Levinson arrives at? What might they be?

Sort out the political implications.
- What results might follow if we had another constitutional convention? What forces would argue for what provisions?
- Would a new convention produce a Constitution better than the one we have? Why or why not?

3.5 A Republic, If We Can Keep It

Bruce Fein, *Washington Times,* 30 July 2002

In marked contrast to Professor Levinson's desire to revamp the Constitution, constitutional lawyer and former Reagan administration official Bruce Fein wants to preserve every aspect of what he calls "our constitutional cathedral." Writing in the *Washington Times,* to which he frequently contributes opinion pieces on legal issues, he treats the Constitution as hallowed ground. His object here is to criticize President George Bush, not for his specific policies but for the way he has gone about enacting them—dismantling the system of checks and balances and violating the founders' intentions that Fein esteems. What are the implications of the principle that the Constitution should be read today in exactly the same way as intended by the founders when they wrote it over 200 years ago?

Fix your remembrance on Sept. 18, 1787. The day before, longheaded delegates to the Constitutional Convention in Philadelphia had given this nation an unprecedented birth of freedom. A written Constitution renounced the monarchies, privileges, and caste-like divides of the Old World. It embraced limited government enshrined by a separation of powers and checks and balances. In lieu of trusting angels, ambition was to counteract ambition to maintain an equilibrium of freedom.

The Founding Fathers also were masters of the human heart and human nature. They knew any constitutional parchment would be brittle if unwritten rules of fairness and restraint were not equally venerated and practiced. Thus, that Sept. 18, as the Philadelphia sun was rising on the infant Constitution, a Mrs. Powell approached Dr. Benjamin Franklin, the eminence grise among the Convention delegates. She inquired, "Well Doctor, what have we got—a republic or a monarchy?" "A republic," replied Franklin, "if you can keep it."

But aren't we, the people, in danger of losing it to an imperial presidency?

Consider the following, not in isolation but as an unmistakable pattern, like the encroachments of Roman emperors on the prerogatives of the Roman Senate.

President George Bush narrowly captures the electoral vote in 2000 with a controversial boost from the United States Supreme Court. He loses the popular vote to Al Gore. Control of the U.S. Senate shifts from Republican to Democrat. The House of Representatives remains Republican, but with a razor-thin majority. Esteemed President Thomas Jefferson had warned against sharp political breaks by exploiting slender majorities. The expectations and interests of losers must be reasonably accommodated to avoid unhealthy shocks to our constitutional system and destabilizing extremes. Moderation and self-restraint

What is an imperial presidency? What are some synonyms for "imperial"?

should be presidential touchstones, not a "take-no-prisoners" strategy of political warfare.

What is the value of moderation and self-restraint?

But has President Bush heeded Mr. Jefferson's time-honored advice? He has brandished unprecedented war-making, secrecy, and law-enforcement powers. He has regularly shipwrecked flagship environmental, energy, health and economic policies inherited from President William Jefferson Clinton.

Most alarming is President Bush's claim of authority to detain any United States citizen in military custody as an illegal combatant for a lifetime on his say-so alone: no right to test that designation in a court of law (with due regard for intelligence sources and methods); no right to question before an independent federal judiciary when, if ever, our war against international terrorism has sufficiently abated to terminate war powers. Moreover, President Bush's Napoleonic arrogation—something neither George Washington, nor Abraham Lincoln, nor Franklin Roosevelt thought necessary to win their wars against foes far more formidable than Osama bin Laden—is advanced without even suspending the writ of habeas corpus (subject to judicial review) as the Constitution permits during emergencies.

Immigration hearings have been ordered closed irrespective of danger to intelligence sources, methods, or national security. Ditto for the identities of detainees held as material witnesses or suspects in terrorism investigations.

President Bush denies a right of congressional oversight or interrogation whatsoever of his national and domestic security advisers, such as Homeland Security Director Tom Ridge, National Security Adviser Condoleezza Rice, or political gurus Karl Rove and Andrew Card. The claim of secrecy reaches far beyond national security into routine matters of budgeting and meetings with erstwhile Enron tycoons. Mr. Bush asserts a right to block disclosures of presidential papers of his predecessors by dint of constitutional prerogative. He has relaxed internal checks against FBI dossiers on the First Amendment activities of citizens under the flag of counterterrorism.

On the domestic policy front, President Bush's hallmark has been sharp U–turns from his predecessor. Environmental standards for clean water, air, and oil and gas exploration have dipped. Endangered species protections have enervated. Wilderness and national forest preserves have been clipped.

The right of workers to withhold political dues from unions has strengthened. Right-to-life inflexibility has been championed in medical research, foreign assistance, and assisted suicide for the terminally ill sanctioned by state referenda in Oregon. Despite his oblations to federalism, the president is proposing a national damages cap on medical malpractice claims arising under state law.

No insinuation or criticism is intended against the right and duty of a president to forge policies that accord with the sentiments of his political base. Indeed, policy changes are what elections should be about. But statesmanship dictates gradualism, which means forgoing Austerlitz-like political triumphs in favor of victory on the installment plan. Human nature balks at jolts. Individuals and businesses legitimately rely upon reasonably stable government. Further, rashness by one party will be answered by rashness in the opposite direction by the other as soon as the reins of power change hands. Domestic tranquility shatters against such violent swings in government.

What does gradualism mean here?

All three branches of government, of course, must bow to self-restraint and moderation to preserve our constitutional cathedral. Thus, the United States Senate deserves scolding for mulishly blocking many of President Bush's gold standard judicial nominees, such as John Roberts, Miguel Estrada, and Mike McConnell. But the president himself is most out of constitutional joint.

In the wake of a crushing 1936 electoral victory, President Roosevelt audaciously championed "court-packing" legislation to enfeeble the Supreme Court. The public and Congress instantly recognized the threat of executive tyranny. The legislation withered. FDR's popularity plunged. Democrats fared poorly in the 1938 midterm elections. Our constitutional balances were preserved.

Isn't now the time for another bravura performance to keep our sacred Republic of which Mr. Franklin spoke? All that has changed since Franklin Roosevelt with Mr. Bush's transgressions against our unwritten Constitution are the players and scenery. Yet Congress, like the Roman Senate, is yawning while the president captures its crown jewels of constitutional power.

Consider the source and the audience.
- The *Washington Times* is a rival paper to the *Washington Post,* but one that usually takes a clearly defined conservative perspective. Why is a conservative paper carrying a critique of President Bush?

Lay out the argument, the values, and the assumptions.
- What is Fein's essential argument about the value of moderation and self-restraint? How do these relate to the constitutional principles of separation of powers and checks and balances?
- What is Fein's standard for good government? Who are his "heroes"?

Uncover the evidence.
- Fein provides lots of evidence of what he sees as Bush's imperial presidency. Is it persuasive? Why or why not?

Evaluate the conclusion.
- Fein feels that the constitutional order itself is in danger here. Is he right? Whose responsibility is it? Who saved the day when FDR tried to pack the Court?
- What does "keeping the republic" mean to Fein?

Sort out the political implications.

• What happens if an imperial presidency is allowed to grow unchecked? Whose job is it to check it? If the majority party in Congress is the same as the president's party, is there any effective check? Are powers still separate?

3.6 *Federalist* No. 51

James Madison, 6 February 1788

Here speaks the main author of the constitutional provisions that have been debated, critiqued, and revered in this chapter's previous selections. *Federalist* No. 51 is James Madison's famous justification of the principles of federalism, separation of powers, and checks and balances. It is based on his notion that if people are too ambitious and self-interested to produce good government, then government will have to be adapted to the realities of human nature. A mechanism must be created by which the product of government will be good, even if the nature of the human beings participating in it cannot be counted on to be so. The solution, according to Madison, is to create a government that prevents one person or one group from obtaining too much power. How does he make human nature, warts and all, work for the public interest in the Constitution? [We present Madison's *Federalist* No. 51, slightly abridged in order to throw his argument about the constitutional protections of liberty into sharper relief.]

In order to lay a due foundation for that separate and distinct exercise of the different powers of government, which to a certain extent, is admitted on all hands to be essential to the preservation of liberty, it is evident that each department should have a will of its own; and consequently should be so constituted, that the members of each should have as little agency as possible in the appointment of the members of the others. Were this principle rigorously adhered to, it would require that all the appointments for the supreme executive, legislative, and judiciary magistracies, should be drawn from the same fountain of authority, the people, through channels, having no communication whatever with one another. Perhaps such a plan of constructing the several departments would be less difficult in practice than in it may in contemplation appear. Some difficulties however, and some additional expense, would attend the execution of it. Some deviations therefore from the principle must be admitted. In the constitution of the judiciary department in particular, it might be inexpedient to insist rigorously on the principle; first, because peculiar qualifications

Why do we bother to separate powers? Why can't we do it completely?

being essential in the members, the primary consideration ought to be to select that mode of choice, which best secures these qualifications; secondly, because the permanent tenure by which the appointments are held in that department, must soon destroy all sense of dependence on the authority conferring them.

It is equally evident that the members of each department should be as little dependent as possible on those of the others, for the emoluments annexed to their offices. Were the executive magistrate, or the judges, not independent of the legislature in this particular, their independence in every other would be merely nominal.

But the great security against a gradual concentration of the several powers in the same department, consists in giving to those who administer each department, the necessary constitutional means, and personal motives, to resist encroachments of the others. The provision for defense must in this, as in all other cases, be made commensurate to the danger of attack. Ambition must be made to counteract ambition. The interest of the man must be connected with the constitutional right of the place. It may be a reflection on human nature, that such devices should be necessary to control the abuses of government. But what is government itself but the greatest of all reflections on human nature? If men were angels, no government would be necessary. If angels were to govern men, neither external nor internal controls on government would be necessary. In framing a government which is to be administered by men over men, the great difficulty lies in this: You must first enable the government to control the governed; and in the next place, oblige it to control itself. A dependence on the people is no doubt the primary control on the government; but experience has taught mankind the necessity of auxiliary precautions.

> What is Madison's view of human nature? Given this view, what is the "great difficulty" that must be addressed if human beings are to govern other human beings?

This policy of supplying by opposite and rival interests, the defect of better motives, might be traced through the whole system of human affairs, private as well as public. We see it particularly displayed in all the subordinate distributions of power; where the constant aim is to divide and arrange the several offices in such a manner as that each may be a check on the other; that the private interest of every individual, may be a sentinel over the public rights. These inventions of prudence cannot be less requisite in the distribution of the supreme powers of the state.

But it is not possible to give each department an equal power of self defense. In republican government the legislative authority, necessarily, predominates. The remedy for this inconvenience is, to divide the legislative into different branches; and to render them by different modes of election, and different principles of action, as little connected with each other, as the nature of their common functions, and their common dependence on the society, will admit. It may even be necessary to guard against dangerous encroachments by still further precautions. As the weight of the legislative authority requires that it should be thus divided, the weakness of the executive may require, on the other hand, that it should be fortified. An absolute negative, on the legislature, appears at first view to be the natural defense with which the executive magistrate should be armed. But perhaps it would be neither altogether safe, nor alone sufficient. On ordinary occasions, it might not be exerted with the requisite firmness, and on extraordinary occasions, it might be prefidiously abused. May not this defect of an absolute negative be supplied, by some qualified connection between this weaker department, and the weaker branch of the stronger department, by which the latter may be led to support the constitutional rights of the former, without being too much detached from the rights of its own department?

If the principles on which these observations are founded be just, as I persuade myself they are, and they be applied as a criterion, to the several state constitutions, and to the federal constitution, it will be found, that if the latter does not perfectly correspond with them, the former are infinitely less able to bear such a test.

There are moreover two considerations particularly applicable to the federal system of America, which place the system in a very interesting point of view.

First. In a single republic, all the power surrendered by the people, is submitted to the administration of a single government; and usurpations are guarded against by a division of the government into distinct and separate departments. In the compound republic of America, the power surrendered by the people, is first divided between distinct governments, and then the portion allotted to each, subdivided among distinct and separate departments. Hence a double security arises to the rights of the people. The different governments will control each other; at the same time that each will be controlled by itself.

> What does Madison mean by a compound republic? How does federalism enhance the principles of separation of powers and checks and balances?

Second. It is of great importance in a republic, not only to guard the society against the oppression of its rulers; but to guard one part of the society against the injustice of the other part. Different interests necessarily exist in different classes of citizens. If a majority be united by a common interest, the rights of the minority will be insecure. There are but two methods of providing against this evil: The one by creating a will in the community independent of the majority, that is, of the society itself, the other by comprehending in the society so many separate descriptions of citizens, as will render an unjust combination of a majority of the whole, very improbable, if not impracticable. The first method prevails in all governments possessing an hereditary or self appointed authority. This at best is but a precarious security; because a power independent of the society may as well espouse the unjust views of the major, as the rightful interests, of the minor party, and may possibly be turned against both parties. The second method will be exemplified in the federal republic of the United States. While all authority in it will be derived from and dependent on the society, the society it-self will be broken into so many parts, inter-ests and classes of citizens, that the rights of individuals or of the minority, will be in little danger from interested combinations of the majority. . . . In the extended republic of the United States, and among the great variety of interests, parties and sects which it embraces, a coalition of a majority of the whole society could seldom take place on any other principles than those of justice and the general good; and there being thus less danger to a minor from the will of the major party, there must be less pretext also, to provide for the security of the former, by introducing into the government a will not de-pendent on the latter; or in other words, a will independent of the society itself. It is no less certain than it is important, notwithstanding the contrary opinions which have been entertained, that the larger the society, provided it lie within a practicable sphere, the more duly capable it will be of self government. And hap-pily for the *republican cause,* the practicable sphere may be carried to a very great extent, by a judicious modification and mixture of the *federal principle.*

> How does Madison think minority rights will be protected in a compound republic? What minorities do you think he is worried about here?

Consider the source and the audience.
- This piece was originally published in a New York newspaper in 1788, at a time when New Yorkers were debating whether or not to ratify the new Constitution. What was its politi-cal purpose? Who was Madison arguing against?

Lay out the argument, the values, and the assumptions.
- What two ways did Madison think the Constitution would undertake to preserve liberty?
- What assumptions did he make about the purpose of government?

Uncover the evidence.
- What sort of evidence did Madison rely on to make his case? Was there any other evi-dence available to him at that time?

Evaluate the conclusion.

- Was Madison right about the best way to preserve liberty in a republic? How would the other authors we've read in this section answer this question?

Sort out the political implications.

- What will the political process be like in a political system that is divided between national and state levels, and at each level between executive, legislative, and judicial branches? Will policymaking be quick and efficient, gradual and judicious, or slow and sluggish? Why?

- How much power do everyday citizens end up having in such a system? Why didn't Madison give us more power?

CHAPTER 4

Civil Liberties

I t's awfully easy to take our freedoms for granted, when no one is trying to take them away. For many Americans, as the twenty-first century dawned, our civil liberties—things like freedom of speech, freedom of religion, due process of law—seemed almost part of the landscape. Certain rights for certain people may have been controversial at times, and there were perennial, irresolvable debates over issues like where the line between church and state should be drawn or whether women have a right to an abortion. Yet as far as the fundamentals went, Americans knew they lived in the freest country in history.

They still do, but since September 11, 2001, the premises and the stakes have changed—and, with them, some of the unalterable freedoms we have been accustomed to. Indeed, it was our very openness and freedom that made us vulnerable to terrorist attack, and many argued that to become less vulnerable we had to be a little less open, a little less free. Individual freedoms often conflict with the common good, and there is an inevitable tension between freedom and security: We could be completely secure if we gave up all of our liberty to a caretaker state, but very few are willing to make that deal.

Our civil liberties are individual freedoms that we possess that government cannot take away. While they exist to empower us, they also exist to limit government. Because they deal with power, both individual and governmental, civil liberties will always be controversial—especially since everyone wants power, there is not enough to go around, and power gained by some people will always mean power lost by others.

In fact, one of the great debates at the time of our Constitution's founding concerned civil liberties—whether that document established a government that was powerful enough to need limiting through the addition of the first ten amendments, or whether it was so weak as it stood that it could not infringe on citizens' lives. Those making the first argument won, of course, and the Bill of Rights became an established part of our constitutional law.

In the United States, we rarely have to resort to violence to solve our conflicts over rights and freedom (although people do occasionally try to take the law into their own hands). There is a consensus, however, that we should look to politics to resolve clashes of rights—specifically to the Supreme Court, with some assistance from the Congress and the president and even the American public, organized into interest groups such as the American Civil Liberties Union or the National Rifle Association.

In this chapter we look at readings that examine several current issues affecting our civil liberties. The first, a *Los Angeles Times* article, is about a man who decided to challenge the appearance of the word "God" in the Pledge of Allegiance, arguing that it violates the First Amendment. First Amendment freedoms are also the subject of the second article, from *The American Prospect,* about a class at the University of North Carolina that assigned freshmen to a book about the Koran. The third selection, from the *National Review Online,* examines some of the post–9/11 security legislation from the standpoint of a civil libertarian who is very wary of placing any limits on liberty. This is followed by a *New York Times* article that borrows from economics for a way to handle the tradeoff between security and liberty. Finally, we look at an excerpt from Alexander Hamilton's *Federalist* No. 84, in which he objects to the addition of the Bill of Rights to our Constitution.

4.1 1 Plaintiff, Against the Grain

Scott Gold and Eric Bailey, *Los Angeles Times,* 27 June 2002

Thomas Jefferson thought there should be a "wall of separation" between church and state, partly to preserve individual liberty and to protect government from organized religion, but also to protect religion from the coercive power of the state. Despite the intentions of the founders, there are many areas where church and state meet and overlap in contemporary American politics. For instance, congressional sessions open with prayer, our paper money proclaims "In God We Trust," and all over the nation, until very recently, the Pledge of Allegiance included the words "one nation, under God." Although the Pledge was written in 1892, with no mention of "God," the word "God" was added in 1954, at the height of the Cold War, to help distinguish Americans from the godless Communists on the other side of the Iron Curtain.

Believing that the new version of the Pledge runs afoul of the separation of church and state, Michael A. Newdow, a doctor and a lawyer in California, sued the federal government. He claimed that his eight-year-old daughter's civil liberties were being infringed when she was forced to say the Pledge of Allegiance with her class, because it violated her First Amendment freedoms. A majority on the federal appeals court agreed with him, holding that use of the word "God" amounts to a government endorsement of religion when the pledge is said in a public school setting. The divided court reaffirmed its ruling in February 2003. (Next stop, the Supreme Court.) Was the court correct in ruling that an atheist has the right to pledge allegiance to his country without violating his personal belief system? Can the full enforcement of the establishment clause constitute a violation of the free exercise clause?

First things first: Michael A. Newdow says he is not a nut. He's an eccentric, for sure, an emergency room physician by training who says he has given up working to "fight the government," an envelope-pushing free-thinker who equates believing in God with believing in Santa Claus.

But Newdow, a 49-year-old single father who lives on the outskirts of Sacramento, also has an undergraduate degree from Brown University, a medical degree from UCLA and a law degree from the University of Michigan.

He has fought repeatedly in court for a strict separation of church and state. And even foes who find his cause misguided—and all of a sudden, there are many—might find his resolve impressive. He estimates that he spent 4,000 hours preparing his own lawsuit arguing that forcing children to pledge allegiance to "one nation, under God" is unconstitutional and marginalizes those who are not religious.

And so, on Wednesday morning, when he won in a federal court, and the collective jaw of the mainstream legal community dropped, Newdow didn't seem to think anything particularly dramatic had happened.

"I don't think it's a very interesting argument. I think it's an unquestionable argument," Newdow said. "Could we say we are 'One nation under Jesus'? Could we say we are 'One nation under David Koresh'? Or Muhammad? No. And we can't say we are 'one nation under God.'"

His community, to put it mildly, does not agree.

Within hours of the 9th Circuit Court of Appeals' decision, the national media descended upon Newdow's two-story, upper-middle-class home, near a crook of the Sacramento River known as "the pocket."

He was quickly forced to buy a second telephone line to his house—primarily to handle the steady influx of obscene messages and death threats that were pouring in.

"You atheist bastard," one woman said on the answering machine. The message was reviewed by a *Times* reporter.

"If you don't like the way this country is, take yourself and your family and get the hell out," the woman continued. She signed off: "This is from America."

Another woman recited the Pledge of Allegiance on the machine, and a man left this message: "I hope you and your daughter go to hell. People are going to get even. I hope you suffer."

Newdow, standing on the hard-wood floors of his kitchen, amid children's toys and stuffed animals and a blackboard that said "ALGAE" in children's writing, was trying to take it all in stride—even doing the dishes as reporters peppered him with questions. But he was clearly stunned by the response to his legal victory.

Why are people reacting to Newdow's actions this way? Is it necessary to believe in God to be a true patriot?

"I wasn't prepared," he said, shaking his head. "And I was stupid not to be prepared."

Except for the toys and the writing scrawled on the blackboard, there was no sign of Newdow's 8-year-old daughter, who will wrap up her second-grade year at an area elementary school next week. Newdow declined to discuss his personal life, though he said he is a single father who wants to protect his daughter by keeping her identity a secret.

"I'm fearful for her. I'm worried," he said. "I'll bet there will be something thrown through my window in the next few days."

Newdow acknowledged that he is, in effect, using his daughter to support his cause. He said as far as he knows, she stands to recite the pledge along with her classmates in school.

"This is more about me than her," he said. "I'd like to keep her out of this."

Most of Newdow's neighbors said they don't support Newdow's cause, but support his right to fight for it.

"I see no fault in saying 'In God we trust,'" said Melvin Holland, a house painter who has lived in the neighborhood for 14 years. "To me, it's mind-boggling that he's doing it."

Told about the obscene messages left on Newdow's answering machine, however, Holland shook his head in disgust.

"That's awful," he said. "Everyone has their right to speak their piece."

Newdow, although he said he wanted to keep details of his personal life private, said he was raised in the Bronx, N.Y., and northern New Jersey. He graduated from Brown University before attending the UCLA Medical School. He worked as an emergency room physician, then returned to school and received a law degree from the University of Michigan. University officials confirmed that Newdow graduated from the colleges.

The balding Newdow, who often answers the phone with a chirpy "Yo," said he has always been an atheist, but a Web site advertising his campaign also describes him as "an average guy."

"What brought me to atheism was the same thing that brought me to stop believing that there was a Santa Claus," he said.

What was it that brought Newdow to stop believing in God?

He was always uncomfortable when asked, along with the rest of the kids, to recite the Pledge of Allegiance in school, he said. In some public school classes, he was also forced to pray.

"I remember it bothered me," he said. "I remember wondering why I had to do that."

Newdow became what he describes as an ordained minister in 1977 through the Universal Life Church, a California organization that has been attacked by mainstream religious institutions for allowing many people to become "ministers," regardless of their beliefs. Even today, the Universal Life Church's Web site advertises that those interested can become ordained ministers "in less than three minutes."

Twenty years later, Newdow says, he launched a religious institution called the First Amendmist Church of True Science, or FACTS.

Newdow initially filed his lawsuit against then–President Clinton and Congress while living in the Fort Lauderdale, Fla., area. When he moved to the Sacramento area in 2000, he said, he lost legal standing in Florida and had to refile the case in Northern California.

He also filed a related case seeking to prohibit President Bush—who once named Jesus when asked for the identity of his favorite political philosopher—from mingling politics and his Christian beliefs.

In that case, filed in federal court in the Sacramento area, Newdow cited Bush's inaugural, during which the Rev. Franklin Graham called upon "the Lord Jesus Christ" for guidance.

Does Bush's freedom of religion entitle him to mingle politics with his Christian beliefs?

Newdow called that a violation of the 1st Amendment, and said the comments clearly showed the government's preference for Christians. That effectively excluded and marginalized members of other religions, Newdow argued.

After federal prosecutors argued that the judicial branch cannot interfere with the other branches of government—namely, the executive branch—a U.S. District Court judge dismissed the case this spring.

"The issue is this: Does government have the right to stick religion in the midst of a pledge, in the midst of society?" Newdow said. "Or anywhere?"

Consider the source and the audience.
- This article appeared in the *L.A. Times*. What is its take on the story? Is this a legal analysis or a human-interest story?
- Does the focus on the individuals involved allow for a full outline of the constitutional issues involved?

Lay out the argument, the values, and the assumptions.
- What are Newdow's religious beliefs? Why does he hold them?
- What does Newdow think is wrong with including the word "God" in the Pledge?

Uncover the evidence.
- What kind of argument is Newdow making? What kinds of evidence are needed to support a constitutional claim?

Evaluate the conclusion.
- What reasons did the callers to Newdow's house give for rejecting Newdow's claim?
- Is it possible to interpret the First Amendment in a way that does not support Newdow? How?

Sort out the political implications.
- Can we enforce the establishment clause part of the First Amendment without stepping on any free exercise clause toes? Are the two parts of the First Amendment compatible?

4.2 Losing Our Religion

Wendy Kaminer, *The American Prospect,* 23 September 2002

The American Prospect is a liberal journal, and the author of this next article pulls no punches about criticizing what she sees as a silly lawsuit filed by conservatives. The lawsuit concerned a summer reading assignment for freshmen at the University of North Carolina that asked the students to read a book about the Koran. According to the lawsuit, the assignment amounted to state-sponsored religion, in violation of the Constitution's First Amendment; constituted "forced indoctrination" of students; and gave a false idea of Islam by not including some of the more violent passages of the Koran. As you can see, the judge dismissed the suit.

In addition to the main set of claims about the academic right of teachers to assign the material they think relevant, there are other arguments to pay attention to here, including an interesting one about the purpose of personal injury lawsuits. What kind of redress should people have if they are injured by a business or a medical procedure? Does the Constitution guarantee a right to sue?

I t's a summer of stupid lawsuits. Food "addicts" are suing McDonald's, Wendy's, Burger King and KFC, claiming that the fast-food industry creates cravings for unhealthy food and fails to provide consumers with nutritional information. (They might as well sue their parents for failing to provide them with common sense.) A female passenger is suing Delta Airlines for negligence, sexual discrimination and intentional affliction of emotional distress, because security agents asked her to hold up a vibrator packed in her mysteriously vibrating suitcase. (If this is her idea of actionable emotional distress and discrimination, you have to wonder how she gets through the day.)

Conservative advocates of tort reform love frivolous cases such as these, overstating their occurrence and using them to promote a misleading image of a legal system overcome by weak, whiny clients and the greedy lawyers who encourage them. In fact, plaintiffs' lawyers who handle personal injury and civil-rights cases often provide the only hope of redress for ordinary people harmed by unsafe or unfair business practices—the ordinary people for whom compassionate conservatives supposedly care.

What view of litigation does this liberal author hold? Does this view help explain why trial lawyers tend to be Democrats and medical doctors tend to be Republicans?

So it's amusing—in fact, it's downright delightful—to report that what may be the summer's stupidest, whiniest lawsuit was initiated by a group of religious conservatives. The Virginia-based Family Policy Network (FPN) sued the University of North Carolina at Chapel Hill (UNC) for asking incoming freshmen to read selections from the Koran and accompanying commentaries by religion professor Michael Sells. Students were also required to write a paper and participate in a discussion about the book; those who found reading about Islam abhorrent were given the option of writing a paper explaining why they chose not to read the book. (The disputed book is *Approaching the Qur'an*, edited and translated by Sells.) The lawsuit (quickly rejected in federal court) was prepared by the American Family Association, with which the FPN is affiliated. It claims that this assignment attempts "to indoctrinate students in religious belief and to promote a particular religion."

> Would the FPN have brought this suit if UNC had been a private school? What does the fact that UNC is a state supported school have to do with the suit?

It seems beyond dispute, however, that this book was assigned for pedagogical, not evangelical, purposes. No sane person would believe that UNC administrators are intent on converting incoming freshmen to Islam or infusing them with particular Islamic values. "We expect Carolina students as part of their education to learn about ideas, philosophies and practices that they never encountered before and that may differ from their own," UNC Chapel Hill Chancellor James Moeser has explained. "We chose [*Approaching the Qu'ran*] because, since September 11, many of us have wondered what the core teachings of Islam really are."

You might think that conservative Christian groups would be among the first to insist that schools have a right (maybe even a responsibility) to teach about religion. You wouldn't expect people who favor official school prayer to balk at academic discussions of religious ideals, except that groups such as the Family Policy Network are interested in preaching, not teaching. In other words, they favor a sectarian approach to religious education in public schools. As FPN President Joe Glover has indicated (in a typically incoherent interview on the Fox News Channel's Hannity & Colmes), he would not object to teaching about Christianity. How, then, does FPN justify opposition to teaching about Islam? Glover complains that Sells' book presents too sympathetic a view of Islam because it omits passages of the Koran that express "hate and vitriol toward Christians and Jews."

Sells explains that his purpose was "not to make a judgment about Islam" but to introduce students to the religion's key theological concepts. If he were preparing a book about the Bible to teach about Christian or Jewish theology, he adds, he would not focus on its many passages filled with hate, vitriol and violence. Rather, he'd omit excerpts from the Book of Joshua, for example, as well as the statement from the gospels that "Jews have the blood of Jesus on their hands," that has been used to persecute Jews down through the centuries.

"I'm not sure whether that's relevant," Glover says, referring to Christian claims that "the Jews killed Christ," as a teenage boy informed me years ago. And

Glover may have an inadvertent point: With religious conservatives enthusiastically supporting Israel, thanks to their mythologies about its role in Armageddon, anti-Semitism on the right, while not exactly irrelevant, has surely become impolitic. In fact, the FPN's lawsuit against UNC included as plaintiffs three anonymous students: one evangelical Christian, one Catholic and one Jew.

This silly case never had much chance of succeeding in federal court, but it may still be a good fundraising opportunity for the FPN and its allies. Already, it's being used to castigate the American Civil Liberties Union (on whose national board I serve) for declining to support the suit. Instead, the North Carolina ACLU affiliate sent a measured letter to the university, asking it to establish guidelines for implementing the assignment and reminding it of the responsibility to teach and not preach, to respect religious privacy and to not stigmatize any students for their beliefs.

> What would a civil libertarian recommend here? Is the ACLU's position consistent with civil libertarian values?

If you're as outraged as some religious conservatives by the ACLU's failure to condemn teaching about world religions, and its refusal to "side with Christians and Jews" in their battle to ensure ignorance of Islam, you can add your name to a petition at www.conservativepetitions.com. "Tell the ACLU to defend Christians and Jews, too," the headline on the Web page screams, with unconscious irony. Does this mean they'll stop calling us the ACLJew?

Consider the source and the audience.

- There's no question that this piece is directed to a liberal audience. What purpose is served by liberal and conservative commentators mocking the other side? Can an argument be both ideological and intellectual?

Lay out the argument, the values, and the assumptions.

- With respect to Kaminer's main argument, what rights does she think teachers have in terms of what they choose to teach? Does she think "anything goes," or are there limits?
- What arguments are made by the group bringing the suit? Why do they think it would be okay to teach the Bible, but not the Koran? What danger do they see?
- What is Kaminer's response to those arguments?

Uncover the evidence.

- Does Kaminer use evidence to support her claims? What rhetorical techniques does she use to move her audience and make her case?

Evaluate the conclusion.

- Has Kaminer succeeded in diminishing the case brought by the FPN? If you didn't agree with her to begin with, would you agree with her now? What are the limitations of making an argument based more on calls to ideology than on factual evidence?

Sort out the political implications.

- What would happen if the curriculum of public colleges were controlled by politics and lawsuits? Who should make those decisions?
- The ACLU agrees to defend civil liberties on anyone's behalf, regardless of ideology, because it sees itself as the protector of liberties, not of particular people. Would it be more effective if it confined itself to liberal or conservative causes? What benefits might come to it from taking a less political approach?

4.3 The Federal Eye

Robert A. Levy, *National Review Online,* 26 November 2002

In the nerve-wracking, horrified days after September 11, 2001, stunned Americans tried to find some kind of answer to their anguished questions: How could such an attack have taken place on U.S. soil? Didn't we see it coming? Could it happen again? Lawmakers—staggered by the enormity of the attacks and the degree to which they seemed to have taken place without warning from the intelligence community, which they had complacently assumed to be the best in the world—rushed to put some kind of legislative roadblocks in the way of such an attack happening again.

Among the legislation passed in the immediate aftermath of September 11 was the anti-terrorism package officially called the Uniting and Strengthening America by Providing Appropriate Tools Required to Intercept and Obstruct Terrorism Act (informally known as the USA PATRIOT Act). Passed slightly more than a month after the attacks, this act, among other things, made it easier for officials to search a person's home or belongings without that person being present, to conduct electronic surveillance through e-mail wiretapping without a judge's previous knowledge, to detain people suspected of terrorist activity, and to monitor private financial transactions and share the data with federal agencies. It coordinated the CIA and the FBI, separated since 1970 to prevent domestic spying, and broadly defined a new crime of "domestic terrorism."

Critics claimed that the USA PATRIOT Act and similar legislation had been passed too hastily—in some cases, by legislators who had not even read it thoroughly, let alone thought carefully about its impact on civil liberties. Supporters said that such concerns were nonsense, that increased security required limits on freedom and was well worth the sacrifice. This article, written over a year after the passage of the act, assesses post–September 11 legislation and practices from the standpoint of a civil libertarian. Civil libertarians, whether liberals or conservatives, believe that government restrictions on our civil liberties are rarely, if ever, justified. Is such absolute protection of civil liberties possible? If it is not, what is the point of being a civil libertarian?

When a former Iran-Contra defendant gets appointed to run a little-known Defense Department operation called "Total Information Awareness," then posts a sign on his office stating that "Knowledge Is Power," civil libertarians, not surprisingly, are exercised. Admiral John Poindexter may be suited for

Why does the notion that "Knowledge Is Power" threaten civil libertarians? Whose knowledge? About what?

the job, but is the job suited for a free society that has, until recently, fastidiously safeguarded the privacy of its citizens?

Reportedly, the new system will use high-tech "data mining" to gather information from multiple databases, link individuals and groups, and share information efficiently. Never mind that Pentagon computer scientists believe that terrorists could easily avoid detection, leaving bureaucrats with about 200 million dossiers on totally innocent Americans—instant access to e-mail, web surfing, and phone records, credit-card and banking transactions, prescription-drug purchases, travel data, and court records.

If Total Information Awareness were the first and only budding threat to civil liberties, opponents might be less apprehensive. But against a backdrop of multiple laws, executive orders, and proposals—all potentially troublesome to hardcore Bill of Rights devotees—our constitutional watchdogs are justifiably uneasy. Here are a few of their grievances:

The USA PATRIOT Act: Ordinarily, advance judicial authorization of executive actions, followed by judicial review to assure that officials haven't misbehaved, shields us from excessive concentrations of power in a single branch of government. Under the PATRIOT Act, however, the executive branch has overwhelming if not exclusive power. Judicial checks and balances are conspicuously absent.

Expansion of the FISA court's authority: The Foreign Intelligence Surveillance Act created a court that approves electronic surveillance of citizens and resident aliens allegedly serving a foreign power. Previously, the FISA court could act if foreign intelligence was the primary purpose of an investigation. Now, foreign intelligence need only be "a significant purpose." That is not a trivial change. It means easier government access to personal and business records, and relaxed authorization of Internet surveillance and wiretaps—even in criminal cases.

Domestic detention of non-citizens: Soon after 9/11, about 1,200 non-citizens were detained in secret without evidence linking a single one of them to al Qaeda. The recurring questions were pretty basic. How many remained in custody? Who were they? What were the charges against them? What was the status of their cases? Where and under what circumstances were they being held? The Justice Department adamantly refused to provide any answers.

Secret INS trials: Hundreds of deportation hearings have been held in secret by the Immigration and Naturalization Service—without a jury, and without access by the defendant to legal counsel. The U.S. Court of Appeals for the Sixth Circuit accused the INS of operating "in virtual secrecy in all matters dealing, even remotely, with national security." The court warned, "Democracies die behind closed doors."

Detention of U.S. citizens: The administration has unilaterally declared that two U.S. citizens are "enemy combatants," whisked them away, detained them indefinitely in a military brig, denied them legal counsel, filed no charges whatever, and prevented them from seeking meaningful judicial review.

> Why do democracies "die behind closed doors"? What is the relationship between democracy and openness?

Monitoring attorney-client communications: Attorney General John Ashcroft, armed only with "reasonable suspicion" that a communication would "facilitate acts of terrorism," invented Justice Department authority to monitor talks between detainees and their lawyers, without a court order, despite constitutional guarantees of an unimpeded right to counsel.

Military tribunals: The Bush executive order on military tribunals fell short in three respects. First, tribunals should be convened only outside the United States. Here, our criminal courts are a perfectly acceptable venue. Second, tribunals must be limited to prosecuting unlawful combatants, not merely someone tangentially related to international terrorism. Third, tribunals should be congressionally authorized, not decreed by the executive branch.

Terrorism Information and Prevention System: TIPS was the administration brainchild that would have transformed us into a nation of busybodies and snoops. About eleven million informants—especially mail carriers, utility employees and others with unique access to private homes—were to help the Justice Department build yet another database containing names of persons not charged with any wrongdoing.

Of course, advocates of expanded executive power remind civil libertarians that President Bush is an honorable man who understands that the Constitution is made of more than tissue paper. That argument is simply not persuasive—even to those who fervently share its underlying premise. The policies that are put in place by this administration are precedent-setting. Bush supporters need to reflect on the same powers in the hands of his predecessor or his successors.

Here's the guiding principle: In the post–9/11 environment, no rational person believes that civil liberties are inviolable. After all, government's primary obligation is to secure the lives of American citizens. But when government begins to chip away at our liberties, we must insist that it jump through a couple of hoops. First, government must offer compelling evidence that its new and intrusive programs will make us safer. Second, government must convince us that there is no less invasive means of attaining the same ends. In too many instances, those dual burdens have not been met.

If administration critics have a single overriding concern about policies adopted in the wake of 9/11, it is this: The president and the attorney general have concentrated too much unchecked authority in the hands of the executive branch—compromising the doctrine of separation of powers, which has been a cornerstone of our Constitution for more than two centuries. Those persons who would unhesitatingly trade off civil liberties in return for national security proclaim that concentrated power is necessary for Americans to remain free. Yet there's an obvious corollary that's too often missed: Unless Americans remain free, they will never be secure.

> What is the relationship between freedom and security? Can we be both completely free and completely secure at the same time?

Consider the source and the audience.

- Levy is writing as a guest columnist in the online edition of *National Review,* a conservative journal. He is a fellow at the Cato Institute, a conservative libertarian think tank. How would the *National Review*'s audience have received this argument? How would conservatives who are *not* civil libertarians respond to the USA PATRIOT Act and the other legislation Levy critiques?

Lay out the argument, the values, and the assumptions.

- What value does Levy seek to protect above all? How does that shape his views on the other values he discusses?
- In what ways, according to Levy, is liberty limited by the legislation and government actions he discusses? How do these laws and actions compromise separation of powers and checks and balances?
- What does Levy mean by saying that the powers being given to the administration are *precedent-setting*? Why should even Bush supporters balk at giving Bush so much power?

Uncover the evidence.

- How does Levy seek to convince his audience that lawmakers and the president are strengthening the executive branch at the expense of civil liberties? Is his list of government actions persuasive?

Evaluate the conclusion.

- Has Levy made the case that government should jump through additional hoops before it takes away Americans' civil liberties?
- Does he address the question of how much liberty he thinks we can safely give up in the name of security?

Sort out the political implications.

- How might a president take advantage of the newly created executive powers that worry Levy?
- We can imagine that the best-case scenario is an honorable government that keeps us safe but minimizes infringements on individual liberty, despite the new laws in place. What's the worst-case scenario?

4.4 Measuring Lost Freedom vs. Security in Dollars

Edmund L. Andrews, *New York Times,* 11 March 2003

In the previous article, civil libertarian Robert Levy bemoaned the inroads made on civil liberties by post–September 11 security legislation, and argued that it should be much harder for government to take such action. This article addresses similar concerns from a novel perspective.

Cost-benefit analysis has long been a method of assessing the effectiveness of public policy. If a policy produces benefits that are more valuable than the costs it imposes, it is evaluated positively. If more than one policy is being considered, the one that imposes the fewest costs gets the edge. This method of analysis is frequently used to evaluate environmental policy, with the cost of regulations to businesses compared to the benefit of the policies to the public. Since it is a lot easier to gauge business costs than to put a price tag on things like clean air and water, this method of analysis does not usually support extensive environmental regulations.

In this article, people from a variety of ideological viewpoints suggest that cost-benefit analysis be applied to the tradeoff between liberty and security that was discussed in the last article. Which side will this approach tend to favor—the regulators or the regulated?

Civil liberties and privacy may be priceless, but they may soon have a price tag.

In an unusual twist on cost-benefit analysis, an economic tool that conservatives have often used to attack environmental regulation, top advisers to President Bush want to weigh the benefits of tighter domestic security against the "costs" of lost privacy and freedom.

"People are willing to accept some burdens, some intrusion on their privacy and some inconvenience," said John Graham, director of regulatory affairs at the White House Office of Management and Budget. "But I want to make sure that people can see these intangible burdens."

In a notice published last month, the budget office asked experts from around the country for ideas on how to measure "indirect costs" like lost time, lost privacy and even lost liberty that might stem from tougher security regulations.

Can we put a price tag on "lost time, lost privacy and even lost liberty"?

The budget office has not challenged any domestic security rules, and officials say they are only beginning to look at how they might measure costs of things like reduced privacy. But officials said they hoped to give federal agencies guidance by the end of the year. And even if many costs cannot be quantified in dollar terms, they say, the mere effort to identify them systematically could prompt agencies to look for less burdensome alternatives.

The issues are not always abstract. American universities are worried that ever-tighter scrutiny of foreign students will cause them to lose market share in foreign students to Australia, Canada and Europe.

Airlines, meanwhile, are eager to increase use of advanced passenger screening systems. Civil rights advocates say the systems would single out some people with particular ethnic backgrounds, but they might also help business fliers whisk through security checkpoints as seemingly low-risk "trusted travelers."

Jarring as it may seem to assign a price on privacy or liberty, the idea has attracted an unusual array of supporters, including Ralph Nader, the consumer advocate and former presidential candidate, who said the approach might expose wrong-headed security regulations.

"As long as they're going to deal with monetary evaluations, I told them they should start asking about the cost of destroying democracy," said Mr. Nader, who lobbied Mitchell E. Daniels Jr., the budget office director, on the issue. "If the value assigned to civil rights and privacy is zero, the natural thing to do is just wipe them out."

Lawyers at the American Civil Liberties Union also support the idea, as do some conservative Republicans who fret about "big government."

Skeptics abound, with some predicting that cost-benefit analysis will bog down domestic security decisions as badly as worries about the spotted owl once bogged down loggers in the Pacific Northwest.

"It may be a waste of time and resources," said Charles Peña, director of defense policy at the Cato Institute, a conservative research organization in Washington. "The last thing you want to do with homeland security is to get mired down in typical bureaucratic debates."

Supporters and critics alike say the effort could open up a new battlefront on domestic security.

The budget office has the power to challenge and sometimes to block regulations if they appear to fail the cost-benefit test.

And given the regulatory costs, whether in the form of mandatory spending on antiterrorist measures or lost customers, many business and organizational groups are likely to have their own reasons for caring about privacy, ease of movement and convenience.

"We already make these kinds of trade-offs all the time," said Bruce Schneier, a security consultant in Sunnyvale, Calif., who is the author of a book due out in September titled *The Security Puzzle.* "What you need to know are the agendas of the different players."

Mr. Graham, a passionate champion of cost-benefit analysis who taught at Harvard before joining the administration, stopped short of saying that government officials might somehow assign a price for costs like lost privacy or convenience.

But he said it was important to analyze such costs, even if they could not be translated into precise dollar amounts. "We can all see that life has changed since Sept. 11," he said in a recent interview in his office in the Old Executive Office Building. "Simply identifying some of these costs will help understand them and get people to think about alternatives that might reduce those costs."

Two of Mr. Graham's colleagues at Harvard have already taken a look at potential trade-offs in a recent paper titled "Sacrificing Civil Liberties to Reduce Terrorism Risk." The authors, W. Kip Viscusi of Harvard Law School and Richard J. Zeckhauser at the Kennedy School of Government, said Harvard law students surveyed were more willing to accept profiling of airline passengers if it meant they could save time in security checks.

Are these Harvard law students the ones who are most likely to be profiled? How might the cost-benefit calculation change for a population of foreign students?

While 44 percent of students said they favored profiling if it saved them 10 minutes, 74 percent were in favor if it saved them an hour.

"Clearly, people are willing to make trade-offs," said Mr. Viscusi, who has been applying cost-benefit analysis to environmental regulations since the early 1980's. Weighing values like privacy or civil liberty against heightened security, he said, could help prevent the security goals from overtaking common sense.

"If you're the homeland security guy, that is the only thing you're going to be looking at and you're going to have tunnel vision," Mr. Viscusi said. "The last tightening of the standard may not have much of a payoff in security but it might have a big cost in civil liberties."

Lawyers at the American Civil Liberties Union also see benefits in treating lost civil liberties as a cost. "Many of the proposals coming out of the Department of Justice would fail the risk-benefit analysis if the costs of lost liberties are weighed in," said Gregory Nojeim, associate director of the A.C.L.U.'s national office. "We think it's necessary to assess the costs of counterterrorism proposals in terms of lost liberties."

Since Sept. 11, 2001, universities have begun providing the government with more detailed information on foreign students and any changes that might invalidate their visas. The Bush administration is also proposing an elaborate new system, linked to security checks at the F.B.I. and C.I.A., under which the government would run background checks on foreign students or foreign teachers who want to do research in potentially sensitive scientific areas.

University officials are increasingly worried that ever-tighter scrutiny will cost them tens of thousands of students a year.

"For decades, we were getting them all, but there has been a sharp increase in competition from Australia, Canada and Europe," said John Vaughn, executive vice president of the Association of American Universities. "If we increase the monitoring of foreign students, with overtones of presumptive guilt, and we increase restrictions on foreigners doing research, these things will have an indirect chilling effect."

The trade-offs are almost certain to escalate. Proposals are circulating for tighter rules on immigration, on customs inspections, on preparation against bioterrorist attacks and on scores of other issues.

Last month, the Justice Department set off a furor among civil rights advocates with the draft of a proposal to expand the powers of the law enforcement authorities.

Though administration officials said the draft was not a formal proposal, its recommendations included invalidating state laws against police spying and imposing a flat ban on using the Freedom of Information Act to identify people detained on suspicions of terrorist involvement.

The domestic security push has in many ways turned the battles of cost-benefit analysis on their head. In the 1980's, consumer advocates like Mr. Nader often denounced cost-benefit analysis as a tool conservatives used to swat down environmental and safety regulations.

But just as business groups once viewed cost-benefit analysis as a way to curb restrictions on their activity, Mr. Nader and civil rights groups see it as a way to curb restrictions on government authorities.

Why are liberals in favor of cost-benefit analysis in this context, through they oppose applying it to environmental policy?

"Even without coming to complete agreement on what we think the cost of lost freedom is, we would all agree that it's not zero," Mr. Nader said. "They are developing dragnet systems of law enforcement that are very inefficient. I'm saying to O.M.B., you guys are the brake. You are the only ones who can bring these guys down to earth."

Consider the source and the audience.

- This article appeared in the *New York Times*. How are the pros and cons of the issue framed here, and how might they be differently framed in a liberal or conservative journal? Can you tell where this author stands?

Lay out the argument, the values, and the assumptions.

- What do advocates of the idea of applying cost-benefit analysis to security policy say in support of this idea? What kinds of costs can be estimated with respect to the reductions of civil liberties that result from security policy? Are such advocates worried about getting everyone to agree on the worth of liberty?
- What do critics of the idea have to say?

Uncover the evidence.

- Does either side have evidence to offer in support of its position? What are the limits of the kinds of poll data that are offered?

Evaluate the conclusion.

- Does the author make the case for cost-benefit analysis, or does he just illuminate the two sides?
- Do you agree with the author that the security-liberty tradeoffs are going to escalate?

Sort out the political implications.

- Whose costs and whose benefits should be taken into account in a policy-evaluation method like this? If different groups are likely to make different calculations about whether a policy was worth the reduction in liberty, who should the government consult?

4.5 *Federalist* No. 84

Alexander Hamilton, *The Federalist Papers*

The original text of the Constitution contained no Bill of Rights, and that would almost be its undoing. Fearful of a strong central government, the Anti-Federalists insisted that they would not vote to ratify the Constitution unless it contained some built-in limitations to its own power. In *Federalist* No. 84, the second-to-last of *The Federalist Papers,* Alexander Hamilton was busy tying up loose ends that had not been dealt with in previous essays. It was here that he chose to rebut the Anti-Federalist claim that a Bill of Rights was needed. It was not necessary, he argued, because many of the state constitutions admired by the Anti-Federalists did not have bills of rights, and in any case the text of the Constitution had many rights built in, among them the protection against the suspension of habeas corpus, the prohibition against bills of attainder and ex post facto laws, and the entitlement to trial by jury.

Hamilton went further than arguing that a Bill of Rights was unnecessary, however. In the excerpt reprinted here, he claimed that it was actually dangerous to liberty. Are we freer or less free than we were at the time of the founding?

It has been several times truly remarked that bills of rights are, in their origin, stipulations between kings and their subjects, abridgements of prerogative in favor of privilege, reservations of rights not surrendered to the prince. Such was MAGNA CHARTA, obtained by the barons, sword in hand, from King John. Such were the subsequent confirmations of that charter by succeeding princes. Such was the PETITION OF RIGHT assented to by Charles I, in the beginning of his reign. Such, also, was the Declaration of Right presented by the Lords and Commons to the Prince of Orange in 1688, and afterwards thrown into the form of an act of parliament called the Bill of Rights. It is evident, therefore, that, according to their primitive signification, they have no application to constitutions professedly founded upon the power of the people, and executed by their immediate representatives and servants. Here, in strictness, the people surrender nothing; and as they retain every thing they have no need of particular reservations. "WE, THE PEOPLE of the United States, to secure the blessings of liberty to ourselves and our posterity, do ORDAIN and ESTABLISH this Constitution for the United States of America." Here is a better recognition of popular rights, than volumes of those aphorisms which make the principal figure in several of our State bills of rights, and which would sound much better in a treatise of ethics than in a constitution of government.

But a minute detail of particular rights is certainly far less applicable to a Constitution like that under consideration, which is merely intended to regulate the general political interests of the nation, than to a constitution which has the regulation of every species of personal and private concerns. If, therefore, the loud clamors against the plan of the convention, on this score, are well founded, no epithets of reprobation will be too strong for the constitution of this State. But the truth is, that both of them contain all which, in relation to their objects, is reasonably to be desired.

I go further, and affirm that bills of rights, in the sense and to the extent in which they are contended for, are not only unnecessary in the proposed Constitution, but would even be dangerous. They would contain various exceptions to powers not granted; and, on this very account, would afford a colorable pretext to claim more than were granted. For why declare that things shall not be done which there is no power to do? Why, for instance, should it be said that the liberty of the press shall not be restrained, when no power is given by which restrictions may be imposed? I will not contend that such a provision would confer a regulating power; but it is evident that it would furnish, to men disposed to usurp, a plausible pretense for claiming that power. They might urge with a semblance of reason, that the Constitution ought not to be charged with the absurdity of providing against the abuse of an authority which was not given, and that the provision against restraining the liberty of the press afforded a clear implication, that a power to prescribe proper regulations concerning it was in-

Do people really not surrender any power under our Constitution? Does it not place any obligations on us?

tended to be vested in the national government. This may serve as a specimen of the numerous handles which would be given to the doctrine of constructive powers, by the indulgence of an injudicious zeal for bills of rights.

On the subject of the liberty of the press, as much as has been said, I cannot forbear adding a remark or two: in the first place, I observe, that there is not a syllable concerning it in the constitution of this State; in the next, I contend, that whatever has been said about it in that of any other State, amounts to nothing. What signifies a declaration, that "the liberty of the press shall be inviolably preserved?" What is the liberty of the press? Who can give it any definition which would not leave the utmost latitude for evasion? I hold it to be impracticable; and from this I infer, that its security, whatever fine declarations may be inserted in any constitution respecting it, must altogether depend on public opinion, and on the general spirit of the people and of the government. And here, after all, as is intimated upon another occasion, must we seek for the only solid basis of all our rights.

There remains but one other view of this matter to conclude the point. The truth is, after all the declamations we have heard, that the Constitution is itself, in every rational sense, and to every useful purpose, A BILL OF RIGHTS. The several bills of rights in Great Britain form its Constitution, and conversely the constitution of each State is its bill of rights. And the proposed Constitution, if adopted, will be the bill of rights of the Union. Is it one object of a bill of rights to declare and specify the political privileges of the citizens in the structure and administration of the government? This is done in the most ample and precise manner in the plan of the convention; comprehending various precautions for the public security, which are not to be found in any of the State constitutions. Is another object of a bill of rights to define certain immunities and modes of proceeding, which are relative to personal and private concerns? This we have seen has also been attended to, in a variety of cases, in the same plan. Adverting therefore to the substantial meaning of a bill of rights, it is absurd to allege that it is not to be found in the work of the convention. It may be said that it does not go far enough, though it will not be easy to make this appear; but it can with no pro-

> The critics of the Constitution did believe it doesn't go far enough in the protection of rights. In what ways does the Bill of Rights go farther?

priety be contended that there is no such thing. It certainly must be immaterial what mode is observed as to the order of declaring the rights of the citizens, if they are to be found in any part of the instrument which establishes the government. And hence it must be apparent, that much of what has been said on this subject rests merely on verbal and nominal distinctions, entirely foreign from the substance of the thing.

Consider the source and the audience.

- Hamilton was directing this essay to staunch opponents of the Constitution, and on this point, at least, they were winning. He was also speaking to citizens of New York who admired their own state constitution. How do these considerations shape the way he framed his argument?

Lay out the argument, the values, and the assumptions.

- How powerful a government does Hamilton believe is established by the Constitution?
- Why does he think a Bill of Rights would be unnecessary?
- Why does he think it would be dangerous? What mischief would be done if the government were told it is not allowed to do things it doesn't have the power to do anyway?

Uncover the evidence.

- Hamilton uses historical evidence to discuss why bills of rights have existed in the past. Does that evidence have anything to do with the present case he is discussing?
- How does he use logic to make the case that a Bill of Rights is dangerous?

Evaluate the conclusion.

- Does Hamilton persuade you that a Bill of Rights will empower government officials to argue that government has all the powers that are not specifically listed in a written Bill of Rights? Does that mean that the burden will be on us to prove that we have any rights other than those listed?

Sort out the political implications.

- Today many Americans (like libertarian Robert Levy in a previous article) argue that we have a right to privacy. People who interpret the Constitution strictly, as do many members of the Bush administration, believe that we have only the rights that are written down in the Constitution. How does this debate relate to Hamilton's argument here?

CHAPTER 5

Civil Rights

I n some ways, for all our lip service to the tenet that "all men are created equal," American history has been a story of exclusion from the very beginning. The early colonies excluded from political power people who were not members of the right church, or who did not have the right amount of land or the right sum of money in their pockets. At various times, we have excluded people from the rights of American citizenship because of the color of their skin, their gender, the country in which they were born, or the language they spoke. Today, groups like the disabled, gays and lesbians, and noncitizens still find themselves excluded from access to some of the basic rights that others in America enjoy. The search for equality in the United States has been a perennial theme of those standing outside the charmed circle of the privileged and the free, fighting hard to get their share of the American dream.

We call the battle for equality in this country a battle for civil rights—citizenship rights guaranteed by the Constitution or, where the Constitution has not been specific enough to protect some groups, by its provisions in the Thirteenth, Fourteenth, Fifteenth, Nineteenth, and Twenty-Sixth Amendments. The struggle for civil rights that produced those amendments and the laws that enforce them has been harrowing and long because so much is at stake. Rights are more than words on paper—they are political power. To deny people the right to do something is to have power over them, and to make them conform to your will. If they gain rights despite your efforts, they have acquired power to stop you from doing what you want. People fight furiously to restrict and to gain rights because they care so deeply about who shall have the power to decide what kind of society we live in— whose will counts and whose does not.

Groups who fight for civil rights—for recognition of their will and inclusion in the system—are handicapped from the start by the fact that, by definition, they are outside the system in significant ways. The initial challenge these groups face is finding an arena in which they can begin their fight. Consider the plight of African Americans after the Civil War. Although slavery was officially over, the southern states had shut blacks out of political power; the justices on the Supreme Court had previously refused to consider them as potential citizens and within several decades would declare that segregation was legal; Congress refused to pass legislation enforcing the newly passed Thirteenth, Fourteenth, and Fifteenth Amendments; and the president, himself a southerner, had no interest in protecting their newfound rights. It took nearly a hundred years, until the composition of the Supreme Court changed sufficiently to be receptive to a brilliant legal strategy mapped out by the National Association for the Advancement of Colored People, before African Americans could get a toehold in the courts, as well as in the political arena where the fight for enforcement of their civil rights could eventually be won. Civil rights struggles are very much about politics, about using the rules of the system to change public opinion, to change the laws, and to change the way the laws are enforced.

In this chapter we look at the civil rights battles still being fought by various groups in the political, legal, and cultural arenas. The first selection, from the *Washington Post,* begins by looking into the question of racial identity. Who gets to decide what group a person belongs to—the person him- or herself, the group, "society," the courts, the legislature? Our second selection, from *People* magazine, focuses on southern high schools that continue to hold separate proms for black and white students. It raises the difficult question of what racism actually is. The third article, from the conservative journal *The American Spectator,* also takes issue with affirmative action's aims to end discrimination and create diversity by arguing that Title IX, the federal legislation that requires educational institutions to give women's sports equal time (and money) relative to men's, does much more harm than good as it is currently understood and implemented. The fourth piece, from the liberal *American Prospect,* looks at a civil rights battle in a much earlier stage than the fight for racial or gender equality. It argues that the gay rights movement won its first battles in the cultural rather than the political arena, and examines its prospects for translating its success there to more concrete forms of power. Finally, for our classic statement about civil rights, we go back to pre–Civil War America, to a brief but powerful speech by Sojourner Truth who used her experience as a slave to take on those critics of women's rights who argued that women are too delicate and fragile to achieve equality with men. All these many years later, as the articles in this chapter make clear, we have still not come to the end of the debate about what racial and gender equality mean, and whether they have been realized in American society.

5.1 People of Color Who Never Felt They Were Black

Racial Label Surprises Many Latino Immigrants

Darryl Fears, *Washington Post,* 26 December 2002

At the end of the 1800s a man named Homer Plessy was arrested for refusing to get off a whites-only railway car in the state of Louisiana. According to Louisiana law, Plessy was a black man even though only one of his eight great-grandparents had been black. Although Plessy's arrest became famous because it led to the Supreme Court case *Plessy v. Ferguson* (1896) in which the Court declared the policy of separate but equal to be constitutional, it is also worth thinking about because it shows us to what degree race is socially constructed—that is, race is what we as a society say it is, as opposed to some quality that people either possess or do not possess.

This article raises fascinating questions about race in America and elsewhere. In a country where racism—institutionalized power inequality based on a perception of racial differences—still affects who gets what, it is important to dig into the question of just how racial differences are perceived. What makes a person black? White? Latino?

A t her small apartment near the National Cathedral in Northwest Washington, Maria Martins quietly watched as an African American friend studied a picture of her mother. "Oh," the friend said, surprise in her voice. "Your mother is white."

She turned to Martins. "But you are black."

That came as news to Martins, a Brazilian who, for 30 years before immigrating to the United States, looked in the mirror saw a *morena*—a woman with caramel-colored skin that is nearly equated with whiteness in Brazil and some other Latin American countries. "I didn't realize I was black until I came here," she said.

That realization has come to hundreds of thousands of dark-complexioned immigrants to the United States from Brazil, Colombia, Panama and other Latin nations with sizable populations of African descent. Although most do not identify themselves as black, they are seen that way as soon as they set foot in North America.

Their reluctance to embrace this definition has left them feeling particularly isolated—shunned by African Americans who believe they are denying their blackness; by white Americans who profile them in stores or on highways; and by lighter-skinned Latinos whose images dominate Spanish-language television all over the world, even though a majority of Latin people have some African or Indian ancestry.

The pressure to accept not only a new language and culture, but also a new racial identity, is a burden some darker-skinned Latinos say they face every day.

"It's overwhelming," said Yvette Modestin, a dark-skinned native of Panama who works as an outreach coordinator in Boston. "There's not a day that I don't have to explain myself."

E. Francisco Lopez, a Venezuelan-born attorney in Washington, said he had not heard the term "minority" before coming to America.

> Who should decide what a person's race is? The group of people who identify as a particular race? The person him- or herself? Other people in society?

"I didn't know what it meant. I didn't accept it because I thought it meant 'less than,'" said Martins, whose father is black. "'Where are you from?' they ask me. I say I'm from Brazil. They say, 'No, you are from Africa.' They make me feel like I am denying who I am."

Exactly who these immigrants are is almost impossible to divine from the 2000 Census. Latinos of African, mestizo and European descent—or any mixture of the three—found it hard to answer the question "What is your racial origin?"

Some of the nation's 35 million Latinos scribbled in the margins that they were Aztec or Mayan. A fraction said they were Indian. Nearly forty-eight percent described themselves as white, and only 2 percent as black. Fully 42 percent said they were "some other race."

Between Black and White

Race matters in Latin America, but it matters differently.

Most South American nations barely have a black presence. In Argentina, Chile, Peru and Bolivia, there are racial tensions, but mostly between indigenous Indians and white descendants of Europeans.

The black presence is stronger along the coasts of two nations that border the Caribbean Sea, Venezuela and Colombia—which included Panama in the 19th century—along with Brazil, which snakes along the Atlantic coast. In many ways, those nations have more in common racially with Puerto Rico, Cuba and the Dominican Republic than they do with the rest of South America.

This black presence is a legacy of slavery, just as it is in the United States. But the experience of race in the United States and in these Latin countries is separated by how slaves and their descendants were treated after slavery was abolished.

In the United States, custom drew a hard line between black and white, and Jim Crow rules kept the races separate. The color line hardened to the point that it was sanctioned in 1896 by the Supreme Court in its decision in *Plessy v. Ferguson,* which held that Homer Plessy, a white-complexioned Louisiana shoemaker, could not ride in the white section of a train because a single ancestor of his was black.

Thus Americans with any discernible African ancestry—whether they identified themselves as black or not—were thrust into one category. One consequence is that dark-complexioned and light-complexioned black people combined to campaign for equal rights, leading to the civil rights movement of the 1960s.

By contrast, the Latin countries with a sizable black presence had more various, and more fluid, experiences of race after slavery.

African slavery is as much a part of Brazil's history as it is of the United States's, said Sheila Walker, a visiting professor of anthropology at Spelman College in Atlanta and editor of the book *African Roots/American Cultures.* Citing the census in Brazil, she said that nation has more people of African descent than any other in the world besides Nigeria, Africa's most populous country.

Brazil stands out in South America for that and other reasons. Unlike most nations there, its people speak Portuguese rather than Spanish, prompting a debate over whether Brazil is part of the Latino diaspora.

Brazilian slavery ended in 1889 by decree, with no civil war and no Jim Crow—and mixing between light and dark-complexioned Indians, Europeans, Africans and mulattoes was common and, in many areas, encouraged. Although discrimination against dark-complexioned Brazilians was clear, class played almost as important a role as race.

In Colombia, said Luis Murillo, a black politician in exile from that country, light-complexioned descendants of Spanish conquistadors and Indians created the "mestizo" race, an ideology that held that all mixed-race people were the same. But it was an illusion, Murillo said: A pecking order "where white people were considered superior and darker people were considered inferior" pervaded Colombia.

> Is it racism if people of one race discriminate against people of the same race because of the lightness or darkness of their skin color?

Murillo said the problem exists throughout Latin American and Spanish-speaking Caribbean countries with noticeable black populations. White Latinos control the governments even in nations with dark-complexioned majorities, he said. And in nations ruled by military juntas and dictators, there are few protests, Murillo said.

In Cuba, a protest by Afro-Cubans led to the arming of the island's white citizens and, ultimately, the massacre of 3,000 to 6,000 black men, women and children in 1912, according to University of Michigan historian Frank Guridy, author of *Race and Politics in Cuba, 1933–34.*

American-influenced Cuba was also home to the Ku Klux Klan Kubano and other anti-black groups before Fidel Castro's revolution. Now, Cuban racism still exists, some say, but black, mulatto and white people mix much more freely. Lopez, the Afro-Venezuelan lawyer, said, "Race doesn't affect us there the way it does here," he said. "It's more of a class thing."

Jose Neinstein, a native white Brazilian and executive director of the Brazilian-American Cultural Institute in Washington, boiled down to the simplest terms how his people are viewed. "In this country," he said, "if you are not quite white, then you are black." But in Brazil, he said, "If you are not quite black, then you are white."

The elite in Brazil, as in most Latin American nations, are educated and white. But many brown and black people also belong in that class. Generally, brown Brazilians, such as Martins, enjoy many privileges of the elite, but are disproportionately represented in Brazilian slums.

Someone with Sidney Poitier's deep chocolate complexion would be considered white if his hair were straight and he made a living in a profession. That might not seem so odd, Brazilians say, when you consider that the fair-complexioned actresses Rashida Jones of the television show "Boston Public" and Lena Horne are identified as black in the United States.

Neinstein remembered talking with a man of Poitier's complexion during a visit to Brazil. "We were discussing ethnicity," Neinstein said, "and I asked him, 'What do you think about this from your perspective as a black man?' He turned his head to me and said, 'I'm not black,'" Neinstein recalled. ". . . It simply paralyzed me. I couldn't ask another question."

By the same token, Neinstein said, he never perceived brown-complexioned people such as Maria Martins, who works at the cultural institute, as black. One day, when an African American custodian in his building referred to one of his brown-skinned secretaries as "the black lady," Neinstein was confused. "I never looked at that woman as black," he said. "It was quite a revelation to me."

Those perceptions come to the United States with the light- and dark-complexioned Latinos who carry them. But here, they collide with two contradictory forces: North American prejudice and African American pride.

"I've Learned to Be Proud"

Vilson DaSilva, a native of Brazil, is a *moreno*. Like his wife, Maria Martins, he was born to a black father and a white mother. But their views on race seem to differ.

During an interview when Martins said she had no idea how they had identified themselves on the 2000 Census form, DaSilva rolled his eyes. "I said we were black," he said.

He is one of a growing number of Latin immigrants of African descent who identify themselves as Afro-Latino, along the same color spectrum as African Americans.

"I've learned to be proud of my color," he said. For that, he thanked African American friends who stand up for equal rights.

An emerging cadre of Latinos in Washington are embracing their African identities and speaking out against what they say is a white Latino establishment, in the U.S. and abroad.

Lopez, the Afro-Venezuelan lawyer, who lives in Columbia Heights, said there was prejudice even in such Hispanic civil rights organizations as the League of United Latin American Citizens, the Mexican-American Legal Defense and Educational Fund and the National Council of La Raza, where, he said, few dark-complexioned Latinos work in the offices or sit on the board. "La Raza? Represent me? Absolutely not," Lopez said.

Charles Kamasaki, an analyst for La Raza, disagreed. "I don't think you can make snap judgments like that," he said. "The way race is played out in Latino organizations is different. There are dark-complexioned people on our board, but I don't know if they identify as Afro-Latino. Our president is mestizo. I would resist the assertion that this organization is excluding anyone because of race."

Yvette Modestin, the black Panamanian who identifies as an Afro-Latina, said that although she accepts her blackness, she's also an immigrant who speaks Spanish. In other words, she's not a black American. "My brother's married to a Mexican," she said. "My brother's been called a sellout by black women while walking down the street with his wife. They are both Latino. They think he married outside his race."

DaSilva agreed that nuances separate African Americans and Afro-Latinos, but he also believes that seeing Latin America through African American eyes gave him a better perspective. Unfortunately, he said, it also made him angrier and more stressed.

When DaSilva returned to Brazil for a visit, he asked questions he had never asked, and got answers that shocked him.

His mother told him why her father didn't speak to her for 18 years: "It was because she married a black man," he said. One day, DaSilva's own father pulled him aside to provide his son some advice. "'You can play around with whoever you want,'" DaSilva recalled his father saying, "'but marry your own kind.'" So DaSilva married Martins, the *morena* of his dreams.

She is dreaming of a world with fewer racial barriers, a world she believes she left in Brazil to be with her husband in Washington.

> Do the old racial categories still hold in this day of immigration and interracial marriages? How should the choices on the census form be worded?

As Martins talked about the nation's various racial blends in her living room, her 18-month-old son sat in front of the television, watching a Disney cartoon called "The Proud Family," about a merged black American and black Latino family. The characters are intelligent, whimsical, thoughtful, funny, with skin tones that range from light to dark brown.

The DaSilvas said they would never see such a show on Latin American TV.

Martins said her perspective on race was slowly conforming to the American view, but it saddened her. She doesn't understand why she can't call a pretty black girl a *negrita*, the way Latin Americans always say it, with affection. She doesn't understand why she has to say she's black, seeming to deny the existence of her mother.

"Sometimes I say she is black on the outside and white on the inside," DaSilva said of his wife, who threw her head back and laughed.

Consider the source and the audience.

- The *Washington Post* reaches a broad audience, but especially the one situated in the nation's multiethnic capital. Would this story be written in the same way for an audience in, say, Idaho?

Lay out the argument, the values, and the assumptions.

- What assumptions are made in this article about how racial identities are constructed?
- What is responsible for the difference in the way that blacks are perceived in the United States and Brazil? Why do we in the United States assume that if you are not quite white, then you are black?
- What happens when the Brazilian perception of race meets what Fears calls "two contradictory forces: North American prejudice and African American pride"?

Uncover the evidence.

- How does Fears support his case that there are different views of race in the United States and other countries?
- How does he use history to explain how these differences came about? Is it effective evidence?

Evaluate the conclusion.

- How would the author answer the question of whether there is more racism in the United States than in Latin America? How would you answer it?

Sort out the political implications.

- If race is socially constructed, what kind of strategy would it take to eliminate racism?

5.2 Black and White Proms

Patrick Rogers, Don Sider, and Lori Rozsa, *People*, 19 May 2003

In the 1950s, the Supreme Court declared that the doctrine of "separate but equal" was unconstitutional. When it came to education, the court ruled in *Brown v. Board of Education,* the very act of separation created inequality, so that separate was unequal, by definition. Black students, forced to go to separate schools, felt inferior and consequently the education they received was inferior.

A half century later, most of us think that the issue of legal segregation of public facilities is dead. As this article from *People* magazine reveals, however, there are still some unsettled gray areas that look like a throwback to a more racist past. At two Georgia high schools, separate junior-senior proms are held for white students and black students, despite black student requests to merge them. The school board in one district allows this situation to continue because, it says, the prom is student organized and funded and hence, not public school business. If the white students prefer a separate prom, should they be allowed to have one?

O n May 9 the dining room of the Dublin, Ga., Elks Lodge will be decked out in purple and silver. Cardboard trees will sprout glittery cardboard diamonds. And just before 8 P.M. about 200 teenagers will arrive in pickup trucks and rented limos for an annual rite of spring: a junior-senior prom for students at Johnson County High School. "I hope I don't fall off my heels," says Carla Rachels, 17, one of the event's organizers. There will be punch and snacks, she says, and a deejay hired to spin until midnight.

But there will be no African-Americans. In a tradition as old as anyone in central Georgia can remember, the black and white students of the high school in Wrightsville, who otherwise mingle in the halls and play on the same sports teams, still go their separate ways on prom night. Many in Johnson County (pop. 8,500) simply accept the status quo. "A really nice black boy asked if we could get together and talk about it. I talked to some of the other white kids about mixing the proms together, and it got shot down," says Rachels. "I'm happy with the way it is." Others aren't so thrilled. "I think there should be one prom," says Tierra Wiley, an African-American junior who attended the black prom on April 19. "All the black kids want it. Some of the white kids too. I think it would be more fun."

> Are blacks and whites deciding to have separate proms because that is the preference of each race, or do whites have proms that exclude blacks, who must then hold their own dances? Does it matter which it is?

Yet no one in the town—not the kids nor their parents or teachers—has made a meaningful move to unite the two dances. "Most people here don't want to stick their necks out," explains Rev. Eugene Allen, a past president of the NAACP in neighboring Laurens County. "A lot of the blacks are comfortable, and they don't want to rock the boat too much." Kathy Cox, Georgia's Superintendent of Schools, thinks the adults have a responsibility to step in to end what she views as a throwback to a divided past. "This is where the school should play a leadership role," she says, "and bridge the gap that still exists between the races."

Since the Johnson County school board has no official control over the proms—they are technically student-organized and student-funded activities— Cox and other state officials are powerless to bring about a change. And administrators at Johnson County High, where the 375-member student body is split evenly among blacks and whites, see no reason to. "We don't get involved," says school principal Roland Thomas. As for whether holding segregated proms could be considered racist, "I'd rather not comment on that," Thomas says.

Though no national figures exist, Johnson is not the only county in the U.S. to host segregated proms. Last year two juniors in Taylor County, Ga.—one white, one black—broke a 31-year tradition of separation by organizing a prom that attracted a mixed group of more than 100 kids. By the time prom season arrived again this year a splinter group of 50 white students in Taylor County had decided to attend another whites-only dance, held May 2 in Columbus. The school's mixed dance will go ahead May 9, says Linda Drains, 35, a child-evaluation specialist at the Georgia Center for Youth and a sponsor of the integrated prom: "It kind of hurt the feelings of the black students when the white kids didn't invite any of them to the prom. I think there's definitely some racism."

If feelings are hurt back in Johnson County, few are airing them openly. "I certainly wouldn't think it's anything racial," said Deidre Ledford, 22, a white Johnson County High grad and editor of *The Johnson Journal* weekly newspaper. "We don't have a racial problem here." Local Sheriff Rusty Oxford agrees—despite two incidents last July in which black citizens reported being stalked by a car carrying two or three men wearing white robes. By the time police arrived, he notes, the alleged stalkers had disappeared and witnesses could not identify the make, year or color of the car.

What does a "racial problem" look like? Do these people have one?

Whether the split proms are racially motivated or not, some see signs of potential change at the school. Since 2000, Johnson County High School reunions have been integrated affairs. And even though they choose to sit separately in the lunch room, black and white kids generally get along. "Fighting racism has been tough in this part of Georgia," says Allen. "Hopefully the generations coming along will be able to change that."

Consider the source and the audience.

- *People* is a popular entertainment journal. It does not cover hard news, but it does look for stories that will have a broad human interest. Why would this story appeal to them?
- How does the magazine's mission to entertain affect the way they present the issue and the underlying question of racism?

Lay out the argument, the values, and the assumptions.

- Is the authors' underlying assumption that having separate proms is normal, or do they think the practice is noteworthy and surprising?
- What do the white students, black students, and school officials all have to say about the practice? What does each group prefer to have happen, and how do they justify their preferences?
- What is racism? Does anyone in the article think that the practice described here is racist?

Uncover the evidence.

- Is there any evidence provided that the two-prom practice is racist, or that it is damaging to students?
- Is there any evidence provided that it is not?

Evaluate the conclusion.

• Do the authors take a position on whether the students who want to hold segregated proms are racist? Are they?
• Does the Supreme Court view that separate cannot be equal apply here?

Sort out the political implications.

• Is this situation comparable to southern school districts that allow prayer in school, claiming that it is okay if the prayer is organized by students and not by the school?
• Is it the same as private clubs (like Augusta National Golf Club) that declare it is their right to discriminate if they want to?

5.3 Tilt! Time's Up for Title IX Sports

Jessica Gavora, *The American Spectator,* May–June 2002

In 1972, Congress passed Title IX of the Educational Amendments, which said that no one can be excluded from participating in sports at an institution supported by federal funds for reasons of gender. Title IX revolutionized the world of girls' athletics. In a relatively short period of time, sports for girls became common in public schools and scholars began to note a variety of side benefits, including higher self-esteem among female students who participate in sports.

Jessica Gavora is highly critical of the way that Title IX has been interpreted and put into effect by policymakers, seeing the effort to put women's sports on a par with men's sports as an intrusive action of big government that has resulted in discrimination against men. Was Title IX intended simply to stop active discrimination against women, or does it require that schools take affirmative action to present women with opportunities to participate in sports?

In the spring of 2001 an ad sponsored by the Independent Women's Forum appeared in UCLA's *Daily Bruin,* offering to expose "the 10 most common feminist myths." Myth number nine—"Gender is a social construction"—was answered thus:

> While environment and socialization do play a significant role in human life, a growing body of research in neuroscience, endocrinology and psychology over the past 40 years suggests there is a biological basis for many sex differences in aptitudes and preferences. Of course, this doesn't mean that women should be prevented from pursuing their goals in any field they choose; what it does suggest is that we should not expect parity in all fields.

The ad's impact on the UCLA campus was immediate and explosive. Rallies were organized. The university women's center demanded that the *Daily Bruin*

What does it mean to say that gender is not socially constructed? How does this idea compare to the claim in Darryl Fears's article that race is a social construction?

"retract" the ad. When the paper's editor defended it as an exercise in free speech, Christie Scott, head of the campus feminist "Clothesline Project," dismissed this rationale as "somewhat cowardly."

"Somewhat cowardly" is the wrong term to apply to the editors of the *Daily Bruin*, but the right term for most participants in the discussion of women's role in American life today. Few topics involve more disinformation and shaving of the truth on the one side and political cowardice on the other. Christina Hoff Sommers—the author of the UCLA ad—Judith Kleinfeld, author, and psychiatrist Sally Satel and others have done an excellent job of uncovering the disinformation and false statistics used by women's advocates to advance their agenda. But they are virtually alone. For far too long, a wittingly or unwittingly gullible media has treated even the most outrageous claims of feminists as fact. The effect has been to give artificial life support to the myth that girls and women are an oppressed minority, clinging weakly to their rights only with the assistance of the full weight and authority of government.

Nowhere is the reality gap wider than in women's sports. Congress did a seemingly simple and laudable thing when it passed Title IX of the Educational Amendments in 1972: "No person in the U.S. shall, on the basis of sex, be excluded from participation in, or denied the benefits of, or be subjected to discrimination under any educational program or activity receiving federal aid."

But as applied to organized sports, Title IX has been interpreted and twisted and bent outside the institutions of our electoral democracy, conforming at last to the shape of unintended consequences: A law designed to end discrimination against women is now causing discrimination against men.

And yet Title IX is remarkably entrenched. Before the new Bush administration even had the chance to appoint a secretary of education, the powerful Women's Sports Foundation fired a shot across the White House bow, vowing to fight "any change that weakens this law and results in unequal treatment of female athletes." And the WSF is just the vanguard of an army of seasoned veterans of the gender wars who stand ready and eager to defend the territory they've gained under Title IX.

To make sure that a risk-averse new Republican president doesn't make the mistake of thinking he can take on the Title IX lobby with impunity, these gender warriors point to the results of a 2000 NBC News/ *Wall Street Journal* poll that seems to show widespread public support for Title IX quotas:

Q: Title IX is a federal law that prohibits high schools and colleges that receive federal funds from discriminating on the basis of gender. Title IX is most commonly invoked to ensure equal opportunities for girls and women in high school and college athletics. Do you approve or disapprove of Title IX as it is described here?

Yes, approve of Title IX: 79%   No, do not approve of Title IX: 14%

Do not know enough about it: 4%   Not sure: 3%

But the issue under Title IX isn't the fair and equal division of resources between men and women: it's an attempt to dictate how men and women should behave. Female athletes have more teams to choose from in colleges and universities today than male athletes. They receive more athletic scholarship aid per capita than male athletes. The battle for "gender equity" is not a battle for resources; if it were, women's groups would have declared victory some time ago. The struggle is about power and ideals.

> What does it mean to say that the battle for "gender equity" is a "struggle . . . about power and ideals"? Does Gavora show that this is the case?

Civil Wrongs

Q: Do you support eliminating men's opportunities to create a 50/50 gender balance in school sports programs?

This is not how the pollsters who conducted the survey for NBC News and *The Wall Street Journal* asked the question. Journalists—even ink-stained veterans— routinely describe compliance with Title IX in terms of the equal sharing of resources between men and women in athletics. The result is that it is rare for a citizen who picks up a newspaper or turns on the television to see coverage of the law that is not glowingly positive. And it is a rare politician or government official who will tell the truth about the law's enforcement today. The first step toward re-leveling the playing field between the sexes in our schools, then, is simply beginning to tell the truth about Title IX.

The reality is that the federal government has enforced a quota standard in Title IX athletics for much of the past decade. This enforcement has been opportunistic; not every school has fallen under scrutiny from the Justice Department's Office of Civil Rights and been forced to cut men's teams, add women's teams or do both to achieve "proportionality." But schools don't need to experience a federal investigation or a lawsuit to know that their athletic departments are not under their control. They've read the "policy interpretations"; they've seen how OCR has treated schools like the University of Wisconsin and Boston University; and they've seen how the courts have ruled on the Brown and Cal State Bakersfield cases. American education has received the message loud and clear.

It is a measure of the power of liberal women's rights activists in academia today that universities are unable—or unwilling—to complain as the federal government micromanages more and more of their affairs in the name of "gender equity." When so-called "women's issues" are on the line, defenders of institutional autonomy like Brown's Vartan Gregorian are distressingly rare. Even among students whose lives are most affected by Title IX quotas, there is little questioning of the need or the rationale for federally mandated gender equity. "Nobody questions the underlying assumptions of Title IX, that male and female students will be equally interested in organized sports and that a lack of proportional numbers must indicate something is 'wrong,'" says Robert Geary, professor of English at James Madison University. "Universities are supposed to be places of inquiry, but some subjects appear closed to scrutiny—too sensitive."

Title IX quotas have never been the subject of debate. They were created outside the electoral process by unelected officials working hand in hand with special interest groups. The first step toward ending gender quotas, then, is to demand the truth from those who insist they don't exist.

Here's the reality. In June 1999 the OCR's Northeast regional office sent a letter to the athletic director and administrators of Central Connecticut State University, warning that they must add 20 female athletes to their sports roster to comply with the federal law. CCSU had already brought the percentage of its athletes who are female from 29 to 49 by dropping men's wrestling and adding women's lacrosse. But females made up 51 percent of the students at CCSU, so OCR insisted that twenty more female athletes were needed—the so-called "proportionality" principal.

Then there's the University of Wisconsin at Madison, which received a similar letter in the fall of 2000. Having labored for a decade to attract women to programs, UWM had achieved near-perfect parity in the spring of that year: 429 athletes on campus were men and 425 were women. Not good enough, said Algis Tamosiunas, director of OCR compliance in Chicago. Because females now constituted a majority of students on the Madison campus (53.1 percent), the school would have to add another 25 women.

Letters like these are routinely sent to schools struggling to stay on the right side of the federal authorities. OCR officials such as Clinton administration's Norma Cantu are being dishonest when they insist that because the regulations don't "require" sex quotas, those who administer the regulations don't work relentlessly to make quotas happen. Proportionality is the threshold test for Title IX compliance in federal regulation. It is the standard adopted by the courts and the only guarantee that a school will not be exposed to a federal investigation or a lawsuit. It is the standard for compliance with Title IX today. To say otherwise is to lie, plain and simple.

Get Smart

The good news is that there are storm clouds gathering on Title IX's horizon. The past decade of gender-based quota expansion in women's sports has also been a time of relative prosperity for colleges and universities. In some cases, this has meant that schools struggling to meet the gender quota in athletics could do so in relatively painless ways, by adding women's sports and/or limiting men's participation by cutting walk-ons. As long as the funds were there, providing the scholarships and building or upgrading facilities for new women's teams were relatively easy.

> *Why is Gavora glad to see the slowing economy and rising budget pressures on universities?*

A slowing economy combined with escalating expenses in athletic programs, however, threatens to change this. Budgets for women's sports are rising faster than those for men's sports, as is spending on scholarships for women. Another financial strain is accommodating the growing desire among athletic directors and fans alike that teams be competitive on the national level. Less and less are sports treated as another part of a well-rounded educational experience; increasingly teams must justify their existence by winning. This compulsion is helping to fuel an "arms race" in spending, not just on big-time football and basketball programs, but on women's teams and men's "non-revenue" sports as well. According to the Chronicle of Higher Education, "nonrevenue" teams in NCAA Division I cost roughly $220,000 on average in 1999–2000. And at big-time football schools, where more money is available, women's teams and men's nonrevenue squads can cost up to half a million dollars apiece.

These exploding costs have already triggered a fresh round of budget cuts. And because women's sports can't be touched, the sacrifice is borne by men's teams. Iowa State University, the University of Kansas and the University of Nebraska have all recently begun major cuts to their men's athletic programs. The bad news for Title IX quota advocates is that rising budget pressures may finally give schools a real incentive to go to court, to argue that women's programs should be fair game as well.

A school that invites a lawsuit by cutting a women's team or refusing to create a new team to meet the gender quota might very well decide to fight back in court rather than be forced to incur costs it can't afford. Alternately, male athletes whose positions are eliminated might decide to take a cue from Duane Naquin, a Boston College senior who was denied entry on the basis of his sex to a class in feminist ethics taught by theology professor Mary Daly; Naquin sued to win his right to coeducation. As that case showed, if there is one thing university administrators fear more than accusations of gender insensitivity, it's lawsuits. In the Daly case and others to come, public interest law firms like the Center for Individual Rights have been effective in reversing the course of sex discrimination in our schools.

Although Title IX preferences have yet to be struck down in a federal district court—and thus be made a prime target for Supreme Court review—creative legal challenges in the right circuits could yield results for fairness and gender-blind policies. "I have no doubt that the Supreme Court will take the case if and when there is a split in the circuit courts," says Maureen Mahoney, who argued

Brown University's case to the Supreme Court. Women's advocates have been careful so far to push for Title IX quotas in liberal district courts that are likely to agree with their version of equity. But according to Mahoney and others, bringing the right challenge in the more conservative Fourth Circuit (which covers Maryland, South Carolina, North Carolina, Virginia and West Virginia) or the Fifth Circuit (including Texas, Louisiana and Mississippi) could bring a judgment that restores the original intent of the law.

The rising cost of fielding intercollegiate athletic teams is also contributing to a reexamination of how sports fit within the mission of the university. All recruited athletes, male or female, receive a preference from college admissions committees. But preferences for female athletes—and arguments for female quotas within athletic programs—are often justified on grounds above and beyond the contribution these women make to sports teams. Make women athletes, we are told, and you make better women. With some justification, women's groups argue that girls who play sports are associated with such positive traits as higher graduation rates, less drug use, higher self-esteem and lower levels of teenage pregnancy.

In *The Game of Life: College Sports and Educational Values,* James Shulman of the Andrew W. Mellon Foundation and former Princeton University president William Bowen examine what kind of students are currently being admitted to schools under athletic preferences. Using the same database that provided the intellectual fodder for Bowen's earlier defense of race-based affirmative action—data on 90,000 students who attended 30 selective colleges and universities in the 1950s, 1970s and 1990s—the authors claim that of all the recipients of affirmative action in colleges and universities today, female athletes are the most preferred. At a representative school in 1999, Shulman and Bowen found that a female who is a member of a minority had a 20 percent admissions advantage, the daughter of an alumnus had a 24 percent advantage, a male athlete had a 48 percent advantage and a female athlete had a 53 percent advantage. That is, a female athlete had a 53 percent better chance of being admitted than a nonathlete with the same SAT score.

And what are schools gaining from this admissions preference? *The Game of Life* sets out purposefully to shoot down the various "myths" of intercollegiate athletics, chief among them, in Shulman and Bowen's view, that athletics builds character. Shulman and Bowen argue that athletes today are less academically prepared, less concerned with scholarship and more financially directed than their fellow students. But what is most interesting about their analysis is their finding that these traits are increasing, among female athletes as well as male. And whereas female athletes were once at least as academically qualified as other female students, they now lag behind. Another benefit frequently cited to justify preferences for female athletes under Title IX is racial and ethnic diversity. But Shulman and Bowen found that Title IX produced gains mainly for white girls, not minorities.

The trend in women's athletics, particularly in the most competitive, high-profile sports, is away from the ideal often claimed by Title IX quota ideologues. Instead of representing the female ideal at the start of the twenty-first century—though, smart, confident and empowered—female athletes are beginning to resemble the dimwitted, half-civilized male athletes of the feminist stereotype. And in such a situation, the rationale that women's preferences under Title IX are justified because they create better students and better citizens becomes hard to sustain.

Couch Potato Blight

Another cloud darkening the future of gender quotas under Title IX is the failure so far of women's sports to attract the fan base and revenue potential that many men's sports enjoy.

The success of Women's World Cup soccer awakened in many women's groups a deep yearning to take women's athletics to the next level, by making it financially viable. The Women's Sports Foundation recently declared a "Brave New World" in which girls and women don't just get a place on the playing field, they get big bucks for playing. "Initially the primary function was opening doors of opportunity," said executive director Donna Lopiano at the WSF's fourteenth annual conference in 2000. "Now, it's exploiting the participation of women in sports in the economic sense, gaining access to assets, program expansion and addressing the continuing problem of girls being discouraged from sports."

The evidence from women's professional athletics, however, is daunting. Five years after the launch of the Women's National Basketball Association and a year after the debut of the Women's United Soccer Association, gender equity may still be more politically profitable than financially rewarding. And it turns out that the social engineers are even more wrong in their contention that men and women are equally interested in watching sports. Many girls and women are enthusiastic participants in sports, but when it comes to being a fan—buying a ticket for a game or watching one on TV—men are still the driving force. According to Lawrence Wenner of Loyola Marymount University in Los Angeles, about 20 percent of men but only 4 to 5 percent of women can be described as "strong, committed" sports fans. Men outnumber women among viewers of major sports telecasts by 2 to 1. They even watch women's sports more than women do.

This gender gap in sportsmania shows up in support for coverage of women's sports in the print media as well. Whereas *Sports Illustrated* goes out each week to about 3.5 million subscribers, *Sports Illustrated for Women* comes out only once every two months, with a circulation of 400,000. Conde Nast gave up on *Women's Sports and Fitness* in 2000 after spending two years and a reported $45 million trying to find an audience.

Lopiano and others rationalize the small crowds at women's sporting events with the argument that the women's sports market needs time to mature, that the female sports fan is an "emerging" fan. In many respects this is true, but the for-profit world of women's professional athletics is very different from the sub-sidized world in which the "gender equity" battle has so far been fought. Finan-cial investors, unlike college administrators, can't be coerced into providing the resources necessary for women's leagues to survive. According to Stefan Fat-sis, sportswriter for *The Wall Street Journal,* several owners of NBA franchises—who also own the local WNBA teams—would rather not have to continue the women's teams, but they have been ordered by NBA commissioner David Stern to "stick with it." Over half of the women's teams are even turning to marketing directly to lesbians through events like "Gay Pride Night." This kind of market-ing, however, carries a risk of alienating some fans. Last year, the WNBA put out a list of married and engaged players, a move seemingly designed to appeal to its fan base of families with children.

Less Is Less

As I write this, the University of Kansas has eliminated its men's swimming and tennis teams, citing financial pressures and federal gender equity requirements. Bucknell University has announced it will drop wrestling and men's crew as varsity sports, eliminating 44 men's positions in order to reach male-female proportionality. Seton Hall, Capital University in Columbus, Ohio, and the Uni-versity of St. Thomas have all dropped their wrestling teams. Iowa State has elim-inated baseball and men's swimming. The University of Nebraska has also axed men's swimming and diving, leaving only four of the schools in the Big 12 con-ference still participating in the sport. The Big 12 is now questioning whether it will continue to stage a men's swimming and diving championship or do away with it altogether, a move that will almost certainly result in the remaining schools eliminating their men's programs.

This denial of opportunity for men is occurring because a group of people with a narrow agenda has worked hard and successfully behind the scenes to make it happen. Driven by the desire to overcome real discrimination against girls and women, activists like Donna Lopiano and Norma Cantu and groups like the Women's Sports Foundation, the National Women's Law Center and the American Association of University Women set out to create preferences for girls and women. They sought out and co-opted friendly government officials. They initiated a shrewd legal strategy when friendly government officials were un-available. Partly through government fiat, partly through a shared ideology, they built a phalanx of promoters and defenders of "gender equity" on college cam-puses and in high schools and grade schools across the country. They wooed their allies and cowed their enemies in Congress and insisted that both parrot their message. They conducted a highly effective and sophisticated media cam-paign. They helped draft regulations and interpretations of regulations and in-terpretations of interpretations of regulations. At each stage in the legal and bureaucratic evolution of Title IX, they out-thought, out-worked and out-cared the people whose opportunities were being destroyed. The edifice of discrimination these activists built is a testament to their commitment.

In the end, of course, it is up to those charged with enforcing our laws to apply Title IX honestly and forthrightly. This is not, needless to say, a politically painless proposition. After some significant rollback of race-based preferences in the 1990s, elected officials and even conservative activists seem to have lost their appetite for battling identity politics. To stand on principle, many seem to believe, is to risk appearing "mean-spirited" in an age when compassion is the opiate of the electorate.

> What does it mean to Gavora to apply Title IX "honestly and forthrightly"? And what does she mean by "compassion is the opiate of the electorate," a takeoff on Karl Marx's famous phrase that "religion is the opiate of the masses"?

Writing about the "conundrum of quotas" in *The Wall Street Journal* in the opening months of the Bush administration, Shelby Steele noted that conservatives have a hard time not appearing mean when they stand on principle on the issue of race because they lack moral authority. "Were conservatives of the last generation fastidious about principles when segregation prevailed as a breach of every known democratic principle, including merit?" wrote Steele.

The equation of race preferences with Title IX sex preferences is not perfect. As we have seen, there are real, innate differences between the sexes, of the kind that cannot be shown to exist between people of different races. Even so, Steele's point can easily be applied to conservatives on the issue of sex today. Conservatives of the last generation certainly did not lead the charge for women's rights—properly understood to be the same rights before the law that men historically have enjoyed. It was liberals, of course, who took the battle for women's rights forward. Eventually they corrupted it into a separatist movement in which women's interests are portrayed to be at odds with those of men. Nonetheless, before feminism took that destructive turn, conservatives did not champion the cause of equality for women, and more often than not they resisted it.

Can we now credibly argue that the principle of gender-blindness be upheld in the laws meant to guarantee it? Liberalism has been suborned on the issue of sex quotas. Can a conservative administration challenge quotas for girls and women without appearing "mean" and losing the thin margin of centrist voters who put it in office—voters who would most likely oppose gender preferences if they knew they existed but who nonetheless distrust conservatives on issues involving women? This is a conundrum of sex quotas every bit as difficult as Shelby Steele's conundrum of race quotas.

The way out of this conundrum is the same as it was in the 1920s, when women struggled for the right to vote, and the same as it was in the 1950s, when blacks encountered segregationists at the schoolhouse door. The way out is to defend the principle of nondiscrimination, even when it is hard. Especially when it is hard.

And liberal feminist groups will make it hard to stand on this principle; they will challenge the moral authority of those who seek to restore the original intent of the law. But the principle of nondiscrimination that is embodied in the original intent of Title IX has stood the test of time. It has allowed girls and women to rise from uncomfortable interlopers to become the dominant force in American education. Conservatives can gain new moral authority by insisting on standing by this principle and resisting a distortion of the law that discriminates against a new group of victims and demeans the very achievements of the girls and women it purports to protect.

Re-leveling the playing field in American education will not be easy. But those who go into this battle have at their side two often underrated assets: First, it's the law. And second, it's the right thing to do.

Consider the source and the audience.
- *The American Spectator* is a conservative journal. How does Gavora's position on Title IX reflect a conservative stance? Does that stance affect her portrayal of opposing views on this subject?

Lay out the argument, the values, and the assumptions.
- What concept of fairness is Gavora applying in this article? How would she like to see Title IX implemented? Why does that view seem more "fair" to her than the current policy?
- What reasons does Gavora give for thinking that the future of Title IX, as thus far implemented, is probably doomed?
- What does Gavora mean when she refers to the goal of "re-leveling the playing field . . . in our schools"?

Uncover the evidence.
- How does Gavora know what the true intent of Title IX is? What evidence does she offer?
- What evidence does she offer to back up her claim that athletics do not actually build character in men or women athletes?
- How does she show that women are not as interested in being sports spectators as men are? How can she tell whether this is the way women are by nature or the way that society has conditioned them to be?

Evaluate the conclusion.
- Gavora claims that the way to true gender blindness is to practice nondiscrimination—not to implement policy meant to make up for past discrimination, since that only discriminates against men in its turn. Is it possible to have a really level playing field when some of the players have for years been held back from gaining the skills necessary to compete?

Sort out the political implications.
- If Title IX is interpreted to mean merely that no one can actively discriminate, but not if men's sports consequently go back to being better funded, will that result be because women really don't want the same opportunities? Will the playing field be level then?

5.4 How the Culture War Was Won

Lesbians and Gay Men Defeated the Right in the 1990s, But Tougher Battles Lie Ahead

E. J. Graff, *The American Prospect,* 21 October 2002

In the chapter thus far, we have looked at civil rights struggles over the issues of race, ethnicity, and gender. In this article from *The American Prospect* we examine a civil rights battle focused on a less visible characteristic—sexual orientation. We argued earlier that civil rights struggles have to be fought initially in the political arenas to which a given group has access. Why were the first gay rights battles won in the arena of popular and political culture? What kinds of battles remain to be fought?

Imagine for a moment that we live in an alternate universe where the United States is openly hostile to lesbians and gay men. How hostile? Well, in this world, the liberal state of Massachusetts bans lesbians and gay men from being foster parents. The only gay person you might find on TV—and you'd have to search hard—is either a lisping hairdresser or a young man tragically dying. Three Maine teenagers confess that they've thrown a young man over a bridge to his death because he's gay, and the national media don't even notice; ditto when hundreds of thousands of lesbians and gay men hold a civil-rights march on the nation's capitol. The U.S. Supreme Court issues a major decision comparing homosexuality to adultery, incest, theft and the use of illegal drugs; the chief justice adds, "To hold that the act of homosexual sodomy is somehow protected as a fundamental right would be to cast aside millennia of moral teaching."

My alternate universe, of course, is the United States just 15 years ago. It's dizzying to try to remember how different attitudes were back then; many American lesbians and gay men feel as if we've since been transported to an entirely different planet. Today, of course, you can scarcely find a TV show without a sympathetic lesbian or gay character, and politicians skirmish for the more than 4 percent of the electorate who identify themselves as lesbian, gay or bisexual. Perhaps most important is the change in lesbians' and gay men's daily lives: Mentioning a same-sex partner in ordinary conversation—to co-workers, doctors, nurses, teachers, contractors, strangers on a plane—no longer feels death-defying, although it hasn't exactly become a yawn.

And yet open contempt toward lesbians and gay men still erupts. This past February, for instance, the Alabama Supreme Court denied a woman custody of her children, using language in its ruling much like that of the 1986 *Bowers v. Hardwick* decision quoted above. Nor have American lesbians and gay men won the most important legislative or court battles. "We haven't won on the military, we haven't won on marriage, we haven't won on the Boy Scouts," says Kevin Cathcart, executive director of the Lambda Legal Defense and Education Fund, "and yet the world is a completely different place."

Why? How, during one of the most conservative periods in American history, at a time when progressives were badly routed on nearly every front, did lesbians and gay men win the culture war? And can an energized lesbian and gay community win the tougher civil-rights battles ahead?

What does Graff mean by "culture war"? What is the role of the media here?

Between 1987 and 1993—the dates of two exhilarating and massive gay-rights marches on Washington—lesbian and gay issues were dragged out of the Ann Landers and home decor columns and onto the front and editorial pages, where they have remained. (Although bisexual and transgendered people are often lumped into the same organizations and acronyms, their causes haven't yet caught up.) Between those two national marches, masses of people came out and lesbian and gay issues emerged as national questions. And as the right wing spewed antigay vitriol, the media crossed over to our side. Why?

Sometimes it takes despair to provoke action. And for despair, AIDS was unbeatable. Until the epidemic, lesbian and gay activists had been the usual motley crew: artsy-lefty types who didn't want to belong to the mainstream anyway or folks who'd been so bashed, blackmailed or ostracized that they felt they had little to lose (and self-respect to gain) by stamping "homo" on their resumes. And until AIDS, lesbians and gay men, like girls and boys at a junior high school dance, kept their political distance: Girls were feminists who worked on issues such as rape or battering or Central America or nuclear disarmament while boys touted (and practiced) sexual freedom. AIDS flushed out passable white gay men, men "for whom gay liberation had meant they could have better party lives—I'm serious!" says John D'Emilio, history professor at the University of Illinois at Chicago and founding director of the National Gay and Lesbian Task Force Policy Institute, "but who wouldn't have thought of going to a gay pride march or a Lambda fundraiser." The prospect of early death concentrated such minds wonderfully. Abruptly, these men's high-level Rolodexes, disposable incomes and insider skills went to work building organizations and lobbying policy makers. Women, meanwhile, started bringing two decades of feminist analysis and women's health organizing to the epidemic. For the first time, they were welcomed instead of driven away by misogyny.

AIDS also broke through to politicians who had dismissed or feared gay issues. Many liberal or moderate legislators believed bills against antigay discrimination were mainly symbolic, according to U.S. Rep. Barney Frank (D-Mass.). But "AIDS was clearly life or death," says Frank. "And when these right-wing assholes—and this did help us—when [Jesse] Helms, [William] Dannemeyer and these fools began to try to interfere with life-saving measures to pursue their prejudice," politicians were startled to see the viciousness aimed regularly at lesbians and gay men.

Even politicians afraid of a backlash in their districts nevertheless felt morally compelled to help. And so on AIDS bills, says Frank, "members [of Congress] voted with us, then braced themselves for the political blow—and it didn't come." Surprise! If you were already known as a liberal or moderate, helping dying gay men didn't subtract any extra votes. As a result, AIDS built good working relationships between legislators, their staffs, and lesbian and gay activists.

In the midst of the AIDS crisis came the 1986 *Bowers v. Hardwick* decision, in which the U.S. Supreme Court voted 5-to-4 to uphold states' rights to ban sodomy. I remember being staggered when *Bowers* was announced; it was hard to grasp that my Supreme Court had just declared me less than a citizen. "*Bowers* was a wake-up call," says Cathcart. "It pushed a lot of gay people to stop pretending that there was justice, that things were fair, that the law didn't have to change." Furious, lesbians and gay men understood—though Harvard law professor Laurence Tribe has suggested that the Supreme Court may not have—

How had the social stigma attached to being gay kept the political base weak?

that the decision was not only insulting but harmful. Anti-sodomy laws allow judges, government officials, employers and others to say that lesbians and gay men, as presumed felons, need not be granted parental custody, immigration status—or simple humanity. Donations to lesbian- and gay-advocacy organizations jumped dramatically.

Read that last sentence carefully: That's right, *Bowers* was a steroids supplement for the lesbian and gay movement. Skinny organizations suddenly bulked up, adding staff and volunteers and tripling efforts. Suddenly they had the muscle to fight and win small but significant battles: rolling back the Massachusetts foster-care ban, defeating Lon Mabon's antigay Oregon ballot initiatives and winning a New York man the right to "inherit" his dead partner's lease to their shared apartment (and setting a breakthrough precedent on the legal meaning of "family"). Each small victory was "like lifting a gag order on some segment of the community," says Cathcart. If you're no longer afraid of losing your children, job, apartment or life, you're freed to volunteer with the gay community center hotline, join the lesbian and gay square-dance group, lobby your state representative or, at the very least, come out to your mother. A new shared subculture began to thrive, complete with a lively lesbian and gay press, pride events, lobbyists and ever more rainbow kitsch.

Then William Jefferson Clinton blasted lesbian and gay issues onto the national stage. "Bill Clinton did more for the cause of gay and lesbian rights than John Kennedy did on race," says Frank. Clinton brilliantly used his bully pulpit on behalf of lesbians and gay men—even while running. A national presidential candidate stood up and talked about gay rights as a righteous, even moral, civil-rights cause. And not in code or in private but in the full light of day. Sound minor? It had never happened before. Lesbians' and gay men's collective jaws dropped. The media—having already gotten a behind-the-scenes education on gay and lesbian issues as their colleagues weakened with AIDS or came out—tentatively followed Clinton's lead. By the time the 1992 Republican convention pushed the culture war onto national TV, attacking lesbians and gay men in language that made our grandmothers cringe, the media declared gay rights "a story."

And Clinton kept it up, appointing openly lesbian and gay men throughout his administration, from the patent office to ambassadorships, and unleashing agencies such as the Department of Justice to help rather than harm lesbian- and gay-advocacy efforts. Even when Clinton badly underestimated American antigay sentiment (as many nongay liberals still do), his ease with gay issues set off a global warming that seems to have permanently changed the cultural climate.

Need it be said that Clinton was far from perfect? His attempt to change the military's policy, firmly blocked by then–Chairman of the Joint Chiefs of Staff Colin Powell, was disastrous. And yet the debate itself was a breakthrough. For the first time, lesbian and gay rights were treated as public-policy issues deserving serious political consideration; gay men and lesbians were discussed not as lisping (or swaggering) jokes but as folks who wanted to serve their country. By the time of the 1993 LGBT (lesbian, gay, bisexual and transgender) March on Washington, that was the story the media chose to run: that homos were not all drag queens or leather men or dykes on bikes or even "transgressive" professors (not that there's anything wrong with those) but also the girls and boys next door.

Surely it's no accident that 1993 was the year that the Hawaii Supreme Court suggested same-sex couples might deserve civil marriage rights. The court eventually bowed to public antagonism, letting die many same-sex couples' dreams of lei-bedecked weddings. But that suggestion set off a nationwide debate that transformed, in many minds, the phrase "same-sex marriage" from an unthinkable oxymoron to an unstoppable eventuality. Yes, Congress passed and Clinton signed the hideously misnamed Defense of Marriage Act in 1996, which banned federal recognition of same-sex marriage just in case any state ever made marriage a possibility. But as with the military debate, that defeat boomeranged. The Jane and Joe Homos, many of whom had never before been activists, mobilized dramatically for marriage rights (despite the distress of certain lesbian and gay politicos who see marriage as a politically retro goal). And the marriage debates have been stereotype busting. If all gay men were really irresponsibly lascivious hedonists racing from one sad anonymous encounter to the next, why would they want to commit themselves to each other for life?

With these debates came innumerable opportunities for lesbians and gay men to tell their individual stories, both in the media and in private. And mainstream minds began to change, with astonishing speed. Frank suggests that's because, unlike any racial, ethnic, class or religious minority, lesbians and gay men were already integrated into the social fabric, albeit invisibly, That's quite different from the experience of, say, African Americans, who had to fight simply to enter various neighborhoods, schools and jobs. "Because of prejudice," says Frank, "black people and white people in America have been living very different lives." Economically, culturally and too often emotionally, that gulf between black and white can still be hard to bridge.

Not so with gay and straight. In families, at school and at work (those three mass socialization experiences), gay and straight folks have long been side by side, as sisters or sons, as vocational-school or Ivy League classmates, as truck drivers or rock stars. And so when lesbians and gay men started coming out, "People learned that a lot of people they liked and respected were gay and lesbian," says Frank. "The average American discovered that he wasn't homophobic: He just thought he was supposed to be."

By the time of Matthew Shepard's hideous death in 1998—only 14 years after Charlie Howard was thrown off a Portland, Maine, bridge to massive media silence and just a decade after Rebecca Wight was shot to death on the Appalachian Trail for kissing her girlfriend—lesbians and gay men were no longer alone in grieving over an antigay hate crime. "Gay people and transgender people are no longer considered fair game," says Cathcart. "The definition of what shocks the conscience has changed."

With the visible emergence of real, ordinary lesbians and gay men, both in person and in the media, bias against us has rapidly crumbled. The poll numbers are enough to bring hope to any progressive heart, even in a time as coldly conservative as ours. In 1988, according to the National Election Survey, only 47 percent of Americans supported laws protecting lesbians and gay men against job discrimination; by 2000, that had jumped to 64 percent (including 56 percent of Republicans). In 1992, the same survey found that only 26 percent supported adoption rights for lesbians and gay men; in 2002, an ABC News poll found that support had jumped to 47 percent. Even on the volatile—and central—question of marriage rights, the issue that most stands for complete equality, there's been a 20-point leap in support. In 1992, the Kaiser Family Foundation found that 27 percent of Americans supported civil marriage rights for same-sex pairs; in 2001, an astonishing 47 percent did. And in a spring 2002 California poll by the firm Decision Research, 75 percent expected that within their lifetimes, same-sex pairs would win civil marriage rights. High-school students favor LGBT rights and same-sex civil marriage in much higher numbers and with even more conviction—suggesting an entirely different political landscape for lesbians and gay men in 20 or 30 years.

Unfortuantely, there's very little that other progressive causes can learn from this cultural victory. "Freedom" is the consumer culture's watchword, an idea propagandized constantly: the freedom to choose one's work and one's love and to enjoy (or suffer) the consequences of one's choices. Cultural acceptance of lesbians and gay men perfectly fits that American social theology, that bedrock belief in liberty and the pursuit of happiness. But that freedom is literally priceless: It requires no new taxes. Tolerance asks for nothing from the public purse and threatens no industry; it requires no changes in hiring practices (except perhaps the rapidly spreading corporate habit of offering domestic-partnership benefits—which, not coincidentally, costs almost nothing). In fact, many companies quickly figured out that an entirely new market segment—middle-class lesbians and gay men—were actually grateful to be winked at in Volkswagen or IKEA or Miller Lite commercials. "Not only does cultural acceptance cost nothing," says Sue Hyde, New England regional organizer for the National Gay and Lesbian Task Force, "but it actually makes the rich richer."

Compare that with anything else on a progressive's wish list: universal health care, a livable minimum wage, progressive taxation, racial equality, environmental preservation, comparable worth, subsidized child care, public housing. These ask Americans not for freedom from one another but responsibility for one another—responsibilities that are most costly for those most likely to vote. "To what extent is the gay and lesbian movement overall a progressive movement?" muses Cathcart. While most self-identified lesbians and gay men are Democrats and many work actively on other progressive issues, there's a reason gay Republicans feel no contradiction between their two group memberships. Liberty and justice based on sexual orientation would redistribute not a penny.

Meanwhile, it's not yet time for the forces of justice to abandon the field; the gay and lesbian cultural victory is still pretty limited. The United States is the last developed country that bans lesbians and gay men from serving openly in the military, keeps sodomy laws on its books and refuses immigration rights to a citizen's foreign-born same-sex partner. And the handful of gay-rights wins are starred with caveats. Only in 1996's *Romer v. Evans* has the Supreme Court voted clearly against antigay animus, and that ruling is very limited. Yes, there's been a tremendous outcry against the Boy Scouts for banning gay leaders, but we actually lost that one in the Supreme Court. Ten states and a host of municipalities have added sexual orientation to their nondiscrimination laws—but mostly where they're least needed. Young people coming out are still on a precarious and lonely perch: The Park Slope, N.Y., or Ann Arbor, Mich., kid with a hip family might do fine, but far too many teens are still beaten, locked in mental hospitals or thrown out on the street when they come out at home or school. Parenting rights for lesbian and gay couples are terrifyingly spotty [See E. J. Graff, "The Other Marriage War, *TAP*, April 8, 2002.]. And only the handful of same-sex couples who live in the state of Vermont—total population 613,000, roughly 0.2 percent of the country—have a pup tent's worth of legal recognition for their unions. And even that temporary roof evaporates if the couple drives to New Hampshire for dinner.

And then there's marriage, without which lesbians and gay men have trouble even burying their dead, much less collecting a loved one's pension or Social Security benefits. Thirty-five states have passed Defense of Marriage Act statutes, which will be tough to undo. Other moral panics have swept the country in times of social change: Anti-miscegenation laws passed after emancipation and the Comstock laws passed in the late 19th century, as birth rates began to drop and as women agitated for education and the vote. Those statutes took between 50 and 100 years (and the brief heyday of the Warren Court) to sweep completely off the books. Right now, it looks possible that the Massachusetts and New Jersey courts might grant marriage rights within the next couple of years. Many of us believe that would guarantee another 50 or so years of court battles over whether those marriages are valid in such states as Alabama, Nebraska and Utah. But then, no sane political observer would have predicted our 1990s cultural victories. Given enough help from our progressive friends, can lesbians and gay men beat the clock? Tune in next decade to find out.

> What are the next ten years likely to mean for gay rights?

Consider the source and the audience.

- Graff is writing for a liberal audience in *The American Prospect,* so she does not need to justify the goals of the gay rights movement but, rather, can discuss progress and strategy. How would such an article be cast in a more ideologically neutral outlet? In a conservative one?

Lay out the argument, the values, and the assumptions.

- What goals and values does Graff assume her audience shares with her?
- What three changes between 1987 and 1993 helped gays and lesbians win the "culture war," despite the general conservatism of the era?
- Why does Graff claim that the cultural acceptance of gays and lesbians was palatable to Americans while other progressive causes were not?

Uncover the evidence.

- What data does Graff cite to back up her claim that the culture war has been won? Is this kind of evidence persuasive?
- Does she supply evidence to support her claim that the cultural acceptance of gays fits with "American social theology"? Does she need to?

Evaluate the conclusion.

- Is Graff right in saying that cultural acceptance of gays has been "priceless" for Americans, allowing it to succeed where other liberal causes have failed? Would social conservatives agree that it has no cost?
- Why does she conclude that cultural acceptance of gays is priceless, yet place racial equality on a list of reforms that are not?

Sort out the political implications.

- What are the limits of cultural acceptance? Are gays likely to move easily from cultural acceptance to a full array of legal rights?

5.5 Ain't I a Woman?

Sojourner Truth, speaking at the Women's Rights Convention in Akron, Ohio, 1851

There were both women and men at the Women's Rights Convention in Akron in 1851. Although many women supported the cause of women's rights, it was an intimidating prospect to stand up and speak to an audience that included many vocal opponents at a time when most women were not used to a public role. Consequently, the convention was dominated by impassioned arguments from men who believed that women were not capable of doing the things men did and were not made equal by God.

Sojourner Truth was an emancipated slave from New York with a commanding presence (contemporary reports put her at almost six feet tall) and a spellbinding speaking voice. When she rose to speak, some women wanted her stopped, fearing that the women's cause would be mixed up with abolitionism in the public's mind and thus be discredited. Nevertheless, the president of the meeting gave her the floor. When she was finished, her listeners found themselves torn between cheers and tears. Though Truth herself has become the stuff of legend, her speech remains today a brief but powerful comment on gender roles. Why are her words so effective?

Well, children, where there is so much racket there must be something out of kilter. I think that 'twixt the negroes of the South and the women at the North, all talking about rights, the white men will be in a fix pretty soon. But what's all this here talking about?

That man over there says that women need to be helped into carriages, and lifted over ditches, and to have the best place everywhere. Nobody ever helps me into carriages, or over mud-puddles, or gives me any best place! And ain't I a woman? Look at me! Look at my arm! I have ploughed and planted, and gathered into barns, and no man could head me! And ain't I a woman? I could work as much and eat as much as a man—when I could get it—and bear the lash as well! And ain't I a woman? I have borne thirteen children, and seen most all sold off to slavery, and when I cried out with my mother's grief, none but Jesus heard me! And ain't I a woman?

Then they talk about this thing in the head; what's this they call it? [member of audience whispers, "intellect"] That's it, honey. What's that got to do with women's rights or negroes' rights? If my cup won't hold but a pint, and yours holds a quart, wouldn't you be mean not to let me have my little half measure full?

Then that little man in black there, he says women can't have as much rights as men, 'cause Christ wasn't a woman! Where did your Christ come from? Where did your Christ come from? From God and a woman! Man had nothing to do with Him.

If the first woman God ever made was strong enough to turn the world upside down all alone, these women together ought to be able to turn it back, and get it right side up again! And now they is asking to do it, the men better let them.

Obliged to you for hearing me, and now old Sojourner ain't got nothing more to say.

Consider the source and the audience.
- How might Sojourner Truth's audience have affected how she presented her message?
- Most contemporary accounts of her speech come to us from her supporters. How might this fact shape the context in which we read her words today?

Lay out the argument, the values, and the assumptions.
- Truth was a slave until New York freed all its slaves in 1828, when she was approximately thirty years old. To what extent did her personal experience fit with the notions that women were too weak and needed too much pampering to be equal to men?
- What idea of equality does she seem to be working with? Does she think *equal* means *identical*?
- What is her image of God? Does God have a gender?

Uncover the evidence.
- What is Truth's evidence that women can be as strong and tough as men? Is it compelling?
- Can she prove God's will? Can her opponents? Can anyone win that part of the argument? If so, how?

Evaluate the conclusion.
- Is Truth's claim that all people should be allowed to develop to their capacity convincing today? Why would anyone ever have opposed it?

Sort out the political implications.
- Truth's contention that the mystique of feminine weakness and delicacy didn't apply to slave women and thus probably didn't apply to white women must have been shocking at the time. Do we still have different expectations of people according to gender and race?

CHAPTER 6

Congress

The Founders' passion for checks and balances reached a high point in their design of the U.S. Congress. Not only is that institution checked by the executive and judicial branches of government, but it is checked and balanced internally as well, by the requirement that both chambers, the large unwieldy House of Representatives and the smaller, more disciplined Senate, agree on all bills that become national law. Though we citizens may fuss and fume over what seems like endless gridlock or legislative log jams, slow, painstaking lawmaking is just what our cautious founders wanted.

In some ways, though, the Congress of today does not look like the founders' ideal. Their hope was that the House of Representatives would be responsive to public opinion and that it would be balanced by the more mature Senate, which would be focused on longer-term issues of the public interest. In truth, members of both institutions are subject to a legislative dilemma. They are torn between two roles—representing the particular interests of their constituencies (either legislative district or state), or engaging in lawmaking that serves the national interest but might not serve their constituency's interest nearly as well. Since the former course is far more likely to lead to their reelection, and reelection is the primary concern of almost every member of Congress, they have every incentive to ignore critical national problems, particularly in the House, where members come up for reelection every two years.

The readings in this chapter touch on some, but by no means all, of the many critical issues concerning legislative politics. The first article, from the *Washington Post*, is about the decision of Representative J. C. Watts (R-OK) to give up not only his leadership position as chairman of the House Republican Conference but also his seat in Congress. This article looks at some of the internal, personal decisions that a member of Congress faces in the course of his career. As the only black Republican member of Congress, Watts felt that his personal decisions were fraught with broader political import. The second article, from *The Chronicle of Higher Education,* looks at pork-barrel spending in colleges and universities—special projects that members of Congress vote to fund in their districts that may not be particularly worthy, at least not to the national taxpayers who foot the bill. The third article, by an *L.A. Times* columnist, examines the effect that massive fundraising and redistricting have had on congressional elections. The fourth piece, from the *New York Times* in the days after the 2002 midterm election, looks at a major consequence of those changes—increasing ideological extremism among members of

Congress. The final selection, a timely reminder of what such extremism can lead to, is a 1950 speech made by Senator Margaret Chase Smith, decrying the incivility and damage to personal liberty that came with the attempt by her colleague Senator Joseph McCarthy to root out what he saw as a Communist threat in American government.

6.1 Fade to White

Jake Tapper, *Washington Post,* 2 January 2003

In 2002, Congressman J. C. Watts (R-OK), decided not to run for reelection. His departure left the Republican Party without a single black representative in Congress. In this article, Jake Tapper interviews J. C. Watts about his membership in the Republican Party, his political experiences in Washington, and his decision to leave politics, at least for now. What were the most significant reasons for the difficulties that Watts faced in his political career?

The empty halls of the Longworth House Office Building echo as Oklahoma Rep. J. C. Watts Jr. makes his way—for one of the last times—to his office.

With Congress in winter recess, much of the Capitol is deserted, its usual hum of committee hearings, press conferences, floor votes and political maneuvering replaced by an unnatural, almost melancholy stillness.

Watts cuts through the gloom in shiny black cowboy boots and a yellow tie that matches his sunny disposition. He's here to tie up loose ends. To pack up. Move on. Bring his high-profile, frustrating years as the country's sole black Republican congressman to an end.

"I don't know where anything is," Watts says with a chuckle as he enters the shambles that was his work space as chairman of the House Republican Conference. "I came here last night, and it looked like a ghost town."

The bookshelves are empty, the University of Oklahoma banners in storage, the mementos long gone. Most of what remains is covered in bubble wrap. A sculpture of an American eagle that once proudly supervised the room is now pushed, face first, against a bare white wall. Two elephants—one black and one white—stare each other down on Watts's desk.

"The most important things are still here," the 45-year-old lawmaker jokes with his press secretary, Kyle Downey. "I got a place to sit," Watts says, patting his black leather chair. "A place to write," he says rapping his desk. "A place to watch ESPN," he laughs, rubbing his TV with his palm. Downey assures his boss, a former star quarterback at Oklahoma, that they fought to keep the cable wired until the very end.

Soon the 108th Congress will be sworn in, and the desk, chair and cable connection will be assigned to someone else.

Watts is ready. Despite being a star within the GOP and holding a coveted leadership position for four years, he was always a solitary figure on Capitol Hill. More outsider than insider, unwilling or unable to master the give and take of building alliances and wielding power.

When he announced his retirement in July, he was fed up, though he didn't come out and say so. Watts has never been one for introspection. And his years as a political lightning rod—hammered by both liberal black Democrats and conservative white Republicans for not following the company line—have only made him more cautious and circumspect.

> What would liberal black congressional Democrats have expected from Watts?

But emotions have a way of spilling out, and, as Watts talks, it becomes clear that a great deal of hurt and anger churn beneath his genial, upbeat veneer.

The topic is golf wunderkind Tiger Woods, under tremendous pressure to boycott the Masters golf tournament because Augusta National Golf Club has no female members.

"Look at what they're doing to Tiger Woods," Watts fumes. "There's no other golfer in America today being asked to do what Tiger is. Being singled out to say, 'You have to act a certain way. You are being held to a different standard than the rest of your colleagues on the PGA Tour.' Tiger's being asked to do something that his association isn't being asked to do! If you're going to ask somebody to boycott the Masters, why not ask the PGA to pull their certification?"

Watts's voice rises in outrage. "It's totally unfair. They're singling him out, not because he's a great golfer. They're singling him out because he's black. . . . I feel like I know exactly what Tiger's going through right now. I suspect I could tell Tiger some stories about my experiences, and he'd say, '"Me, too.'"

He pounds the table for emphasis. He's endured all sorts of indignities trying to build bridges between blacks and Republicans—efforts that often left him isolated from both groups. His staffers look at him, perhaps afraid that in these closing days he's going to say what he truly feels, really let go about what his eight years in Washington were like.

He doesn't. By the afternoon, in fact, Watts is standing before television cameras to defend a far different target of racial crossfire than Tiger Woods: Mississippi Sen. Trent Lott. The Senate's incoming majority leader has been hit with a storm of criticism for praising Sen. Strom Thurmond's 1948 presidential campaign at Thurmond's 100th birthday party. Since Thurmond ran as a Dixiecrat defender of segregation, plenty of people consider Lott's remarks an outrageous endorsement of the days of Jim Crow and racial oppression. He's being slammed not only by liberal Democrats like Al Gore, Jesse Jackson and Al Sharpton, but by the conservative *Wall Street Journal* editorial page and the Family Research Council.

Watts initially sees the controversy as a cynical Washington game, one that trivializes the issue of race by focusing on some ill-conceived remarks at a banquet rather than on larger matters of economic inequity and failing schools. For an hour he tells one reporter after another that he has worked closely with Lott and never seen any evidence of racism. Lott has assured him, Watts says, that he didn't mean the comments in the way they are being interpreted. Watts believes him, despite Lott's record opposing civil rights legislation, the Rev. Martin Luther King Jr. holiday and affirmative action, and despite his willingness to speak to segregationist groups.

Watts is the man of the hour. Producers and correspondents from Fox News, CNN, ABC, CBS and NBC queue up to get their sound bites.

"Isn't the congressman concerned about being labeled an Uncle Tom?" one reporter asks Downey, who retorts: "And that would be different from the last eight years how?"

From the moment he arrived in Washington, Julius Caesar Watts Jr. has been a political curiosity. Even his late father, Buddy, had trouble figuring out how his son had wound up a Republican. "A black man voting for the Republicans," he was often quoted as saying, "makes about as much sense as a chicken voting for Colonel Sanders."

Such distrust is widespread in the African American community. Despite sporadic efforts by the GOP to woo black voters, Democrats routinely win 90 percent of the African American vote in national elections. And the ranks of elected black Republicans remain pitifully small. Of the 9,040 blacks elected to public office across the country in 2000, only 50 were Republican, according to the Joint Center for Political and Economic Studies, a Washington think tank that studies black political participation.

The conservative fold does include some prominent—and powerful—blacks: Supreme Court Justice Clarence Thomas, Secretary of State Colin Powell, National Security Adviser Condoleezza Rice. But they remain rare. And, in the minds of some in the liberal black establishment, suspect.

Watts, the fifth of Buddy and Helen's six children, certainly didn't start out as a conservative. Pretty much everyone he knew in his tiny, hardscrabble hometown of Eufaula, Okla., was a Democrat, including his father, a farmer and Baptist minister who served on the town council, and his uncle Wade, who headed the state chapter of the National Association for the Advancement of Colored People.

The civil rights struggle wasn't something Watts studied in textbooks. It was something he witnessed firsthand when the public schools were being desegregated in rural Oklahoma. The racism was open and debilitating. Once, as a boy, he yelled at a teacher: "You think because we're black that you can treat us like dogs!"

At the University of Oklahoma, Watts became a star quarterback, leading the Sooners to Orange Bowl victories [in] 1980 and 1981 as the most valuable player in both games. But he wasn't drafted as a quarterback by the National Football League, which, at that time, remained the almost exclusive domain of white quarterbacks. Watts had to settle for the Canadian Football League. After six seasons in Ottawa and Toronto, he wound up back in Oklahoma, where the Republicans began courting him.

Watts, who'd grown up poor, liked the party's message of self-reliance. He liked Don Nickles, the state's Republican senator. He also thought liberal policies had failed to help the black community and that Democrats took the black vote for granted.

When he switched parties in 1989 to run for a seat on the Oklahoma Corporation Commission, it was considered a coup for the GOP. The party had been trying to make inroads with black voters since at least 1978, when Republican National Chairman William Brock hired black consultants to develop a program for minorities and asked Jesse Jackson to come speak to the RNC. The outreach hadn't had much impact.

But GOP leaders were convinced that Watts, a handsome young football hero and a charismatic public speaker, could help the party connect with African American voters and improve its image with suburban white swing voters as well. Republicans embraced him eagerly—too eagerly, his father and uncle thought.

Though Watts had voted for Michael Dukakis in 1988 and had served as a state regulatory commissioner for less than two years, he was asked to nominate George H. W. Bush for president at the 1992 Republican National Convention.

His election to the U.S. House of Representatives in 1994 made Watts the first black Republican congressman from a Southern state in 120 years. Republicans were jubilant and jetted Watts around the country for speeches and fundraisers. His name was perennially bandied about as a possible vice presidential candidate. At the 1996 Republican National Convention, the attention was so overwhelming that he had to have police escorts just to be able to walk across the convention floor. Everybody wanted their picture taken with him. The following year, Watts delivered the GOP's rebuttal to President Clinton's State of the Union speech.

Heady stuff, though it didn't protect him from the sneers of black Democrats. People like Jackson and Sharpton dismissed Watts as a sellout, a GOP poster boy for diversity. Others were offended by his refusal to join the Congressional Black Caucus, which he regarded as a Democratic club that forced its members to march in lockstep.

Watts doesn't pretend that his skin color had nothing to do with his meteoric rise. "The fact is," he acknowledges, "when you're the majority party you have to consider how the head table looks at the banquet. It's just a fact, just a reality in politics." Watts saw himself as a trailblazer, not a token.

"Is it tokenism to say I think more black men should be schoolteachers?" he asks. "No—I think it matters." In second grade he was one of two black kids to integrate all-white Jefferson Davis Elementary School. From that point on, he didn't see a black teacher until his sophomore year in high school. "That's not symbolism," he insists. "These things are important. I take great pride when I see

General Powell giving a briefing. Black kids know where to look to find the wrong kinds of role models."

Being the only black guy in the room wasn't easy, though Watts usually treated it with eye-rolling good humor. When party leaders asked him to appear at welfare reform press conferences, he'd privately remark that since a majority of those on welfare were white, he didn't really see the point in his attendance. But more often than not, he'd show up.

Sometimes in the halls of Congress, a clueless colleague would make a point of introducing him to a black constituent, as if the constituent and Watts had to be long-lost friends, members of some club who might slap-five. Watts would grin and bear it.

Far more damaging were Watts's tangles with House Majority Whip Tom DeLay, his frustration at his lack of clout within the Republican leadership and his growing sense that he wasn't being treated with the same respect as other House leaders.

All of it, say those who know him well, took a psychic toll. His wife, Frankie, had never moved to the capital, preferring to stay in Norman, Okla., with their five children. (Watts also has a sixth child, who was born when he was 17 and was raised by his uncle.) Watts flew back to Oklahoma almost every weekend to see his family. In truth, he was more comfortable there anyway.

A devout Christian and part-time Baptist preacher, Watts doesn't drink, doesn't smoke and doesn't have much of an appetite for the capital's party circuit. He bonded with staffers while watching reruns of his beloved "Andy Griffith Show," but he never developed the kind of close personal ties that give Congress its clubby atmosphere.

"I can see why people might say, 'It's not easy to get to know J. C.,'" says Watts, who admits that he doesn't confide in people. "It's one of my weaknesses. I don't open up to people and tell them personal things. It's just not my nature."

Watts had colleagues, but not friends. He was lonely in Washington, says one senior GOP leadership aide: "I mean, J. C. isn't a white guy with black skin. He's a black guy."

Now the black guy is going, leaving Congress bereft of even one elected African American Republican voice for the first time since 1990. It is a worrisome development for a party trying to sell itself as the home of compassionate conservatism. Every bit as damaging, in its own way, as public nostalgia for segregation.

It was a dozen years between the defeat of Sen. Edward Brooke (R-Mass.) in 1978 and the election of Rep. Gary Franks (R-Conn.) in 1990; before that, it was 32 years in the wilderness.

"I think for any caucus on any level to be absent the black perspective is a deficiency," says the Rev. DeForest

> What does Watts's departure mean for the Republican Party's efforts to reach out to blacks?

"Buster" Soaries, a black Republican who lost a race against Rep. Rush Holt (D-N.J.) in November.

"There are racial dynamics to everything," he says, and whites can stumble into offensive statements without even realizing it. Sometimes "it gets down to a certain word in a press release that the majority just misses but the minority community picks up on it." Soaries has spent a great deal of time explaining the loaded term "state's rights" to young white Republicans. "They're thinking of a conservative model of a government construct, but if you say it to black people they're thinking George Wallace or Mississippi and those states that wanted the right to continue with segregation." Without Watts, Republicans in Congress will have to work hard to bring non-elected black Republicans into their process, Soaries says.

Jim Dyke, a spokesman for the RNC, says that Chairman Marc Racicot is doing just that. "He is adamant about these outreach efforts," says Dyke, who points out that the party holds regular events like one in Charlotte, N.C., last August featuring second-tier black Bush administration officials. And while November didn't prove fruitful for either Soaries or Las Vegas City Councilwoman Lynette Boggs McDonald—a black Republican who lost her bid to unseat Rep. Shelley Berkley (D-Nev.)—Dyke points out that other African American Republicans won, including Maryland Lt.-Gov.-elect Michael Steele.

"As far as the farm team goes," McDonald says, "it's stronger than it's ever been."

Democrats, of course, don't buy it. They've long questioned the sincerity of Republican efforts to win over black voters, labeling the outreach all talk and no action. They point out that the vice chair of the RNC's New Majority Council, launched with great fanfare several years ago to court black voters, resigned in 2000, saying that the RNC didn't stand for more than "the oratory of inclusion."

Soaries reports that "some Republicans were a little nervous because of my potential appeal to black voters, because if black voters turned out in large numbers for me, many Republicans were afraid that would help other Democrats in other races." He was stunned when some Republican officials urged him to not campaign in black areas.

Watts, too, recalls that before his 1990 race for Oklahoma corporation commissioner, a prominent state Republican predicted that Watts would be a disaster for the rest of the GOP ticket. Blacks, the Republican reasoned, would turn out in huge numbers for Watts, but vote Democratic for every other office.

Watts considers this a "sick, pathetic theory," but it continues to hold sway with some Republicans, and he acknowledges that it may be part of the reason the party hasn't made minority outreach a higher priority. The lack of strong commitment exasperates Watts. Republican Strom Thurmond, Watts points out, won 22 percent of the black vote in his last Senate race in South Carolina. If a former segregationist can do that in the South, Watts argues, there's no reason why the national GOP can't do the same.

There are other cracks in the black Democratic fortress, Watts adds. In a poll released by the Joint Center for Political and Economic Studies in October, 63 percent of blacks identified themselves as Democrats, down from 74 percent two years ago. The number of blacks who identified themselves as Republicans grew from 4 percent to 10 percent. And for the first time, Colin Powell scored a higher approval rating on civil rights than Jesse Jackson.

But David Bositis, a senior researcher for the think tank, doesn't believe any of this has translated into more black votes for the Republican Party: "It's just not there. The fact is George Bush got the lowest percentage of the black vote of any Republican since Goldwater."

If Watts's mission was to build bridges between blacks and Republicans, he has failed, Bositis says. "The party hasn't changed. There's some moves within the party to change, but it hasn't changed. And Trent Lott's a perfect example of it."

Watts's real legacy wasn't making the GOP more attractive to blacks, Bositis says. It was keeping the party from making itself less attractive.

In 1996, the revolution that had swept Republicans to power in the House was in full swing, and conservatives were on a tear. With most of the "Contract With America" already passed into law, they set their sights on dismantling affirmative action.

Franks, the only other black Republican in Congress, and Rep. Charles Canady of Florida introduced a bill to eliminate racial preferences designed to make up for past discrimination against minorities. They called the proposed legislation the Civil Rights Act of 1996. It was a hot issue. While affirmative action had broad and vociferous support within the black community and among many Democrats, many Republicans argued that racial preferences of any kind made it impossible to achieve a colorblind society.

Watts had reservations about affirmative action, too, but absent an alternative, a "Plan B," he decided to oppose Canady and Franks. Just as his family's self-reliance ultimately led him to support welfare reform, Watts's personal experiences led him to conclude that the United States was not yet ready to end affirmative action altogether. Much had changed from his childhood days when Watts had to sit in the balcony at the Eufaula Theater. But racism hadn't disappeared. Driving his Chevy Blazer in Oklahoma one day, Watts had been pulled over by the police six different times. The sole reason, he believed, was his skin color.

Watts worked for weeks to arrange a private meeting with then–House Speaker Newt Gingrich. One afternoon, he finally found himself in Gingrich's office. On the wall hung an immense portrait of the Rev. Martin Luther King Jr., who appeared to be watching as Watts asked Gingrich to kill the Canady-Franks bill. Doing anything less, Watts said, would send a signal that the GOP believed racism no longer existed in America. Politically, the party hadn't laid the groundwork for such a move, Watts argued. And what were the Republicans proposing other than just ending affirmative action?

"Look, in principle, I don't agree with affirmative action," Watts said. "But in practice, we still don't have a level playing field." It was an emotional issue for Watts. "I don't know, Newt, I'm thinking with my heart here, not my head."

Gingrich listened, then leaned forward and touched Watts's arm. "That's why I like having you around, J. C.," he said. "Don't ever stop listening to your heart. I need your heart."

Gingrich told Franks to pull his bill.

But the next year, Canady continued his crusade without Franks, who had been defeated at the polls. Canady and the other backers of the bill knew they needed Watts's support to make their case that race was no longer an issue in America—an irony not lost on the party's only black congressman.

They brought in Ward Connerly, a conservative African American for whom ending racial preferences had become a raison d'etre, to try to persuade Watts. The meeting got a bit tense.

"Affirmative action isn't the problem," Watts remembers telling Connerly. "Lousy education for black kids is the problem. Until you fix these schools don't talk to me about equal opportunity."

This time, though, the bill seemed headed for a vote on the House floor. Then something surprising happened: When the House Judiciary Committee took up the bill, eight Republicans didn't show up and four Republicans moved to kill the bill. Watts strongly suspects Gingrich was at work behind the scenes.

The party of Lincoln had, in effect, endorsed the need for affirmative action— or least acknowledged that America had yet to reach its colorblind promise. And J. C. Watts's voice had been heard.

Watts ran for chairman of the House Republican Conference in 1998, a time of tremendous turmoil on Capitol Hill. President Clinton was being impeached, and Gingrich had survived a coup attempt by fellow Republicans.

The Republicans desperately needed to soften their strident image, and, as conference chair, Watts would handle communications for the team. Calm, affable and compassionate, he was able to take down conference Chairman John Boehner, a Republican from Ohio who'd been one of the participants in the failed coup.

On his 41st birthday, Watts became the fourth-ranking Republican in the House, putting him on track for even bigger things. But he soon found himself at odds with one of the Hill's most formidable political pit bulls: Tom DeLay.

A former pest exterminator from Texas nicknamed "the Hammer," DeLay didn't have much use for anyone who wasn't part of his bare-knuckles, vote-gathering machine. And Watts wasn't.

"Have you ever seen the movie 'A Few Good Men'?" Watts asks as he ruminates about DeLay and the whip's frequent run-ins with the media. At the film's climax, a young lieutenant played by Tom Cruise needles Jack Nicholson's Col. Nathan Jessup into his courtroom confession. "When Colonel Jessup was on the stand down in the stretch there, and Cruise knew he was going to convict him?

The reason he knew he would convict him is, he knew Jessup had too much pride to lie. He said, 'Did you order the Code Red?' and Jessup said, 'You're damn right I ordered the Code Red!'"

Watts smiles, letting the analogy hang there. It's an interesting comparison, considering the villainous Nicholson character is a man who took the Marine Corps code to extremes.

"Tom's a very proud conservative," Watts observes. "He knows one way, he's very hard-charging."

And in 1999, it was clear that DeLay was charging right for him. That summer, DeLay's office distributed an array of communications materials to the House Republican Conference, publicly doing Watts's job for him. Then, in December, conservative syndicated columnist Robert Novak wrote that "dissatisfaction" with Watts as conference chair was "being voiced by his congressional colleagues, including other members of the party leadership."

Watts, who considered resigning or retiring then, says the criticism of his performance was unfair. Elected conference chairman in November 1998, "I didn't get a staff and budget until the middle of March," Watts says. "And everybody was saying, 'Oh, he's gotten off to a rocky start,' but I didn't have the ability to do the job I was elected to do."

He was used to the Uncle Tom broadsides from the Jacksons and Sharptons of the world. But public sniping [at] "other members of the party leadership," as Novak put it, that was too much. "There was, I am convinced, an orchestrated effort to cause me problems and to keep me from doing my job," Watts says.

DeLay's office didn't return numerous phone calls to comment for this article. But a Republican source describes DeLay's thinking this way: "Tom's very frustrated when the message doesn't get out. Tom wants the whole team to work together, and he wants the message part to work. . . . 'Just do the job. If you're going to do the job, great. If you're not and you want help, we're here to help. If you're not and you don't want help, then we're going to do the job.'"

Watts eventually appealed to House Speaker Dennis Hastert for support and got it, but he remained frustrated. Some came to view him as petulant. He "threatened to quit leadership half a dozen times that I know of," one Republican says. "He's very high maintenance."

It took a long time for Watts to come to terms with how betrayed he felt. He didn't understand, at first, "the dynamics of the leadership table, the challenges, even some games being played at that time, some turf grabbing," Watts says. "I was naive in thinking that 'Gosh, we all wear the same colored jersey, we're all going to be one big happy family and we're all going to work as a team for the cause.'"

"Being at the leadership table is often like the company that keeps two sets of books, one public set of books and one private set of books, and I just never got into that and never wanted to get into it."

Even so, late in 2001, when House Majority Leader Dick Armey announced he would retire at the end of 2002, Watts considered running for Armey's leadership job. His opponent would be Tom DeLay. Watts asked some of his colleagues to "keep their powder dry" while he took a couple of months to contemplate a run. It was a naive request. While Watts was mulling his future, DeLay began button-holing colleagues. Though the election was still months away, DeLay quickly nailed down enough votes to assure victory. The Hammer would be the next leader.

For months last year, the Pentagon had been considering killing the $11 billion Crusader artillery program, which Defense Secretary Donald Rumsfeld considered a Cold War relic not worthy of 21st-century warfare. Watts was one of its principal defenders: The weapon system was to be partially assembled in Elgin, Okla., and used for training at Fort Sill, both of which lie in Watts's district.

Generally the pet projects of congressional leaders are sacrosanct. But President Bush made it clear that he would veto any defense appropriations bill that continued funding the Crusader.

Watts didn't seem to have much clout with the Bush administration, despite having been one of Bush's earliest supporters. He couldn't even get the administration to return his phone calls.

"I had been trying to call Don Rumsfeld for probably six weeks," Watts recalls. "And finally, after about a month, I got a call back from [Deputy Defense Secretary Paul] Wolfowitz." He told Watts that the Pentagon was studying the issue, and things could go either way. "We may end up canceling the program," Wolfowitz told Watts in late April, "but, you know, we may end up building more."

On the morning of May 8, Watts received call after call from people who'd heard that Rumsfeld was announcing the program's demise at 2 P.M. No one from the administration called. News of the program's imminent death appeared on the Associated Press wire. Still no call.

Finally, at around noon, Wolfowitz phoned to give Watts the news everyone already knew. Watts was furious. He told Wolfowitz and eventually Rumsfeld that the way the administration had treated him was "indecent and totally unprofessional."

"Such a thing, it gnaws at you," says one of Watts's closest allies, Rep. Christopher Shays (R-Conn.). "You think, 'My gosh, I'm an active supporter of the president, the fourth-ranking Republican in the House. And more than that: I'm the only African American Republican in Congress and, as such, am asked to do so much for my party—to go around the country and raise money. And they don't even give me the courtesy of a heads-up?' It's gross."

When Bush came to speak to the 223-member House Republican Conference the following week, its chairman didn't show up. Everyone knew why Watts had stiffed the president. He felt he hadn't been treated with the same respect another member of the House leadership would have received. "I doubt it would have happened to anybody in the top three," Watts says, still bristling at the memory.

But beyond the slight—which administration officials privately acknowledge was an unintended screw-up—lies something more telling about Watts: his inability, or unwillingness, to wheel and deal. In Washington, that's how power bases are built, careers propelled and Crusaders saved.

Many people involved were surprised by his feeble response to the attack on the Crusader. Why hadn't Watts tried to work a deal with leadership and appropriators? they asked. Why hadn't he cozied up to members of the House Armed Services Committee or rallied a team to back him on this? Where was his coalition?

"He has absolutely no interest in doing those things," says a Republican who knows Watts well. "It's yucky kind of work in his mind."

"He's not one of the old, traditional guys who go around slapping backs, the good ol' boys," agrees one of his biggest Democratic fans, Rep. John Lewis (Ga.). "That's not his style."

Watts doesn't disagree with the assessment that he's no wheeler-dealer. His straightforwardness, he maintains, has "been my strength." But he acknowledges that he doesn't "ask people for things very well. I don't like feeling like I owe people something."

Even before the Crusader mess, Watts had been weighing whether his life on the Hill and its accompanying frustrations were worth the time away from Frankie and the kids, three of whom are still living at home. It was time, Watts decided, to stop shuttling between Oklahoma and Washington.

Top Republicans, including Bush, Hastert and Vice President Cheney, took turns trying to talk Watts into staying. They were joined by several black Democrats, who'd come to appreciate having Watts on the opposite side of the aisle.

> *What kind of people are best suited to a career in Congress? Are these the kind of people we want as public servants?*

"I hate to see him go," said South Carolina Rep. James Clyburn. "J. C. is someone who really has been quietly but very forcefully doing a lot of good."

Civil rights legend Rosa Parks, who refused to give up her seat to a white man on an Alabama bus in 1955, also wrote to Watts, asking him to reconsider his decision. "If you can," she said in her letter, "please remain as a pioneer on the Republicans' side until others come to assist you. I am glad I stayed in my seat."

But Watts had made up his mind. He wants to start a public relations firm with offices in both Oklahoma and Washington, to preach and give speeches, to serve on corporate boards. He's already written an autobiography, *What Color Is a Conservative?* (which blasts the Jackson/Sharpton crowd but contains few harsh words about Republicans who didn't appreciate what he brought to the table). Maybe someday he'll return to politics, Watts says. Just not now.

The Bookers Are Calling

Everyone, it seems, wants Watts's take on Trent Lott, who is under increasing pressure to resign as Senate Republican leader. Watts agrees to appear on NBC's "Meet the Press" with Tim Russert, the top-rated Sunday morning talk show. By 7:30 A.M. Central time on December 15, he arrives at the University of Oklahoma satellite studio in Norman, where he has done live feeds for years. He'll be paired on the show with his friend, Rep. John Lewis.

Many of Lewis's colleagues in the Congressional Black Caucus are calling for Lott's head. Oklahoma's Don Nickles, the second-ranking Senate Republican and a man Watts has admired for two decades, is questioning Lott's viability. Colin Powell and Condoleezza Rice have declined to lift a finger on Lott's behalf. President Bush has repudiated Lott's words and done little to come to his aid.

But Watts can't bring himself to join the growing chorus of Lott bashers, though he will eventually suggest that it might be better for Lott to step down. With Russert, he simply acknowledges the damage Lott has done to the GOP's standing with black voters. He says he has talked to Lott several times during the past week, and he has urged the senator to go beyond apologies. "We can't be about symbolism from here on in," Watts tells Russert. "We have to be about substance. That was my advice, and those were my comments to the senator."

It's not a particularly strong defense of Lott, nor is it a particularly strong performance by Watts. There's a noticeable weariness in his voice.

When the controversy first broke, Watts fixated on the way Lott was being savaged by liberals and the media. And he identified with him because of it. As the furor has worn on, however, Watts finds himself offended not only by the details of Lott's segregationist-coddling past but also by the posturing of the senator's conservative critics. They are worried, they say, about the impact of Lott's comments on the party's outreach toward African Americans.

What outreach? Watts wonders. For a long time, he says, he has been the only congressional Republican actually doing outreach instead of just talking about it. Outreach? Where have you been for the past eight years? Watts wonders.

Once again, his long-simmering resentment of liberal exploitation of racial issues for political gain is at war with his frustration at his party's tone-deafness and lip service about inclusion. Watts is trying to straddle a fault line that Lott has turned into a chasm.

It was there when he entered the House eight years ago. And it is there as he leaves. Now it's someone else's turn to bridge the thorny politics of Capitol Hill, race and Republicanism.

Watts finishes talking to Russert and takes off his mike. He is guest-preaching this morning at a Methodist church about 90 minutes away from Norman—and light-years away from Washington. The soon-to-be ex-congressman gets into his Blazer and drives away.

Consider the source and the audience.

• This article, by political reporter Jake Tapper, appeared in the *Washington Post,* where it was sure to be read by political insiders as well as the general public. Does that fact affect the content or tone of the article?

Lay out the argument, the values, and the assumptions.

• What do Tapper's goals seem to be in writing this article? Is he sympathetic to Watts? To Watts's critics?

• What does Watts seem to think caused the difficulties he faced in Congress? What do his critics think were his biggest problems? Can these two interpretations be reconciled?

• How much effect did Watts's race have on his political fortunes?

Uncover the evidence.

• Tapper interviews Watts, his allies in Congress, and his enemies. Are there voices that he should have included but didn't?

• Are there limits to this kind of evidence?

Evaluate the conclusion.

• Clearly, J. C. Watts and his supporters on the one hand and his detractors on the other have conclusions about what happened to Watts's congressional career. What does Tapper's view appear to be?

• What conclusions do you yourself draw about this matter? What do you think is the source of the Republicans' difficulties with the race issue?

Sort out the political implications.

• What impact will the difficulties the Republicans have had in attracting and keeping black candidates for public office have on the party's future?

• From a practical standpoint, how can the Republicans reach out more effectively to racial minorities?

6.2 Another Record Year for Academic Pork

Jeffrey Brainard, *The Chronicle of Higher Education,* 27 September 2002

Here Jeffrey Brainard looks at some of the consequences of pork-barrel spending on higher education. Pork is congressional spending that is earmarked for projects in a particular congressperson's district. It may benefit the district, but it generally has no real benefit for the public at large, whose tax dollars go to pay for the project. Frequently, pork is slipped into bills on other issues and gets passed without the rigorous debate, hearings, and scrutiny that other spending bills are subject to. Members of Congress love pork because it raises their credit with their constituents, who like to see their representatives "bring home the bacon." Does the practice of pork-barrel spending do anything to help the country as a whole?

Continuing a six-year upward trend, Congress showered money on colleges for pork-barrel projects this year, as the amount grew by 10 percent and reached the largest total ever.

For the 2002 fiscal year, which ends September 30, Congress directed federal agencies to award at least $1.837-billion to projects involving specific universities and colleges, according to an analysis by *The Chronicle.* That total is $169-million higher than last year's and a fivefold increase since 1996. It is the highest since *The Chronicle* began its annual survey of such spending, in 1989.

Although Congress provided more money for the directed grants, known as earmarks, than it did last year, the median earmark actually decreased, to $550,000 from $625,000 in 2001, as lawmakers shared the wealth with a larger number of institutions and projects. In all, a record 668 institutions got earmarks. That represents a 27-percent increase over the previous year, and shows that colleges increasingly see their Congressional representatives as conduits for federal funds for campus projects.

Why are colleges looking increasingly to members of Congress to supply money for research projects? Where else could they get these funds?

The directed grants paid for an eclectic mix of research, construction, and teaching projects, including research by the Stevens Institute of Technology on land mines, the construction of a dormitory at the Citadel, and a project to archive documents electronically at the University of Mississippi's National Library of the Accounting Profession.

The largest single earmark this year, for $20-million, went to Auburn University, to help finance construction of the university's Center for Transportation Technology, where researchers will develop analytical approaches to vehicle safety and to highway design and construction.

The pork-barrel projects are controversial because they depend on the political influence and seniority of the lawmakers who secure them, and circumvent the open, peer-reviewed competitions that federal agencies typically use to award money for such projects. In those competitions, winners are chosen by agency employees who are experts in the particular fields of research or education being financed.

In contrast, members of Congress and their aides choose recipients of the directed grants based on their own judgments, often after lobbying by the colleges seeking the money. As a result, the funds may support projects that are of relatively poor quality or do not serve national priorities, say some experts on federal research spending and officials in the Bush administration.

But lawmakers and college officials, who for the most part support earmarking, counter that the practice helps worthy projects that agency experts and peer reviewers have wrongly dismissed or misjudged.

Despite the controversy, the past year brought few signs that the brakes will be applied to pork-barrel spending anytime soon. President Bush's budget director, Mitchell E. Daniels Jr., at first challenged Congress to restrain its appetite for pork, but he encountered such bruising opposition that he ran up a white flag of surrender this summer.

Nor did the federal government's worsening fiscal health restrain lawmakers. After four years of surpluses, the government is expected to run a deficit of $157-million in 2002, as taxes were cut and spending increased on anti-terrorism measures. A deficit was forecast before lawmakers finished work last fall on the 2002 budget.

"I think it's been clear for some time that this genie was out of the bottle, and nobody was going to put it back," says Robert M. Rosenzweig, a former president of the Association of American Universities, a group of 63 of the largest research universities in the United States and Canada.

Congress "can't resist" earmarks, he says, noting that lawmakers are elected "to serve their constituents." He calls the directed funds "a natural part of our political system, and a highly dysfunctional [one] as it applies to R&D."

Unhealthy Spending Level

Some scholars of federal spending say the total amount of earmarked funds for research has grown to an unhealthy level. Of the 2002 total, $1.359-billion, or 74 percent, financed research projects and $236-million, or 13 percent, went for research-related construction or equipment, according to *The Chronicle*'s analysis. The combined total of earmarked funds designated for research-related activities, $1.595-billion, represented 8 percent of the $19.879-billion that the federal government spent on academic research projects, buildings, and equipment in 2000, the last year for which figures were available.

"I think some warning lights should be going off at that level" of earmarked funds, says David M. Hart, an associate professor of public policy at Harvard University, who studies the relationship between science and the government. "It's a worrisome number, and maybe a call to arms." Although some research projects supported by earmarks may be worthy, he says, there is little evidence to prove it.

For their part, officials at universities that receive earmarks call them an antidote to flaws in the peer-review system, which they argue is dominated by the large research institutions that already got most of the competitively awarded funds. The officials charge that the peer-review panels are controlled by scientists from large universities who look out for one another and are biased against newer, smaller research institutions.

Colleges in economically depressed regions also see earmarked funds for research projects as key tools to try to jump-start technology-oriented businesses and create jobs.

The continued rise in academic earmarks for the 2002 fiscal year was fueled partly by the federal government's response to the September 11 terrorist attacks.

Those events united President Bush and Congress behind significantly increased spending to strengthen national defense and to fight terrorists abroad. In that atmosphere, previous concerns about controlling federal spending and avoiding a budget deficit dissipated. In 2002, federal discretionary spending—the part of the budget not automatically devoted by law to programs like Social Security and Medicare—rose by 13 percent.

The rise in earmarks was "part of a breakdown in budget discipline across the board," Mr. Hart says.

For 2002, the spending bill that finances the Defense Department attracted more earmarked dollars than any other. It is also the single largest appropriations bill of the 13 that Congress passes annually to finance the activities of the federal government.

Lawmakers finished the spending plan for the 2002 fiscal year three months after the September 11 attacks. As the final appropriations bills were hammered out, some colleges recognized and responded to the government's new spending priorities. They secured earmarked funds for a wealth of academic research and training projects aimed at combating terrorism and defending against chemical, biological, and nuclear attacks. Congress provided $116-million to universities for 35 such projects in 2002, nearly double the $60-million it awarded in the 2001 fiscal year, *The Chronicle* found.

Some of that money went to relatively small colleges represented by powerful members of Congress. St. Petersburg College, a two-year institution in Florida, got $2.6-million for its National Terrorism Preparedness Institute, through the support of its local congressman, C. W. (Bill) Young, chairman of the Appropriations Committee in the U.S. House of Representatives. The institute trains emergency workers to deal with attacks involving weapons of mass destruction.

Sen. John McCain, an Arizona Republican who is one of the few Congressional critics of the set-asides, complained last fall that earmarks for research and weapons were gobbling up money that was badly needed to raise low pay and remedy operational deficiencies in the military. But the Senate passed the defense-spending measure, 94 to 2.

Relative to the giant overall defense budget—$351-billion this year—the research earmarks are "sofa change" and attract little attention at the Pentagon, says Christopher Hellman, a senior analyst at the Center for Defense Information, a nonprofit organization here that studies military issues and opposes earmarks. And as a possible war with Iraq looms, "questioning [earmarks] done in the name of national security is a lot harder than [challenging] things like agriculture subsidies," he says.

> *The article says that John McCain is "one of the few Congressional critics" of this practice. Why don't more members of Congress raise their voices against it?*

Even so, when Congress last year asked Defense Department officials for their views of the military value of some projects that later received earmarks, the evaluations were less than glowing.

Each year, as staff members of the House and Senate Appropriations Committees prepare the defense-spending bill, they routinely ask Pentagon officials to comment on some of the research projects that the committees are considering for earmarks. Through a Freedom of Information Act request, *The Chronicle* obtained copies of the Defense Department's responses, which were prepared last year before Congress completed the 2002 budget.

Among other details, the committees asked the Defense Department to rate projects on their military value. *The Chronicle* received responses on 97 projects involving universities. The Pentagon ranked just 5 of them as of high value, 29 as medium, and the rest as low. (Those numbers do not include projects in the Air Force, which was the only Pentagon branch that denied *The Chronicle*'s request. The denial is under appeal.)

With President Bush needing lawmakers' support for his domestic and foreign policies, political analysts say he cannot afford to alienate members of Congress by going after their pet projects.

But for a time last year, Mr. Bush's budget director, Mr. Daniels, did just that. He poked fun at lawmakers who supported the projects, saying, "Their motto is, 'Don't just stand there, spend something.' This is the only way they feel relevant."

Lawmakers in both parties were quick to defend their prerogatives, and several lashed out at Mr. Daniels personally, in unusually harsh terms, for overstepping his bounds. Sen. Robert C. Byrd, a West Virginia Democrat who heads the Senate Appropriations Committee and is a scholar of the Roman Senate, called him "our little Caesar."

By July of this year, a chastened Mr. Daniels had conceded. "We've made what we think is the good-government point," he told *Congressional Quarterly*. "We think [earmarking] does lead to poor decision-making, but enough said. We do have bigger fish to fry."

Mr. Daniels said he would be satisfied if Congress observed the overall spending limits set by the White House, although those remain short of what the Senate's Democratic leaders support. If reaching a compromise means that the administration will have to tolerate earmarks, Mr. Daniels said, "so be it."

Select Group

Even with few constraints on pork-barrel spending, not all colleges shared equally in Congress's largess. The pattern of earmarks in 2002 shows that when Congress doles out money for such projects, a select class of lawmakers—the members of the powerful appropriations panels in the Senate and House—send especially large shares back to their home states.

Eight of the 10 states that received the most earmarked funds that were not shared with any partners had lawmakers who led appropriations committees or subcommittees last year, *The Chronicle* found.

In contrast, only one state among the 10 that received the least earmarked funds, Vermont, had such representation. Sen. Patrick Leahy, a Vermont Democrat, heads a subcommittee that sets spending for aid to other nations.

The takeover of the Senate last year by Democrats appears to have resulted in more earmarks flowing to colleges in states with senators of that party. Democrats had last controlled the chamber in 1994, and the 2002 budget was the first passed by Congress after the leadership switch.

In 2002, 13 states moved up by at least five spots in the rankings. Seven of those 13 states have Democratic senators who last year became leaders of appropriations subcommittees. (They were Iowa, Louisiana, Maryland, Nevada, North Dakota, South Carolina, and Wisconsin.) Three of the other states—Connecticut, Georgia, and South Dakota—have two Democratic senators. Sen. Tim Johnson of South Dakota, a member of the Senate Appropriations Committee who is in a tight race for re-election, has boasted to voters of his ability to bring home the bacon. The Democrats' one-vote majority in the Senate hangs in the balance.

Eleven states fell by at least five places in 2002. Five of those states share among them a total of seven Democratic senators, only one of whom, Richard J. Durbin of Illinois, heads an appropriations subcommittee. The other six states were each represented by two Republican senators.

Still, party control is not always a prerequisite to pork; earmarking remains bipartisan. Even while Republicans controlled both chambers of Congress for six years, their Democratic colleagues steadily got earmarks for projects, in some cases covering multiple years.

One such project is the Large Millimeter Telescope, a 16-story-high radio telescope being built on a mountain peak in Mexico. The telescope is a joint effort between researchers there and at the University of Massachusetts at Amherst. The project has received about $25-million in Defense Department earmarks since 1994.

However, it was not included on a list of priority astronomical projects drawn up by National Academy of Sciences panels in 1991 and again in 2001.

A principal sponsor of the earmarks has been U.S. Rep. John W. Olver, a Massachusetts Democrat who is a member of the House Appropriations Committee and a former assistant professor of chemistry at the university.

Low-Quality Projects

Many other projects have received Congressionally earmarked money for years. But a new study appears to support criticisms that research financed through earmarks tends to be of relatively low quality.

The study . . . , by A. Abigail Payne, an assistant professor of economics at the University of Illinois at Chicago, is believed to be the first to examine the effect of earmarked funds on research productivity. Ms. Payne measured research quality by studying 120 major research universities that had received earmarked funds between 1981 and 1998, relying in part on numbers from *The Chronicle*'s annual surveys.

Ms. Payne tracked the total number of academic papers published by those universities' faculty members in scholarly journals and the number of citations by other scholars to those papers.

She then compared the changes in the number of articles published and the number of citations per paper between 1981 and 1998, after controlling for factors other than earmarks that could have affected differences among the universities' publication rates over time.

She found that for the average level of earmarked funds given to an institution, the average number of articles published increased from 8 to 14 percent over that period. However, the average citations per paper declined by at least 9 percent.

That decline may partly reflect that earmarked funds are typically directed to support applied research, not basic research, Ms. Payne says, "and therefore promote activities that do not result in widely cited academic publications. Whether this is a good use of federal funding is a question that should be explored in future research."

Whatever the actual value of earmarked research, colleges' appetite for the money may not soon be sated.

Members of Congress will continue to try to oblige their constituents, predicts Mr. Hart of Harvard. If earmarked funds for colleges are to be restrained, "I think the universities have to take the first step," he adds. "It's their integrity that gets damaged if funds are misspent. They have to be the guardians of the system" of peer review.

Whose job is it to stop the pork in higher education?

However, Mr. Rosenzweig, the former Association of American Universities president who now is a consultant for colleges, doubts that such an effort will work. As the association's president from 1983 to 1993, he tried to persuade the members to voluntarily refrain from seeking earmarks, in order to support the peer-review model for distributing research funds.

But more and more members of the association continued to get earmarks anyway. In 2002, all but five of the group's 61 domestic members received at least one.

"Of all of the things I have done in my professional career, and the battles I have taken on, I have never failed as dismally as in the battle over earmarks," Mr. Rosenzweig says. "I don't think I persuaded anybody."

Consider the source and the audience.

• This article is written for *The Chronicle of Higher Education*. How does that fact shape the article's focus? How could you find out about pork-barrel spending in other areas?

Lay out the argument, the values, and the assumptions.

• What is the author's basic attitude toward the increased pork-barrel spending in higher education?

• What are the three central arguments against academic pork that the author cites?

• Is there a more general argument to be made against pork-barrel spending? Any to be made in its favor?

Uncover the evidence.

• What kinds of evidence does Brainard base his story on?

• What other sources could Brainard have tapped? If he had interviewed more members of Congress who favor pork-barrel spending, would that have changed the way you see the issue?

Evaluate the conclusion.

• Brainard's sources seem to be pessimistic about the chances of slowing or eliminating the practice of earmarking funds for colleges and universities. Based on what you know and have read about Congress, is that pessimism warranted?

Sort out the political implications.

• If the White House is unable to reign in congressional spending and continues to support tax cuts, what is the U.S. budgetary situation likely to be in the future? Is there anything wrong with a government running a deficit?

• Whose responsibility is fiscal responsibility? The president's? Congress's? The voters'?

6.3 Close Races Go the Way of Rotary Phones, Newt Gingrich

Ronald Brownstein, *Los Angeles Times,* 15 April 2002

The founders designed the House of Representatives to be responsive to changes in public opinion—presumably if there were a tremendous shift in policy preferences over a two-year period, the entire composition of the House could change from election to election. Here Brownstein argues that something has gone amiss with the founders' plans, something that "should have Madison turning in his grave." Is there anything the founders could have done to prevent the trends that Brownstein notes?

In designing the new American government, the founders expected tremors in public opinion to rattle the windows in the House of Representatives before anyplace else. James Madison, in "The Federalist Papers," insisted that of all the government's branches, the House most needed "an immediate dependence on, and intimate sympathy with, the people." To stay attuned to the people, Madison believed House members had to stay accountable to the people, with frequent elections that he considered the only way to ensure that "dependence and sympathy."

Two hundred fifteen years later, House members still stand for election every two years.

They just don't face much risk anymore that they will lose those elections.

Perversely, the House has become the arm of government that is now arguably the most insulated from shifts in the public mood. Throughout the 1990s, almost three-fourths of the 435 House seats never changed hands

> *How did Madison and his colleagues design the House so that it would be most responsive to shifts in the popular will?*

between the parties, calculates independent political analyst Rhodes Cook. The signs point toward even less turnover in the years ahead. Even this far from election day, it appears that only about four dozen House seats may generate plausible races this year. By this fall, experts on both sides expect the number of truly competitive contests to drop to as few as two dozen.

It's a trend that should have Madison turning in his grave. "It's outrageous," says Mark Gersh, Washington director of the National Committee for an Effective Congress, a leading liberal political action committee. "The political trends are muted with this many noncompetitive seats, because even if the public wants to express an opinion about what is going on in Congress, they can't. It is really a perversion of democracy."

Partly, the death of competition in the House can be explained by natural causes. In recent years, many of the most competitive seats were held by members caught, in effect, behind enemy lines: Southern Democrats holding seats voting Republican for president, or Northeastern Republicans in the opposite position. As voters have harmonized their votes for president and Congress, many of those legislators have now been replaced with representatives more unambiguously in tune with the district's dominant ideology. That evolution has taken many of those districts out of play.

> *How did it happen that some members of Congress were "caught . . . behind enemy lines"?*

But far less benign factors have also contributed to the collapse in competition. One is money. In the 2000 election, the average House incumbent raised almost six times as much as his or her opponent. A financial disadvantage isn't always fatal in Senate races because those contests attract enough media attention to let challengers become known, even if they can't match the incumbent's television budget. But House races usually draw less coverage than high school baseball games. That means House challengers without the money to buy advertising are almost always doomed.

Just as important in the muffling of competition has been redistricting. That's the process where states, once every 10 years, redraw the lines of congressional districts after the census maps the new distribution of population.

This year's redistricting is likely to be remembered as a bipartisan monument to back-scratching. In a few states where one party controlled the state legislature and the governorship, it used that leverage to draw maps that will tilt several congressional seats in its direction. Most often, though, the two parties colluded to protect incumbents, creating districts so heavily Republican or Democratic that the other party has little chance of ever taking them.

The most dramatic example is in California. In the 1990s, about one-fifth of the state's congressional districts changed hands between the parties at least once. But Gary Jacobson, a political scientist at UC San Diego, says the state's 53 districts now all lean so heavily toward one side or the other, it's possible *none* will change partisan control until the next redistricting, 10 years from now.

And California isn't alone. "It is going to be true all over the country," says former Republican National Committee general counsel Benjamin Ginsberg, who consults with state Republican parties on redistricting. "If there are two dozen seats at play in any election [nationwide], it is going to be a lot."

That prospect has several implications, none of them healthy. First it means that absent some major unpredictable event—a recession, a big scandal—there won't be enough truly competitive seats to give either party more than a slim majority in the House. "They are locked into narrow margins," says Ginsberg.

> What does "healthy" mean in this context? Whose health is Brownstein concerned with?

That will make governing tough. Governing will get even tougher as more House members represent seats so safe that they don't have to consider the views of voters outside their own base. That allows—indeed encourages—them to embrace purist ideological positions, which impedes compromise.

It is probably no coincidence that legislators were more willing to cross party lines on key issues when more of them had to run in competitive districts. Twenty years ago, members of Congress sided with their own party on about three-fourths of major votes, according to *Congressional Quarterly*. On average since 1995, Democrats have voted with their own party 83% of the time, and Republicans 88%. An excess of safe seats is transforming Congress into "Crossfire."

The heaviest price for shrinking competition will be paid by voters, especially moderate voters not firmly aligned with either party. Those swing voters will be dissected and courted and coddled in presidential elections and statewide races for governor or senator. But in most House districts, they can be safely ignored because the result is guaranteed by the die-hard partisans around them. Indeed, the overwhelming majority of Americans who vote this fall will cast ballots in House races where one candidate is so likely to win that individual voters have no realistic chance of changing the outcome. That's a mockery of Madison's vision of the people's house and a bipartisan assault on the right to cast a meaningful vote.

Consider the source and the audience.
- Brownstein writes a regular column for the *Los Angeles Times*. How does a columnist's job differ from a straight news reporter's? What impact is that likely to have on what he has to say?

Lay out the argument, the values, and the assumptions.
- Brownstein sometimes uses language that reveals a clear preference for how House elections should operate. What do you make of his use of words like *benign*, *perversion*, *healthy*, and *mockery*?
- What are the three root causes of the perversion of democracy that Brownstein sees taking place?
- What is the likely consequence of these political trends? Who does Brownstein think will be hurt by them the most?

Uncover the evidence.
- What evidence does Brownstein offer that the problem he describes is indeed occurring?
- What evidence does he offer of its negative consequences? Is there other evidence he could provide?

Evaluate the conclusion.
- Are there consequences of the decreasing competitiveness of House elections other than the ones that Brownstein notes?
- Is the decreasing competitiveness of elections necessarily thwarting the people's will?

Sort out the political implications.
- If we wanted to counteract the trends that Brownstein notes, what political reforms would be necessary?

6.4 In the House, at Least, Moderation Is No Virtue

Robin Toner, *New York Times,* 17 November 2002

Public opinion polls tell us that most Americans place themselves in the middle of the ideological scale—not too liberal, not too conservative. The same cannot be said of their representatives in Congress, however— the people elected to Congress are increasingly being found at the ends of the ideological spectrum. This *New York Times* article looks at the signs of this trend in the House of Representatives. How would the increasingly safe elections that we read about in the Brownstein article contribute to this trend? If the major challenge a candidate faces is in the primary, what impact would that have on how ideological the candidate is?

It seemed, to many Republicans, too good to be true: Representative Nancy Pelosi, an archetypal San Francisco Democrat, assumed the leadership of the House Democrats last week. Republicans cheerfully revived all the old stereotypes of the loony left—the latte-drinking, culturally alien, soft-on-national-defense limousine liberals.

In all the chortling, a few political realities got lost. Yes, Ms. Pelosi is a liberal's liberal, with a rating from Americans for Democratic Action of 100 percent and a district that gave just 15 percent of its presidential vote to George W. Bush. But she is no more of a liberal than Representative Tom DeLay, the new majority leader of the Republicans, is a conservative, with his zero ratings from the A.D.A. and the League of Conservation Voters. The two representatives represent the heart of their parties' caucuses in the House with far more ideological purity than either party would like to admit.

Why do people on each side of the political spectrum like to call attention to their opponents' "extremism"?

"It's perfectly symmetrical," said Charles Cook, an independent expert on Congressional elections. "I don't know that San Francisco is any further from the ideological 50-yard line than Sugar Land, Tex., is," he added, referring to the hometown of Mr. DeLay.

In fact, the ascension of Ms. Pelosi and Mr. DeLay reflects a long-running trend in Congress, particularly in the House. While presidential candidates race to the center, Congressional candidates often head the other way.

Congressional Republicans have grown more consistently conservative, and Congressional Democrats more consistently liberal, over the past 30 years, scholars said. Not surprisingly, their leaders come from that base, said Ross K. Baker, an expert on Congress at Rutgers University. "She's drawn fire for being some outlier, but she's not," he added of Ms. Pelosi.

The ideological polarization on Capitol Hill was most apparent in 1994, when Newt Gingrich took control of the House and claimed a mandate for revolutionary change. His party lost seats in the next two elections, in part because Democrats were able to campaign against him as a conservative extremist.

Since then, leaders of both parties have grown far more savvy about the image they project. Republican leaders were carefully pledging to reach across the aisle and build bipartisan coalitions last week, while Ms. Pelosi was arguing, with a centrist's smile, "It's not about left and right." As she noted at one point, "I'm a liberal Democrat, but I'm a conservative Catholic—put that into the mix."

But the fact remains that the Congressional wings of both parties have grown further apart, particularly as the South has realigned to the Republicans over the last three decades, thinning the ranks of conservative Southern Democrats on Capitol Hill. Party unity scores, a measure of how often members vote with the majority of their party, were substantially higher in recent years than they were 30 years ago, according to an analysis by *Congressional Quarterly*. The philosophical divisions between the two parties are acutely apparent when the debate turns to issues like the role of government and health care.

The reasons for the great divide in the House are partly structural. While presidential candidates are forced to focus on swing voters in big states, House members are often elected from politically safe districts where their chief concern may be a challenge in the primary—not the general election.

> Is it just the congressional wings of the party that have grown apart, or are the parties themselves getting more extreme?

This lack of competition was strikingly apparent this year, the first election following the 2000 census, when, as after every census, Congressional district lines have been redrawn and more challengers should be willing to take on an incumbent.

But this year, redistricting became, in many states, an exercise in protecting incumbents. As a result, Charles Cook listed just 45 races—out of 435 in the House—as competitive in October; at the same time 10 years ago, there were 151 competitive races. Only 25 incumbents won with less than 55 percent of the vote, according to another dependent analyst, Rhodes Cook.

There are still moderates in both parties, elected from districts that could go either way. Moreover, the Senate elections were fiercely competitive this year, and the new Republican leadership there, while conservative, has promised to pay careful attention to the needs of their moderates. Those leaders are, after all, keenly aware of the cost of a defection, given that Senator James M. Jeffords's departure last year cost them their majority.

But the ultimate counterweight to the Congressional parties may be the president or, in the case of the Democrats, the nominee. It is not hard to imagine some tension between conservatives on Capitol Hill and a White House focused on re-election in 2004 and the battleground states that will decide it. In a similar situation in 1996, President Clinton famously "triangulated," and found a third way by maneuvering between two polarized parties.

> Why would the Democratic nominee for president pull the party back toward the middle? Why would a presidential candidate be less extreme than a member of Congress?

As for the Democrats, even those who praised Ms. Pelosi said her days as the main voice and image of the party will be numbered. "Nancy Pelosi is going to be like most other minority leaders in the end," said Peter Hart, a Democratic pollster. "They can help shape and direct the message of the party, but they are not the message of the party—that will be created by the nominee."

Al From, the leader of the Democratic Leadership Council, which is devoted to pushing the party to the center, argued that the party's presidential candidate is who really matters. "Bob Michel didn't define the Republican Party," alluding to the Republican House leader in the early 1980's. "Ronald Reagan did. Gephardt and Foley didn't define the Democratic Party in 1992. Bill Clinton did."

This doesn't stop Republicans from trying to make the most of their San Francisco Democrat.

"We've gotten fuzzy about our ability to remind people what it means to be a national Democrat," said Bill McInturff, a Republican pollster. "And Nancy Pelosi's voting record offers a real opportunity in a lot of Southern and border South districts to remind people of what it means."

On the other hand, a few Democrats remembered when Republicans took aim at another Democratic symbol on Capitol Hill—Thomas P. O'Neill Jr., whom they cast as an overweight caricature of Democratic excess. The Democrats scored big gains in the following election.

Consider the source and the audience.
- What kind of perspective would you expect this *New York Times* story to take? Is it evenhanded?

Lay out the argument, the values, and the assumptions.
- Do the experts Toner cites think that Pelosi's strong liberalism is unusual?
- Why does Toner think that many congressional representatives tend to be more extreme in their views than most Americans?
- How (and why) do most presidential candidates counterbalance the extremism of members of Congress?

Uncover the evidence.
- Does Toner's reliance on experts satisfy you? To be balanced, does he need to include some sources who claim that one party is more extreme than the other?

Evaluate the conclusion.
- Do presidential races tend to bring parties back to the center? How could you find out?

Sort out the political implications.
- If increasingly safe districts result in more ideologically extreme parties in Congress, how is this likely to affect legislators' abilities to get things done?
- If it is the more extreme primary voters who are choosing these more ideological representatives, do moderate Americans have a voice in Congress?

6.5 Declaration of Conscience

Margaret Chase Smith, Speech on the Senate Floor, 1 June 1950

We have read articles in this chapter that argue that Congress is getting more ideologically divided, its members more extreme in their views than the majority of the population. Democrats accuse Republicans of being racists and elitist warmongers, Republicans accuse Democrats of being big spenders and un-American peaceniks. In a closely divided, already partisan Congress, the post–September 11 pressures of fear, war, and antiterrorist zeal have sharpened ideological differences and heightened existing animosities.

It's hard to imagine, however, a time as rancorous in U.S. legislative history as the 1950s, also a time of national fear and unease, when Republican Senator Joe McCarthy used the Senate as a platform for rooting out anyone he thought had Communist sympathies. As a result of his frequently unsubstantiated accusations and innuendo, many people lost reputations, jobs, and security. Democrats and Republicans accused each other of being too soft on communism or too restrictive of civil liberties.

Clearly, while congressional politics may seem partisan and nasty in the early years of the twenty-first century, it is not a new phenomenon. Nor is the kind of integrity and concern for the national good over partisan self-interest that led Republican Senator Margaret Chase Smith (the first woman to have been elected to both the House and the Senate) to break with her party and make this speech on the Senate floor condemning the politics of personal destruction. Following Chase's speech, others gathered to condemn McCarthy, including journalists like Edward R. Murrow, and McCarthy was officially censured by the Senate in 1954. How could one go about building such a bridge between acrimonious partisans in Congress today?

I would like to speak briefly and simply about a serious national condition. It is a national feeling of fear and frustration that could result in national suicide and the end of everything that we Americans hold dear. It is a condition that comes from the lack of effective leadership in either the Legislative Branch or the Executive Branch of our Government.

That leadership is so lacking that serious and responsible proposals are being made that national advisory commissions be appointed to provide such critically needed leadership.

I speak as briefly as possible because too much harm has already been done with irresponsible words of bitterness and selfish political opportunism. I speak as simply as possible because the issue is too great to be obscured by eloquence. I speak simply and briefly in the hope that my words will be taken to heart.

> Why does Smith bother to note that she speaks as a Republican, a woman, a senator, and an American, when surely her audience is aware of all four aspects of her identity?

I speak as a Republican. I speak as a woman. I speak as a United States Senator. I speak as an American.

The United States Senate has long enjoyed worldwide respect as the greatest deliberative body in the world. But recently that deliberative character has too often been debased to the level of a forum of hate and character assassination sheltered by the shield of congressional immunity.

It is ironical that we Senators can in debate in the Senate directly or indirectly, by any form of words, impute to any American who is not a Senator any conduct or motive unworthy or unbecoming an American—and without that non-Senator American having any legal redress against us—yet if we say the same thing in the Senate about our colleagues we can be stopped on the grounds of being out of order.

It is strange that we can verbally attack anyone else without restraint and with full protection and yet we hold ourselves above the same type of criticism here on the Senate Floor. Surely the United States Senate is big enough to take self-criticism and self-appraisal. Surely we should be able to take the same kind of character attacks that we "dish out" to outsiders.

I think that it is high time for the United States Senate and its members to do some soul-searching—for us to weigh our consciences—on the manner in which we are performing our duty to the people of America—on the manner in which we are using or abusing our individual powers and privileges.

I think that it is high time that we remembered that we have sworn to uphold and defend the Constitution. I think that it is high time that we remembered that the Constitution, as amended, speaks not only of the freedom of speech but also of trial by jury instead of trial by accusation.

Whether it be a criminal prosecution in court or a character prosecution in the Senate, there is little practical distinction when the life of a person has been ruined.

Those of us who shout the loudest about Americanism in making character assassinations are all too frequently those who, by our own words and acts, ignore some of the basic principles of Americanism:

The right to criticize;
The right to hold unpopular beliefs;
The right to protest;
The right of independent thought.

The exercise of these rights should not cost one single American citizen his reputation or his right to a livelihood nor should he be in danger of losing his reputation or livelihood merely because he happens to know someone who holds unpopular beliefs. Who of us doesn't? Otherwise none of us could call our souls our own. Otherwise thought control would have set in.

The American people are sick and tired of being afraid to speak their minds lest they be politically smeared as "Communists" or "Fascists" by their opponents. Freedom of speech is not what it used to be in America. It has been so abused by some that it is not exercised by others.

The American people are sick and tired of seeing innocent people smeared and guilty people whitewashed. But there have been enough proved cases such as the Amerasia case, the Hiss case, the Coplon case, the Gold case, to cause nationwide distrust and suspicion that there may be something to the unproved, sensational accusations.

As a Republican, I say to my colleagues on this side of the aisle that the Republican Party faces a challenge today that is not unlike the challenge that it faced back in Lincoln's day. The Republican Party so successfully met that challenge that it emerged from the Civil War as the champion of a united nation—in addition to being a Party that unrelentingly fought loose spending and loose programs.

Today our country is being psychologically divided by the confusion and the suspicions that are bred in the United States Senate to spread like cancerous tentacles of "know nothing, suspect everything" attitudes. Today we have a Democratic Administration that has developed a mania for loose spending and loose programs. History is repeating itself—and the Republican Party again has the opportunity to emerge as the champion of unity and prudence.

The record of the present Democratic Administration has provided us with sufficient campaign issues without the necessity to resorting to political smears. America is rapidly losing its position as leader of the world simply because the Democratic Administration has pitifully failed to provide effective leadership.

The Democratic Administration has completely confused the American people by its daily contradictory grave warnings and optimistic assurances—that show the people that our Democratic Administration has no idea of where it is going.

The Democratic Administration has greatly lost the confidence of the American people by its complacency to the threat of communism here at home and the leak of vital secrets to Russia through key officials of the Democratic Administration. There are enough proved cases to make this point without diluting our criticism with unproved charges.

Surely these are sufficient reasons to make it clear to the American people that it is time for a change and that a Republican victory is necessary to the security of this country. Surely it is clear that this nation will continue to suffer as long as it is governed by the present ineffective Democratic Administration.

Yet to displace it with a Republican regime embracing a philosophy that lacks

> What's wrong with winning a Republican victory on the "Four Horsemen of Calumny"? Why doesn't Smith justify any means to the end she wants?

political integrity or intellectual honesty would prove equally disastrous to this nation. The nation sorely needs a Republican victory. But I don't want to see the Republican Party ride to political victory on the Four Horsemen of Calumny— Fear, Ignorance, Bigotry, and Smear.

I doubt if the Republican Party could—simply because I don't believe the American people will uphold any political party that puts political exploitation above national interest. Surely we Republicans aren't that desperate for victory.

I don't want to see the Republican Party win that way. While it might be a fleeting victory for the Republican Party, it would be a more lasting defeat for the American people. Surely it would ultimately be suicide for the Republican Party, and the two-party system that has protected our American liberties from the dictatorship of a one-party system.

As members of the Minority Party, we do not have the primary authority to formulate the policy of our Government. But we do have the responsibility of rendering constructive criticism, of clarifying issues, of allaying fears by acting as responsible citizens.

As a woman, I wonder how the mothers, wives, sisters, and daughters feel about the way in which members of their families have been politically mangled in Senate debate—and I use the word "debate" advisedly.

As a United States Senator, I am not proud of the way in which the Senate has been made a publicity platform for irresponsible sensationalism. I am not proud of the reckless abandon in which unproved charges have been hurled from this side of the aisle. I am not proud of the obviously staged, undignified counter-charges that have been attempted in retaliation from the other side of the aisle.

I don't like the way the Senate has been made a rendezvous for vilification, for selfish political gain at the sacrifice of individual reputations and national unity. I am not proud of the way we smear outsiders from the Floor of the Senate and hide behind the cloak of congressional immunity and still place ourselves beyond criticism on the Floor of the Senate.

As an American, I am shocked at the way Republicans and Democrats alike are playing directly into the Communist design of "confuse, divide, and conquer." As an American, I don't want a Democratic Administration "whitewash" or "coverup" any more than I want a Republican smear or witch hunt.

As an American, I condemn a Republican "Fascist" just as much as I condemn a Democrat "Communist." I condemn a Democrat "Fascist" just as much as I condemn a Republican "Communist." They are equally dangerous to you and me and to our country. As an American, I want to see our nation recapture the strength and unity it once had when we fought the enemy instead of ourselves.

It is with these thoughts that I have drafted what I call a "Declaration of Conscience." I am gratified that Senator Tobey, Senator Aiken, Senator Morse, Senator Ives,

How does infighting weaken a nation? How does focusing on a common enemy make it stronger?

Senator Thye, and Senator Hendrickson have concurred in that declaration and have authorized me to announce their concurrence.

Consider the source and the audience.
- This is a speech on the Senate floor made by a woman junior senator (the only woman in the Senate at the time), criticizing a colleague from her own party (whom she never mentions by name). How might these circumstances have affected her credibility with her other colleagues and the way the speech was perceived?

Lay out the argument, the values, and the assumptions.
- Why does Smith call this speech a "Declaration of Conscience"? What does she reveal explicitly about her basic values here—for instance, in terms of what it means to be an American, what is her view of the public interest and what values are more important than winning? What does she reveal about her values by her willingness to take McCarthy on when her other colleagues remained silent?
- How does Smith think the Senate should conduct itself? Why?
- What does Smith think are proper grounds for criticizing the Democrats, and how does she think that criticism is undermined by the Senate's behavior?

Uncover the evidence.
- What kinds of evidence does Smith use to support her claims? Why were her claims about what Americans want persuasive even in the days before there was extensive polling evidence to back her up?
- How does she use historical evidence to support her views?

Evaluate the conclusion.
- What does Smith imply are the proper limits of partisanship? Should the effort to advance one's own party's fortunes stop? How can partisanship be balanced against the public interest?

Sort out the political implications.
- Are there any parallels between McCarthyism and the effort today to brand dissenters and government critics as unpatriotic?
- What would this speech sound like coming from a Democrat or a Republican today? What vision of the public interest could be offered to offset partisan views?

CHAPTER · 7

The Presidency

Since the New Deal, in the 1930s, we have come to have increasingly huge expectations of our presidents to solve our problems and ensure us the good life, while giving them limited constitutional power to do the things we demand. In addition, we expect them to fill two roles: to be both head of government—a sort of "politician-in-chief," passing legislation and leading his party—and head of state, guiding the government through difficult times, and symbolizing all that is good and unifying in America.

Different presidents respond to these conflicting demands in different ways, but all of them are forced to confront a tough truth. If they do not have sufficient popularity with the public to convince Congress not to cross them, they will not have the leverage to get their laws passed and their appointments approved. In many ways, the chief resource of the American president, on which he depends to shape the country and its institutions in the direction he desires, is his power to persuade, and to control the way the media portrays him (which in turn affects his standing with the public).

Many commentators believed that the presidency of George W. Bush, which began so ignominiously with the contested election of 2000, would last only one term, that his tentative electoral victory had denied him the mandate that would persuade the public to endorse his policies and enable him to govern effectively. Almost from the start, however, he confounded his critics.

The events of 2001, particularly the terror attacks on September 11, convinced the public that he did indeed have what it would take to lead during difficult times. With the support of his soaring approval ratings, Bush began to craft a presidency along stronger lines than we had seen since the days of Richard Nixon. Arguing that since Watergate the power of the office had been nibbled away by Congress (and its stature diminished by White House occupants of whom they did not approve), the Bush administration set out to create an executive branch arguably more powerful than any we had previously seen.

In this chapter we look at several dimensions of the Bush presidency. We begin with a profile of Brett Kavanaugh, a Republican lawyer who has had a singular role in the legal debates over presidential power. The second article is an editorial taking issue with a Bush executive order overriding a law that requires presidential papers to be made public after twelve years, except in cases of national security concerns. The third, written before the start of the Iraq war, examines the delicate balance of the relationships presidents have with Congress over the issue of declaring war, and urges Bush to heed the experience of those who came before him. The fourth article is an analysis of Bush's leadership style, looking to see how well he fulfilled his promise to be "a uniter, not a divider" in Washington, and asking what strategies are justified in the name of getting passed the policies that one values. Finally, we turn to Abraham Lincoln, who also makes an "ends justify the means" argument about presidential power. In this speech excerpt he explains to Congress why he was defying a ruling from a Supreme Court justice that his suspension of habeas corpus during wartime was unconstitutional.

7.1 Whitewater Lawyer Turns Proponent of Presidential Power

Dana Milbank, *Washington Post* 15 October 2002

Our founders, fresh from the domination of King George III, were so apprehensive about creating a strong executive that they gave the new office of the American presidency only limited constitutional power. Much of what presidents have or have not been able to do since then has depended on their ability to persuade Congress, the Supreme Court, and the American people to loosen their constitutional reins. Increasingly, presidents hire batteries of lawyers to help them make their case for a strengthened presidency, just as their opponents hire legal assistance to weaken it.

Recently, one man has found himself on the front lines of both sides of this issue. This *Washington Post* article looks at Brett Kavanaugh's legal work over the last decade and tries to assess whether he is driven by constitutional principle or political ideology. With a Constitution as unclear as ours is about presidential power, is it possible to take politics out of the question of how much power the president should have?

W here there is controversy, there is Brett Kavanaugh.

The legal fight after Vincent Foster's suicide? Kavanaugh led it.

The Starr report on Bill Clinton and Monica Lewinsky? Kavanaugh co-wrote it.

President Bush's order limiting the release of presidential papers? Kavanaugh drafted it.

The probe of Clinton's pardon of Marc Rich? Kavanaugh was in the thick of it.

The hotly contested judicial nominations of Priscilla Owens and Miguel Estrada? Kavanaugh coordinated them.

Indeed, for the past eight years, Kavanaugh, 37, has had a hand in virtually every high-profile legal battle involving

What do all these issues— investigations into a presidential aide's suicide and a president's alleged ethical and criminal behavior, the issuance of executive orders, the exercise of a presidential pardon, and the nomination of candidates to the federal courts— have in common?

presidential power. But for Bethesda native Kavanaugh, there's an intriguing twist: As a lawyer working for Kenneth Starr during the Whitewater investigation, he was devoted to restricting the powers of the president. Now, as a lawyer in the Bush White House, he is devoted to expanding the chief executive's powers. Within a few years, Kavanaugh's work has gone from being described as "a serious blow to the presidency," as Clinton lawyer Lloyd Cutler put it, to promoting an "imperial presidency," as Rep. Henry A. Waxman (D-Calif.) put it.

The political opposition sees rank hypocrisy. "Kavanaugh, who once defended Starr's insatiable appetite for information on presidential doings as being not about politics but about the sanctity of the law, has apparently changed his tune," according to the liberal *Nation* magazine. "The ironies abound." A cynical view of Kavanaugh's actions would be that he bases his legal reasoning on his conservative views—that he supports broad powers for a Republican president and circumscribed powers for a Democratic president. A more charitable explanation is that Kavanaugh is merely a good lawyer, forcefully representing the best interests of his client at the moment. Asked about Kavanaugh's ideology, Craig Lerner, a former colleague from the Whitewater investigation, replied: "He's a terrific lawyer."

Kavanaugh declined to be quoted in this article, but his administration colleagues say he has been consistent in the positions he took for Starr and now for Bush. Under Starr, they say, he was seeking to rein in presidential privileges in a criminal matter; as a counsel to Bush, he is seeking to defend presidential privileges in civil matters.

> What's the difference between a civil and a criminal matter? Are all criminal matters equally serious? Are all civil questions less consequential?

"The need for information in criminal proceedings is a trump card," said another former Starr lieutenant now in the Bush administration. "In civil litigation, a president gets the benefit of the doubt a lot more."

For the dozen former Starr underlings with high-level jobs in or appointments by the Bush administration—including two in the White House and three in the Justice Department—that explanation is something of a personal rationale. The real test will come if the Bush administration is facing a criminal probe. "You might have to reassess based on what Brett does at that point," the former Starr colleague said.

For a man with such a record of controversial cases, Kavanaugh has few enemies. Even legal opponents find him charming, and his friends say he has none of the hard edges of an ideologue. "I don't view him as a hard-core right-wing Republican, said Doug Gansler, a Democrat who is the Maryland state's attorney in Montgomery County. "He's seemingly much more moderate than his writings and words would suggest."

Mark Tuohey, who as a Starr deputy in 1994 and 1995 hired Kavanaugh, said he's "never viewed Brett as somebody of ideological purity. I always felt very comfortable that Brett looked at things through a legal prism, not a political prism." Still, said Tuohey, a Vinson & Elkins partner and self-described Democrat, it would be hard to say that the anti-Clinton work Kavanaugh did for Starr is ideologically consistent with the pro-Bush work he's now doing. "I think it's a stretch," Tuohey said.

After college and law school at Yale, Kavanaugh clerked for federal appellate judge Alex Kozinski and Supreme Court Justice Anthony M. Kennedy, and worked briefly at President George H. W. Bush's Justice Department. In between and after stints on the Whitewater investigation, Kavanaugh spent about three years at Starr's firm, Kirkland & Ellis.

For Starr, Kavanaugh went to the Supreme Court in the Foster case, arguing, unsuccessfully, that the lawyer-client confidentiality expires at death. He represented Starr in efforts to get Hillary Clinton's notes related to the Foster matter, to get lawyer Bruce Lindsey's notes in the Lewinsky affair, and to get testimony from Secret Service agents. His greatest fame, though, came as an author of the Starr report—the legal piece, not the explicit narrative.

In the White House, Kavanaugh developed an executive order related to the Presidential Records Act, giving former presidents and their families more power to prevent the release of presidential papers. The order infuriated historians, and an effort to overturn it is underway in Congress.

Kavanaugh was also at the center of efforts to prevent Congress from getting access to Clinton's pardon records and to documents related to the 1996 Clinton fundraising investigation. He's found himself at the center of Bush's judicial selections and a fight with the Senate Governmental Affairs committee over the administration's Enron documents. And he is involved in the liability provisions in the terrorism insurance legislation that have set off a fight on Capitol Hill.

> Why would Kavanaugh try to protect Clinton's pardon records? Do his efforts in this regard have anything to do with the fact that the issue arose after Bush was president? Whose presidency is strengthened by his efforts?

Still, Kavanaugh finds time to speak at occasional gatherings of the Federalist Society, a club of elite conservative lawyers. But for those who see that as evidence he's an ideologue, Kavanaugh also belongs to the American Bar Association—the organization Kavanaugh's office has removed from the judicial selection process.

Consider the source and the audience.

- The *Washington Post* likes to cover stories that interest Washington insiders. Does that fact help explain why they have done this story on a man whom most Americans have never heard of? Does knowing about people who have jobs like Kavanaugh's help us to understand the way the American political system works?

Lay out the argument, the values, and the assumptions.

- What kinds of things did Kavanaugh do to try to weaken Clinton's power? To strengthen Bush's?

- Consider the two arguments here—the one made by defenders of Kavanaugh's role, the other one made by critics. What is the basic assumption shared by both sides about the role that politics ought to play or not to play in legal arguments about presidential power? Does it make a difference if Kavanaugh is a hypocrite?

- Why do both sides point out that Kavanaugh does not seem to be an extreme ideologue? What picture of the man emerges, and how does that seem related to the arguments made about him? Why did Kavanaugh himself refuse to be interviewed?

Uncover the evidence.

- How does each side seek to support its claims about Kavanaugh?

- Would an interview with Kavanaugh have helped either side, or would it have been irrelevant?

Evaluate the conclusion.

- Does one's conclusion about Kavanaugh's role necessarily depend on whether one likes Clinton or Bush?

- Why does the author dwell on all the contradictions in Kavanaugh's personal and professional life? What is his conclusion?

Sort out the political implications.

- Should the power of the presidency vary according to whether or not we like the person in office? Should it vary at all?

- Is the presidency today too strong, too weak, or just right? Why?

7.2 An Executive Order: Hiding Presidential Papers

Editorial, *San Francisco Chronicle*, 11 November 2001

This editorial, from the *San Francisco Chronicle*, takes on an executive order issued by President Bush in November 2001 (drafted, by the way, by Brett Kavanaugh, the man profiled in the previous selection in this chapter). Claiming national security concerns, the executive order runs counter to the Presidential Records Act passed by Congress in 1978 to regulate the disclosure of former presidents' papers. The executive order essentially gives the sitting president as well as former presidents the right to override the law in determining when their papers must be released. The author of the editorial looks at possible reasons for and consequences of this action by the Bush administration. What limits should be placed on a president's ability to counteract congressional legislation?

"A popular government without popular information or the means of acquiring it, is but a prologue to a farce or a tragedy or perhaps both. Knowledge will forever govern ignorance, and a people who mean to be their own governors, must arm themselves with the power knowledge gives."—James Madison, father of the Constitution.

President Bush's sudden move to restrict public access to presidential papers has ignited a firestorm of protest from archivists, historians and journalists.

Should you care? Yes, and here's why. Although most of us will never use presidential archives, we depend on historians and journalists who need these documents to write our political history, to scrutinize the public record and to keep the past honest. In short, a free and democratic society requires open archives.

We fought long and hard for public access to governmental records. In the aftermath of the Vietnam War and the Watergate scandal, the public grew weary of hearing half-truths and outright lies from government officials. In 1974, Congress passed the Freedom of Information Act, which guaranteed citizens access to public information.

> How does the access of journalists and historians to presidential archives directly benefit U.S. citizens?

Four years later, the Presidential Records Act, which defied Richard Nixon's last attempt to conceal his papers and tape recordings, stated that presidential records are the property of the government and do not belong to former presidents. In a spirit of compromise, the act guaranteed public access to papers 12 years after a president has left office.

Last January, former President Reagan's most sensitive records became available for public scrutiny. The Bush administration, however, delayed the release of some 68,000 records three times.

Then, on Nov. 1, President Bush issued an executive order that gives himself— as well as former presidents—the right to veto requests to open any presidential records. Even if a former president wants his records to be released, the executive order permits Bush to exercise executive privilege. It also gives him and former presidents an indefinite amount of time to ponder any requests.

Bush's executive order openly violates the Presidential Records Act passed by Congress in 1978.

In defending the executive order, the White House has argued that these new restrictions balance public access with "national security concerns."

But few archivists, journalists or historians believe that national security has anything to do with Bush's executive order. That is because national security documents are already excluded from public scrutiny.

Bruce Craig, director of the National Coordinating Committee for the Promotion of History, an umbrella group that represents more than 60 organizations, says, "These claims have no bearing on national security, or on information that may be of use to terrorists."

Steven Aftergood of the Federation of American Scientists agrees. "We are not talking about protecting national security information of properly classified documents."

Those who study the presidency and political decision-making are rightly outraged. Hugh Davis Graham, a presidential historian at Vanderbilt University, charges the Bush administration with trying to "reverse an act of Congress with an executive order." Thomas S. Blanton, executive director of the National Security Archive, notes that "The Presidential Records Act was designed to shift power over presidential records to the government and ultimately to the citizens. This shifts the power back."

Former President Clinton also opposes the new order; he wants the public to have full access to his papers.

What, then, prompted Bush to issue such a controversial executive order?

Critics note that, aside from Bill Clinton, the 1978 act will affect the presidential papers of Ronald Reagan, Bush's father, George H. W. Bush, as well as the vice-presidential papers in each administration.

What kinds of information, they ask, might President Bush wish to protect from public scrutiny?

Anna Nelson, an historian at American University, is hardly alone in suspecting that the White House is worried about what the Reagan and Bush papers may reveal about officials who worked in those administrations and are now part of George W. Bush's inner circle. They include, for example, Secretary of State Colin Powell, Vice President Dick Cheney, White House Chief of Staff Andrew Card, and Budget Director Mitch Daniel Jr.

"There may in fact be embarrassing documents," concedes White House counsel Alberto Gonzales, "but that would not be considered a legitimate reason to withhold archives from historians and journalists."

If not embarrassing moments, then what?

There is, of course, no end to growing speculation. That is the problem with trying to suppress information. It inevitably raises the question, "What is he trying to hide?"

> Is it fair to ask "What is he trying to hide?" under these circumstances?

Consider, for example, the Iran-Contra scandal that tainted the Reagan administration. In order to finance opposition to the Sandinista government in Nicaragua, certain high-level administration officials sold weapons to Iran. This was illegal. But despite a huge public scandal, no government official ever went to prison. At the time, some suspected that then–Vice President George Bush, a previous head of the CIA, knew more than he let on about the illegal Iran-Contra scheme. The elder Bush, however, always protested that he "was out of the loop."

Still, other historians think that the current Bush White House, deeply im-mersed in the war on terrorism, may be worried about fresh revelations that de-tail the Reagan administration's strong financial support of the Taliban as they rose to power.

Although the president may have hoped that this executive order might go unnoticed, the backlash is already fierce. Archivists and historians have accused the White House of using heightened public interest in national security as an excuse for quashing access to presidential papers. Members of both political par-ties have also condemned Bush's attempt to suppress public information. Last week, Rep. Steven Horn, R-Long Beach, chairman of the House Government Reform Committee, even held hearings on the executive order.

To deny the public's right to presidential papers is a violation of the law—as well as the spirit of a democratic society. President Bush should rescind his ex-ecutive order immediately. If not, Congress should act quickly to overturn this high-handed order.

At stake is nothing less than the public's right to know how our democracy works—in the past, as well as in the present.

Consider the source and the audience.

- The *San Francisco Chronicle* is published in a liberal community and is likely to have a liberal readership. Editorials taking this stance appeared in newspapers around the coun-try, however. Why would both liberal and conservative newspapers be likely to oppose this executive order? Who would support it?

Lay out the argument, the values, and the assumptions.

- Why does this editorial begin by invoking James Madison? What is the chief principle motivating this editorial?
- What does the editorial writer think of the executive order? What harm is it likely to do?
- Why does the writer think Bush chose to issue this order?

Uncover the evidence.

- Does the writer offer evidence for the claim that democracies depend on governmental openness and freedom of information? Does he or she need to?
- Does the writer offer evidence for the speculation about what Bush might be "trying to hide"? Is the point to prove a particular motive? Or to show that when information is missing, many motives look plausible?

Evaluate the conclusion.

- Is it likely that democracies will fail if the public is kept in the dark about how they work?
- Is this executive order a significant step toward keeping the public in the dark?

Sort out the political implications.

- Why hasn't Congress overturned this order?
- How did the events of September 11, 2001, and the flurry of political activity that followed, help to keep this executive order off the public's radar screen?

7.3 Ask First, Shoot Later

Gordon Silverstein, *New Republic Online,* 5 September 2002

Although the president is commander in chief of the U.S. armed forces, the Constitution assigns Congress the power to declare war. Despite that fact, Congress has declared war only five times in our history. Every other time, including the conflict in Vietnam, Congress has passed legislation to allow the president to send troops abroad but has not taken responsibility for participation in wartime decisions.

This article, by a political science professor writing in the *New Republic Online,* considers the consequences of what he sees as a constitutional failure, and warns that unlike previous presidents (including his own father) President Bush should seek congressional approval for the Iraq war that is more than "just a formality." Shortly after this article appeared, Congress passed a resolution giving Bush authority to take military action in Iraq. The resolution was broader and even less specific than the one that Bush's father got in 1991. Why did the founders want the president's and Congress's war-related responsibilities to check each other?

President Bush's announcement that he will "seek approval" from Congress before launching a preemptive strike against Iraq suggests that he may have stopped listening to his lawyers and started paying attention to the Constitution. Or does it? It all depends upon the meaning of the word "approval."

If by "approval," President Bush (the younger) means to follow the example of President Bush (the elder) and present Congress with an opportunity to get on board or get out of the way, then his plan will only serve to enhance congressional credit-claiming for any successful war effort, and continue to insure that the president alone takes the heat if the policy fails to accomplish its goals.

On the other hand, if by "approval" President Bush actually means to force Congress to play its constitutional role as a full partner in the decision to risk American blood and treasure overseas, then he may be able to break away from the self-destructive tendency presidents have had since World War II to try to assert prerogative control over the decision to go to war.

> Why does Silverstein call the president's tendency to go it alone "self-destructive"?

The Constitution is ambiguous about many things. But it is quite clear about war. Only Congress can raise and support armies and navies—and only Congress can declare a war that will send those armies and navies into harm's way.

Despite the constitutional clarity, presidents regularly try to claim these and other powers that are assigned by the Constitution to Congress. This shouldn't be surprising. It is the nature of our system that the people who end up behind the desk in the Oval Office tend to be people who like power and don't like sharing it. What seems more surprising is that members of Congress have been so willing to let this happen.

James Madison designed his constitution to use human ambition, greed, and ego to counteract human ambition, greed, and ego. Indeed, the genius of the constitution is the way in which it harnesses human vices to keep the system safe from human vice. As Madison put it in *The Federalist Papers,* the personal interests of the individual politician must be connected "with the constitutional rights of the place." If presidents care about presidential power and members of Congress care about congressional power, the rest will take care of itself. When each side struggled with the other, the result would be something like a well-balanced tug-of-war. And while they were struggling with each other, it would be safe for the rest of us to go about our daily lives.

At least, that's how it was supposed to work. Unfortunately, something different has been happening in the modern era. Presidents since World War II seem to be following the blueprint, grabbing and protecting all the power they can. But Congress appears to be doing the opposite: It appears to be giving away its power or, at the very least, surrendering it without a fight. Have members of Congress become less selfish? Hardly. They've simply come to realize that power brings with it responsibility—and that's something they'd rather not have when it comes to controversial wars.

> What do members of Congress gain by avoiding responsibility? What do they lose?

Korea was "Truman's War." The escalation and devastation of Vietnam will forever be linked to Lyndon Johnson. Richard Nixon was elected in 1968 in part because he had a "secret plan" to end the war in Vietnam, a war that was still raging when he left office prematurely in 1974. It was Jimmy Carter's administration that crashed and burned in the deserts of Iran. And when Bill Clinton sent troops to Bosnia in 1995, legislators passed resolutions supporting the troops and condemning their commander-in-chief. The troops could stay—but their blood would be on Clinton's hands.

When President Bush (the elder) turned to Congress for "support" on January 8, 1991—five months after Iraq had invaded Kuwait, and just three days before the president's January 15 deadline for Iraqi withdrawal—more than 500,000 American troops had already been deployed to the Persian Gulf and national prestige and credibility were on the line. Congress had no choice. Its approval was assured. Which is why the effort to force Iraq out of Kuwait, although a military success, was a constitutional failure. Congress failed to play its role while the president let it happen—indeed, he made sure it would.

Maybe President Bush (the younger) can learn from his father's mistake—and the similar mistakes of every president since Harry Truman. Forcing Congress to play a full role in this decision, and not merely giving legislators a chance to offer their "approval," will give the war greater legitimacy in the eyes of the public. And it will prevent members of Congress from undercutting the war effort—and the president's authority as commander-in-chief—the moment the first casualties start to roll in. As Arthur Vandenberg, the long-time chairman of the Senate

Foreign Relations Committee in the 1950s, often said, if you want Congress in on the crash landings, you'd better have them in on the take-offs as well. It may seem politically risky to put the war to a vote now when there is still a chance Congress could say no, or could insist on a real role in the decision, but in the long run it's far more risky to accept a meaningless vote as happened in 1991.

Of course, maybe President Bush hasn't learned from his father's mistake. Maybe he intends to do exactly what his father did: To mass troops and prepare for war until it is a fait accompli, thereby relegating Congress to its now-familiar role as mere accessory-after-the-fact. That's why Congress should demand that President Bush go beyond his promise to conduct a wide-ranging debate, and make Congress a full partner in any decision to go to war.

Members of Congress who have enjoyed short-term benefits from shirking their constitutional responsibilities when it comes to war and emergency powers may be reluctant to accept them now. But those eyeing a long career on Capitol Hill need to realize that it's actually in their institutional self-interest to assert themselves in this debate. No one who voted to support the first President Bush in 1991 ever imagined that they had signed a check that would still be good eleven years later. But now White House lawyers insist that the 1991 vote is sufficient authorization for a new war—just as many in the executive branch cite other half-hearted authorizations, like the Formosa Straits resolution in 1955, the Mideast resolution in 1957, the Tonkin Gulf Resolution of 1964, the Senate's breast-beating vote to "support the troops" in Bosnia in 1995, and the similarly cynical House vote on deployments to Kosovo in 1999.

> *What does Silverstein think is wrong with a "half-hearted" congressional resolution?*

Members of Congress tend to think about life in a two-year cycle (six years for senators). But each time Congress delegates power to the president, or even merely fails to assert its own prerogatives against the president's claim to exclusive power, they have actually made it both politically and legally harder for some future Congress to get that power back.

Politically, a simple way to think about this is that it takes just 50 percent plus one in each house of Congress to give power away but—assuming a president likes getting power, and vetoes any attempt by Congress to take it back later—it takes two-thirds of each house to override that veto. This produces a political ratchet effect: It's much easier to give power away than it is to get that power back again.

There is a legal ratchet effect as well. Courts can reverse precedents. But when Congress gives away its own powers or tolerates the president's hand in their cookie jar over and over again, judges who are already reluctant to intervene in questions of war and peace become increasingly unwilling to save legislators from their own mistakes.

There will likely come a time when a future Congress actually does want to play a full role in deciding when to get in (or out of) war. But between the political ratchet and the legal precedents, they will find that those who filled their chairs in the past have undermined their ability to exercise their constitutional power.

Whether he did so because of mounting criticism or simply because he thinks it's the right thing to do, President Bush has taken an important first step by agreeing to seek congressional approval. But that approval needs to be more than a formality. It's in the president's own best interests to follow the constitutional blueprint—and, more important, it's also in the nation's best interests.

Consider the source and the audience.

- This article appears in the online version of a liberal opinion magazine. It is written by an expert on the role of the presidency in foreign policy. How might those two factors affect the content of the article?

Lay out the argument, the values, and the assumptions.

- What does the author think is the ideal way for the president and Congress to work together in military matters? Why does he cite *Federalist* No. 51?
- What incentives do Congress and the president have to depart from that ideal? Who carries more blame? What are the consequences for the domestic balance of power and the health of our system?
- What does the author urge President Bush to do with respect to the Iraq War? Congress?

Uncover the evidence.

- The author cites a number of historical instances in which Congress has shirked its responsibility and the president has assumed too much power. Does he successfully show what the consequences of these instances have been?

Evaluate the conclusion.

- Is the power in American politics shifting from the Congress to the president, as the author claims?

Sort out the political implications.

- How would the author evaluate the congressional resolution that passed in October 2002?
- Now that the war in Iraq is officially over, has our experience in that war borne out the author's expectations?

7.4 Bush Moves by Refusing to Budge

Ronald Brownstein, *Los Angeles Times,* 2 March 2003

George W. Bush ran for president on the promise of being a "uniter, not a divider." More than halfway through his first term, however, the country has solidified along the Red America/Blue America split we saw on electoral maps on election night 2000. This article, by *LA Times* veteran political reporter Ron Brownstein, analyzes Bush's leadership style and looks for reasons why the expectations that Bush would be a consensus builder have fallen so far short of the mark. Does the responsibility to build consensus belong to Bush or to congressional Democrats? Who sets the tone in Washington?

From his law office in the small Texas town of Henderson, former Democratic state Rep. Paul Sadler barely recognizes George W. Bush anymore.

When Bush served as Texas governor, Sadler probably negotiated with him more extensively than any other Democrat in the Legislature, forging agreements on difficult issues from education reform to taxes. Through that partnership, Sadler came to see Bush as a conciliator committed to building consensus across party lines.

Now, as he watches Bush operate in Washington, Sadler sees "a harder edge."

"Almost all of us who had dealt with Bush, who were chairmen of committees or worked with him in Texas, have noticed the difference," Sadler says. "There has not been that collaborative spirit. I don't know if he's changed since Texas or the Democrats are different in Washington, or maybe it's both. But he is not the centrist as president that he was as governor."

How might the Democrats in Washington be different from those in Texas? Why would that difference affect Bush's leadership style?

At home and abroad, Bush has surprised friends and critics with the ambition of his presidential agenda—and the forceful, often confrontational, manner in which he has pursued it.

From a deal-maker in Texas, he has morphed into a back-breaker in Washington. With Congress and allies abroad, he has displayed a pugnacious style of leadership, advancing boldly ideological ideas that test the boundaries of consensus. He often has accepted compromise only when it appeared that he had no other choice.

"I remember describing Bush as an incrementalist when he was down here, and he was," said Bruce Buchanan, a professor of government at the University of Texas. "He was not throwing the long pass. He was not a policy ideologue by any stretch of the imagination. Now all of a sudden he's this guy who is deeply and passionately committed to a heavily substantive ideological agenda."

This approach has brought Bush many successes, from a major 2001 tax cut to the United Nations resolution that returned arms inspectors to Iraq. But it also has produced a more polarizing presidency than his record in Texas, or his rhetoric in the 2000 campaign, might have predicted.

Bush advisors believe that by showing his commitment to bold change, he reinforces an image as a strong leader that could become his greatest asset for re-election. But Democrats believe Bush is unnecessarily dividing Congress and the country in ways that could threaten his legislative agenda and his prospects for a second term.

In 2000, Bush pledged to govern as a "uniter, not a divider" who would "change the tone in Washington." On one level, he has succeeded—personal animosity between the parties isn't as intense as it was between congressional Republicans and President Clinton. But the policy differences between the two sides may be even wider than in the Clinton years.

Party-line voting in Congress has reached a new peak. According to *Congressional Quarterly*, Republicans went with their party on nearly 90% of the votes during Bush's first two years, while Democrats voted with their party nearly 86% of the time.

And despite the public's impulse to rally around the commander in chief in an unsettling age of global terrorism, opinion about Bush's performance and priorities is at least as polarized as it was about Clinton's. In the most recent poll conducted for *The Times*, 95% of Republicans said they approved of Bush's performance, while just 28% of Democrats agreed.

These centrifugal tendencies predate Bush's presidency. Party-line voting has increased steadily in Congress over the last 30 years. So has the gap between the president's approval rating among voters from his own party and those from the opposition, said Matthew Dowd, director of polling at the Republican National Committee.

Yet Bush's decisions have, in most respects, accelerated these trends.

The administration worked closely with Democrats on Bush's education reform bill and the legislative response to the Sept. 11 terrorist attacks. And on issues such as campaign finance reform, corporate accounting reform and the federalization of airport security workers, he eventually acquiesced when bipartisan congressional majorities insisted on a course he had resisted.

But mostly, Bush has pursued as hard a line in pushing his goals with Congress as he has with the world over Iraq. His intent was clear even before he took office.

Shortly after the 2000 election, Nick Calio, the first White House director of leg-

What does it mean to say "we will not negotiate with ourselves"? What are the implications of this statement for the way Bush chooses to govern?

islative affairs, went to see Bush in Texas. When Calio started to walk through concessions he might have to make to pass the tax cut bill, Bush cut him off. "Nicky," he said, "we will not negotiate with ourselves, ever."

It's a promise Bush has kept with a vengeance.

From his initial tax cut through a huge second round of tax reductions he has proposed this year, to his energy plan, his staunchly conservative judicial nominations and his new plans to restructure Medicare and Medicaid, Bush has consistently offered proposals that excite conservatives while holding little appeal even to centrist Democrats. Several moderate Republicans also have recoiled at elements of his new tax cut plan, and he's been forced to back off his initial Medicare plan after objections from both parties.

"What you get now from Bush is a sense that this is a White House determined to squeeze every last bit of political advantage out of every situation," says Will Marshall, president of the Progressive Policy Institute, a centrist Democratic think tank.

Indeed, centrist Democrats open to accommodation with Bush have complained that the White House has shown too little interest in working with them.

Moderate Sen. John B. Breaux (D-La.), who often has tried to operate as a bridge between the parties, has expressed frustration about being shut out on Medicare reform efforts, an issue where he has offered ideas similar to Bush's.

"There's been less negotiation on the policies that they are trying to push forward domestically—health care and taxes—than there has been in the past," Breaux says.

Many Bush advisors acknowledge pursuing a hardball approach, but argue they are applying lessons from President Reagan on how to move the policy debate in their direction.

"Reagan's approach was you push hard; Democrats come out against you; it seemed to be polarizing," said one senior White House aide. "But Reagan held firm, aggressively pushed his position, and at the last minute cut a deal if he had to. Many times Democrats, at least some Democrats, came with him—and Reagan got the legislation he wanted."

Key to this vision has been maximizing Republican unity. Bush's core legislative strategy has been to pass bills that track his preferences through the GOP-controlled House.

Then the White House tries to get whatever it can through the Senate, hoping to tilt the final product further in its direction in House-Senate negotiations.

That model worked in mid-2001 when the final bill produced a $1.35-trillion tax cut, about $200 billion more than the Senate had passed.

But after Democrats seized Senate control when Vermont's James F. Jeffords quit the GOP to become an independent, Bush's approach proved a recipe for stalemate on a series of issues.

Although the House passed measures Bush backed to reform health maintenance organizations, provide prescription drugs for seniors, increase government cooperation with religious charities and set a new energy policy, no bill ever reached him on those issues—either because the House and Senate could not agree or because the Senate deadlocked along party lines.

In all four cases, Democrats complained that the White House made little effort to resolve the disagreements.

In talks over HMO reform, for instance, Senate advocates of the bill say administration officials did little more than recite insurance industry objections to the measure.

"What the hell do we care what the insurance industry thinks?" Sen. John Edwards (D-N.C.), one of the bill's key sponsors, grumbled to Sen. John McCain (R-Ariz.) in one session.

Bush's hands-off attitude marked a stark contrast with his earlier pattern. In Texas, Bush was renowned for bringing together legislators from both parties and asking what it would take to reach a deal. "That was constantly our conversation," Sadler said.

But Senate Minority Leader Tom Daschle (D-S.D.) has told friends he has only rarely had such pragmatic conversations with Bush. In turn, White House aides said that even when the administration moved toward Daschle's position, the Democrat demanded more.

Most Bush advisors say it's not possible to re-create the consensual approach he used in Texas because the environment in Washington is much more partisan.

Somewhat wistfully, Bush on several occasions told Calio, "In Texas, everybody was a lot friendlier and a lot more interested in the result than the process."

And some Senate Republicans, such as Finance Committee Chairman Charles E. Grassley of Iowa, note that the administration, even if not typically working with Democrats, has not objected when they have done so.

On the morning after the Senate approved the final version of the 2001 tax bill with 12 Democratic votes, Bush called Grassley at 8:15 A.M. "I knew you were good," Grassley said Bush told him, "but I didn't know you were that good."

> What is the tradeoff between polarization and a demonstration of resolve all about? What does the Bush administration believe it has to gain in this tradeoff?

Yet it is also clear that given the choice between making concessions that create a broader bipartisan majority and narrowly passing a bill that more closely tracks his preferences, Bush will choose the latter, White House aides agree.

The aides believe his hard-line approach energizes the GOP base—his approval rating among Republicans exceeds even Reagan's—and reinforces his image as a strong, decisive leader. In effect, many of Bush's key advisors see polarization as an acceptable cost for the demonstration of resolve and vision.

Buchanan, the Texas professor, sees these assumptions as a key to Bush's different approach at the national level.

While the limited powers of the Texas governorship encourage a mediator's role, he says, the White House appears to have concluded that Bush's greatest form of leverage is his ability to change the parameters of debate with bold initiatives.

Some friends and foes also see in Bush a growing confidence after the Sept. 11 attacks in his own beliefs, which leads him to view domestic issues in the same black-and-white terms he has used to frame the war against terrorism.

The political risk is that this approach portrays Bush to swing voters as too rigid or too ideological. In polls, his presidency is dividing not only Democrats from Republicans, but drawing a bright line down the electorate's center. In the recent poll by *The Times,* 62% of independents who consider themselves conservative said they were inclined to support Bush in 2004; but just 24% of liberal-to-moderate independents agreed.

> Is the goal of Bush getting his way on substantive issues worth the deterioration of the national political process?

As political storms gather at home, Bush seems as unaffected as he does by the international turmoil over Iraq.

"In general, he is more a goal-oriented person than a process-oriented person," the senior White House aide said. "We are pursuing policies we believe are in the best interest of the country, which in the end will redound to his benefit. If that makes the process more contentious and polarized than we'd like, I think it is an acceptable price to pay."

Consider the source and the audience.
- Brownstein is a well-known political reporter for a reputable national paper. What kind of sources is he likely to be able to tap into for a story like this?
- Would a liberal or conservative journal present this issue any differently?

Lay out the argument, the values, and the assumptions.
- What is Brownstein's basic argument about Bush's leadership style in Texas as opposed to the White House?
- What do Bush's advisors see as the benefits of his current style? What do Democrats see as its drawback?
- What reasons for Bush's changed role are offered by the people Brownstein talks to?

Uncover the evidence.

- Brownstein offers data to support his claim that America is divided along partisan lines. Do these data show that the divide is due to Bush? Are there additional data that would help?
- Brownstein talks to a number of people about Bush's leadership style and its effects on national politics. Is his selection of sources balanced? Is there anyone else you'd like to hear from?

Evaluate the conclusion.

- Do any of the people Brownstein talks to, even among Bush's supporters, contest the claim that Bush's leadership style is more contentious and polarizing than they expected?
- Are the Democrats right in saying that ultimately his failure to reach out to them will damage the country?
- Are Bush supporters right in saying that the gains in achieving Bush's goals justify the increased political polarization?

Sort out the political implications.

- What are the political implications of the "ends justify the means" argument made by Bush's supporters in this context? What is the national interest here—in substantive policy goals geared to one party's base or in policy driven by national political consensus?
- Can we expect to see Bush turn back to the ideological middle and the model of consensus politics as the 2004 election approaches?

7.5 Excerpt from Speech to Congress

Abraham Lincoln, 15 September 1863

In a list of restrictions on the powers of Congress, Article I, Section 9 of the U.S. Constitution says, "The Privilege of the Writ of Habeas Corpus shall not be suspended, unless when in Cases of Rebellion or Invasion the public Safety may require it." Habeas corpus, meaning literally "to have the body," is a way of protecting someone from being arrested and held for political reasons. A judge can issue a writ of habeas corpus and have the prisoner delivered before him, to inquire into the legality of the charge. For some people this writ is so essential to our notion of due process of law that they call it the "writ of liberty."

As the Civil War began, President Abraham Lincoln struggled to suppress the rebellion in the southern states and the activities of its northern sympathizers in the Democratic Party. In April 1861 he was fearful that the state of Maryland, leaning toward secession, would act to prevent the federal army from passing through the state. To control what he believed to be the subversive speech and actions of Maryland politicians, he suspended the writ of habeas corpus.

John Merryman was arrested in May of the same year. U.S. Supreme Court Justice Roger B. Taney issued a writ of habeas corpus to the military to show cause for Merryman's arrest. Under Lincoln's orders, the military refused. Taney issued a judgment saying that under the Constitution only Congress had the power to suspend the writ, and that by taking that power on himself, Lincoln was taking not only the legislative power, but also the judicial power, to arrest and imprison without due process of law. Taney granted that he could not enforce his judgment against the power of the military but said that if the military were allowed to take judicial power in that way, then the people of the United States had ceased to live under the rule of law.

On July 4, Lincoln appeared before Congress and, among other things, attempted to defend his assumption of the power to suspend habeas corpus and his defiance of the Supreme Court ordering him to stop. The following is an excerpt from his speech.

Obviously we have survived what Taney saw as an overzealous power grab. Although Lincoln expanded the suspension of habeas corpus in 1862, Congress finally acted to approve it in 1863 and it remained suspended until a Supreme Court ruling in 1866 (*Ex Parte Milligan*) officially restored it. What did Lincoln risk in defying the Supreme Court? Was it worth it?

Soon after the first call for militia it was considered a duty to authorize the commanding general in proper cases according to his discretion, to suspend the privilege of the writ of habeas corpus, or in other words to arrest and detain, without resort to the ordinary processes and forms of law, such individuals as he might deem dangerous to the public safety. This authority has purposely been exercised but very sparingly. Nevertheless the legality and propriety of what has been done under it are questioned and the attention of the country has been called to the proposition that one who is sworn to "take care that the laws be faithfully executed" should not himself violate them. Of course some consideration was given to the questions of power and propriety before this matter was acted upon. The whole of the laws which were required to be faithfully executed were being resisted and failing of execution in nearly one-third of the States. Must they be allowed to finally fail of execution, even had it been perfectly clear that by the use of the means necessary to their execution some single law, made in such extreme tenderness of the citizen's liberty that practically it relieves more of the guilty than of the innocent, should to a very limited extent be violated? To state the question more directly, are all the laws but one to go unexecuted and the Government itself go to pieces lest that one be violated? Even in such a case would not the official oath be broken if the Government should be overthrown, when it was believed that disregarding the single law would tend to preserve it? But it was not believed that this question was presented. It was not believed that any law was violated. The provision of the Constitution that "the privilege of the writ of habeas corpus shall not be suspended unless when in cases of rebellion or invasion the public safety may require it," is equivalent to a provision—is a provision—that such privilege may be suspended when in cases of rebellion or invasion the public safety does require it. It was decided that we

> What does this characterization of the writ of habeas corpus mean? What does Lincoln mean that it is "made in such extreme tenderness of the citizen's liberty that practically it relieves more of the guilty than of the innocent?"

have a case of rebellion, and that the public safety does require the qualified suspension of the privilege of the writ which was authorized to be made. Now, it is insisted that Congress and not the Executive is vested with this power. But the Constitution itself is silent as to which, or who, is to exercise the power; and as the provision was plainly made for a dangerous emergency, it cannot be believed the framers of the instrument intended that in every case the danger should run its course until Congress could be called together, the very assembling of which might be prevented, as was intended in this case, by the rebellion.

Consider the source and the audience.

- Lincoln is speaking to Congress under a state of emergency. How does that fact affect the terms in which he casts his argument? When does urgency become panic? How far should it be resisted?

Lay out the argument, the values, and the assumptions.

- What is Lincoln's essential purpose here, which he believes justifies some reduction in due process? What does he see as the tradeoff facing him as executor of the laws?
- Why doesn't he mention the name of the person who has challenged his actions?
- How does he reason that the founders must not have intended members of Congress to be the ones to decide whether habeas corpus should be suspended?

Uncover the evidence.

- What does a reading of the Constitution tell us about this matter? Is the Constitution indeed silent?

Evaluate the conclusion.

- How persuasive is the "ends justify the means" argument in this context? What are its limits? Are there any means that are not justified by a worthy end?

Sort out the political implications.

- Is Lincoln's argument relevant to the acquiring of additional power by the Bush administration? What are the similarities between the two situations? What are the differences?

CHAPTER 8

The Bureaucracy

Bureaucracy. We may love to hate it—but we can't live without it.

No other part of American government is so often mocked and maligned, yet touches our lives more frequently or more directly. The job of American government in the twenty-first century is vast, and the people who do that job—who deliver our mail, approve our student loan checks, examine our tax returns, register us to vote, issue our drivers' licenses, direct airport security, buy fighter jets, determine what intersections should have stoplights, even the people who decide how much arsenic can safely be in our drinking water—are all federal, state, or local government employees, also known as bureaucrats.

A bureaucracy is really no more than a hierarchical organization (meaning that power flows from the top down), governed by explicit rules, where workers specialize in particular tasks and advance by merit. It is decisionmaking by experts and specialists, where those with less power defer to those with more, and everyone defers to the rules. What it especially is *not* is democratic. Democratic decisions are made when we want to take account of as many views as possible, or to serve the broadest possible interests. Democracy is often slow and cumbersome, and certainly not very efficient. We would never want to decide democratically about whether to approve a new cancer drug, for instance, because most of us don't know enough to make a very good job of it, and by the time we all finished making our views heard, several people would no doubt have died waiting for the drug's approval.

Although it's difficult for Americans to accept, democracy is not always an appropriate decisionmaking technique. Bureaucracy sometimes does a much better job. But the things that make bureaucracy good at what it does—the expert decisions made behind closed doors, the lack of accountability to the public, the huge number of rules and massive amounts of paperwork (known as red tape) that help to ensure that bureaucrats treat all people the same—also make it ripe for criticism by an impatient and suspicious public. And that, perhaps, is the best check of all on a bureaucracy that, although subject to executive approval and legislative oversight, still wields a great deal of power without having to answer directly to the American voters.

In this chapter we present five selections that show the bureaucracy from various perspectives. The first article reports on an artist who, frustrated with the system of highways signs in L.A. that repeatedly confused him and sent him the wrong way, decided to ignore regular bureaucratic channels and take matters into his own hands. The second article describes what happens when Congress allocates money to solve a public problem but fails to put into effect safeguards that would ensure that the money it spends actually solves the problem. The third article is about a serious problem that bureaucracies face—their tendency to develop their own culture where it becomes unacceptable to police themselves sufficiently to ensure that they do a good job. The fourth selection, about Bush's call for a Department of Homeland Security, discusses the difficulties faced in combining preexisting agencies into new ones, as bureaucrats battle over turf and lines of authority, and over who wins and who loses in such a major government restructuring. Finally, our classic selection is a speech by President Harry Truman in 1945 calling for the creation of a Department of Defense—echoing many of the Homeland Security arguments, but also differing in some interesting ways.

8.1 In Artist's Freeway Prank, Form Followed Function

Unauthorized Addition to Sign Went Unnoticed for Months. No Charges Planned.

Hugo Martin, *Los Angeles Times,* 9 May 2002

This article appeared in the *Los Angeles Times,* a mainstream big-city daily newspaper. It is a straight piece of reporting, not a news analysis or editorial. The argument here is being made not by the author but, rather, by the subject of the piece. It is the story of one individual's actions, but it raises all kinds of political questions. On the one hand, it seems admirable and heroic for one individual to challenge the unwieldy tangle of public bureaucracy. Americans love to hear stories that tell them "Yes, you can fight City Hall." On the other hand, we inevitably wonder, "What if everyone decided to take such matters into his or her own hands?" How would the system work then?

What more could an artist want?

An unusual medium. A chance to take a jab at the establishment. An almost endless audience, speeding to see the work.

Richard Ankrom created that enviable milieu above an unlikely canvas—the Harbor Freeway in downtown Los Angeles.

For two years, the rail-thin artist planned and prepared for his most ambitious project, a piece that would be seen by more than 150,000 motorists per day on the freeway, near 3rd Street.

With friends documenting his every move on camera, Ankrom clandestinely installed the finished product on a gray August morning. For nine months, no one noticed. It even failed to catch the eye of California Department of Transportation officials.

And that is exactly what Ankrom hoped for.

The 46-year-old Los Angeles artist designed, built and installed an addition to an overhead freeway sign—to exact state specifications—to help guide motorists on the sometimes confusing transition to the northbound Golden State Freeway a couple miles farther north.

He installed his handiwork in broad daylight, dressed in a hard hat and orange reflective vest to avoid raising suspicion. He even chopped off his shoulder-length blond hair to fit the role of a blue-collar freeway worker.

The point of the project, said Ankrom, was to show that art has a place in modern society—even on a busy, impersonal freeway. He also wanted to prove that one highly disciplined individual can make a difference.

What were Ankrom's political goals?

Embarrassed Caltrans officials, who learned of the bogus sign from a local newspaper column, concede that the sign could be a help. They will leave it in place, for now. The transportation agency doesn't plan to press charges, for trespassing or tampering with state property.

Why didn't the counterfeit sign get noticed?

"The experts are saying that Mr. Ankrom did a fantastic job," conceded Caltrans spokeswoman Jeanne Bonfilio. "They thought it was an internal job."

Ankrom's work has also won praise from some in the art world.

Mat Gleason, publisher of the Los Angeles art magazine *Coagula,* learned about the project a few months ago. He calls it "terrific" because it shows that art can "benefit people and at the same time the bureaucracy a little."

The idea for the sign came to Ankrom back in 1999, when he found himself repeatedly getting lost trying to find the ramp to the north Golden State after the Harbor becomes the Pasadena Freeway. (The sharp left-lane exit sneaks up on drivers at the end of a series of four tunnels.)

He thought about complaining to Caltrans. But he figured his suggestion would get lost in the huge state bureaucracy. Instead, Ankrom decided to take matters into his own hands by adding a simple "North 5" to an existing sign.

Why didn't Ankrom go through official channels? On whose authority did he decide his actions needed to be taken?

"It needed to be done," he said from his downtown loft. "It's not like it was something that was intentionally wrong."

It didn't hurt that his work is displayed before 150,000 people daily. On an average day, even the Louvre gets only one-tenth that many visitors. He also didn't mind that his "guerrilla public service" made Caltrans look a bit foolish. "They are left with egg on their faces," he said.

Ankrom had planned to wait until August—a year after the installation—to reveal his forgery via video at an art show. But a photographer friend leaked the story.

From his tiny Brewery Art Complex loft, Ankrom said he tries to use his work to comment on current trends. The Seattle native fabricates hatchets embedded with roses and produces neon-illuminated laser guns. To pay the bills, he is also a freelance sign maker.

The expertise he gained in both fields helped him pull off the perfect counterfeit job.

He closely studied existing freeway signs, matching color swatches and downloading specifications from the Federal Highway Administration's Web site.

His biggest challenge was finding reflective buttons resembling those on Interstate signs—a dilemma finally resolved when he discovered a replica sold by a company in Tacoma, Wash.

The video he made of the entire process shows Ankrom snapping digital photos of existing Golden State Freeway signs and projecting the images onto paper, before tracing them onto a sheet of aluminum. He cut and painted the aluminum sign and even "aged" it with a layer of gray.

Ankrom affixed a contractor-style logo on the side of his pickup truck to add authenticity during the project. But closer examination might have raised suspicions. It read: Aesthetic De Construction. He even printed up a bogus work order, just in case he was stopped by police. "I tried to make this airtight, because I didn't want anything to go wrong," he said.

In early August, Ankrom launched the final phase of his project. After friends were in place with video and still cameras, one gave the all-clear signal via walkie-talkie: "Move in rubber ducky."

He made short work of the final installation—climbing up the sign and hanging over speeding traffic to install his addition. The main challenge was avoiding the razor wire on the way up.

Ankrom said he's not surprised that Caltrans isn't pressing charges, adding, "It wasn't straight-out vandalism."

For now, department officials say they will merely inspect the elements of Ankrom's sign to make sure they are securely fastened. They may be replaced in a few months as part of a program to retrofit all freeway signs with new, highly reflective models.

Caltrans officials had discussed adding more directional signs, but the agency spokeswoman said she is not sure why the department never followed through.

Why wasn't it vandalism? What if a less skilled person had decided to change the sign? What if the sign change had caused an accident?

Ankrom said he would like Caltrans to return the work. "If they want to keep it up there, that is fine too," he said. "Hopefully it will help people out, which was the whole point."

Consider the source and the audience.

- What does it mean that the source is a major-circulation, western-city newspaper?

Lay out the argument, the values, and the assumptions.

- What did Ankrom think he was doing? What were his political goals, and why did he think he was justified in pursuing them? (For our present purposes, we can set aside his artistic goals.)
- Can you put Ankrom's argument into general terms, so that it would apply to other people in other situations?
- What can you tell about Ankrom's worldview and the values that underlie his thinking about this issue?

Uncover the evidence.

- Does Ankrom offer any evidence to support his claim that his actions are justified?

Evaluate the conclusion.

- Are Ankrom's actions justified? Can you imagine coming to the opposite conclusion? Which is more persuasive? Why?

Sort out the political implications.

- Did Ankrom's actions cause any harm? Could they have? What if everyone behaved this way?

8.2 AIDS Incorporated

How Federal AIDS Money Ended Up Funding Psychic Hotlines, Neiman Marcus, and Flirting Classes

Wayne Turner, *Washington Monthly,* April 2001

This article comes from the *Washington Monthly,* a journal that is proud of its record of crusading against abuses of government power. Its author is a co-founder of ACT UP (the AIDS Coalition to Unleash Power). He makes a much clearer argument than we found in the first article in this chapter, and he offers more objective evidence, in the form of numerous examples. As you read, stay focused on the basic argument and the role that different political interests play in it. Who has power, and who does not? How do those without try to get it?

"You must help us against these, these THIEVES!" demanded Jose Colon loudly, as a dozen or so members of Congress stared curiously from their dais. This was unusual testimony at an AIDS-funding hearing.

> Who are the "thieves"? What exactly does "accountability in the use of federal AIDS funds" mean? Who should be accountable to whom?

Colon's 10-minute address to the U.S. House of Representatives Commerce Subcommittee on Health and Environment last July marked the end of a long, painful journey. Colon, along with countless others, has been fighting for accountability in the use of federal AIDS funds. For him, that fight is deeply personal. Colon is living with AIDS; his partner of 17 years, Aramis, died in 1991, not from AIDS, but from neglect.

Colon, a resident of Puerto Rico, recalled for the committee how Aramis had contracted an opportunistic infection in his lungs and had sought treatment from a federally funded clinic, the San Juan AIDS Institute. Yet, Aramis was never able to get an appointment with his assigned doctor. Eventually, the infection overwhelmed him, and he ended up hospitalized.

Aramis' physician from the Institute, Dr. Jorge Garib, paid just one brief visit to his patient at the hospital, declaring, "You know you have a pneumonia that kills."

Then Dr. Garib abruptly left the hospital room, and never returned. Several months later, Aramis died.

On the day Colon presented his testimony, a federal judge in San Juan sentenced Garib to the maximum 10 years in prison for his involvement in an embezzlement scandal at the AIDS clinic that rocked Puerto Rico and sent shock waves all the way to Washington.

During Garib's trial, and the trials of several other Institute officials, prosecutors outlined a paper trail of dummy corporations, off-shore bank accounts, payments for luxury cars, jet skis, cash pay-offs to the Institute's political benefactors, and for Dr. Garib, a personal maid—all using $2.2 million in federal AIDS funds.

Even the governor of Puerto Rico, Pedro Rosselló, was twice subpoenaed to testify, though he has not been indicted. A prosecution witness claimed Rosselló supervised the transfer of $250,000 in a shoe box from the Institute to support his 1992 election campaign.

Rosselló, who decided not to seek re-election, continues to deny involvement in the scandal. Yet prior to his election as governor, Rosselló ran the San Juan health department, administering the federal AIDS grants and hand-selecting the very AIDS Institute directors who now stand convicted of fraud.

The San Juan AIDS scandal was many years in the making, but the people responsible for ensuring that AIDS money is well spent did little but sit by and watch. A member of the Puerto Rican legislature, Rep. David Noriega Rodriguez, presented substantial evidence of AIDS fraud in a report to U.S. Health and Human Services Secretary Donna Shalala in May 1993, but received only a form letter in return.

The feds' indifference continued for years. According to the *San Juan Star,* Lawrence Poole, an HHS official responsible for monitoring federal funds distributed under the Ryan White CARE Act, admitted under oath in 1999 that his department continually paid millions of dollars to the Institute without ever receiving an accounting or financial report.

It took courthouse vigils in San Juan to force action on behalf of the victims. Colon and Anselmo Fonseca, who also lost his partner to AIDS, together formed Pacientes de SIDA Pro Politica Sana (AIDS Patients for Sane Policies) to demand more accountability in the use of federal AIDS funds for the poor.

At first, they were criticized for drawing attention to the scandal, mostly by employees of other AIDS agencies who feared the scandal could taint their own organizations. Despite political pressure, and even anonymous threats of violence, their numbers grew as more victims of the scandal stepped forward.

For these patients and family members who watched their loved ones die, the five convictions and seven guilty pleas won by the U.S. Attorney's Office in Puerto Rico are little consolation.

The activists attempting to expose such funding abuses in Puerto Rico and elsewhere have been met with stony silence and even outright hostility, mostly from those who are supposed to be their strongest allies in the fight against AIDS.

Their experience shows that after a hard-fought 20 years, the AIDS epidemic has finally become a sacred cow. It is immune from budget cuts; even the Republican-controlled Congress has steadily increased federal AIDS funding, at times well beyond the Clinton administration's request. The Ryan White CARE Act, a $1.7 billion program, was unanimously reauthorized by the 106th Congress last year.

Named 10 years ago in memory of a teenager who died from AIDS, the act was originally conceived to provide emergency relief to low-income people with HIV and AIDS, to provide doctor's visits, medications, food banks, emergency assistance, and other survival services.

Yet lawmakers and the administration have done little to ensure that the money actually helps patients. Lax oversight of federal AIDS programs has permitted a rash of abuses from San Francisco to San Juan. While the money keeps rolling in to bloated nonprofit and government AIDS agencies, many patients continue to suffer with low-quality care, or no services at all.

Fraud Cases Mount

When Colon and his colleagues began citing the San Juan case as symptomatic of larger problems with federal AIDS funding, many Washington policy makers and AIDS organizations simply dismissed it as an isolated incident. Even worse, some hinted that it was just those "corrupt Puerto Ricans." AIDS groups who have taken great pains to stake out a benevolent image still refuse to acknowledge that the number of "isolated incidents" of fraud, mismanagement, and abuse of AIDS funds are increasing nationwide.

What's the author's purpose in providing so much supporting evidence?

Just a few examples:
- In Texas, the FBI is currently probing a South Dallas AIDS clinic that mis-spent tens of thousands of federal dollars intended to benefit poor African Americans. A county audit of the former Margaret K. Wright Clinic discov-ered that shopping sprees to Neiman Marcus, home appliances, and psy-chic phone-line calls had all been billed to the Ryan White CARE Act.

The Wright clinic has been the sole source of AIDS services in North Texas for low-income African Americans, who comprise the region's highest percentage of AIDS cases. "The FBI also is investigating allegations that the clinic bought ex-pensive AIDS drugs that remain unaccounted for and applied federal funds toward treatment of patients who might not have existed," wrote the *Dallas Morning News* last year.

- Corey White, a bookkeeper for Central Florida United AIDS Resources in Orlando, Fla., was sentenced to 37 months in jail for embezzling more than $500,000 from the group, which provides assistance to AIDS patients needing housing and medications. According to investigators, White spent the funds on Disney tickets, hotels, and restaurants. Some months her credit card bills exceeded $25,000.

- In North Carolina, the State Bureau of Investigation (SBI) is probing a Johnston County AIDS organization after an audit revealed that James Wise, the director of Drugs and AIDS Prevention Among African-Americans (DAPAA), kept 10 percent of all Medicaid payments to DAPAA as personal compensation, and wrote himself checks totaling $13,300, according to the Associated Press (AP). "Between June 1996 and October 1997, DAPAA ob-tained $15,380 from another AIDS agency by saying the money would pay the rent for DAPAA clients at specific properties. Wise arranged to have the checks made out to his mother, who did not own the properties."

The SBI is also investigating Wise's wife, Janet, the assistant chief of the state's HIV/STD prevention section, who awarded $684,291 to DAPAA between 1993 and 1997.

- Years of complaints finally led to a state audit of the Los Angeles County AIDS housing program, funded by the Federal Housing Opportunities for People with AIDS (HOPWA).

The May audit showed that a whopping $21.8 million in federal grants to house homeless people with AIDS had accumulated since 1993 and remained unspent.

Michael Weinstein, president of the AIDS Healthcare Foundation, told the AP, "The program is in shambles . . . and every dollar wasted is costing a life."

- AIDServe Indiana, the only state-wide agency providing assistance to pa-tients with HIV/AIDS, "mismanaged hundreds of thousands of dollars, with devastating consequences for sick people," according to an investiga-tion last year by the *Indianapolis Star.* While administrators diverted funds to help cover salaries and other operating costs, AIDServe owed thousands of dollars to dozens of landlords, pharmacies, doctors and dentists throughout Indiana. "Some are refusing to provide vital medical care, housing, and life-saving drugs to patients until they get their money," the *Star* reported.

The *Star* documented the plight of AIDS patients hounded by creditors for unpaid medical bills, facing eviction notices from their homes, or living under bridges. The State Health Department canceled all contracts in November and is now conducting a full audit of the group's finances. $175,000 raised during last October's AIDS Walk was seized by Fifth Third Bank in February to pay for an overdue loan to AIDServe, according to the *Star.*

AIDServe Indiana's president and chief executive officer, Mark St. John, wrote an op-ed last June defending AIDServe and urging the general assembly to increase the group's funding. Five months later, St. John resigned, admitting that funds had been mismanaged. The organization shut down in November.

Conferences or Junkets?

The Washington adage that it's often the legal things that are the most scandalous applies all too accurately to federal AIDS funding. AIDS has spawned a rash of conferences that are little more than taxpayer-financed vacation junkets. The annual exodus every March to the AIDS Update Conference in San Francisco is unabashedly referred to as "Spring Break" by employees of East Coast AIDS service organizations.

This unique AIDS industry perk is finally receiving some attention. *The Washington Post* last year exposed an AIDS "conference" held in St. Thomas, Virgin Islands, at the Marriott Frenchman's Reef Resort Hotel.

The conference was convened by Joe O'Neill, the head of the HIV/AIDS Bureau at the Health Resources Services Administration—responsible for monitoring federal AIDS funds earmarked for patient care—who urged the invitation-only participants to attend the Caribbean confab using their Ryan White funding.

Although the conference was supposed to highlight HIV/AIDS in poor, developing areas, no local physicians, public health officials, or patients were invited. A *Virgin Islands Daily News* reporter was ejected from the conference cocktail party reception, along with his photographer.

While the clients of AIDServe Indiana faced eviction from their homes, HRSA's O'Neill found the time and resources to attend another conference in Rio de Janeiro, held between the beaches of Ipanema and Copacabana no less, and flew to London in December, just in time for holiday shopping.

Yet O'Neill told a congressional subcommittee last July that his department lacked the resources to adequately monitor and detect AIDS funding scandals.

Indeed, reported instances of funding abuses in North Carolina, Florida, California, Texas, Puerto Rico, and Indiana were all uncovered, not by HRSA, but by local auditors, journalists, and community activists.

Cap Salaries, Not Services

Service providers often justify the conferences and trips to the beach as an entitlement to compensate for their status as "underpaid" poverty workers. Yet the administrators of some AIDS charities earn more than mayors, governors, and members of Congress.

The head of the San Francisco AIDS Foundation, Pat Christen, tops the list, earning more than $200,000 a year, according to the group's 1999 tax forms. In the District of Columbia, the area's second largest AIDS service provider, Food and Friends, paid $163,111 to its executive director, Craig Shniderman, in 1998, the most recent year for which documents are available.

One D.C. clinic continued paying its well-compensated director even after he resigned to become a city council member. When Jim Graham resigned as executive director of Whitman-Walker Clinic, he saw his $186,453 annual salary cut by more than half. Clinic officials came to Graham's rescue, with a $70,000 consulting contract. The *Washington City Paper* blew the whistle on the secret deal in February 1999, and the contract was withdrawn due to conflict-of-interest rules.

Graham did end up with a consolation prize of sorts. The clinic, which has waiting lists for its services, donated a roomful of designer Stickley office furniture to the new councilmember, because Graham couldn't tolerate his government-issued desks.

The cushy positions of some AIDS executives stand in stark contrast to the subsistence living of many HIV/AIDS patients, whose disability income can range between $500–$700 per month. Gaining access to services provided through the government can often be a Herculean task.

Programs like Medicaid or food stamps require applicants to appear in person and, in places like D.C., waiting in line can take all day. There is little accommodation for those with fevers, nausea, vomiting, weakness, and other symptoms of HIV.

This daily struggle for survival is only confounded by the intricate maze of repetitious forms, red tape, paperwork, and waiting lists created by the AIDS service providers.

Instead of streamlining operations, however, the AIDS service industry has created yet another layer of jobs. Several cities, including D.C., invented a new service category called "Access Advocates," employees to assist patients confronting the vast AIDS bureaucracy in gaining access to "Case Managers," employees assigned to assist patients confronting the vast AIDS bureaucracy.

There is a method to this madness. Groups receiving funds have a strong incentive to invest more in staff and overhead than in patient care, so that they are ready for the next grant cycle where infrastructure counts more than effectiveness.

San Francisco's *Bay Area Reporter* wrote last year about a man with AIDS suffering from chronic diarrhea, Terry Leone. Leone was denied a 95-cent adult diaper as he left San Francisco General Hospital and traveled home on a bus, soaked in his own excrement. He did have five CARE-paid case managers who, instead of giving him a diaper, sent letters insisting he return in person to their offices to fill out forms to be "recertified" as a client. Leone didn't live long enough to meet the agencies' bureaucratic requirements. He died five months later.

Foxes Guarding the Hen House

AIDS agencies' burdensome emphasis on paperwork, often in lieu of services, is not surprising. People living with HIV/AIDS have little say in how their CARE dollars are spent.

When the Ryan White Act was first drafted in 1990, Congress created Title I planning councils, composed of locally appointed community members, to establish critical service priorities and oversee the allocation of federal dollars.

The councils were then mandated to reflect the demographics of the local infected population by including at least 35 percent people living with HIV/AIDS—an important win for AIDS activists who have long insisted that affected communities are their own best advocates.

The promise of full community participation and oversight in the allocation of federal funds never materialized, however. For the past 10 years, planning councils have been packed almost entirely with salaried employees, board members, and consultants to groups receiving Ryan White funds. They determine everything from funding priorities to who gets approved to join the council.

Council meetings can often resemble an episode of "Survivor," especially when the time comes to divide up the money. Competition is cut-throat, as members fight for their own service categories, sometimes forming alliances with other providers. It's usually clients who get voted off the island. Out of the 60 appointees on the D.C. planning council, there have been as few as three non-aligned members, i.e., people who aren't board members or employees of groups receiving the funds. Conflict-of-interest rules are rarely enforced, so that what could be an effective body of local watchdogs has become more like a group of hungry foxes guarding the hen house.

Health Care for Dead People

The annual local wrangling over who gets the biggest helping at the AIDS gravy train was mirrored last year during congressional re-authorization, pitting large, entrenched first-wave cities against new areas facing the rising tide of the AIDS epidemic.

Since 1990, Ryan White funds have been distributed according to a complicated formula that counts the cumulative number of AIDS cases within a jurisdiction, not the current number of living clients. As a result, San Francisco, which experienced a devastating death toll early in the epidemic, still receives twice the funds, per patient ($5,980), than other cities with a comparable caseload such as

Chicago ($3,123) and the District of Columbia ($2,869), according to a General Accounting Office (GAO) report last year.

"The U.S. taxpayer has been funding health care services for dead people," said GAO Assistant Director Jerry Fastrup at last year's congressional hearing on the Ryan White CARE Act.

Funding inequities particularly impact African-American and other minority communities now facing the full brunt of the AIDS epidemic. HIV/AIDS patients in 17 states are on waiting lists or have restricted access to potentially life-saving medications under the AIDS Drug Assistance Program.

While thousands of patients have no access to life-saving pills, the CARE Act subsidizes frills programs such as San Francisco's AIDS Health Project, which, with $977,701 in Ryan White grants for FY 2000, features flirting classes and HIV bowling nights. In New York, the nation's oldest and largest AIDS service organization, the Gay Men's Health Crisis, provides hair styling and art classes.

Patients vs. Providers

A grassroots network of activists is fighting for greater equity in the distribution of AIDS funds and other reforms so that resources are targeted where they're needed most. The argument that geography should not determine an HIV/AIDS patient's ability to access medication and other services, however, faces fierce opposition.

After two decades of the epidemic, the bulk of the AIDS movements' political muscle is concentrated, not with patient groups, but with firms lobbying for AIDS service providers. Nonprofit AIDS agencies have invested millions of dollars in operations like AIDS Action and the CAEAR Coalition (Cities Advocating Emergency AIDS Response).

To compete with states and second-wave cities for funding, the CAEAR coalition hired a consulting firm called the Sheridan Group. The Sheridan Group coincidentally, operates AIDSPAC, a political action committee that raises millions of dollars for federal candidates.

Not surprisingly, the bulk of AIDSPAC money goes to pay the Sheridan Group for its consulting services. The few campaign contributions AIDSPAC made were earmarked for CAEAR coalition allies, such as Rep. Nancy Pelosi (D-Calif.) and Sen. Edward Kennedy (D-Mass.). Both defended the specialized funding given to certain cities at the expense of HIV/AIDS patients living elsewhere.

The mass marches that once characterized AIDS funding battles in Congress didn't materialize last year during the Ryan White reauthorization. Paid industry lobbyists made their usual rounds on Capitol Hill in their Gucci loafers, pleading poverty on behalf of AIDS victims. The only opposition facing this well-oiled machine came from within.

Open warfare broke out over who gets the most money. San Francisco fought with Los Angeles, big cities with smaller cities; states fought the cities and each other, and rural areas fought urban areas.

Meanwhile, a loose-knit coalition of patient activists emerged with their own proposals, designed to bring greater accountability to the $1.7 billion federal program. Foremost among these was a proposal to cap salaries of top AIDS executives, so that no administrator of groups receiving Ryan White funds would receive a compensation package greater than that of the chief elected official of the jurisdiction wherein the group resided. In a city like D.C., where the mayor earns approximately $110,000 per year, the executive salaries of the area's leading AIDS providers would be cut by more than a third.

Such a proposal proved sufficient to unite the warring factions among service providers as only Sen. Jesse Helms could. Even a compromise version requiring just a public list of the top AIDS earners was quashed in committee.

With no PAC money, and the vigorous opposition of industry lobbyists, AIDS activists had an uphill battle to include reforms to the CARE Act. They found an unusual ally: conservative Dr. Tom Coburn (R-Okla.), co-author of the Ryan White CARE Act in the House. He was joined by Rep. Henry Waxman (D-Calif.) in incorporating accountability measures, proposed by patient activists, in the final version of the reauthorization.

These reforms require more consumers on planning councils, whose meetings would be opened to the public. New council members would receive training to ensure their effective participation, and a random sample of all Ryan White CARE Act programs will be audited annually by the federal government. These modest provisions, activists hope, will help strengthen patient participation and oversight at both the local and federal levels.

> Who did Congress intend AIDS groups to be accountable to, and who are they accountable to in reality?

Challenges Ahead

Those who implement the CARE Act now need to place a greater priority on patients' needs, instead of the money-hungry AIDS industry. Turning that hope into reality poses significant challenges, however.

Congress, by finally providing oversight, can prove its commitment to AIDS victim by measuring their program's effectiveness, and not just its annual appropriation. Likewise, the mainstream media, now accustomed to featuring feel-good stories on fundraising events like the AIDS Rides, should follow their counterparts in the gay press by scrutinizing where the millions of dollars raised actually go.

Finally, people living with HIV and AIDS face the ultimate challenge, particularly those without health insurance and living in poverty. They can be the most effective watchdogs, yet their voices are so often silenced by a paternalistic AIDS care delivery system that seems to have forgotten just who it is meant to serve.

Consider the source and the audience.
- Do the kind of journal and the likely audience of this piece have any impact on the way the argument is presented?

Lay out the argument, the values, and the assumptions.
- Be clear about Turner's basic argument about AIDS funding. Why is there no accountability? What power relationships support the status quo?
- What kinds of values does Turner promote? Who does he think the winners here should be?
- Does he give any weight to arguments from the other side? Should he?

Uncover the evidence.
- Turner cites loads of evidence. Is it persuasive? Should there be more? Less?

Evaluate the conclusion.
- Is the problem Turner sees real? Will the reforms fix it?

Sort out the political implications.
- Was there any way to avoid what happened with AIDS funding? How much of what Turner saw might be present in other bureaucracies?

8.3 FBI CYA

The Problem the Bureau Still Hasn't Fixed

Scott Shuger, *Slate,* 30 May 2002

This article comes from an online journal called *Slate,* owned by Microsoft (but usually scrupulous about disclosing that fact to readers if any conflict of interest arises). *Slate's* style is more informal and edgier than traditional news sources (FBI CYA, for instance, stands for FBI Cover Your Ass—not a typical headline from, say, the *New York Times*). Its arguments are up-front and provocative.

Shuger's analysis appeared right after the FBI announced plans to reorganize in the wake of a number of accusations, including one from FBI agent Coleen Rowley, that it had missed the boat in warning U.S. officials and citizens of the September 11 attacks on New York and Washington, D.C. Basically, he says, its organization is not the FBI's primary problem. What is? Can it be solved? Is it likely to be?

The post–9/11 reorganization plan the FBI announced yesterday may indeed remedy some of the shortcomings that enabled the WTC/Pentagon plotters to succeed. Some 500 agents will be reassigned to anti-terrorism duty, computers will be upgraded, and special counterterror response "flying squads" and a new intelligence office will be formed. But these reforms don't address the FBI's historically biggest weakness: its obsession with its own image.

Since both the flying squads and the intel office will be based in Washington, D.C., the new changes only further consolidate FBI HQ's control over

Where does whistleblower Rowley say the FBI's problems are located?

counterterrorism efforts. In her *j'accuse* memo to FBI Director Robert Mueller, longtime FBI agent and attorney Coleen Rowley anticipates this key flaw: "The Phoenix, Minneapolis and Paris Legal Attache Offices reacted remarkably, exhibiting keen perception and prioritization skills regarding the terrorist threats they uncovered or were made aware of pre–September 11th. The same cannot be said for the FBI Headquarters' bureaucracy and you want to expand that?!"

Rowley lays out some perceptive reasons why centralization has been bad for the FBI: 1) Overseeing aggressive operations that don't pan out (as, for example, at Ruby Ridge and Waco) has usually been career-ending, so FBI managers tend to avoid all "unnecessary" decisions. 2) Headquarters is dominated by managers, many of them failed street agents, on 18-month ticket-punching tours too short for them to master the details and trends in the areas they supervise. But

What task does Shuger say occupies FBI headquarters—and with what consequences?

Rowley doesn't note another aspect of the Bureau's overcentralization, one that's caused it to blow many big cases over the years: It's fostered by the Bureau's obsession with its image, because relentless image control requires a strong central hand. And if making sure the FBI comes out looking good is job No. 1, then truly effective law enforcement—which would require openly admitting mistakes and working with other agencies—is not.

The cult of appearances at the FBI was originated, of course, by founding Director J. Edgar Hoover, who ran the show for 48 years. It was Hoover who promulgated the notion that all FBI agents were either lawyers or accountants at a time when only a small percentage of them were; it was he who came in to make highly publicized personal "arrests" of big-time gangsters already surrounded by street agents (Public Enemy No. 1 Alvin Karpas) or delivered by a reporter (Lepke Buchhalter, the head of Murder Inc., served up by Walter Winchell). It was he who responded to press criticisms about a dearth of black agents by instantly dubbing his chauffeur one. And it was Hoover who expressed his awareness of the FBI's failure to properly monitor Lee Harvey Oswald upon his return from Russia, not in his public testimony before the Warren Commission, but only in scribbled comments on the margins of a secret FBI memo. Hoover censured or put on probation more than a dozen agents for Oswald-related failures—but without ever publicly acknowledging this.

It's striking how strongly this legacy has endured in the three decades since Hoover's death in office. When things go wrong, the Bureau's instinct is still the same—to misplace blame and refuse help from other agencies. To wit:

- When one of the FBI's own scientists, Frederic Whitehurst, complained about quality control problems in the Bureau's crime lab—later verified by the Justice Department—problems that jeopardized hundreds of prosecutions, the Bureau reacted not by adopting the reforms Whitehurst suggested, but by suspending and then transferring him.

- During the Waco standoff, senior FBI officials ignored the warnings issued by the Bureau's own behavioral specialists that David Koresh posed a serious suicide risk and didn't consult with outside experts on cults.
- When the FBI investigated the Oklahoma City bombing, it excluded other agencies, including bomb experts from the Bureau of Alcohol, Tobacco, and Firearms, both at the blast site and when it raided a farm where it was believed Timothy McVeigh and Terry Nichols built practice bombs.
- After the bombing at Atlanta's Summer Olympics, the FBI once again stiffed the ATF. This time it shipped all the evidence to its own problem-riddled lab, ignoring the ATF's lab right in Atlanta, which had solved a similar high-profile bombing case. And the Bureau used press leaks to wrongly finger security guard Richard Jewell as the prime suspect. So grudging was the FBI's admission that it had goofed on Jewell that it waited months to develop the evidence in the backpack the real bomber left behind and to release a tape to the public of the anonymous 911 call warning about the bomb before it went off. The case is still open.

Are there conclusions that can be drawn from these mistakes other than the ones that Shuger arrives at?

  Then–FBI Director Louis Freeh later endorsed a Justice Department report finding that field agents in the case "made a major error in judgment"—even though it was Freeh who personally ordered that Jewell be read his *Miranda* rights when he came in voluntarily for an interview.
- In the FBI's investigation of the possible theft of nuclear secrets from the Los Alamos lab, agents mistakenly focused entirely on Wen Ho Lee, thereby ignoring many other leads. It probably didn't help that even though, according to a Justice Department report, the Bureau didn't have analysts of its own with enough knowledge of weaponry and computers, it didn't reach out to competent outside experts. Nevertheless, Lee was arrested on espionage charges and was denied bail based in large part on assurances made by Freeh and other agents about the solidity of the case.
- Even after the capture of CIA traitor Aldrich Ames in 1994, the Bureau failed to adopt the CIA's practice of regular mandatory polygraph tests for agents. And despite some troubling evidence that one of the FBI's own, Robert Hanssen, was spying for the Soviet Union and Russia, the Bureau mistakenly ignored him and focused instead on a CIA officer.

This egregious track record will not be improved upon in the terrorism sphere simply by moving some agents around and creating some new places to move them to. Some of the right heads have to roll, too. And this means the FBI's near-ancient commitment to damage control has got to go. In Hoover's FBI, or Freeh's, the supervisors at HQ who ignored or downplayed warnings from the field about radical Arab hijackers might get quiet rebukes, but they would stay in place (and might even get bonuses) where they would continue to threaten public safety. And whistle-blowers like Rowley would probably get out, or punished, or at the very least never get promoted again.

There is exactly one way the Bureau can show now that it has really changed—by firing those supervisors, promoting Rowley, and calling for a public independent investigation of its counterterror foul-ups.

Consider the source and the audience.
- Is the fact that *Slate* is an online journal likely to affect its content? How? Who are its readers likely to be?

Lay out the argument, the values, and the assumptions.
- Shuger makes an explicit argument here. What is it? What is the main thing he does not like about FBI culture?
- How does Shuger think the FBI should be run? What role should whistleblowers like Rowley have? What values does Shuger think are important?
- Can you extend Shuger's argument about bureaucratic culture and the role of whistleblowers beyond the FBI?

Uncover the evidence.
- What kind of evidence does Shuger offer to support his argument? Is it open to other interpretations? Could he have found other kinds of evidence to support his contention?

Evaluate the conclusion.
- Shuger is very positive about what needs to be done to fix the FBI and what's wrong with its plans to fix itself. Is he right? Does he give you enough information to decide?

Sort out the political implications.
- If bureaucracy and democracy do not work well together, what chances are there for Shuger's plans to be truly effective? How pervasive might this problem be?

8.4 *All Things Considered*

Transcript, National Public Radio, 7 June 2002

This is a transcript from *All Things Considered,* a show that airs every evening on National Public Radio (NPR) and is supported by taxpayer dollars, listener contributions, and corporate donations. The segment presented here includes several interviews with experts on the subject of President Bush's proposal to make a new cabinet-level Department of Homeland Security by combining and reorganizing various existing agencies. It provides several different perspectives on who stands to win and who to lose in the reorganization process.

We do not see a single argument here but, rather, a weaving together of several arguments, made by the different guests. Remember that someone at NPR picked which people to interview, so the combination tells you something about the overall NPR perspective. Here's some background on the people who appear on the show: Bush, of course, is president of the United States. Democratic senators Joe Lieberman and Bob Graham are chairs of Senate committees with major roles in the restructuring. (Democrats are featured here because they were the ones in leadership positions at the time of Bush's proposal.) Paul Light is a scholar at the Brookings Institution, a non-profit organization that evaluates government performance. David Corn is an editor at *The Nation,* a journal that takes a liberal point of view, and David Brooks is an editor at *The Weekly Standard,* a conservative journal. It is interesting to note that the experts here are journalists—professional political observers—being interviewed by other journalists.

JOHN YDSTIE, host: From NPR News, this is *All Things Considered.* I'm John Ydstie.

ROBERT SIEGEL, host: And I'm Robert Siegel. President Bush today began an intense lobbying campaign to win passage of his plan to reorganize the government's homeland security efforts. The president's request that Congress merge several different agencies into a new Department of Homeland Security has been generally well received on Capitol Hill. But as NPR's Pam Fessler reports, lawmakers won't see the fine print for another two weeks or more, and they're warning that such a huge reorganization will be difficult.

PAM FESSLER reporting: President Bush met first thing this morning with a bi-partisan group of congressional leaders who are key to getting his new homeland security plan enacted. The president said he knows lots of people will be fighting to protect their turf in the weeks and months ahead, but that he is optimistic.

President GEORGE W. BUSH: That's what this meeting is all about is the beginning of winning the turf battle. I think most members of Congress understand the need to act.

> What "turf battle" is Bush talking about? What does "turf battle" mean in a bureaucratic context? What turf of his own might Bush want to claim?

FESSLER: In fact, many on Capitol Hill have been calling for such a reorganization for months. They say the current White House Office of Homeland Security lacks the power needs to ensure the nation's safety. The president, who earlier resisted moves to create a new agency, said he's actually been considering such a change for a while. He said he just needed time after September 11th to figure out if it was the best thing to do. Today, the president said the sooner his plan can be enacted, the better.

Pres. BUSH: To this end, I'm going to direct Tom Ridge to testify before Congress about the need for the establishment of this Cabinet agency.

FESSLER: His refusal earlier to allow Ridge, a presidential adviser, to testify on Capitol Hill was one of the main reasons members of Congress have been seeking a Cabinet-level homeland defense agency where the secretary would have to testify.

Lawmakers who attended the White House meeting said everyone now seems to be on the same page. Democrat Joseph Lieberman of Connecticut chairs the Senate Governmental Affairs Committee, which will have jurisdiction over the reorganization plan. Lieberman said he expects some opposition, but he dismissed complaints that trying to coordinate work that now involves 100 different government agencies will only divert energy from ongoing homeland defense programs.

Senator JOSEPH LIEBERMAN (Democrat, Connecticut): I would say to those who would argue that getting together to better organize to protect the American people at home is a distraction for those involved is really just an excuse for doing nothing and accepting less than the American people deserve.

FESSLER: Under the president's plan, the new department would include some of the biggest agencies that now deal with one aspect or another of homeland defense. These include the Customs Service, the Coast Guard, the Immigration and Naturalization Service, the new Transportation Security Administration and the Federal Emergency Management Agency; and it will involve 170,000 government employees. Senate Intelligence Committee Chairman Bob Graham of Florida said the CIA and the FBI will continue to be independent, but that the intelligence information they collect will be fed into a new analytical unit in the homeland security agency.

Senator BOB GRAHAM (Democrat, Florida): Where you will have the chance of putting all of that material before one human being who, hopefully, is imaginative and creative and can see what it means and act upon what it means.

What political turf do Lieberman and Graham want to claim?

FESSLER: But Graham also has his own proposal to create an Office of Counterterrorism inside the White House, and Lieberman said that might be one of the changes Congress will consider to the president's plan. Other changes are also likely, but so far, there are few specifics about how the reorganization will work. Paul Light of the Brookings Institution cautions that it will be far more difficult than anyone can imagine.

What is the show implying when it emphasizes Light's argument that the agencies to be merged have different bureaucratic cultures and identities and serve different interests?

Mr. PAUL LIGHT (Brookings Institution): They've got to find a building, and that's not easy to do. They're going to have to design a flag, they're going to have to design stationery. You think that's easy, or you think that's trivial, but it's all part of building an identity in a common culture.

FESSLER: And that, he says, is crucial because right now many of the agencies the president wants to merge have long traditions of independence and very different missions.

Mr. LIGHT: Secret Service serves the president. Coast Guard serves boaters, law enforcement, even sea turtles. The Federal Emergency Management Administration serves victims of disaster.

FESSLER: Light says it's possible to pull all these entities into one agency with everyone working toward a common goal, but that it could take years. The president would like the new agency up and running by January 1st. Pam Fessler, NPR News, Washington.

JOHN YDSTIE, host: With me in the studio to sift through the homeland security reorganization are David Corn, Washington editor of *The Nation,* and David Brooks, senior editor at *The Weekly Standard.* Gentlemen, welcome.

Mr. DAVID BROOKS (Senior Editor, *The Weekly Standard*): Good to be here.

Mr. DAVID CORN (Washington Editor, *The Nation*): Hello.

YDSTIE: The biggest reorganization since the Truman era. Who are the winners and losers here? David Corn, start with you.

Mr. CORN: Well, the old saying is that "God is in the details." There literally are millions, if not tens of millions of details to be worked out on this reorganization plan. Hard to see how it's going to happen in the next three months. I think a big winner, though, is President Bush—this puts him out ahead of the story when he had been falling behind and he had a flip-flop on his support for this, and it I think takes a lot of the oxygen out of all the other politics that might otherwise be occurring on Capitol Hill. So it's going to be very hard for the Democrats, who are looking for an agenda to push going into the elections in November, to get much steam up on anything else while we're going through this massive reorganization.

YDSTIE: David Brooks, would you agree with that?

Mr. BROOKS: I basically agree. I think certainly the winners were any caffeine makers 'cause worthwhile bureaucratic reshuffling is not exactly the most exciting thing; but we are all excited by it. Certainly the losers were the Cabinet secretaries, aside from the new one who is going to be created. One of the interesting ways this was done was that the White House staff, really seven or 10 people, met together in a secret cabal for about 10 days, put together this whole plan. And the reason they did that was because if they let it go public, then every Cabinet secretary on earth would be approaching President Bush with some three-ring binder saying, "There's a reason I should keep the Secret Service in my Treasury Department." And Bush would have to fend off all these guys. The Bush administration—secrecy is its middle name, but it did this quite ruthlessly, and so lots of agencies lose lots of power, lots of little private armies, lots of money.

YDSTIE: Quite remarkable that this was kept secret until the very last minute.

Mr. CORN: You have to take your hat off to them. I'm not a big fan of secrecy, and they've done it across the board in so many other issues, but it was quite stunning that they could put together this giant plan, go back, you know, to the old New Deal days and you think about FDR bringing in, you know, tens

Both editors note that the reorganization plans were made secretly by the Bush administration. What were the reasons for the secrecy, and what were some of the political costs?

and twenties and hundreds of people to work on all the various alphabet agencies. These guys really did it on the back of an envelope, and that's why we're still waiting for a lot of details.

And I think while there was a tactical reason for doing this, it certainly would have maybe served the administration in another way had it actually reached out to the Democrats who had been pushing this, and Republicans on the Hill, too, like J. C. Watts, and saying, "Let's sit down and work this out together," rather than say, "No, no, no," to this and then, "Oh, by the way, we're jumping ahead of you." You know, Bush came to Washington saying he wanted to change the tone, but there's not very much tone changing when you act with such secrecy.

YDSTIE: It is interesting that this appears to be a move towards a sort of top-down military-type hierarchy as opposed to the kind of decentralized business plan model that's been popular in recent years. Is that a direct response to 9/11, and are we going to see more of it? David Brooks.

Mr. BROOKS: Yeah, I think it is. I think the correct comparison Bush really drew was to Harry Truman. At the beginning of the Cold War, you really did need fundamental restructuring in a more militaristic manner, and the same way here, restructuring it to face the war on terror. The essential thing that caused all this was Tom Ridge coming to office and finding he was toothless, that when, say, the anthrax thing hit, he couldn't coordinate the various health agencies, couldn't get them to do what he wanted aside from begging and pleading because they didn't answer to him. So finally, there will be somebody in the Cabinet to whom they do answer, whether happily or not, that he will control their budget. So there will be some central authority figure.

YDSTIE: David Corn, is this return to big government, big agencies a good thing?

Mr. CORN: Well, I'm hoping it works out for the best. I think there are a lot of hurdles to overcome. You take an agency like FEMA;* FEMA is going to be put into this new superagency. FEMA primarily works on hurricanes 364 days a year, and then if a terrorist event happens, then is called into that. So now they're going to be part of an agency where the number-one priority is not their chief mission, and they're going to be working and answering to people who may not care much about hurricanes and floods in the Midwest and so on. So it remains to be seen how that culture is going to fit in with the overarching culture of this new agency, and I think you're going to have questions down the line of that sort. I'm very interested in how they're going to handle

---

*Editor's note: FEMA is the Federal Emergency Management Agency.

the intelligence side of this. One of the four major components is intelligence coordination analysis, and that's something that the director of Central Intelligence is already supposed to be doing but isn't, and is this going to add another bureaucratic player to the intelligence community mix, or actually impose some order upon it? We won't know for a long time about that.

YDSTIE: Any thoughts on that, David? What about the intelligence component of this new Cabinet department?

Mr. BROOKS: Clearly the weakest part of the whole agency because, first of all, this agency will not be able to investigate people; that'll be up to the FBI. They won't even be able to see the raw FBI files; they'll only be able to see the processed stuff which, if—pre–September 11th that would have told you nothing because the important information was left out. And then they won't be able to arrest people. So you've really got a straight line within the FBI from investigation to arresting, and then off on the side somewhere is this new agency where the information will supposedly flow. But it seems to me in the real world of bureaucratic life, the information will flow, if it flows at all, on the straight line in the FBI.

> How do these intelligence concerns relate to the "turf battle"?

YDSTIE: Of course, there were some cynics who said it wasn't any coincidence that President Bush unveiled this plan on the very day that the Senate Judiciary Committee began its public televised hearings looking into the apparent intelligence failures that preceded September 11th. Is that a fair analysis?

Mr. CORN: I'm not sure they were trying to divert attention from that particular hearing. I was actually at the judiciary hearing yesterday morning and, you know, the beepers and cell phones started going off at 10 A.M. as the hearing was taking off, and you saw one reporter after another sort of leaving to do the stories in preparation for the speech that night. So it certainly had that impact. I think overall, the White House was obviously concerned that in the media and in the sort of political landscape, you know, it was getting trumped by these stories. It looked like it, you know, hadn't been on the ball before September 11th, and there was a lot of momentum building behind the plans in Congress to go ahead and do this for . . .

YDSTIE: In fact, there was a quote from some administration source suggesting that President Bush had said, "Better to do it ourselves than have it done to us." And so they put this plan out instead of getting one that the Congress had hatched.

David, what's your sense about the cynics and diverting attention from the headlines? Was that—I mean, this certainly came up very quickly.

Mr. BROOKS: It is interesting how Bush flip-flopped on this. Just a month ago, he was saying we didn't need another Cabinet agency. But this—they sometimes project the image of omniscience and omnipotence, but the Bushes historically,

especially in Texas, were very quick to hop on somebody else's good idea, claim credit for it and declare
victory.

YDSTIE: David Brooks of *The Weekly Standard,* and David
Corn of *The Nation,* thank you both very much.

Mr. BROOKS: Thank you.

What are these guests
saying about Bush's
political motivations?
Relate that back to the
turf theme.

Consider the source and the audience.
- Who is the likely audience for NPR? How might that shape the complexity and sophistica-
  tion of the coverage?

Lay out the argument, the values, and the assumptions.
- The president, the senators, and the various experts all made separate arguments about
  government reorganization. What are they?
- Is *All Things Considered* implying an overall argument by virtue of the views it includes?
  What might that be? What views do you think the show has left out? Why?

Uncover the evidence.
- Given the nature of the interview (many voices, limited space), much of the evidence is
  summarized and implied. Were there places where you would have liked to see more?
  How much was merely asserted, and how much was supported?
- What was *ATC's* evidence for its overall position? Are the interviews offered as evidence of
  anything?

Evaluate the conclusion.
- Is there an overall conclusion here about political power and government reorganization?
  What is it? How persuasive is the conclusion?

Sort out the political implications.
- This interview is about bureaucratic turf battles, but it also shows people actually staking
  out their political turf. Is change possible under these conditions? What general lessons
  about politics are suggested here?

8.5 Special Message to the Congress Recommending the Establishment of a Department of National Defense

Harry S Truman, 19 December 1945

We saw in the preceding NPR transcript some of the kinds of concerns that arise when government attempts to reorganize existing units to better accomplish a goal that has been made urgent
by current events. That the Bush administration was not the first to face this challenge is apparent
in the following speech, given by President Harry Truman over half a century ago.

Truman is calling here for combining the different branches of the military, previously managed
by the War Department and the Department of the Navy, under a single command in the form of

a new Department of Defense. As with the Department of Homeland Security, this move involved restructuring existing government departments, with all the associated turf battles and disputes. In this speech, Truman lays out the case for why such a move was necessary. (We reprint only the first part of his long speech here.) What did this bureaucratic move have in common with the more recent creation of the Department of Homeland Security? How is it different?

To the Congress of the United States:

In my message of September 6, 1945, I stated that I would communicate with the Congress from time to time during the current session with respect to a comprehensive and continuous program of national security. I pointed out the necessity of making timely preparation for the Nation's long-range security now—while we are still mindful of what it has cost us in this war to have been unprepared.

On October 23, 1945, as part of that program, there was for your consideration a proposal for universal military training. It was based upon the necessities of maintaining a well-trained citizenry which could be quickly mobilized in time of need in support of a small professional military establishment. Long and extensive hearings have now been held by the Congress on this recommendation. I think that the proposal, in principle, has met with the overwhelming approval of the people of the United States.

We are discharging our armed forces now at the rate of 1,500,000 a month. We can with fairness no longer look to the veterans of this war for any future military service. It is essential therefore that universal training be instituted at the earliest possible moment to provide a reserve upon which we can draw if, unhappily, it should become necessary. A grave responsibility will rest upon the Congress if it continues to delay this most important and urgent measure.

Today, again in the interest of national security and world peace, I make this further recommendation to you. I recommend that the Congress adopt legislation combining the War and Navy Departments into one single Department of National Defense. Such unification is another essential step—along with universal training—in the development of a comprehensive and continuous program for our future safety and for the peace and security of the world.

One of the lessons which have most clearly come from the costly and dangerous experience of this war is that there must be unified direction of land, sea and air forces at home as well as in all other parts of the world where our Armed Forces are serving.

We did not have that kind of direction when we were attacked four years ago—and we certainly paid a high price for not having it.

In 1941, we had two completely independent organizations with no well-established

> What kinds of problems would be caused by going to war without a unified command structure?

habits of collaboration and cooperation between them. If disputes arose, if there was failure to agree on a question of planning or a question of action, only the President of the United States could make a decision effective on both. Besides, in 1941, the air power of the United States was not organized on a par with the ground and sea forces.

Our expedient for meeting these defects was the creation of the Joint Chiefs of Staff. On this Committee sat the President's Chief of Staff and the chiefs of the land forces, the naval forces, and the air forces. Under the Joint Chiefs were organized a number of committees bringing together personnel of the three services for joint strategic planning and for coordination of operations. This kind of coordination was better than no coordination at all, but it was in no sense a unified command.

In the theaters of operation, meanwhile, we went further in the direction of unity by establishing unified commands. We came to the conclusion—soon confirmed by experience—that any extended military effort required overall coordinated control in order to get the most out of the three armed forces. Had we not early in the war adopted this principle of a unified command for operations, our efforts, no matter how heroic, might have failed.

But we never had comparable unified direction or command in Washington. And even in the field, our unity of operations was greatly impaired by the differences in training, in doctrine, in communication systems, and in supply and distribution systems, that stemmed from the division of leadership in Washington.

It is true, we were able to win in spite of these handicaps. But it is now time to take stock, to discard obsolete organizational forms and to provide for the future the soundest, the most effective and the most economical kind of structure for our armed forces of which this most powerful Nation is capable.

I urge this as the best means of keeping the peace.

No nation now doubts the good will of the United States for maintenance of a lasting peace in the world. Our purpose is shown by our efforts to establish an effective United Nations Organization. But all nations—and particularly those unfortunate nations which have felt the heel of the Nazis, the Fascists or the Japs—know that desire for peace is futile unless there is also enough strength ready and willing to enforce that desire in any emergency. Among the things that have encouraged aggression and the spread of war in the past have been the unwillingness of the United States realistically to face this fact, and her refusal to fortify her aims of peace before the forces of aggression could gather in strength.

Now that our enemies have surrendered it has again become all too apparent that a portion of the American people are anxious to forget all about the war, and particularly to forget all the unpleasant factors which are required to prevent future wars.

Whether we like it or not, we must all recognize that the victory which we have won has placed upon the American people the continuing burden of responsibility for world leadership. The future peace of the world will depend in

large part upon whether or not the United States shows that it is really determined to continue in its role as a leader among nations. It will depend upon
whether or not the United States is willing to maintain the physical strength necessary to act as a safeguard against any future aggressor. Together with the other
United Nations, we must be willing to make the sacrifices necessary to protect
the world from future aggressive warfare. In short, we must be prepared to maintain in constant and immediate readiness sufficient military strength to convince
any future potential aggressor that this Nation, in its determination for a lasting
peace, means business.

We would be taking a grave risk with the national security if we did not move
now to overcome permanently the present imperfections in our defense organization. However great was the need for coordination and unified command in
World War II, it is sure to be greater if there is any future aggression against
world peace. Technological developments have made the Armed Services much
more dependent upon each other than ever before. The boundaries that once
separated the Army's battlefield from the Navy's battlefield have been virtually
erased. If there is ever going to be another global conflict, it is sure to take place
simultaneously on land and sea and in the air, with weapons of ever greater
speed and range. Our combat forces must work together in one team as they
have never been required to work together in the past.

We must assume, further, that another war would strike much more suddenly
than the last, and that it would strike directly at the United States. We cannot expect to be given the opportunity again to experiment in organization and in
ways of teamwork while the fighting proceeds. True preparedness now means
preparedness not alone in armaments and numbers of men, but preparedness
in organization also. It means establishing in peacetime the kind of military organization which will be able to meet the test of sudden attack quickly and without having to improvise radical readjustment in structure and habits.

The basic question is what organization will provide the most effective employment of our military resources in time of war and the most effective means
for maintaining peace. The manner in which we make this transition in the size,
composition, and organization of the armed forces will determine the efficiency
and cost of our national defense for many years to come.

Improvements have been made since 1941 by the President in the organization of the War and Navy Departments, under the War Powers Act. Unless the
Congress acts before these powers lapse, these Departments will revert to their
prewar organizational status. This would be a grievous mistake.

The Joint Chiefs of Staff are not a unified command. It is a committee which
must depend for its success upon the voluntary cooperation of its member agencies. During the war period of extreme national danger, there was, of course, a
high degree of cooperation. In peacetime the situation will be different. It must
not be taken for granted that the Joint Chiefs of Staff as now constituted will be
as effective in the apportionment of peacetime resources as they have been in

the determination of war plans and in their execution. As national defense appropriations grow tighter, and as conflicting interests make themselves felt in major issues of policy and strategy, unanimous agreements will become more difficult to reach.

It was obviously impossible in the midst of conflict to reorganize the armed forces of the United States along the lines here suggested. Now that our enemies have surrendered, I urge the Congress to proceed to bring about a reorganization of the management of the Armed Forces. . . .

I recommend that the reorganization of the armed services be along the following broad lines:

(1) There should be a single Department of National Defense. This Department should be charged with the full responsibility for armed national security. It should consist of the armed and civilian forces that are now included within the War and Navy Departments.

Truman refers elsewhere to the civilian command of the military as "one of the most fundamental of our democratic concepts." Why?

(2) The head of this Department should be a civilian, a member of the President's cabinet, to be designated as the Secretary of National Defense. Under him there should be a civilian Under Secretary and several civilian Assistant Secretaries.

(3) There should be three coordinated branches of the Department of National Defense: one for the land forces, one for the naval forces, and one for the air forces, each under an Assistant Secretary. The Navy should, of course, retain its own carrier, ship, and water-based aviation, which has proved so necessary for efficient fleet operation. And, of course, the Marine Corps should be continued as an integral part of the Navy.

(4) The Under Secretary and the remaining Assistant Secretaries should be available for assignment to whatever duties the President and the Secretary may determine from time to time.

(5) The President and the Secretary should be provided with ample authority to establish central coordinating and service organizations, both military and civilian, where these are found to be necessary. Some of these might be placed under Assistant Secretaries, some might be organized as central service organizations, and some might be organized in a top military staff to integrate the military leadership of the department. I do not believe that we can specify at this time the exact nature of these organizations. They must be developed over a pe-

riod of time by the President and the Secretary as a normal part of their executive responsibilities. Sufficient strength in these department-wide elements of the department, as opposed to the separate Service elements, will insure that real unification is ultimately obtained. The President and the Secretary should not be limited in their authority to establish department-wide coordinating and service organizations.

(6) There should be a Chief of Staff of the Department of National Defense. There should also be a commander for each of the three component branches—Army, Navy, and Air.

(7) The Chief of Staff and the commanders of the three coordinate branches of the Department should together constitute an advisory body to the Secretary of National Defense and to the President. There should be nothing to prevent the President, the Secretary, and other civilian authorities from communicating with the commanders of any of the components of the Department on such vital matters as basic military strategy and policy and the division of the budget. Furthermore, the key staff positions in the Department should be filled with officers drawn from all the services, so that the thinking of the Department would not be dominated by any one or two of the services.

As an additional precaution, it would be wise if the post of Chief of Staff were rotated among the several services, whenever practicable and advisable, at least during the period of evolution of the new unified Department. The tenure of the individual officer designated to serve as Chief of Staff should be relatively short—two or three years—and should not, except in time of a war emergency declared by the Congress, be extended beyond that period.

Unification of the services must be looked upon as a long-term job. We all recognize that there will be many complications and difficulties. Legislation of the character outlined will provide us with the objective, and with the initial means whereby forward-looking leadership in the Department, both military and civilian, can bring real unification into being. Unification is much more than a matter of organization. It will require new viewpoints, new doctrine, and new habits of thinking throughout the departmental structure. But in the comparative leisure of peacetime, and utilizing the skill and experience of our staff and field commanders who brought us victory, we should start at once to achieve the most efficient instrument of national safety.

Once a unified department has been established, other steps necessary to the formulation of a comprehensive national security program can be taken with greater ease. Much more than a beginning has already been made in achieving consistent political and military policy through the establishment of the State-War-Navy Coordinating Committee. With respect to military research, I have in a previous message to the Congress proposed the establishment of a federal research agency, among whose responsibilities should be the promotion and coordination of fundamental research pertaining to the defense and security of the Nation. The development of a coordinated, government-wide intelligence system is in process. As the advisability of additional action to insure a broad and coordinated program of national security becomes clear, I shall make appropriate recommendations or take the necessary action to that end.

The American people have all been enlightened and gratified by the free discussion which has taken place within the Services and before the committees of the Senate and the House of Representatives. The Congress, the people, and the President have benefited from a clarification of the issues that could have been provided in no other way. But however strong the opposition that has been expressed by some of our outstanding senior officers and civilians, I can assure the Congress that once unification has been determined upon as the policy of this nation, there is no officer or civilian in any Service who will not contribute his utmost to make the unification a success.

> Why is it important to have free discussion among the public about this kind of government reorganization? How does such discussion increase the legitimacy of the bureaucratic change in question?

I make these recommendations in the full realization that we are undertaking a task of greatest difficulty. But I am certain that when the task is accomplished, we shall have a military establishment far better adapted to carrying out its share of our national program for achieving peace and security.

Harry S Truman

Consider the source and the audience.

- Truman is speaking to Congress and also, indirectly, to the American public. How does that affect the way he frames the issue and the stakes he emphasizes?

Lay out the argument, the values, and the assumptions.

- How does Truman view America's role in the world and the kind of threats that are likely to be levied against it?
- Why does he feel that the United States could not count on another victory of the sort it won in World War II? What were the flaws in the existing military command structure?
- What would increase America's ability to provide security for its own citizens and its chances of continuing its leadership role in the world? Why?

Uncover the evidence.

- Does Truman offer real examples of problems under the existing military structure to support his case?
- How does he use logic, examples of changes in the military, and the threat of possible future defeat as support for the kind of change he wants to bring about?

Evaluate the conclusion.

- Was Truman right in saying that combining the two Departments was sufficient to offset the kinds of problems he foresaw? Has our military history since World War II borne that out?

Sort out the political implications.

- What would be the situation today if we were trying to conduct the war on terror with two unlinked Departments of War and Navy?
- Are the arguments for combining those Departments analogous to politicians' arguments for creating a single Department of Homeland Security?

CHAPTER 9

The Courts

Trying to persuade New Yorkers that they had nothing to fear from the proposed Constitution, founder Alexander Hamilton wrote in *The Federalist Papers* that the judicial branch was not a threat to liberty since it possessed the power neither of the purse nor the sword. Unable to raise money or troops, insulated from political pressure and public opinion by lifetime tenure, it would be the "least dangerous branch" of the new government.

While the original Supreme Court was an institution of so little prestige that President George Washington had trouble finding qualified people who were willing to sit on it, today's Court is a monument of political power that has made decisions as central as whether someone has the right to die, to speak freely, to have an abortion, or to go to the public school of his or her choice. In 2000, it took on the ultimate political role of kingmaker, when a 5–4 Republican majority decided the closely contested presidential election in favor of George Bush.

In this chapter we deal with complicated and abstract issues that focus on the political power of the courts. The overarching theme in all these issues is that, contrary to Hamilton's claims, the courts are powerful and political institutions; they are deeply involved in divvying up scarce resources, choosing who gets to have their way about the kind of society we live in, and ruling on the most fundamental issues: who lives, who dies, and who gets to decide.

The articles in this chapter are selected to help you see how these abstract concepts play out in the political world. The first selection is a TV interview with a man who decided to bill a court for his time when he was asked to hold himself ready to do jury duty, a civic obligation most of us will face at some time in our lives. This selection highlights the difficulty of balancing our self-interest and our public interest. The second selection is a National Public Radio interview with several people who speculate on the different sorts of people Bush and Gore would have appointed to the Supreme Court, and debate whether justices ought to follow the Constitution literally or interpret it more flexibly. The third examines the increasingly contentious process of Senate confirmation of presidential nominations for the federal bench. The fourth looks behind the scenes of the Court's controversial decision in *Bush v. Gore*. Finally, we turn to *The Federalist Papers* themselves, for Hamilton's original explanation of why the judiciary is the least dangerous branch of government. Would he be surprised by the judicial politics of today?

9.1 Interview with David Williamson

Greta Van Susteren, *Fox on the Record with Greta Van Susteren,* 4 September 2002

Meet David Williamson, software consultant and irate citizen. Summoned by the court to be available for jury duty during the month of August, Williamson took matters into his own hands. Deciding that the $40 per day jury wages would not compensate him for time lost, he billed the court at his consultancy rate of $100 an hour, for twenty-one eight-hour days. Unamused, the judge threatened him with a contempt of court citation.

In this Fox excerpt, legal analyst Greta Van Susteren interviews the man about his jury duty experience. Most Americans can be sure of being called for jury duty at some point in their lives, and for many it can be a lengthy, tedious, and costly experience. While Williamson's response may seem extreme, many Americans share his frustration, with the result that they frequently find excuses not to fulfill what amounts to one of the few real civic responsibilities we as Americans have. Before we write off Williamson as an ingrate or celebrate him as a hero, consider what the court system could do to make the obligation to sit on a jury more palatable to citizens. After all, our Constitution guarantees us a trial by jury. What if there were not enough juries to go around?

VAN SUSTEREN: Many Americans have tried to get out of jury duty at one time or another, but, instead of making an excuse, our next guest sent a federal court in Texas a bill for his time, a bill for more than $16,000.

That apparently, didn't sit so well with the judge who struck back with a notice to show cause why he should not be held in contempt, writing, "Although Mr. Williamson could live in a country which does not require jury service, such as Iraq, Cuba, North Korea, Russia, Mr. Williamson wants the benefits of [an] American citizen but, apparently, without fulfilling the responsibility."

David Williamson joins us from San Antonio, Texas.

Welcome, David.

DAVID WILLIAMSON, $100-AN-HOUR JUROR: Thank you, ma'am. It's nice to be here.

VAN SUSTEREN: All right. All right, David. It seems like you picked a fight with a federal judge. And what happened?

> What is the judge saying here about the relationship of the rights we have as Americans and the responsibilities we bear to the system?

WILLIAMSON: Well, I was summoned for jury duty, and, during the process of being summoned—and I was explaining to him why it would be a hardship for me to spend a long time in jury duty. I asked him for a reprieve or an excuse.

And the clerk sent back a—an excuse—a letter telling me I was excused, but she also told me to hold my entire month of August open for them. And I'm a consultant, I don't work for a company, and so a month without the ability to do any work is a month without revenue.

So I figured this . . .

VAN SUSTEREN: All right, Let me back up for a second. Was [this] the first time you'd been summoned for jury duty?

WILLIAMSON: No, ma'am. This was about the third time that I had been summoned for jury duty, and, each time, I had explained to them the hardship it would create and asked them to be rescheduled.

I'd also asked in letters—several letters to—if I could sit with somebody and schedule a time where it would be convenient for them and me to come and do jury duty. I never tried to get out of jury duty.

VAN SUSTEREN: All right. The judge wasn't particularly amused, and so he sent— to say it politely. He sent you a show cause order, means that you better get down here, pal, or you're in big trouble, and I'm going to send the sheriffs out to pick you up. What happened? Did you show up in court on the show cause hearing?

WILLIAMSON: Well, the show cause order contained two clauses. One was—is I could either go to court and explain to him why I didn't want—in his words, why I didn't want to go to court—or didn't want to do jury duty, or the second one is—the second part of the show cause order said that I could purge myself of the entire show cause order by showing up and—just showing up for jury duty, and I sent him a reply back explaining to him that that's exactly what I would do.

VAN SUSTEREN: And, of course, I have seen the reply. You a little pushed his buttons and tweaked him. It isn't quite so low-key because, in your letter, you even put the definition of "arrogance" from the Webster dictionary, right?

WILLIAMSON: Oh, yes, ma'am. I . . .

VAN SUSTEREN: OK. So you were . . .

WILLIAMSON: You know . . .

VAN SUSTEREN: You were pitching right back at the judge, right?

WILLIAMSON: Sure. You know, this—this is a free country, and we have the right to question leaders, you know, to paraphrase a movie, but we have [the] right to question those guys, and the judge is a leader like the president is and just like everybody else. He's an authority figure. So I have the right to question him and the right to express my opinion.

Williamson says he was exercising his right as a citizen to question authority. What are the limits of such a right?

VAN SUSTEREN: All right. So you—so you show up. And what happens when you walk through the courthouse doors?

WILLIAMSON: Well, my intent was to go to serve jury duty and just purge myself of the order because I figured I'd made him just a little bit unhappy, and, as I walked through the metal detectors, I was met by two federal marshals, and they escorted me into the courtroom and sat me at the table. . . .

VAN SUSTEREN: So what—so what happened? I mean, what's the ultimate—what's the end of this story?

WILLIAMSON: Oh, well, the end of the story is—is that I have done my jury duty, and—which I never didn't want to do in the first place. I've done my jury duty, and I thankfully don't have to be called again for another two years, at least to his court, and I have resubmitted my invoice.

VAN SUSTEREN: For how much?

WILLIAMSON: Well, $16,800—800 and some odd dollars. . . .

VAN SUSTEREN: Do you think you'll ever get paid the amount of money for this invoice?

WILLIAMSON: I sure hope so. I—you know, this—the court ordered me basically to not do any work for an entire month. I took that as a contract, and so I explained that to them.

If it wasn't a contract, I think that they should send me a letter back saying, "No, that wasn't our intent," and all they would have to do was just say, "We're planning on you being there the end of the week—or the end of the month or the middle of the month or whatever," so I could plan my time.

I do a lot of business outside the City of San Antonio.

> Could the court have done something to make this experience easier on Williamson, such as not requiring him to hold an entire month in reserve?

VAN SUSTEREN: All right. David, listen, I'll tell you what. If the judge does pay you, I hope you'll let us know. I think you'll probably be the first ever to get paid, but it's not—it's a pretty high bill.

But thank you very much for joining us. And don't charge us for your time tonight.

WILLIAMSON: OK. This one's on me.

VAN SUSTEREN: Oh, good. It's on the house. Thank you. All right.

WILLIAMSON: Thank you. Yes, ma'am.

Consider the source and the audience.

- Although Greta Van Susteren's role is that of neutral legal analyst, making complex legal issues intelligible for a general audience, Fox itself tends to promote a more conservative point of view. Would Williamson's citizen protest be more likely to resonate with conservatives or with liberals? Why?

Lay out the argument, the values, and the assumptions.

- What exactly does Williamson claim about jury duty? He says he is happy to serve, but under what conditions? Is his attitude consistent with the purpose of jury duty?
- He clearly values his freedoms as an American. What can we infer that he believes about the corresponding responsibilities of citizenship?

Uncover the evidence.

- Does Williamson offer any evidence for his claims? Did he, for instance, consult a lawyer to see if his summons for jury duty constituted a contract? Does he indicate that he tried in any other way to get the court to be more specific about when he was to show up?

Evaluate the conclusion.

- Williamson arrives at the conclusion that since the court told him to hold himself ready to serve during the month of August, the court owes him for his time during that period. He responded by billing the court. How else could he have made his point that the court's sweeping request for him to remain available for a month was inconvenient and costly to him? How effective were his actions?

Sort out the political implications.

- Experts agree that some courts are not very efficient or reasonable in their efforts to get citizens to sit on jury duty, and many citizens balk. How might they go about inspiring more cooperation among potential jurors?
- What should our public service cost us? What's reasonable? How much do we owe back for the considerable freedoms we enjoy?

9.2 Look at Presidential Politics and the Supreme Court

Melinda Penkava, *Talk of the Nation,* National Public Radio, 1 November 2000

This is an excerpt from a National Public Radio show, aired just before the 2000 presidential election, on what impact a Gore or Bush victory would have had on the composition of the Supreme Court. Unlike the previous interview, this one involves multiple participants, which makes it trickier for a listener and even a reader to follow the various strands of argument. You might try jotting down the names of the NPR expert (Nina Totenberg), the conservative guest (Clint Bolick), and the liberal guest (Ralph Neas) and keeping track of their arguments so you can see if they make sense.

It is worth paying the extra attention in this case, because the concepts being debated are central to understanding the Supreme Court. What different definitions are given to the concepts of strict constructionism and judicial activism, and what role do they play in American politics? The speakers use these terms in different ways, so be clear on what they mean. What policy stands are likely to be taken by a judge appointed by a Republican president as opposed to those taken by a Democratic appointee?

MELINDA PENKAVA, host: It's Talk of the Nation. I'm Melinda Penkava in for Juan Williams. Next Tuesday when we choose our next president, we may also be choosing the direction of the U.S. Supreme Court for a period much longer than the next president's term in office. Here's why. It's been six years since a Supreme Court justice has been appointed, the longest period in the last 100 years. Two justices are older than 75 and retirement seems imminent and the next president could be appointing one, two, even three justices before 2004. And that could undo the balance that now exists between conservatives, moderates and liberals on the high court.

So the Supreme Court is at a fork in the road. Whether the court heads left or right depends on who is tapped to be a justice. And that decision rests with the next president, presumably George W. Bush or Al Gore. And both have given signals of the type of justices they would appoint.

Governor GEORGE W. BUSH (Republican, Presidential Candidate): I'll put competent judges on the bench, people who will strictly interpret the Constitution and will not use the bench to write social policy. And that's going to be a big difference between my opponent and me. I believe that the judges ought not to take the place of the legislative branch of government, that they're appointed for life and that they ought to look at the Constitution as sacred. They shouldn't misuse their bench. I don't believe in liberal activist judges. I believe in strict constructionists. And those are the kind of judges I will appoint.

> *What are the essential differences in the views expressed by Bush and Gore? What makes one conservative and one liberal?*

Vice President AL GORE (Democrat, Presidential Candidate): In my view, the Constitution ought to be interpreted as a document that grows with our country and our history. And I believe, for example, that there is a right of privacy in the Fourth Amendment. And when the phrase "strict constructionist" is used and when the names of Scalia and Thomas are used as benchmarks for who would be appointed, those are code words, and nobody should mistake this, for saying that the governor would appoint people who would overturn *Roe v. Wade.*

PENKAVA: Abortion is mentioned most often as hanging in the balance, but there is much more in play with the next Supreme Court nominations. With just six days to go till the election, we look today at what the Supreme Court might do depending on whether it is Al Gore or George W. Bush who are making the appointments.

Joining us here in Studio 3A are Nina Totenberg, NPR's legal affairs correspondent, Clint Bolick, who is vice president and director of litigation at the Institute for Justice, and Ralph Neas, who is president of People for the American Way.

Well, the words "strict constructionist" came up in both the candidates' replies to that question during the debate and so I would like to devote some time to that. Nina, where are we going with this strict constructionist? Can we agree on what the definition is here?

NINA TOTENBERG (NPR Legal Affairs Correspondent): Well, yes and no. I mean, it was first used as far as I know by President Nixon and when he said it, he meant more or less law and order judges. And it came to mean much more than that. I think it's fair to say it is a code word for a judge who interprets the Constitution in an extremely—narrow has a sort of pejorative tone to it and I don't mean it to, but in the legal profession they call it an originalist way, meaning as the framers of the Constitution would have intended it and understood it at the time it was adopted.

The contrary view is that the country changes. I guess the most obvious example of that is wire tapping didn't exist at the time the Constitution was framed and the country changes. Its mores change. Abortion was simply not done at the time of the beginning of the Constitution was written because, among other things, it was too dangerous for women. So what does it mean to have a guaranteed right to be free from unreasonable search and seizure? Does that imply a right of privacy? For example, the non-strict constructionist would say, "Yes, it does." The strict constructionist would say, "No, it doesn't."

With these candidates, though, I think there's less mystery than we might think because they've told us who their role models are. And pressed on the subject, Governor Bush has said his role model for a Supreme Court justice is Antonin Scalia or Clarence Thomas, the two most conservative members of the court, strict constructionists by anybody's definition, originalists. And Vice President Gore has said that his model, it was Thurgood Marshall, the first African-American to serve on the court, who was clearly a more liberal justice than any justice currently sitting, including the two Clinton nominees.

PENKAVA: Mm-hmm. And, Clint Bolick, this is what you would like to see happen.

Mr. CLINT BOLICK (Institute for Justice): Oh, absolutely. And I do think there are certainly differences that can take place among strict constructionists. For example, I consider myself one but I very much believe that privacy is protected by the Constitution. But what we mean by this term, "strict constructionist," is a judge who feels bound by the rule of law. That the Constitution does change in terms of the circumstances to which it applies, but the principles don't change and a judge is not free to substitute his or her principles for the principles that are in our organic law. Now the way to do that is to change the Constitution, not just to change the judges.

So for example, there was an era of liberal court activism for many years in this country in which judges were doing things like creating welfare entitlements, like imposing racial quotas and forced busing, like letting criminals out on technicalities. That was an era that was not a strict constructionist era. That was an era of activism and over the last 10 or 15 years, we have a court that really does hew to the rule of law very closely. It protects individual liberties, but at the same time it feels itself bound by law and by precedent, And I think most Americans feel very good about the court that we have right now.

PENKAVA: But there is this balance and some might say an uneasy balance right now on the court because it is moderate, liberal, conservative there and just changing one justice, two justices, would that alter things, Ralph Neas?

Mr. RALPH NEAS (President, People for the American Way): Melinda, let me first discuss strict constructionism. Nina was correct in part. Strict constructionism actually goes back to 1955. Strict constructionism started then, those opposed to *Brown vs. Board of Education* and desegregating our nation's schools. It certainly arose during the Nixon years in the criminal law capacity, and then after *Roe vs. Wade* with respect to abortion rights, it really became, again, the rallying cry of those who elected to turn back the clock, not just on abortion rights, but civil rights, the environment, etc., etc.

Right now we have a conservative court, a court that on a lot of issues is 5-to-4, resurrecting the doctrine of state's rights, trumping many of the civil rights laws—for example, the Age Discrimination Act in Employment that was passed in the 1970s. The disability rights laws now are threatened. But what we're afraid of, and this is what you were getting to in your comment, one or two more right-wing justices in the mold of Antonin Scalia and Clarence Thomas, we could have 100 Supreme Court precedents overturned affecting not just *Roe vs. Wade* and abortion rights, the environment, gun control, campaign finance reform, civil rights, religious liberty. It goes on and on and on. This is why we say this is the most important national issue, the future of the Supreme Court, in the most important national election since 1932.

PENKAVA: Mm-hmm. Nina?

TOTENBERG: Well, I think the discussion about who's a strict constructionist and who's for hewing to the principles of law is almost—it's just a discussion almost not worth having because if you—either side can make the case. But if you look at the current court, which is, as both these gentlemen have said, split 5-to-4 in more than a quarter of its decisions last term, in the last five years it has struck down more than a dozen I think state and federal laws, which is—you know, by anybody's definition, it is not deferring to democracy. Right? It says, "Hello, legislatures, state or federal, you passed a law and we're telling you you can't have that law because it's unconstitutional." Now some of those are liberal laws and some of those are conservative laws. Some of them are so-called partial-birth abortion laws. Some of them are—one federal one was the Communications Decency Act.

> What is at stake for each side in being able to claim to be the party that "hews to the principles of law"?

I mean, so the job of the Supreme Court is to say when the legislature has stepped over the line. And at almost any juncture, either liberals or conservatives can make the argument that the existing court is an activist court because when it lives up to that expectation, it is saying to the legislature, "You can't do this. What your constituents wanted you to do, you can't do. The Constitution says you can't do it. Majoritarian rule doesn't work here. The principles of the Constitution trump it.

PENKAVA: I wonder if "activist" is a label that some people throw at it if it's a decision they don't like."

Mr. BOLICK: Well, Nina, I think, is not really following what I would consider to be what a strict constructionist judge is. A strict constructionist judge is not one who sits back and lets the legislature do anything. The Constitution is a document that limits government power. And simply deferring to democracy is not what a strict constructionist judge does. Well, let me give you a specific example. Take the area of school desegregation, for example. A judge who believes in the rule of law strikes down segregation as unconstitutional, in violation of the principle of equal protection of the law.

A liberal activist judge takes over the school system and runs it for 50 years, getting into the minutia of really legislative and executive functions. That's the difference.

A judge judges. A judge declares a law unconstitutional or constitutional, but a judge does not engage in legislative or executive functions such as imposing taxes, such as deciding what teachers will be hired where and those sorts of things that really enrage people, and appropriately so because they're simply not judicial functions. And that's the difference.

I agree with Ralph. This is the sleeper issue in the campaign. Not only the Supreme Court but Bill Clinton has appointed roughly half of the federal judges across the board, so we're at the tipping point, not just on the Supreme Court but the federal judiciary as a whole. We're one vote away from going back to a liberal activist court and I think that's the real impact of this election.

PENKAVA: Ralph Neas?

Mr. NEAS: The Gallup poll came out about a week or so ago, I'm not sure how much of a sleeper issue it is anymore. The future of the Supreme Court ranked ahead of the Middle East, it ranked ahead of the stock market. Seventy-two percent of the American people now say it's either extremely important or very important, for good reason.

PENKAVA: Now were those people who were Independent and hadn't . . .

Mr. NEAS: Registered voters.

PENKAVA: Oh, just all registered voters.

Mr. NEAS: Registered voters.

PENKAVA: OK.

Mr. NEAS: But I want to make this point. It is an activist court. I think all nine of them are activists and the conservatives are in charge right now. There have been 23 acts of Congress invalidated in the last four or five years—four or five a year. In the previous 200 years or 183, one per year. This is a court that has an agenda and anyone who cares about abortion rights, anyone who cares about the environment or civil rights or religious liberty should be absolutely terrified at the prospect of a president who says that Scalia and Thomas are his favorite justices. One or two more Scalias or Thomases and we'll have fundamental rights and liberties that we've accepted and taken for granted for decades vanish overnight.

> What is the argument over "activism" about? Does it actually mean something, or was Penkava right when she said earlier that both sides are using it to signal decisions they don't like?

TOTENBERG: Well, you know, I think that it's a very interesting thing. As a person who writes these stories every eight years about the Supreme Court, now this is going to really be very important and the next president will be picking justices. And usually nobody pays any attention except my editors. This year, they pay attention and, you know, there's polling data that shows it is an issue. Whether it's a determinative issue, I don't know. I asked Frank Luntz to include some Supreme Court questions in some focus groups that he did with independent voters. And for example on the one he did at the Republican convention with Independent voters, the issue cut always against Bush and for Gore. That means that, in this particular case, four out of 36 people who were at this focus group, all of whom classified themselves as either Independents or Republican-leaning Independents, said they were worried about the future of the court and it was making them more likely to vote for Al Gore. But it is the base, normally, that cares about this issue: the lefties and the righties.

PENKAVA: Now we're seeing a few in the middle maybe—that may be their determining factor. Nina, thanks for joining us. I know you have to get back to a story right now.

TOTENBERG: Thank you.

PENKAVA: NPR's legal affairs correspondent Nina Totenberg. . . .

PENKAVA: But there is—as I understand it, there is a level of federal judges, appointees, from previous administrations, conservatives, who are strict constructionists and, for instance, have ruled that the Clean Water Act that the EPA was trying to impose was—they couldn't do that because Congress had given the EPA authority it shouldn't have given it. And as I understand, they didn't define what, you know, protecting public health meant. And I wonder if that can qualify as activism on the other side as well here. I mean, because it seems like people would say, "Well, you know, public health is so people are able to drink water that's clean."

Mr. BOLICK: Well, here's . . .

PENKAVA: Are they not activists on the right, then?

Mr. BOLICK: What happens is that you have a Congress that is also very activist and in many instances Congress says, "We're going to pass vague laws or laws that exceed our authority and just see whether the courts have the guts to strike them down." It's very important that courts act in holding Congress within its delegated powers. This is actually a huge issue of difference between the Republican appointees or some of the Republican appointees to the court and President Clinton's appointees to the court. We've looked at the voting records of the various justices over the years and in cases that present individual liberties against federal government power, exactly the kind of case that you're talking about, Justice Ginsburg, a Clinton appointee, has voted to strike down government power in only 13 percent of the cases and Breyer in 0 percent of the cases. That to me is a judge who is giving far too much deference to government and far too little protection to individual liberties.

PENKAVA: And I'm guessing, Ralph Neas, that you might say that there's a difference between a judge telling exactly what the quota has to be and a judge saying let's strike down the Clean Water Act?

Mr. NEAS: There are definitely activists right now on the right. But let's establish a fundamental fact. Since 1950, more than 70 percent of the Supreme Court justices have been appointed by Republicans. We've had a Republican Court for 50 years. Seventy-seven percent of the justices now are Republican. But those Republican justices and Democratic justices have looked at the Constitution, they've looked at original intent, they've looked at the legislative history, but they've also seen the Constitution as an evolving document. Principles, yes, but there is a flexibility that our Founding Fathers intended. And what we've had over this 50 years is a revolution, a bloodless revolution with respect to the social justice in this country, whether it's abortion rights, whether it's civil rights, whether it's the environment or privacy.

What Clint Bolick wants, what George W. Bush wants, what Jerry Falwell and Pat Robertson want is to overturn 40 or 50 years' worth of precedence. That's their definition of strict constructionism. That's what we face. We've got the clearest choice with respect to presidential candidates, Ralph Nader notwithstanding. There is a chasm between these two candidates and what George W. Bush and the right want to do is upend the social justice progress of the last five decades.

PENKAVA: Clint?

Mr. BOLICK: That's a pretty strong statement.

Mr. NEAS: Yes.

Mr. BOLICK: Conservatives tend to be much more deferential to precedent than liberal judges do and I think this court is as well. Where we are right now, I think that most Americans like the court that they have right now. But where we are really close to a real revolution is going back to the era of the '60s and the '70s. For example, on issues of civil rights. This vote is one—this court is one vote away, only one, from upholding racial preferences carte blanche, from upholding racial gerrymandering, from striking down private property rights protections that are very, very essential. And also on criminal issues, this court has preserved the Miranda right but at the same time you don't see judges today going around letting people off on technicalities.

Many of the Clinton appointees have done exactly that and it's provoked a great deal of appropriate irritation on the part of people seeing judges doing things like that.

PENKAVA: Well, I want to get back to the race. You know, a second ago, Ralph Neas, you mentioned Ralph Nader and he's made the comment that there's—it's no great shakes, what happens there. I think he even went so far as to say that *Roe vs. Wade* even if it were overturned, you know, the states could still allow abortion. So is Ralph Nader really bringing much to the table on this kind of discussion?

Mr. NEAS: As a friend of Ralph's for a quarter of a century and someone who came to public service in large measure because of Ralph Nader, I can't tell you how disappointed I am in him. His statements are absolutely outrageous and irresponsible with respect to *Roe vs. Wade* and he said recently there has been no retrenchment on civil rights since the Dred Scott decision, which would come as a surprise to post-reconstruction in the 19th century and the Reagan-Bush years and the middle of this last century. So I'm not sure what Ralph is thinking. He's certainly not thinking clearly or accurately. There is a tremendous difference between Gore and Bush on the Supreme Court. And on the Supreme Court issue alone, anyone thinking of voting for Ralph Nader should think about protecting the Constitution and fully realize that we could lose everything that Ralph Nader did over the last 25 or 30 years as well as the Constitution rights and liberties that so many million of Americans depend on.

Consider the source and the audience.

- Who is most likely to listen to a news show on National Public Radio? What kind of audience is the show serving, and how might that affect its content?

Lay out the argument, the values, and the assumptions.

- There are several different arguments being made here by different speakers. Try to isolate them and see what's involved.
- What is Nina Totenberg's role here? What values does she bring to her appearance on the show? What does she have to say about strict constructionism and judicial activism?
- What is Bolick's role? What are his values? (See the Institute for Justice website at *http:// www.ij.org.*) Why does he adhere to an understanding of activism that is essentially the opposite of strict constructionism—activism as moving beyond the specific intentions of the founders?
- How about Neas? What are his role and values? (See the People for the American Way web site at *http://www.pfaw.org.*) Why does he broaden the definition of activism to include a proactive judicial role of overturning what legislatures do?
- Despite the dispute between Bolick and Neas over who is really an activist justice, can you figure out how each one thinks a justice should rule and what the role of the Supreme Court should be?

Uncover the evidence.

- What is really the issue between these two men? What kinds of evidence do they provide to support their claims? Would other evidence be necessary to convince you that one or the other is right, or is this really a debate about value preferences that is not subject to factual proof?

Evaluate the conclusion.

- What difference does it make which definition of activism one accepts?
- What do *you* think the role of the Supreme Court justice should be?

Sort out the political implications.

- How would a Court appointed by someone with Bush's views differ from one appointed by someone with Gore's? What do you think the effect of Bush's appointments to the Court is likely to be?

9.3 Obstruction of Judges

Jeffrey Rosen, *New York Times Magazine,* 11 August 2002

The Constitution gives the Senate the job of approving presidential nominees to the federal judiciary from the Supreme Court on down. This article is about the growing trend in the last twenty years for senators to subject nominees to the federal appeals courts to the same stringent ideological tests that they have been applying to Supreme Court nominees since the 1970s. The result of this practice is that when the president and the majority party in the Senate are from different parties, many nominees can be blocked. The same concerns we read about in the last selection—

about whether the Constitution should be read strictly or flexibly, and whether judges should take an active role in overturning the laws of legislatures and making policy—come into play in these decisions. Are such concerns relevant at the appellate level? Are there "litmus tests" that should be given to potential judges? What are the consequences of using them?

Allen Snyder and John Roberts are two of the most respected appellate lawyers in Washington. They were at the top of their classes at Harvard Law School, and they went on to clerk for Justice William Rehnquist on the Supreme Court. Both ended up at the glamorous law firm Hogan & Hartson, where they became partners as well as friends, advising each other about ethical issues and preparing each other for arguments before the Supreme Court. In recognition of their exceptional talents, they were nominated by the president to sit on the U.S. Court of Appeals for the District of Columbia Circuit, widely viewed as the second most important court in the nation.

Roberts, a Republican, was nominated by the first President Bush; Snyder, a Democrat, was nominated by President Clinton. But neither nominee made it through the Senate, and together they stand as examples—call them exhibits A and B—of a crisis that has paralyzed the judicial nomination process for more than a decade. Roberts was nominated by Bush in January 1992. The Senate, controlled at the time by the Democrats, refused to give him a hearing, and his nomination lapsed with Bush's defeat that November. In September 1999, Clinton nominated Snyder; the Senate, back in the hands of Republicans, refused to bring his nomination to a vote. Last May, the second President Bush renominated Roberts to the seat he was denied a decade ago—but just when Senate Republicans were on the verge of scheduling a hearing, James Jeffords of Vermont renounced the G.O.P., and the Democrats took control once again. Now more than a year has passed since Roberts's second nomination, and the Judiciary Committee has still not scheduled a hearing and is in no rush to do so. "I can't tell you," Senator Charles Schumer said when I asked if Roberts would get a hearing. "I think it's the intention to have hearings on most of the nominees, although we're not going to be stampeded. What the ideologues want to do is stampede us."

The confirmation process for federal judges is in something of a meltdown. Appellate nominations are now provoking a level of partisan warfare that used to be reserved for the Supreme Court. In a fit of recriminations, Democrats and Republicans are blaming each other for changing the rules of the game. James Buckley, a former judge on the D.C. Circuit, recently wrote an op-ed column in *The Wall Street Journal* accusing Senate Democrats of "obstruction of justice" for refusing to grant hearings to President Bush's appellate nominees. "This extraordinary inaction is having a significant effect on the court's ability to handle its workload," he wrote. Democrats made identical charges against Republicans during the Clinton years.

Already this year the Democrats have rejected one Bush nominee, Charles Pickering, and are now trying to defeat another, Priscilla Owen, largely because of concerns about *Roe v. Wade*. And the recent decision by a federal appeals court in California striking down the Pledge of Allegiance has only fanned the partisan flames. "This highlights what the fight over federal judges is all about," said the Senate minority leader, Trent Lott.

Despite the suggestion of Republicans, the federal appeals courts are not yet paralyzed by the slowdown of the confirmation process, which began during the first Bush administration. The U.S. Court of Appeals for the D.C. Circuit, which had 12 judges at its peak, has been able to function with four standing vacancies. (Indeed, Republicans argued during the Clinton years that the court had too little work to occupy 10 judges.) And the Pledge of Allegiance decision—written by a Nixon appointee—will almost certainly be reversed.

Like the fight over abortion, however, the Pledge of Allegiance decision is a symptom of a broader dysfunction in American politics: the legalization of the culture wars. That phenomenon, which is at the heart of the breakdown of the confirmation process, has its roots in the 1980's, when an army of interest groups on the left and on the right were created to lobby the courts for victories over cultural disputes that each side was unable to win in the legislatures. Right-wing groups resolved to use the courts to restrict Congress's power to pass anti-discrimination laws, affirmative action and environmental regulations, while left-wing groups pledged to extend the logic of *Roe v. Wade* to protect gay rights, the right to die and other forms of personal autonomy.

> This idea of fighting culture wars in the courts is an important one for Rosen's argument. What exactly does he mean?

These groups cut their teeth on Supreme Court nominations, especially the conflagrations over Robert Bork and Clarence Thomas. But now there hasn't been a Supreme Court vacancy for eight years—the longest period since the beginning of the 19th century. Biding their time until the next Supreme Court explosion, the interest groups have been working to justify their continued existence by turning their vast screening machinery on the lower federal courts. Both sides have urged sympathetic senators to treat each nominee to the federal appellate courts as a Supreme Court justice in miniature, and to ask the nominees not merely whether they would follow Supreme Court precedents like *Roe v. Wade* but also whether they personally agree with them.

This strategy makes no sense. Unlike Supreme Court justices, lower-court judges are required to apply Supreme Court precedents, rather than second-guess them. By treating every appellate-court nomination as a dress rehearsal for a Supreme Court battle to come, the Senate and the interest groups have created the misleading impression that lower-court judges are more polarized and less constrained than they actually are. In fact, on the best functioning appellate courts, there are clear right and wrong answers in most cases that judges, Democrats and Republicans alike, can identify after careful study of the complicated facts and relevant precedents. By subjecting lower-court nominees to brutalizing confirmation hearings in the Supreme Court style, the Senate is contributing to the Clarence Thomas syndrome, which occurs when a judge is so scarred and embittered by his confirmation ordeal that he becomes radicalized on the bench, castigating his opponents and rewarding his supporters. In short, by exaggerating the stakes in the lower-court nomination battles, interest groups on both sides may be encouraging the appointment of judges who will fulfill their worst fears.

As a case study in the way that nominees on both sides are being caricatured by the confirmation process, I arranged to meet with Allen Snyder and with John Roberts. Snyder, who is 56, is based at home these days; after his nomination died in the Senate in 2000, he resigned his partnership at Hogan and took early retirement.

Quiet and mild-mannered, Snyder exudes moderation and weighs his words carefully. But he is clearly still frustrated by the fact that the opposition to him was almost entirely masked. "As a nominee, you get virtually no information as to what's going on," he said in a conversation at Hogan & Hartson. "I got a call the afternoon before that I was getting a hearing the very next morning." Snyder's hearing in May 2000, eight months after he was nominated, was something of a lovefest. Though he was nominated by Clinton, he had the support of several influential conservatives, including his former boss, Chief Justice Rehnquist, and Robert Bork, who worked with him on behalf of Netscape in the Justice Department's suit against Microsoft. At the hearing, whose chairman was Senator Arlen Specter of Pennsylvania, Snyder proclaimed his devotion to judicial restraint. "Senator Specter congratulated me on how well things had gone and told me he was confident I would be confirmed and told me I would be a great judge," Snyder recalls. "And then the committee never took a vote."

A week after the hearing, *The Wall Street Journal* wrote a vicious editorial attacking Senator Orrin Hatch for having granted Snyder a hearing in the first place. Titled "A G.O.P. Judicial Debacle?" the editorial's only charge against Snyder was that he served as a lawyer for Bruce Lindsey, President Clinton's White House counsel. Calling the nomination Snyder's reward for "counseling the consigliere," the editorial pointed out that "conservatives still hold a 6–4 ideological edge on the D.C. Circuit on most issues" and that Snyder's confirmation might mean "a 5–5 split that could haunt the first year of a Bush Presidency." Blaming the Democrats for having "established a precedent for sitting on election-year nominees" by denying a hearing to John Roberts in 1992, the editorial concluded, "If Senator Hatch lacks the backbone, we suspect the nomination could still be stopped with the right phone call—to Senate Majority Leader

Trent Lott from George W. Bush." Shortly after, Snyder was told that Lott had decided to kill his nomination.

"I think what happened to John Roberts and others caused there to be a sense of payback," Snyder says.

A few days after meeting Snyder, I returned to the 13th floor of Hogan & Hartson to meet Roberts. If Snyder is quiet and gently formal, Roberts, 47, is boyish and ebullient. Although he felt frustrated and out-of-sorts during the wait for a hearing during his first nomination, now, during his second, he is 10 years older and resolved to be more patient, fully aware of the uncertainties ahead. The Democrats have not yet decided whether they will give Roberts a hearing. And even if he does get a hearing, his candidacy has been thrown into further question by the Democrats' decision to make each confirmation a referendum on a single case: *Roe v. Wade.*

In 1990, when he was a deputy solicitor general, Roberts signed a brief in a case about abortion financing that included a footnote calling for *Roe v. Wade* to be overturned, the Bush administration's official position at the time. "I think that raises very serious questions about where he is on this issue," I was told by Kate Michelman, the head of the National Abortion and Reproductive Rights Action League. Was it really fair, I asked, to hold Roberts accountable for defending the Bush administration's position, which was after all his job? "I think Roberts is going to have to speak directly as to whether or not he believes that the Constitution protects the right to choose," Michelman replied, "and if not, then I think he should not sit on the bench."

Michelman's challenge—that all Bush's judicial nominees must swear a loyalty oath not merely to accept *Roe* but personally to embrace it—is one that several Democratic senators on the Judiciary Committee have taken up. Several of the Democrats say they are haunted by the example of Clarence Thomas, who swore at his confirmation hearing that he believed that the Constitution protects a right to privacy and then promptly voted to overturn *Roe v. Wade.* To avoid a repeat of this, Senate Democrats have decided to ask nominees not merely whether they would apply *Roe v. Wade* in the future but whether they have questioned it in the past.

In the case of Priscilla Owen, a nominee to the federal appeals court in Texas, the Democrats' concerns are arguably justified: even President Bush's White House counsel, Alberto Gonzales, called Owen's attempt to narrow a Texas law allowing minors to have abortions without their parents' consent "an unconscionable act of judicial activism" when he was a colleague of Owen's in Texas. But the Democrats have also opposed other nominees who had no clear judicial record on abortion. During the confirmation hearing earlier this year for Charles Pickering, whom the Judiciary Committee ultimately rejected, Senator Maria Cantwell of Washington State pressed Pickering to explain where, precisely, he found a right to privacy in the Constitution. "My personal view is immaterial and irrelevant," Pickering responded, adding that he would follow *Roe v. Wade.* (The exchange shook a conservative friend of mine. "She wanted to know what was in Pickering's soul, he marveled.)

Many lawyers and law professors—on both sides of the abortion issue, Democratic as well as Republican—view *Roe* as a loosely reasoned decision that failed to explain convincingly why the Constitution protects the right to choose during the first trimester of pregnancy. Nevertheless, after the Supreme Court reaffirmed *Roe* in 1992, not even the most conservative lower-court judge in the country has refused to apply it for a simple reason: lower-court judges are required to follow Supreme Court precedents whether they like them or not.

> Why are the Democrats and Republicans using *Roe v. Wade* and the issue of abortion as a screening test for judicial nominees?

By putting abortion at the center of the lower-court nomination battles, the Democrats seem more interested in placating liberal interest groups than in examining the issues that the lower-court judges actually decide. "Kate Michelman is very helpful to us in identifying problems with nominees," says a Democratic Senate staff member, "and in deciding who is vulnerable."

But the Democrats' extremism on the abortion question is matched by the extremism of the right. The man who has been called the leading judicial attack dog on the right is Thomas Jipping. He recently moved from the Free Congress Foundation to a group called the Concerned Women for America, whose mission is to "bring Biblical principles into all levels of public policy." This means outlawing abortion, promoting school prayer and fighting all pornography and obscenity. Jipping defines a judicial activist as anyone who accepts three decades of Supreme Court precedent in abortion cases. "This entire abortion area is just an exercise in judicial invention," he told me. "I have not heard of a Clinton nominee who embraced judicial restraint."

Taking an even more combative view of the culture wars, Robert Bork, the rejected Supreme Court nominee, recently wrote a polemic in *The New Criterion* urging conservatives to relitigate the entire 20th century. Describing a pitched battle between the "traditionalists" and the "emancipationists," Bork wrote that the courts, and especially the Supreme Court, are "the enemy of traditional culture," in areas including "speech, religion, abortion, sexuality, welfare, public education and much else." "It is not too much to say," Bork argued, "that the suffocating vulgarity of popular culture is in large measure the work of the court."

Bork is living in a dystopian time warp. As sociologists like Alan Wolfe and Francis Fukuyama have demonstrated, social conservatives largely lost the culture wars in the 1990's not because of the Supreme Court but because of MTV, the Internet, the expansion of sexual equality and other democratizing forces of popular culture. Nevertheless, because a minority of extreme Republican and

Democratic interest groups and judges refuse to accept the Supreme Court's relatively moderate compromises on abortion and religion, our confirmation battles continue to be fought over the most extreme positions in the culture wars, which the American people have already rejected.

This is particularly true on the court to which Roberts and Snyder were nominated. The U.S. Court of Appeals for the D.C. Circuit hasn't heard an important abortion-rights case in living memory. Instead, the D.C. Circuit focuses on the less sexy but no less important issues concerning the limitations of federal power and the boundaries of the regulatory state. There is a pitched battle among liberal and conservative judges, from the Supreme Court on down, about whether the Constitution imposes meaningful limits on Congress's ability to regulate the environment, the workplace and affirmative action. Here it is the Republicans who want to use the courts to strike down laws passed by legislatures and the Democrats who are defending judicial restraint. For this reason, Senator Schumer has vowed to ask all Bush nominees what they think of the Supreme Court's recent decisions limiting the scope of federal power. Schumer argues plausibly that since President Clinton, by and large, appointed moderate rather than extremist Democrats to the appellate courts, the Senate should ensure balance by screening out extremist Republicans.

Asking the nominees their views about federalism is a more appropriate way of smoking out extremists than grilling them about *Roe v. Wade.* But even when it comes to the debates over federalism, the D.C. Circuit today is far less polarized than the confirmation battles it has ignited might suggest. Eleven years ago, when I was a law clerk for Abner Mikva, then the chief judge of the D.C. Circuit, the liberal and conservative judges were at one another's throats. On the left and on the right, a few of the judges had strong ideological agendas and aggressive personalities, and this combination led them to fight constantly over internecine issues.

Over the past decade, however, the personalities on both the D.C. Circuit and the legal landscape in America have mellowed. Many of the most bruising legal battles in the culture wars have been settled by the Supreme Court: now that the justices have significantly restricted the discretion of lower courts in cases involving criminals' rights, for example, there is far less for lower-court judges to fight about. In fact, an alliance between libertarian Republicans and libertarian Democrats has produced important victories for privacy and free expression since Sept. 11.

Moreover, President Clinton's appointments to the D.C. Circuit have won the respect of their conservative colleagues for their personal as well as their judicial moderation. Because the judges now trust one another enough to reason together, fewer than 3 percent of the cases between 1995 and 2001 provoked any dissenting opinions at all. In an impressive sign of the court's bipartisanship and mutual trust, all seven judges joined together last June to find Microsoft liable for antitrust violations.

Federal courts, as it happens, are very much like university faculties: small groups of prima donnas, often with too much time on their hands, whose political dynamics can be shaped as much by personalities as by reasoned arguments. On a small court, the addition of one or two disruptive figures can change the dynamics of the entire group, causing Democrats and Republicans to gravitate toward increasingly extreme positions in order to signal their allegiance to one side or the other. Once a court has been polarized, moreover, it can easily deteriorate into a group of squabbling children. The U.S. Court of Appeals for the Sixth Circuit demonstrated this tendency in its recent opinion upholding the University of Michigan Law School's affirmative action program. One of the dissenting judges published a remarkable appendix accusing the chief judge of having cherry-picked the judges on an earlier panel to reach a predetermined result.

The D.C. Circuit at the moment is one of the best-functioning courts in the country. It would be bad for the law and bad for the future of the regulatory state if President Bush's successful nominees were so embittered by their confirmation ordeals that, like Clarence Thomas, they arrived on the court in the mood for payback. Instead of flyspecking their views about *Roe v. Wade* therefore, it would make more sense for the Senate to explore whether nominees like John Roberts have the judicial temperament and personal humility to defer to Congress and to apply the Supreme Court's precedents. Judicial temperament is often hard to predict; but for what it's worth, I was struck in a wide-ranging conversation by Roberts's sense of humor, apparent modesty and above all his Jimmy Stewart–like reverence for the ideal of law shaped by reasoned argument rather than by ideology. "If I were inclined to do something that I would find politically satisfying and that I didn't feel I could adequately defend in an opinion," Roberts told me, "it would embarrass me to put that out in front of" the Clinton appointees on the court, whom he has known for years and respects.

> What danger for the courts does Rosen see in putting a nominee through a grueling and rancorous confirmation process?

After talking to Roberts and Snyder, in fact, I had the impression that they would agree in more cases than they disagreed, and that both had the sheer legal ability that sometimes distinguishes judges who care about working to identify the right answer from those who are driven by ideological agendas.

"John is one of the most brilliant minds in this or probably any other city, and he clearly meets anybody's tests for qualifications and legal background," Snyder says.

"I can't see much difference in terms of how Allen and I would approach cases," Roberts says. "He thinks there is an answer, and the harder you work, the more likely you are to get it, and to get it right. I think we share that." The Senate—and the nation—may never find that out.

Consider the source and the audience.

- This article appeared in the *New York Times Magazine.* Although Rosen is the legal writer for the *New Republic,* a liberal opinion magazine, the *Times* serves a more general audience. How is this fact reflected in Rosen's tone and conclusions?

Lay out the argument, the values, and the assumptions.

- What is Rosen's main goal here? What kind of tone would he like to see on courts such as the U.S. Court of Appeals for the D.C. Circuit?
- Why does he think that tone is in danger?
- How does he think it can be preserved?

Uncover the evidence.

- What different kinds of evidence does Rosen assemble to make his case? Is it a persuasive combination? What if Snyder and Roberts were less likable guys and more ideologically extreme? Would that have damaged Rosen's argument?

Evaluate the conclusion.

- Who does Rosen hold responsible for the way judicial confirmations do or do not proceed today? Is he right?

Sort out the political implications.

- If the trend discussed by Rosen continues, what is it likely to mean for our court system?
- Why do senators listen to interest groups anyway? Can that be changed? How?

9.4 The Truth Behind the Pillars

The Final Act: They Cultivate an Olympian Air, But the Justices Are Quite Human—and Can Be Quite Political

Evan Thomas and Michael Isikoff, *Newsweek,* 25 December 2000

For those who weren't paying attention in the days after the 2000 presidential election, here's what happened. Al Gore, the winner of the popular vote by about half a million votes, was virtually tied with George W. Bush for the electoral votes in Florida that would give one of them the edge in the electoral college. With Florida's vote so close that it triggered an automatic recount, and with many reports of election irregularities, the election was too close to call. When Florida Secretary of State Katherine Harris finally declared that Bush had won the state's election, Gore went to court to seek a recount. The Florida Supreme Court ruled that a recount should go ahead. Bush appealed to the U.S. Supreme Court to stop it. To the surprise of many, in a 5–4 decision a bare majority of the Court's members, all of whom were committed to the principle of states' rights, overturned the Florida high court, and effectively awarded the presidency to Bush.

Endless second-guessing has followed. Was there a constitutional basis for the decision? Was the majority, Republicans all, merely exercising its political preferences? Would a decision, unjustifiable on legal grounds, have been warranted by the desire to preempt a constitutional crisis? The Supreme Court's deliberations are secret. What follows are two *Newsweek* reporters' efforts to ferret out the truth about *Bush v. Gore.*

Supreme Court Justice Sandra Day O'Connor and her husband, John, a Washington lawyer, have long been comfortable on the cocktail and charity-ball circuit. So at an election-night party on Nov. 7, surrounded for the most part by friends and familiar acquaintances, she let her guard drop for a moment when she heard the first critical returns shortly before 8 P.M. Sitting in her hostess's den, staring at a small black-and-white television set, she visibly started when CBS anchor Dan Rather called Florida for Al Gore. "This is terrible," she exclaimed. She explained to another partygoer that Gore's reported victory in Florida meant that the election was "over," since Gore had already carried two other swing states, Michigan and Illinois.

Moments later, with an air of obvious disgust, she rose to get a plate of food, leaving it to her husband to explain her somewhat uncharacteristic outburst. John O'Connor said his wife was upset because they wanted to retire to Arizona, and a Gore win meant they'd have to wait another four years. O'Connor, the former Republican majority leader of the Arizona State Senate and a 1981 Ronald Reagan appointee, did not want a Democrat to name her successor. Two witnesses described this extraordinary scene to *Newsweek*. Responding through a spokesman at the high court, O'Connor had no comment. O'Connor had no way of knowing, as she watched the early returns, that election night would end in deadlock and confusion—or that five weeks later she would play a direct and decisive role in the election of George W. Bush. O'Connor could not possibly have foreseen that she would be one of two swing votes in the court's 5–4 decision ending the manual recount in Florida and forcing Al Gore to finally concede defeat. But her remarks will fuel criticism that the justices not only "follow the election returns," as the old saying goes, but, in the case of *George W. Bush v. Albert Gore Jr.*, sought to influence them.

Since the high court is supposed to be above politics, guaranteeing a government of laws, not men, partisanship is a base charge to level against a justice. Even the most caustic critics last week were reluctant to directly accuse individual justices of putting narrow party interests before constitutional principle. Speaking carefully (he will have to face the justices again in future cases), Harvard law professor Laurence Tribe danced around the question last week in an interview with *Newsweek*. The court's opinion was "peculiar and bizarre," said Tribe, who argued on Gore's behalf the first time the high court considered the case two weeks ago. The justices, he said elliptically, were "driven by something other than what was visible on the face of the opinions."

But what? It is a tricky business to read the minds of Supreme Court justices, who operate in one of the last truly secret precincts in Washington. From hints and sometimes murky signals, one must try to divine the true motivations of the High Nine. Was the court's judgment derived from established legal and constitutional principle? Or were a majority of the justices "result-oriented," searching for a high-minded philosophical rationale to paper over their political leanings? It is more than an idle guessing game. The court just decided the presidential election, and may have exposed itself to questions that could undermine its legitimacy. A *Newsweek* reconstruction sheds light on the conflicting forces and elusive motives at play behind the curtain of the nation's highest court.

The court's majority was clearly aware of the perils of entering what one long-ago justice once called "the political thicket." "None are more conscious of the vital limits on judicial authority than are the members of this court," declared the unsigned majority opinion, as if the anonymous authors were eager to shed "our unsought responsibility to resolve the federal and constitutional issues the judicial system has been forced to resolve." And yet, the court's majority—supposedly judicial conservatives all, with a high regard for states' rights and an avowed distaste for interventions by the federal judiciary—reached down to stop the Florida courts from carrying out their electoral duties ordained by the Constitution. Even Bush's own lawyer, Ted Olson, was surprised when the high court issued an unusual emergency order to stop the manual ballot recount in Florida on Dec. 9.

What's "the political thicket"? Why should the Court stay out of it?

In its final decision last week, the court found that the different standards used by the various Florida counties to count ballots—those dimpled, indented and hanging chads—violated the rights of voters to have their ballots counted equally and fairly. Sounds reasonable, but some court watchers regarded the high court's stated grounds for reversing the Florida Supreme Court with suspicion.

Curiously for a court that often preaches "judicial restraint," seven of the nine justices based their opinions on a clause of the Constitution that has been the single best tool of judicial activists for the past half century: the "equal protection" clause of the 14th Amendment to the Constitution. Long dormant until it was rediscovered by the liberal Warren Court in the 1960s, the 132-year-old equal-protection clause (passed to guarantee against racial discrimination after the Civil War) became a kind of all-purpose tool used by judicial activists to strike down any "state action" that seemed unfair. Since unfairness abounds in everyday life, the equal-protection clause is a potentially limitless invitation to meddling by judges. Indeed, the court seemed to be perhaps inadvertently opening the door to a whole new class of lawsuits challenging election procedures on grounds of unfairness. No wonder, then, that Justice John Paul Stevens chastised his brethren in a scathing dissent not so subtly impugning their motives. The court's action in *Bush v. Gore* he wrote, "can only lend credence to the most cynical appraisal of the work of judges throughout the land."

Here's that concept of judicial activism versus restraint again. What does it mean here?

Stevens is himself a case study in the mysteries of the court. Though a Republican Midwesterner and a Ford appointee, he surprised his backers by joining the liberal wing of the court. He is now considered a champion of causes favored by Democrats, like the right to abortion and affirmative action. Yet the bow-tied jurist is so determined to stay above the fray that he has spoken out against the recent practice of swearing in justices at the White House. Too political, says Stevens, who these days only irregularly shows up at his own chambers in Washington, preferring to draft opinions from his retirement home in Florida.

Other justices, too, seem to relish their aloofness from the political scene, in ways at once grand and quirky. The high court's weekly conferences are truly private. The junior justice, Stephen Breyer, answers the door and serves coffee, and the room is swept periodically for electronic bugs. When other government offices close down in snowstorms, the Supreme Court almost always stays open. Chief Justice William Rehnquist, a former military meteorologist, apparently likes to be above the weather as well as politics. State of the Union addresses are required appointments for lawmakers, cabinet officers, diplomats, the top brass—but at President Clinton's last SOTU, not a single one of the nine justices showed up. (A spokesman blamed "travel changes and minor illness.")

The justices refuse to allow cameras in the Supreme Court, and when their ruling in *Bush v. Gore* was announced last week, they had already gone home for the night. A clerk handed out printed copies—65 pages, six separate opinions—to panting reporters. When Governor Bush anxiously called his headquarters on his mobile phone, eager to know if he had just won the presidency, his campaign chairman, Don Evans, was forced to say, "We'll have to call you back."

The next morning one of the justices, Clarence Thomas, gave an especially pointed—some might say defensive—account of the court's Olympian detachment. Speaking to a group of high-school students, he referred to the houses of Congress, located in the Capitol across the street from the court, as "entirely different worlds. . . . We happen to be in the same city. We may as well be on entirely different planets." Politicians, he declared, "have no influence on us. The last political act we engage in is confirmation. That is the last act. And I have yet to hear any discussion, in nine years, of partisan politics in this—among members of this court." Thomas is regarded as a somewhat extreme example of aloofness. He's said he does not read newspapers, except for the sports pages, and he almost never speaks up during oral arguments, the court's one semipublic outing. The only glimpse he offered of his role in *Bush v. Gore* was to indicate that in the rush to hand down a decision he pulled his first "all-nighter" since law school.

At least Thomas's name appeared in the court's opinions, joining Rehnquist and Justice Antonin Scalia in a separate opinion arguing that the Florida Supreme Court had violated state law by ordering a recount. The

> What do you think about all this secrecy? Should the Court be required to make its deliberations public, especially in cases where it makes decisions with clear political consequences?

name of the likely author of the majority opinion—Justice Anthony Kennedy—was entirely missing from court documents. Kennedy might have had some help from O'Connor, but court watchers can only guess, since her name is also absent. The opinion was labeled "per curiam," meaning "by the court." Normally, per curiam opinions are unanimous and uncontroversial. Kennedy's (and/or O'Connor's) will be the source of controversy and debate for years.

Kennedy is regarded as one of the court's swing votes, a moderate Republican who, like O'Connor, has made majorities for both liberal and conservative rulings. A Reagan appointee—considered less controversial than Robert Bork, whose appointment he took after Bork was rejected by the U.S. Senate in 1987—Kennedy has a somewhat grandiose sense of his own role. He allowed a reporter from *California Lawyer* magazine to observe him just before he took the bench to announce a momentous abortion decision, *Planned Parenthood of Southeastern Pennsylvania v. Casey,* in June 1992. The reporter described Kennedy moodily staring out the window. "Sometimes you don't know if you're Caesar about to cross the Rubicon or Captain Queeg cutting your own towline," Kennedy mused aloud. He asked to be left alone, telling the reporter, "I need to brood. . . . I generally brood, as all of us do on the bench, just before we go on. It's a moment of quiet around here to search your soul and your conscience."

Kennedy's decision in *Casey* reaffirming the court's 1973 decision in *Roe v. Wade* guaranteeing women the right to choose an abortion, infuriated the court's conservatives. They suspected that he had been somehow manipulated by the court's liberal wing. At an end-of-the-year skit by the high court's clerks, he was gently mocked as "Flipper." (Clerks from the chambers of the conservative justices played the theme song from the old TV show, "They call him Flipper, Flipper. . . .") Kennedy is now said to be sensitive to any suggestion that he is a pawn of other justices. There were rumors last week that Justice David Souter, another centrist, was quietly lobbying Kennedy to allow the Florida voting to go forward. A shy bachelor with an aversion to incandescent light, Souter does not seem like much of a glad-hander or arm-twister. A clerk recalls finding him in his darkened chambers reading with a small desk lamp. "It was like wandering into a room with Miss Havisham," the clerk reported. But Souter is brilliant and persuasive, and he was said to be trying to bring Kennedy around to his point of view: that the Florida Supreme Court be given at least until Dec. 18 to adopt a uniform vote-counting standard. That narrow window might have given Florida a chance to finish a statewide manual recount—which might well have pushed Gore ahead of Bush.

But then what? If the Florida Supreme Court ordered the secretary of state, Katherine Harris, to certify Democratic electors for Gore, the GOP-dominated state legislature seemed determined to appoint its own set of Republican electors for Bush. Congress would then have had to choose. But the Republicans in the House were likely to reject the Gore electors, and the Senate—divided

50–50, with Vice President Al Gore casting the tie-breaking vote on his own behalf—would almost surely reject the Bush electors. What then? In one scenario, the whole mess would go back to Florida for the governor to decide—Gov. Jeb Bush.

At some point on this chaotic journey, the U.S. Supreme Court was bound to be drawn back into the fray, perhaps to decide if George W. Bush could, in effect, be elected by his own brother. It was the prospect of such an electoral circus (with the justices in the role of ringmasters) that may, in the end, have forced the Supreme Court's intercession last week. However high-handed the justices appeared, they might have looked far worse trying to referee a true constitutional crisis in January.

Not a word was uttered about this potential car wreck in the court's decisions. But at least one politician who is close to Justice Scalia, Sen. Robert Torricelli of New Jersey, believes that the court was trying to save the nation from an ugly deadlock. Torricelli, who is friendly with Scalia from an Italian-American group in Washington (they have gone on camping and rafting trips together with other prominent Italian-Americans), has a feel for the court's internal dynamics. As Torricelli saw it, Scalia and the other justices peered into the abyss and then fashioned an opinion to avoid it. The New Jersey senator told *Newsweek* that his "disappointment" in the defeat of his fellow Democrat Al Gore was coupled with "gratitude that the nation dodged a bullet."

And Justice O'Connor's role? She is not likely to hold forth on her personal views any time soon. Scholars will long debate the court's reasoning and motivations. But one lesson is clear to presidential candidates. On Dec. 9, when the Supreme Court stopped the counting in Florida, shouts of glee broke out in the offices occupied by Bush's legal team in Tallahassee. "It was like we had just won the high-school basketball game after the last-second Hail Mary shot at the buzzer," said a participant. A top Bush adviser wandered by the desk of Timothy Flanagan, one of Bush's lawyers. "Do you think," Flanagan asked, "that Governor Bush understands now, how important the Supreme Court is—and how important it is to pick the right people?"

Consider the source and the audience.
- This is an article from *Newsweek,* a weekly magazine for a mass audience. *Newsweek* is owned by the *Washington Post.* What is the likely goal of the author in this article?

Lay out the argument, the values, and the assumptions.
- What is Thomas and Isikoff's main argument here? What is the value of debunking myths about the Supreme Court justices being above politics?
- What kind of values drive the sort of political exposé that the authors engage in? Investigative journalist objectivity? The public's right to know? Political cynicism?

Uncover the evidence.

- How much of the evidence here is concrete, and how much is speculative? What are writers to do when so much of what they want to discover is secret? To what extent are they justified in drawing inferences about motive from actions and words on other topics?

Evaluate the conclusion.

- What do the authors want us to take away from this story? Is it a reminder of the political power of the "least dangerous branch," a warning to pay attention to what the justices say and do, a suggestion to look closely at the relationship between the presidency and the courts, or all of the above?

Sort out the political implications.

- Do you agree with the authors' attempt to make public what the justices prefer to keep secret? How would judicial politics be different if the justices had to make their intentions and political values known?

9.5 *Federalist* No. 78

Alexander Hamilton, *The Federalist Papers*

Thus far we have read a number of articles and transcripts that deal with the increasing power and political nature of the courts. Yet, as we noted in the introduction to this chapter, Hamilton claimed that the judiciary would be the least dangerous branch of government because it was the least powerful. Have things changed, or could we have anticipated the power of today's courts from Hamilton's own arguments?

This essay is fascinating, but it needs careful reading—several subarguments require some unraveling before we can be clear about Hamilton's thesis. The basic task he undertakes here is to justify why judges in federal courts should be appointed to hold their offices on good behavior—essentially that they be appointed for life unless they do something really wrong. (The conditions for impeaching a judge are the same as for impeaching a president—the commitment of high crimes and misdemeanors.) Hamilton first declares that the judiciary is the least powerful branch of the federal government, seeming to suggest that giving lifetime appointments to an institution that is not very powerful is not all that threatening in the first place. Then he embarks on a far more controversial argument. Federal judges require lifetime tenure to keep them politically independent from the other two branches not because they are not powerful but because they are the only ones who hold in their hands the power to determine if the laws of Congress violate the will of the people as expressed in the Constitution. Does Hamilton's famous justification of *judicial review,* a power that does not appear in the Constitution itself, contradict any aspect of what he said about the judiciary being the weakest branch of government?

To the People of the State of New York:
    WE PROCEED now to an examination of the judiciary department of the proposed government.

In unfolding the defects of the existing Confederation, the utility and necessity of a federal judicature have been clearly pointed out. It is the less necessary to recapitulate the considerations there urged, as the propriety of the institution in the abstract is not disputed; the only questions which have been raised being relative to the manner of constituting it, and to its extent. To these points, therefore, our observations shall be confined.

The manner of constituting it seems to embrace these several objects: 1st. The mode of appointing the judges. 2d. The tenure by which they are to hold their places. 3d. The partition of the judiciary authority between different courts, and their relations to each other.

First. As to the mode of appointing the judges; this is the same with that of appointing the officers of the Union in general, and has been so fully discussed in the two last numbers, that nothing can be said here which would not be useless repetition.

Second. As to the tenure by which the judges are to hold their places; this chiefly concerns their duration in office; the provisions for their support; the precautions for their responsibility.

According to the plan of the convention, all judges who may be appointed by the United States are to hold their offices DURING GOOD BEHAVIOR; which is conformable to the most approved of the State constitutions and among the rest, to that of this State. Its propriety having been drawn into question by the adversaries of that plan, is no light symptom of the rage for objection, which disorders their imaginations and judgments. The standard of good behavior for the continuance in office of the judicial magistracy, is certainly one of the most valuable of the modern improvements in the practice of government. In a monarchy it is an excellent barrier to the despotism of the prince; in a republic it is a no less excellent barrier to the encroachments and oppressions of the representative body. And it is the best expedient which can be devised in any government, to secure a steady, upright, and impartial administration of the laws.

Whoever attentively considers the different departments of power must perceive, that, in a government in which they are separated from each other, the judiciary, from the nature of its functions, will always be the least dangerous to the political rights of the Constitution; because it will be least in a capacity to annoy or injure them. The Executive not only dispenses the honors, but holds the sword of the community. The legislature not only commands the purse, but prescribes the rules by which the duties and rights of every citizen are to be regulated. The judiciary, on the contrary, has no influence over either the sword or the purse; no direction either of the strength or of the wealth of the society; and can take no active resolution whatever. It may truly be said to have neither FORCE nor

WILL, but merely judgment; and must ultimately depend upon the aid of the executive arm even for the efficacy of its judgments.

This simple view of the matter suggests several important consequences. It proves incontestably, that the judiciary is beyond comparison the weakest of the three departments of power;[1] that it can never attack with success either of the other two; and that all possible care is requisite to enable it to defend itself against their attacks. It equally proves, that though individual oppression may now and then proceed from the courts of justice, the general liberty of the people can never be endangered from that quarter; I mean so long as the judiciary remains truly distinct from both the legislature and the Executive. For I agree, that "there is no liberty, if the power of judging be not separated from the legislative and executive powers.[2] And it proves, in the last place, that as liberty can have nothing to fear from the judiciary alone, but would have every thing to fear from its union with either of the other departments; that as all the effects of such a union must ensue from a dependence of the former on the latter, notwithstanding a nominal and apparent separation; that as, from the natural feebleness of the judiciary, it is in continual jeopardy of being overpowered, awed, or influenced by its co-ordinate branches; and that as nothing can contribute so much to its firmness and independence as permanency in office, this quality may therefore be justly regarded as an indispensable ingredient in its constitution, and, in a great measure, as the citadel of the public justice and the public security.

> Has Hamilton proved "incontestably" that the judiciary is the weakest of the three branches of government? Are the sword and the purse the only powers we need to worry about?

The complete independence of the courts of justice is peculiarly essential in a limited Constitution. By a limited Constitution, I understand one which contains certain specified exceptions to the legislative authority; such, for instance as that it shall pass no bills of attainder, no ex-post-facto laws, and the like. Limitations of this kind can be preserved in practice no other way than through the medium of courts of justice, whose duty it must be to declare all acts contrary to the manifest tenor of the Constitution void. Without this, all the reservations of particular rights or privileges would amount to nothing.

Some perplexity respecting the rights of the courts to pronounce legislative acts void, because contrary to the Constitution, has arisen from an imagination that the doctrine would imply a superiority of the judiciary to the legislative power. It is urged that the authority which can declare the acts of another void must necessarily be superior to the one whose acts may be declared void. As this doctrine is of great importance in all the American constitutions, a brief discussion of the ground on which it rests cannot be unacceptable.

There is no position which depends on clearer principles, than that every act of a delegated authority, contrary to the tenor of the commission under which it is exercised, is void. No legislative act, therefore, contrary to the Constitution, can be valid. To deny this, would be to affirm, that the deputy is greater than his principal; that the servant is above his master; that the representatives of the people are superior to the people themselves; that men acting by virtue of powers, may do not only what their powers do not authorize, but what they forbid.

If it be said that the legislative body are themselves the constitutional judges of their own powers, and that the construction they put upon them is conclusive upon the other departments, it may be answered, that this cannot be the natural presumption, where it is not to be collected from any particular provisions in the Constitution. It is not otherwise to be supposed, that the Constitution could intend to enable the representatives of the people to substitute their WILL to that of their constituents. It is far more rational to suppose, that the courts were designed to be an intermediate body between the people and the legislature, in order, among other things, to keep the latter within the limits assigned to their authority. The interpretation of the laws is the proper and peculiar province of the courts. A constitution is, in fact, and must be regarded by the judges, as a fundamental law. It therefore belongs to them to ascertain its meaning, as well as the meaning of any particular act proceeding from the legislative body. If there should happen to be an irreconcilable variance between the two, that which has the superior obligation and validity ought, of course, to be preferred; or, in other words, the Constitution ought to be preferred to the statute, the intention of the people to the intention of their agents.

Nor does this conclusion by any means suppose a superiority of the judicial to the legislative power. It only supposes that the power of the people is superior to both; and that where the will of the legislature, declared in its statutes, stands in opposition to that of the people, declared in the Constitution, the judges ought to be governed by the latter rather than the former. They ought to regulate their decisions by the fundamental laws, rather than by those which are not fundamental.

This exercise of judicial discretion, in determining between two contradictory laws, is exemplified in a familiar instance. It not uncommonly happens, that there are two statutes existing at one time, clashing in whole or in part with each other, and neither of them containing any repealing clause or expression. In such a case, it is the province of the courts to liquidate and fix their meaning and operation. So far as they can, by any fair construction, be reconciled to each other, reason and law conspire to dictate that this should be done; where this is impracticable, it be-

> If Hamilton really believes that judicial review merely supports the will of the people rather than empowering the courts, why isn't judicial review actually in the Constitution?

comes a matter of necessity to give effect to one, in exclusion of the other. The rule which has obtained in the courts for determining their relative validity is, that the last in order of time shall be preferred to the first. But this is a mere rule of construction, not derived from any positive law, but from the nature and reason of the thing. It is a rule not enjoined upon the courts by legislative provision, but adopted by themselves, as consonant to truth and propriety, for the direction of their conduct as interpreters of the law. They thought it reasonable, that between the interfering acts of an EQUAL authority, that which was the last indication of its will should have the preference.

But in regard to the interfering acts of a superior and subordinate authority, of an original and derivative power, the nature and reason of the thing indicate the converse of that rule as proper to be followed. They teach us that the prior act of a superior ought to be preferred to the subsequent act of an inferior and subordinate authority; and that accordingly, whenever a particular statute contravenes the Constitution, it will be the duty of the judicial tribunals to adhere to the latter and disregard the former.

It can be of no weight to say that the courts, on the pretense of a repugnancy, may substitute their own pleasure to the constitutional intentions of the legislature. This might as well happen in the case of two contradictory statutes; or it might as well happen in every adjudication upon any single statute. The courts must declare the sense of the law; and if they should be disposed to exercise WILL instead of JUDGMENT, the consequence would equally be the substitution of their pleasure to that of the legislative body. The observation, if it prove any thing, would prove that there ought to be no judges distinct from that body.

If, then, the courts of justice are to be considered as the bulwarks of a limited Constitution against legislative encroachments, this consideration will afford a strong argument for the permanent tenure of judicial offices, since nothing will contribute so much as this to that independent spirit in the judges which must be essential to the faithful performance of so arduous a duty.

This independence of the judges is equally requisite to guard the Constitution and the rights of individuals from the effects of those ill humors, which the arts of designing men, or the influence of particular conjunctures, sometimes disseminate among the people themselves, and which, though they speedily give place to better information, and more deliberate reflection, have a tendency, in the meantime, to occasion dangerous innovations in the government, and serious oppressions of the minor party in the community. Though I trust the friends of the proposed Constitution will never concur with its enemies,[3] in questioning that fundamental principle of republican government, which admits the right of the people to alter or abolish the established Constitution, whenever they find it inconsistent with their happiness, yet it is not to be inferred from this principle, that the representatives of the people, whenever a momentary inclination happens to lay hold of a majority of their constituents, incompatible with the provisions in the existing Constitution, would, on that account, be justifiable in a violation of those provisions; or that the courts would be under a greater obligation to connive at infractions in this shape, than when they had proceeded wholly from the cabals of the representative body. Until the people have, by some solemn and authoritative act, annulled or changed the established form, it is binding upon themselves collectively, as well as individually; and no presumption, or even knowledge, of their sentiments, can warrant their representatives in a departure from it, prior to such an act. But it is easy to see, that it would require an uncommon portion of fortitude in the judges to do their duty as faithful guardians of the Constitution, where legislative invasions of it had been instigated by the major voice of the community.

But it is not with a view to infractions of the Constitution only, that the independence of the judges may be an essential safeguard against the effects of occasional ill humors in the society. These sometimes extend no farther than to the injury of the private rights of particular classes of citizens, by unjust and partial laws. Here also the firmness of the judicial magistracy is of vast importance in mitigating the severity and confining the operation of such laws. It not only serves to moderate the immediate mischiefs of those which may have been passed, but it operates as a check upon the legislative body in passing them; who, perceiving that obstacles to the success of iniquitous intention are to be expected from the scruples of the courts, are in a manner compelled, by the very motives of the injustice they meditate, to qualify their attempts. This is a circumstance calculated to have more influence upon the character of our governments, than but few may be aware of. The benefits of the integrity and moderation of the judiciary have already been felt in more States than one; and though they may have displeased those whose sinister expectations they may have disappointed, they must have commanded the esteem and applause of all the virtuous and disinterested. Considerate men, of every description, ought to prize whatever will tend to beget or fortify that temper in the courts: as no man can be sure that he may not be to-morrow the victim of a spirit of injustice, by which he may be a gainer to-day. And every man must now feel, that the inevitable tendency of such a spirit is to sap the foundations of public and private confidence, and to introduce in its stead universal distrust and distress.

That inflexible and uniform adherence to the rights of the Constitution, and of individuals, which we perceive to be indispensable in the courts of justice, can certainly not be expected from judges who hold their offices by a temporary commission. Periodical appointments, however regulated, or by whomsoever made, would, in some way or other, be fatal to their necessary independence. If the power of making them was committed either to the Executive or legislature, there would be danger of an improper complaisance to the branch which possessed it; if to both, there would be an unwillingness to hazard the displeasure of either; if to the people, or to persons chosen by them for the special purpose, there would be too great a disposition to consult popularity, to justify a reliance that nothing would be consulted but the Constitution and the laws.

There is yet a further and a weightier reason for the permanency of the judicial offices, which is deducible from the nature of the qualifications they require. It has been frequently remarked, with great propriety, that a voluminous code of laws is one of the inconveniences necessarily connected with the advantages of a free government. To avoid an arbitrary discretion in the courts, it is indispensable that they should be bound down by strict rules and precedents, which serve to define and point out their duty in every particular case that comes before them; and it will readily be conceived from the variety of controversies which grow out of the folly and wickedness of mankind, that the records of those precedents must unavoidably swell to a very considerable bulk, and must demand long and laborious study to acquire a competent knowledge of them. Hence it is, that there can be but few men in the society who will have sufficient skill in the laws to qualify them for the stations of judges. And making the proper deductions for the ordinary depravity of human nature, the number must be still smaller of those who unite the requisite integrity with the requisite knowledge. These considerations apprise us, that the government can have no great option between fit character; and that a temporary duration in office, which would naturally discourage such characters from quitting a lucrative line of practice to accept a seat on the bench, would have a tendency to throw the administration of justice into hands less able, and less well qualified, to conduct it with utility and dignity. In the present circumstances of this country, and in those in which it is likely to be for a long time to come, the disadvantages on this score would be greater than they may at first sight appear; but it must be confessed, that they are far inferior to those which present themselves under the other aspects of the subject.

Is it really possible that we would run out of qualified people to appoint to the courts if we did not give them lifetime jobs?

Upon the whole, there can be no room to doubt that the convention acted wisely in copying from the models of those constitutions which have established GOOD BEHAVIOR as the tenure of their judicial offices, in point of duration; and that so far from being blamable on this account, their plan would have been inexcusably defective, if it had wanted this important feature of good government. The experience of Great Britain affords an illustrious comment on the excellence of the institution.

PUBLIUS.

---

[1] The celebrated Montesquieu, speaking of them, says: "Of the three powers above mentioned, the judiciary is next to nothing." "Spirit of Laws." vol. i., page 186.

[2] Idem, page 181.

[3] Vide "Protest of the Minority of the Convention of Pennsylvania," Martin's Speech, etc.

Consider the source and the audience.

- Hamilton is writing to audiences who are skeptical of the power in the new Constitution he wants them to ratify. Article III of the Constitution, setting out the judiciary, is among the briefest and least specific of the constitutional provisions precisely because so many people objected to a strong and powerful federal court system. How is this factor likely to shape the arguments he makes here?

Lay out the argument, the values, and the assumptions.

- We know from a variety of sources that Hamilton was an advocate of a strong federal government. In this essay, how does he balance his own preferences with the necessity to persuade people who fear a strong government?
- What are Hamilton's major arguments for lifetime tenure of federal judges?
- Why does he think that judicial review does not unduly elevate the Court over the legislature?
- How does he think judges can be kept from exercising their will rather than their judgment?

Uncover the evidence.

- Does Hamilton provide any evidence to support his arguments? What are the advantages and limitations of relying on logic and rhetoric to support one's argument?

Evaluate the conclusion.

- Hamilton believes that there "can be no room to doubt" that federal judges should be appointed for life, and he incidentally believes that it is okay to give them the power to strike down the laws passed by Congress if they do not, in their judgment, conform to the Constitution. Has he made his case?
- Is his argument consistent with his initial contention that the courts will constitute the least dangerous and weakest branch of government?

Sort out the political implications.

- In what ways does judicial politics today depart from Hamilton's plan? Is the judiciary truly independent of the other two branches? Does politics intrude, despite Hamilton's precaution of providing lifetime tenure?
- What would Hamilton think about the Supreme Court's ruling in *Bush v. Gore*?

CHAPTER 10

Public Opinion

How much should public opinion count in a democracy? Do we want our representatives to be slaves to what we say we want? Do we think they should ignore us and steer their own course? When Bill Clinton was running for president, he was nicknamed "Slick Willie" for his practice of changing his issue stances according to the polls. Eight years later, George Bush promised that his administration would not be run by pollsters because, he said, true leaders make up their own minds and are not swayed by public opinion. The difference in these two leadership styles boils down to a difference over a fundamental question of democracy: Should what citizens think matter to their representatives, or should those representatives follow their own judgment and consciences?

People who support Bush's view on this issue claim that people are too ignorant, busy, or irrational to have opinions of the quality that we want represented in government, and that our representatives are better qualified to know what we want. Opponents of that view claim that no one is better qualified than the American public to decide what Americans want, and that the essence of democracy is responsiveness to public opinion. Many social scientists claim that even though people are busy and do not focus on politics on a daily basis, they still gather enough information to make informed choices about the things that affect their interests.

Regardless of whether they think public opinion ought to matter, most politicians act as if it does matter. Elected officials, after all, have to contend with what the public thinks during elections, even if they disregard polls at other times. And, as it turns out, few politicians disregard polls altogether. Even George W. Bush has a polling staff that helps him gauge the public mood, craft messages, and test ideas.

Indeed, nationwide, pollsters have gotten into the habit of asking Americans what they think about a wide variety of issues, and have scientifically honed the instruments with which they measure their opinions. They do this for lots of reasons: Marketers want to find out what consumers want to buy, politicians want to know what voters want them to do, and everyday Americans want to know what their neighbors and colleagues are up to. There is no denying that in American politics today, polling is big business.

In this chapter we look at several articles that show the debates surrounding the role of public opinion polls in democratic governance. First, to bring the issue close to home, we consider an article that examines the changing political beliefs of college freshmen over time. The next article, from *The American Spectator,* a conservative opnion journal, laments the ignorance of the American public on a host of issues and is pessimistic about its effect on public policy. The third article, by the man in charge of the Pew Research Center for the People and the Press, which conducts its own polls, addresses the responsibility the media and politicians have for educating the public on complex issues. In the *Washington Monthly,* an investigative, anti-establishment journal, Joshua Green compares the polling efforts of Clinton and Bush and their role in each administration. Finally, we turn to George Gallup, the father of opinion polling in America, for the classic defense of public opinion's role in democratic government.

10.1 Poll Says College Students Lean Left

UCLA Survey Finds Highest Percentage of Politically Liberal Students Since Early '70s

Rebecca Trounson, *Los Angeles Times,* 28 January 2002

What goes on in the minds of college freshmen? Are they liberal? Conservative? Religious? Academically engaged? Community minded? Stressed out? You may know many college freshmen (indeed, you may even be one), but if you know the answers to these questions, chances are your knowledge is anecdotally based. That is, you probably only know what you've heard through conversation, gossip, and rumor.

Public opinion polls give us a way to learn what large categories of people are thinking about in a way that goes beyond hearsay. This article reports on a yearly poll of college freshmen that tells us scientifically what goes on in their heads. Even if these poll results are completely different from the way you think, does that mean they are invalid?

More college freshmen today describe themselves as politically liberal than at any time since the Vietnam War, a nationwide survey by UCLA researchers has found.

A resurgence of liberalism among U.S. freshmen also is reflected in their shifting attitudes on a range of hot-button political and social issues, according to survey results released today.

"It's a real change, a broad-based trend toward greater liberalism on almost every issue we look at," said Alexander W. Astin, a UCLA education professor who started the survey, the nation's largest, in 1966.

The researchers measured "liberalism" by asking students to describe their political views and to take positions on certain benchmark issues.

For instance, a record proportion—57.9%—believe that gay couples should have the legal right to marry. The highest portion in two decades—32.2%—say the death penalty should be abolished. And more than a third—the highest rate

These issues are largely social. What other kinds of issues would you like to see the results on before you judge how liberal or conservative students are?

since 1980—say marijuana should be legalized, although 75% also say employers should be allowed to require drug testing of workers and applicants.

Still, about half of the class of 2005, in line with their recent predecessors, view themselves as "middle of the road" politically. And 20.7% consider themselves conservative or "far right," while 29.9%—the highest figure since 1975—say they are liberal or "far left."

The latter figure has risen steadily since 1996, said Linda Sax, an education professor and director of the 36th annual survey. But it pales compared with the peak year in 1971, at the height of the anti–Vietnam War fervor, when 40.9% of those polled called themselves liberal.

The American Freshman Survey, based this year on responses from 281,064 students at 421 four-year colleges and universities, is the nation's oldest and most comprehensive assessment of student attitudes. It is a joint project of UCLA's Higher Education Research Institute and the American Council on Education, based in Washington.

Freshmen usually fill out questionnaires during orientation or the first week of classes, so their answers often reflect more on their high school experiences than on those in college.

Almost all of this year's forms were completed before Sept. 11, so any changes in student attitudes as a result of the terrorist attacks on the World Trade Center and the Pentagon would be reflected in next year's results, survey directors said.

What impact do you think September 11 would have had on student opinion?

Among the more striking findings of this year's poll was a reversal in a long slide toward political apathy on college campuses, probably attributable to the dramatic 2000 presidential contest, Sax said.

A growing, though still small, percentage of students now say they frequently discuss politics and that it is important to them to keep up to date with political affairs. And a record 47.5%—three times greater than when the question was first asked in 1966—said they participated in organized demonstrations in the previous year.

Contrary to common perception, Astin said, there are more demonstrations now—albeit smaller protests—than during the era best known for student activism.

"They feel freer [to protest], and there's an environment that's acceptable," he said.

ULCA freshman Ricardo Gutierrez, who took part in a recent campus rally to support lower tuition for illegal immigrants, explained that students "need to be involved if we want laws passed that we agree with."

"It's important to show people what we think," said Gutierrez, 18, who is from Lamont, near Bakersfield. He said he tries to keep up with political issues.

Not all agreed. UCLA freshman Nate Skrzypczak said he paid close attention during the presidential race, then quickly returned to what he called his "usual disinterested self."

"I don't see that [politics] really directly affects anyone," said the 18-year-old from San Diego. "It just doesn't have that big an impact on my life."

Whether or not they are politically involved, many college freshmen are anything but disengaged when it comes to community service. This year's class reported record levels of volunteerism, with 82.6% saying they had done some volunteer work in the last year.

Although many high schools require community service for graduation, and it can boost the prospects for a college applicant, Astin said the desire to help appears to go well beyond that.

Despite continuing evidence that today's students are relatively materialistic—73.6% said they want to be very well off financially—they also seem to want to find an outlet for what Astin called their "higher selves."

"They're much more inclined to express their concerns about other people," he said, in contrast to previous generations of students.

Volunteering "helps get your mind off yourself," said Christie Tedmon, a UCLA freshman and a member of its top-ranked gymnastics team. During high school in Sacramento, Tedmon joined many of her classmates in helping repair the homes of elderly people and also volunteered at a local hospital.

"We owe it to the community to help out a little," she said.

Patrick Hamo, 18, spent many hours in high school tutoring disadvantaged children in a Glendale program started by his older brother. "It really opens your eyes," the UCLA freshman said. "It makes you realize how much you can do."

Other trends emerged in this year's survey:

- Of this year's freshmen, 70% said they had socialized with someone of another racial or ethnic group in the last year—the highest rate since the survey began.
- Fewer students than before—19.5%—said they believed racial discrimination was "no longer a major problem" in the United States, and fewer thought affirmative action in college admissions should be abolished.
- A record 15.8% of freshmen said they have no religious preference, up slightly from last year and more than double the figure in 1966.
- More students than ever appear to be academically disengaged. A record 41.1% said they were frequently bored in class, and only 34.9% reported spending at least six hours a week hitting the books as high school seniors.

What is likely to be the consequence of such high levels of academic disengagement for the future of America's workforce?

In 1987, when the question was first asked, 47% said they studied at least six hours each week.

- This year's students continue to show signs of stress, worrying about completing all the tasks confronting them. A gender gap persists, with more than twice as many young women—36.6%—as young men—17.4%—reporting feeling "frequently overwhelmed by all I have to do."

These students never really get a chance to calm down," Sax said, especially in the final, frenzied years of high school. "They're multi-tasking on everything at once, trying to build these strong resumes before they even get into college."

Consider the source and the audience.
- This is a *Los Angeles Times* piece covering a University of California–Los Angeles poll. Would other newspapers cover this poll differently?

Lay out the argument, the values, and the assumptions.
- The author, Rebecca Trounson, is reporting the conclusions of education professors who conduct a survey. The professors are not so much making an argument as they are drawing conclusions from the data. What are their views about the 2001–2002 crop of college freshmen?
- What do you think they mean by "real change"?

Uncover the evidence.
- What is the American Freshman Survey? How can you find out more about its results?
- What factors might limit the usefulness of these poll results?
- What other kinds of evidence can you look for to corroborate the evidence of this poll?

Evaluate the conclusion.
- If all the results reported here are sound, how big a leftward shift are we really talking about?
- What trends would be bringing it about?

Sort out the political implications.
- If the findings here are accurate, what changes could we expect to see in American politics?

10.2 Party On, Dudes!

Ignorance Is the Curse of the Information Age

Matthew Robinson, *The American Spectator,* March/April 2002

This article bemoans what its author sees as the ignorance of the American public and its general unfitness for the task of self-governance. In a way, he is writing about all of us. As you read the article, poll yourself. Do you think the Constitution guarantees you a job? Do you know who Alexander Hamilton is? Can you identify the Chief Justice of the U.S. Supreme Court? Do you know what DNA is? Do you know who won the battle of Yorktown? Can you correctly estimate the proportion of the U.S. populaton that is homeless or the number of abortions performed every year?

How important is this kind of knowledge to the ability to formulate opinions on public matters and to understand one's own political interests? If we do not all match the democratic ideal of interested and informed citizens, should our opinions count?

A lmost any look at what the average citizen knows about politics is bound to be discouraging. Political scientists are nearly unanimous on the subject of voter ignorance. The average American citizen not only lacks basic knowledge but also holds beliefs that are contradictory and inconsistent. Here is a small sample of what Americans "know":

Nearly one-third of Americans (29 percent) think the Constitution guarantees a job. Forty-two percent think it guarantees health care. And 75 percent think it guarantees a high school education.

Forty-five percent think the communist tenet "from each according to his abilities, to each according to his needs" is part of the U.S. Constitution.

More Americans recognize the Nike advertising slogan "Just Do It" than know where the right to "life, liberty, and the pursuit of happiness" is set forth (79 percent versus 47 percent). 90 percent know that Bill Gates is the founder of the company that created the Windows operating system. Just over half (53 percent) correctly identified Alexander Hamilton as a Founding Father.

Fewer than half of adults (47 percent) can name their own Representative in Congress. Fewer than half of voters could identify whether their congressman voted for the use of force in the Persian Gulf War.

Just 30 percent of adults could name Newt Gingrich as the congressman who led Republican congressional candidates in signing the Contract with America. Six months after the GOP took Congress, 64 percent admitted they did not know.

A 1998 poll by the Pew Research Center for the People and the Press showed that 56 percent of Americans could not name a single Democratic candidate for president; 63 percent knew the name "Bush," but it wasn't clear that voters connected the name to George W. Bush.

According to a January 2000 Gallup poll, 66 percent of Americans could correctly name Regis Philbin when asked who hosts *Who Wants to Be a Millionaire,* but only 6 percent could correctly name Dennis Hastert when asked to name the Speaker of the House of Representatives in Washington.

Political scientists Michael X. Delli Carpini and Scott Keeter studied 3,700 questions surveying the public's political knowledge from the 1930's to the present. They discovered that people tend to remember or identify trivial details about political leaders, focusing on personalities or simply latching onto the policies that the press plays up. For example, the most commonly known fact about George Bush while he was president was that he hated broccoli, and during the 1992 presidential campaign, although 89 percent of the public knew that Vice President Quayle was feuding with the television character Murphy Brown, only 19 percent could characterize Bill Clinton's record on the environment.

Their findings demonstrate the full absurdity of public knowledge: More people could identify Judge Wapner (the longtime host of the television series *The People's Court*) than could identify Chief Justices Warren Burger or William Rehnquist. More people had heard of John Lennon than of Karl Marx. More Americans could identify comedian-actor Bill Cosby than could name either of their U.S. senators. More people knew who said, "What's up, Doc," "Hi ho, Silver," or "Come up and see me sometime" than "Give me liberty or give me death," "The only thing we have to fear is fear itself," or "Speak softly and carry a big stick." More people knew that Pete Rose was accused of gambling than could name any of the five U.S. senators accused in the late 1980s of unethical conduct in the savings and loan scandal.

In 1986, the National Election Survey found that almost 24 percent of the general public did not know who George Bush was or that he was in his second term as vice president of the United States. "People at this level of inattentiveness can have only the haziest idea of the policy alternatives about which pollsters regularly ask, and such ideas as they do have must often be relatively innocent of the effects of exposure to elite discourse," writes UCLA political science professor John R. Zaller.

All of this would appear to be part of a broader trend of public ignorance that extends far beyond politics. Lack of knowledge on simple matters can reach staggering levels. In a 1996 study by the National Science Foundation, fewer than half of American adults polled (47 percent) knew that the earth takes one year to orbit the sun. Only about 9 percent could describe in their own words what a molecule is, and only 21 percent knew what DNA is.

Esoteric information? That's hard to say. One simple science-related question that has grown to have major political importance is whether police ought to genetically tag convicted criminals in the hopes of linking them to unsolved crimes. In other words, should police track the DNA of a convicted burglar to see if he is guilty of other crimes? Obviously issues of privacy and government power are relevant here. Yet how can a poll about this issue make sense if the citizenry doesn't understand the scientific terms of debate? Asking an evaluative question seems pointless.

The next generation of voters—those who will undoubtedly be asked to answer even tougher questions about politics and science—are hardly doing any better on the basics. A 2000 study by the American Council of Trustees and Alumni found that 81 percent of seniors at the nation's fifty-five top colleges scored a D or F on high school–level history exams. It turns out that most college seniors—including those from such elite universities as Harvard, Stanford, and the University of California—do not know the men or ideas that have shaped American freedom. Here are just a few examples from *Losing America's Memory: Historical Illiteracy in the 21st Century,* focusing on people's lack of knowledge about our First Citizen—the man whose respect for the laws of the infant republic set the standard for virtue and restraint in office.

> Robinson switches from talking about citizens answering public opinion polls to talking about voters voting. Do his conclusions about the uselessness of polls extend to elections?

Barely one in three students knew that George Washington was the American general at the battle of Yorktown—the battle that won the war for independence.

Only 42 percent could identify Washington with the line "First in war, first in peace, first in the hearts of his countrymen."

Only a little more than half knew that Washington's farewell address warned against permanent alliances with foreign governments.

And when it comes to actually explaining the ideas that preserve freedom and restrain government, the college seniors performed just as miserably.

More than one in three were clueless about the division of power set forth in the U.S. Constitution.

Only 22 percent of these seniors could identify the source of the phrase "government of the people, by the people, and for the people" (from Lincoln's Gettysburg Address).

Yet 99 percent of college seniors knew the crude cartoon characters Beavis and Butthead, and 98 percent could identify gangsta rapper Snoop Doggy Dogg.

Apparent ignorance of basic civics can be especially dangerous. Americans often "project" power onto institutions with little understanding of the Constitution or the law. Almost six of ten Americans (59 percent) think the president, not Congress, has the power to declare war. Thirty-five percent of Americans believe the president has the power to adjourn Congress at his will. Almost half (49 percent) think he has the power to suspend the Constitution (49 percent). And six in ten think the chief executive appoints judges to the federal courts without the approval of the Senate.

Some political scientists charge that American ignorance tends to help institutions and parties in power. That is hardly the active vigilance by the citizenry that the founders advocated. Political scientists continue to debate the role of ignorance and the future of democracy when voters are so woefully ignorant. As journalist Christopher Shea writes, "Clearly, voter ignorance poses problems for democratic theory: Politicians, the representatives of the people, are being elected by people who do not know their names or their platforms. Elites are committing the nation to major treaties and sweeping policies that most voters don't even know exist."

Professors Delli Carpini and Keeter discovered, for example, that most Americans make fundamental errors on some of the most contested and heavily covered political questions. "Americans grossly overestimate the average profit made by American corporations, the percentage of the U.S. population that is poor or homeless, and the percentage of the world population that is malnourished," they write. "And, despite twelve years of antiabortion administrations, Americans substantially underestimate the number of abortions performed every year."

With most voters unable to even name their congressperson or senators during an election year, the clear winner is the establishment candidate. Studies by Larry Bartels at Princeton University show that mere name recognition is enough to give incumbents a 5-percentage-point advantage over challengers: Most voters in the election booth can't identify a single position of the incumbent, but if they've seen the candidate's name before, that can be enough to secure their vote. (In many cases, voters can't even recognize the names of incumbents.)

Media polls are typically searching in vain for hard-nosed public opinion that simply isn't there. Polls force people to say they are leaning toward a particular candidate, but when voters are asked the more open-ended question "Whom do you favor for the presidency?" the number of undecided voters rises. The mere practice, in polling, of naming the candidates yields results that convey a false sense of what voters know. When Harvard's "Vanishing Voter Project" asked voters their presidential preferences without giving the names of candidates, they routinely found that the number of undecided voters was much higher than in media polls. Just three weeks before the 2000 election, 14 percent of voters still hadn't made up their minds.

Even when polling covers subjects on which a person should have direct knowledge, it can yield misleading results because of basic ignorance. The nonpartisan Center for Studying Health System Change (HSC) found that how people rate their health care is attributable to the type of plan they *think* they are in more than their actual health insurance. The center asked twenty thousand privately insured people what they thought of their coverage, their doctor, and their treatment. But instead of just taking their opinions and impressions, the center also looked at what coverage each respondent actually had.

Nearly a quarter of Americans misidentified the coverage they had. Eleven percent didn't know they were in an HMO, and another 13 percent thought they were in an HMO but were *not*. Yet when people believed they were in a much-maligned HMO (even when they actually had another kind of insurance), their perceived satisfaction with their health care was lower than that of people who believed they had non-HMO coverage (even when they were in an HMO). Similarly, on nearly all ten measures studied by the center, those HMO enrollees who thought they had a different kind of insurance gave satisfaction ratings similar to those who actually had those other kinds of insurance.

Once center researchers adjusted for incorrect self-identification, the differences between HMO and non-HMO enrollees nearly vanished. Even on something as personal as health care, citizens display a striking and debilitating ignorance that quietly undermines many polling results.

After looking at the carnage of polls that test voter knowledge rather than impressions, James L. Payne concluded in his 1991 book *The Culture of Spending:*

> Surveys have repeatedly found that voters are remarkably ignorant about even simple, dramatic features of the political landscape. The vast majority of voters cannot recall the names of congressional candidates in the most recent election; they cannot use the labels "liberal" and "conservative" meaningfully; they do not know which party controls Congress; they are wildly wrong about elementary facts about the federal budget; and they do not know how their congressmen vote on even quite salient policy questions. In other words, they are generally incapable of rewarding or punishing their congressman for his action on spending bills.

Ignorance of basic facts such as a candidate's name or position isn't the only reason to question the efficacy of polling in such a dispiriting universe. Because polls have become "players in the political process," their influence is felt in the policy realm, undercutting efforts to educate because they assume respondents' knowledge and focus on the horse race. Is it correct to say that Americans oppose or support various policies when they don't even have a grasp of basic facts relating to those policies? For instance, in 1995, GrassRoots Research found that 83 percent of those polled underestimated the average family's tax burden. Taxes for a four-person family earning $35,000 are 54 percent higher than most people think. Naturally when practical-minded Americans look at political issues, their perceptions of reality influence which solutions they find acceptable. If they perceive that there are fewer abortions or lower taxes than there really are, these misperceptions may affect the kinds of policy prescriptions they endorse. They might change their views if introduced to the facts. In this sense, the unreflective reporting on public opinion about these policy issues is deceptive.

The Wall Street Journal editorial page provides another example of how ignorance affects public debate. Media reports during the 1995 struggle between the

Republicans in Congress and the Clinton White House continually asserted that the public strongly opposed the GOP's efforts to slow the growth of Medicare spending. A poll by Public Opinion Strategies asked one thousand Americans not what they felt but what they actually *knew* about the GOP plan. Twenty-seven percent said they thought the GOP would cut Medicare spending by $4,000 per recipient. Almost one in four (24 percent) said it would keep spending the same. Another 25 percent didn't know. Only 22 percent knew the correct answer: The plan would increase spending to $6,700 per recipient.

Public Opinion's pollsters then told respondents that true result of the GOP plan and explained: "[U]nder the plan that recently passed by Congress, spending on Medicare will increase 45 percent over the next seven years, which is twice the projected rate of inflation." How did such hard facts change public opinion about Medicare solutions? Six of ten Americans said that the GOP's proposed Medicare spending was too *high*. Another 29 percent said it was about right. Only 2 percent said it was too *low*.

Indeed polling and the media may gain their ability to influence results from voter ignorance. When a polling question introduces new facts (or any facts at all), voters are presented with a reframed political issue and thus may have a new opinion. Voters are continually asked about higher spending, new programs, and the best way to solve social ills with government spending. But how does the knowledge base (or lack of knowledge) affect the results of a polling question? That is simply unknown. When asked in a June 2000 *Washington Post* poll how much money the federal government gives to the nation's public schools, only 31 percent chose the correct answer. Although only 10 percent admitted to not knowing the correct answer, fully 60 percent of registered voters claimed they knew but were wrong. Is there any doubt that voters' knowledge, or lack thereof, affects the debate about whether to raise school spending to ever higher levels?

What are the particular issues that interest Robinson? Why is it the misperception of taxation levels, abortion rates, and school spending that concerns him? Would we all agree if only we had the correct facts?

Reporters often claim that the public supports various policies, and they use such sentiment as an indicator of the electoral prospects of favored candidates. But this, too, can be misleading. Take, for instance, the results of a survey taken by The Polling Company for the Center for Security Policy about the Strategic Defense Initiative. Some 54 percent of respondents thought that the U.S. military had the capability to destroy a ballistic missile before it could hit an American city and do damage. Another 20 percent didn't know or refused to answer. Only 27 percent correctly said that the U. S. military could not destroy a missile.

What's interesting is that although 70 percent of those polled said they were concerned about the possibility of ballistic missile attack, the actual level of ignorance was very high. The Polling Company went on to tell those polled that "government documents indicate that the U. S. military cannot destroy even a single incoming missile." The responses were interesting. Nearly one in five said they were "shocked and angry" by the revelation. Another 28 percent said they were "very surprised," and 17 percent were "somewhat surprised." Only 22 percent said they were "not surprised at all." Finally 14 percent were "skeptical because [they] believe that the documents are inaccurate."

Beyond simply skewing poll results, ignorance is actually amplified by polling. Perhaps the most amazing example of the extent of ignorance can be found in Larry Sabato's 1981 book *The Rise of Political Consultants*. Citizens were asked: "Some people say the 1975 Public Affairs Act should be repealed. Do you agree or disagree that it should be repealed?" Nearly one in four (24 percent) said they wanted it repealed. Another 19 percent wanted it to remain in effect. Fifty-seven percent didn't know what should be done. What's interesting is that there was no such thing as the 1975 Public Affairs Act. But for 43 percent of those polled, simply asking that question was enough to create public opinion.

Ignorance can threaten even the most democratic institutions and safeguards. In September 1997, the Center for Media and Public Affairs conducted one of the largest surveys ever on American views of the Fourth Estate. Fully 84 percent of Americans are willing to "turn to the government to require that the news media give equal coverage to all sides of controversial issues." Seven in ten back court-imposed fines for inaccurate or biased reporting. And just over half (53 percent) think that journalists should be licensed. Based on sheer numbers—in the absence of the rule of law and dedication to the Bill of Rights—there is enough support to put curbs on the free speech that most journalists (rightly) consider one of the most important bulwarks of liberty.

In an era when Americans have neither the time nor the interest to track politics closely, the power of the pollster to shape public opinion is almost unparalleled when united with the media agenda.

For elected leaders, voter ignorance is something they have to confront when they attempt to make a case for new policies or reforms. But for the media, ignorance isn't an obstacle. It's an opportunity for those asking the questions—whether pollster or media polling director—to drive debate. As more time is devoted to media pundits, journalists, and pollsters, and less to candidates and leaders, the effect is a negative one: Public opinion becomes more important as arbiter for the chattering classes. But in a knowledge vacuum, public opinion also becomes more plastic and more subject to manipulation, however well intentioned.

Pollsters often try to bridge the gap in public knowledge by providing basic definitions of terms as part of their questions. But this presents a new problem: By writing the questions, pollsters are put in a position of power, particularly when those questions will be used in a media story. The story—if the poll is the story—is limited by the questions asked, the definitions supplied, and the answers that respondents are given to choose from.

The elevation of opinion without context or reference to knowledge exacerbates a problem of modern democracies. Self-expression may work in NEA-funded art, but it robs the political process of the communication and discussion that marries compromise with principle. Clearly "opinion" isn't the appropriate word for the melange of impressions and sentiment that are presented as the public's beliefs in countless newspaper and television stories. If poll respondents lack a solid grasp of the facts, surveys give us little more than narcissistic opinion.

As intelligent and precise thinking declines, all that remains is a chaos of ideologies in which the lowest human appetites rule. In her essay "Truth and Politics," historian Hannah Arendt writes: "Facts inform opinions, and opinions, inspired by different interests and passions, can differ widely and still be legitimate as long as they respect factual truth. Freedom of opinion is a farce unless factual information is guaranteed and facts themselves are not in dispute."

If ignorance is rife in a republic, what do polls and the constant media attention to them do to deliberative democracy? As Hamilton put it, American government is based on "reflection and choice." Modern-day radical egalitarians—journalists and pollsters who believe that polls are the definitive voice of the people—may applaud the ability of the most uninformed citizen to be heard, but few if any of these champions of polling ever write about or discuss the implications of ignorance to a representative democracy. This is the dirtiest secret of polling.

Absent from most polling stories is the honest disclosure that American ignorance is driving public affairs. Basic ignorance of civic questions gives us reason to doubt the veracity of most polls. Were Americans armed with strongly held opinions and well-grounded knowledge of civic matters, they would not be open to manipulation by the wording of polls. This is one of the strongest reasons to question the effect of polls on representative government.

In what ways does public opinion drive public affairs?

Pollsters assume and often control the presentation of the relevant facts. As a blunt instrument, the pollster's questions fail to explore what the contrary data may be. This is one reason that public opinion can differ so widely from one poll to another. When the citizens of a republic lack basic knowledge of political facts and cannot process ideas critically, uninformed opinion becomes even more potent in driving people. Worse, when the media fail to think critically about the lines of dispute on political questions, polls that are supposed to explore opinion will simplify and even mislead political leaders as well as the electorate.

When the media drive opinion by constant polling, the assumption of an educated public undermines the process of public deliberation that actually educates voters. Ideas are no longer honed, language isn't refined, and debate is truncated. The common ground needed for compromise and peaceful action is eroded because the discussion about facts and the parameters of the question are lost. In the frenzy to judge who wins and who loses, the media erode what it is to be a democracy. Moments of change become opportunities for spin, not for new, bold responses to the exigencies of history.

Not only are polls influenced, shaped, and even dominated by voter ignorance, but so is political debate. The evidence shows that ignorance is being projected into public debate because of the pervasiveness of polls. Polls are leading to the democratization of ignorance in the public square by ratifying ill-formed opinions, with the march of the mob instigated by an impatient and unreflective media. Polls—especially in an age marked by their proliferation—are serving as broadcasting towers of ignorance.

Political science professor Rogan Kersh notes, "Public ignorance and apathy toward most policy matters have been constant (or have grown worse) for over three decades. Yet the same period has seen increasing reliance on finely tuned instruments for measuring popular opinion, and more vigorous applications of the results in policy making." And here is the paradox in the Age of Polls: Pollsters and political scientists are still unclear about the full consequences of running a republic on the basis of opinion polls. The cost of voter ignorance is high, especially in a nation with a vast and sprawling government that, even for the most plugged-in elites, is too complicated to understand. Media polling that does not properly inform viewers and readers of its limitations serves only to give the facade of a healthy democracy, while consultants, wordsmiths, and polling units gently massage questions, set the news agenda, and then selectively report results. It is like the marionette player who claims (however invisible the strings) that the puppet moves on his own.

Consider the source and the audience.
- Matthew Robinson is an editor at *The American Spectator*, a conservative opinion journal. How might the conservative nature of the journal affect the evaluation of public opinion presented here?

Lay out the argument, the values, and the assumptions.
- What is Robinson's view of how democracy should work? Is there a place for public opinion polls in his view? For voting? What views should be represented?
- Robinson believes that American public discourse is in trouble because of unscrupulous pollsters, shoddy journalism, and ignorant voters. Are polls influenced by voter ignorance, or is voter ignorance a product of manipulative polls?
- Does Robinson show a link between voter ignorance and bad public policy? Do voters need the information he believes they don't have in order to make sound political decisions?

Uncover the evidence.

- Robinson's chief concern is voter ignorance, and he cites a lot of poll evidence and scholarly opinion to illustrate it. Do we need to know anything more about the polling evidence he cites in order to evaluate it?
- Does Robinson provide evidence that voter ignorance and irresponsible polling actually drive public affairs?

Evaluate the conclusion.

- Robinson makes a number of observations about the American voter. Are the conclusions he draws from them clear? Do they necessarily follow from his assumptions and evidence?

Sort out the political implications.

- If Robinson were writing the rules, what role would the American public play in U.S. government? What role would the media play?

10.3 Simply Put, the Public's View Can't Be Simply Put

Andrew Kohut, *Washington Post,* 29 September 2002

The Robinson article lamented public ignorance and took the media to task for manipulating polls and sending flawed messages to policymakers about what the public wants. This *Washington Post* column on opinion about what was then a possible war with Iraq explains that the fault may be not in the public or in the polls, but in the complexity of public opinion on important issues.

Ask a pollster if there is public support for war with Iraq and the answer is likely to be "yes." Ask reporters doing man-in-the-street interviews or traveling around the country, and they are likely to say "no." As *New York Times* columnist Tom Friedman wrote on Sept. 18, "Don't believe the polls that a majority of Americans favor a military strike against Iraq. It is just not true."

Who's right here? From my vantage point, they both are. And therein lies the problem—and the challenge—in understanding the public's will on this important issue.

Public opinion about a potential war with Iraq does not lend itself to an easy thumbs-up, thumbs-down characterization. Almost all national surveys this year have found a broad base of potential support for using military force to rid the world of Saddam Hussein. In mid-September, for example, the Pew Research Center found that 64 percent favor taking military action to end the Iraqi president's rule. But when pollsters go beyond this initial question, they find lots of qualifications and caveats. Respondents' concerns about the lack of allied backing and the prospect of heavy casualties reduce general support levels dramatically. Complicating the picture further, as many as four in 10 Americans still have not seriously considered the issue of war with Iraq. The polls also find that Americans may not ultimately judge a war with Iraq only on the basis of an initial military victory. For all that, there appears to be enough potential backing for President Bush to successfully sell war to the American public, as his father did 11 years ago. But he hasn't closed the deal.

Such a complex picture of public opinion is not what headline writers long for, nor is it easy material for the cable chat-show circuit. Press references rarely go beyond something along the lines of "the latest polls show a majority of Americans support a possible invasion of Iraq." So it's little wonder that both sides in the debate about Iraq have laid claim to public backing for their point of view.

Why doesn't media coverage of polls reveal the complexity that Kohut talks about?

The basis for potential backing for a war in Iraq stems from the strong support for the use of military force following the Sept. 11, 2001, attacks. In contrast, the public kicked and screamed about every intervention by the Clinton administration, whether in the distant Balkans or nearby Haiti. The Clinton White House got as much support as could be hoped for the air war in Kosovo, but over the short course of that campaign, Clinton's approval ratings fell more than they did over the entire span of the Monica Lewinsky scandal.

The attacks of Sept. 11 changed all that. Support for a defense spending hike hit a 25-year high, fueled by female support, as the once yawning gender gap on military issues narrowed significantly. More than 70 percent of men and women backed sending troops to Afghanistan, even at the risk of casualties. And our polling has found that 58 percent of the public supports combating terrorism by using military force against countries attempting to develop nuclear weapons.

Is the post–September 11 reduction in the gender gap likely to last, or to extend to nonmilitary issues?

Given the new public mandate—protect us—it is not surprising that the idea of military action against Saddam Hussein has gotten such a positive reaction over the past year. He's a bad guy from a dangerous part of the world who wants to do us harm, say Americans. The latest CBS News national poll found that 77 percent think Hussein already possesses weapons of mass destruction, 61 percent believe he wants to use them against us and 51 percent say he was involved in the Sept. 11 attacks.

In the first polls after 9/11, support for using force against Iraq was at the 70 percent level. It fell to the low fifties in August, when some prominent Republicans voiced their concerns. However, public support has since rebounded: An average of this month's major national poll results finds more than 60 percent backing military action.

At the same time, the polls consistently find less than majority support when a tag line such as "even if it means thousands of casualties" is added to the question.

This is a bit of an unfair test, because most of these questions mention only the cost of a war, not the benefit that might be achieved by such national sacrifice. It is always difficult to predict how the public will react to actual casualties. On the one hand, Americans know that war inevitably risks the lives of soldiers and civilians, and this is implicit in support for military action. On the other, they have grown accustomed to light American losses in military engagements.

The lack of allied backing is an even bigger drain on support for the use of force than the prospect of casualties. Our most recent poll found that 64 percent generally favor military action against Iraq, but that withers to 33 percent if our allies do not join us.

The first President Bush faced the same challenge, but turned public opinion to his favor with the November 1990 U.N. Security Council resolution demanding an Iraqi pullout from Kuwait. Prior to that resolution, Gallup found just 37 percent of the public favored going to war with Iraq. After the decision, majorities of the public favored going to war in every Gallup survey. Indeed, by January 1991 the only public tension was not over whether to go, but when.

What role might presidential polling have played in the preparation of Bush's U.N. speech that so dramatically changed public opinion?

It is unlikely that this President Bush will persuade the public to go to war without a coalition of traditional allies. In fact, the importance of the United Nations was underscored by public reaction to Bush's U.N. speech earlier this month. After his appearance there, the percentage of Americans who think that he has explained clearly what's at stake for the United States in Iraq rose from 37 percent to 52 percent. This was a step in the right direction for the president, but it still pales in comparison with the 77 percent who thought his father had a clear rationale for using force against Iraq in the fall of 1990.

While the current President Bush's approach is a work in progress, so is the public's thinking. Since his U.N. speech, an increasing number of respondents say they have thought a great deal about the issue—55 percent, up from 46 percent in August. But that is still below the 66 percent who had given careful thought to the question of war or peace on the eve of the Gulf War.

Part of this deliberative process may well raise the question of what will constitute a successful outcome in Iraq. We were surprised when our Sept. 11 anniversary polling found that, despite the quick rout of the Taliban in Afghanistan, relatively few Americans described that war as a success; fully 70 percent said it is too early to tell. Accordingly, two-thirds of our respondents believed we should keep forces in Afghanistan to maintain the peace. And a growing majority think that the U.S. will have to help rebuild the country.

No doubt, many Americans have the same vision of the end game in Iraq should U.S. forces quickly dispatch Hussein's troops. Both CBS and Pew surveys find Americans expecting that, unlike the Gulf War, the U.S. involvement in Iraq will be lengthy.

Al Gore and Tom Daschle's vocal criticism this past week of the Bush policy may encourage further public reflection and help influence how America makes up its mind in coming months. So far, a plurality of the public believes that Congress has asked too few questions about Bush's intentions. A dozen years ago, support for the Persian Gulf War deepened following a sometimes contentious debate. Today's polls do agree on one point: A conflicted public would welcome a comparable airing of the pros and cons of the Bush administration's Iraq policy.

Consider the source and the audience.
- Andrew Kohut is the director of the Pew Research Center for the People and the Press, a nonprofit, public interest research institute. How might his position affect his argument?

Lay out the argument, the values, and the assumptions.
- How does Kohut feel about the value of polling? Is he optimistic or pessimistic about the capabilities of the American public to understand a complex issue?
- Why don't the media capture the complexity and conflict within public opinion on a subject like war with Iraq?
- What does Kohut imply about the relationship between how the public feels about war and what the president and Congress do about it?

Uncover the evidence.
- Does Kohut's polling data support the claim he is making?

Evaluate the conclusion.
- Is Kohut right in saying that a confused public would welcome public debate on the issue of war?

Sort out the political implications.
- What should or could public officials do to help a conflicted public sort out the options and risks involved in a complex issue like war?
- Why didn't Congress more vigorously debate the possibility of war in the fall of 2002?

10.4 The Other War Room

President Bush Doesn't Believe in Polling—Just Ask His Pollsters

Joshua Green, *Washington Monthly,* April 2002

This selection further examines the degree to which public policy is guided by public opinion, this time with respect to polls conducted not by the media but by presidential administrations. As we noted, Bill Clinton was famous for his polling activities, and he was often accused by his opponents of being too "poll-driven"—that is, too willing to change his policies according to what his pollsters told him the American people wanted to hear. President Bush ran, in part, on his independence from polls in formulating his policy stances. This article doesn't dispute that fact, but it argues that Bush uses polls too. How does Bush's poll use differ from Clinton's?

On a Friday afternoon late last year, press secretaries from every recent administration gathered in the Ward Room of the White House at the invitation of Ari Fleischer, press secretary to President Bush. There was no agenda. It was just one of those unexpectedly nice things that seemed to transpire during the brief period after September 11 when people thought of themselves as Americans first and Democrats and Republicans second. Over a lunch of crab cakes and steak, Republicans such as Fleischer and Marlin Fitzwater traded war stories with Joe Lockhart, Mike McCurry, and assorted other Democrats. Halfway through lunch, President Bush dropped by unexpectedly and launched into an impromptu briefing of his own, ticking off the items on his agenda until he arrived at the question of whether it was preferable to issue vague warnings of possible terrorist threats or to stay quietly vigilant so as not to alarm people. At this point, former Clinton press secretary Dee Dee Myers piped up, "What do the poll numbers say?" All eyes turned to Bush. Without missing a beat, the famous Bush smirk crossed the president's face and he replied, "In this White House, Dee Dee, we don't poll on something as important as national security."

This wasn't a stray comment, but a glimpse of a larger strategy that has served Bush extremely well since he first launched his campaign for president—the myth that his administration doesn't use polling. As Bush endlessly insisted on the campaign trail, he governs "based upon principle and not polls and focus groups."

It's not hard to understand the appeal of this tactic. Ever since the Clinton administration's well-noted excesses—calling on pollsters to help determine vacation spots and family pets—polling has become a kind of shorthand for everything people dislike about Washington politics. "Pollsters have developed a reputation as Machiavellian plotters whose job it is to think up ways to exploit the public," says Andrew Kohut, director of the Pew Research Center for the People and the Press. Announcing that one ignores polls, then, is an easy way of conveying an impression of leadership, judgment, and substance. No one has recognized and used this to such calculated effect as Bush. When he announced he would "bring a new tone to Washington," he just as easily could have said he'd banish pollsters from the White House without any loss of effect. One of the most dependable poll results is that people don't like polling.

But in fact, the Bush administration is a frequent consumer of polls, though it takes extraordinary measures to appear that it isn't. This administration, unlike Clinton's, rarely uses poll results to ply reporters or congressional leaders for support. "It's rare to even hear talk of it unless you give a Bush guy a couple of drinks," says one White House reporter. But Republican National Committee filings show that Bush actually uses polls much more than he lets on, in ways both similar and dissimilar to Clinton. Like Clinton, Bush is most inclined to use polls when he's struggling. It's no coincidence that the administration did its heaviest polling last summer, after the poorly received rollout of its energy plan, and amid much talk of the "smallness" of the presidency. A *Washington Monthly* analysis of Republican National Committee disbursement filings revealed that Bush's principal pollsters received $346,000 in direct payments in 2001. Add to that the multiple boutique polling firms the administration regularly employs for specialized and targeted polls and the figure is closer to $1 million. That's about half the amount Clinton spent during his first year; but while Clinton used polling to craft popular policies, Bush uses polling to spin unpopular ones— arguably a much more cynical undertaking.

> *How does Green know about the differences between Bush's and Clinton's use of polls?*

Bush's principal pollster, Jan van Lohuizen, and his focus-group guru, Fred Steeper, are the best-kept secrets in Washington. Both are respected but low-key, proficient but tight-lipped, and, unlike such larger-than-life Clinton pollsters as Dick Morris and Mark Penn, happy to remain anonymous. They toil in the background, poll-testing the words and phrases the president uses to sell his policies to an often-skeptical public; they're the Bush administration's Cinderella. "In terms of the modern presidency" says Ron Faucheux, editor of *Campaigns & Elections*, "van Lohuizen is the lowest-profile pollster we've ever had." But as Bush shifts his focus back toward a domestic agenda, he'll be relying on his pollsters more than ever.

Bush's Brain

On the last day of February, the Bush administration kicked off its renewed initiative to privatize Social Security in a speech before the National Summit on Retirement Savings in Washington, D.C. Rather than address "Social Security," Bush opted to speak about "retirement security." And during the brief speech he repeated the words "choice" (three times), "compound interest" (four times), "opportunity" (nine times) and "savings" (18 times). These words were not chosen lightly. The repetition was prompted by polls and focus groups. During the campaign, Steeper honed and refined Bush's message on Social Security (with key words such as "choice," "control," and "higher returns"), measuring it against Al Gore's attack through polls and focus groups ("Wall Street roulette," "bankruptcy" and "break the contract"). Steeper discovered that respondents preferred Bush's position by 50 percent to 38 percent, despite the conventional wisdom that tampering with Social Security is political suicide. He learned, as he explained to an academic conference last February, that "there's a great deal of cynicism about the federal government being able to do anything right, which translated to the federal government not having the ability to properly invest people's Social Security dollars." By couching Bush's rhetoric in poll-tested phrases that reinforced this notion, and adding others that stress the benefits of privatization, he was able to capitalize on what most observers had considered to be a significant political disadvantage. (Independent polls generally find that when fully apprised of Bush's plan, including the risks, most voters don't support it.)

This is typical of how the Bush administration uses polls: Policies are chosen beforehand, polls used to spin them. Because many of Bush's policies aren't necessarily popular with a majority of voters, Steeper and van Lohuizen's job essentially consists of finding words to sell them to the public. Take, for instance, the Bush energy plan. When administration officials unveiled it last May, they repeatedly described it as "balanced" and "comprehensive," and stressed Bush's "leadership" and use of "modern" methods to prevent environmental damage. As *Time* magazine's Jay Carney and John Dickerson revealed, van Lohuizen had poll-tested pitch phrases for weeks before arriving at these as the most likely to conciliate a skeptical public. (Again, independent polls showed weak voter support for the Bush plan.) And the "education recession" Bush trumpeted throughout the campaign? Another triumph of opinion research. Same with "school choice," the "death tax," and the "wealth-generating private accounts" you'll soon hear more about when the Social Security debate heats up. Even the much-lauded national service initiative Bush proposed in his State of the Union address was the product of focus grouping. Though publicly Bush prides himself on never looking in the mirror (that's "leadership"), privately, he's not quite so secure. His pollsters have even conducted favorability ratings on Ari Fleischer and Karen Hughes.

Bush's public opinion operation is split between Washington, D.C., where van Lohuizen's firm, Voter/Consumer Research, orchestrates the primary polling, and Southfield, Mich., where Steeper's firm, Market Strategies, runs focus groups. What the two have in common is Karl Rove. Like many in the administration, Steeper was a veteran of the first Bush presidency, and had worked with Rove on campaigns in Illinois and Missouri. Van Lohuizen has been part of the Bush team since 1991, when Rove hired him to work on a campaign to raise the local sales tax in Arlington, Texas, in order to finance a new baseball stadium for Bush's Texas Rangers.

Like previous presidential pollsters, van Lohuizen also serves corporate clients, including Wal-Mart, Qwest, Anheuser-Busch, and Microsoft. And like his predecessors, this presents potential conflicts of interest. For example, van Lohuizen polls for Americans for Technology Leadership, a Microsoft-backed advocacy group that commissioned a van Lohuizen poll last July purporting to show strong public support for ending the government's suit against the company. At the time, Bush's Justice Department was deciding to do just that. Clinton pollster Mark Penn also did work for Microsoft and Clinton took heat for it. Bush has avoided criticism because few people realize he even *has* a pollster.

The nerve center of the Bush polling operation is a 185-station phone bank in Houston through which van Lohuizen conducts short national polls to track Bush's "attributes," and longer polls on specific topics about once a month. These are complemented by Steeper's focus groups.

One real difference between Bush and Clinton is that, while Clinton was the first to read any poll, Bush maintains several degrees of separation from his pollsters. Both report to Matthew Dowd, the administration's chief of polling, stationed at the RNC, who then reports to Rove. "Rove is a voracious consumer of polls," says a Republican pollster. "He gets it, sifts through it, analyzes it, and gives the president the bottom line." In other words, when it comes to polling, Rove serves as Bush's brain.

What is the significance of Bush maintaining "several degrees of separation" from his pollsters? What role does Karl Rove play in the Bush administration?

Poll Vault

The practice of presidents poll-testing their message dates back to John F. Kennedy, who wished to pursue a civil rights agenda but knew that he would have to articulate it in words that the American public in the 1960s would accept. Alarm about being known to use polls is just as old. Kennedy was so afraid of being discovered that he kept the polling data locked in a safe in the office of his brother, the attorney general. Lyndon Johnson polled more heavily than Kennedy did and learned, through polling, that allowing Vietnam to become an issue in 1964 could cost him re-election. Richard Nixon brought polling—and paranoia over polling—to a new level, believing that his appeal to voters was his reputation as a skilled policymaker, and that if people discovered the extent to which he was polling, they would view him as "slick" and desert him. So he kept his poll data in a safe in his home. But though presidents considered it shameful, polling became an important tool for governing well. Nixon was smart enough to make good use of his polls, once opting to ban oil drilling off the California coast after polling revealed it to be highly unpopular with voters. Jimmy Carter's pollster, Pat Caddell, was the first rock-star pollster, partying with celebrities and cultivating a high-profile image as the president's Svengali (an image considerably tarnished when Caddell's polling for another client, Coca-Cola, became the rationale for the disastrous "New Coke" campaign in the 1980s).

Ronald Reagan polled obsessively throughout his presidency. His pollster, Richard Wirthlin, went so far as to conduct them "before Reagan was inaugurated, while he was being inaugurated, and the day after he was inaugurated," says an administration veteran. He was the first to use polls to sell a right-wing agenda to the country, but he knew enough to retreat when polls indicated that he couldn't win a fight. (Wirthlin's polls convinced Reagan not to cut Social Security, as he'd planned.) By contrast, his successor, George H.W. Bush, practically eschewed polls altogether. "There was a reaction against using polls because they reacted against everything Reagan," says Ron Hinckley, a Bush pollster. "They wanted to put their own name on everything. But their efforts to not be like Reagan took them into a framework of dealing with things that ultimately proved fatal." Indeed, in his first two years in office, Bush is said to have conducted just two polls. Even at Bush's highest point—after the Gulf War, when his approval rating stood at 88 percent—Hinckley says that his economic numbers were in the 40s. "We were in a hell of a lot of trouble," he says, "and nobody wanted to listen."

Bill Clinton, of course, polled like no other president. In addition to polling more often and in greater detail than his predecessors, he put unprecedented faith in his pollsters, elevating them to the status of senior advisers. His tendency to obsess over polls disconcerted even those closest to him, and his over-reliance on polls led to some devastating errors, such as following a Morris poll showing that voters wouldn't accept a candid acknowledgment of his relationship with Monica Lewinsky. But the truth about Clinton's use of polls is more nuanced than is generally understood.

Early in his administration, Clinton drifted away from the centrist agenda he campaigned on and staked out policy positions that appealed to his base. Like Reagan, he polled on how best to sell them to the American people. Healthcare reform is the most instructive example. Describing Clinton's handling of healthcare reform in their book *Politicians Don't Pander: Political Manipulation and the Loss of Democratic Responsiveness*, political scientists Lawrence R. Jacobs and Robert Y. Shapiro conclude: "The fundamental political mistake committed by Bill Clinton and his aides was in grossly overestimating the capacity of a president to 'win' public opinion and to use public support as leverage to overcome known political obstacles—from an ideologically divided Congress to hostile interest groups." The authors call this kind of poll-tested message "crafted talk." Clinton learned its shortcomings firsthand and modified his subsequent use of polls. He fired his pollster, Stanley Greenberg, in favor of centrist pollsters such as Dick Morris and Mark Penn. Though widely ridiculed for it in the press, after the disastrous midterm elections in 1994, Clinton began responding to voters' wishes, moving toward the political center.

Oftentimes these were largely symbolic nuggets like supporting school uniforms or choosing Christopher Reeve to speak at the 1996 Democratic National Convention (Reeve outpolled Walter Cronkite and John F. Kennedy, Jr.). But they also included important policies such as reforming welfare, balancing the budget, and putting 100,000 new police officers on the streets. Many of these centrist policies initially met strong resistance from congressional Democrats, the agencies, and interest groups, as well as liberals within the White House. But the fact that the policies polled well became a powerful tool of persuasion for Clinton and his centrist aides to use. Nor was Clinton afraid to act in spite of the polls, which he did on Bosnia, Haiti, the Mexican bailout, and affirmative action. Indeed, according to senior aides, it was forbidden to discuss foreign policy in the weekly polling meeting Clinton held in the White House residence. (Although, in a priceless irony, Clinton was sufficiently worried about appearing to be poll-driven that Morris drafted a list for him of the "unpopular actions you have taken despite polls.")

"The Circle is Tight"

When George W. Bush launched his campaign for president, he did so with two prevailing thoughts in mind: to avoid his father's mistakes and to distinguish himself from Bill Clinton. To satisfy the first, Bush needed a tax cut to rival the one being offered by Steve Forbes, at the time considered Bush's most formidable rival for the GOP nomination. But to satisfy the second, Bush needed to engage in some tricky maneuvering. A van Lohuizen poll conducted in late 1998 showed tax cuts to be "the least popular choice" on his agenda among swing voters. So Bush faced a dilemma: He had to sell Americans a tax cut most didn't want, using a poll-crafted sales pitch he didn't want them to know about. In speeches, Bush started listing the tax cut after more popular items like saving Social Security and education. In March 2001, with support still flagging, he began pitching "tax cuts and debt relief" rather than just tax cuts—his polling showed that the public was much more interested in the latter. After plenty of creative math and more poll-tested phrases, Bush's tax cut finally won passage (a larger one, in fact, than he'd been offering in '98).

In a way, Bush's approach to polling is the opposite of Clinton's. He uses polls but conceals that fact, and, instead of polling to ensure that new policies have broad public support, takes policies favored by his conservative base and polls on how to make them seem palatable to mainstream voters. This pattern extends to the entire administration. Whereas Clinton's polling data were regularly circulated among the staff, Bush limits his to the handful of senior advisers who attend Rove's "strategy meetings." According to White House aides, the subject is rarely broached with the president or at other senior staff meetings. "The circle is tight," Matthew Dowd, Bush's chief of polling, testifies. "Very tight." As with Kennedy and Nixon, the Bush administration keeps its polling data under lock and key. Reagan circulated favorable polling data widely among congressional

Republicans in an effort to build support. Clinton did likewise and extended this tactic to the media, using polls as political currency to persuade reporters that he was on the right side of an issue. "You don't see it like you did in the Dick Wirthlin days," says a top Republican congressman. "The White House pollster won't meet with the caucus to go through poll data. It just doesn't happen." Says a White House reporter, "The Clinton folks couldn't wait to call you up and share polling data, and Democratic pollsters who worked for the White House were always calling you to talk about it. But there's a general dictate under Bush that they don't use polls to tell them what to think." This policy extends to the president's pollsters, who are discouraged from identifying themselves as such. The strategy seems to be working. A brief, unscientific survey of White House reporters revealed that most couldn't name van Lohuizen as the Bush's primary pollster (most guessed Dowd, who doesn't actually poll). For his part, van Lohuizen sounded genuinely alarmed when I contacted him.

Crafted Talk

It's no mystery why the Bush administration keeps its polling operation in a secure, undisclosed location. Survey after survey shows that voters don't want a president slavishly following polls—they want "leadership" (another word that crops up in Bush's speeches with suspicious frequency). So it's with undisguised relish that Dowd tells me, "It was true during the campaign, it's true now. We don't poll policy positions. Ever."

> Why is it seen as "slick" for a politician to listen to polls and do what people want, and as "leadership" for a politician to do what he wants, regardless of what the public says?

But voters don't like a president to ignore their desires either. One of the abiding tensions in any democracy is between the need for leaders to respond to public opinion but also to be willing to act in ways that run counter to it. Good presidents strike the right balance. And polls, rightly used, help them do it.

But used the wrong way, polls become a way to cheat the system and evade this tension altogether. As Jacobs and Shapiro explain in *Politicians Don't Pander,* with the exception of the latter Clinton years, presidents since 1980 have increasingly used polls to come up with the "crafted talk" that makes their partisan, interest-group-driven policies seem more mainstream than they really are. Consider the Republican stimulus plan unveiled last winter: So heavily did it tilt toward corporate interests that focus group participants refused to believe that it was real—yet Bush pitched it for months as a "jobs" package.

Presidents, of course, must occasionally break with public opinion. But there's a thin line between being principled and being elitist. For many years, Democrats hurt themselves and the country by presuming they knew better than voters when it came to things like welfare, crime, and tax increases. Clinton used polling to help Democrats break this habit. Bush is more intent on using it to facilitate the GOP's own peculiar political elitism—the conviction that coddling corporations and cutting taxes for the rich will help the country, regardless of the fact that a majority of voters disagree.

Bush's attempt to slip a conservative agenda past a moderate public could come back to hurt him, especially now that his high approval ratings might tempt him to overreach. Recent history shows that poll-tested messages are often easy to parry. During the debate over Clinton's healthcare plan, for instance, Republican opponents launched their own poll-tested counterattack, the famous "Harry and Louise" ads, which were broadcast mainly on airport cable networks such as "CNN Airport" where well-traveled congressmen would be sure to spot them and assume they were ubiquitous. Because lawmakers and voters never fully bought Clinton's policy, it couldn't withstand the carefully tested GOP rebuttal.

A similar fate befell the GOP when it took over Congress in 1995, after campaigning on a list of promises dubbed the "Contract With America." As several pollsters and political scientists have since pointed out, the Contract's policies were heavily geared toward the party's conservative base but didn't register with voters—things like corporate tax cuts and limiting the right to sue. The GOP's strategy was to win over the press and the public with poll-tested "power phrases." Education vouchers, for instance, were promoted as a way of "strengthening rights of parents in their children's education," and Republicans were instructed by RNC chairman Haley Barbour to repeat such phrases "until you vomit." But when it came to proposals such as cutting Medicare, Republicans discovered that their confidence in being able to move public opinion—"preserving" and "protecting" Medicare—was misplaced. Clinton successfully branded them as "extremists," and this proposal, along with many of the Contract's provisions, never made it beyond the House.

Like so many other Republican ideas, Barbour's has been reborn under Bush. "What's happened over time is that there's a lot more polling on spin," says Jacobs. "That's exactly where Bush is right now. He's not polling to find out issues that the public supports so that he can respond to their substantive interests. He's polling on presentation. To those of us who study it, most of his major policy statements come off as completely poll concocted." Should this continue, the administration that condemns polling so righteously may not like what the polls wind up saying.

Consider the source and the audience.

- The *Washington Monthly* is an independent investigative political journal that prides itself on its ability to take on both liberals and conservatives, and whose mission statement makes clear its goal of influencing Washington insiders. How does this article fit that profile?

Lay out the argument, the values, and the assumptions.

- What does Green believe the role of public opinion ought to be in a democracy? How does he differ here from Matthew Robinson (the author of the second article in this chapter)?
- When should a president listen to public opinion, and when should he not? What role can polls play here?
- Is there a legitimate way for politicians to use public opinion and an illegitimate one?

Uncover the evidence.

- Where does Green go to investigate public opinion gathering in the Bush administration? Given how "tight the circle is," how can he know what he claims to know?
- Whether or not Bush uses polls is a matter for factual investigation. What kind of evidence does Green rely on to support his claim that Bush uses polls to "spin" policy stances he has already taken and make them palatable to the public?

Evaluate the conclusion.

- What are the differences between Green's conclusion and Robinson's? What role does each think public opinion plays in policymaking, and who does each hold responsible for the manipulation of public opinion?
- Is Green right in saying that those who manipulate public opinion to advance a more extreme ideological agenda will be vulnerable to attack from moderate opponents more in tune with the public?

Sort out the political implications.

- What does it mean for the future of democracy if more polls are being done to "spin" policy than to create and direct it?

10.5 Will the Polls Destroy Representative Democracy?

George Horace Gallup and Saul Forbes Rae, *The Pulse of Democracy,* 1940

This selection is a concluding chapter of a book that polling pioneer George Horace Gallup co-authored about the role of polls in democracy. Counter to some of the articles we have read in this chapter, this is a classic statement of confidence in the American people particularly, and in the central role of public opinion in a democracy generally. Gallup's book was written in 1940; are his arguments still relevant today?

Another accusation leveled at the modern polls is based on the assumption that they intensify the "band-wagon" instinct in legislators and undermine the American system of representative government. "Ours is a representative democracy," a newspaper editorial suggested soon after the polls had become prominent in 1936, "in which it is properly assumed that those who are chosen to be representatives will think for themselves, use their best judgment individually, and take the unpopular side of an argument whenever they are sincerely convinced that the unpopular side is in the long run in the best interests of the country."

The point has been made more recently by a student of public opinion. "If our representatives were told," it has been written, "that 62% of the people favored payment of the soldier's bonus or 65% favored killing the World Court Treaty, the desire of many of them to be re-elected would lead them to respond to such statistics by voting for or against a measure not because they considered it wise or stupid but because they wanted to be in accord with what was pictured to them as the will of the electorate."[1]

Beyond such criticisms, and at the root of many objections to the polls of public opinion, lies a fundamental conflict between two opposed views of the democratic process and what it means. This conflict is not new—it is older than American political theory itself. It concerns the relationship between representative government and direct democracy, between the judgments of small exclusive groups and the opinions of the great mass of the people. Many theorists who criticize the polls do so because they fear that giving too much power to the people will reduce the representative to the role of rubber stamp. A modern restatement of this attitude may be found in an article written by Colonel O. R. Maguire in the November, 1939, issue of the *United States Law Review.*[2]

> What exactly are the two views of the democratic process that Gallup and Rae discuss? Follow their definition of these positions closely.

Colonel Maguire quotes James Madison: ". . . pure democracies . . . have ever been spectacles of turbulence and contention; have ever been found incompatible with personal security or the rights of property; and have in general been as short in their lives as they have been violent in their deaths."

To support these statements made by an eighteenth-century conservative who feared the dangers of "too much democracy," Maguire insists that the ordinary man is incapable of being a responsible citizen, and leans heavily on the antidemocratic psychological generalizations of Ross, Tarde, and Le Bon. He follows James Madison and the English Conservative, Edmund Burke, in upholding the conception of representative government under which a body of carefully chosen, disinterested public representatives "whose wisdom may best discern the true interest of their country, and whose patriotism and love of justice will be least likely to sacrifice it to temporary or partial considerations," interpret the real will of the people. Under such conditions, it is argued, "it may well happen that the public voice, pronounced by the representatives of the people, will be more consonant to the public good than if pronounced by the people themselves, convened for that purpose." The polls are condemned because, in his view, they invite judgments on which the people are ignorant and ill-informed, on which discussion must be left to representatives and specialists. Finally, a grim picture is drawn of the excesses that will follow the growth of "direct democracy": ". . . the straw ballot will undermine and discourage the influence of able and conscientious public men and elevate to power the demagogue who will go to the greatest extremes in taking from those who have and giving to those who have not, until there has been realized the prophecy of Thomas Babington Macaulay that America will be as fearfully plundered from within by her own people in the twentieth century as Rome was plundered from without by the Gauls and Vandals."

This case against government by public opinion reveals suspicion not only of the public-opinion surveys, but also of the mass of the people. By and large, the thesis that the people are unfit to rule, and that they must be led by their natural superiors—the legislators and the experts—differs only in degree, and not in essence, from the view urged by Mussolini and Hitler that the people are mere "ballot cattle," whose votes are useful not because they represent a valuable guide to policy, but merely because they provide "proof" of the mass support on which the superior regime is based. It must not be forgotten that the dictators, too, urge that the common people, because of their numbers, their lack of training, their stupidity and gullibility, must be kept as far away as possible from the elite whose task it is to formulate laws for the mass blindly to obey.

Many previous statements and charges of just this kind can be found throughout history. Every despot has claimed that the people were incapable of ruling themselves, and by implication decided that only certain privileged leaders were fit for the legislative task. They have argued that "the best" should rule—but at different times and in different places the judgments as to who constituted "the best" have been completely contradictory. In Burke's England or Madison's America, it was the peerage or the stable wealthier classes—"the good, the wise, and the rich." In Soviet Russia, the representatives of the proletariat constitute "the best."

But the history of autocracy has paid eloquent testimony to the truth of Lord Acton's conclusion that "Power corrupts—absolute power corrupts absolutely." The possible danger of what has been called "the never-ending audacity of elected persons" emphasizes the need for modifying executive power by the contribution of the needs and aspirations of the common people. This is the essence of the democratic conception: political societies are most secure when deeply rooted in the political activity and interest of the mass of the people and least secure when social judgment is the prerogative of the chosen few.

The American tradition of political thought has tried to reconcile these two points of view. Since the beginning of the country's history, political theorists have disagreed on the extent to which the people and their opinions could play a part in the political decision.

"Men by their constitutions," wrote Jefferson, "are naturally divided into two parties: 1.—Those who fear and distrust the people and wish to draw all powers from them into the hands of the higher classes; 2.—Those who identify themselves with the people, have confidence in them, cherish and consider them as the most wise depository of the public interests."[3] Jefferson himself believed that the people were less likely to misgovern themselves than any small exclusive group, and for this reason urged that public opinion should be the decisive and ultimate force in American politics.

> Are the two parties that Thomas Jefferson said people are "naturally divided into" relevant to the two major parties today?

His opponents have followed Alexander Hamilton, whose antidemocratic ideas provide an armory for present-day conservatives. "All communities divide themselves into the few and the many," Hamilton declared. "The first are the rich and well-born, the others are the mass of the people. The voice of the people has been said to be the Voice of God; and however generally this maxim has been quoted and believed, it is not true in fact. The people seldom judge or determine right." Those who have followed the Federalist philosophy have largely been concerned with the liberties and property of the minority and have continually urged the necessity of building checks against the people's power.

Those who favor rule of "the best," through the gifted representative, and those who desire to give the common people more power are frequently at loggerheads because their arguments do not meet each other. The need exists to find the right balance between the kind of mass judgments and comments obtained by the public-opinion polls and the opinions of legislators. Both extreme views contain a kernel of truth. No one would deny that we need the best and the wisest in the key positions of our political life. But the democrat is right in demanding that these leaders be subject to check by the opinions of the mass of the people. He is right in refusing to let these persons rule irresponsibly. For in its most extreme form, the criticism that opposes any effort, like the modern polls, to make the people more articulate, that inveighs against the perils of a "direct democracy," leads directly to antidemocratic government. If it is argued that legislators understand better than the people what the people want, it is but a short step to give legislators the power to decree what the people *ought* to want. Few tendencies could be more dangerous. When a special group is entrusted with the task of determining the values for a whole community, we have gone a long way from democracy, representative or any other kind.

The debate hinges to some extent on which particular theory of the representatives' role is accepted. There is the view which the English Conservative, Edmund Burke, advanced in the eighteenth century to the electors of Bristol: "His unbiased opinion, his mature judgment, his enlightened conscience, he ought not to sacrifice to you; to any man, or to any set of men living. These he does not derive from your pleasure. They are a trust from Providence, for the abuse of which he is deeply answerable. Your representative owes you, not his industry only, but his judgment; and he betrays instead of serving you, if he sacrifices it to your opinion." This view has been restated more sharply in the words of the Southern Senator who is reported to have told a state delegation: "Not for hell and a brown mule will I bind myself to your wishes." But, on the other hand, it must be remembered that the electors of Bristol rejected Burke after his address, and that there are many in our own day who take the view that one of the legislator's chief tasks in a democracy must be to "represent."

Unless he is to be the easy prey of special interests and antisocial pressure, he must have access to the expression of a truly "public" opinion, containing the views of all the groups in our complex society. For free expression of public opinion is not merely a right which the masses are fortunate to possess—it is as vital for the leaders as for the people. In no other way can the legislators know what the people they represent want, what kinds of legislation are possible, what the people think about existing laws, or how serious the opposition may be to a particular political proposal. A rigid dictatorship, or any organization of political society which forbids the people to express their own attitudes, is dangerous not only to the people, but also to the leaders themselves, since they never know whether they are sitting in an easy chair or on top of a volcano. *People who live differently think differently.* In order that their experience be incorporated into political rules under which they are to live, their thinking must be included in the main body of ideas involved in the process of final decisions. That is why the surveys take care to include those on relief as well as those who draw their income from investments, young as well as old, men and women of all sorts from every section of the country, in the sample public.

Another form which the case against the people takes is the argument that we are living today in a society so complex and so technical that its problems cannot be trusted to the people or their representatives, but must be turned over to experts. It has been urged that only those who know *how* to legislate should have the power of decreeing what type of legislation *ought* to exist. The Technocracy movement put this view squarely before the American public. If it is true, it means that the kind of mass value judgments secured by the polls and surveys is quite useless in political life. It means that the people and their representatives must abdicate before the trained economist, the social worker, the expert in public finance, in tariffs, in rural problems, in foreign affairs. These learned persons, the argument runs, are the only ones who know and understand the facts therefore, they alone are competent to decide on matters of policy.

There is something tempting about the view that the people should be led by an aristocracy of specialists. But Americans have learned something from the experience of the past decade. They have learned, in the first place, that experts do not always agree about the solutions for the ills of our times. "Ask six economists their opinion on unemployment," an English wag has suggested, "and you will get seven different answers—two from Mr. John Maynard Keynes."

The point is obviously exaggerated. Certainly today a vast body of useful, applicable knowledge has been built up by economists and other specialists— knowledge which is sorely needed to remedy the ills of our time. But all that experts can do, even assuming we can get them to agree about what need be done, is to tell *how* we can act.

The objectives, the ends, the basic values of policy must still be decided. The economist can suggest what action is to be taken if a certain goal is to be reached. He, speaking purely as an economist, cannot say what final goal *should* be reached. The lawyer can administer and interpret the country's laws. He cannot say what those laws should be. The social worker can suggest ways of aiding the aged. He cannot say that aiding aged persons is desirable. The expert's function is invaluable, but its value lies in judging the means—not the ends—of public policy.

Thus the expert and his techniques are sorely needed. Perhaps Great Britain has gone even further than the United States in relating expert opinion to democratic government. The technique of the Royal Commission, and the other methods of organizing special knowledge, are extremely valuable ways of focusing the attention of the general public on specific evils and on solutions of them. In these Commissions, expert opinion is brought to bear, and opportunities for collective deliberation are created for those with special knowledge of political and economic questions. But even these Royal Commissions must remain ineffective until the general public has passed judgment on whether or not their recommendations should be implemented into legislation.

As a corollary of this view that expert opinion can bear only on specific questions of means, on the technical methods by which solutions are to be achieved, we must agree that most people do not and, in the nature of things, cannot have the necessary knowledge to judge the intimate details of policy. Repeated testing by means of the poll technique reveals that they cannot be expected to have opinions or intelligent judgments about details of monetary policy, of treaty making, or on other questions involving highly specialized knowledge. There are things which cannot be done by public opinion, just as there are things which can only be done by public opinion. "The people who are the power entitled to say what they want," Bryce wrote, "are less qualified to say how, and in what form, they are to obtain it; or in other words, public opinion can determine ends, but is less fit to examine and select means to those ends."[4]

> What is it that experts are best at, and what is public opinion best at?

All this may be granted to the critics. But having urged the need for representatives and experts, we still need to keep these legislators and experts in touch with the public and its opinions. We still have need of declarations of attitudes from those who live under the laws and regulations administered by the experts. For only the man on relief can tell the administrator how it feels to be on relief. Only the small businessman can express his attitude on the economic questions which complicate his existence. Only women voters can explain their views on marriage and divorce. Only all these groups, taken together, can formulate the general objectives and tendencies which their experience makes them feel would be best for the common welfare. For the ultimate values of politics and economics, the judgments on which public policy is based, do not come from special knowledge or from intelligence alone. *They are compounded from the day-to-day experience of the men and women who together make up the society we live in.*

That is why public-opinion polls are important today. Instead of being attempts to sabotage representative government, kidnap the members of Congress, and substitute the taxi driver for the expert in politics, as some critics insist, public-opinion research is a necessary and valuable aid to truly representative government. The continuous studies of public opinion will merely *supplement,* not destroy, the work of representatives. What is evident here is that representatives will be better able to represent if they have an accurate measure of the wishes, aspirations, and needs of different groups within the general public, rather than the kind of distorted picture sent them by telegram enthusiasts and overzealous pressure groups who claim to speak for all the people, but actually speak only for themselves. Public-opinion surveys will provide legislators with a new instrument for estimating trends of opinion, and minimize the chances of their being fooled by clamoring minorities. For the alternative to these surveys, it must be remembered, is not a perfect and still silence in which the Ideal Legislator and the Perfect Expert can commune on desirable policies. It is the real world of competing pressures, vociferous demonstrations, and the stale cries of party politics.

Does this mean that constant soundings of public opinion will inevitably substitute demagogery for statesmanship? The contrary is more likely. The demagogue is no unfamiliar object. He was not created by the modern opinion surveys. He thrives, not when the people have power, facts, information, but when the people are insecure, gullible, see and hear only one side of the case. The demagogue, like any propagandist of untruths, finds his natural habitat where there is no method of checking on the truth or falsity of his case. To distinguish demagogues from democratic leaders, the people must know the facts, and must act upon them.

Is this element secured by having no measurement of public opinion, or by having frequent, accurate measurement? When local Caesars rise to claim a large popular support for their plans and schemes, is it not better to be able to refer to some more tangible index of their true status than their own claims and speeches? The poll measurements have, more than once, served in the past to expose the claims of false prophets.

As the polls develop in accuracy, and as their returns become more widely accepted, public officials and the people themselves will probably become more critical in distinguishing between the currents of opinion which command the genuine support of a large section of the public and the spurious claims of the pressure groups. The new methods of estimating public opinion are not revolutionary—they merely supplement the various intuitive and haphazard indices available to the legislator with a direct, systematic description of public opinion. Politicians who introduced the technique of political canvassing and door-to-door surveys on the eve of elections, to discover the voting intentions and opinions of the public in their own districts, can hardly fail to acknowledge the value of canvassing the people to hear their opinions, not only on candidates, but on issues as well. It is simply a question of substituting more precise methods for methods based on impressions. Certainly people knew it was cold long before the invention of the thermometer, but the thermometer has helped them to know exactly how cold it is, and how the temperature varies at different points of time. In the same way, politicians and legislators employed methods for measuring the attitudes of the public in the past, but the introduction of the sampling referendum allows their estimates to be made against the background of tested knowledge.

Will the polls of the future become so accurate that legislators will automatically follow their dictates? If this happened would it mean rule by a kind of "mobocracy"? To the first point, it may be suggested that although great accuracy can be achieved through careful polling, no poll can be completely accurate in every single instance over a long period of time. In every sampling result there is a small margin of error which must never be overlooked in interpreting the results. The answer to the second question depends essentially on the nature of the judgments which people make, and on the competence of the majority to act as a directive force in politics.

There has always been a fear of the majority at the back of the minds of many intelligent critics of the polls. Ever since the time of Alexis de Tocqueville, the phrase, "tyranny of the majority," has been used widely by critics of democratic procedure, fearful lest the sheer weight of numbers should crush intelligent minorities and suppress the criticism that comes from small associations which refuse to conform to the majority view. It has been asserted that the same tendencies to a wanton use of power which exist in a despotism may also exist in a society where the will of the majority is the supreme sovereign power.

What protection exists against this abuse of power by a majority scornful of its weaker critics and intolerant of dissenting opinions? The sages of 1787 were fully aware of the danger, and accordingly created in the Bill of Rights provisions whereby specific guarantees—free speech, free association, and open debate— were laid down to ensure the protection of the rights of dissident minorities.

Obviously, such legal provisions cannot guarantee that a self-governing community will never make mistakes, or that the majority will always urge right policies. No democratic state can ever be *certain* of these things. Our own history provides abundant evidence pointing to the conclusion that the majority can commit blunders, and can become intolerant of intelligent minority points of view. But popular government has never rested on the belief that such things *cannot* happen. On the contrary, it rests on the sure knowledge that they *can* and *do* happen, and further, that they can and do happen in autocracies—with infinitely more disastrous consequences. The democratic idea implies awareness that the people *can* be wrong—but it attempts to build conditions within which error may be discovered and through which truth may become more widely available. It recognizes that people can make crucial mistakes when they do not have access to the facts, when the facts to which they have access are so distorted through the spread of propaganda and half-truths as to be useless, or when their lives are so insecure as to provide a breeding ground for violence and extremes.

> What does it mean to say that "the democratic idea implies awareness that the people can be wrong"? What's the check on their being wrong?

It is important to remember that while the seismograph does not create earthquakes, this instrument may one day help to alleviate such catastrophes by charting the place of their occurrence, their strength, and so enabling those interested in controlling the effects of such disasters to obtain more knowledge of their causes. Similarly, the polls do not create the sources of irrationalism and potential chaos in our society. What they can do is to give the people and the legislators a picture of existing tendencies, knowledge of which may save democracy from rushing over the edge of the precipice.

The antidote for "mobocracy" is not the suppression of public opinion, but the maintenance of a free tribunal of public opinion to which rival protagonists can make their appeals. Only in this atmosphere of give-and-take of rival points of view can democratic methods produce intelligent results. "The clash and conflict of argument bring out the strength and weakness of every case," it has been truly said, "and that which is sound tends to prevail. Let the cynic say what he will. Man is not an irrational animal. Truth usually wins in the long run, though the obsessions of self-interest or prejudice or ignorance may long delay its victory."

There is a powerful incentive to expose the forces which prevent the victory of truth, for there is real value in the social judgments that are reached through widespread discussion and debate. Although democratic solutions may not be the "ideally best," yet they have the fundamental merit of being solutions which the people and their representatives have worked out in co-operation. There is value in the method of trial and error, for the only way people will ever learn to govern themselves is by governing themselves.

Thus the faith to which the democrat holds is not found so much in the inherent wisdom of majorities as in the value of rule by the majority principle. The democrat need not depend upon a mystic "general will" continually operating to direct society toward the "good life." He merely has to agree that the best way of settling conflicts in political life is by some settled rule of action, and that, empirically, this lies in the majority principle. For when the majority is finally convinced, the laws are immeasurably more stable than they would be were they carried out in flagrant opposition to its wishes. In the long run, only laws which are backed by public opinion can command obedience.

"The risk of the majority principle," it has been said "is the least dangerous, and the stakes the highest, of all forms of political organization. It is the risk least separable made from the process of government itself. When you have made the commonwealth reasonably safe against raids by oligarchies or depredations by individual megalomaniacs; when you have provided the best mechanisms you can contrive for the succession to power, and have hedged both majorities and minorities about with constitutional safeguards of their own devising, then you have done all that the art of politics can ever do. For the rest, insurance against majority tyranny will depend on the health of your economic institutions, the wisdom of your educational process, the whole ethos and vitality of your culture.[5] In short, the democrat does not have to believe that man is infinitely perfectible, or that he is infinitely a fool. He merely has to realize that under some conditions men judge wisely and act decently, while under other conditions they act blindly and cruelly. His job is to see that the second set of conditions never develops, and to maximize the conditions which enable men to govern themselves peacefully and wisely.

The "tryanny of the majority" has never been America's biggest problem. It is as great a danger to contemplate the "tyranny of the minority," who operate under cover of the Bill of Rights to secure ends in the interests of a small group. The real tyranny in America will not come from a better knowledge of how majorities feel about the questions of the day which press for solution. Tyranny come from ignorance of the power and wants of the opposition. Tyranny arises when the media of information are closed, not when they are open for all to use.

The best guarantee for the maintenance of a vigorous democratic life lies not in concealing what people think, but in trying to find out what their ultimate purposes are, and in seeking to incorporate these purposes in legislation. It demands exposing the weakness of democracy as well as its values. Above all, it is posited on the belief that political institutions are not perfect, that they must be modified to meet changing conditions, and that a new age demands new political techniques.

[1] Smith, C. W., *Public Opinion in a Democracy,* New York, 1939, p. 411.

[2] Maguire, O. R., "The Republican Form of Government and the Straw Poll—an Examination," *U.S. Law Review,* November, 1939.

[3] Agar, Herbert, *Pursuit of Happiness,* p. 42.

[4] Bryce, James, *The American Commonwealth,* p. 347.

[5] Lerner, Max, *It Is Later Than You Think,* 1938, p. 111.

Consider the source and the audience.

- Gallup was writing a book to showcase his science of polling and its possibilities. Would that fact affect his message?

Lay out the argument, the values, and the assumptions.

- Which of the two views of the democratic process that Gallup and Rae discuss do they adhere to?
- What is public opinion capable of doing, and what are its limitations?
- What is the worst form of government that Gallup and Rae can imagine? How do they think the monitoring of public opinion can help avert that form of government?

Uncover the evidence.

- Where do Gallup and Rae draw the evidence for their argument? Are historical example and philosophical principle sufficient to make their case? Is there any kind of empirical evidence they could offer?

Evaluate the conclusion.

- Is democracy doomed if it is not based on the public's own determination of what it wants?
- Can public opinion be an effective check on the dangers inherent in democracy?

Sort out the political implications.

- How much democracy would Gallup and Rae favor? What role do they see for polls? What would they think of the uses to which polling is put today?

CHAPTER 11

Political Parties

The U.S. Constitution is silent on the subject of political parties, but our founders were not. Madison warned against the dangers of factional divisions among the population in *The Federalist Papers* and George Washington echoed that warning when he left office after serving two terms as the first president of the new nation. And yet, parties were present in the early days of the republic, and they are present today.

Defined as groups that unite under a common label to control government and to promote their ideas and policies, parties have become an integral part of the American political system. Two parties in particular, the Democrats and the Republicans, have dominated the political scene for approximately one hundred and fifty years.

Defenders of parties say that they strengthen American democracy, serving to recruit candidates, define their policy agendas, and run their campaigns, as well as providing a link between voters and the people they elect, greater political accountability, and continuity and stability in government. Some people go so far as to say that it is political parties that make democracy possible.[1]

Critics, however, say that the parties are captives of special interests, that their divisive partisanship turns voters off, that they narrow voters' political choices, that they provide a haven for corruption, and that they are driven by an untouchable elite. Some critics want to do away with parties altogether; others want to change the rules to empower more parties; still others want to reduce the power of all parties.

The selections in this chapter look at some central issues in the study of political parties: whether the parties stand for different things, how groups align themselves with parties, how parties' efforts to gain and maintain power lead them to take particular stands on issues, what role the party plays, what would happen if we had no parties, the limits of a two-party system, and whether parties endanger democracy. We begin with a chapter from a book written by Vermont Senator Jim Jeffords, who turned party politics upside-down in 2001 when he changed his party affiliation from Republican to Independent and, in the process, turned control of the Senate over to the Democrats. The second piece begins with a discussion of Republicans' efforts in 2000 to portray themselves as a party of diversity, and asks how the party of Lincoln ever lost the black vote in the first place. The third selection,

---

[1] E. E. Schattschneider, *Party Government* (New York: Farrar and Rinehart, Inc., 1942).

from the *New York Times,* looks at efforts by New York's mayor to join a rising trend in the United States toward getting rid of party labels in municipal elections and city government. Fourth is an essay by Ralph Nader, the Green Party nominee for president in 2000, who, frustrated at his exclusion from the presidential debates, highlights what he sees as the evils for American voters of having a party system where the rules are made by the two dominant parties to keep themselves in power. Finally, we look at a classic, George Washington's Farewell Address, in which he celebrates American government but points out the pitfalls he sees before it, chief of which is the danger of partisan division.

11.1 Obscure Senator, Small State

James M. Jeffords, *My Declaration of Independence,* 2001

In the wake of the 2000 election, the Senate was evenly divided (50/50) between Republicans and Democrats. The rules of the Senate decree that in the case of a tie, the vice-president casts the tie-breaking vote. In 2001, the vice-president was Dick Cheney, a Republican, and so when the Senate voted on who should lead the Senate, the Republicans could command a majority of the votes. Republican Senator Trent Lott held the post of Senate Majority Leader; Democratic Senator Tom Daschle was Minority Leader.

All that changed in May 2001, when a Republican senator from the tiny state of Vermont left his party to become an Independent and agreed to vote for Daschle for the leadership post. Jim Jeffords' discomfort with the direction of his party led him to single-handedly give control of the Senate to the Democrats, who held it until the Republicans were voted back into power in the 2002 midterm elections.

While Democrats cheered and welcomed him, and most of his constituents in Vermont supported his decision, Republicans were stunned. Since the majority party in the Senate controls the committee chairs as well as the majority leader's seat, many Republicans were out of power as a result of Jeffords' action. What could he have been thinking, they wondered, to have taken so momentous a step? The following excerpt is the first chapter of a small book Jeffords wrote about his decision, in which he answers that question and recounts the actual moment in which he knew his decision was final.

I must have walked the corridors of National Airport, now named Reagan National, seven or eight hundred times heading home to Vermont. Though people may imagine the life of a Senator as somewhat distant and glorious, for much of our lives we are first cousins of the traveling salesman. Marriages fail, children suffer, and friends are lost. If this time my mood was on the gloomy side, it was because I had just left a meeting where I had very likely lost a few more friends. It was easily the toughest meeting of the thousands I have had during my three decades in politics.

I was heading for Burlington, Vermont, the trip I had made so many times before, but tonight's eight o'clock flight was anything but routine. Although I had yet to fully appreciate this fact, the people at the airline had, and I had been steered by the airline's personnel to a VIP lounge just beyond the security checkpoint.

It seemed like the first half hour in days that I had a chance to catch my breath. The morning papers scattered about the room had given the story of my considering leaving front-page coverage with photos. The television was running the story almost constantly. Even the business news gave it play, attributing some of the movement in the stock market to speculation about my pending announcement.

My press secretary, Erik Smulson, had been so deluged by phone calls from reporters and producers that this was his first chance to see what was going on around us. Like me, he was amazed by the wall-to-wall coverage. Erik's job had been transformed over the past few days from trying to generate news to trying to contain it at some manageable level.

As the flight's departure time neared, we left the lounge and headed down the corridor to Gate 35A, the low-tech launching pad for the jets and prop planes headed for the small cities of the East Coast. I soon realized why the airline staff had intervened. A hundred yards away, dozens of reporters had staked out the little gate, with TV cameras and microphones pointed my way. This was not going to be another milk run to Burlington.

Before I reached the press, I got my first taste that my deliberations had pierced the veil of public indifference that often attends what Congress does or does not do. On both sides of the broad aisle, passengers awaiting their flight stood on their chairs and started cheering and applauding, while others pushed forward to shake my hand. This for someone who a few days before may have ranked about 99th on the U.S. Senate celebrity scale.

People don't much care what Congress does, and in a democracy, that can be a very good thing. There are, and should be, more important things in people's lives than who a Senator from a small state might be, or what he might do. But here were scores of people who not only recognized me but also approved of what they thought I would be doing the next day in Vermont, who literally wanted to reach out and touch me. It was extraordinary that the glare of media attention in just a few days had thrust me before people's eyes in a way that was flattering but not entirely comfortable. How had what I thought or done to that point so touched these people?

> Is it a good thing if people don't care what Congress does? Can it also be a bad thing? What does Jeffords mean here?

After running the press gauntlet, something I had some practice in after the past few days, my wife Liz, Erik, my chief of staff, Susan Russ, and I rode a shuttle bus out across the tarmac to the plane.

I had tried throughout the past few days to keep a level head about me, but my family and staff took no chances. Lest I had invested too much meaning into the reception I had just received, Susan pointed out that the people cheering me were waiting for a plane to Boston, hardly a political cross section of the country.

Our plane was a small jet, three seats across, which was a blessing for the Vermont delegation in Congress compared to the small props connecting through Pittsburgh or LaGuardia that used to be our only alternative. The flight usually had a Vermont flavor—a few students from the University, an engineer from IBM, a state employee or two heading home from a conference in Washington, sometimes even Ben or Jerry. It is pretty common to know a few people on the trip; such is the size of my state.

But tonight the press had commandeered it. Within a few minutes of announcing at midday that I would travel to Vermont to make a statement the next day, the seats were sold out (which is not saying all that much, I suppose). UVM may have been represented on the flight, but so were the network news shows, newspapers from London, Dallas, Los Angeles, and Tokyo, and camera crews from who knows where.

But it was not all strangers. The father of my former state director was on the flight, though I have to admit it was awkward seeing him. His daughter had left my office and with my support had won a job in the new Bush Administration, as head of the Vermont–New Hampshire USDA Rural Development office. Hers is one of a handful of jobs in a state that a Senator can have a role in filling when the President is from the same party. She is immensely qualified and a good Republican, but who could know her fate at that point? Would my candidates for the Vermont U.S. Attorney, U.S. Marshal, and Farm Service Agency Director jobs be at risk as well? Yet more people whose lives my decision would touch.

> Here is the practice of patronage, still alive and well. How can the ability to fill jobs that is contingent on one's good standing with the president affect one's ability to make independent decisions?

My wife Liz, one of the people most affected, was seated next to me on the plane. While normally as voluble as I am quiet, she had little to say as we settled in for the flight. Over the past week, we had said about all there was to say on the topic of my party affiliation.

Liz is an independent soul, but she has to be labeled a liberal. How else do you describe someone who was an early supporter of Reverend Jesse Jackson's bid for the presidency, and who put up a yard sign for the Democrat running for Governor the same year I was running as a Republican for the U.S. Senate?

In the instant and sometimes inaccurate analysis that characterized much of the coverage of my decision, Liz was rumored by some to have been the catalyst for my switch, when in fact the opposite was true. She thought it was a bad idea, said so repeatedly and in very unvarnished terms, but gave me tremendous support once she realized my decision was close to being made. She is not one to stand meekly by her man. But I think she realized the anguish I was enduring and wanted me to do what I thought was right.

It may be hard to understand if you are fed a steady diet of caricatures, but the Senate consists of real people, many of whom have personalities as magnetic as their political views can be repellent. I thought Liz would be the last to place much stock in the relationships you can develop in Washington. I traveled home to Vermont almost every weekend. She chose to spend most of her time there, leaving our home on the back side of Killington Mountain only once or twice a year to visit Washington, D.C. But she found, as I did, that political views do not always provide a window on someone's personality. Senator Jesse Helms and his wife, Dorothy, would not agree with Liz on many issues, but they are two of the nicest people you could ever meet.

Is it possible to divorce political views from your opinion of a person? I think so, and I could not function in the Senate otherwise. How corrosive it would be to constantly recalibrate your approach to an individual based on whether you agreed or disagreed on the last vote.

A conservative Republican lobbyist who once spent much of a weekend with Liz and me remarked of her afterward that he had never so thoroughly enjoyed a person with whom he so completely disagreed. My response was "Me, too." It got a good laugh, but in fact Liz and my views are not that far apart, and on the issue of my switch we had made our peace. I had explained to Liz again and again why I was thinking of casting off my Republican label. But she couldn't shake the hurt it would cause our friends, whom she was fond of despite being political opposites.

She also questioned why I would make such a decision so late in my career and whether it would overshadow all else. Neither of us could know how the public, and particularly Vermonters, would receive it. Would I be seen in a harsh light, as petulant or prideful, or could people come to understand my reasoning? What kind of repercussions would flow from it? And as Liz knew better than anyone else, rocky relations with the Republican Party were nothing new; indeed, they have characterized my entire political career in Vermont and Washington, D.C. We had coped with it for thirty years. Why now?

The explanations I had given her were much the same as those I had provided in my meeting a few hours earlier in the Capitol.

At the behest of John Warner, the senior Senator from Virginia and the picture of a southern gentleman, I had joined a small group of Senators in the Vice President's Room, a small, ornate ceremonial office off the floor of the Senate chamber, just before leaving for the airport. John is a tremendously decent and honorable man, and it is almost impossible to say no to him. The room is controlled by the President of the Senate—the role assigned by the Constitution to the Vice President of the United States, Dick Cheney. It had become familiar surroundings over the past few weeks.

Though I agreed to join my colleagues, I knew it would be miserable. How do you explain abandoning your allegiance to the Republican Party to a group of people that will be hurt both personally and professionally?

One of the people in the room, Senator Chuck Grassley of Iowa, came to the Congress with me in January of 1975. The two of us washed up into the House of Representatives in the midst of the Democratic tidal wave caused by Watergate. Voters elected 75 Democrats that fall, and only 17 Republicans. Thanks to my two terms as an active Attorney General in Vermont, I had eked out a narrow 53 percent victory.

Chuck was hobbling around on crutches from a sports injury, and I wore a neck brace from being rear-ended in my car in the last weeks of the campaign. As we walked down the center aisle of the House, probably still more than a little amazed at our surroundings, one Democratic wag remarked, "There's two we almost got."

Chuck and I served on the House Agriculture Committee for years, and he preceded me to the U.S. Senate in 1981. He had slowly worked his way up the seniority ladder so that finally, in January 2001, he became the chairman of a major committee, the powerful Senate Committee on Finance, for the first time in his congressional career.

As we sat in the Vice President's Room, the question Chuck and everyone asked was "How could you do this to us?" They would lose the power some of them had acquired only a few months prior. And while the power of a chairmanship in an evenly divided Senate is far from absolute, it is still considerable. With it, they had hoped to advance the causes and dreams that were as important to them as mine to me.

By the end of the meeting I had tears in my eyes, as did many of the Senators sitting around me. It was gut-wrenching trying to explain what impelled me to think of leaving the party, handing control of the Senate to the Democrats and wresting it from my friends and colleagues. By the time I left the meeting, I had agreed to rethink whether I really could decide the course of the Senate by myself. It was the first time in the past ten days that I had genuine second thoughts.

> What were Jeffords' second thoughts based on—principle, personal ties, or ethical considerations?

I sat on the plane, inches from Liz, but entirely alone. How could I arrogate to myself this power, when I had been elected by fewer than 200,000 people in Vermont? How could I exact such a price from my friends? I turned these questions over again and again in my head as we made the 90-minute flight to Vermont. There were no easy answers.

But I knew that if I went ahead, I would have to deliver the speech of my life the next morning. So I worked on the speech draft, reading and rereading the text, adding a few words here, marking for a break there.

My critics are right about one thing. I am not God's gift to oratory. I envy those of my colleagues who could talk a dog off a meat wagon. But that's not me. The *Vermont Owner's Manual,* by Frank Bryan and Bill Mares, is a small humor book on Vermont that tries to explain the state to natives and newcomers alike. In its section on which laws are to be taken seriously and which are not, it describes a twenty-minute high school graduation speech by our governor as a misdemeanor, and the same by me as a felony.

Fortunately Vermont is a small enough place that people can know you for your deeds as well as your words. You can still engage in retail politics, walking down Main Street, working the crowds at the county fairs, and greeting people outside the plant gate. At one point a question on a political survey showed that a third of the voters had met me or attended a meeting I had spoken at. (I'm hoping they are not the third that consistently voted against me.) It is also a state that is fiercely independent. While there is no party registration, polls show about half the state's voters consider themselves independents, with the remainder splitting their allegiances between the two major parties.

The more I went over the speech, the more I thought about the reasoning behind it. Just as my colleagues couldn't understand how I could go ahead and switch, I couldn't understand how I could stay a Republican.

The budget and tax battles of the spring had brought home to me how wide a gulf had come to separate me from national Republican orthodoxy. While I thought we should use much of the surplus for addressing pressing domestic spending needs, such as education and child care and health care, few of my Republican colleagues saw these as high priorities. This view was based on their belief that the best government is the least government, and that as many surplus dollars as possible should be returned to the taxpayer.

I understand that view, but do not subscribe to it. It seems to me that a healthy skepticism of government ought to be leavened with an appreciation for what it can do and for what people cannot do for themselves. As Franklin Roosevelt once remarked, "Better the occasional faults of a government that lives in a spirit of charity than the consistent omissions of a government frozen in the ice of its own indifference."

Low-wage and even middle-class working parents simply cannot afford decent child care, yet research is making it abundantly clear that these early years in a child's life are both critical and largely irretrievable. Every other industrialized nation fully furnishes such care as part of the public school system. In our country, state and local governments are forced to bear ever larger costs for educating our children with special needs because the federal government has never made good on its promise to fund 40 percent of the costs of special education. And without a prodigious investment of additional funds, we will never help the more than 40 million Americans who lack health insurance.

This is an argument I can make to my constituents in Vermont and the vast majority will agree that we should invest more in our children, even if it means forgoing a share of a tax cut. Indeed, it is exactly the argument I made to

Vermont voters in the fall of 2000 when I ran for reelection and won close to two-thirds of their votes. But for many of my Republican colleagues in Washington, this argument makes no sense. Throughout the spring, as I voiced my concerns in Republican meetings, I met with rolled eyes of disbelief more often than nodding heads of agreement.

I was a tangle of emotions on the flight home to Vermont. The tug of war between my allegiance to my friends in the Senate and remaining true to my own beliefs yielded no clear victor. I was beat, my emotions were still raw, and my thoughts were still somewhat unsettled.

But as the plane began its descent above the Champlain Valley into the familiar hills of Vermont, I knew the next day I would break with the party I had supported throughout my adult life. My first allegiance had to be not to my colleagues, but to my constituents and my conscience. The makeup of the Senate is not created by national referendum, but by thirty-three or so individual races in very different states every two years. As I had made clear in my Senate campaign six years before, my contract was not with America, but with Vermont.

I had tried to effect change within the party. I had tried to accommodate my beliefs to the party as a whole. I had tried to be fair to those with whom I had formed friendships over the decades. And I had tried to balance my decision against the impact it would have on my colleagues, my family, and my staff, many of whom would soon be thrown out of work. But in the end, I had to be true to what I thought was right, and leave the consequences to sort themselves out in the days ahead.

Consider the source and the audience.
- What might Jeffords' motives have been in writing a book recounting and explaining his reasons for switching parties?
- How would you read a book written by Jeffords on this subject differently from one written by a journalist, or by a political opponent?

Lay out the argument, the values, and the assumptions.
- What is Jeffords' chief goal in writing this book?
- Consider the kinds of values and concerns that were important to him in making his decision. What considerations drove him to follow through, and what considerations gave him pause? Which were ultimately most important to him?

Uncover the evidence.
- This is an essay of personal experience, not an academic argument, so the role played by evidence is slightly different from that seen in other readings. What kinds of evidence convinced Jeffords that his decision was the right one?

Evaluate the conclusion.
- For Jeffords, his obligation to his constituents and the principles he believed in trumped his feelings of friendship for members of his party. What seems to be absent here is any commitment to the principles of the Republican Party itself. Should that have played a larger role?

Sort out the political implications.
- What would happen if other members of Congress switched parties at will? Consider what would happen to Congress, but also what would happen to the members who switched. Why has Jeffords received so much support from his constituents?

11.2 The Party of Lincoln . . .

But Not of Hayes, Harrison, Hoover, Eisenhower, Nixon, Reagan, or Bush

David Greenberg, *Slate*, 10 August 2000

David Greenberg writes a column for the electronic journal *Slate* called "History Lesson" in which he covers the historical background of contemporary political events. Greenberg, a Ph.D. in history and a fellow at Columbia University, wrote this piece after the 2000 Republican Party convention, during which the Republicans celebrated their links to Abraham Lincoln and made a point of portraying their party as one of diversity.

The Republicans are indeed the party of Lincoln, but as Greenberg points out, since the electoral realignment of the 1930s, most African Americans have voted for the Democrats. That pattern continued to hold true in the 2000 election. Even after the Republicans' televised effort to reach out to minority voters, and after George W. Bush made clear before the election his intention to appoint African Americans, including Colin Powell and Condoleezza Rice, to his administration, Democratic nominee Al Gore received 90 percent of the black votes cast.

Republicans have worked to change this voting pattern, hoping their stances on school vouchers and faith-based initiatives would appeal to black voters. Democrats, knowing that their political viability depends on their continued appeal to minorities, fight back by emphasizing their position on policies that support families economically and extend civil rights. In this article, Greenberg looks at how the shift in electoral allegiance initially took place and suggests what might need to be done to reverse it.

Now that its convention is over, will the Republican Party keep pretending that it likes black people? As the Philadelphia story would have it, attracting black voters simply means returning to a proud history from which the GOP has only recently deviated. In truth, the history of the Republican Party's relationship with blacks is one of a bright start followed by a gradual but steady decline.

In 1854, the Republican Party was founded mainly to end slavery, and for two decades it honorably promoted African-American

> This is a pretty provocative question. What does Greenberg imply when he says that the Republican Party is "pretending that it likes black people"?

equality. Its first presidential nominee, pioneer James C. Frémont, took a staunch anti-slavery stand in 1856 and ran well, paving the way for Abraham Lincoln's election four years later. Lincoln was no radical. He believed white men superior to blacks and opposed the outright abolition of slavery. But he wanted to stop slavery's westward expansion in the hope that it would die out—a position that won him endorsements from leading African-Americans such as Frederick Douglass and 40 percent of the overall vote, enough for victory in a four-way race.

After the Civil War, the "Radical Republicans," who oversaw the Reconstruction of the South, brought blacks into electoral politics. Blacks naturally joined the GOP rather than the white supremacist Southern Democrats. In these golden years, black Republicans got the vote and even won elective office (Mississippi elected the nation's first African-American senator in 1870). Led by the GOP, the nation ratified the 13th, 14th, and 15th Amendments, which ended slavery and gave black men full citizenship and the franchise.

The GOP's abandonment of African-Americans commenced with the presidential election of 1876. The party had already been subordinating its agenda of black equality to that of cultivating Northern industrialists when Ohio Republican Rutherford B. Hayes, to resolve a contested election, agreed to the notorious Compromise of 1876. In exchange for their support, Hayes promised Southern Democrats to withdraw federal troops from the South and to let them treat blacks as they pleased. Almost immediately, white supremacist, or "redeemer" Democrats regained power, heralding the reign of Jim Crow. Ironically, the compromise also crippled black Republicanism, as state Republican parties, to compete for white votes, engaged in racial me-tooism, purging blacks from the party or shunting them into "Black and Tan" delegations whose legitimacy was not always recognized.

By the Progressive Era, both the Republicans and the Democrats were generally uninterested in helping African-Americans. One issue that couldn't be ignored—though the parties tried—was the horror of lynching, which had become rampant in the post-Reconstruction South. Anti-lynching laws marked the last major civil rights issue on which Republicans were out in front.

In 1920 Leonidas Dyer, a Missouri Republican from a largely black St. Louis district, introduced an anti-lynching bill, which the new Republican president, Warren Harding, endorsed. The House passed it in January 1922 (231–199, with only 17 Republicans opposing and eight Northern or border-state Democrats in support). Yet even though they controlled the Senate too, the GOP couldn't, or wouldn't, pull out the stops to pass the law. While Majority Leader Henry Cabot Lodge of Massachusetts supported the bill, the powerful Idaho Republican William Borah opposed it as meddling in states' rights and helped Southern Democrats kill it. The Borah-Lodge rift foretold a schism in the GOP between Northeastern liberals and a Midwestern and Western Old Guard that would later scramble the party's racial politics.

Meanwhile, blacks were fleeing the South for Northern cities. There, the Democrats' political machines delivered services and patronage to immigrants in exchange for their votes, and Democratic bosses shrewdly absorbed blacks into their system. In contrast, Republicans missed another opportunity. Their machines (yes, they existed too) reacted coolly to black voters' demands and to black politicians' ambitions—leading many to leave the party.

The realignment crystallized under President Franklin Roosevelt. In 1932, FDR won just 23 percent of the black vote. Yet he swiftly bolstered his black support. Gestures such as consulting a "black cabinet" of unofficial African-American advisers surely helped, but more important were his economic relief programs. The Depression hit black Americans disproportionately hard, and FDR's relief programs, such as the Civilian Conservation Corps and the Public Works Administration, gave them much-needed aid and jobs. A popular song among Depression-era blacks made it plain:

> What does the word "realignment" mean here?

Roosevelt! You're my man!
When the time come I ain't got a cent
You buy my groceries
And pay my rent.

Mr. Roosevelt, you're my man!

In Congress, meanwhile, Northern and Western Democrats took the lead on progressive racial legislation; it was two Democratic senators who in 1934 introduced the next major anti-lynching bill. Between 1932 and 1936, writes historian Nancy J. Weiss in *Farewell to the Party of Lincoln: Black Politics in the Age of FDR,* "Roosevelt and the New Deal changed the voting habits of black Americans in ways that have lasted to our own time."

Some Republicans still grasped desperately for black ballots. In an ideologically divided party, liberal leaders, such as presidential nominees Wendell Willkie and Thomas Dewey, incorporated pro-civil-rights language into the platforms. But their efforts paled next to Harry Truman's. Truman, the strongest civil rights president the nation had seen, won 70 percent of the black vote in 1948 with a bold, progressive racial agenda. He supported a Fair Employment Practices Commission to fight job discrimination and desegregated the military by executive order.

By the 1950s racial liberalism in the GOP was fading fast. Dwight Eisenhower, a conservative (though not a reactionary) on race, opposed Truman on key issues. In 1945 Eisenhower testified before Congress against integrating the military, and as president he resisted reviving the FEPC. He opposed the 1954 Supreme Court decision *Brown vs. Board of Education,* which ruled that segregated public schools were unconstitutional. (Bowing to the inevitable, the 1956 GOP platform endorsed Brown.) Ike remarked that "you cannot change people's hearts merely by laws"—repeatedly justifying his inaction in the face of rising demands for civil rights laws.

(At last week's convention, Bush adviser Condoleezza Rice said the Alabama Republican Party of 1952 registered her father to vote when the Democrats wouldn't. That may be true, but in much of the deep South then the GOP was virtually nonexistent. In Georgia, writes the historian Taylor Branch, "Barry Goldwater had trouble drawing crowds to fill even barber shops.")

Entering the 1960 election the Democrats, behind such leaders as Hubert Humphrey of Minnesota and Herbert Lehman of New York, had become the unquestioned party of civil rights. Richard Nixon, who always overestimated his own popularity with blacks, still hoped to fare well—Jackie Robinson, for one, endorsed him—and he probably had a stronger civil rights record than John F. Kennedy. But JFK courted the black vote, famously phoning Martin Luther King Jr.'s wife, Coretta, when the civil rights leader was jailed. Kennedy would have commanded the black vote anyway, but the closeness of the election led analysts to mythologize the phone call as critical.

The battle over the 1964 Civil Rights Act marked the last hurrah for racial liberalism within the GOP. President Lyndon Johnson, Attorney General Robert Kennedy, and the liberal Democrats decided the time was ripe to pass a bill with teeth, their Southern party-mates be damned. While the Republican leadership took a wait-and-see position, younger GOP congressmen such as New York's John Lindsay (who later became a Democrat) and Maryland's Charles Mathias worked on the bill, helping it to passage in the House over Southern opposition.

In the Senate, Southern Democrats predictably undertook a filibuster, which boded ill. Never had civil advocates mustered the two-thirds supermajority needed to close off debate.[*] At first, few Republican senators were willing to vote to end the filibuster, believing strongly in states' rights. But behind the scenes Vice President Hubert Humphrey negotiated with Minority Leader Everett Dirksen of Illinois, a supporter of the bill. Humphrey claimed that he courted Dirksen as avidly as he had wooed his wife, Muriel. Dirksen promised to round up enough Republican holdouts if Humphrey would attach amendments paying lip service to state and local control. The deal was struck, and after more than two months the Senate voted 71–29 for cloture, with six Republicans joining 23 Southern Democrats in opposition (44 Democrats and 27 Republicans voted aye).

> This is the second time Greenberg has mentioned Republicans' commitment to states' rights. How would such a commitment rule out Republican support for civil rights in the South?

---

[*] Sixty votes are needed to end a filibuster.

Sen. Richard Russell of Georgia, the Democrat who led the opposition, said Dirksen had "killed off a rapidly growing Republican Party in the South." But Russell had it backward. Significantly, the opponents of the 1964 law included the GOP's future leaders, including Arizona Sen. Barry Goldwater and Texas Senate aspirant George H. W. Bush. They knew their electoral success depended on conservative support in the South and West.

Goldwater's "Operation Dixie" in his 1964 presidential race may have meant surrendering the black vote; LBJ won 94 percent that year. But it bore fruit four years later. Richard Nixon's successful "Southern Strategy" of 1968 became the blueprint for Ronald Reagan's Southern inroads and Lee Atwater and George Bush's Willie Hortonism. So, if George W. Bush, running under the guidance of Atwater's protégé Karl Rove, can reverse that trend it will be more than a change in his party's line. He will be declaring, truly, that this is not his father's Republican Party.

Consider the source and the audience.

- *Slate* is an online journal, whose writers and audience include both Democrats and Republicans. In what ways does this audience appeal to both sides?
- Does the fact that the author is an historian give him any more authority than if he were a regular journalist? What are the strengths and weaknesses of an historical approach?

Lay out the argument, the values, and the assumptions.

- What does Greenberg believe that understanding the past can do for our understanding of the present?
- Does he see the historical actions of the two parties in terms of "right vs. wrong" or in terms of a struggle for political support and power?
- How did the Democrats win the support of black voters in the 1930s? Why, in Greenberg's view, did the Republicans abandon the attempt to woo them back, especially in the 1960s?

Uncover the evidence.

- What kind of evidence do historians rely on? Is it beyond dispute, or open to interpretation?
- Does Greenberg make any claims that require additional evidence to back them up?

Evaluate the conclusion.

- Is Greenberg right in saying that the Republican Party has come to power on a conservative southern power base that precludes it from reaching out to blacks?
- Does he spend adequate time exploring such issues as the conflict between states' rights and civil rights?

Sort out the political implications.

- In what ways has President George W. Bush succeeded in changing the racial stance and strategy of "his father's Republican Party"? In what ways has he failed?

11.3 To the Faithful, "Nonpartisan" Is a 4-Letter Word

Jonathan P. Hicks, *New York Times,* 26 August 2002

Although our founders had strong reservations about political parties, which do not appear in the Constitution, it is hard for those of us in twenty-first century America to imagine doing without them. New York City Mayor Michael Bloomberg didn't have that trouble, though, in the summer of 2002 when he tried to get an amendment on the ballot that would have abolished parties for municipal elections. If he had been successful (the movement was abandoned well before election day) he would have been following the trend in three-quarters of American cities and one state legislature (Nebraska) of preventing candidates from running for office under the labels of Republican or Democrat.

In New York City, people love their parties, and they were sharply opposed to giving them up. This *New York Times* article explores their arguments against the move to nonpartisan elections, and Bloomberg's for favoring them.

One night a month, Theresa Brown takes large bags of chicken wings and a variety of other ingredients and prepares dinner for several hundred members of the 57th Assembly District Democratic Organization, a highly active political club in the Fort Greene section of Brooklyn.

For Ms. Brown, a cheerful great-grandmother whose age is "not yet 60," cooking for the meeting the last Thursday of every month is not a duty, but a reflection of her devotion. "I've been involved in Democratic politics for longer than I can remember," said Ms. Brown, who seems constantly to be working on some local campaign and is also in charge of the club's newsletters, which are mailed to 800 people several times a year.

"For me, it's not just politics," she said. "It's a lot more than that. It's a place that's, well, like family."

In Ms. Brown's eyes, that makes Mayor Michael R. Bloomberg something of a home wrecker. She sees the Republican mayor's plan to put an amendment on the ballot this November to eliminate partisan elections in New York City as nothing less than the dismantling of a way of life she has come to cherish.

Though not everyone feels this way, she speaks for many of the foot soldiers and party faithful—the people who wear the buttons, who pass out the campaign literature at subway stations at dawn and who make the telephone calls for candidates when they get home from work. To them, Mr. Bloomberg's proposal is not an academic exercise, nor does it accomplish any real political purpose.

"I don't see how it enhances the way elections are held," said Walter T. Mosley, a member of the Thurgood Marshall Democratic Club in Crown Heights, Brooklyn. As an aide to Assemblyman Clarence Norman Jr., the Brooklyn Democratic Party chairman, Mr. Mosley has firsthand experience with the details of party politics in Brooklyn.

"Parties play a fundamental role in shaping the political debate," he said. "If anything, they give clarification to a race. It gives a people a sense of the agenda and goals of a candidate."

Mr. Bloomberg argues that the influence of the Democratic and Republican Parties limits participation in elections, and that political ideology has no place in municipal government. The mayor, who was a registered Democrat just a short time before joining the Republican Party and running for mayor, has said he thinks a wider range of people would be attracted to politics if the role of the party were eliminated.

How his proposal would work is not clear; the concept is being reviewed by the Charter Revision Commission established by the mayor. However, some in the Bloomberg administration suggest there is a model in how the city holds special elections to fill vacancies on the City Council after resignations or deaths.

Those elections are nonpartisan, meaning candidates cannot run under the labels of the major political parties. Instead, they select other labels—such as "Experience First" or "United Neighborhoods"—to appear with their names on the ballot.

How one would get on the ballot in the first place or how many signatures would be required for a ballot spot—and from whom—has not been worked out.

Still, the angst over the mayor's proposals has more to do with emotion than details. Several political scientists suggest, however, that the change will not necessarily hurt the parties or their people.

In a trend that started out West, about 75 percent of all American cities have switched to nonpartisan elections, according to the National League of Cities.

In the major cities with nonpartisan elections, the party role is often diminished, but political organizations nonetheless thrive because state and national races are as lively as ever.

What is it about the culture or politics of the western United States that might have given rise to the start of the trend toward nonpartisan elections?

"It's certainly true that there are some political leaders who no longer have control of the process when cities change to having nonpartisan elections, but there still is a lot of party activity that continues to go on," said Jeffrey B. Lewis, an assistant professor of political science at the University of California at Los Angeles.

And Professor Lewis said any loss of party power could not be blamed solely on a change in local rules. "It's difficult to say whether the political parties lose their strength because of nonpartisan elections, because they were thought to be losing their strength anyway," he said. "And how do you measure that?"

New York City, however, remains a bastion of partisanship, particularly for Democrats. Although the city has elected two Republican mayors in a row and is in a state with a two-term Republican governor, New York's United States senators are Democrats, and registered Democrats in the city continue to outnumber registered Republicans five to one.

But not all the resistance to Mr. Bloomberg's proposal has come from Democrats.

"I don't support the idea of nonpartisan elections," said Vincent M. Ignizio, a leader in the Republican Party in Staten Island.

"There is a philosophy associated with my enrollment with a national, state and local party," Mr. Ignizio said. "And when an elected official speaks, he espouses that philosophy. It's a notice to the public that there are certain principles that you stand for."

> How does the fact that parties are seen as standing for certain principles help to clarify political debate?

Mr. Ignizio, who has worked on virtually every significant Republican race in Staten Island in the last few years, suggested that changes in campaign finance laws and the adoption of term-limit laws have already achieved the mayor's goal of opening up the elective process.

"The system has never been more open than it is now," he said. "The way it works now, if you have five people who are willing to go out and get signatures on your behalf, you can get on the ballot. The parties give the people a stronger voice."

Rank-and-file party loyalists also voice many of the same objections made by other critics of the mayor's proposal, the most common being that Mr. Bloomberg is rushing the process, leaving too little time for the change to be adequately studied. For it to appear for voter approval on the November ballot, the Charter Revision Commission must complete its work, including hearings throughout the city, by Sept. 6.

Despite their attempts to halt it, many of the party faithful say they expect the issue to be on the ballot in November. So the monthly meetings of the political clubs and the most casual conversations between active party people are full of discussions about a possible nonpartisan future.

> This article seems to be focused on the effects of nonpartisanship on political parties. What effects might it have on city government?

Would it be as devastating to the parties as many of them expect? Political scientists point out that the parties would still be active in the legislative, statewide and national elections. Some also suggest that the parties would maintain substantial influence in municipal elections. Even now, in those special elections to fill the unexpired terms of City Council members, traditional party activists and leaders often wield considerable clout.

"It very well may strengthen the role of party organizations," said Evan Stavisky, a political consultant who usually works with Democratic candidates in New York City.

"It would open up the process to more candidates," he said. "But the candidates who emerge and are successful are the ones generally who have the money and endorsements. So, the role of a party might well be strengthened under that system."

Still, habit and lifestyle are difficult to change. Thus there is much concern and confusion at the Bushwick United Democratic Club, a Brooklyn political institution where there seems to be a meeting a night to plan campaign strategy for one local candidate or another.

"I don't really know what to make of it," said Demrys Reyna, while sitting at a computer designing campaign literature at the club's headquarters. "But all I know is, I don't see what's wrong with keeping things the way they are."

Consider the source and the audience.

- The *New York Times* is writing for a homegrown audience here. Would the article have been written differently if it were directed to a western state, for instance?

Lay out the argument, the values, and the assumptions.

- There are two competing arguments in this piece: Bloomberg's anti-party argument and his opponents' pro-party argument. How might Mayor Bloomberg's unusual partisan history shape his views on the evils or blessings of party? Why does he think the parties' influence on politics is bad?
- What role does party play in the lives of Bloomberg's opponents that might shape their views about it? Why do they defend the role of party?

Uncover the evidence.

- Does this article achieve enough depth in its exploration of the evidence behind each argument? What would such evidence look like?

Evaluate the conclusion.

- Does either side provide a convincing case? Since there are cities that have nonpartisan elections, how could we use their experience to test the conclusions here?

Sort out the political implications.

- Can you speculate about how differently politics might proceed without parties? How would voters choose candidates if they could not rely on party labels? What difference would it make to the behavior of lawmakers if they did not run and were not organized by party?

11.4 Why Voters Will Lose Out in Tuesday's Debate

Ralph Nader, *Boston Globe,* 30 September 2000

Months before Gore voters would call him a "spoiler" for his role in George Bush's 2000 election victory, Ralph Nader, the Green Party candidate, was just trying to get into the race. In this op-ed piece in the *Boston Globe* he spoke out against being excluded from the upcoming presidential debate between the two major party candidates, and argued that it was the voters who were going to be the true losers. Do voters lose out in a two-party system? How?

F our years ago a majority of eligible voters, in effect, cast their ballots for "none of the above" in the presidential election. As a result, President Clinton was returned to office in 1996 by only slightly less than 25 percent of the electorate.

Democracy is in a serious crisis when more than 94 million voters stay at home and turn their backs on the precious right to select the people who will lead the nation. Commanding the money, the media, and the access to both the ballots and debates, the Republican and Democratic parties have designed and enforced a closed system that largely shuts out new parties and new ways to strengthen our democracy. One result has been a decline in voter turnout, a citizenry that increasingly has lost control of its government, and a nation in which a few wealthy and powerful corporations dictate public policy that does not benefit the majority of Americans.

> Does Nader know that the strength of the two-party system has caused a decline in turnout? Why else might turnout have declined?

The two major parties will parade their candidates before the nation in the first presidential debates of this century at the University of Massachusetts at Boston on Tuesday night. On the stage will be two more "look-alike" candidates speaking to a narrow set of issues and avoiding any utterances that might step on the toes of their major corporate donors, who have carefully divided the campaign loot between the two parties.

Absent will be candidates who speak about what to do regarding the excessive concentration of power by big business over our governments, our workplace, marketplace, and environment.

It is not the candidates but the citizenry who will lose out Tuesday night as George W. Bush and Al Gore are allowed to sidestep issues that are important to millions of Americans and the solutions that would improve their lives.

Subject matters that will be avoided by Bush and Gore include: corporate welfare giveaways that could be better used to provide for human needs; weak enforcement against corporate crime, fraud and abuse; restrictive labor laws that are keeping tens of millions of low-wage workers from forming trade unions; media concentration; racism; renewable energy; full public funding of election campaigns; universal, accessible health insurance for all Americans; and the renegotiation of global trade treaties with labor, environmental and consumer rights standards that pull communities up rather than pushing them down.

What role does Nader think a third-party candidate can play in the debate?

Instead, viewers will be watching a ritualistic debate by two hereditary politicians financed by corporate cash. It is little surprise that the Commission on Presidential Debates, created and controlled by the Democratic and Republican parties, has chosen to lock significant third-party candidates out of the debates and a national television audience.

Sadly, some commentators have endorsed the exclusion of my Green Party candidacy, which uniquely advocates new tools of democracy based on a long record of achievement.

The Republican and Democratic parties are not an enshrined duopoly in our Constitution. Our society should never let them, by default, control the "Khyber Pass" to tens of millions of voters who will watch these debates. A large majority of the American people want to have leading third-party candidates in the debates.

Nader calls for the admission of "significant" third-party candidates to the debate. What does "significant" mean here? Would Nader deny some candidates the right to participate? Who?

Anyone who discounts the value of debates in gaining public support has only to look at Minnesota. There, Jesse Ventura, a former professional wrestler, was mired in third place in the gubernatorial race with poll numbers in single digits. But he was given a place in the debates, and that exposure vaulted him into the governor's chair.

The Minnesota experience weighs heavily on the Democratic and Republican parties. The major-party machines, with their handpicked commission serving as the sole referee, are not about to give up their monopoly control of the debates.

Despite the machinations of the two major parties and their corporate campaign paymasters, citizens still can have the final say in a democracy. If enough people deny them their votes, sooner or later the political machine will have to give up their key to their gated domain.

American democracy does not belong to the decayed Democratic and Republican parties. It belongs to the people, and they should reclaim and rebuild it for themselves and for future generations.

Consider the source and the audience.

- Nader is writing in the *Boston Globe* the weekend before the presidential debates are scheduled to be held at the University of Massachusetts in Boston. Why not write in the *New York Times,* or some paper with a broader circulation?

Lay out the argument, the values, and the assumptions.

- What societal ills does Nader blame on the two-party system? Is this assumption of blame justified? What purpose of Nader's is served by it?
- What are Nader's political values? Is he liberal, conservative, or something else?
- Why does Nader think the two-party system cannot or will not address the issues he cares about?

Uncover the evidence.

- What evidence does Nader offer to support the causal link he sees between the two-party system, on the one hand, and low voter turnout and popular disaffection with politics on the other? Can the claim stand without evidence?
- What evidence does Nader offer in support of his contention that he should be allowed to participate in the debate? Are polling data and Nader's other political experiences convincing here?

Evaluate the conclusion.

- Does Nader make his case that he should be allowed to participate in the debate? Why or why not? Does he leave unanswered any concerns that should be addressed?

Sort out the political implications.

- How many people can participate in a debate before it loses its usefulness in helping the audience see the differences between and strengths and weaknesses of the candidates? If we are all but certain that one of two people will be chosen president, does it make any sense to admit a third person to the debate? What about a fourth, or a fifth? Where do we draw the line? What kind of yardstick should we use?

11.5 Farewell Address

George Washington, 17 September 1796

On the brink of leaving office, President George Washington prepared this address to the nation he had led since its birth. Eager to retire (this address was originally intended to mark his departure four years earlier but he was persuaded to stay on), he was also anxious to point out to the young nation where danger might lie in its future. Chief among his concerns were political parties, fiscal responsibility, and foreign policy.

Here we excerpt Washington's remarks with respect to parties since, contrary to many modern observers, he saw party as an evil influence on politics and government. Like his colleague James Madison who, with Alexander Hamilton, helped prepare earlier drafts of this address, he feared factional forces that would divide the nation against itself. The founders had tried to keep parties out of their new Constitution, and Washington was concerned that geographical and ideological divisions were admitting them through the back door. They had the potential, he believed, to spell doom for the fledgling republic. That the republic still stands is not to say that his argument has no merit, for many of his concerns find an echo in present-day politics.

Friends and Citizens:

The period for a new election of a citizen to administer the executive government of the United States being not far distant, and the time actually arrived when your thoughts must be employed in designating the person who is to be clothed with that important trust, it appears to me proper, especially as it may conduce to a more distinct expression of the public voice, that I should now apprise you of the resolution I have formed, to decline being considered among the number of those out of whom a choice is to be made. . . .

The impressions with which I first undertook the arduous trust were explained on the proper occasion. In the discharge of this trust, I will only say that I have, with good intentions, contributed towards the organization and administration of the government the best exertions of which a very fallible judgment was capable. Not unconscious in the outset of the inferiority of my qualifications, experience in my own eyes, perhaps still more in the eyes of others, has strengthened the motives to diffidence of myself; and every day the increasing weight of years admonishes me more and more that the shade of retirement is as necessary to me as it will be welcome. Satisfied that if any circumstances have given peculiar value to my services, they were temporary, I have the consolation to believe that, while choice and prudence invite me to quit the political scene, patriotism does not forbid it. . . .

Here, perhaps, I ought to stop. But a solicitude for your welfare, which cannot end but with my life, and the apprehension of danger, natural to that solicitude, urge me, on an occasion like the present, to offer to your solemn contemplation, and to recommend to your frequent review, some sentiments which are the result of much reflection, of no inconsiderable observation, and which appear to me all-important to the permanency of your felicity as a people. These will be offered to you with the more freedom, as you can only see in them the disinterested warnings of a parting friend, who can possibly have no personal motive to bias his counsel. Nor can I forget, as an encouragement to it, your indulgent reception of my sentiments on a former and not dissimilar occasion.

Interwoven as is the love of liberty with every ligament of your hearts, no recommendation of mine is necessary to fortify or confirm the attachment.

The unity of government which constitutes you one people is also now dear to you. It is justly so, for it is a main pillar in the edifice of your real independence, the support of your tranquility at home, your peace abroad; of your safety; of your prosperity; of that very liberty which you so highly prize. But as it is easy to foresee that, from different causes and from different quarters, much pains will

What value does political unity hold for Washington?

be taken, many artifices employed to weaken in your minds the conviction of this truth; as this is the point in your political fortress against which the batteries of internal and external enemies will be most constantly and actively (though often covertly and insidiously) directed, it is of infinite moment that you should properly estimate the immense value of your national union to your collective and individual happiness; that you should cherish a cordial, habitual, and immovable attachment to it; accustoming yourselves to think and speak of it as of the palladium of your political safety and prosperity; watching for its preservation with jealous anxiety; discountenancing whatever may suggest even a suspicion that it can in any event be abandoned; and indignantly frowning upon the first dawning of every attempt to alienate any portion of our country from the rest, or to enfeeble the sacred ties which now link together the various parts.

For this you have every inducement of sympathy and interest. Citizens, by birth or choice, of a common country, that country has a right to concentrate your affections. The name of American, which belongs to you in your national capacity, must always exalt the just pride of patriotism more than any appellation derived from local discriminations. With slight shades of difference, you have the same religion, manners, habits, and political principles. You have in a common cause fought and triumphed together; the independence and liberty you possess are the work of joint counsels, and joint efforts of common dangers, sufferings, and successes.

But these considerations, however powerfully they address themselves to your sensibility, are greatly outweighed by those which apply more immediately to your interest. Here every portion of our country finds the most commanding motives for carefully guarding and preserving the union of the whole.

The North, in an unrestrained intercourse with the South, protected by the equal laws of a common government, finds in the productions of the latter great additional resources of maritime and commercial enterprise and precious materials of manufacturing industry. The South, in the same intercourse, benefiting by the agency of the North, sees its agriculture grow and its commerce expand. Turning partly into its own channels the seamen of the North, it finds its particular navigation invigorated; and, while it contributes, in different ways, to nourish and increase the general mass of the national navigation, it looks forward to the protection of a maritime strength, to which itself is unequally adapted. The East, in a like intercourse with the West, already finds, and in the progressive improvement of interior communications by land and water, will more and more find a valuable vent for the commodities which it brings from abroad, or manufactures at home. The West derives from the East supplies requisite to its growth and comfort, and, what is perhaps of still greater consequence, it must of necessity owe the secure enjoyment of indispensable outlets for its own productions to the weight, influence, and the future maritime strength of the Atlantic side of the Union, directed by an indissoluble community of interest as one nation. Any other tenure by which the West can hold this essential advantage, whether derived from its own separate strength, or from an apostate and unnatural connection with any foreign power, must be intrinsically precarious.

While, then, every part of our country thus feels an immediate and particular interest in union, all the parts combined cannot fail to find in the united mass of means and efforts greater strength, greater resource, proportionably greater security from external danger, a less frequent interruption of their peace by foreign nations; and, what is of inestimable value, they must derive from union an exemption from those broils and wars between themselves, which so frequently afflict neighboring countries not tied together by the same governments, which their own rival ships alone would be sufficient to produce, but which opposite foreign alliances, attachments, and intrigues would stimulate and embitter. Hence, likewise, they will avoid the necessity of those overgrown military establishments which, under any form of government, are inauspicious to liberty, and which are to be regarded as particularly hostile to republican liberty. In this sense it is that your union ought to be considered as a main prop of your liberty, and that the love of the one ought to endear to you the preservation of the other.

These considerations speak a persuasive language to every reflecting and virtuous mind, and exhibit the continuance of the Union as a primary object of patriotic desire. Is there a doubt whether a common government can embrace so large a sphere? Let experience solve it. To listen to mere speculation in such a case were criminal. We are authorized to hope that a proper organization of the whole with the auxiliary agency of governments for the respective subdivisions, will afford a happy issue to the experiment. It is well worth a fair and full experiment. With such powerful and obvious motives to union, affecting all parts of our country, while experience shall not have demonstrated its impracticability, there will always be reason to distrust the patriotism of those who in any quarter may endeavor to weaken its bands.

In contemplating the causes which may disturb our Union, it occurs as [a] matter of serious concern that any ground should have been furnished for characterizing parties by geographical discriminations, Northern and Southern, Atlantic and Western; whence designing men may endeavor to excite a belief that there is a real difference of local interests and views. One of the expedients of party to acquire influence within particular districts is to misrepresent the opinions and aims of other districts. You cannot shield yourselves too much against the jealousies and heartburnings which spring from these misrepresentations; they tend to render alien to each other those who ought to be bound together by fraternal affection. The inhabitants of our Western country have lately had a useful lesson on this head; they have seen, in the negotiation by the Executive, and in the unanimous ratification by the Senate, of the treaty with Spain, and in the universal satisfaction at that event, throughout the United States, a decisive proof how unfounded were the suspicions propagated among them of a policy in the General Government and in the Atlantic States unfriendly to their interests in regard to the Mississippi; they have been witnesses to the formation of two treaties, that with Great Britain, and that with Spain, which secure to them everything they could desire, in respect to our foreign relations, towards confirming their prosperity. Will it not be their wisdom to rely for the preservation of these advantages on the Union by which they were procured? Will they not henceforth be deaf to those advisers, if such there are, who would sever them from their brethren and connect them with aliens?

To the efficacy and permanency of your Union, a government for the whole is indispensable. No alliance, however strict, between the parts can be an adequate substitute; they must inevitably experience the infractions and interruptions which all alliances in all times have experienced. Sensible of this momentous truth, you have improved upon your first essay, by the adoption of a constitution of government better calculated than your former for an intimate union, and for the efficacious management of your common concerns. This government, the offspring of our own choice, uninfluenced and unawed, adopted upon full investigation and mature deliberation, completely free in its principles, in the distribution of its powers, uniting security with energy, and containing within itself a provision for its own amendment, has a just claim to your confidence and your support. Respect for its authority, compliance with its laws, acquiescence in its measures, are duties enjoined by the fundamental maxims of true liberty. The basis of our political systems is the right of the people to make and to alter their constitutions of government. But the Constitution which at any time exists, till changed by an explicit and authentic act of the whole people, is sacredly obligatory upon all. The very idea of the power and the right of the people to establish government presupposes the duty of every individual to obey the established government.

All obstructions to the execution of the laws, all combinations and associations, under whatever plausible character, with the real design to direct, control, counteract, or awe the regular deliberation and action of the constituted authorities, are destructive of this fundamental principle, and of fatal tendency. They serve to organize faction, to give it an artificial and extraordinary force; to put, in the place of the delegated will of the nation the will of a party, often a small but artful and enterprising minority of the community; and, according to the alternate triumphs of different parties, to make the public administration the mirror of the ill-concerted and incongruous projects of faction, rather than the organ of consistent and wholesome plans digested by common counsels and modified by mutual interests.

> What definition of party is Washington using?

However combinations or associations of the above description may now and then answer popular ends, they are likely, in the course of time and things, to become potent engines, by which cunning, ambitious, and unprincipled men will be enabled to subvert the power of the people and to usurp for themselves the reins of government, destroying afterwards the very engines which have lifted them to unjust dominion.

Towards the preservation of your government, and the permanency of your present happy state, it is requisite, not only that you steadily discountenance irregular oppositions to its acknowledged authority, but also that you resist with care the spirit of innovation upon its principles, however specious the pretexts. One method of assault may be to effect, in the forms of the Constitution, alterations which will impair the energy of the system, and thus to undermine what cannot be directly overthrown. In all the changes to which you may be invited, remember that time and habit are at least as necessary to fix the true character of governments as of other human institutions; that experience is the surest standard by which to test the real tendency of the existing constitution of a country; that facility in changes, upon the credit of mere hypothesis and opinion, exposes to perpetual change, from the endless variety of hypothesis and opinion; and remember, especially, that for the efficient management of your common interests, in a country so extensive as ours, a government of as much vigor as is consistent with the perfect security of liberty is indispensable. Liberty itself will find in such a government, with powers properly distributed and adjusted, its surest guardian. It is, indeed, little else than a name, where the government is too feeble to withstand the enterprises of faction, to confine each member of the society within the limits prescribed by the laws, and to maintain all in the secure and tranquil enjoyment of the rights of person and property.

I have already intimated to you the danger of parties in the State, with particular reference to the founding of them on geographical discriminations. Let me now take a more comprehensive view, and warn you in the most solemn manner against the baneful effects of the spirit of party generally.

This spirit, unfortunately, is inseparable from our nature, having its root in the strongest passions of the human mind. It exists under different shapes in all governments, more or less stifled, controlled, or repressed; but, in those of the popular form, it is seen in its greatest rankness, and is truly their worst enemy.

The alternate domination of one faction over another, sharpened by the spirit of revenge, natural to party dissension, which in different ages and countries has perpetrated the most horrid enormities, is itself a frightful despotism. But this leads at length to a more formal and permanent despotism. The disorders and miseries which result gradually incline the minds of men to seek security and repose in the absolute power of an individual; and sooner or later the chief of some prevailing faction, more able or more fortunate than his competitors, turns this disposition to the purposes of his own elevation, on the ruins of public liberty.

Without looking forward to an extremity of this kind (which nevertheless ought not to be entirely out of sight), the common and continual mischiefs of the spirit of party are sufficient to make it the interest and duty of a wise people to discourage and restrain it.

It serves always to distract the public councils and enfeeble the public administration. It agitates the community with ill-founded jealousies and false alarms, kindles the animosity of one part against another, foments occasionally riot and insurrection. It opens the door to foreign influence and corruption, which finds a facilitated access to the government itself through the channels of party passions. Thus the policy and the will of one country are subjected to the policy and will of another.

There is an opinion that parties in free countries are useful checks upon the administration of the government and serve to keep alive the spirit of liberty. This within certain limits is probably true; and in governments of a monarchical cast, patriotism may look with indulgence, if not with favor, upon the spirit of party. But in those of the popular character, in governments purely elective, it is a spirit not to be encouraged. From their natural tendency, it is certain there will always be enough of that spirit for every salutary purpose. And there being constant danger of excess, the effort ought to be by force of public opinion, to mitigate and assuage it. A fire not to be quenched, it demands a uniform vigilance to prevent its bursting into a flame, lest, instead of warming, it should consume. . . .

Why is it that parties can preserve liberty in monarchies but destroy liberty in democracies?

Consider the source and the audience.
- Although this address was never actually given by Washington in person, it was clearly intended to be. To whom is Washington primarily addressing his words—the American public? Fellow politicians? Political adversaries?

Lay out the argument, the values, and the assumptions.
- What are Washington's basic assumptions about human nature? What is the link between human nature and parties?
- What values does he believe government should protect above all?
- In what ways does he think parties threaten those values?

Uncover the evidence.
- What evidence does Washington provide to support his contention that a unified country is a good thing?
- Is that evidence sufficient to convince people that parties are consequently bad, or should he have provided something more?

Evaluate the conclusion.
- Washington makes a powerful logical and rhetorical case. Are passion, logic, and eloquence enough to convince you?
- What does Washington want Americans to do about the dangers of party?

Sort out the political implications.
- In what ways do modern-day politics support or weaken Washington's contention? Would he think that his fears had been realized, or that they were unnecessary?

CHAPTER · **12**

Interest Groups

rench philosopher Alexis de Tocqueville, writing about American culture and government during his trip to the United States in the early 1830s, noted that "Americans of all ages, all conditions, and all dispositions, constantly form associations. They not only have commercial and manufacturing companies, in which all take part, but associations of a thousand other kinds—religious, moral, serious, futile, general, or restricted, enormous or diminutive."[1] Tocqueville's observation, made more than 150 years ago, still applies today. In fact, while we often criticize Americans for their lack of political engagement, more than 80 percent of us belong to at least one interest group.[2] An interest group is simply an organization of individuals who share a common political goal and unite for the purposes of influencing government decisions.

Indeed, one theory of representative democracy notes the incredible importance of interest groups in our society. Believers in pluralist democracy argue that, while individually we may not have much power to influence government, our voices are magnified through our membership in interest groups. Representatives may discount our single vote, or ignore our single letter, but they are likely to listen to the Sierra Club, the National Rifle Association, or the American Association of Retired Persons when their professional representatives, known as lobbyists, come to call.

We may be, as Tocqueville wrote, a country of "joiners," but that doesn't necessarily mean we hold interest groups in the highest regard. Our founders were quite wary of factions (their term for interest groups) because they feared it would then be easy for a majority to suppress the minority. James Madison makes this argument very persuasively in *Federalist* No. 10, included in this chapter. Today, when there are more interest groups than at any other time in our history, citizens often view interest groups as defenders of "special interests"—interests that, as far as Madison was concerned, do not represent the general public good. Interest groups such as the National Rifle Association and the Association of Trial Lawyers of America seem to have immense influence with elected officials, but their views are not necessarily consistent with the majority of the public. We also are skeptical of the

---

1. Tocqueville, Alexis de, *Democracy in America,* Richard D. Heffner, ed. (New York: New American Library, 1956), p. 198.

2. *The Public Perspective,* April–May 1995.

role of interest groups in elections, and we fear that interest group money buys or unduly influences elected officials' votes. While political scientists haven't conclusively demonstrated this to be true, they have found substantial evidence that money buys access, which could indirectly influence votes.

The articles in this chapter examine several different aspects of interest groups and social movements. The first looks at the active role a college student has played in campus protests and the price he has had to pay for his involvement. The next two articles deal with the role of interest groups in elections: Lonnae O'Neal Parker, writing in the magazine *Essence,* discusses the development of a political action committee (PAC)—the fundraising arm of an interest group—designed to help elect black females. And Sheryl Gay Stolberg, writing in the *New York Times,* looks at the ways powerful interest groups try to influence legislation on an issue near and dear to their hearts. In the fourth selection, Bill Hogan, a writer for *Mother Jones* magazine, criticizes the efforts of interest group lobbyists—those whose job it is to persuade elected officials to support the groups' positions—post-9/11. Finally, we close with Madison's famous *Federalist* No. 10, in which he warns against the negative effects of factions.

12.1 "My Life Is Shaped by the Border"

Student Activist Faces Fallout from Mideast Protest

Tanya Schevitz, *San Francisco Chronicle,* 18 November 2002

Interest groups organize around a common interest to try to influence public policy. Usually they work through the system, directly or indirectly targeting government as the focus of their efforts. Sometimes groups, such as African Americans in the 1950s and 1960s, or women at the turn of the century, have difficulty getting into the system to work to bring about the change they value. When an interest group is unable to work within the political system, we usually call it a social movement. Such groups may use nonviolent civil disobedience or more active forms of demonstration. As we see here, the line between freedom of speech and assembly and breaking the law can be hard to draw. Those actors who want to keep a group outside the system have every incentive to define their efforts as law breaking; the social movement itself usually claims the protection of the First Amendment.

The sit-ins during the 1960s, for example, were a major success in forcing department stores to integrate their lunch counters. Throughout the South (and even in parts of the North), African Americans—in this case, mostly college students—ignored integration laws by refusing to give up their seats. In many instances, they were arrested. In the end, however, the protests forced many stores to change their policies. Civil disobedience also played a major role on college campuses as students protested the Vietnam War. While controversial, civil disobedience is a classic example of political participation.

The following article from the *San Francisco Chronicle* documents the plight of a UC Berkeley student who faces severe punishment because of his involvement in campus protests aimed at altering university policy. Where should the line be drawn between free speech and criminal activity in these cases?

Roberto Hernandez remembers looking out the window of his San Ysidro elementary classroom and seeing the Border Patrol chasing people "who look like me" across the playground.

When he got older, he was often stopped by the Border Patrol near his San Diego County home, even though he had a green card.

"The military checkpoints are much worse in Palestine," he says, "but for me there is a natural link there."

These days, Hernandez's strong feelings about the Israeli-Palestinian quagmire have gotten him in big trouble at his school, UC Berkeley.

What is the power of seeing what happens to "people 'who look like me'"? How did such "consciousness raising" bring Hernandez to his position on the Palestinian question?

Hernandez was one of 79 protesters arrested during an April 9 demonstration held by the Students for Justice in Palestine, as part of a campaign to force the university to divest from companies with business ties to Israel.

While the Alameda County District Attorney's office did not file criminal charges against those arrested, the university is pursuing campus disciplinary charges against Hernandez and 31 other students.

Hernandez will face a campus hearing Wednesday—a battle that students characterize as a free speech issue but one that the university considers a simple matter of protecting other students' rights to an education.

The university has put a hold on Hernandez's degree, which is preventing him from officially graduating and enrolling in his graduate program. That means he isn't a student and cannot collect the fellowship he was relying on to pay tuition and living expenses.

"Everything in my life, my politics, is shaped and changed by the border," said Hernandez, 23, who grew up as a Mexican citizen just seven blocks from the U.S.-Mexican border.

From one perspective, Roberto Hernandez personifies the traditional American success story. His parents are poor immigrants from Guadalajara and Chiapas who have little education.

But he made it to UC Berkeley and excelled throughout his undergraduate years, getting involved in the campus community, and earning a campus fellowship and a spot in Berkeley's doctoral program in ethnic studies.

University officials paint quite a different portrait: a rabble-rouser who attends virtually every campus protest and who jeopardized his future by participating in a takeover of Wheeler Hall last spring.

Hernandez, they say, not only defied the rules by occupying a campus building but also bit a campus police officer while he was being arrested.

And they say that Hernandez and the other students arrested were warned repeatedly against disrupting the "academic mission" of the campus and that they have a right to pursue disciplinary charges dealing with the campus code of conduct.

UC administrators are seeking up to a year's suspension for each of the students.

But Hernandez, who became a U.S. citizen two years ago, says he is just following the values his mother instilled in him. His mother was so proud of her Mexican heritage that when she went into labor with him, she traveled to a hospital across the border to retain the family's "Mexican nationality."

Although she had just an eighth-grade education, his mother was always active in his school, organizing other parents to improve things and encouraging Hernandez and his sister to get involved.

"My mom brought me up to be involved in the schools," he said, "but it became larger than that."

He became politicized at age 13, when he got swept up in his first "real demonstration," a 1992 protest of the celebration of the 500th anniversary of Christopher Columbus' "discovery" of America.

"It was so huge, and it was beautiful. Five thousand people coming together to say no, to take a stand," he said. "That was the beginning for me. It had never really clicked for me before. Until that point, I was confused and full of rage, but I didn't know how to channel it."

> How do social movements and interest groups help to channel emotions like rage and frustration? What sorts of people would be encouraged to join for such benefits?

He began protesting police and Border Patrol brutality and providing support and security to the Pastors for Peace caravans headed with food and supplies to Cuba.

In ninth grade, he wrote a paper on what it means to be an American and received an F for writing of America as a continent, including Mexico. He then joined MEChA, a Chicano student group, for support.

He was involved in the campaign against Proposition 187, organizing student walkouts to protest the measure to deprive undocumented workers of education and health and welfare services. (The measure was approved but has since been halted by the courts.)

From then on, he was active on every state proposition affecting minorities, including Proposition 209, which eliminated the use of race in university admissions.

"I think back now not in terms of time, but in terms of propositions," he said.

He was admitted to UC Berkeley in the last year that affirmative action was in place and isn't ashamed to say he probably benefited from the use of racial preferences.

"Affirmative action only opens the door," he said. "We have to work our a— off and earn our degree."

His apartment is one of an intellectually and politically engaged student, with a bed crowded into the corner of a tiny room filled with eight towering bookshelves packed with books, mostly about minority issues. The walls are papered with Mexican flags, posters of Che Guevara and announcements of political demonstrations.

"People know of my place here as a mini-Chicano resource center," Hernandez said. "I don't have formal library cards, but people do come check out books here."

Even in his academic life at UC Berkeley, he focused on political issues that arose from his upbringing. He has researched the social, political and cultural aspects of the border and the functionality of borders internationally.

Hernandez admits he is involved in a lot of campus political actions but says it is because he has been frustrated every time he has tried to work within the system. He served as a student senator on campus but found his agenda thwarted by politics and partisanship, he said.

What mainstream interest groups began as social movements because of similar frustrations?

"I try these other formal means of enacting change, but a lot of times we came up against these roadblocks," he said.

Hernandez has been arrested before, during a September 2001 protest of a *Daily Californian* cartoon that many considered racist and anti-Muslim. The charges were dropped.

And he was involved in the highly publicized 1999 demonstrations, where students demanded increased support for the ethnic studies program by fasting and camping outside Chancellor Robert Berdahl's office.

But he says his participation is always peaceful. He says the university is targeting him because he is so politically active.

Hernandez's professors—and even a University of California regent who knows him—believe the university is overreacting to this latest incident because of political pressures that label any criticism of Israel as anti-Semitic.

The entire ethnic studies department signed a letter of support for Hernandez.

"To see this kid get trashed this way, I just can't see it," said UC Regent Alfredo Terrazas, who first met Hernandez in 1998 at a scholarship fund-raising event by the Chicano Latino Alumni Club. "For him, it is devastating for his career. For the university, it is a shame. And we lose an individual in the Latino community who I really believe is going to be a leader."

Campus spokeswoman Janet Gilmore says that the university's disciplinary charges have nothing to do with politics and that pro-Palestinian students who were merely protesting and marching around campus have not faced any charges.

"Clearly, there is not an effort to stop them from exercising their free speech," Gilmore said.

For Hernandez, political dissent could come at a price he was not prepared to pay.

"I wasn't expecting the university to come down on us as hard as they have," he said.

Consider the source and the audience.

- The *San Francisco Chronicle* is one of two major newspapers in the Bay Area, located near the University of California at Berkeley. This is clearly a local story for the *Chronicle*—but does it also have a more general relevance?

Lay out the argument, the values, and the assumptions.

- How has Hernandez's background influenced his values? What changes does he want to bring about? Why does he feel that more "traditional" forms of participation have not been effective? How does he think the university should respond to his actions?
- How does the University of California view Hernandez's behavior? What does it consider its "academic mission" to be, and how does Hernandez damage this mission?
- One of Hernandez's supporters says that the loss of Hernandez is a shame for the university. What contribution might Hernandez be making to the university? What could be the costs of suspending him?

Uncover the evidence.

- Is there any kind of evidence that either side could provide to back its arguments, or is this just a case of opposing viewpoints? How do the conflicting interests here shape the way the two sides interpret events?

Evaluate the conclusion.

- Why would the university react so harshly to these students? What is at stake for them?
- What is at stake for Hernandez? Were there other avenues open to him to achieve his ends?

Sort out the political implications.

- Can universities promote free speech and academic freedom without disrupting students' educations? What rights do students have to express their views? What can they do if they feel that their rights are being violated?
- How might this campus climate affect students who want to demonstrate in favor of or against military action around the world?

12.2 Money, Power, Respect

The Black Woman's Vote Can Often Determine the Outcome of an Election, Yet When It Comes to Political Power, We Aren't Getting Our Due: A New Political Action Committee Aims to Change That

Lonnae O'Neal Parker, *Essence,* February 2003

An obvious way for interest groups to try to influence government policy is to attempt to get sympathetic officials elected in the first place by donating money to the candidates' campaigns. By law, however, interest groups are not allowed to donate money directly to candidates or political parties. In order to do so, they must create a political action committee (PAC), which is basically the fundraising arm of an interest group (or of an individual or political party). PACs were created by election law reform in the 1970s so that it would be possible to trace the money in electoral politics, thereby helping the public become aware of who was giving how much to whom. Like all campaign donors, PACs are limited in terms of the amounts of money they can contribute directly to candidates, but collectively they can come to wield considerable power.

Due to the importance of money in campaigns, PACs have grown enormously in number over the last twenty years, as have the money amounts that PACs contribute. With the campaign finance reform in 2002 that eliminates soft-money donations to candidates (unlimited contributions that could be made to parties), some speculate that PACs' skills in raising hard (regulated) money will become even more important. Because it seems as if everyone has a PAC these days, groups who do not might feel that their interests are not being adequately represented. The following article, from *Essence* magazine, discusses the creation of a new PAC by African American women who hope to increase their voices in the government arena. What does the race to form PACs tell us about the role of money in American politics? Why do these women think that merely turning out to vote is not sufficient to increase their political power?

They banded together to launch the first national Black women's political action committee. The participants included women who've long been fighting for political power: Dr. Dorothy I. Height, president emerita of the National Council of Negro Women; Marianne Spraggins, president and CEO of Atlanta Life Insurance Company Investment Advisers (ALICIA); Eddie Bernice Johnson of the Congressional Black Caucus; Alma Brown, a senior vice-president of Chevy Chase Bank and widow of former Secretary of Commerce Ron Brown; Congresswoman Lois DeBerry (D-Memphis); Joy Atkinson, a founder of the Los Angeles African American Women's Political Action Committee (LAAAWPAC).

Never before had so many Black women convened from all corners of the country with this singular objective: to forge a political legacy. "Politics affects everything we do from the cradle to the grave, including the quality of the water we drink," says Julianne Malveaux, economist, writer and PAC board member. "We can't afford not to be involved."

As more than 80 women filed into the dining area at the National Council of Negro Women headquarters in Washington, D.C., last September, the room crackled with excitement. "This is our PAC," said California Congresswoman Barbara Lee. "Our time has come!"

Corporations, unions and other special-interest groups have typically formed PACs to raise money for candidates who will further their interests. This new group, called Women Building for the Future or The Future PAC, "is dedicated to building a national network of support and funding that progressive Black women candidates need to launch effective campaigns and win elections,"

> Do African American candidates have to be elected in order for the interests of African Americans to be represented?

explains Gwen Moore, chair of the organization and a former California assem-blywoman who has worked on the national scene, as well as with state legislators and local elected officials. "The Future PAC aims to put in office African-Ameri-can women who will develop policies and programs that will improve the lives of African-American people."

The group's founders have the political savvy and connections to move this goal forward. They include chair Alice Huffman, president of the California NAACP, who has 14 years experience managing a multimillion-dollar PAC, and Celestine Palmer, a founder of the LAAAWPAC. Lottie Shackelford, the former mayor of Little Rock, Arkansas, is also a founder, along with Minyon Moore, a po-litical strategist and public-affairs consultant who is a former chief operating officer of the Democratic National Party, as well as the assistant to former Presi-dent Clinton and director of political affairs and public liaison for both Clinton administrations.

While Blacks have traditionally gained political power through grassroots ac-tivism, organizers of this effort say The Future PAC represents the next step in our political maturity. "We have to get in on the front end of the process," says Marianne Spraggins, the group's finance chair. "We must determine not only whom to vote for, but who is going to run and if they are serving our interests."

"It's time for Black women to become bigger players in the political process," says Donna L. Brazile, the foremost African-American campaign manager in the country who led the Gore presidential campaign and worked on the Clinton-Gore presidential campaigns in 1992 and 1996 and on Jesse Jackson's historic bid for the presidency in 1984. "Black women are the most loyal and consistent voters in American politics. Without us, there would be no Senator Zell Miller of Georgia or Hillary Clinton of New York."

Brazile, who's also chairwoman of the Democratic National Committee's Vot-ing Rights Institute, cites the 2000 presidential election, in which 67 percent of Black women participated, as another example of our political might. "Without the support of Black women, the race wouldn't have been as close as it was," she points out. "There would have been no need to recount the votes in Florida." But Brazile says our loyalty has largely gone unrewarded. "We're not underrep-resented in political office," she says. "Underrepresentation would signal we were in the pipeline. We're invisible."

The statistics are startling. There are no Black senators or Black governors, and of the 76 women in Congress, only 13 are Black. And few Black women have been chosen for such influential positions as Secretary of State. . . . The Future PAC's organizers want to see Black women reap the rewards that their numbers, spending power and tax dollars deserve. "People treat us like we're waiting for a handout," Brazile says. "But elected officials wouldn't be there unless we voted for them. We've got to stop giving away our vote. We need a return on our investment."

The idea for The Future PAC took shape last spring after the tenth anniversary celebration of the LAAAWPAC. Founded by Celestine Palmer and others, the group has helped elect more than two dozen Black women to national, state and local offices, including Congresswoman Barbara Lee (D-Calif.) and Congresswoman Diane E. Watson (D-Calif.). Palmer and Susan L. Taylor, editorial director of *Essence* and keynote speaker at the Los Angeles event, seized the opportunity to bring together a group of women who could establish a political action committee on a national level. "It's so difficult for Black women candidates to raise money," says Taylor, who is also a Future PAC founder. "I felt that *Essence* should and could play a role in helping involve more sisters in the political process as well as electing to office progressive Black women who will fight for the critical needs of our people."

What does it mean to look at voting as an investment on which a return is due?

With her experience helping several candidates outside of California, including former Illinois Senator Carol Moseley-Braun, Palmer agreed that the time was right for a national group. "We could see the value in trying to get women from all over the country to participate," she says.

Veteran politicians like Congresswoman Eddie Bernice Johnson (D-Texas) are eager to see The Future PAC succeed. "I've been a lot of firsts," she says, referring to her political career, "but I don't want to be the last." Johnson says Blacks generally support campaigns in every way except fund-raising. The financial backing she has received, she adds, has largely been from the same people. "I ran for the first time 30 years ago and people would give me a $3 check or dollar bills," Johnson explains. "It has been appreciated, but it takes thousands of people giving that amount to finance a campaign." Spraggins adds, "Black women cannot get elected without money and, collectively, we control a lot of it, so we have to channel our energy and resources into our candidates."

Because of recent reforms in campaign-finance laws limiting the amount of soft money (contributions not directly used to elect a candidate but for party-building activities like get-out-the-vote drives) corporations and individuals can donate, political action committees will become even more important. With issues like education, health care and economic development in play, organizers say The Future PAC needs to begin raising money as soon as possible. "We're going to support as many good, progressive Black female candidates as we can," says Minyon Moore.

Why does this PAC seek to support "progressive" candidates? Would it support a black female Republican candidate?

Although the committee will court big donations, organizers say all contributions are welcome. "This movement is trying to embrace everything that's important to African-American women in the political process," adds Moore, one of the most visible and well-respected young people in politics. She hopes the word goes out to working-, middle- and upper-class Black women. "Whether you have $5, $50 or $500, your voice must be heard."

Isisara Bey, vice-president of corporate affairs for Sony Music Entertainment, Inc., brought optimism—and a check—to the event. "We're making a bid for a higher level of power," she said. Michelle Anderson Lee, chief of staff for Pennsylvania Congressman Chaka Fattah, agreed. "This will make folks take us seriously," Lee said. "And that's what it's all about."

Consider the source and the audience.

- *Essence* is a magazine devoted to lifestyle issues that targets African American women. The editorial director of *Essence* is a founder of The Future PAC. Is there a conflict of interest here? Why would a media outlet take such an overtly political role?

Lay out the argument, the values, and the assumptions.

- Why do the founders of The Future PAC believe there is a need for the PAC? What kind of theory of representation are they working with here?
- In what ways does their model of electoral power go beyond a focus on the voter? What are the "steps of political maturity" the author speaks of?
- How do these women think they are being hurt not having a PAC devoted to the interests of African American women? What are they fighting for?

Uncover the evidence.

- What evidence do the founders of The Future PAC provide to support their claim that black women are underrepresented among elected officials?

Evaluate the conclusion.

- This article, written in the excitement of The Future PAC's creation, is optimistic about the prospects of black women gaining the financial clout to make their voices heard in American politics. What kinds of concerns might offset that optimism?

Sort out the political implications.

- If The Future PAC succeeds in putting more black women into the ranks of elected politicians, what effects might this be expected to have on the African American community?

12.3 Lobbyists on Both Sides Duel in the Medical Malpractice Debate

Sheryl Gay Stolberg, *New York Times,* 12 March 2003

There are few issues on which Congress is not lobbied by powerful interest groups. Nowhere can this be seen more clearly than in the debate over capping awards for medical malpractice, an issue Congress took up in 2003. Some of Washington's largest and most influential interest groups, such as the American Medical Association and the Association of Trial Lawyers of America, have invested substantial time and money trying to convince members of Congress to support their position.

In this *New York Times* article, we see lobbyists employing a variety of the techniques and strategies at their disposal—lobbying Congress directly by providing testimony and campaign contributions as well as indirectly by attempting to sway public opinion. Are these interest group activities consistent with democratic principles?

F ew people noticed the lobbyist hovering in the background when Mary Rasar came to the Capitol last week to tell the story of her father's death.

With three Republican senators by her side, and a gaggle of reporters before her, Ms. Rasar recounted how her father was injured in a car accident in Las Vegas the day after high liability premiums forced the local trauma center to close. He died in an emergency room—"a tragic, tragic story," said Senator John Ensign, Republican of Nevada, vowing to press for caps on jury awards in malpractice cases.

Their joint appearance was arranged by the lobbyist, William Nixon, as another salvo in a war of dueling images in the medical malpractice debate. For weeks, trial lawyers and consumer groups fighting against caps have been bringing malpractice victims to the Capitol—including a 17-year-old girl whose face had been ruined by botched surgeries and a woman whose breasts had been removed unnecessarily after a doctor wrongly diagnosed cancer. So Mr. Nixon, who represents hospitals, fired back with Ms. Rasar.

What effect are these testimonies expected to have on members of Congress, the media, and the public?

"The point," he said, "is to demonstrate that there are legitimate victims on both sides."

With the House expected on Thursday to take up legislation imposing a $250,000 cap on "pain and suffering" awards in malpractice cases, and the Senate planning to tackle medical liability later this month, lobbyists on both sides have been working at a fever pitch. The bill is expected to pass the House, but will probably face difficulty in the Senate, where some prominent Republicans say it must include an exception for egregious cases like that of Jésica Santillán, the 17-year-old who died after receiving a heart and lung of the wrong blood type.

Limiting jury awards has long been a high priority for Republicans and business interests, who believe malpractice legislation could open the door to a broader tort reform agenda. President Bush has been attacking trial lawyers—and, by extension, the Democrats they support—for "frivolous lawsuits," and he has invited a dozen House members to the White House on Wednesday to try to increase support for the House measure. With the president's backing and Republicans' running both the House and Senate, proponents say their goal is within reach.

"This is the first time in a decade that there has been an opportunity for real legal reform," said Karen Ignagni, president of the American Association of

Health Plans, which represents managed care organizations. "All the key actors in the health care system are now united."

Mr. Nixon's client, the Coalition for Affordable and Reliable Health Care, is a perfect example. It was founded last September by the Baylor Health Care System in Texas and several other hospitals with one goal, overhauling malpractice law to bring down insurance premiums. "For the first time," he said, "they feel they are in striking distance."

The debate has also made for new lobbying alliances on Capitol Hill, and shattered some old ones. Last year, the American Medical Association, which represents doctors, was working hand in hand with the Association of Trial Lawyers of America—and against Ms. Ignagni's group—to promote legislation enabling patients to sue their health insurers. Now, the A.M.A. has joined with the insurance industry. Lobbyists for the trial lawyers complain they cannot get the doctors to talk to them.

> Why would the American Medical Association have sided with the Association of Trial Lawyers of America on one issue but opposed them on another? How is the AMA's interests served both by allowing patients to sue insurers and by capping malpractice awards?

Dr. Donald A. Palmisano, the A.M.A.'s president-elect, says revamping liability laws is the association's No. 1 legislative priority. He recalled meeting President Bush in July in High Point, N.C., on the day the president gave his first speech on the topic.

"He looked right at me and he said, 'We can get medical liability reform now if you will go to the grass roots,'" Dr. Palmisano said.

To that end, the association is trying to raise $15 million for a nationwide media campaign. Doctors around the country have rallied to the cause, waging a series of highly publicized walkouts and protests. Though local chapters have been behind the rallies, Dr. Palmisano has been flying around the country to attend them. The powerful images have not been lost on lawmakers.

"They've demonstrated with their feet," said Representative Billy Tauzin, the Louisiana Republican who is chairman of the House Energy and Commerce Committee, which last week sent the malpractice bill to the full House for a vote.

Mr. Tauzin was among several Republicans, including President Bush, who addressed more than 600 doctors last week at the A.M.A.'s National Advocacy Conference. Over breakfast of eggs, toast, peaches and sausage, the doctor-lobbyists, who later fanned out across Capitol Hill, got some friendly advice from Senator Bill Frist—the Republican leader and a heart transplant surgeon.

Do not be satisfied with seeing Congressional staffs, Dr. Frist advised, adding, "Say, 'I just want to see the senator for two minutes.'"

In addition to the war of images, there has been a war of words and numbers, with proponents trying to link high liability premiums to high jury awards, and opponents trying to disprove a link, in part by citing studies showing the influence of larger economic trends on insurance costs. Last week, Tommy G.

Thompson, the secretary of health and human services, announced a new study that found "the main factor causing the crisis is the rise in mega-awards and settlements," including jury awards that can exceed $1 million. Opponents responded with their own statistics, from the government's National Practitioner Data Bank, showing the average jury verdict, far from being in the millions, is roughly $400,000 and the average settlement about $200,000.

"It's like an escalating arms race, but with disinformation," said Jamie Court, executive director of the Foundation for Taxpayer and Consumer Rights, the advocacy group that put out the lower figures. "There is so much floating information around that no one knows what to believe, and almost every statistic becomes useless."

Also floating around, this being Washington, is money. Proponents of malpractice change include some of Washington's most powerful and well-financed lobbies. According to the Center for Responsive Politics, which tracks campaign spending, the A.M.A. contributed $2.7 million to candidates in the 2002 election cycle, with 60 percent going to Republicans. The American Hospital Association, which strongly backs malpractice law changes, gave $1.9 million, 53 percent of it to Republicans.

What groups have been involved in this lobbying process overall? Whom do they represent? Is anyone left out?

But the opponents are also well financed. The trial lawyers contributed $3.7 million in the 2002 election cycle, 89 percent of it to Democrats.

"I've been working this for 20 years, and it has often seemed very close," said Linda Lipsen, who is running the trial lawyers' lobbying effort. Recently, the group brought 120 members to Washington to knock on lawmakers' doors. "It's very arduous," Ms. Lipsen said, "but we feel like if we can tell the story of the patients that our lawyers represent, the justice system should prevail."

And so, almost daily, those stories are being told. Last month, the Center for Justice and Democracy, a consumer group, brought 30 victims of medical malpractice to Washington, and staged a "rump hearing" before Democrats on the House Judiciary Committee. The patients ran the gamut, from a man whose right lung was removed after doctors discovered a tumor in the left lung to Linda McDougal, the woman who underwent an unnecessary double mastectomy after pathologists erroneously diagnosed breast cancer.

On Wednesday, the day before the House is scheduled to vote, the trial lawyers will be bringing Ms. McDougal back to the Capitol, for an appearance with the minority leader of the Senate, Tom Daschle, and his counterpart in the House, Nancy Pelosi. But Mr. Nixon, the hospital lobbyist, is ready. He is bringing back Ms. Rasar, for an appearance with Speaker J. Dennis Hastert.

Consider the source and the audience.
- Does this *New York Times* story provide evenhanded treatment of the issue of capping medical malpractice awards? How might a more partisan outlet portray the issue?

Lay out the argument, the values, and the assumptions.
- What is the issue of capping damages for pain and suffering in malpractice suits all about?
- What is at stake for the various groups involved (doctors, hospitals, insurance companies, lawyers, consumers)? What arguments does each group make? How does each group attempt to get its way?
- What overall picture does this article give of lobbying's role in American lawmaking?

Uncover the evidence.
- What evidence does each side have to support its arguments? Is it persuasive?
- Whom do the sides have to convince? What will it take to do that?

Evaluate the conclusion.
- Is there a right answer here? If so, who has it? If not, why not?
- Does the author of the article seem to draw any conclusions about the lobbying process?

Sort out the political implications.
- Are any important voices left unheard in this process? Is interest group pluralism democratic? Why or why not?
- Based on the example here, how much power does money seem to have in the legislative process? Should money have this much influence in determining the winners and losers in American politics?

12.4 Star-Spangled Lobbyists

Rushing to Enlist in the War on Terrorism, Corporate Lobbyists Are Doing Their Patriotic Duty by Seeking Federal Handouts for Everything from Bison Meat to Chauffeured Limousines

Bill Hogan, *Mother Jones,* March–April 2002

The previous two articles discussed efforts by PACs to get like-minded individuals elected to office. The job of an interest group doesn't stop once elections are over, however. If anything, its job is just beginning. Interest groups must fight to make sure Congress does not ignore their needs. Interest groups hire lobbyists whose sole task is to work the corridors of the Capitol, take part in the Washington social scene, and meet privately with elected officials and their staffs to push the interests of the group. The following article, by Bill Hogan in *Mother Jones* magazine, criticizes the efforts of the lobbying industry after September 11. This article focuses on the excesses of the lobbying industry. What positive roles do interest groups perform in American politics?

On Sept. 19, eight days after the terrorist attacks on New York and Washington, Senator Frank Murkowski took to the Senate floor to deny reports that he was trying to affix an amendment containing one of his pet proposals to a fast-moving defense bill. Murkowski, a Republican from Alaska, said he resented any suggestion that he was exploiting a national military emergency to slip through a measure that would open the Arctic National Wildlife Refuge (ANWR) to energy exploration and development. "That is certainly not the case," a plainly agitated Murkowski told his colleagues. "It would be inappropriate and in poor taste."

Just hours later, however, one of Murkowski's key allies in the Senate did exactly what Murkowski said he would not do. Republican James Inhofe of Oklahoma introduced an amendment—drawn verbatim from an energy bill that Murkowski had written six months earlier—to permit drilling for oil and natural gas in ANWR's environmentally sensitive coastal plain. And two days later, Murkowski's reticence to link ANWR to the events of Sept. 11 had apparently evaporated. "I think we've got an issue here whose time has come," he told reporters. Soon he was couching his pronouncements in the twin themes of antiterrorism and national security. "Mideast oil funds terrorism," he declared. "If there was a terrorist attack on our oil supply, such as an attack on tankers in the Strait of Hormuz, there would be a significant blow to our national security." The ANWR amendment was ultimately removed from the defense appropriations bill, but Murkowski vowed to attach what he now called the "Homeland Energy Security Act" to other legislation.

Murkowski was not the only elected official trying to slip industry-backed items into unrelated emergency measures. In the wake of Sept. 11, scores of Capitol Hill lawmakers, Washington lobbyists, trade associations, and interest groups rushed to repackage their old proposals in national security wrapping. Bald opportunism and the political exploitation of tragedy is nothing new in the nation's capital, but what's happened in the months since the terrorist attacks may well show Washington at its worst. "I think that this was more shameless than anything else I've ever seen in Washington," says Ronald Utt, a senior research fellow at the Heritage Foundation, a conservative Washington think tank.

Television producer Bill Moyers, in a speech to a group of environmental funders, put a more venal cast on the latest lobbying tactics. "It didn't take long for the wartime opportunists—the mercenaries of Washington, the lobbyists, lawyers, and political fundraisers—to crawl out of their offices on K Street to grab what they can for their clients," he said. "In the wake of this awful tragedy wrought by terrorism, they are cashing in."

Consider, for example, the lobbying strategy of the nation's beleaguered steel industry. The smoke had not yet cleared from the wreckage of the World Trade Center when the nation's big steelmakers and their allies in Washington began invoking the terrorist

> Why do we find it so distasteful and repulsive to see people cashing in on tragedy? Would this behavior seem less awful if no one had died in the September 11 attacks?

attacks to bolster their arguments for direct subsidies, as well as further restrictions on imports of less-costly foreign steel. "Without steel, we cannot guarantee our national security," said Senator Jay Rockefeller, a Democrat from West Virginia. "Without steel, we cannot build from our tragedy." (Without steel, Rockefeller might have added, the two political parties and their congressional candidates would have been about $2.7 million poorer in the 2000 elections.)

"Absolute baloney," Robert Crandall, a senior fellow at the Brookings Institution, says of the argument that propping up the domestic steel industry is vital to the national security. One or two steel mills, he maintains, could produce all the steel plate needed for shipbuilding and other critical defense industries.

National security arguments were even used to advance a farm-subsidy bill worth $167 billion. Before Sept. 11, the bill was titled the Agriculture Act of 2001. After the terrorist attacks, it was renamed the Farm Security Act of 2001. On Sept. 24, the growers of more than 20 federally subsidized agriculture commodities sent a letter to Capitol Hill lawmakers in which they said that the attacks had "bolstered the argument that food production is vital to the national interest." No doubt their message got through: The producers of these and other commodities had poured more than $58 million into the 2000 elections. On October 5, the measure passed the House by a vote of 291 to 120.

Similar arguments were advanced by the manufacturers of traffic signs, barricades, and other equipment, who gamely recast their perennial plea for more federal highway-safety spending in a national security framework. A spokesman for the 1,800-member American Traffic Safety Services Association said that increased federal spending on highway signs and other traffic-routing devices would help motorists flee cities faster and more safely during a terrorist attack. Rob Dingess, the association's director of government relations, pointed out that the evacuation of many federal facilities following the attack on the Pentagon left the nation's capital in gridlock. "If a second plane had come into that city," Dingess said, "you would almost have had to helicopter people to fight fire or evacuate people."

Then there was the American Bus Association, which represents nearly a thousand private companies that provide intercity bus and motorcoach service. The trade group has been lobbying for legislation that would provide $400 million "to improve bus security and safety." The legislation is important, the association insists, because it would help bus companies retain drivers who, in the wake of Sept. 11, have come to fear potential terrorist attacks.

But the most labored stretch may have come from the National Taxpayers Union, a conservative advocacy group that touted a cut in capital-gains taxes as a national security initiative. Eric Schlecht, the organization's director of congressional relations, maintains that lowering taxes for the rich would flood the coffers of the IRS with more money. "By reducing the rate at which capital gains are taxed," he says, "President Bush and Congress could help revitalize the sagging economy and bring new revenues to Washington—decidedly aiding our war against terrorism."

Washington has always been a city of wretched excesses, but never have so many lobbyists for so many different special interests so blatantly wrapped their requests for subsidies, tax breaks, and other forms of federal largesse in patriotic packaging. "No self-respecting lobbyist in Washington has resisted the temptation to reframe the exact arguments they were making before September 11 into a post–Sept. 11 response to terror," observes Rep. Edward Markey (D-Mass.). "There is no issue—none—where they aren't doing it."

The feeding frenzy was kicked off by the airline industry's drive for a fast-track bailout in the days immediately after the terrorist attacks. By Sept. 22, the airlines had sealed an especially sweet deal: $5 billion in cash, plus another $10 billion in loan guarantees based on their pre–Sept. 11 market share rather than their post–Sept. 11 losses. The airlines also won protection from any lawsuits arising from the attacks, a provision of the bailout that may ultimately cost taxpayers many additional billions.

> What would have been the effect on the nation if the airline industry had collapsed in the wake of the attack? Whose job is it to be sure that this industry didn't collapse? Do any of the airlines have legitimate claims on the government?

The success of the airlines inspired the insurance industry to follow suit. On Sept. 21, during a private meeting at the White House arranged by the American Insurance Association, 16 insurance executives informed President George Bush and Commerce Secretary Donald Evans that the industry would be able to pay all the claims—estimated at $40 billion to $75 billion—arising from what's expected to be the costliest disaster in the nation's history. During a brief "photo op," the executives assured Bush that the insurance industry, with its $3 trillion in assets in the United States alone, wouldn't need federal help.

When the cameras were gone, however, the executives—led by CEOs Maurice Greenberg of American International Group and Robert O'Connell of Massachusetts Mutual Life Insurance—got down to the real business at hand. They bluntly pressed Bush and Evans for legislation that would shift the lion's share of liability for future terrorist attacks to the federal government. Furthermore, Greenberg reportedly asked the White House for its help in keeping claim disputes related to the World Trade Center disaster confined to a federal court in Manhattan—and thereby out of state courts, where insurers could potentially be liable for additional millions, if not billions, in punitive damages. If the White House failed to act, the insurers warned, the industry would refuse to cover damage from future terrorist attacks, potentially triggering a full-scale financial crisis.

The executives in the industry's delegation were anything but strangers to their White House hosts. In particular, Greenberg and O'Connell had been among the elite group of fundraisers known as "Pioneers" who raised at least $100,000 for Bush's presidential campaign under the direction of his finance chairman, Donald Evans. In all, the insurance industry had invested nearly $1.6 million to elect Bush, and Greenberg's company and two industry trade associations had chipped in $100,000 apiece to underwrite his inaugural celebration. The industry had also pumped more than $20 million into Republican and Democratic soft-money accounts since 1999—corporate checks bearing such names as Chubb, CNA, Hartford, Kemper, Travelers, and Zurich, all of whom had representatives at the White House meeting.

The White House was quick to respond to the industry's request. On October 15, it unveiled a plan to cap the industry's liability in 2002 by agreeing to use public funds to pay all but $12 billion of the first $100 billion in future terrorism-related claims. The plan would also limit the industry's liability to $23 billion in 2003 and $35 billion in 2004.

In November, the House voted along party lines to approve the plan, which had been introduced as the "Terrorism Risk Protection Act" by Rep. Michael Oxley, a Republican from Ohio. Oxley was clearly the right lawmaker for the job: Even with Election Day more than a year away, he'd already collected more than $34,000 in contributions from insurance-industry interests.

The plan to shift the cost of any future terrorist attacks to taxpayers later stalled in the Senate, but the early successes of the airline and insurance industries emboldened other businesses to think big. "If you start saying, 'Well, the airlines have been hurt because nobody wants to fly on airplanes any longer,' there are literally hundreds of industries that could make that exact same claim," says Stephen Moore, a senior fellow at the Cato Institute, a free-market-oriented think tank. "It starts with the airlines, and then it's insurance businesses, and then it's the entertainment industry, and tourism, and then, of course, the Las Vegas casinos. It just becomes a parade of special-interest groups down Pennsylvania Avenue that have their hands out. This is the quintessence of corporate welfare." . . .

Indeed, as both the Senate and House crafted huge economic-stimulus bills in November, lobbyists from nearly every industry scurried to get a piece of the action. "As soon as there was an announcement of an aid package, people started coming out of the woodwork," acknowledged James Albertine, president of the American League of Lobbyists. "There are a lot of industries that will be looking at the pot of gold. The federal government is spending more and, obviously, there will be some winners. There's lots of opportunities and it cuts across all industries. It's pretty much open season."

Barely a month after the terrorist attacks, Rep. Jim Moran, a Democrat whose Virginia congressional district includes Reagan National Airport, bluntly summed up the attitude of both lawmakers and lobbyists. "It's an open grab bag," he said, "so let's grab."

In a few cases, the lobbying free-for-all proved too brazen even by Washington standards. In November, lobbyist Howard Marlowe scored a modest but impressive victory for the nation's seaside resorts, persuading Congress that it was vital for national security to spend a record $135 million to shore up public beaches with sand—nearly $50 million more for beach "nourishment" than the Bush administration had requested. Emboldened by their success, Marlowe's clients immediately made a pitch for additional subsidies. "America needs to make a major commitment to its energy and water infrastructure, both for security and economic reasons," the American Shore and Beach Preservation Association urged lawmakers. "Protecting the nation's coastline is also vitally important to ensure the recovery of the American economy."

This time around, though, the appeal went nowhere. "We haven't gotten anything yet, and I don't think we will," says Marlowe, who concedes that the lobbying frenzy has gotten out of hand. "It gets to the point where you don't want to be associated with it," he says. "So many people saw opportunity in the wake of tragedy that it's definitely gotten unseemly."

Perhaps the most unseemly proposal of all was the juicy platter of corporate tax breaks that formed the centerpiece of the economic-stimulus plan put forward by House Republicans. The GOP plan called for almost doubling the amount that companies can write off for capital expenses they haven't yet incurred, allowing corporations that rely on loopholes to pay no taxes at all, and providing immediate rebates for any alternative-minimum taxes they have paid since 1986. The congressional Joint Committee on Taxation estimated that the bill would trigger nearly $13 billion in rebates, with nearly a third going to just 16 Fortune 500 firms. The legislation also proposed making permanent a provision that allows multinational corporations to shelter their U.S. profits from taxation by shifting them, on paper, to offshore tax havens. The provision was included even after an administration official conceded that the measure—which would cost taxpayers $21 billion over 10 years—would have "zero stimulative effect."

> *Could any lobbyists risk not being associated with the post-9/11 feeding frenzy? Would they have been doing their jobs effectively for their clients if they had missed a big chance to secure significant government contributions?*

Much of the lobbying for the tax breaks was orchestrated by Kenneth Kies, a partner at the accounting and lobbying firm of PricewaterhouseCoopers who previously worked on Capitol Hill as staff director of the Joint Committee on Taxation. Like other lobbyists, Kies suggested to reporters that he was only trying to do his patriotic duty by bolstering the bottom lines of some of the nation's wealthiest corporations. "I wouldn't be doing the job—not necessarily for my clients—but for my country," he told the *New York Times*, "if I wasn't being helpful in terms of offering ideas that can be helpful in stimulating the economy."

But many didn't find the ideas very helpful—especially when Republicans balked at extending direct assistance to workers struggling to pay for health insurance. "The House bill was a public-relations disaster, because it really read

Kies is an example of a person taking advantage of the revolving door between public service and the lobbying industry. How might his public and private positions have constituted a conflict of interest?

like it was written by K Street corporate lobbyists," says Stephen Moore of the Cato Institute, the free-market think tank. "And unfortunately, the truth is that it was largely written by K Street corporate lobbyists." With Senate Democrats refusing to sign on to the tax breaks, the stimulus package failed to win approval before Congress adjourned at the end of the year.

But despite the political setback, many seasoned observers say the lobbying landscape in Washington has shifted dramatically since Sept. 11. The corporate tax breaks are back on the table, they say, as industry lobbyists intent on raiding the federal treasury continue to sell their proposals by waving the flag or stirring public fears of future attacks. "Lobbyists are in the business of asking for things," says the Heritage Foundation's Ronald Utt. "And they adjust their message to whatever they think will sell. Right now that's national security, economic stimulus, and disaster relief, and so they link what they want to one of those—better yet, to all three."

Even the Bush administration is now playing the name game: Early this year White House spokesmen started referring to the president's economic-stimulus package as an "economic security" plan.

"You know, this stuff never goes away," says Robert McIntyre, director of Citizens for Tax Justice, a Washington-based watchdog organization. "They never close down K Street."

Consider the source and the audience.

- *Mother Jones* prides itself on being a nonprofit magazine that is committed to issues of progressivism and social justice. How would it define "social justice"? Where can we see its liberal bent?

Lay out the argument, the values, and the assumptions.

- Why does Hogan take the lobbying industry to task? What broadly held values is he appealing to in order to condemn its behavior? What does he see as the conflict between national tragedy and greed, patriotism and profit?
- How do the airline, steel, agriculture, and insurance industries, among many others, frame their appeals for money in terms of national security? Do they feel this behavior is justified? Why?

Uncover the evidence.

- Hogan provides example after example of lobbyists trying to secure funds from the government, under what he considers to be the guise of "homeland security." Does it help that he can cite members of the lobbying industry who themselves have qualms about their own behavior?
- Does he pay any attention to legitimate claims for post-9/11 government money? Does he have to?

Evaluate the conclusion.

- Why does Hogan consider the efforts by people to couch tax cuts and tax breaks as "necessary for national security" to be more egregious than the other offenses he cites? Is he up-front about the values that lead him to make those claims? Is he himself using the national tragedy of 9/11 to score his own ideological points?
- How do you think most lobbyists would respond to Hogan's article? Would they think it was a fair description of the industry?

Sort out the political implications.

- What would have happened had all politicians taken (and stuck to) the attitude expressed by Murkowski in the first paragraph?
- How should the lobbying industry have responded after 9/11? At what point would it have been seen as acceptable for lobbyists to begin pushing their claims?

12.5 *Federalist* No. 10

James Madison, *The Federalist Papers*

Of all *The Federalist Papers,* perhaps none has received as much scrutiny and discussion as Madison's *Federalist* No. 10. Whereas supporters of pluralist democracy—a theory of representative democracy that holds that citizen membership in groups is the key to political power—argue that interest groups are an essential component of a republic, Madison claims that the formation of interest groups—or factions, as he calls them—can potentially threaten the very health of a society. In *Federalist* No. 10, Madison argues that the proposed new republic offers the perfect opportunity to control "the violence of faction" while, at the same time, not limiting individual freedoms. How does Madison's view of factions in 1787 compare with our view of interest groups today?

To the People of the State of New York:

Among the numerous advantages promised by a well constructed Union, none deserves to be more accurately developed than its tendency to break and control the violence of faction. The friend of popular governments never finds himself so much alarmed for their character and fate, as when he contemplates their propensity to this dangerous vice. He will not fail, therefore, to set a due value on any plan which, without violating the principles to which he is attached, provides a proper cure for it. The instability, injustice, and confusion introduced into the public councils, have, in truth, been the mortal diseases under which popular governments have everywhere perished; as they continue to be the favorite and fruitful topics from which the adversaries to liberty derive their most specious declamations. The valuable improvements made by the American constitutions on the popular models, both ancient and modern, cannot certainly be too much admired; but it would be an unwarrantable partiality, to contend that they have as effectually obviated the danger on this side, as was wished and expected. Complaints are everywhere heard from our most considerate and virtuous citizens, equally the friends of public and private faith, and of public and personal liberty, that our governments are too unstable, that the public good is disregarded in the conflicts of rival parties, and that measures are too often decided, not according to the rules of justice and the rights of the minor party, but by the superior force of an interested and overbearing majority. However anxiously we may wish that these complaints had no foundation, the evidence, of known facts will not permit us to deny that they are in some degree true. It will be found, indeed, on a candid review of our situation, that some of the distresses under which we labor have been erroneously charged on the operation of our governments; but it will be found, at the same time, that other causes will not alone account for many of our heaviest misfortunes; and, particularly, for that prevailing and increasing distrust of public engagements, and alarm for private rights, which are echoed from one end of the continent to the other. These must be chiefly, if not wholly, effects of the unsteadiness and injustice with which a factious spirit has tainted our public administrations.

By a faction, I understand a number of citizens, whether amounting to a majority or a minority of the whole, who are united and actuated by some common impulse of passion, or of interest, adversed to the rights of other citizens, or to the permanent and aggregate interests of the community.

There are two methods of curing the mischiefs of faction: the one, by removing its causes; the other, by controlling its effects.

There are again two methods of removing the causes of faction: the one, by destroying the liberty which is essential to its existence; the other, by giving to every citizen the same opinions, the same passions, and the same interests.

It could never be more truly said than of the first remedy, that it was worse than the disease. Liberty is to faction what air is to fire, an aliment without which it instantly expires. But it could not be less folly to abolish liberty, which is essential to political life, because it nourishes faction, than it would be to wish the annihilation of air, which is essential to animal life, because it imparts to fire its destructive agency.

The second expedient is as impracticable as the first would be unwise. As long as the reason of man continues fallible, and he is at liberty to exercise it, different opinions will be formed. As long as the connection subsists between his reason and his self-love, his opinions and his passions will have a reciprocal influence on each other; and the former will be objects to which the latter will attach themselves. The diversity in the faculties of men, from which the rights of property originate, is not less an insuperable obstacle to a uniformity of interests. The protection of these faculties is the first object of government. From the protection of different and unequal faculties of acquiring property, the possession of different degrees and kinds of property immediately results; and from the influence of these on the sentiments and views of the respective proprietors, ensues a division of the society into different interests and parties.

The latent causes of faction are thus sown in the nature of man; and we see them everywhere brought into different degrees of activity, according to the different circumstances of civil society. A zeal for different opinions concerning religion, concerning government, and many other points, as well of speculation as of practice; an attachment to different leaders ambitiously contending for preeminence and power; or to persons of other descriptions whose fortunes have been interesting to the human passions, have, in turn, divided mankind into parties, inflamed them with mutual animosity, and rendered them much more disposed to vex and oppress each other than to co-operate for their common good. So strong is this propensity of mankind to fall into mutual animosities, that where no substantial occasion presents itself, the most frivolous and fanciful distinctions have been sufficient to kindle their unfriendly passions and excite their most violent conflicts. But the most common and durable source of factions has been the various and unequal distribution of property. Those who hold and those who are without property have ever formed distinct interests in society. Those who are creditors, and those who are debtors, fall under a like discrimination. A landed interest, a manufacturing interest, a mercantile interest, a moneyed interest, with many lesser interests, grow up of necessity in civilized nations, and divide them into different classes, actuated by different sentiments and views. The regulation of these various and interfering interests forms the principal task of modern legislation, and involves the spirit of party and faction in the necessary and ordinary operations of the government.

> What is Madison's view of human nature? If this is what people are like, what is government's job with respect to them?

No man is allowed to be a judge in his own cause, because his interest would certainly bias his judgment, and, not improbably, corrupt his integrity. With equal, nay with greater reason, a body of men are unfit to be both judges and parties at the same time; yet what are many of the most important acts of legislation, but so many judicial determinations, not indeed concerning the rights of single persons, but concerning the rights of large bodies of citizens? And what are the different classes of legislators but advocates and parties to the causes which they determine? Is a law proposed concerning private debts? It is a question to which the creditors are parties on one side and the debtors on the other. Justice ought to hold the balance between them. Yet the parties are, and must be, themselves the judges; and the most numerous party, or, in other words, the most powerful faction must be expected to prevail. Shall domestic manufactures be encouraged, and in what degree, by restrictions on foreign manufactures? are questions which would be differently decided by the landed and the manufacturing classes, and probably by neither with a sole regard to justice and the public good. The apportionment of taxes on the various descriptions of property is an act which seems to require the most exact impartiality; yet there is, perhaps, no legislative act in which greater opportunity and temptation are given to a predominant party to trample on the rules of justice. Every shilling with which they overburden the inferior number, is a shilling saved to their own pockets.

It is in vain to say that enlightened statesmen will be able to adjust these clashing interests, and render them all subservient to the public good. Enlightened statesmen will not always be at the helm. Nor, in many cases, can such an adjustment be made at all without taking into view indirect and remote considerations, which will rarely prevail over the immediate interest which one party may find in disregarding the rights of another or the good of the whole.

The inference to which we are brought is, that the CAUSES of faction cannot be removed, and that relief is only to be sought in the means of controlling its EFFECTS.

If a faction consists of less than a majority, relief is supplied by the republican principle, which enables the majority to defeat its sinister views by regular vote. It may clog the administration, it may convulse the society; but it will be unable to execute and mask its violence under the forms of the Constitution. When a majority is included in a faction, the form of popular government, on the other hand, enables it to sacrifice to its ruling passion or interest both the public good and the rights of other citizens. To secure the public good and private rights against the danger of such a faction, and at the same time to preserve the spirit and the form of popular government, is then the great object to which our inquiries are directed. Let me add that it is the great desideratum by which this form of government can be rescued from the opprobrium under which it has so long labored, and be recommended to the esteem and adoption of mankind.

Why isn't Madison worried about minority factions? Why are majority factions the chief danger?

By what means is this object attainable? Evidently by one of two only. Either the existence of the same passion or interest in a majority at the same time must be prevented, or the majority, having such coexistent passion or interest, must be rendered, by their number and local situation, unable to concert and carry into effect schemes of oppression. If the impulse and the opportunity be suffered to coincide, we well know that neither moral nor religious motives can be relied on as an adequate control. They are not found to be such on the injustice and violence of individuals, and lose their efficacy in proportion to the number combined together, that is, in proportion as their efficacy becomes needful.

From this view of the subject it may be concluded that a pure democracy, by which I mean a society consisting of a small number of citizens, who assemble and administer the government in person, can admit of no cure for the mischiefs of faction. A common passion or interest will, in almost every case, be felt by a majority of the whole; a communication and concert result from the form of government itself; and there is nothing to check the inducements to sacrifice the weaker party or an obnoxious individual. Hence it is that such democracies have ever been spectacles of turbulence and contention; have ever been found incompatible with personal security or the rights of property; and have in general been as short in their lives as they have been violent in their deaths. Theoretic politicians, who have patronized this species of government, have erroneously supposed that by reducing mankind to a perfect equality in their political rights, they would, at the same time, be perfectly equalized and assimilated in their possessions, their opinions, and their passions.

A republic, by which I mean a government in which the scheme of representation takes place, opens a different prospect, and promises the cure for which we are seeking. Let us examine the points in which it varies from pure democracy, and we shall comprehend both the nature of the cure and the efficacy which it must derive from the Union.

The two great points of difference between a democracy and a republic are: first, the delegation of the government, in the latter, to a small number of citizens elected by the rest; secondly, the greater number of citizens, and greater sphere of country, over which the latter may be extended.

> What exactly is the difference, in Madison's view, between a republic and a democracy?

The effect of the first difference is, on the one hand, to refine and enlarge the public views, by passing them through the medium of a chosen body of citizens, whose wisdom may best discern the true interest of their country, and whose patriotism and love of justice will be least likely to sacrifice it to temporary or partial considerations. Under such a regulation, it may well happen that the public voice, pronounced by the representatives of the people, will be more consonant to the public good than if pronounced by the people themselves, convened for the purpose. On the other hand, the effect may be inverted. Men of factious tempers, of local prejudices, or of sinister designs, may, by intrigue, by corruption, or by other means, first obtain the suffrages, and then betray the interests, of the people. The question resulting is, whether small or extensive republics are more favorable to the election of proper guardians of the public weal; and it is clearly decided in favor of the latter by two obvious considerations:

In the first place, it is to be remarked that, however small the republic may be, the representatives must be raised to a certain number, in order to guard against the cabals of a few; and that, however large it may be, they must be limited to a certain number, in order to guard against the confusion of a multitude. Hence, the number of representatives in the two cases not being in proportion to that of the two constituents, and being proportionally greater in the small republic, it follows that, if the proportion of fit characters be not less in the large than in the small republic, the former will present a greater option, and consequently a greater probability of a fit choice.

In the next place, as each representative will be chosen by a greater number of citizens in the large than in the small republic, it will be more difficult for un-worthy candidates to practice with success the vicious arts by which elections are too often carried; and the suffrages of the people being more free, will be more likely to centre in men who possess the most attractive merit and the most diffusive and established characters.

It must be confessed that in this, as in most other cases, there is a mean, on both sides of which inconveniences will be found to lie. By enlarging too much the number of electors, you render the representatives too little acquainted with all their local circumstances and lesser interests; as by reducing it too much, you render him unduly attached to these, and too little fit to comprehend and pursue great and national objects. The federal Constitution forms a happy combination in this respect; the great and aggregate interests being referred to the national, the local and particular to the State legislatures.

The other point of difference is, the greater number of citizens and extent of territory which may be brought within the compass of republican than of democratic government; and it is this circumstance principally which renders factious combinations less to be dreaded in the former than in the latter. The smaller the society, the fewer probably will be the distinct parties and interests composing it; the fewer the distinct parties and interests, the more frequently will a majority be found of the same party; and the smaller the number of individuals composing a majority, and the smaller the compass within which they are placed, the more easily will they concert and execute their plans of oppression. Extend the sphere, and you take in a greater variety of parties and interests; you make it less probable that a majority of the whole will have a common motive to invade the rights of other citizens; or if such a common motive exists, it will be more difficult for all who feel it to discover their own strength, and to act in unison with each other. Besides other impediments, it may be remarked that, where there is a consciousness of unjust or dishonorable purposes, communication is always checked by distrust in proportion to the number whose concurrence is necessary.

Hence, it clearly appears, that the same advantage which a republic has over a democracy, in controlling the effects of faction, is enjoyed by a large over a small republic,—is enjoyed by the Union over the States composing it. Does the advantage consist in the substitution of representatives whose enlightened views and virtuous sentiments render them superior to local prejudices and schemes of injustice? It will not be denied that the representation of the Union will be most likely to possess these requisite endowments. Does it consist in the greater security afforded by a greater variety of parties, against the event of any one party being able to outnumber and oppress the rest? In an equal degree does the increased variety of parties comprised within the Union, increase this security?

Does it, in fine, consist in the greater obstacles opposed to the concert and accomplishment of the secret wishes of an unjust and interested majority? Here, again, the extent of the Union gives it the most palpable advantage.

The influence of factious leaders may kindle a flame within their particular States, but will be unable to spread a general conflagration through the other States. A religious sect may degenerate into a political faction in a part of the Confederacy; but the variety of sects dispersed over the entire face of it must secure the national councils against any danger from that source. A rage for paper money, for an abolition of debts, for an equal division of property, or for any other improper or wicked project, will be less apt to pervade the whole body of the Union than a particular member of it; in the same proportion as such a malady is more likely to taint a particular county or district, than an entire State.

In the extent and proper structure of the Union, therefore, we behold a republican remedy for the diseases most incident to republican government. And according to the degree of pleasure and pride we feel in being republicans, ought to be our zeal in cherishing the spirit and supporting the character of Federalists.

PUBLIUS.

> What does Madison mean by the famous phrase "a republican remedy for the diseases most incident to republican government"? Why are factions more likely in a republic? How does a republic help to contain them?

Consider the source and the audience.

- *Federalist* No. 10 was an editorial, written anonymously under the name "Publius," in an effort to get the citizens of New York to sign on to the Constitution. *Federalist* No. 10 was especially aimed at people who feared the possibilities for corruption in a large country. How does that fact affect how Madison couches his arguments about factions?

Lay out the argument, the values, and the assumptions.

- What does Madison believe are the root causes of factions?
- Why does Madison think factions are problematic?
- Does Madison want to control the causes of factions or the effects of them—and why? What's the difference? Why does he think the root causes of factions cannot be controlled, but the effects of factions can?
- How, in Madison's view, will the new republic contain the dangers of factions? What is the key role that its size will play?

Uncover the evidence.

- Does Madison provide any evidence to support his arguments, or are they all theory driven? Is there any type of evidence he could have added to make his argument more persuasive?

Evaluate the conclusion.

- Hindsight is 20/20. Historical works allow us to go back and ask "Was the author right?" Was he? Has the Constitution limited the power of factions?
- Even if Madison was right—specifically, in saying that the Constitution would control the effects of factions—was his premise correct? Are factions bad? What good, if any, can come from them?

Sort out the political implications.

- Conditions have changed since Madison's day. With phones, e-mails, and fax machines, we can now get in touch with someone on the other side of the country in seconds. The landmass of the United States is significantly larger than when Madison was writing; yet, in a sense, the country is much smaller today. Does the shrinking of America negate the force of Madison's argument about the containment of the ill effects of factions?
- What would Madison say if he could come back today? Would he think his expectations in *Federalist* No. 10 had been borne out? Would he be pleased or displeased? Why?

CHAPTER 13

Voting and Elections

Elections are at the very heart of a representative democracy, based on the principle that the public interest is best served by many individuals each choosing those leaders they feel will make decisions in their particular interests. Politics is about power, after all. It's about winners and losers, and nowhere is this more evident than in elections in the United States. Parties, interest groups, individuals, and candidates throw hundreds of millions of dollars into campaigns for one reason: so their team (or at least their candidate) will win and their interests will be served.

Because winning is what really counts in electoral politics, campaigns have become more expensive, more negative, and more long-lived. Political consulting has become a lucrative business. Today's candidates have not only policy advisors but campaign strategists, pollsters, opposition researchers, and speechwriters all working to put, and keep, the candidate in office.

Even with the rise of candidate-centered elections, we still measure who wins and who loses based on how well the two major parties do. The importance of winning means that parties must have a strategy. There may be small policy differences among party members, but the party needs a message. It must make clear what it stands for and what it will do if it wins. The party that has the more effective, persuasive message normally will set the agenda for the next few years.

All campaign strategy is created with voters in mind. Who votes? Who doesn't? How will the candidate do among women voters? African Americans? The poor? The educated? The first major theory of voting, developed in the 1940s, held that campaigns don't matter because we simply vote with the groups with which we identify. If we are wealthy, we vote Republican. If we come from a blue-collar family, we vote Democratic. If we are Protestant, we vote Republican. If we are Jewish, we vote Democratic. While more recently many political scientists have criticized this theory of voting, campaigns still devise their strategies as if it were valid. During the next election, pay attention. You will surely hear pundits make such comments as "Candidate X must win at least 60 percent of the white vote to be successful" or "Candidate Y is really struggling with women. If he can't improve women's perceptions of him, he will lose." Candidates constantly alter their strategies to make them more appealing to certain groups that are essential for them to win. They can't rest on their laurels; they must continually try to expand that winning electoral coalition.

Obviously campaign strategy depends on who the voters are. But just as important may be who the voters aren't, and unfortunately most of us aren't voters. The United States prides itself on being the model democracy—the one that others should look to as an example. But in this model democracy, only about half of all eligible voters will cast their ballots in a presidential election. This percentage gets even worse when we look at midterm elections where voter turnout hovers around 35 percent or at primaries and caucuses where turnout is even less. In 1996, only 915 people came to the Wyoming Republican caucus meeting! And in contrast to the Olympic medal count, in which the United States prides itself on finishing toward the top, few people seem to care that we consistently rank near the very bottom of the list regarding voter turnout in industrialized countries.

The selections in this chapter examine questions from a campaign's point of view, a voter's point of view, and, finally, a candidate's point of view. The first article, from the *New York Times,* discusses the role a close advisor to President Bush played in crafting the successful Republican campaign strategy during the 2002 midterm elections. The second article, also from the *Times,* is written by a conservative media commentator, Tucker Carlson, who criticizes the Democratic Party for its inability to put forth a compelling alternative to President Bush's agenda. Next, from *The American Spectator,* John Fund examines a proposal to lower the costs of voting—same-day voter registration—and argues that it will do more harm than good. Fourth, Tony Mauro in *USA Today* takes on the newly passed campaign-finance reform and challenges it on constitutional grounds. Finally, we conclude with the concession speech by one of the most famous electoral losers of the last few years—former Vice-President Al Gore, who shows how elections promote stability when all agree on the rules of the game, even when they dislike the outcome.

13.1 The Strategist

Republicans Say Rove Was Mastermind of Big Victory

Elisabeth Bumiller and David E. Sanger, *New York Times,* 7 November 2002

In the run-up to the 2002 midterm elections, the Democrats were feeling hopeful that they would hold their small majority in the Senate and perhaps even take control of the House of Representatives. Their hopes were not unreasonable. After all, the president's party traditionally loses seats in the midterm elections (only once, in 1998, had it happened otherwise since 1934) and many polls in the week before the election showed the Democrats doing well. Consequently, the Democrats were stunned when, after the smoke cleared on Election Day, it was the Republicans who had picked up seats in the House and who regained control of the Senate.

In the days and weeks after the election, there would be many explanations for the election results, among them the claim that it was the Democrats' own fault for not offering a serious alternative to Republican policy and for failing to energize their supporters. The search for an explanation began the very day after the election, however, when this *New York Times* article addressed the notion that it was not so much a Democratic loss that had to be explained as it was a Republican victory—a victory that was largely attributable to the efforts of one man, President George W. Bush's political advisor, Karl Rove. How much impact can the actions of a single person have on a complex political outcome?

H is name was not on any ballot but Karl Rove, the West Wing mastermind who has plotted for years to bring George W. Bush and the Republican Party to dominance, emerged as one of the biggest winners in the midterm elections of 2002.

More than anyone, Mr. Rove urged a president who hates to travel to campaign relentlessly for Republican candidates. And more than anyone, he urged that president to put the prestige of the White House on the line for the Republican Party and his own re-election in 2004.

"Karl clearly has a disposition where he likes to take risks, and George Bush trusts him implicitly," said Rich Bond, the former chairman of the Republican National Committee. "Karl laid out a very plausible scenario on investment of political capital, and Bush went with it. He has now gotten the upper hand, and it was a move that will go down in history."

It was Mr. Rove who insisted that the president devote the last five days before the election on a 10,000-mile, 17-city, 15-state blitz, and campaign as if his political life depended on it. It was Mr. Rove who insisted that Mr. Bush make a political stop in Minnesota only nine days after the death of Senator Paul Wellstone and campaign for Mr. Wellstone's opponent, even after Mr. Bush had skipped the late senator's funeral.

> What is "political capital"? How does a politician accumulate it, and how does he or she "cash it in"?

Mr. Rove also helped refine the part of Mr. Bush's stump speech that has drawn some of the biggest applause around the country: his vow to "hunt down these cold-blooded killers one by one." More recently, it was Mr. Rove who devised Mr. Bush's criticism of Democrats for using union rules to hold up creation of a new Department of Homeland Security.

Mr. Rove's reputation as a powerful and imperious political adviser to Mr. Bush is already well established in Washington. But even those in top Republican political circles said today that they were taken aback by Mr. Rove's relentlessness and gutsiness in sending out the president on the last weekend before the election to races where Democrats were leading—and where Mr. Bush might have been blamed had the Republicans lost. Mr. Rove declined to be interviewed for this article.

"They went to races not where they were already close to winning to get the credit; they went to races to create the opportunity to win," said Bill McInturff, the pollster for Saxby Chambliss, the Republican who won a surprise victory for Senate in Georgia over the incumbent, Max Cleland.

Mr. Bush made two stops in Georgia on Saturday, three days before the election, when Mr. Chambliss was down by as much as 7 percentage points in Mr. McInturff's poll. By Sunday, not even 24 hours after Mr. Bush fired up enormous crowds at Republican rallies in Marietta and Savannah, Mr. McInturff said his polling showed that Mr. Chambliss had bounced up to even with Mr. Cleland.

Republicans and Democrats agreed today that Mr. Bush's last five-day push, the most extensive of any president, was critical to the outcome, and that Mr. Rove had correctly foreseen that it would rally Mr. Bush's core supporters. "It took the oxygen out of all other issues," said Kenneth M. Duberstein, a former chief of staff to Ronald Reagan. "When the president comes into a state, all the news is dominated by the president and Air Force One."

Was there anything the Democrats could have done to keep media attention on the issues they cared about once the presidential entourage had arrived in town?

In Minnesota, where Mr. Bush touched down on Sunday, Mr. Rove showed his fiercest determination to fight to the end. In the immediate aftermath of Mr. Wellstone's death, some senior Bush advisers questioned whether it was appropriate for the president to make another campaign stop in the state, but Mr. Rove said that the race was too crucial to bypass—and that the other side had no right to cry politics when a memorial service for Mr. Wellstone evolved into a Democratic rally.

Nonetheless, it was Mr. Rove who recommended that Mr. Bush open his stump speech in St. Paul with a respectful tribute to Mr. Wellstone.

Republicans credit Mr. Rove for planning the strategy for the 2002 election almost from the first day that Mr. Bush became president. After the debacle of the 2000 election, when the Supreme Court propelled a candidate who had lost the popular vote into the White House, Mr. Rove foresaw, Republicans say, that he had no time to waste in expanding his client's narrow mandate.

Why did Rove's effort go back as far as 2001? How did he figure a big 2002 victory would make up for the narrowly contested 2000 election?

So in the early spring of 2001, Mr. Rove set out to make Republican gains with early and aggressive recruiting of candidates for critical House and Senate races and a major fund-raising push. White House advisers said he essentially controlled the Republican National Committee from the White House.

By late March this year, as Mr. Bush began a record-breaking fund-raising odyssey across the United States that ultimately brought in more than $140 million for Republicans, Mr. Rove had already deployed his deputy, the White House political director Ken Mehlman, to work with the national committee to find consultants for important Congressional races. In the past, Republicans have sent plenty of money, but usually waited until after Labor Day to dispatch their professionals to needy campaigns.

"Generally speaking, the R.N.C. has functioned as an A.T.M. machine," said Wayne L. Berman, a longtime Republican fund-raiser and lobbyist. "In this case, they functioned like a McKinsey-like consulting firm."

Republicans said today that Mr. Rove had also worked hard to keep the small army of party pollsters and consultants who are hired by Congressional campaigns happy and connected. True, they said, Mr. Rove has a reputation for hot-tempered behavior—and even for berating members of Congress who do not hew to the administration line—but his White House political operation, led by Mr. Mehlman, does not.

"The White House political shop has created enormous good will in the Republican family because of the way they used the president, and because of their dealings with people," said Mr. McInturff, Representative Chambliss's pollster, adding that Mr. Rove and company also tried to keep a lid on what outside consultants said to reporters.

"But even when I've gotten my occasional call of, 'Gee, we can't help but wonder why you said X,'" Mr. McInturff said, "they've done that in a gentlemanly tenor, like having a friendly conversation within the family."

Other Republicans said today that while Mr. Rove may be considered the political genius of the moment, he has made some big mistakes in the past. Most notably, Mr. Rove's pick for governor of California, Richard J. Riordan, lost by a huge margin in the Republican primary earlier this year to a political neophyte, Bill Simon Jr., who then lost to the incumbent Gray Davis on Tuesday night. Last year, Senator James M. Jeffords defected from the Republicans, leaving the Senate to turn Democratic on Mr. Rove's watch.

White House advisers also say that while Mr. Rove has a powerful influence on the president's schedule, it is Mr. Bush who makes the decisions in the end, and that the president's political instincts are at least as good as those of Mr. Rove. As the White House prepared for the five-day campaign blitz, one adviser said, "everybody understood the states we had to go to, so it was just a matter of configuring it in a way that was acceptable to the president."

Nonetheless, Mr. Rove acknowledged his outsized role in the White House, and the animosity he can engender, in an interview with ABC News broadcast on Monday.

"If we win, it'll be because of the president, and the quality of our candidates and our campaigns," Mr. Rove said. "If we lose, it'll be because of me."

Consider the source and the audience.

- Elizabeth Bumiller covers the White House for the *Times*. How does that fact affect where she looks for an answer to the question of why Republican congressional candidates performed so well in the election?

Lay out the argument, the values, and the assumptions.

- Why do the reporters and their sources believe that the Republicans won their victory on Election Day?
- What were the components of the strategy that they believe is responsible? Whose strategy was it, and what role did it require of the White House at the various stages of planning?
- What risks were involved in the strategy? Why did it work?

Uncover the evidence.

- What evidence do the reporters have for concluding that the strategy they cite was responsible for the victory? Did they talk to Democrats as well as Republicans?
- How do we know what Rove's role was in devising the Republican strategy? Who were the reporters' sources? Who else might they have talked to?

Evaluate the conclusion.

- Does Rove deserve all the credit he is given for the Republican victories? What other explanations could be considered?

Sort out the political implications.

- How much power should a presidential adviser like Rove have? Who are the other "White House advisers" cited in the article, and why are they anxious to point out that Rove merely advises Bush and that the president's political instincts are "at least as good as those of Mr. Rove"?
- How active a role should the president play in an election in which he is not on the ballot? What risks does he take by campaigning?

13.2 Memo to the Democrats: Quit Being Losers!

Tucker Carlson, *New York Times Magazine,* 19 January 2003

As the previous article made clear, the results of the 2002 midterm elections caught the Democrats unaware. This was the second straight election that left the party disappointed and frustrated at its inability to get a convincing message out to the American public. The Bumiller and Sanger article indicated that the Democrats' problem was a well-executed strategy by Republican Karl Rove, but many critics, on both the left and the right, also blamed the party's poor performance on the lack of a strong leader and a clear message. Tucker Carlson, a conservative commentator and co-host of the CNN show *Crossfire,* provides Democrats with a blueprint for what he believes to be an effective electoral strategy. Why do you think the Democrats have had such difficulty crafting a message?

This fall, for the second time in a row, the Democratic Party lost an election it should have won. Democrats offered no rationale for why they should be running the country and no vision for how they would run it. The party got the drubbing it deserved. I enjoyed watching.

But at the same time, I found the Democrats' distress faintly unsettling. One-party government makes me nervous. It's too efficient. There isn't enough grid-lock. Worst of all, the arguments tend to be boring. Like drunks and children, ineffectual political parties make for frustrating debate partners. Even if you're wrong, you still beat them. Every country deserves at least two functioning parties. With that in mind, I have some ideas for how Democrats can help their party be taken seriously again. Why should Democrats listen to advice from someone who represents the right on a television talk show? Partly because there are lessons worth learning from the many years Republicans spent as the minority party and partly because, why not? Nothing else seems to be working.

> Why does Carlson, a conservative, claim to want the Democrats to do better? What's the problem with one-party government?

For Democrats to win back Congress and the White House in 2004, they must: a) arrange for the current president to mess up horribly, preferably by losing a war or driving the economy into stagflation, and b) pick a national political leader with the stature, political skill and clarity of vision to take advantage of the opportunity. None of this will be easy. More than anything, it will require luck, the most underrated factor in politics. That may take awhile.

In the meantime, Democrats should forget about running on economic issues alone. In the months before the midterm elections, the entire Democratic strategy seemed to consist of criticizing Bush's economic policy by insulting Harvey Pitt, the former chairman of the Securities and Exchange Commission. Not only was this a lame argument; it was bad politics. Did any voter really believe that the health of the economy hangs on staff changes at the S.E.C.? Did the average person even know who Harvey Pitt was?

In general, Democrats have spent relatively little time over the past two years telling voters why Bush's policies are bad for the country. They've attacked Bush the man quite a bit, but when was the last time you heard an elected Democrat explain precisely, with numbers, not slogans, how the Bush tax cuts have damaged the economy? Do you know anything about the Democratic economic stimulus plan? Is there one? And what exactly do the Democrats think about fighting terrorism and the coming war with Iraq? They need to figure it out quickly.

Democrats won't start winning elections until they convince the public that they're capable of responding vigorously to threats from abroad. At this point voters are skeptical. A *USA Today*/CNN/Gallup poll taken the week of the midterms showed Republicans beating Democrats by 30 points on the question Which party is "tough enough on terrorism"? Numbers like these mean political death, but so far Democrats haven't even tried to overcome them. "If we try and make defense, foreign policy, the overriding issue," Representative Martin Frost of Texas told fellow Democrats in the fall, "we will lose, because the country is with the president on that issue."

In other words, nod when Bush talks about Iraq, then change the subject to taxes. The hope is that 2004 will be a replay of 1992, when the Democrats were able to neutralize the president's foreign policy success with attacks on his economic stewardship. But 2004 won't be 1992. Of course, if there's a recession, the Democrats should blame Bush for it and exploit it for all it's worth. But around the next election, American forces, and America itself, will still be at risk. Recession or not, war is likely to be the overriding issue. The Democratic Party needs something to say about it.

Ideally, Democrats would campaign on fresh, new, daring ideas about America's role in the world. In real life, fresh, new, daring ideas are rare. Even when you find them, it takes years to refine a crackpot theory into a workable policy. Democrats would be better off stealing Bush's positions, then making them stronger—becoming more Bush than Bush.

There's nothing embarrassing about this. Appropriating the rhetoric of your enemies is among the oldest traditions in politics. Bill Clinton used Republican language and symbols to transform his party's image from soft on crime to ferociously pro-law enforcement. As a candidate, Clinton executed a brain-damaged criminal. As president, he promised more cops, signed a crime bill and in general talked like John Walsh.

These days almost all Democrats are law-and-order Democrats. Relatively few with national aspirations even oppose capital punishment. One of the few who does is Senator John Kerry of Massachusetts (though since Sept. 11, Kerry has said he would make an exception for terrorists). Last year, I asked Kerry about it. Yes, I oppose the death penalty, he said. On the other hand, "I have killed people in war—personally." Kerry may be liberal, but he'd like you to know that he's a Schwarzenegger liberal.

The Democratic Party needs to establish this same sort of tougher-than-thou credibility on foreign policy. The problem is that "Democrats are really freaked out by anti-Americanism," says Peter Beinart, editor of *The New Republic*. "They're a little like Canadians in that they have difficulty going to sleep at night knowing that people hate them." Fighting terrorism requires exerting American power. Exerting power makes people hate you. Hence the Democrats' bind. Beinart recommends "a Sister Souljah moment

Why is it that fighting terrorism "makes people hate you"? Can it be done in a way that does not?

with the U.N.," a high-profile news event that Democrats can use to show they really don't care what France thinks.

That might help. So would amping up the rhetoric in the war on terrorism. Democrats cringed when Bush used cowboy language to describe the fight against Al Qaeda. They'd be smart to come out with their own, bloodthirstier version: "I won't rest until Osama bin Laden's head is resting—on a stake." Try that as a slogan. Out-gunsling Bush.

Kerry, my pick for the most promising of the Democratic candidates, has been moving in this direction. The fighting in Afghanistan was just cooling off when Kerry declared the operation in Tora Bora a disaster. Kerry turned out to be right, but what was interesting was his diagnosis: not enough force. The Pentagon, he said, should have used American soldiers, rather than local militia, to chase Al Qaeda into the mountains. The mission failed because the military was too timid, too afraid to risk American lives. When was the last time you heard a Democrat say that?

When it comes to guarding America, Democrats should prove they're more vigilant than the president. They can do it in obvious ways—more money for port security—and in not so obvious ones, like tightening border controls, an issue on which Bush, who has pledged to increase immigration, is vulnerable. Democrats can't hope to take a tougher position on Iraq than the president has. But they can outflank him on the rest of the Middle East. In a debate over foreign policy, Democrats have one advantage over Bush: they can sound as bellicose as they like without actually having to conduct diplomacy. They should remind voters that Hamas and Hezbollah still exist, still hate America and still pose an arguably greater threat to the United States than Saddam Hussein does. They should take a harder line on Syria, Iran, Pakistan and Saudi Arabia, all of which have received a temporary pass while America's attention has been focused on Iraq. The next time the Bush administration allows North Korean missiles to pass unmolested to their destination in Yemen, Dick Gephardt should stage a protest in front of the Pentagon.

From there he should head to the steps of the Department of Energy, to unveil his party's plan to develop alternative energy sources. Cynics will expect the usual dopey "No Nukes, Go Solar" slogans of the 70's. Gephardt should surprise them by framing the issue from the right, as a matter of urgent national security: energy independence as a weapon in the war against terrorism. He ought to make open-minded noises about nuclear power, just to prove he's serious. In the months after Sept. 11, Gephardt called for another Manhattan Project to develop new energy sources, like hydrogen fuel cells. He hasn't said much about it since. He should.

And he should hurry. It can't be long before the president comes out with his own plan to develop alternatives to fossil fuels. Imagine it: an oilman pledges to wean America from oil. It's brilliant. Bush will do it. He isn't stupid. Which is something else Democrats ought to remember.

Democrats have a lot of planning to do. The great thing about being in the minority is that you have the time to think deeply about how government should be run. Ideas become important when you're out of power, mostly because they're all you have.

Just ask the Republicans. The G.O.P. lost control of Congress during the Great Depression and didn't regain it for any length of time until the Clinton administration. At its nadir, during the 75th Congress, the Republican Party held just 105 seats in the entire legislative branch, 89 in the House and 16 in the Senate. For 60 years Republicans had some free time on their hands. They used it to decide what they believed. Between Barry Goldwater's defeat and Ronald Reagan's victory, the Republican Party arrived at a kind of ideological clarity. Republicans decided they were against Communism and for smaller government. Reagan's 1980 campaign ads were some of the least confusing ever made: strong defense, lower taxes. Lower taxes, strong defense. You couldn't miss the message, and voters didn't.

A pair of bullet points do not make a governing agenda, of course. But then, a lot of the time those who govern don't make the governing agenda. This is the problem with wielding political power in Washington: the job is so demanding and complicated and immediate that the big picture gets tiny. Ideas get lost. "The urgent overwhelms the important," in the words of Ed Feulner, longtime president of the Heritage Foundation.

The aim of the Heritage Foundation and other conservative think tanks is to help Republicans keep track of the important details. In 1980, Feulner and others at Heritage produced a blueprint to help Reagan run the executive branch, a 3,000-page book called "Mandate for Leadership." No one claims that Reagan read the whole thing, but someone in the White House apparently did. Among the 2,000 recommendations in "Mandate for Leadership" was advice on handling labor disputes with air-traffic controllers. Heritage's position was, Don't tolerate strikes.

Over the past 20 years, virtually every big Republican idea and many small ones—school choice, welfare reform, enterprise zones, Social Security privatization—have originated in think tanks, rather than on Capitol Hill. Think tanks have sponsored some of the most important conservative books and published some of the best conservative magazines.

By the time the Republicans took over Congress in 1994, there were scores of conservative think tanks ready to help them govern. One of these was the Project for the Republican Future, a tiny operation run by William Kristol, Dan Quayle's former chief of staff. In January 1994, Kristol decided to derail the Clinton health care plan. He and his staff issued a position paper titled "How to Oppose the Health Plan—and Why." Aimed at Republicans on the Hill, the paper contended that any compromise with the president on health care would be bad for American medicine and bad for the G.O.P. Kristol argued that Republicans should stonewall Clinton while presenting their own less severe alternatives for reform. Kristol's memo gave Republicans heart. They resisted the Clinton health plan, HillaryCare failed and by the election it was Democrats who were suffering.

Democrats often complain that conservatives benefit from a privately financed parallel political establishment. They're right. And they should build their own.

And while they're at it, they ought to rediscover their sense of humor. Liberals used to be funny. They edited magazines like *National Lampoon*. They had a claim on cool. Then something happened. They became sour and earnest and neurotic about secondhand smoke. The Democratic Party became the that's-not-funny-young-man party, the party of no fun. *National Lampoon* folded. At least one of its editors became a conservative and started writing for *The American Spectator*.

If you began reading *The American Spectator* in the mid-90's, you probably remember it for obsessive, slightly kooky (sometimes very kooky) investigative journalism that wasn't all that interesting unless you hated Bill Clinton for a living. But before Clinton, believe it or not, it was a very funny magazine. In the summer of 1989, *The Spectator* published an article titled "A Call for a New McCarthyism," by P. J. O'Rourke, late of *National Lampoon*. O'Rourke opened by conceding that the liberals were absolutely right, that the Reagan years had in fact been a replay of the darkest days of the 1950's. "Indeed," he wrote, "we are experiencing anew many of the pleasures and benefits of that excellent decade: a salubrious prudery, a sensible avariciousness, a healthy dose of social conformity, a much-needed narrowing of minds and a return to common-sense American political troglodytism." According to O'Rourke, the only thing missing from the 80's was a good old-fashioned witch hunt. So he started one: "The fun part of McCarthyism is, as it always was, making out the enemies list." O'Rourke's list included "fuzzy-minded one-worlders, pasty-faced peace creeps and bleeding-heart bed-wetters" like Sting and Susan Sarandon and Amy Carter.

O'Rourke wrote the article for the same reason the Fox News Channel calls itself "fair and balanced"—to drive liberals crazy. It worked. Years later, when the essay was expanded into a book, an outraged reviewer at *Library Journal* huffed that O'Rourke was trying to revive "the ghosts of Joe McCarthy and Richard Nixon." Bait taken.

It's both the job and the privilege of the minority party to gleefully torment its more powerful opponents. Democrats seem to have forgotten this. Ever read *The American Prospect?* The closest thing to humor in a recent issue is an account of how the media were mean and unfair to Al Gore during the last election. It's a serious article. The comedy is purely unintentional.

For politicians, humor is freedom. Late last year, Al Gore finally seemed to learn this. But it was too late. Hours after his winning appearance on "Saturday Night Live," he retired from politics. For most of his career, Gore suffered from the opposite problem: he was a terrible straight man. He never seemed to be telling the truth, even when he may have been. He came off as a dissembler, and this as much as anything doomed his 2000 presidential bid.

Is straightforward language always the same as honesty? If "straight talk" is as successful as Carlson believes, why don't more candidates speak from the heart?

Democrats have forgotten how much the public loves straightforward language. Voters love it even more than accurate language. I first became convinced of this in the spring of 1999, when I went to Austin, Tex., to profile George W. Bush. The day I arrived, Bush held a news conference to explain his views on the war in Kosovo. He proceeded to mangle almost every word. Bush referred to "Mylo-sovack" (commonly known as Milosevic), then talked at some length about the "Kosovanians" and our allies "the Grecians." I was shocked. This may work in Texas, I thought, but the rest of the country won't tolerate this level of inarticulateness in a presidential candidate.

As it turned out, the rest of the country didn't care. If anything, voters interpreted Bush's dyslexia as candor. At least he's not slick was the idea. After a decade of Clinton-Gore, that's how desperate the public was for an honest candidate.

Will the Democrats get one in 2004? To find out, I called Howard Dean, the former longtime governor of Vermont and newly announced candidate for the White House. Parties are often revived by insurgents from within them—Reagan, Gingrich—and Dean is nothing if not an insurgent. Plus, I'd heard that he's a straight-shooter.

He is. While other candidates divulge their positions on uncomfortable social issues almost parenthetically, Dean leads with his. He is for needle exchanges, unrestricted abortion and civil unions between homosexuals, and he's happy to tell you about it. Most politicians squirm at the mention of partial-birth abortion. Not Dean. "Partial-birth abortion is a manufactured issue," he says. "It's expletive. Partial-birth abortion essentially doesn't exist." And even if it does, "it isn't any of Congress's business."

Dean isn't surprised by the Trent Lott scandal. The Republican Party is fundamentally hostile to blacks and Hispanics, he says, riddled as it is with "institutional racism." It's also full of liars. "I find the Republican Party pretty bankrupt intellectually," Dean says, adding that he doesn't read anything written by conservatives. Nothing? "No." Are there any conservatives who are intellectually honest? "I don't think so. I can't think of any." He sounds cheery as he says this.

Dean's tone has changed a few hours later when he calls back and leaves this message: "Tucker, this is Howard Dean. I was talking to some staff folks after I got off the phone with you, and they were worried about my term 'institutional racism.' Probably that might have been not the right word to use. I was a little nervous now that the word 'racist' was such a charged word that it might have been better if I talked about 'intolerance' and 'divisiveness.' If you could give me a call back, that would be great."

Damn. The consultants. They've gotten to him already. Dean hasn't even had a chance to say anything truly outrageous, and already the campaign professionals, sworn enemies of colorful language, are telling him to tone it down, advising him to dilute his essential Howard Dean-ness. Fire them, I thought. Send them back to Washington before it's too late.

Of course, in a deeper sense, it's already too late. Dean, like the other Democrats running for president in 2004 is unlikely to become president, consultants or not. Which is all the more reason to run an honest campaign. Relax. Say what you think. Tell an off-color joke now and then. Have a good time. No one wants to watch a suffering candidate. Voters will like you if you like what you're doing. You probably won't win the election. You might as well enjoy running.

Consider the source and the audience.

- As we noted, Tucker Carlson is a conservative news commentator who is the co-host of CNN's *Crossfire*, a show where liberals and conservatives debate contemporary issues. What kinds of motives would lead Carlson to write an article like this? Why would the more liberal *New York Times* want to publish it?

Lay out the argument, the values, and the assumptions.

- What value does Carlson see in having two vigorous political parties?
- What does he think the Democrats did wrong in the 2000 and 2002 elections?
- What six actions does he think they should undertake in order to be a winning party in 2004?
- Does he think the Democrats will win if they follow his advice? If not, why not, and why bother?

Uncover the evidence.

- On whose experience does Carlson base his advice to the Democrats? Does what works for one party necessarily work for another?
- Where else might Carlson look for lessons for the Democrats?

Evaluate the conclusion.

- Carlson seems to believe that the Democrats will need a lot of luck to prevail against Bush in 2004. If it is true that the deck is stacked against them, why were so many Democrats lining up to take him on?
- Is Carlson right that politics should be fun? Why does it so often seem not to be?

Sort out the political implications.

- If the Democrats' fortunes do not turn in 2004, what will be the political impact of more years of "one-party government"? How will this outcome affect domestic policy? Foreign policy? The courts?
- Why is it left to a conservative to make these prescriptions for the Democrats? Why don't they make such arguments for themselves?

13.3 Sunshine Voters

John H. Fund, *The American Spectator,* July–August 2002

As we discussed earlier, the United States prides itself on being the world's greatest democracy. But if one aspect of being a model democracy is participating in elections, America has room for a lot of improvement. Voter turnout in the United States lags far behind that of most of the world's other democracies.

One explanation people give for America's poor voter turnout is that there are too many costs to voting. It is difficult to get off work. We might have to wait in line. We may get lost on the way to the polling precinct. And in all states but North Dakota, we must register before qualifying to vote. Accordingly, some states have tried to lower the costs of voting by implementing same-day voter registration. Instead of having to be registered to vote fifteen or thirty days before the election, as some states require, with same-day voter registration, people can just walk into the precinct on Election Day and vote. This essay from *The American Spectator* takes issue with such reform. Is low voter turnout really a problem that needs to be solved?

> The people who cast the votes decide nothing. The people who count the votes decide everything.
>
> —*attributed to Joseph Stalin*

In the wake of the Florida election mess, many proposals have been made to clean up our sloppy election systems and make it easier for people to vote. Some of those changes—increasing voter education and retiring antiquated machines—make sense. But another idea—to allow people who aren't registered to vote to cast ballots on Election Day—could create chaos eclipsing Florida's infamous chads. Nonetheless, the idea is being pushed by two young Democratic millionaire sugar daddies. They have ponied up big bucks to put same-day voter registration initiatives on the ballot this November in California and Colorado.

Are "cleaning up our sloppy election systems" and "[making] it easier for people to vote" the same problem for Fund? Whose voting would he like to make easier?

Same-day registration, which allows people to walk into a polling place on Election Day and vote on the spot, has long been used in the small states of Idaho, Wyoming, New Hampshire and Maine. But in those states many people know their neighbors, and the risk of fraud is minimal. In Minnesota and Wisconsin, the two larger states where it's now used, problems have developed. Anecdotal reports often surface in Minnesota of college students floating from precinct to precinct casting ballots. In Wisconsin, in a truly rich example of liberal hypocrisy, a New York socialite working for Al Gore pleaded guilty to fraud in the 2000 presidential race when she admitted to bribing the homeless with cigarettes, after they'd been given rides to polling places in order to vote. At least 3,500 Wisconsin voters who were sent confirmation for their Election Day registration had them returned by the post office as undeliverable. Al Gore wound up winning the state by only 5,700 votes, out of 2.5 million cast.

But those pushing to expand same-day registration to other states dismiss such problems as trivial. They argue that pre-election registration deadlines—15 days in California, 30 days in Colorado—contribute to declining voter participation, because unregistered voters who don't become interested in an election until the last minute are frozen out.

Rob McKay, a philanthropist whose father built the Taco Bell restaurant empire, has placed an initiative on California's November ballot to require same-day registration. He plans on spending up to $8 million on the campaign. He insists his motivations are nonpartisan, although he acknowledges he is a registered Democrat and won't disagree with those who say his measure will help Democratic get-out-the-vote efforts.

> Why does Fund claim that same-day voter registration is more likely to help Democrats than Republicans?

It's a safe bet that same-day voter registration would make California's loosey-goosey polling places all the more chaotic. Lisalee Anne Wells, who has worked polling places in Long Beach, says that with "polling places now going unattended, others with staff but no paperwork and the typical staffer a distracted part-timer, the notion that voter registration should be added to Election Day is laughable."

County officials in California agree. Steve Weir, the voter registrar of Contra Costa County, says the initiative "adds complications, and the one thing California elections officials agree on unanimously is that elections have gotten too complicated, and so we're going to make mistakes." In his county he estimates that he would have to spend $75,000 to recruit an additional worker for each of its 800 polling places in order to register voters on Election Day.

In Colorado, a same-day voter registration initiative is being pushed by 27-year-old Jared Polis, a dot-com millionaire who in 2000 spent over $1 million of his own money to get elected to the state board of education, a nonpaying position. Now he is spending even more to tout the idea that Colorado is somehow putting insuperable barriers to voting by requiring registration in advance.

Even the normally liberal *Denver Post* is cool to Mr. Polis' idea. It recently editorialized that "the idea of registering on Election Day would gladden the hearts of New York City's old Tammany Hall tigers, who routinely shifted battalions of voters from precinct to precinct in pursuit of their 'vote early, vote often' philosophy."

Indeed, the untold story of Florida's 2000 election controversy was the number of suspect ballots that could have affected the outcome. The *Miami Herald* reviewed a third of Florida's counties and found that more than 1,200 votes were cast illegally by felons. In addition, in Duval County alone, 499 votes were cast by unregistered voters. Cora Thigpen, aged 90, admitted to voting for Al Gore and being proud of it: "If I had voted a half-dozen times, I would have voted every time for Al Gore." Let's not make it easier for voters like Ms. Thigpen to show their devotion.

The history of voter registration is rife with stories of fraud and outrageous disenfranchisement. As the liberal writers Frances Fox Piven and Richard Cloward have pointed out, political machines like Tammany Hall and Richard Daley's Chicago swelled voter rolls with the names of the dead. Poll taxes, literacy tests and other obstacles were used until the 1960s to discourage voting among immigrants in the North and blacks in the South.

Is there any relationship between poll taxes and literacy tests, on the one hand, and same-day voter registration, on the other? What is Fund trying to claim here?

Given this history of abuse, it makes sense to tread carefully when millionaires put forward pet political causes such as same-day registration. It is a recipe for bedlam at the polls, greater voter cynicism about the integrity of elections and the throwing of more contested races into the courts. The last thing we want is another Florida. But that's exactly what same-day registration would make more likely.

Consider the source and the audience.

- *The American Spectator* is a conservative news magazine that prides itself on challenging political correctness. How might the magazine's mission influence the views in this essay?

Lay out the argument, the values, and the assumptions.

- What problem does Fund identify as needing solving? Is low voter turnout the circumstance he wants to change, or is he concerned with making sure that the people who already vote run into fewer difficulties?
- Why does same-day voter registration worry Fund?
- Who does he seem to think would likely remain unregistered come Election Day? Would he want to make it easier for these people to vote?

Uncover the evidence.

- Fund provides anecdotal evidence for his claims. How persuasive are those examples?
- Is there other evidence he could provide? What else might we want to know about the experience of Idaho, Wyoming, New Hampshire, and Maine?
- Why would the experience of Florida be relevant to his argument? Why does he cite it?

Evaluate the conclusion.

- Is Fund's argument against same-day voter registration a strong one? What arguments could one make in response?

Sort out the political implications.

- What might be the political outcome of making voting much easier? Would one party benefit over the other, as Fund fears?
- How easy should voting be? If we could get everyone to vote on Election Day, would we want to do that?

13.4 Campaign Bill to Kids: Take a Hike

Tony Mauro, *USA Today,* 20 March 2002

When it comes to elections, money talks—loud and clear. However intelligent, dynamic, charismatic, and good-looking a candidate may be, if she doesn't have money, she is not going to win. Where money plays such a central role, there is a high potential for corruption—for buying political favors, influence, and power. Politicians, who have a considerable conflict of interest in this matter since they are the primary beneficiaries of money in politics, have passed laws to limit corruption—but loopholes still exist.

Previous campaign finance legislation in the 1970s had limited the amount of direct (hard-money) contributions that individuals and groups could make to candidates' campaigns. However, it had left a loophole for soft money—money that people were allowed to give to parties in unlimited amounts for grassroots party building activities, such as voter registration drives and generic party advertising. Frequently such unlimited money ended up being spent to support the very candidates whose campaign contributions were supposed to be limited by the law.

In 2002, Congress finally passed—and the president signed—a new campaign-finance reform bill that had been pushed for years by Senators John McCain (R-AZ) and Russ Feingold (D-WI). Two aspects of that bill were especially controversial. First, the bill banned soft-money contributions, although loopholes still remained. Second, the bill restricted issue advocacy ads—ads that discuss a candidate's record on a specific issue, but cannot explicitly advocate voting for that person—thirty days before a primary and sixty days before a general election. Many, including Tony Mauro in this *USA Today* article, argue that this is a violation of free speech.

Mauro focuses his attention, however, on another provision of the bill that he believes is unconstitutional—the rarely discussed provision that prohibits children under the age of eighteen from donating money to any candidate or political party. What should the role of children be in politics? How much of a voice should they have?

The high school students have returned to the U.S. Capitol, visiting the offices of their representatives, crowding into committee hearings, all of them eager to—or at least assigned to—learn more about Congress.

I wonder how many of these students are aware that Congress is about to dis them, big time.

The Senate is starting debate on campaign-finance reform, and tucked deep into the bill it is debating is a provision that would forbid anyone age 17 or under from making contributions to a political candidate or party. (The House of Representatives passed it last month as Section 318 of H.R. 2356, if you want to look it up.)

In one 29-word sentence, Congress would cut an entire generation out of a crucial part of the political process. Adults can give a candidate up to $1,000 per election ($2,000 if these reform measures are signed into law), but under this section, a 17-year-old could not donate a dime. A 16-year-old who wants to put $10 toward a candidate he or she thinks highly of would be violating the law. Members of a high school Young Republican club who want to give their lunch money to the GOP wouldn't be able to do so.

The provision has gotten almost no attention in the public discussion of the Shays-Meehan bill that contains it. But it warrants debate in the halls of Congress—and in the halls of high schools. Not only does it have First Amendment implications for young people, but it also symbolizes how, in the name of reform, good intentions can run amok.

Why have the media devoted so little attention to this provision? Would children be aware of it even if the media covered it more thoroughly?

What are the "good intentions" behind this ban on youthful donations? The answer is clear: The aim is to block an end run around the ceiling on campaign contributions for adults. Adults who want to contribute more than the limit allows simply have each of their children donate money as well. Studies cited by the Center for Responsive Politics indicate that a large percentage of donations given by those who list their occupations as "student" are for $1,000 and are given to the same candidates who have received money from the students' parents.

What's wrong with allowing parents to donate money to candidates in their kids' names?

But why target young people alone, and why cut them out so completely? Someone intent on evading the legal limits could use neighbors, friends—or even offspring who are over 17—to execute the same trick. Yet, it is only children who are excluded.

A separate federal law already on the books forbids anyone from knowingly making a contribution in someone else's name—a law that seems to take care of the fraud problem pretty neatly, without going after children as a group.

No matter what the motive is, this provision tells young people that they are too immature, too unimportant, to be part of the political system they will inherit in only a few short years. That sort of paternalism is an insult to the young people I've seen over the years (including my daughter Emily) who know a lot more about how things work than Congress seems to think.

Young people also have a lot more control over their own money than in past generations. Donating $50 to a congressional candidate seems to be at least as responsible a spending choice as a lot of others that youths make, so why discourage it by law? If President Bush can ask American young people to send money to kids in Afghanistan, why is Congress about to tell kids they can't send money to political candidates back home?

More fundamentally, it seems to be a flat-out violation of the First Amendment. The Supreme Court has long viewed the money used in political campaigns as a form of free expression. And 33 years ago, the Supreme Court in the *Tinker* case proclaimed that students do not "shed their constitutional rights to freedom of speech or expression at the schoolhouse gate."

That noble principle would surely protect young people who participate in a local campaign to increase the school budget. It should also protect young people who want to help candidates for Congress or the White House. Kids have always helped political candidates by licking envelopes or handing out buttons. They should be able to donate their money as well as their time.

Do children share all the same rights that adults have? Should they?

This is not the only well-intentioned part of the campaign-finance legislation that appears to violate the First Amendment. The most infamous is the provision that bars unions, corporations and advocacy groups from certain kinds of issue advertising within 60 days of a federal election. That is a clear ban on speech at a time when the speech would be most important. It will probably be dead on arrival at any court where it is challenged.

You might say that Congress is doing young people a favor by prohibiting them from donating to political campaigns. Why should they become part of the sleazy money machine that has overwhelmed the system? But shielding them from politics won't help at all. Young people might as well become part of the process as soon as possible. Maybe then they can figure out a better way to fix it—certainly, a better way than Congress has found so far.

13.5 Concession Speech

Al Gore, 13 December 2000

In this chapter we have looked at elections from the perspective of the campaign strategist, the political pundit, the reformer, and the constitutional analyst. Before we close we ought to look as well at elections from the perspective of the candidate—in this case, a losing candidate who at one time had reason to consider himself the winner.

Elections serve lots of purposes in democratic society: They give people a voice in their government, they lend legitimacy to leadership change, they offer an alternative to fighting in the streets when people disagree. Another function of elections is to provide political stability. The 2000 presidential election was unusual on several counts. We had a state's election results contested, amid accusations of fraud and misleading ballot design; that state's supreme court was overruled by the U.S. Supreme Court in the matter of recounts; and the results of that contested state election gave an electoral college victory to a candidate who had lost the popular vote. To top it off, the governor of the state in question was the brother of the candidate who was eventually declared the winner. In many societies, such a series of events could have led to rioting, violence, or revolution. But in the United States, where there is commitment to the Constitution and to the idea of procedural justice (that is, if the rules are fair, then the results will be fair), the outcome, though distressing to many, was accepted by most.

Among the disappointed was Vice-President Al Gore, who believed that he would have won the election in Florida if all the votes had been counted, and who knew that he had won the popular vote in any case. The night of the election, he had called George W. Bush to concede, only to be told afterward that the networks had erred in projecting Bush the winner in Florida, and that this state was still in play. He called Bush back and retracted his concession. Over a month later, he finally phoned Bush again.

How did the country manage to go on after this as if nothing, really, had happened, with a majority of voters, including some of those who had voted for Gore, giving Bush high approval ratings as he came into office? How do elections serve to legitimate results as odd as this one?

G ood evening.

Just moments ago, I spoke with George W. Bush and congratulated him on becoming the 43rd president of the United States, and I promised him that I wouldn't call him back this time.

I offered to meet with him as soon as possible so that we can start to heal the divisions of the campaign and the contest through which we just passed.

Almost a century and a half ago, Senator Stephen Douglas told Abraham Lincoln, who had just defeated him for the presidency, "Partisan feeling must yield to patriotism. I'm with you, Mr. President, and God bless you."

Well, in that same spirit, I say to President-elect Bush that what remains of partisan rancor must now be put aside, and may God bless his stewardship of this country.

Neither he nor I anticipated this long and difficult road. Certainly neither of us wanted it to happen. Yet it came, and now it has ended, resolved, as it must be resolved, through the honored institutions of our democracy.

Over the library of one of our great law schools is inscribed the motto, "Not under man but under God and law." That's the ruling principle of American freedom, the source of our democratic liberties. I've tried to make it my guide throughout this contest as it has guided America's deliberations of all the complex issues of the past five weeks.

Now the U.S. Supreme Court has spoken. Let there be no doubt, while I strongly disagree with the court's decision, I accept it. I accept the finality of this outcome which will be ratified next Monday in the Electoral

What does it mean to be under law, not man? How would Gore's behavior have been different if he had placed his own view of what was right over the law's?

College. And tonight, for the sake of our unity of the people and the strength of our democracy, I offer my concession.

I also accept my responsibility, which I will discharge unconditionally, to honor the new president elect and do everything possible to help him bring Americans together in fulfillment of the great vision that our Declaration of Independence defines and that our Constitution affirms and defends.

Let me say how grateful I am to all those who supported me and supported the cause for which we have fought. Tipper and I feel a deep gratitude to Joe and Hadassah Lieberman who brought passion and high purpose to our partnership and opened new doors, not just for our campaign but for our country.

This has been an extraordinary election. But in one of God's unforeseen paths, this belatedly broken impasse can point us all to a new common ground, for its very closeness can serve to remind us that we are one people with a shared history and a shared destiny.

Indeed, that history gives us many examples of contests as hotly debated, as fiercely fought, with their own challenges to the popular will.

What's the point of invoking history here? What purpose does it serve?

Other disputes have dragged on for weeks before reaching resolution. And each time, both the victor and the vanquished have accepted the result peacefully and in the spirit of reconciliation.

So let it be with us.

I know that many of my supporters are disappointed. I am too. But our disappointment must be overcome by our love of country.

And I say to our fellow members of the world community, let no one see this contest as a sign of American weakness. The strength of American democracy is shown most clearly through the difficulties it can overcome.

Some have expressed concern that the unusual nature of this election might hamper the next president in the conduct of his office. I do not believe it need be so.

President-elect Bush inherits a nation whose citizens will be ready to assist him in the conduct of his large responsibilities.

I personally will be at his disposal, and I call on all Americans—I particularly urge all who stood with us to unite behind our next president. This is America. Just as we fight hard when the stakes are high, we close ranks and come together when the contest is done.

And while there will be time enough to debate our continuing differences, now is the time to recognize that that which unites us is greater than that which divides us.

While we yet hold and do not yield our opposing beliefs, there is a higher duty than the one we owe to political party. This is America and we put country before party. We will stand together behind our new president.

As for what I'll do next, I don't know the answer to that one yet. Like many of you, I'm looking forward to spending the holidays with family and old friends. I know I'll spend time in Tennessee and mend some fences, literally and figuratively.

Some have asked whether I have any regrets and I do have one regret: that I didn't get the chance to stay and fight for the American people over the next four years, especially for those who need burdens lifted and barriers removed, especially for those who feel their voices have not been heard. I heard you and I will not forget.

I've seen America in this campaign and I like what I see. It's worth fighting for and that's a fight I'll never stop.

As for the battle that ends tonight, I do believe as my father once said, that no matter how hard the loss, defeat might serve as well as victory to shape the soul and let the glory out.

> Gore's father was a senator who once lost an important election. Why does Gore mention him here? How does defeat "shape the soul"?

So for me this campaign ends as it began: with the love of Tipper and our family; with faith in God and in the country I have been so proud to serve, from Vietnam to the vice presidency; and with gratitude to our truly tireless campaign staff and volunteers, including all those who worked so hard in Florida for the last 36 days.

Now the political struggle is over and we turn again to the unending struggle for the common good of all Americans and for those multitudes around the world who look to us for leadership in the cause of freedom.

In the words of our great hymn, "America, America": "Let us crown thy good with brotherhood, from sea to shining sea."

And now, my friends, in a phrase I once addressed to others, it's time for me to go.

Thank you and good night, and God bless America.

Consider the source and the audience.

- Gore is speaking to several audiences here. Who are they? Why does he address "our fellow members of the world community"?
- At the time, Gore was certainly considering a run for the presidency in the future. How might that have shaped his message?
- How could he have used this speech to rally supporters if he had wanted to?

Lay out the argument, the values, and the assumptions.

- What personal values of Gore's become apparent in this speech? How do they affect his political views?
- What is Gore's view of the common good here? How does that differ from partisan advantage, and when should the former take precedence over the latter?
- When should a political outcome be accepted even when one doesn't like it? How do the "honored institutions of our democracy" help to resolve contests like this? In what context does he refer to the Supreme Court and the electoral college?

Uncover the evidence.

- What kinds of evidence does Gore use to support his argument that the result of the election process should be accepted even if one doesn't agree with it, and that George W. Bush is the legitimate president of the United States?

Evaluate the conclusion.

- Did Gore's use of symbolism and references to history, law, and religion convince supporters to accept the election result?
- Did they convince the world that the United States was a stable and solid nation?
- Did they convince the nation to put the trauma of the partisan backbiting behind it and move on?

Sort out the political implications.

- Many electoral reforms were debated following the election, but few were enacted. Who would have resisted reform, and why?
- Why was there little serious and sustained call for reform of the electoral college following the election?

CHAPTER 14

The Media

O f all the things that have changed in the United States since the country's founding, it is perhaps the media that have changed the most. Whereas once we got our news, often months old, from weekly papers and in Sunday sermons, we can now access worldwide news in real time on devices we carry in our pockets. We have truly experienced a revolution in communication in the last one hundred years.

In a democratic society, access to accurate timely news is essential so that we can make informed decisions at the voting booth but also so that we can keep tabs on what government does, and keep our representatives honest. Free speech and press freedom were some of the key values preserved by the framers, who knew that a stifled press could not work to protect any other of our liberties.

The threat to press freedom that the authors of the Constitution were concerned about was the government—and they had reason to be concerned. During colonial times, printers had to get government approval for the work they turned out. Even after independence, the newspaper business was often subsidized by politicians in exchange for favorable coverage. It was not until mass circulation papers acquired some measure of financial independence that journalistic objectivity and detachment from political patronage became economically feasible and, in fact, commercially savvy. The effort to appeal to a broad audience was enhanced if a paper did not risk alienating part of that audience by taking up controversial political positions.

The objectivity spawned by mass circulation papers is jealously guarded today by partisans on both sides of the ideological spectrum who eagerly scan the media's output for signs of liberal or conservative bias. We know that, on average, journalists tend to be slightly more liberal than the average American, and media owners and editorial writers slightly more conservative. Most Americans, however, are amply armed to deflect any political bias that sneaks into the media because we bring our own ideological filters to the business of reading the paper and watching the news.

We are less primed to watch for the effects of other kinds of pressures on the media that may have a more serious influence on the news that we get. Today, the media are part of corporate America, where the drive for profits helps define the news and the way it is presented and packaged. In addition to the commercial pressures coming from their corporate owners, journalists have to contend with the efforts of politicians to control the way they are presented by the media and, since

September 11, 2001, with a vocal element that sees criticism of President Bush and the war on terrorism as inherently "un-American." All these forces can make the public job of the journalist—to provide accurate and timely news to citizens and to maintain a check on government—increasingly difficult.

The articles in this chapter deal with some of the pressures faced by journalists today. The first piece, from the liberal journal *The Nation,* chronicles the solitary efforts of cartoonist Aaron McGruder to keep a critical and skeptical eye on the Bush administration in the days after September 11. From the *Columbia Journalism Review,* the second article examines one of McGruder's chief critics, the Media Research Center, which took as its post–September 11 mission the job of cracking down on media voices that failed to engage in "home team sports reporting" about Bush and the war on terrorism. Margo Hammond, in the *St. Petersburg Times,* reviews a book that argues that the media bias we need to watch for is financial in nature. The *New York Times'* Frank Rich looks at the aging network news anchors and argues that the network news has an important civic role to play in American culture. Finally, we look backward in time to the arguments made by media giant William Randolph Hearst, about the evils of government-controlled newspapers.

14.1 Huey Freeman: American Hero

Sure, He's a Cartoon Character, But It Still Takes Courage to Speak Out

John Nichols, *The Nation,* 28 January 2002

Although often overlooked in the lineup of contemporary media figures, political cartoonists are journalists every bit as serious as those who pen editorials or sit in front of the camera. They convey information, news, and points of view, work under deadline pressure, and worry about censorship and editorial judgments to the same extent as their in-print or on-camera counterparts. Here is the story of one political cartoonist's decision to face the potential wrath of editors, newspaper owners, and readers alike to tell a story about the war on terrorism that he believed had to be told. Should cartoons be treated differently from any other journalistic product?

O n Thanksgiving Day 2001, with the United States in the midst of what polls identify as one of the most popular wars in history and with President Bush's approval ratings hovering around 90 percent, more than 20 million American households opened their daily newspapers to see a little black kid named Huey Freeman leading the pre-turkey prayer.

"Ahem," began the unsmiling youth. "In this time of war against Osama bin Laden and the oppressive Taliban regime, we are thankful that OUR leader isn't the spoiled son of a powerful politician from a wealthy oil family who is supported by religious fundamentalists, operates through clandestine organizations, has no respect for the democratic electoral process, bombs innocents, and uses war to deny people their civil liberties. Amen."

In the whole of American media that day, Huey's was certainly the most pointed and, no doubt, the most effective dissent from the patriotism that dare not speak its mind. And it was not the only day when the self-proclaimed "radical scholar" skewered George W. Bush, Attorney General John Ashcroft, the Defense Department, dithering Democrats, frenzied flag-wavers and scaremongering television anchors in what since September 11 has been the most biting and consistent critique of the war and its discontents in the nation's mass media.

The creation of 27-year-old cartoonist Aaron McGruder, Huey Freeman appears daily in *The Boondocks,* a comic strip featured in 250 of America's largest newspapers, including the *Washington Post, Dallas Morning News, Chicago Tribune, Los Angeles Times* and *Philadelphia Inquirer.* "There are a lot of newspapers where Aaron's comic strip probably is the only consistent voice of dissent," says Pulitzer Prize–winning cartoonist Joel Pett, whose editorial-page cartoons for the Lexington, Kentucky, *Herald-Leader* have raised tough questions about the suffering of Afghan civilians and the role the United States has played in spreading terror. "I think that not only is he doing good stuff, the fact that he is on those comics pages makes it important in a way that none of the rest of us could accomplish. He's hooking a whole group of people. He's getting ideas out to people who don't always read the opinion pages. And he's influencing a lot of young people about how it's OK to question their government and the media. When you think about it, what he has done since September 11 has just been incredible."

> What difference does it make if a cartoonist's work appears in the comic pages or the editorial pages? Is it perceived differently? Is it subject to different standards? Does it impose different obligations on the cartoonist?

In recent weeks, McGruder's Huey has grumbled about how it may no longer be legal in John Ashcroft's America to ask whether George W. Bush was actually elected; hiked atop a mountain to yell, "For goodness sake people, it's a recession! Save money this Christmas!"; and repeatedly expressed the view that "Dick Cheney is just plain creepy." And he has listened in disbelief to an "announcement" from the Attorney General that went: "I would like to reassure Congress that my proposed Turban Surveillance Act, which would allow the FBI to covertly plant listening devices in the headgear of suspected terrorists, is in no way meant to single out Arab or Muslim Americans."

At a time when most comedians are still pulling their punchlines, McGruder has gotten plenty of laughs at the expense of the Bush Administration and its policies. But not everyone has been amused. In early October the cartoonist had Huey call the FBI's antiterrorist hotline to report that he had the names of Americans who trained and financed Osama bin Laden. When the FBI agent said that, yes, he wanted the names, Huey began, "All right, let's see, the first one is Reagan. That's R-E-A-G. . . ." This series of strips was pulled from the New York *Daily News* and *Newsday* and shuffled off comics pages at other papers. Editors were quick to deny they were censoring *The Boondocks,* claiming they simply thought McGruder had gotten a little too political. McGruder played the controversy into more laughs. He produced an inane new strip featuring talking patriotic symbols, launching it with a satirical editor's note: "Due to the inappropriate political content of this feature in recent weeks, it is being replaced by 'The Adventures of Flagee and Ribbon,' which we hope will help children understand the complexities of current events. United we stand." Ribbon then declares, "Hey, Flagee, there's a lot of evil out there," to which his compatriot replies, "That's right, Ribbon. Good thing America kicks a lot of *@#!"

McGruder, whose cartoon began appearing nationally in April 1999, says he did not set out to make Huey the nation's No. 1 dissenter. Yes, *The Boondocks*—which recounts the experiences of Huey and his younger brother, Riley, inner-city youths who move with great trepidation to the suburbs—has always been controversial. Bitingly blunt in its examination of race and class issues, *The Boondocks* has made more waves more often than any nationally syndicated comic strip since Garry Trudeau's *Doonesbury* characters declared Nixon aides "Guilty! Guilty! Guilty!" in the Watergate era. "It even got pulled from the Buffalo paper for something involving Santa Claus," recalls McGruder, who grew up listening to rap artists Public Enemy and KRS-One, idolized Berkeley Breathed's politically pointed *Bloom County* comic strip, took an African-American studies degree from the University of Maryland and started drawing cartoons for the hip-hop magazine *The Source.*

But the cartoonist knew that the controversy he would stir in the weeks after September 11 would be different from any he had provoked before. What he did not know was that, unlike Trudeau in the Watergate era, he and his preteen characters would challenge a popular President and his policies with little cover from allies in the media or Congress. "Sometimes, I do look around and say to myself, 'Gee, I'm the only one saying some of these things.' That can make you a little paranoid. But I don't think that's a reflection on me so much as it is a reflection on how narrow the discussion has become in most of the media today. The media has become so conglomerated that there really are very few avenues left for people to express dissent," says McGruder. Well aware that he is a young cartoonist—as opposed to a senator or veteran television commentator—McGruder is the

Was McGruder just the only one saying these things, or was he the only one thinking them? If others thought them too, why did so few speak up?

first to note, "I should not be the guy right now. I should not be the one who is standing out here saying, 'Hold it. This doesn't make any sense. . . . There are a lot of people who do this so much better than I do. I just have the distribution and the opportunity."

When the terrorist planes hit the World Trade Center and the Pentagon, McGruder was not thinking about the next turn in his career path; rather, he was doing what Huey and the other *Boondocks* kids do a lot of: watching television. "I watched five straight days of television. I was shocked by what happened. But I was also shocked by the simplistic nature of a lot of the commentary—this whole 'good' versus 'evil' analysis that sounded like something from fifth grade. And I started to recognize that this was going to be a defining moment in my career," recalls McGruder, who acknowledges that Huey tends to channel his most passionately held views. "I decided that I was going to risk throwing my career away. I absolutely thought that was the risk I was taking."

Why take the risk?

"*The Boondocks* is not an alternative weekly strip. This is not a website strip. This is in the *Washington Post*," he explains. "It just seemed like nobody else was going to say the things that needed to be said in the places where I had an opportunity to raise questions about the war—in newspapers that millions of people read every day."

McGruder is not the only cartoonist upholding the craft's honorable tradition of tweaking the powerful. Despite pressure from many editors to narrow the discourse—because, in the words of *Soup to Nutz* cartoonist and National Cartoonist Society spokesman Rick Stromoski, "sales and subscriptions are down, and papers are afraid of offending their communities and losing even more readers"—a number of editorial-page cartoonists have poked and prodded more than most mainstream journalists. Pulitzer Prize–winner Steve Benson has created a tremendous stir in Phoenix, where his cartoons for the conservative *Arizona Republic* have attacked "war fever" and mocked superpatriots; angry readers have condemned Benson for what one described as "a vile tirade upon the people of the United States." Kentucky's Joel Pett has wondered aloud whether the antiterrorist cause might be better served by more food drops and fewer bombs. The *Philadelphia Inquirer*'s Tony Auth, the *Philadelphia Daily News*'s Signe Wilkinson and the *Sacramento Bee*'s Rex Babin have savaged the Bush Administration's assaults on civil liberties and decision to rely on military tribunals. And, though far gentler than in his heyday, Trudeau has used his *Doonesbury* strip—which often appears on editorial pages—to address anti-Arab stereotyping, slack media coverage and the dubious alliances made between the United States and Afghan warlords.

Gary Huck and Mike Konopacki, whose cartoons frequently appear in labor-union publications, have dissected war profiteering by corporations. Ted Rall, who is published in alternative weeklies and a growing number of daily papers, has exposed the excesses of corporate America (one of his cartoons, titled "America's business leaders consider their role in the war," features an executive crowing, "I laid off thousands of people and scored a bailout"); in addition, Rall has filed some of the best war reporting from Afghanistan by an American journalist. And no one has skewered the mindless patriotism of the media better than Dan Perkins, whose Tom Tomorrow strip coined the phrase "We must dismantle our democracy in order to save it."

But while many editorial cartoons are syndicated, none reach the audience that *The Boondocks* does daily. Thus when Huey started raising a ruckus, a lot of people noticed. One night last fall, when the LA-based cartoonist was visiting his parents in Maryland, McGruder sat down with Mom and Dad to watch a segment on ABCs *Nightline* portray him as one of America's most controversial commentators. Despite his off-message message, offers keep coming McGruder's way from Hollywood; he's developing an animated version of *The Boondocks* that's expected to show up as a network series this fall, and he's writing movie scripts—including one about George W. Bush's theft of the 2000 election. "If we can get it made, it will be a miracle," jokes McGruder, who calls Bush "our almost-elected leader." Weighing the continued success of *The Boondocks* and his Hollywood options against the recent controversy, McGruder says, "I can't say I've suffered. A few papers pulled [the strip] but most of them haven't. And the publicity has just drawn attention to what I'm doing."

Indeed, McGruder wonders why so few successful artists speak out about race, class, war and Bush's court-ordered presidency. "I understand that in a capitalist society, anger at the system is a luxury. But some people are on top of the system. Why don't they speak out?" he asks. "The only time I really get upset is when I see someone like Oprah [Winfrey], who has the money, who has the power, and I think, 'What is holding you back from changing the world, from changing the world in a drastic way?'" Adds McGruder, who has frequently used *The Boondocks* to criticize African-American celebrities who take the cautious route, "Some of these people clearly decided, at some point, not to take any risks. I can't do that." So Huey Freeman refuses to shut up. "I'm going to stay cynical, resist this bandwagon war," the cartoon character told his pal Caesar in a recent strip. "Sure, my kind may be obsolete. But so what?"

Actually, McGruder says, he doesn't believe Huey's thinking—or his own—to be obsolete, or even all that radical. "I really think that what I am doing with *The Boondocks* is common sense. It's just that when no one in a position to be heard is speaking out, common sense seems radical," he says, sounding distinctly like Huey as he adds, "How's that for irony: We live in a time when common-sense statements seem radical."

Is McGruder's work the voice of common sense or of radical political criticism?

Consider the source and the audience.

• *The Nation* is a liberal opinion journal. Does this article reflect that fact? How would the theme be different if Huey Freeman were covered in the *National Review* or on Rush Limbaugh's radio show?

Lay out the argument, the values, and the assumptions.

• What does Nichols seem to believe is a main purpose of the media? How about McGruder?

• What moral obligations does McGruder believe come with his job? Does he believe that his career should take precedence over his principles, or vice versa?

• Why, in Nichols' view, don't more mainstream journalists take on the American war on terror? Why does he believe they should?

Uncover the evidence.

• What evidence does Nichols use to back up his claim about the mainstream media?

• Does McGruder offer any evidence to support his moral argument? Does he need to?

Evaluate the conclusion.

• Is McGruder's stance an admirable one or an unpatriotic one? Is he right in saying that he is just speaking "common sense"?

Sort out the political implications.

• What if public opinion succeeded in silencing voices such as McGruder's? Would we be a stronger or weaker nation?

• Is it possible to disagree with McGruder's opinions and still support his right to air them?

14.2 Framing the Flag

Michael Scherer, *Columbia Journalism Review,* March–April 2002

In the previous article we met Aaron McGruder, creator of the outspoken Huey Freeman comic strip. Not surprisingly, McGruder has frequently found himself the target of this next article's subject, the Media Research Center (MRC). In the *Columbia Journalism Review,* Michael Scherer examines the practice of the MRC, which is dedicated to rooting out what it sees as a liberal bias in the media—defined, since September 11, 2001, as "interfering with America's war on terrorism or trying to undermine the authority of President Bush." Conservatives have long been critical of the so-called political correctness movement for inhibiting free speech. Is the MRC's mission fundamentally different?

One month after the first U.S. bombing of Kabul, Fox News correspondent Brit Hume delivered a short but stinging report on his nightly broadcast. "Over at ABC News, where the wearing of American flag lapel pins is banned," said Hume, his own pin firmly in place, "Peter Jennings and his team have devoted far more time to the coverage of civilian casualties in Afghanistan than either of their broadcast network competitors."

Citing a new study, Hume said that ABC spent exactly fifteen minutes, forty-four seconds covering these casualties over the previous several weeks, nearly twice the time spent at NBC and about four times as much as CBS. The implication was clear: war coverage on ABC, free patriotic accoutrements, was quite possibly drifting from the national interest.

> **Why is reporting enemy casualties a disloyal act?**

For the Media Research Center, the conservative watchdog that authored the report, Hume's dispatch represented yet another success in its campaign to hew reporters to open support for the war. Already the nation's most vocal critic of the media's perceived liberal bias, the center took on a "new and vital mission" in the months following the attacks on Washington and New York, according to its founder, L. Brent Bozell III. "We are training our guns on any media outlet or any reporter interfering with America's war on terrorism or trying to undermine the authority of President Bush," he wrote in a recent fundraising letter.

In terms of mainstream media exposure, the center has enjoyed significant success in its new role, often framing the discussions of journalistic objectivity. Between September 11 and December 31, MRC reports and staff members were quoted eighty separate times by major news outlets in the Nexis database. This included eleven interviews and citations on Fox News, CNN, and CNNfn. Bozell even made it onto Imus in the Morning in February.

"The fact that we have been received reasonably well during this period is good for us," says Rich Noyes, the center's director of media research. "I think you can tell when we are raising good questions."

Those questions often concerned the patriotic credentials of top broadcast news reporters, producers, and executives. The center praised Rather, Brokaw, and Russert for editorializing their support of the war; it chastised journalists who kept a greater editorial distance. "What we were looking for was home-team sports reporting," Noyes explains.

> **What different perspectives would we normally look for in a political reporter versus a sports reporter?**

In practice, the center defined the home team as the Bush administration and its policies. Journalists and pundits who challenged them were tarred with the epithet "political activist," or in the case of the cartoonist Aaron McGruder, "America-hater." In one report, the center took Peter Jennings to task for suggesting on a talk show that Americans respect different views of patriotism. The center's editorial response: "Unlike Jennings, who is still a Canadian citizen, we are Americans."

After CNN submitted six questions to an alleged representative of Osama bin Laden, the *Los Angeles Times* quoted Bozell calling the questions a "slap in the face of the American people." *The Boston Globe* and *The Christian Science Monitor* reported on the center's criticism of Reuters and the BBC for swearing off the term "terrorist." The center also spread the word about ABC News president David Westin's equivocation over whether the Pentagon had been a "legitimate military target," eliciting a prompt apology from the network chief and a flurry of embarrassing press coverage. "They put stuff out there and either it speaks for itself or it doesn't" said Hume, who worked at ABC News for twenty-three years before joining Fox. "The value of these people is their research."

Some media watchers agree. "Senior network executives tend to dismiss the center a bit too reflexively," said Howard Kurtz, media reporter for CNN and *The Washington Post*. "This is clearly because the organization has such a conservative agenda, but that doesn't mean their barbs aren't hitting the mark sometimes."

In many ways, Bozell's group has continued the mission begun in 1969 by Reed Irvine's Accuracy in Media, which helped found MRC in 1987 by sharing its mailing list. But Bozell, a syndicated columnist who served as finance director in Patrick Buchanan's 1992 presidential campaign, has developed a much larger organization. Funded by such conservative groups as the Sarah Scaife Foundation, his center boasted an income of $15 million in 2000, more than eighteen times as much as Fairness and Accuracy in Reporting, the largest liberal media watchdog.

Why is an antiwar position "liberal"? Would a conservative oppose a war?

From September 11 until Christmas, a staff of eight full-time researchers recorded and reviewed all the broadcasts on CBS, NBC, ABC, CNN, MSNBC, and Fox News, said Noyes. Any possible evidence of "liberal bias" or wavering support of the military mission was flagged for distribution through the group's Web page, e-mail list, and "Notable Quotables," a biweekly newsletter delivered free to many of the nation's newsrooms.

While the center's direct impact on those newsrooms is difficult to measure, television coverage has been far more supportive of the Bush administration's policies than have newspaper reports. In November, for instance, a new study by the Project for Excellence in Journalism found that 54 percent of broadcast segments "entirely" supported official U.S. viewpoints, compared with 23 percent of applicable newspaper coverage.

At CNN, NBC, MSNBC, and ABC, reporters and producers said that while they are aware of the center's criticisms, they keep partisan assaults from influencing their news judgment. Still, says Tom Nagorski, the foreign news editor at ABC, "I suppose in a subtle way it's in the back of your mind." For supporters of the Media Research Center, that may be all they can ask.

Consider the source and the audience.

- The *Columbia Journalism Review* is published by the Columbia University School of Journalism with the intent to monitor the profession of American journalism. Its commentators are on the watch for limits on objectivity and freedom of the press. What kind of view are they likely to hold of the MRC?

Lay out the argument, the values, and the assumptions.

- Can you determine Scherer's view of how the profession of journalism should be practiced? How is he likely to feel about the kinds of restrictions the MRC wants to put on the press?
- What kinds of values does the MRC promote? Why does it believe that the restrictions it wants the media to practice are justified? What are the consequences of free criticism of the government's war efforts?

Uncover the evidence.

- Scherer cites some evidence that the MRC is having the effect it wants in silencing government criticism. Is this evidence persuasive?
- Does the MRC offer evidence about why criticism of Bush or the war on terrorism is detrimental?

Evaluate the conclusion.

- Scherer expects his audience to reject the argument and the actions of the MRC. Does he give reasons for this rejection, or does it seem self-evident to him? Does his argument satisfy you?

Sort out the political implications.

- If the media censor themselves because they don't want to be criticized and accused of disloyalty, is that outcome the same as if the government censored them? Are the consequences of these two scenarios different?

14.3 The Real Media Bias: Profits

Margo Hammond, *St. Petersburg Times,* 24 February 2002

Liberals fret about the growing conservative media presence in America; conservatives howl about a liberal mainstream press. But many less ideological critics say they are both wrong. The bias is not partisan or political—it's corporate. Here a *St. Petersburg Times* reporter reviews a book by two *Washington Post* editors who claim that the problem with the media today is that they don't find it profitable to show hard news. Should consumers or journalists decide what people ought to listen to and read?

In *Bias: A CBS Insider Exposes How the Media Distort the News,* a book that has been on the *New York Times* bestseller list for the past 10 weeks, former CBS reporter and producer Bernard Goldberg argues that the quality of the news we receive has declined. Why? Because of a liberal bias in the media.

Now this week in a new book, two journalists coming from what most fans of Goldberg's book would consider the very bastion of liberal bias offer their own indictment of journalism. But don't expect a rebuttal of Goldberg's thesis. In *News About the News: Journalism in Peril,* Leonard Downie Jr., the executive editor of the *Washington Post,* and Robert Kaiser, a *Post* associate editor, are not interested in whether the press is liberal—or conservative, for that matter.

Their operative word is profits.

The real bias in media these days is not ideological but financial, as Downie and Kaiser amply demonstrate through a careful examination of newspapers, local stations and national networks. Too often, news decisions are subjected solely to an accounting test: "Does it make money?" That's an ominous trend for our society. In a democracy, giving the media the role of watchdog is one of the best ways to hold government and powerful institutions accountable for their actions. News matters. But fewer and fewer media institutions are engaging in it, say Downie and Kaiser.

Can the media be biased both ideologically and financially?

Newspapers have shrunk their reporting staff and the space they devote to news. Very few have bureaus in their state capitols. The staffs of local television stations have been cut to the bone. National television networks have closed their foreign bureaus. Cable stations offer endless chatter and little substance.

All these decisions have sprung out of a media world which increasingly is in the hands of mega-corporate interests. In other words, most news organizations, which once served to keep tabs on those in power, are now powerhouses themselves. They are concerned not with public service, which they see as too costly, but with filling up air time (and newsprint) as cheaply as possible.

That means instead of hiring investigative reporters to keep politicians honest, newspapers settle for expanded lifestyle sections that please advertisers. Instead of reporting on what government is doing, local stations offer "action news," segments that appear to be investigative reports ("Pollution in the Rivers, Tune in at 5") but which are really pre-packaged formulas bought from consultants. Instead of in-depth reports from abroad, national networks and cable stations offer up endless entertainment features and talk shows that shed more heat than light.

Crammed with celebrity interviews, disaster and crime reports, punditry and manufactured news, the media is not so much an arsenal against ignorance. It's becoming a weapon of mass distraction.

What were the benefits of locally owned media?

It wasn't always this way, as Downie and Kaiser point out. For most of the first two centuries of American history, the country's newspapers were deeply rooted local institutions. So were television stations. "Some were public-spirited, others merely provincial, but everyone in town knew who the owner was and where to find him," they write. Now, "most newspapers, television networks and local television and radio stations belong to giant, publicly owned corporations far removed from the communities they serve."

And don't think this will change any time soon. With the ruling last week that paves the way for cable operators to own television networks, the concentration of media ownership into the hands of a few entertainment monopolies will only become more intense. And with it will come even more quarterly profit pressures from Wall Street.

"Media owners are accustomed to profit margins that would be impossible in most traditional industries," write Downie and Kaiser. "For General Motors, a profit margin of 5 percent of total revenue would mark a very good year, but the Tribune Company of Chicago, which owns newspapers and television stations located all across the country, wants a 30 percent margin. Many local television stations expect to keep 50 percent of their revenue as profit. Protecting such high profits can easily undermine the notion that journalism is a public service."

Downie and Kaiser are not opposed to news organizations making money, mind you. They receive their paychecks, after all, from the *Washington Post,* whose profit margins regularly exceed 15 percent and often go above 20 percent of total revenues (their own figures). But at the *Post,* they argue, those increased profits have not been made at the expense of serious news gathering. It is when newspapers are willing to sacrifice quality to meet the increasing demands of stockholders for more profits that the larger society stands to lose.

"Newspapers must get better, not worse, to retain the loyalty of readers, and thus the dollars of advertisers," they write. "If they fail to get better, newspapers will continue to shrink—in size, in quality, in importance. This would be tragic, because no other news medium can fill the role that good newspapers play in informing the country."

If that sounds like a bias toward print journalism, it is. Freely admitting they are not the best people to criticize the *Post,* the two *Post* veterans do take note of their own newspaper's deserved reputation for journalistic excellence. They also praise the newspaper that writes my paycheck—the *St. Petersburg Times*—pointing out that its unique financial structure (it is independently owned by a local nonprofit media institute) allows it to be "run for the public's benefit." On the other hand, they bemoan what they call the "profit-driven big chains" such as Gannett and Knight-Ridder, and the tendency of even well-respected newspapers to blur the lines between advertising and news. They take the *Los Angeles Times,* for example, to task for its notorious deal with the Staples Center, in which the newspaper shared advertising revenues from a Sunday magazine that purported to be news. The *Times* case was so egregious that its own editors later published a report critical of the newspaper's Staples decisions.

Downie and Kaiser's most vitriolic attacks, however, are reserved for the electronic media, particularly local television. "The owners and managers of local television stations feel little obligation to provide coverage of government, politics or civic affairs in return for the free airwaves they use, or the First Amendment protections they enjoy," they write. Whatever happened to the notion of public service?

There was, of course, a time last fall when it looked like that notion might be revived. During the days and weeks that followed Sept. 11, news organizations seemed to forget about profits and concentrated on serving the public. Television networks suspended commercials. Newspapers put out extra editions and expanded their news holes to accommodate badly sought after information about terrorism here and abroad.

Will such newfound interest in serious news last? Will the owners of news organizations now be convinced that it is in their best interest to encourage better journalism and spend more money on covering the news? Downie and Kaiser, who were finishing up their book just after the terrorist attacks, were cautiously hopeful. But the bulk of their research, obviously completed well before Sept. 11, indicates that it will be an uphill battle.

> Do the media have an obligation to serve the public? Is that different from entertaining them? Did they have an obligation to the public on September 11?

CBS' Goldberg is certainly skeptical. "On September 11, 2001, America's royalty, the TV news anchors, got it right," he wrote in a brief note added to his best-seller *Bias* after the terrorist attacks. "But it shouldn't take a national catastrophe of unparalleled magnitude to get the news without the usual biases."

Goldberg and other media critics continue to lay the blame for media mediocrity on the press' liberal or conservative bias. But in criticizing the media elites, Goldberg could have just stopped after the phrase "to get the news." The more pressing problem is not whether the news we get is slanted, right or left. It's whether we get any news at all.

Consider the source and the audience.

- As Hammond admits, the book she is reviewing by Downie and Kaiser is very complimentary toward the paper she writes for. Might that fact affect her portrayal of the book's argument? Or, might the fact that her paper is independently owned make it more likely to give fair coverage to their thesis?
- What Hammond has written is a book review. What are the advantages of reading a review, and what limitations does it have?

Lay out the argument, the values, and the assumptions.

- What do Downie and Kaiser see as the main purpose of journalism?
- Why do they think the contemporary media are not fulfilling that purpose?
- If they are right about both those things, what is the likely consequence of this failure of journalism to do what they say is its job?

Uncover the evidence.
- What evidence does Hammond offer in support of Downie's and Kaiser's claims?
- What kind of evidence would you hope to see in their book?

Evaluate the conclusion.
- Does democracy require a "watchdog" to keep a check on those in power?
- Are Downie and Kaiser right in saying that journalists have an obligation to act as that government watchdog, or are the media free to be an entertainment industry if their shareholders want them to be?

Sort out the political implications.
- If it's unprofitable to print or broadcast news, is that because most people don't want to read or hear it? If so, should the media give people what they want, or what it is good for them to have?
- If the authors are right and current trends continue, what happens to democracy?

14.4 The Weight of an Anchor

In the Twilight of Brokaw, Jennings, and Rather, It Is Not at All Clear That the Nightly News Program Is History: Why Network News Still Matters

Frank Rich, *New York Times Magazine,* 19 May 2002

In this giddy age of electronic media innovation, when one can have the news custom-delivered to a device in one's pocket, let alone tune into a talk radio show that echoes one's own political predilections or watch breaking news on cable 24/7, it is popular to talk about the death of the old-fashioned nightly network news show. Are the network anchors stodgy gray figures from an outmoded past? Here Frank Rich argues to the contrary. In fact, he claims, they serve a purpose in our civic culture that not one of the snazzy new inventions has managed to replace. Is there a future for the network news?

I t can't be fun to be told repeatedly that you are obsolete, dying, soon to be relegated to TV's Hall of Fame like such other once ubiquitous but now half-forgotten golden oldies as "Kukla, Fran & Ollie." So pity, at least for a moment, the plight of three of the most widely known and highly paid stars in the vast American information firmament: the network news anchormen. Their nightly newscasts, which collectively commanded 84 percent of the viewing audience in 1981, now attract only 43 percent of the pie. Those Americans who do tune in, with a median age ranging from 56 (NBC) to 60 (CBS), are regarded as a step or two from the grave by the youth-centric standards of a medium that worships the 18–24 demographic. Whatever the news each night on NBC's "Nightly News," CBS's "Evening News" and ABC's "World News Tonight," the commercials on the three broadcasts amount to a grim virtual tour of a medicine cabinet largely for the aging, the infirm, the impotent and the incontinent: Plavix, Pepcid, Nexium, Ditropan, Caltrate, Viagra and Depends.

The anchors themselves, all of whom have been on their thrones continuously since the early 1980's, may look preternaturally well preserved, but they are even closer to geezerdom than their typical viewer, with Dan Rather now 70, Peter Jennings 63 and Tom Brokaw 62. They must endure constant taunting by fellow journalists who make sport of anticipating their exit, a drumbeat that has become louder than ever in the aftermath of Disney's foiled effort this year to displace another fixture of anchordom, the 62-year-old Ted Koppel. This newspaper, like others, has written flatly of "the coming disappearance" of the evening news. The nation's TV columns are jumpy with speculation that Jennings, whose contract is up for renewal, may have to take a salary cut (most unlikely), that Rather's new contract signals he will someday shift from anchoring to another CBS News role (possible, but far from imminent) and that Brokaw, now negotiating his NBC future, will formalize a transition to his zealous heir apparent, Brian Williams (maybe, but well-placed sources at the network say Brokaw will extend at least through the 2004 election). Whoever leaves when, the No. 1 cliché among media critics is that we're watching the "last hurrah" of network news anchors as we have known them for nearly half a century. Or as Roger Ailes, the impresario of cable's swash-buckling Fox News Channel, puts it somewhat less delicately about the anchor roles played by Tom, Peter and Dan, "They're dinosaurs, and when they're gone, it's extinction."

The anchors hear the buzz. "We had our picture taken for *TV Guide* recently," Brokaw said when I asked him about the relentless dinosaur talk. "It was one of those quasi-awkward moments—the three of us were standing there in this kind of stilted pose. So I leaned into the camera and said: 'We'd like to welcome you to the anchorman's nursing home. We have great soft food and a fine array of nurses, and if you've just come here, we'll make an arrangement for all of you to join us on the porch as, well, we go into the future.'"

How could the twin American institutions of the anchor and the evening news have fallen into such seeming decrepitude and peril? The standard rap cites these factors: the fractionallization of the TV audience in the 500-channel cable-satellite media universe; the fierce and ever-expanding competition of cable news, as led by Ailes and Fox; the postmodern news-grazing habits of the young, who turn to such antiestablishment sources as the Internet and Jon Stewart's "Daily Show" for their information fix; the revolutions in American life that have rendered the progressively earlier

Do these reasons for the projected extinction of the nightly network news make sense? Do you ever watch the network news shows? Why or why not?

nightly news time slot (as early as 5:30 in some markets) a nonstarter for the modern family; the bottom-line-*Überalles* imperatives of the networks' latest set of gargantuan corporate owners; and the content and nature of the broadcasts themselves.

Take away the ads and promos, and there are only about 20 minutes for actual news on each night's evening news. In a media-saturated world where many have already scanned the headlines on cable or the Web during the workday, much of that precious time is given over to features pitched to boomers. "The evening news should be news," Walter Cronkite, now 85, said when I talked with him over lunch at the Four Seasons. Cronkite still wears CBS "eye" cuff links but is less than pleased about what has happened to the franchise that he more than any-one elevated into iconic status. "Those feature stories—'Eye on America,' your kitchen and mine, your back porch and mine, your garbage pail and mine—it's not bad stuff. But *not,* for God's sake, in the national news! *Not* on the front page! They're taking that time from the major news they should be covering."

For some, the idea of the anchor—an omniscient father figure decreeing "that's the way it was" from behind an imposing desk—has itself become a relic of an American hierarchy that will soon be gone with the wind. "The customer is king now," says Sir Howard Stringer, the longtime CBS News executive who cur-rently runs the Sony Corporation of America. "The viewer chooses how he gets his information, news and entertainment. It's a form of empowerment: I'll get my news in my own way, thank you very much."

Nor do many believe that the current anchors can be replicated, even were that worth doing. "When you think of Cronkite, you think of him crawling around on his belly with a typewriter in World War II," Ailes says, recalling the CBS news-man's legendary early career as a U.P.I. war correspondent whose exploits in-cluded crash-landing into the Battle of the Bulge. "Dan was at the Kennedy assassination. Jennings was a foreign correspondent. I have respect for these people. They've *been* there." Their likely successors, the prevailing view has it, could never boast the same authority. The decline in momentous stories to cover after the fall of the Berlin Wall, as well as the overall cutback in network news budgets and foreign bureaus, stilled the assembly line that once minted anchors.

When Cronkite was preparing to depart, there were at least three heavyweight contenders for his seat at CBS alone: Rather, Roger Mudd and Charles Kurault. In the new succession sweepstakes, the A list at all three networks combined has dwindled to Williams, 43, at NBC and John Roberts, 45, at CBS. (At ABC, the principal sub for Jennings, Charles Gibson, 59, is ensconced at "Good Morning America.") Though they have done duty overseas, few think of them as battle-seasoned.

"I think Brian Williams has been to New Jersey," Ailes says. "He's a perfectly fine news reader, a good guy, pretty smart. But you can't invent gravitas." While Ailes doesn't think the evening news "will die a sudden death" when the big three anchors leave, he can picture a fast meltdown. "They'll give John Roberts

13 weeks," he says with characteristic theatrical hyperbole, "and if he doesn't get the age demographics, the ratings or more ad dollars, they'll take him out back and shoot him. And he'll end up the lead anchor in Detroit for the rest of his life."

Yet there are some strong abstainers to the Twilight of the Anchors orthodoxy, starting with the heads of the Big Three network news divisions, who unequivocally dismiss reports of the death of both the anchorman and the evening news. "If you listen to Roger Ailes say it loudly enough and often enough, it sounds plausible," says David Westin, the president of ABC News. "But if you look at the curve for prime-time entertainment at the networks, the audience is in steeper decline than it is for news, including for demographics. And no one says prime-time entertainment is going to go anywhere."

Just look at the numbers, say Westin and company. The combined audience of the three nightly network broadcasts, even in their reduced state, is still larger than that of most prime-time entertainments—30 million viewers each night versus 24 million for a No. 1 sitcom like "Friends." (Not bad for 6:30.) Despite all the hype, the combined prime-time audience for all three cable news networks is three million—or one-tenth the viewership of the evening news, and with no younger demographics (median age at CNN, 58; at Fox, 56).

Then why this constant talk that we're at the end of an era? "It's a *Schadenfreude* frenzy on the part of print reporters and cable people, all triggered by Disney's Mickey Mouse treatment of Ted Koppel," says Andrew Heyward, the president of CBS News. "Cable wants to believe that it's the future and we're the past. Print wants to believe we're dumber, shallower and bizarrely richer."

He may just have a point. Cable news is better at self-promotion than at drawing network-size audiences. Some print journalists do resent the fame and wealth of TV news stars whom they tend to regard as glib actors reading from "My Weekly Reader"–level scripts. Almost everyone predicting the demise of the evening news does have an investment in its demise. If the mass network audience that still gathers for the Big Three disperses, might not the niche alternatives, like cable news channels and newspapers, inherit the earth? Maybe. But wishing can't make it so, and the constantly chanted mantra that the network anchor and evening news are on their way out may, in fact, be dead wrong.

In the middle of the story about the End of TV News as We Know It are the anchors themselves. They certainly occupy a strange position in the American scheme of status. Not quite movie stars, not quite officialdom, they are more famous than most movie stars and more powerful than most politicians. They have their own idiosyncratic gestalt. Though they come from unpretentious backgrounds—Brokaw and Rather are émigrés from small towns and the working class; Jennings didn't finish high school—they dress like captains of industry for their nightly broadcasts: bespoke suits, spread-collar shirts and power ties. "On assignment," they wear costumes from stock—Rather in a flak jacket to cover the Middle East; Brokaw in a parka for the Olympics. For many Americans, the anchors designate a news event as serious simply by lending it their presence, even if that decision sometimes seems to have more to do with personal image–tending than with journalism. (After their over-the-top anchoring binge at Princess Di's funeral, they had little choice but to cover Mother Teresa's soon after, although there was no earthly, as opposed to heavenly, reason for them to do so.) Lest anyone think they are less intellectual than their print colleagues, they all write books, or in some cases co-write them—a literary output (most conspicuously Brokaw's "Greatest Generation" series) that can achieve the kind of instant best-sellerdom that can drive full-time noncelebrity authors to drink.

Each of the three has his own specific star persona, as rigidly projected to the public through the years as those of Hollywood's studio-era royalty. Rather is the folksy (to a scripted fault to his detractors), tightly wound, slightly weird one—with a tendency to get into scrapes, especially with Republican administrations. Jennings is the brainy perfectionist—an effete, controlling egomaniac to his critics. The relatively easygoing, low-maintenance Brokaw is by common consent the "most normal" of the trio, though those who don't warm to him find him facile. To their respective fans, both Rather and Brokaw are "America's anchors." Jennings is Canadian, which to his fans makes him almost as Bohemian as a beret-wearing Left Bank intellectual in this bland context.

They are as competitive as gladiators. Early in his newscast each night, Jennings flips a switch at his anchor desk allowing him to watch a split-screen monitor that shows him what stories the other two are leading with. The point of this competitive zeal may seem arcane to anyone outside the television industry. The current difference in audience among the evening-news programs is hardly earthshaking—ranging this season to date from 10.9 million viewers (NBC) to 10.4 million (ABC) to 9.2 million (CBS)—and may have less to do with the quality of the look-alike shows than with the overall ratings vicissitudes of the networks themselves, both at the national and local levels.

In the hothouse of the network-news industry itself, however, there is a constant undertow of bitchiness, as if the three men were squaring off in a new election for prom king every single night. While I was reporting this article, staff members at the other two networks made sure, sotto voce, that I knew that Rather was on vacation the week during which Brokaw and Jennings went to Beirut to cover the Arab summit. But Brokaw and Jennings were foiled a week later when they were back in Manhattan and Rather belatedly showed up in the Middle East, just in time to be at the front as violence between the Israelis and Palestinians worsened. When Rather subsequently appeared on CNN's "Larry King Live" to talk about how he had just missed being the victim of a bombing ("Danger is my business," he told King, and not for the first time), wags at NBC and ABC clucked that he was grandstanding. But within days, Jennings, too, was expounding with Larry King—after which he was one-upped by Brokaw, who took off for Baghdad.

Do the three anchors ever compare notes about this strange elite club of which they are the sole members, or are they too competitive even for that? "What does happen is we have conversations," Rather says—usually to confer about joint appearances at charitable or civic events. There are occasional congratulatory calls and "in a rare instance" polite exchanges about mild beefs. "Once in a very great while, though I can't remember the last time it happened, it's not unheard of to have lunch," Rather says. "But it doesn't happen as often as once a year."

The anchors do have some sense of humor about their elevated celebrity. When I asked Rather how he had succeeded in retrieving a favorite chair that had been earmarked for destruction along with the rest of his office furnishings following its post–Sept. 11 contamination by anthrax, he took a practiced comedian's pause, grinned and said, "By throwing an anchor tantrum." Jennings says: "I see no reason why we should not be objects of fun and, on occasion, derision. Print reporters cannot resist hair-spray jokes, and we tell our own, of course. You're out on location, and you're in the middle of a damn hurricane, and I always tell people, pay close attention: the only thing not moving is the anchorman's hair."

As the sole evening-news anchor who has been divorced, dated in public and remarried, Jennings has at times had to suffer through racy tabloid mockery as well. And the perks? "The one thing that has always stunned me is the anchorperson's ability to get a table in a restaurant," he says, though you suspect he might be able to come up with a few more impressive examples, like instant access to world leaders as well as maître d's.

Each of the anchors makes a point of saying that he never aspired to be an anchor per se, only a newsman. Still, Brokaw recalls being struck by the growing power of anchors as he and they started to come of age in the 50's. "I used to say, boy, that's the job I think would be great," he says. "And it was in part because it was this phenomenon at the time. It was a kind of new status job in America. It was interesting. It was important. It paid well. I remember reading that David Brinkley and his wife decided on the spur of the moment to go down to Miami Beach for the weekend, and they were able to get a hotel. And I thought, Yeah, that's pretty good. And you could meet anyone you wanted to. I was a total political junkie, and I thought, Wow, this is the Mel Allen of news and politics."

Being an anchor can be "a tough job," Jennings says, "but I'm, God knows, unbelievably well remunerated for it." (He is thought to be at the high end of an anchor pay scale ranging between $7 million and $10 million a year.) Yet the roots of this august calling are far more humble than most of today's viewers could imagine; at first the job was neither tough nor lucrative. . . .

It was in 1963 that the network anchors as we define them today were born: a man (and still almost always a man) who is at once an authoritative reporter, a

Why is the nightly network news such a "man's world"? Why have there been no women anchors among the evening Big Three, despite successes like Katie Couric's with the morning news?

cool news reader and the nation's emotional proxy at history's events. All these elements converged in Walter Cronkite, who had just succeeded [Douglas] Edwards as anchor. Cronkite's evening news was the first to expand from 15 minutes to a half-hour (over the objections of CBS's affiliates), the first in which the anchor assumed the powers (and title) of managing editor and the first to unfold in a "newsroom-studio" in which the anchor sat at a horseshoe desk while nameless writers and editors clattered at typewriters on the periphery of the image. . . . The Kennedy assassination did the rest. For the first time, network news offered four days' blanket coverage of a news event, with the anchor at the eye of the harrowing storm. To this day, the moment when Cronkite, after announcing the president's death, took off his glasses and ever-so-slightly lost it, remains the cathartic peak of the story for the millions who were watching.

Leading the country through shock and grief as much as through a journalistic narrative, the anchor, as recalibrated by Cronkite, became, in the words of Harrison E. Salisbury of *The Times*, "a father figure to a country that seems to be looking for one." Polls found Cronkite to be "the most trusted man" in the country. He remained that steadying fixture through the civic paroxysms of the Vietnam War and Watergate. When, after the Tet offensive of 1968, the anchor returned from Vietnam to pronounce the war unwinnable, Lyndon Johnson famously told his aides, "If I've lost Cronkite, I've lost Middle America."

In those days, says Howard Stringer, who first went to work for CBS in 1968, "we were the flagship newscast. We could beat *The Times* on a story and make front-page news. During Vietnam and Watergate, the evening news was so powerful you could legitimize the interpretation of events. When Walter said the Vietnam War was over, it was *over*."

Even so, anchors were not yet fabulously paid. When I asked Cronkite if he had missed the big money in anchoring, he scrunched his eyes and lowered his voice into a theatrical mock sob. "Yes, I did," he said and then added, "I frequently call myself the Mickey Mantle of network news." The big-money era in TV news was, in fact, inaugurated with his abdication as anchor. When Roone Arledge, who had previously revolutionized ABC Sports, took over the perennially third-place, talent-poor ABC News, he decided to catapult it into the game by adding stars that would have to be poached from the far-deeper ranks of the other network-news divisions. Show-biz tactics begat show-biz salaries. In 1981, he made an unprecedented $2 million offer to Rather to jump networks, which not only pressured CBS to promote him to succeed Cronkite as anchor sooner than it (or

Cronkite) had planned but also raised the salary structure exponentially across the industry for the top on-air talents in network news. The level of compensation for stars has continued on a stratospheric trajectory ever since—even as new owners stripped network news divisions of hundreds of jobs and even as the audience declined and aged. It was as cable arrived in the late 1970's, offering other choices in the early evening, that the young in particular began to peel away. The median age of the evening news viewership hit the 50's by the 1980's.

It is a measure of how the evening news has fallen in status since then that some of the biggest news stars can be found on the network morning shows, which, with their steadily growing and more demographically desirable audiences, are generating larger revenue. "All ABC News cares about—all of the energy—is to have 'Good Morning America' beat the 'Today' show," says one major player in ABC's news division. "That's where the power is now." Today the highest-paid news personality at NBC, or any network, is Katie Couric. She is believed to make $13 million to $15 million a year as co-anchor of the "Today" show, the same job that was considered merely a stepping stone to the big time back when Brokaw had it before ascending to "Nightly News" anchor 20 years ago.

Though the three anchors may not pal around, they agree about much. Indeed, their responses to my questions differed little more than their nightly newscasts do. They are as political as any politicians. They are as one in describing how their job is most often misperceived by outsiders. "I think they think that we show up at 6 o'clock and put on some makeup and read out loud," Brokaw says, laughing. "Even among my friends, there is still a lot of that." Asked to define exactly what he does on a typical day at home base, Jennings delineated a routine that is more or less echoed by his peers: "For most of my day, I work as an editor. For part of the day, I'm a rewrite man. For part of the day, I am a reporter or a producer. For part of almost every day, I am a semi-member of management, trying to help develop new correspondents. Part of the day, I am, sad to say, a P.R. man for the company—I go out and carry the ABC flag at functions. Oh, and then at the end of the day, I'm a news reader for half an hour." . . .

Rather, Jennings and Brokaw came up through a system that held out anchoring as the ultimate prize. Now the rules of the game are changing, and they are still playing by the old ones, while the new kids on the block, the brash upstarts of Fox and company, grab the limelight without paying their dues.

But when I sit down to talk to Rather about the other half of anchoring—managing the nonstop coverage of a breaking news story—I get another impression entirely. The topic is Sept. 11, and he is energized. Sept. 11 had proved to be a day on which the audience returned en masse to the three networks for their continuous news coverage, abandoning the boys and girls of cable and reaffirming the trust they still place in the Big Three anchors in a crisis.

"There are so many more things about 9/11 to talk about than this," Rather said. "But in our small little world, even in this building, so many people had bought into the idea that cable was that little shop of horrors that they doubted the audience would come. I don't say this in my self-serving way, but I never doubted it. The viewer must have a sense that the anchor has seen enough of life, enough of news, to be trusted with this storm, this hurricane of fact, rumor, information, misinformation, interviews, new reports coming in to sort through. On big breaking news, there is no place to hide. It's where experience is leveraged.

"When we're at our best, there is in that role the ability to help knit the country together, to give the country a sense of shared experience. I've never particularly liked the metaphor, but in a time when it's very difficult to find anything approaching a national hearth, people are looking for that kind of national hearth. And if the anchor does his or her job anywhere at or near our best, we have the ability to do that. It took me a long time to come to grips with the symbolic nature of the job. But like it or not, people key off you. If in your inner core you think of yourself as the holder of a trust, not in any arrogant or conceited way but in a very humble way, not a word generally associated with anchors, then I think that that gets through the glass. It's the very essence of being an effective anchor."

Though Rather didn't have a moment on Sept. 11 comparable to Cronkite's welling up during the Kennedy assassination, he found an updated way to do so some days later, when he cried openly not on his own broadcast but on David Letterman's, a venue befitting a cultural era when a late-night comic is as significant a standard-bearer for a network brand, if not more so, than the evening-news anchor.

Later I would talk with Al Artiz, the CBS News producer whose voice was literally in Rather's ear for many of the 17 hours he spent continuously on the air after the attack on the World Trade Center. To Artiz, Rather's job that day, like Cronkite's on Nov. 22, 1963, was rife with dangers; it was paramount that an anchor not foment hysteria by relaying any rumors or other "bad information" to an already jumpy, shellshocked nation. "He was at his best ever," Artiz said. "They all were, and they would say it about each other."

It's true—they all were. And many viewers didn't want to take the risk of turning to the personalities of cable on Sept. 11, 2001, when separating fact from fiction mattered more than it had for most Americans in their lifetimes. From the Big Three anchors, there was little possibility of recklessness. After a decade of O.J. and Monica, they were at the center of the media map again. "Very good friends of mine," recalls Brokaw, "some of them quite critical of what it is that we do, and strangers as well, said, My God, you were so important to me that day. And I said: Yeah, but it wasn't me. It was about the information. You could come to me and say he's going to tell me what's factual as opposed to the hysteria in the air. Because it could have very quickly become an 'Oh, my God' day. 'Oh, my God' *this.* 'Oh, my God' *that.*"

Jennings, whose coverage of Sept. 11 helped ABC to win the Peabody Award, says: "The first day, I did 17 hours. If your concentration wavers for just a second, you're going to miss something. The job of the anchorperson then is to sit there and knit the whole thing together and give it perspective and give it context and know what questions to ask and know who to bring in, who to put onstage. And when to get them onstage and when to get them offstage. And to not get in the way of those dimensions of the story that don't need a lot of chatter. And the answer to how you do that is mileage. Had I not had that experience, that would have been the longest, most difficult, most horrendous day of my life professionally. Just couldn't have done it."

But if Sept. 11 validated the value of the anchors to the culture in covering a story of seismic magnitude, could that value accrue to the next crop? None of the Big Three's potential successors has that much mileage. "I've always thought anchors were like chained tigers," says Howard Stringer, who worked at CBS with both Cronkite and Rather. "They earned their stripes reporting stories, traveling the world over, knocking down doors. The danger of the next generation is that they're almost professional anchors: they don't want to go to the field. More and more journalists think it's a bit more fun sitting in front of a teleprompter and being self-important than being in Afghanistan. After the fall of Kuwait, the first volunteers at CBS to go to Baghdad were Dan Rather, Mike Wallace and Ed Bradley. Think of the median age! The young recruits had to be strapped to the jeep."

Stringer and Cronkite both find that when they address journalism schools, they can immediately pick out who wants to be an anchor these days—Ken dolls whose main qualification is that they look like anchors. "I look around the crowd," Cronkite says, "and see who wants to be an anchorperson, not a journalist. The women are all blond, and so are the men. The few serious journalists look like they got out of bed a little late; they ask questions about the coverage. The others ask: 'How can I get a job? How can I'—and here Cronkite lets loose with a most un-Cronkite-like sneer—'establish my credentials?'"

Roger Ailes of Fox, who says he would put Cronkite on his network today were he available, concurs. "There are news anchors and news actors," he says. As an example, he cites Ashleigh Banfield, a star of war coverage on a rival cable channel, MSNBC. (Though Fox's own Geraldo Rivera, I would argue, is the master of this trade.) "If you turn down the sound, it's like watching Tom Mix movies. It's all about her, performing the news. She's a news actress, and that's terrifying. It's like a theater actor can tell when an actor breaks character: you know when they're not in the moment."

Yet some considered Brokaw and Rather too young and gravitas-deficient when they initially took over from John Chancellor and

> Does it matter whether the news is presented by an anchor or an actor? What difference does it make to the news you get? Or to what Rich calls the "symbolic nature of the job"?

Cronkite. Neal Shapiro, the president of NBC News, says: "The doctor I go to may no longer be older than I am, but I still go to the doctor. And people will still go to the anchors. As long as they're really good, their age doesn't matter."

What does matter—though few in the business will concede it—is how they look. Being blond may not be a requirement, but all pending evening-news anchors are not only men but, like the incumbents, handsome in the same way. Jennings jokes about how he was handed an early stint as the ABC anchor in the mid-1960's (when he was in his mid-20's) because it was "the Gidget era" and, he says, "I had all my hair and all my teeth." But not that much has changed. Hair and teeth still matter. Discernible ethnicity is a no-no on the front line of the evening news. ABC's short-lived, long-ago efforts to install either nonwhite or nonmale anchors in the 1970's—Barbara Walters and Max Robinson—proved dead ends. Male anchors who don't fit the mold, much like female anchors, get substitute and weekend anchoring slots, Sunday shows like "Meet the Press," prime-time magazine gigs and "Nightline." . . .

But what about the substance? Last summer, Dan Rather, perhaps the most persistent critic of television news among the anchors, wrapped up his report on President Bush's national address about stem-cell research by encouraging his viewers to read the story in "one of the better newspapers tomorrow" since "it's the kind of subject that, frankly, radio and television have some difficulty with because it requires such depth into the complexities of it."

Maybe the most substantive argument for the evening news's survival is civic, not journalistic. "I do not subscribe to the view that you have all the news you need from cable by 6 at night," says ABC's emeritus news czar, Roone Arledge, who, by his count, has watched "a lot of television" while coping with illness in recent years. "So much of the cable world is people yelling at each other all the time and trying to get attention." If more and more Americans customize their news intake to their own individual interests—whether through broadband or TV time-shifting technology like TiVo—the mass audience splinters into millions of individual audiences. "The founding fathers had a town meeting in mind where we'd develop a rough consensus," says Heyward, who sees the evening news as playing that town-meeting role. "An audience of one is a different model. How do we have a national dialogue on which to base decisions for democracy?" The hope at organizations like CBS is that Americans will turn en masse to the news brands they trust when they have to, just as they did on Sept. 11. "Maybe the hearth of the evening news will grow more important," Heyward says. "There's a human desire to gather around the fire—there always has been."

But it is not just the idea of the hearth that is durable; nearly as enduring are the formats of mass culture. The novel hasn't changed much since the 19th century. TV sitcoms in 2002 are structured much as they were from the start of the medium, as are late-night talk shows, game shows and prime-time dramas. Heyward points out that even when MTV jazzes it up, its format for hard news is the standard one: "It's still anchors leading into packages by reporters."

The form is so powerful that the turnover in cast members may not matter. Though the broadcast networks have toyed with a deeper hourlong evening newscast for decades, it has never materialized, perhaps out of an instinctive sense that the mass public wants a half-hour evening news—no more, no less. The minority that wants a serious news hour or more can gravitate to PBS or NPR. Those who want continuing, incremental coverage of a breaking story can go to CNN or perhaps MSNBC (when, and if, it figures out its identity). Those who want a highly opinionated, 24-hour op-ed page can go to Fox. Those who want a comic take on the headlines can go to Comedy Central. Those who want the depth of a newspaper will either read it on paper or on the Web or check out the cable channel with which it has aligned (as *The Wall Street Journal* has with CNBC and *The Times* with the Discovery Channel). A thousand niches will bloom—thus far with audiences numbering at most in the very low single-digit millions for even the most popular of them. The networks' evening news may continue to soar far above, smaller than it once was but still profitable and with any one of the three broadcasts drawing four or five times the viewers of either Jim Lehrer or Bill O'Reilly.

Yes, the network news audience is old, but it has been for the past 25 years—and is constantly being replenished from the ranks of the formerly young. That viewership may remain loyal even if the anchors cease to be father figures or journalists but are simply plausibly intelligent messengers who show up at the same time each night and don't yell like the guys on "Crossfire" and its countless variants.

It is, after all, a comfort to know that a complicated world can be distilled into a compact and reliable daily report that, for the most part, goes down as easily as the prescription pills that are hawked in between the segments. Turn on cable TV news in the evening, and you're told that the world is about to end, over and over into the night. The evening news, in a triumph of form over content, re-stores order in a discrete half-hour. In our new, information-saturated century, there may be less need than ever for the news in the evening news. But there may be just as big a market as ever, if not more so, for its illusion of peace.

Consider the source and the audience.
- Here again is the *New York Times,* itself known as the "old gray lady" of the news world. Might that fact affect the evaluation of the nightly news in this article?
- Author Frank Rich is a middle-aged former drama critic and now political commentator for the *Times.* Might a younger person have come to a different conclusion?

Lay out the argument, the values, and the assumptions.
- Can you tell from this article what Rich's views on the role of the journalist are?
- What does Rich think is the value of the nightly news? How does he describe its symbolic role? In what ways does he think it enhances democracy in America?

Uncover the evidence.

- Is Rich arguing that the nightly news *is* alive and well, or that it *should be,* or both? What different kinds of evidence are required for each claim?
- What is Rich's evidence for his claim that the network news is not doing as badly as its critics claim?
- What is Rich's evidence for his claim that there is a democratic value to the nightly news beyond simply disseminating current events?

Evaluate the conclusion.

- Is Rich right in making the empirical claim that network news *is* surviving?
- Is he right in making the normative claim that it *should* survive—that there is an important civic function to the evening network news? Can that function be performed by other news sources, or is it unique to the nightly network coverage?

Sort out the political implications.

- What does it mean for the political world if Rich is right about the role the news should play but wrong about its viability in a modern world? Is there anything else in our mass culture that could fulfill the civic function of the news?

14.5 Mr. Hearst Answers High School Girl's Query

William Randolph Hearst, *San Francisco Examiner,* 8 October 1935

In times of war and national insecurity there are many pressures on the media, both from within government and without, to control its coverage of national affairs. In the days immediately after the September 11 terrorist attacks, President Bush's press secretary told a questioner that people needed to be very careful about what they said. Although he later retracted the statement, it was clear that he was warning people to be cautious about their comments on the government's anti-terror efforts. Journalists covering the war in Afghanistan said that there were tighter limits on the information available to them than in previous military actions they had covered. During wartime there are security concerns that obviously demand secrecy, but governments also have an incentive to use national security as an excuse to control the information and images that go out to the public. The Vietnam War is a lesson in what public opinion can do to a war effort that people do not approve of.

Media censorship is an issue that pertains not only to the war on terror, as demonstrated by this editorial letter by William Randolph Hearst, the great newspaper publisher and editor. Hearst was often blamed for contributing to the sensationalism of the news in the early decades of the last century, but, in fact, that gossipy, exaggerated, human-interest form of journalism allowed newspapers to garner sufficiently large circulations that they could afford to free themselves from the government financial support (and control) they had required before the Civil War. In this letter, written in response to a high school girl's question, Hearst makes clear that he thinks the worst fate that can befall the news is to be government controlled. Are his arguments valid today?

There is no such thing and can be no such thing as government control of NEWSPAPERS.

There may be and there is government control of publications, including daily papers.

But daily papers cease to be NEWSPAPERS as soon as they come under governmental control.

Please observe Germany and Russia and Italy, and all the nations where governments control the daily press.

Papers in such countries print only what the Government wants them to print.

The Government suppresses anything which it does not want printed; and if the editor prints anything which the Government does not approve, he goes to jail and the paper is compelled to suspend publication.

Consequently the public never get the full facts about anything.

They never get the actual NEWS.

They always get just one side of every question,—and that is the government side.

When I was last in England, I met an old friend who was London correspondent for what had once been a great German newspaper. He said:

"I have been relieved of my post and am going back to Germany."

"Good heavens," I said, "what have you done?"

"Oh," he said, "I have not done anything, but I cannot send any news from London. My editor says that he is not allowed to print any more news from or about England excepting what the German Government gives him to print.

"He cannot print the real news. He must print what the Government desires to have the people believe. Consequently he says he has no need for a news correspondent. The foreign office of the Government hands him his so-called foreign news."

Again, when I was in Germany, a paper was closed up and its editor deprived of the privilege of ever again editing a paper because he had printed in his paper some absolutely true account of occurrences that the Government did not want printed.

In Russia the same conditions prevail in more aggravated form, and more drastic degree. Editors who do

> *What was going on in Germany in the 1930s that the government would want to control?*

> *Why does the public need full facts? Why is freedom of the press valuable?*

not print what the Government wants or who print what the Government does not want are sent to Siberia or shot.

Under such circumstances, there cannot be any real news or any real newspapers.

Consequently the people never know the TRUTH.

In a despotism perhaps this does not matter much.

It would not do the people any good if they did know the truth. They could not do anything about it. The iron heel of a military dictator is on their necks.

But in a democracy the people MUST know the facts, and must know all sides of all questions.

Good government in a democracy depends upon the enlightenment of the electorate. They cannot vote right unless they are completely informed.

They must have the right to read not merely one newspaper but many newspapers, and get all the facts and shades of opinion.

Free speech and free publication are the cornerstones of democracy—the keystones of liberty.

The first step towards tyranny is the suppression of free speech, and the government control of the press.

When the Government controls the press the people no longer get true accounts of what their Government is doing; and the successive steps to tyranny come quickly and surely.

Therefore, those who advocate government control of the press advocate the downfall of democracy and the end of liberty.

> *Are there circumstances or conditions under which government control of the press is justified? If so, where do we draw the line?*

Consider the source and the audience.

- This letter appeared on the front page of Hearst's *San Francisco Examiner.* What does the front-page placement of a letter better suited for the editorial pages tell us about how Hearst regarded his message?

Lay out the argument, the values, and the assumptions.

- What is the relationship between Hearst's key values of truth and democracy? Can we have one without the other?
- What does he see as the citizen's role in democratic government? What happens if citizens are unable to perform that role?
- Would Hearst think that there are ever times when it is allowable to have government control of the press? What would happen if we did?

Uncover the evidence.

• Is Hearst's use of comparative examples persuasive? Is what happens in Germany or Russia relevant to what happens in the United States? Why or why not?

Evaluate the conclusion.

• Hearst is uncompromising in his conclusions on this subject. Is he unnecessarily harsh, or is government censorship an all-or-nothing proposition? What would he think would happen once the door to government control was opened?

Sort out the political implications.

• Are there any conditions under which censorship is permissible? When? How do we avoid setting a precedent?

CHAPTER 15

Domestic Policy

So far we have spent a good deal of time looking at governmental actors and processes, the who and the how of politics. In this chapter we turn our attention to the *what*. What is it that government does with all the personnel, resources, and rules at its disposal? What is at stake in the nitty-gritty political struggles we have examined in this book?

When all is said and done, what government does (or doesn't do) is called policy. What the U.S. government does here in the United States is domestic policy; what it does in other countries is foreign policy (the subject of our next chapter). Domestic policies can concern anything government decides is its business—transportation, drugs, security, defense, welfare, education, regulating the economy, or protecting the environment. The potential list is endless.

Some of the biggest political battles in the United States are about deciding what is government's business and, if something is an appropriate target for government action, which level of government should act. Historically the U.S. federal government had only a limited policymaking role. The Great Depression of the 1930s changed that dramatically, however, as people demanded that government do something to regulate the ailing economy, get them back to work, and provide some security for them. President Franklin Roosevelt's New Deal offered a way out of many of the social ills that plagued the country after the Depression, and it ushered in a new era of American policymaking.

Since the New Deal, in general (though in politics there are always exceptions), Democrats tend to approve a larger role for the federal government in solving social problems, and they tend to take an expansive idea of what a social problem is. They are often reluctant to leave problems in the hands of the states, fearing uneven or inadequate responses. Republicans, on the other hand, generally believe that problems should be solved first at the individual level, and then at the state level, with federal action a last resort except for such policy areas as national defense and domestic security.

Members of the two parties also differ in their constituencies, so they are often at odds about whom they think government action should assist. To give just a few examples, Democrats tend to respond to issues affecting workers, minorities, and the environment, while Republicans are more responsive to issues affecting business, religious conservatives, and the military. Another way to think about this is to consider three kinds of policies: *distributive policies,* those that benefit targeted portions of the population (homeowners, for instance, or students, or veterans) and are paid for by all taxpayers; *redistributive policies,* which shift resources from the wealthier part of the population to the less well off; and *regulatory policies,* which seek to restrict or change the actions of a business or individual. While both parties frequently support distributive policies (though they do not always agree on the groups who should be assisted), Democrats tend to favor redistributive policies, which Republicans are more likely to oppose. Democrats also favor regulation of business, while Republicans are more likely to favor regulation of personal/ religious life.

Policymaking is very tricky for lawmakers. Not only do they have to agree on the problem to be solved and on how to solve it, but they need to monitor the policy once it is made to see if the solution works and to be sure that it does not cause new, unexpected problems. All kinds of political actors are joined in the enterprise of policymaking—members of Congress, but also the president, the bureaucracy, the courts, and groups of interested citizens along with their professional organizers and lobbyists. Policymaking is the main job of American government, and all the available political resources come to be involved in it.

The selections in this chapter look at a variety of different policies. The first article, from the *Los Angeles Times,* discusses the plight of an honor student who unknowingly violated the school's "zero-tolerance" policy regarding weapons on campus. This story raises important questions about balancing the regulation of individual behavior with the protection of civil liberties, and about the unintended consequences of a well-intentioned law. The second article, from the online journal *Slate,* also focuses on regulation. It criticizes President Bush's logging policy as being both bad for the environment *and* bad for business. Kate O'Beirne's article, from the *National Review,* addresses the efforts of the Bush administration to encourage people to get married as a method of improving child welfare. The *Wall Street Journal* editorial looks at tax policy, and makes an argument about how the tax burden should be distributed in America. Finally, we provide a transcript of a radio address by President Franklin Roosevelt detailing his actions and plans for combating high unemployment during the Great Depression. In this speech we can see FDR redefining the role of government, setting the stage for many of the policy debates we have today.

15.1 Zero Tolerance Lets a Student's Future Hang on a Knife's Edge

A Utensil Fell into Taylor Hess' Pickup, Dropping Him into a Storm over School Policy

Barry Siegel, *Los Angeles Times,* 11 August 2002

In the aftermath of a wave of school violence that hit a horrible climax with the 1999 Columbine High School shootings, several states and localities decided to clean up their schools by enacting "zero-tolerance" laws designed to keep weapons off campus. These laws meant that any transgression of the rules, no matter how seemingly insignificant or unintentional, would result in a student's expulsion.

The following article from the *Los Angeles Times* shows that the best intentions can result in unexpected consequences that can return to haunt policymakers. This story profiles an honor student who was expelled for unknowingly bringing a butter knife to school. Although he was eventually readmitted to school, the case raised many questions. Why are "zero-tolerance" policies attractive to policymakers? What are their limitations? How can lawmakers control the unforeseen consequences of the policies they make?

No big deal. That's what 16-year-old Taylor Hess thought, watching the assistant principal walk into his fourth-period class.

For Taylor, life was good, couldn't be better. He was an honors student. He was a star on the varsity swim team. That morning, he'd risen at 5:30 for practice. It was agonizing, diving into the school pool before sunrise, but Taylor liked getting something done early. He also liked the individuality of his sport, how in swimming you can only blame yourself.

The assistant principal, he now realized, was looking at him. In fact, Nathaniel Hearne was pointing at him. "Get your car keys," Hearne said. "Come with me."

Taylor still thought, no big deal. Maybe he'd left his headlights on. Maybe he'd parked where he shouldn't.

"A knife has been spotted in your pickup," Hearne said.

He'd gone camping with friends on Saturday, Taylor told him. Maybe someone left a machete in the truck.

"OK," Hearne said. "We'll find out."

In the parking lot, beside the 1993 cranberry red Ford Ranger he'd worked all summer to buy, Taylor saw Alan Goss, the Hurst city policeman assigned full time to L.D. Bell High. He also saw two private security officers holding a pair of dogs trained to find drugs and weapons.

Taylor looked at the bed of his pickup. It wasn't a machete after all, but an unserrated bread knife with a round point. A long bread knife, a good 10 inches long, lying right out in the open.

Now it clicked. That's my grandma's kitchen knife, Taylor explained. She had a stroke, we had to move her to assisted living, put her stuff in our garage. Last night we took it all to Goodwill. This must have fallen out of a box. I'll lock it up in the cab. Or you can keep it. Or you can call my parents to come get it.

The others just kept staring at the knife. Taylor thought they looked confused, like they didn't know what to do.

"Is it sharp?" Hearne finally asked.

Officer Goss ran his finger along the blade. "It's fairly sharp in a couple of spots."

Hearne slipped the knife inside his sport coat. Taylor walked with him back to class, wondering what his punishment might be. Saturday detention hall, maybe. He'd never pulled D hall before, never been in any trouble.

"Get your stuff and come to my office," Hearne said. "I've got to warn you, Taylor, this is a pretty serious thing."

Beginnings at Columbine

The Hurst-Euless-Bedford Independent School District, about 12 miles west of Dallas, resembles so many others that have fashioned zero-tolerance policies to combat mounting fears of campus violence. For most districts, it began in 1994 with the federal Gun-Free Schools Act, which required all schools receiving federal aid to expel students who bring firearms to campus. Many states and school boards, appalled by the shootings that culminated in the 1999 Columbine High School massacre in Colorado, adopted policies even wider and tougher than the federal law. Everything from paper guns to nail files became weapons, everything from second-grade kisses to Tylenol tablets cause for expulsion. In countless rule books, "shall" and "must" replaced administrative discretion.

There'd been crazy situations ever since: Eighth-graders arrested for bringing "purple cocaine"—grape Kool-Aid—in lunch boxes; a sixth-grader suspended for bringing a toy ax as part of his Halloween fireman costume; a boy expelled for having a "hit list" that turned out to be his birthday party guests. Pundits clucked and civil rights lawyers protested, but for the most part, parents liked the changes, in fact campaigned for them. They wanted more rules, stricter rules. They also wanted consistency. They wanted students treated equally.

> How does "zero tolerance" achieve consistency and equality?

Jim Short, the principal of L.D. Bell High, understood all this as he sat at his desk on Monday afternoon, Feb. 25. Just minutes before, they'd found Taylor Hess' knife. Short's heart told him to ignore the matter. He knew Taylor well, thought him a great kid, a terrific young man. He believed the boy's story, he understood what had happened. He didn't believe Taylor had done anything wrong. Yet as principal, Short didn't think he could turn a blind eye.

Before him he had the Texas Education Code's Chapter 37 and his own school district's student code of conduct. They both told him the same thing: He had no latitude. There it was in the state code: A student shall be expelled . . . if the student on school property . . . possesses an illegal knife. There it was in the district code: Student will be expelled for a full calendar year. . . .

Nothing got people's attention more quickly than weapons on campus. Short appreciated this. He was 50 years old. For 26 years, he'd worked in the Abilene, Texas, schools, the last 15 as a principal, before coming to L.D. Bell this year. He knew schools could be dangerous places. An Abilene teacher had been shot on campus. Kids were good generally, but some just didn't care. If Short ignored an infraction, it could blow up in his face. If he ignored Taylor Hess' knife, people would hear about it. Then he'd be assailed for paying no heed to a big carving knife. He had to follow the rules.

Still—Short had a sick feeling. He kept asking himself, what did he expect Taylor to have done differently?

At 2 p.m. that day, Short met with five assistant principals and the Hurst police officer, Alan Goss. They traded opinions without reaching a consensus. Most, even while hoping Taylor might win a later appeal, thought the state and district codes mandated expulsion.

We don't make the laws, the way Officer Goss saw it. Their hands were tied. If he were working as a street cop, if he had pulled Taylor over and seen an illegal knife in his pickup, Goss had discretion on whether even to write a report. He'd probably let him go with a warning. But he couldn't do that on school grounds. Not under the district's zero-tolerance policy.

Short found himself sounding the most liberal. Yet he saw his colleagues' viewpoints. It seemed to him they were honorable people with different opinions. Honorable people who all left the meeting with long faces.

More voices soon chimed in. The Texas Education Agency advised that the district had to proceed against Taylor. A county prosecuting attorney said yes, this was a case he'd accept, this was a violation of the penal code.

That made a difference. Officer Goss had been expecting the prosecuting attorney to say no, don't bring it to me. Expecting—and hoping.

At 2:40 p.m., Taylor Hess, summoned from his 11th-grade advanced-placement chemistry class, stepped into the principal's office. This will all blow over, he'd been telling himself. If no one else knows, they can let it pass. He didn't feel guilty or anxious, the way you did when you knew you'd messed up. Besides, he had a history with this principal. Jim Short had been supportive of the swim team. He'd sat around with them, talking to Taylor, congratulating him for being regional backstroke champ. Short knew him, knew what kind of kid he was.

A non-event. That's what all this was, Taylor figured. A non-event.

He explained again, telling Short about his grandma's stroke, packing up her stuff, driving to Goodwill. Short appeared to believe him but still looked mighty serious. When Taylor stopped talking, Short said, "Taylor, are you aware this calls for mandatory expulsion?"

Parents' Disbelief

Robert and Gay Hess, Taylor's parents, have an unspoken rule. She doesn't call him at work unless it's urgent. She's a physical therapist's assistant at North Hills Hospital; he's a customer service manager for American Eagle airline at the Dallas–Fort Worth airport. At 3 p.m. that Monday, his pager beeped while he sat in a staff meeting. He bolted from the room to call his wife.

"You're not going to believe this," she began, sounding distraught. Taylor's principal had just phoned her. She'd realized right off what this was about. She'd explained everything to Jim Short. He'd appreciated her account, Gay thought. After all, she'd corroborated Taylor's story without knowing what Taylor had told them. Yet Gay didn't think she'd swayed the principal. This is very serious, he'd kept telling her. This is very serious.

Robert Hess tried to calm his wife. He was good at solving problems and easing tension. That's what he did all day with aggravated airline travelers. He could fix this. It was a bread knife, after all. Taylor obviously never even saw it. They were all grown-ups, weren't they?

"The school district has competent leaders," Robert told Gay. "Surely they will be fair and logical."

Late that day, he called Jim Short's office and arranged to meet with him the next afternoon. During dinner, the Hess family—Taylor has one older brother, Jordan, 17, then an L.D. Bell senior—talked things over. Gay thought it ironic that their family had always wanted to make schools safer; she'd never expected it would backfire on them. Taylor thought, this just shows that no good deed goes unpunished.

Robert Hess' mind drifted to Sunday, to their hours in the garage packing up his mother Rose's stuff. Going through everything had sparked such memories. The glassware, for instance. He was 46 now, yet there were glasses he remembered drinking from as a child, glasses his mom had used to serve Kool-Aid at Cub Scout meetings. She must have kept them, he imagined, because they took her back to a time when she was a young, beautiful woman with small children. Now 80, she sat in assisted living, unaware of Taylor's plight, for they'd chosen not to upset her.

It was funny. Robert and Gay had debated about the cutlery set. Gay had decided not to keep it, so it went into a box. Dusk fell before they finished. In the dark, Robert and Taylor drove a mile to the Goodwill center, bouncing along on the Ranger's old springs. The night drop-off area was poorly lighted, so they could barely see as they unloaded. They worked fast, eager to get home.

Don't worry, Robert Hess told his family now. Maybe Taylor will have to write an essay. Something like that. Something that fits the event.

A Word Study

Again and again, Principal Jim Short flipped through the penal code, the state code, the school code. He asked himself, how do you define "possession"? He studied the words: "knowingly" . . . "willingly" . . . "recklessly." The first two didn't apply, but "recklessly"—there were those in the district, both below and above him, who thought Taylor's conduct reckless.

Another word drew Short's attention: "shall." Shall be expelled, not "may" be expelled. . . .

Ten years ago, he would have handled the Taylor Hess situation by himself. No longer. Now Short had to talk to his district supervisors, who talked to the district superintendent, Gene Buinger. People in Buinger's office had to talk to the Texas Education Agency and local police authorities. The rules and codes kept evolving. Although the federal Gun-Free Schools Act had allowed them "case by case" flexibility, the state refined and the districts refined even further. It was Texas that required expulsion of a student with an "illegal knife," but it was Short's own district that insisted the expulsion be for a full year.

Some school administrators found it insulting or preposterous to lose personal discretion. Zero-tolerance panels at school board conferences often drew overflow crowds. There was always talk of the foolish cases. In recent years in Short's district, there'd been half a dozen as perplexing as Taylor Hess', half a dozen where district Supt. Buinger believed the punishment had been excessive. "Feel-good legislation" is what Buinger called the state laws; legislation that is "supposed to solve, but deep down, everyone knows it just addresses issues superficially."

Still, Buinger had to admit—zero-tolerance rules made life easier. They eased the burden. By applying consistency instead of subjective judgment, you had support for your actions rather than claims of discrimination. If Jim Short disregarded the Taylor Hess case and six months later a different principal responded another way with, say, a Latino student, you would surely hear cries about prejudice.

What are the advantages and disadvantages of allowing administrative discretion in enforcing rules?

That, above all, was why Short's supervisors wanted firm formulas. Their school district was in transition, undergoing "a change in demographics." It was one-third minority now, mostly Latino. There was a distinct and growing gap between poorer and more affluent students. For people to have faith in the school system, they had to believe everyone was being treated equally.

Deep down, despite his unease, Jim Short agreed. He had to admit: He derived a certain comfort in not having discretion. He could lean on that. He could then say he followed the formula.

As arranged, Robert Hess appeared in his office at 2:15 P.M. on Tuesday. Assistant Principal Nathaniel Hearne joined them. So did the Hurst police officer, Alan Goss. Hess sat down, ready to settle this as he did most problems. Right off, though, Short handed him a letter and asked him to sign a receipt for it.

For the first time, Hess began to feel a little nervous. "Wait a minute," he said. "Let me read it."

This letter is to notify you that your son, Ryan Taylor Hess, is being considered for expulsion from L.D. Bell High School. . . . We have scheduled a Due Process Hearing for Friday, March 1 at 9:00 A.M. . . .

Hess' nervousness grew. This looked more significant than he'd expected. He asked, "Would I be overreacting if I brought an attorney?"

"I can't say," Short told him. "But if you do, you need to notify us so we have ours too."

The principal felt he owed it to Hess to be truthful. Short himself would preside at the due process hearing, he explained. He'd be following the code of conduct. It would be unlikely that he'd be able to recommend anything but expulsion.

Hess, normally easy with conversation, sat speechless. OK, he thought, OK. This has gone a step or two further than he'd expected. But surely they'd resolve this at the hearing. They just needed to prepare; they just needed to get ready.

They needed to do one other thing, Robert Hess decided. They needed to call a lawyer.

Quizzing the Educators

A door at the rear of the principal's office leads into a private conference room. There everyone gathered at 9 A.M. Friday, settling around a rectangular table. On the table, a tape recorder turned silently. Facing the Hess family now, along with Short, Hearne and Goss, was Dianne Byrnes, who directs the district's "alternative education programs" for problem kids.

This wouldn't be adversarial, Short had advised. Yet it seemed that way to the Hesses. Taylor felt numb, in shock, ready for anything. He talked little, trying instead to grasp what was going on. Same with his mother, who couldn't believe this was even happening. Mainly, Robert Hess spoke for the family.

He'd been preparing for two days, studying the codes, scouring the Internet, consulting an attorney, drafting specific questions for each person present. Whoever loses his temper, he reminded himself, is at a disadvantage. So he spoke politely, without a hint of antagonism, something that Short noted and appreciated. Yet as they walked through the facts of the case, Hess poured on the questions, unrelenting.

You don't have the knife or a photo of the knife at this hearing? You don't have a copy of the police report? You're sitting here today without any of the evidence? Do you really think these proceedings are fair? Do you really feel you're following the spirit of the law? Do any of you in the least doubt the truth of Taylor's explanation? What are your feelings about the school district's zero-tolerance policies? How do you feel about what you're doing to Taylor?

Dianne Byrnes, who wrote the district's code of conduct and spends most of her time on matters of discipline, took the hardest line. Her stance made the Hess family feel uncomfortable. "Taylor did have a knife visible in his truck . . . ," she said. "Taylor did put students at risk. . . . The spirit of the law is to ensure the safety of students. . . . I think there was a risk factor."

Jim Short sounded much more ambivalent. Where Byrnes resisted questions about personal feelings, he responded. He thought zero-tolerance policies "a two-edged sword." They made it possible for him to "look myself in the mirror and know that I treated the students as equally as I possibly could." On the other hand, the policies "make you feel like you lose some judgment." So it was for him "a love-hate thing."

Short turned to Hess. "I don't know if that answers your question."

Hess said, "Yes, you answered it eloquently. I can appreciate how frustrating it must be to have your hands tied."

Short sighed. "I'd be lying if I said any aspect of this is pleasant. This is a sorrowful experience."

As they talked, Hess kept looking for signs. No one else had files or questions or evidence. They've already made their decision, he concluded. Reading their body language, he believed he saw people eager to go. To him, Dianne Byrnes seemed particularly antsy, glancing often at her watch. She had another appointment, she declared finally. They would have to postpone this hearing.

"No," Robert Hess said. "We're not through."

Short eventually sided with Hess. At 11 A.M., two hours into the hearing, Dianne Byrnes left. Hess seized the opportunity. Again he asked Short how he felt.

"Miserable," the principal said, with a rueful laugh. "How's that?" He paused. "There's not a good feeling in my body about this."

Half an hour later, they all rose. Short usually ruled right away in these situations, but not today. "I want to think about this over the weekend," he told the Hess family.

Doing the "Right Thing"

Late on Monday afternoon, Robert Hess called the L.D. Bell office. "I need another day," Jim Short told him. "I want to make sure we do the right thing for Taylor and for the student population of Bell High."

Hess' heart sank. Right thing for the student population. Oh my God, he thought. They're going to expel Taylor.

That night he warned his family. Taylor reeled. He'd been in turmoil for a week. Like his principal, he'd been wondering why he hadn't just denied any knowledge of the knife. It hadn't occurred to him, though. There'd been no reason to lie. Besides, he'd always been taught to tell the truth.

Taylor had career plans. He wanted to get a private pilot's license; he wanted to study aeronautical engineering. Now what would happen? Taylor couldn't help but think this whole thing made the school administrators look cowardly. Nobody was asking, what should we do? Instead, everyone was asking, what do we have to do?

The call from Short finally came at 3:15 P.M. Tuesday. "I've decided to expel Taylor," the principal told Robert Hess. "You can appeal. I encourage you to appeal. If you do, I'll be one of Taylor's biggest advocates." Short also asked, "Do you want me to tell Taylor, or should you?"

"We'll both tell him," Hess said. "I'm on my way there." . . .

In Short's office, Hess and the principal swapped letters.

Legalese filled Short's: "This is to inform you of my decision to recommend expulsion of Ryan Taylor Hess from L.D. Bell High School."

Hess' cited a federal appellate court ruling in another zero-tolerance case: A school administrator that executed such an action could be held personally liable and would not have the luxury of his qualified immunity.

Hess vainly implored Short to reconsider. Hess said, "Mr. Short, the only thing that can happen from this point on is, this could get bigger and uglier."

Short replied, "I'll try not to take that as a threat." Yet to himself, he thought: This man is just being an advocate for his child. I would do exactly the same.

They called Taylor in. He'd been waiting in the anteroom, summoned once again from his advanced-placement chemistry class. Short explained his decision. Taylor felt gut-punched, stung with pain. All my hard work shot to hell, he thought. Honors classes, the swim team, all a waste of time. He held his tongue, though. Jim Short thought him amazingly courteous.

The principal let Taylor stay at L.D. Bell for two more days, Wednesday and Thursday. Taylor told all his friends now, after keeping things mostly to himself. A couple of teachers had him get up, explain to the class. He asked his English teacher to spread the word wider, to tell other students. Taylor preferred that everyone hear the true story rather than think he'd gone and stabbed someone. . . .

Debate Goes Public

On the Thursday afternoon of spring break, district Supt. Gene Buinger arrived home to find a note on his front door. It was from Monica Mendoza, a reporter for the *Fort Worth Star-Telegram*. Robert Hess had contacted her, she advised, and had provided her a tape recording of Taylor's due process hearing. She'd be writing a story for the Sunday paper. Did Buinger want to respond?

Buinger had heard about the Taylor Hess case. There were 20,000 students in his district, though, 30 schools in all, so he didn't have a complete grasp of the matter. His first response to the reporter's note was surprise—surprise that the Hess family had gone to a newspaper. In his 20 years as a superintendent, that had never happened. Most parents didn't want the notoriety. The Hesses were waiving lots of confidentiality rights.

That didn't mean Buinger believed he could waive confidentiality. He declined to comment to the reporter, explaining that federal law prevented him from responding. Then he braced himself for the article.

Jim Short's phone rang at 4:30 that Sunday morning. You going to call off school? an anonymous voice inquired. Short didn't know what the man was talking about. He was still in bed and hadn't seen the newspaper. The caller explained: They're going to have lots of sharp pencils out.

By 10 that morning, the onslaught had begun, mostly directed at Short. Phone calls, e-mails, radio talk shows, TV cameras, CNN, NBC—from all quarters, pundits and outraged citizens were lambasting him. He'd never imagined being the subject of radio talk shows; he'd never grasped the full might of the Internet.

Zero tolerance is a cop-out. Here my tax dollars are paying a principal to not use his judgment. . . . Ludicrous . . . I am so disgusted. . . . Not only insane, but cruel and unnecessary. . . . Any administrator who supports this should resign immediately. . . .

Other messages scared Short even more. The loudest voices came not from civil libertarians but from the antigovernment, right-to-bear-arms crowd. Free men are armed, slaves are disarmed. The Constitution guarantees the right of the people to bear arms. . . . You're just a bunch of left-wing nazi indoctrinators. . . . Take away the arms and you break a nation.

Most damaging of all were the Hess family's comments. They were doing back-to-back interviews now, filling TV screens by the hour. It had been their attorney's idea to contact the news media. They agreed, seeing no other alternative, but called only the one Fort Worth reporter. They'd not expected the enormous response. They'd not realized that people would sense this could happen to their own kids, to anyone. The feedback felt good to the Hess family, but also scary. "We're just regular working folks," Robert Hess kept saying. "We're not used to TV trucks and reporters outside our door. This feels so alien."

> Why did Robert Hess choose to follow this media strategy? What were the advantages of "going public"? Would all students trapped in Taylor Hess' situation have access to the same strategy?

All the same, they handled it with aplomb. Hess observed that "an act of being a good Samaritan now has this fine young man expelled from school. . . . Having zero tolerance doesn't mean having zero judgment or zero rights." Taylor, amid bashful shrugs, said, "Somehow a knife had to fall out. A fork couldn't fall out, a spoon couldn't fall out. . . . It's criminal trespass if I go on campus, which means I can't see my brother graduate."

Gene Buinger and Jim Short realized there was no way to look good. Truth was, they didn't feel good. Buinger thought of his old Marine adage: There's a time when you have to stand at attention and take it.

By Tuesday, though, he'd decided to respond. The school district called a news conference for 2 P.M., timed to make the evening news. Buinger still wouldn't discuss the details of the Hess case, but he wanted to explain the state laws and district codes that mandated their zero-tolerance policy. With printed handouts and a big-screen PowerPoint presentation, he emphasized the "musts" and "shalls."

"We're very limited in what we can do," he said. "I understand the public's frustration. I'm frustrated too. . . . Individuals opposed to such policies should take their concerns to their respective state legislators."

Watching from the back of the hall, Robert Hess thought Buinger handled himself well. The superintendent had said something about possibly being able to shorten the expulsion because the offense involved a knife, not a gun. Hess sensed that Buinger was trying to find a way out.

The outcry wouldn't stop, though. Hess couldn't believe the momentum. The national newspapers were calling him now, alerted by a story distributed by Associated Press. The school district was getting crucified. The Hurst Police Department had backed away, deciding not to file a complaint with the county prosecutor. So had the Texas Education Agency, telling AP that local districts did have discretion, that "every case has to be looked at individually."

Enough, the Hess family resolved. For Taylor, the first couple of times on TV had been neat, but the back-to-back interviews lost their sparkle real quick. For his father, it began to feel like piling on. When would it just become cruel? It wasn't his intent to ruin the school system, to hurt these people's careers. He just wanted Taylor back in school.

He would turn down further interviews, Hess decided. He'd take all the reporters' phone numbers, stick them in his hip pocket. If his family lost their appeal, scheduled for Thursday at 11 A.M., he could always pull them out again.

By Wednesday night, that didn't seem likely. Early in the evening, the phone rang at the Hess home. It was an assistant superintendent in Gene Buinger's office. Would the Hesses be agreeable to a 9 A.M. meeting, he wondered, before the scheduled appeal? The district had some ideas. The district thought matters maybe could be resolved.

Finding a Way to Bend

In the end, it all came down to what had been lacking, to what everyone said the law didn't allow: personal judgment.

The federal Gun-Free Schools Act had always included a clause specifying that state laws "shall" allow school superintendents to modify expulsion requirements. The Texas Education Agency, in a letter to district administrators, had made clear that the term of expulsions "may be reduced from the statutory one year." Yet it was the Hurst-Euless-Bedford district's own code that governed in the Hess case—and like many others across the country, the HEB district had handcuffed itself by mandating inflexible one-year expulsions.

Now, one day before the Hesses' appeal, Gene Buinger decided to remove the self-imposed handcuffs. He'd simply waive district policy; he'd rescind the expulsion. Following a conversation with the Texas Education Agency's school safety division, he thought he could do that, especially since the police had never filed a complaint. And if he could do that, why even hold an appeal hearing?

When the Hesses arrived at his office on Friday morning, Buinger began to explain his plan. Just then, however, an assistant came in carrying a newly arrived fax from the state agency's legal department. No, the fax advised, Buinger couldn't rescind the expulsion. He could only reduce the expulsion to time served.

Buinger wasn't sure whether the Hesses would buy this. He shared with them the conflicting advice he'd received. This does call for expulsion, he said, but we can adjust the amount of time. Is that OK with you?

Robert Hess had a typed list of conditions. "Yes," he said. "If we can agree on these."

The Hesses wanted Taylor readmitted immediately to L.D. Bell, his record expunged of any reference to the expulsion, tutorials to help him catch up on missed classes and a public announcement of the resolution. Buinger's staff readily agreed, but since it was already Thursday, they thought Taylor should come back to Bell on Monday.

No, Robert Hess said. Tomorrow.

Applause greeted the announcement, at an 11 A.M. joint news conference, that Taylor Hess would be returning to L.D. Bell the next morning. Taylor said it hadn't been "a pleasant experience, but I hold no personal grudges." Robert Hess said, "What I was hoping for is exactly what I got." Gene Buinger said, "Zero-tolerance policies have become excessive. . . . The school board is now undertaking a complete review of district policy. We want to give as much discretion as possible to local administrators so we don't have to repeat this situation."

In time, the district would revise its policy, among other things ending the mandatory one-year term for expulsions. All that remained unresolved were the fundamental reasons for zero-tolerance policies in the first place. Gene Buinger knew as much; he knew that if another student had lifted the knife from Taylor's pickup and used it in an altercation, they would have endured an even more impassioned response. He knew also what he would hear in the next knife-on-campus case: I want the same as Taylor Hess. If I don't get the same, it's discrimination.

There were no simple answers. Still, returning to L.D. Bell after the final news conference, Jim Short saw one thing clearly. This day happened to be the occasion for another random security sweep of the campus, complete with drug-sniffing dogs. There they were, out on the parking lot, just as they were the morning they spotted Taylor's knife. This crew had never found drugs, hardly ever weapons. Littering and tardiness had been the biggest problems at Bell all year.

"No thank you," Short told the dog handlers. "You're not going to do this today. Stay out of the parking lot. Stay out of our classes."

Consider the source and the audience.

- Why would a national newspaper like the *Los Angeles Times* run a story about a small town in Texas?
- This is a human-interest story with lots of personal detail. How does that fact affect your feelings about it? Can you tell where the author's sympathies lie?

Lay out the argument, the values, and the assumptions.

- The people advocating zero-tolerance laws and those opposing them are both concerned about "fairness," but they define it differently. What are the two definitions of "fairness" at work here?
- How do values like safety, flexibility, due process, and equality figure into the arguments made by each side? What tradeoffs among them does each side make?

Uncover the evidence.

- How does Siegel know what happened, who thought what, and who said what to whom? What motives might his sources have had in talking to him?
- What evidence do the two sides bring to bear in making their cases for and against the policy?

Evaluate the conclusion.

- The advocates of zero tolerance believe that schools can be safe, and students treated fairly, only if all transgressions of the no-weapons rule are swiftly and evenly met with expulsion. Opponents also want safety and fairness, but they want administrators to be able to use discretion in applying sanctions. Can either side get what it wants?
- What are the implications of this article for zero-tolerance policies? Are such implications clearly stated?

Sort out the political implications.

- Ultimately, even with a zero-tolerance policy in place, Taylor Hess was treated differently due to the individual circumstances of his case, his own personal merits, and the advantages his family could bring to his defense. What is the lesson here for the makers of zero-tolerance policies?

15.2 Dead Wood

The Lousy Economics of Bush's Forest Policy

Douglas Gantenbein, *Slate,* 4 December 2002

Republicans are generally thought to be the pro-business party and when business interests clash with environmental concerns, it is business that is supposed to come out on top. In a regular *Slate* feature called "Hey, Wait a Minute: The Conventional Wisdom Debunked," journalist Douglas Gantenbein challenges the rationale of a recent Bush administration forestry proposal as being not only bad for the environment but bad for business as well. What does he think is the true motivation for Bush's policy?

One day before Thanksgiving, when the only environmental issue anyone was paying attention to was turkey depopulation, the Bush administration quietly declared an enormous change in how the government will manage its 192 million acres of national forests. Billed as a way to "streamline" planning in the forests, the Bush proposal would, among other things:

- Allow local forest managers to decide if logging and grazing deserve as much weight as protecting animals or birds;
- drop a 25-year-old requirement that forest-management plans contain detailed environmental impact statements;
- set the stage for reducing requirements that the Forest Service protect plant and animal diversity in the forests.

It's perhaps true, as Forest Service officials claim, that current forest-management rules are too complex and costly to administer. But if so, it's equally true that the proposed rule changes are essentially an effort to open national forests to more logging than they have seen in years.

How will these proposals open the national forests to more logging?

Among those with fingerprints on the proposal is Mark Rey, the undersecretary of agriculture who runs the Forest Service. Rey was a longtime foe of logging regulations on national forests, primarily as vice president of the American Forest and Paper Association, an industry trade group that bitterly fought logging cutbacks during the early '90s. "This is a timber industry proposal, pure and simple," Charles Wilkinson, a University of Colorado law professor, told the *Denver Post.*

But the real problem with the logging changes is not that they are pro-timber industry, it's that they are economic nonsense. It's curious that an administration that is so business-friendly would take measures that actually would hurt business, let alone dozens of small towns across the West. But that's exactly what would happen.

For starters, the last thing the United States needs right now is more lumber. Despite the continued housing boom, lumber itself is as cheap as it has ever been. Two years ago, for instance, the lumber required to build a new home might have cost about $12,000. Today that same lumber package would run about $7,500.

Despite a tariff on Canadian lumber, wood from north of the border is inexpensive and plentiful. The continued strength of the U.S. dollar, meanwhile, has encouraged timber imports from Europe. At the same time, the strong dollar has discouraged exports to Japan, which once bought millions of board feet per year taken from private U.S. timberlands (exports of logs from national forests are banned). That privately owned timber also is finding its way onto the U.S. market, adding to the glut.

And on a per-capita basis, Americans simply use less wood than they once did. Today new homes are built with big pieces of wood made by gluing together little pieces of wood, a process that saves big, mature trees from the chainsaw. Some "wood" isn't even wood—many homes now have siding made with a mix of concrete and sawdust. In many new homes, the only traditional sawn lumber may be the cheap 2-by-4 studs used for framing, and sometimes steel studs replace even those.

More important, the proposals represent an archaic understanding of the Western economy. The policy is designed to help a West traumatized by the spotted owl and salmon logging cutbacks of the '90s. But this West doesn't need the help.

Logging is an extractive industry. Even during boom times, lumber towns never really prospered. They didn't attract other businesses or investment because they were designed to be more or less temporary, since they were mowing down their chief resource: trees.

For many parts of the West, it was only when logging was curtailed in the late '80s and early '90s that things picked up. That's because standing trees—which attract tourists, well-heeled fly-fishers, and retirees looking for a home in the country—are worth more than cut trees. Thomas Power, an economist with the University of Montana, says that by the late '90s, eight of 10 national forests in Montana generated three times as much income from tourism and recreation as they did from cutting down trees.

Typical of the West's new economic order are companies such as North Fork Anglers, founded by fishing guide Tim Wade in Cody, Wyo., in 1984. Today the shop employs 15 retail employees and guides and hosts as many as 400 fishers a year who pay $150 a day for the privilege of wetting a line, fill Cody's hotel rooms and restaurants, and add to the coffers of United and Delta airlines. Moreover, Wade's company is theoretically permanent. It is not destroying the rivers. Loggers, by contrast, are paid to decimate the very thing that keeps them employed.

But perhaps the Bush administration's rule changes really are not about economics. In conservative circles logging is a bellwether issue, a club with which to beat Bill Clinton, the Sierra Club, and the heavy hand of government in general. Logging is a kind of religious issue: Conservatives take it on faith that cutting down trees is good for business. But the economics of the West during the past 20 years argues that it isn't.

> In what way would the West have been traumatized by environmental policy in a Democratic era, what Gantenbein refers to as "the spotted owl and salmon logging cutbacks of the '90s"? How would the Bush policy ease that "trauma"?

> From the context, what does "bellwether" seem to mean? Although its modern meaning is "trend setting," it comes from the word for a sheep with a bell around its neck that leads the rest of the flock. Does Gantenbein mean this word in its neutral or its more negative sense?

Consider the source and the audience.

- As we know, *Slate* is a journal with an ideological mix. The column this article appeared in is specifically dedicated to turning the conventional wisdom upside down. How does it claim to do that here?

Lay out the argument, the values, and the assumptions.

- What are the two main reasons why Gantenbein thinks Bush's proposals are "economic nonsense"?
- Is Gantenbein sympathetic to the loggers or to the environmentalists? What can you tell about his values?
- What does Gantenbein suggest is the real motivation for Bush's policy?

Uncover the evidence.

- What different kinds of evidence does Gantenbein provide? Are economic data, expert testimony, and anecdotal examples enough? Would any additional evidence strengthen his case?

Evaluate the conclusion.

- Does Gantenbein's reasons why Bush's proposal are "economic nonsense" make sense?
- If Gantenbein's evaluation of the logging industry and the Western economy are correct, does it follow that Bush's proposal is bad for the economy?
- If the answer to that is "yes," does it mean that Gantenbein's ideological explanation must be correct?

Sort out the political implications.

- If the person who runs the Forest Service in the Bush administration is a former employee of a logging industry trade group, what kind of forestry policy would we expect to see made? What kinds of people would a Democratic president be likely to appoint to such a post?

15.3 Altared States

Bush Tries to Promote Marriage Through Welfare Reform

Kate O'Beirne, *National Review,* 6 May 2002

The United States has long had an uneasy relationship with welfare policy. Compared with other advanced industrial countries, it has offered relatively meager benefits available only to those who pass stringent means tests. Means tests require potential welfare recipients to prove that they are sufficiently poor and unable to provide for themselves before they can receive government assistance. U.S. welfare has been criticized for being demeaning and degrading to recipients, on the one hand, and for discouraging marriage and offering no incentives to get people back to work, on the other. Reform in 1996 aimed to remove at least some of these objections—in part, by requiring recipients to get a job and limiting the period of time they can collect benefits. As a result of the reforms and the economic prosperity of the 1990s, the number of people on welfare declined.

This article by Kate O'Beirne addresses an argument frequently made by some conservative critics of U.S. welfare policy, including President Bush, that government ought to actively encourage marriage as a way of alleviating the problem of child poverty. Should government action tackle a private concern like marriage? What problems are fair game for government action and which ones should be off-limits?

The experience of decades makes clear that welfare and non-marriage go together like a horse and carriage. Forty percent of children with single mothers are poor—five times the rate of children with married parents—so President Bush proposes that the federal government get into the business of promoting marriage in order to reduce welfare dependency. In the next round of reform, the president declares, "stable families should be the central goal of American welfare policy."

Predictably, the initiative has been condemned by the government-friendly Left: *The American Prospect*'s Robert Kuttner has derided its goal as "shotgun welfare betrothals." Also not surprisingly, a recent Pew Research Center poll found that marriage-friendly conservatives object to government meddling in this private relationship: Almost 80 percent of Americans—and 60 percent of "highly committed" white evangelicals—object to the government's encouraging people to marry. This latest example of Bush's activist conservative agenda is meeting the same fate as its predecessor, the plan to increase the role of faith-based charities by federally funding their good works: Liberals are objecting to the goal, and conservatives have reservations about the means.

> What does O'Beirne mean when she says that liberals object to the goal and conservatives to the means?

The 1996 welfare reform has shown remarkable success in putting welfare recipients to work: The rolls are down by over 50 percent, and three-quarters of single mothers are now employed. But there has been only modest success in achieving the reform law's other key goal: the reduction of out-of-wedlock births and the "formation and encouragement of two-parent families." Only a handful of states have heeded Washington's call to implement programs aimed at promoting marriage among the poor. West Virginia pays a $100 monthly bonus to married welfare families, while Michigan and Utah offer classes and videos on marriage and parenting skills. Oklahoma has the most ambitious program, involving churches, social-service agencies, and the business community in extolling the importance of marriage and the harmful effects of divorce. (It's too early to tell whether there has been any payoff from these state efforts.) The administration now proposes setting aside $300 million to induce other states to launch their own experiments to encourage "healthy, two-parent married families."

Conservatives—and many liberals—can at least agree on what the problem is: The evidence that children are far better off being raised by their married, biological parents is overwhelming. Studies consistently show that children living in broken or never-formed families are more likely to have emotional and behavioral problems, fail in school, be physically abused, be involved in crime, and wind up on welfare as adults. Children have clearly suffered as a result of a federal welfare system that for decades subsidized single parents and penalized marriage. With subsidies

> <u>Do</u> conservatives and many liberals agree on what the problem is? How should we decide what social problems need to be addressed?

inevitably increasing the behavior Washington was paying for, and modern cultural norms dictating that no stigma attach to illegitimacy and single motherhood, the number of out-of-wedlock births soared.

The media image notwithstanding, unmarried mothers are far more likely to be high-schoolers than Wall Street lawyers haunted by the ticking of their biological clocks. Although teen pregnancy and birth rates have declined over the past ten years, the U.S. still has the highest rates of teen pregnancy and birth in the fully industrialized world. Four out of ten all-American girls become pregnant at least once before they celebrate their 20th birthdays. About 80 percent of teen mothers are unmarried, and 75 percent are on welfare within five years.

Early, unmarried motherhood typically gives birth to poverty and welfare dependency. Half of all welfare recipients had their first baby as a teenager. Robert Rector of the Heritage Foundation logically concludes that the "collapse of marriage is the principal cause of child poverty." He estimates that federal and state spending in means-tested aid for single-parent families amounts to about $150 billion a year. Rector also recognizes the inherent anti-marriage bias in means-tested welfare programs that offer cash and services to low-income single mothers, and that reduce benefits upon marriage to a working husband.

Because he doesn't see Washington dismantling this means-tested welfare system anytime soon, Rector thinks it's about time the federal government spent a fraction of what it spends on single-parent families on an effort to reduce the number of such families. But here's where it gets complicated: How exactly does the government expect $300 million to counteract the anti-marriage effects of the $150 billion it spends on means-tested programs? No one knows. Ron Haskins of the Brookings Institution, a veteran welfare analyst who is advising the administration on welfare reform, explains, "We know that marriage is important, but we don't know how to promote it, so we want to put money out and see what we learn."

The hope is that just as the welfare culture was shifted toward an appreciation of the importance of work and self-sufficiency, it can also be taught to value the benefits of marriage. A comprehensive study of the 1996 reform by the Nelson A. Rockefeller Institute of Government marvels at the success of state welfare agencies in adopting the "work first" demands of the law. Welfare offices are adorned with banners proclaiming, "Welcome Job Seekers!" and "Life Works If You Work First." But the researchers caution that state workers—who have little trouble demanding that others work—are likely to be less enthusiastic in touting the importance of marriage. A New York City official pointed out: "Ninety percent of our workers are themselves single parents and identify on that point with their clients."

Can government legislate values?

Isabel Sawhill, Haskins's colleague at the Brookings Institution and president of the National Campaign to Prevent Teen Pregnancy, doesn't dispute the demon-

strable benefits for children of having married parents, but thinks that the failure
to marry is not the problem. She notes that 90 percent of American women are
married by the age of 45, but women in their mid-twenties are more likely to have
children than to be married—so Sawhill believes that the problem that must be addressed is early childbearing. Rather than encourage marriage, she says, we should
"stop people from having babies before they get married."

Research shows that this is a plausible idea: Teen marriages are especially unstable, and once a woman becomes a single mother her prospects for marriage
to anyone other than the baby's father are slim. Sawhill advocates that welfare offices keep doing what they're doing; she cites evidence that the demands that
young mothers work, and that young men pay child support, have already contributed to the (modest) decline in the number of single-parent families.

Making welfare more demanding has the indirect—but quite logical—effect
of making single motherhood less appealing. Indeed, as we have learned, the attempt to discourage single motherhood is *always* indirect: The proponents of
marriage, beginning with President Bush, dare not extol its benefits without first
paying tribute to the nobility of single mothers. There is no taste for the hard
truths, even among the boosters of wedded bliss. But until the culture is willing
to stigmatize unmarried sex and the irresponsibility of single mothers who risk
damaging their children by failing to marry before giving birth, it's difficult to
see how the number of illegitimate (whoops!) children then will be significantly
reduced. If single mothers bore the social stigma of smokers, children would be
far better off.

Consider the source and the audience.

- The *National Review* is a conservative journal. Is there a single conservative view represented here? What disagreements among conservatives does O'Beirne reveal?

Lay out the argument, the values, and the assumptions.

- O'Beirne assumes some common values among her readers. What are they?
- What "hard truths" does she think need to be acknowledged?
- What role does she think government should play in solving the problem of child welfare?
  What roles does she reject? Why?

Uncover the evidence.

- O'Beirne mentions lots of evidence and research. What additional information would
  allow us to evaluate that evidence?
- Is her evidence open to more than one interpretation? Do we have enough information
  to tell?

Evaluate the conclusion.

- Is it government's business to encourage people to marry? Is active encouragement the
  same as removing obstacles?
- If government does nothing to encourage people to marry, is that a policy choice in and of
  itself?

Sort out the political implications.

• What would it be like to live under a government that did the things that O'Beirne wants it to do? If it were up to policymakers to encourage people to marry, what other tasks might they undertake?

15.4 The Non-Taxpaying Class

Editorial, *Wall Street Journal,* 20 November 2002

Here's a brief lesson on taxes: Like many countries the United States has a progressive income tax, which means that the more you make, the higher the tax rate your marginal income (the amount over a certain level) is subject to. For instance, a head of household with a taxable income of $350,000/year pays 10 percent on the first $10,000; 15 percent on the income from $10,000 to $37,450; 27 percent on the income from $37,451 to $96,700; 30 percent on the income from $96,701 to $156,600; 35 percent on the income from $156,601 to $307,050; and 38.6 percent on all income over $307,051. A person who makes only $30,000 a year, on the other hand, is never taxed above the 15 percent rate.

On the other hand, payroll taxes, such as the amount we pay for Social Security and Medicare, are not progressive. Everyone pays exactly the same percentage of their income up to $87,000 (in 2003). Payroll taxes are regressive, meaning that those with less than $87,000 in wages pay a higher percentage of their income in payroll tax than do those with wages of more than $87,000. Some of the working poor get a percentage of this back in the form of the "earned income tax credit."

In this *Wall Street Journal* editorial, the author is arguing that poor people do not pay enough taxes—that the tax burden is borne disproportionately by the rich. This argument was made by a number of conservative commentators, including some in the Bush administration, immediately before Bush released his 2003 economic plan, which proposed to eliminate the estate tax and the dividend tax—two taxes that predominantly affect the very well-to-do. What would be their motivation for making this argument at that time?

The stars look to be in perfect alignment for tax relief. With a GOP majority in both houses of Congress, the Bush Administration is making eager and energetic noises, and the economy is in what Fed Chairman Greenspan calls a soft spot.

But as the Republicans construct their tax plan, there is a large and underappreciated fact they would do well to keep in mind. Over the past decade or so, fewer and fewer Americans have been paying income taxes and still fewer have been paying a significant percentage of income in taxes. While we would opt for a perfect world in which everybody paid far less in taxes, our increasingly two-tiered tax system is undermining the political consensus for cutting taxes at all.

Even the barest of glances at tax data reveal a system that is steeply progressive. Tax revenue has been increasingly squeezed out of top earners. According to the most recent data, from 1999, the richest—with income above half a million dollars—constituted 0.5% of taxpayers but accounted for 28% of total tax revenue. Simply put, a tiny group of people (553,380) were responsible for more than one-quarter of the income tax take of $877 billion.

Well, maybe you're saying—so what? They can afford it. Then take a look at those who aren't Richie Rich. The most recent data from the IRS, in 2000, show that the top 5% coughed up more than half of total tax revenue. Specifically, we are talking about folks with adjusted gross incomes of $128,336 and higher being responsible for 56% of the tax take. Eyebrows raised? There's more. The top 50% of taxpayers accounted for almost all income tax revenue—96% of the total take.

> The author says that people besides "Richie Rich"—for instance those with adjusted gross incomes of $128,336 and higher—are taxed unfairly. What is the _Journal's_ definition of a rich person?

These numbers are more arresting when compared with the situation 14 years earlier. In 1986, the top 1% paid 26% of revenue, the top 5% was responsible for 42% and the top half contributed 93%. And what about the bottom half of taxpayers? They accounted for 7% of the total in 1986 but only 4% in 2000.

This skewed reality is the result of a growing number of absolutely legal escape hatches. Consider what happens to those in the lowest bracket. Say a person earns $12,000. After subtracting the personal exemption, the standard deduction and assuming no tax credits, then applying the 10% rate of the lowest bracket, the person ends up paying a little less than 4% of income in taxes. It ain't peanuts, but not enough to get his or her blood boiling with tax rage.

> Why does the author want the poorer taxpayer's blood to boil?

Of course, lower-income workers are on the hook for the payroll tax—but a sizable group slip free from even that net tax liability via the refundable earned income tax credit. ("Refundable" means even if your net income tax liability is zero, the government still writes you a check.)*

---

*The earned income tax credit is a refundable credit for low-income workers; it is determined by income and family size. To qualify in 2002, earned income and adjusted gross income must be less than $33,178 for filers with more than one qualifying child ($34,178 for "married filing jointly"); $29,201 for filers with one qualifying child ($30,201 for "married filing jointly"); and $11,060 for filers without a qualifying child ($12,060 for "married filing jointly"). There are many restrictions—for example, the credit does not apply to married couples who file separately, to these who exclude foreign income, or to individuals who have more than $2,550 in investment income—and claims are heavily audited by the IRS.

These numbers represent only people who have a positive adjusted gross income. In 1999, there were 127 million tax filers, 94.5 million of whom showed an income tax liability. That is, 26% had no liability at all. The actual number of people filing without paying comes to 16 million (after subtracting those getting earned income tax credits and thus, presumably, still somewhat sensitive to tax rates). So almost 13% of all workers have no tax liability and so are indifferent to income tax rates. And that doesn't include another 16.5 million who have some income but don't file at all.

Who are these lucky duckies? They are the beneficiaries of tax policies that have expanded the personal exemption and standard deduction and targeted certain voter groups by introducing a welter of tax credits for things like child care and education. When these escape hatches are figured against income, the result is either a zero liability or a liability that represents a tiny percentage of income. The 1986 tax reform, for example, with its giant increase in the personal exemption and standard deduction, took six to seven million people off the tax rolls.

Are Americans with incomes so low that they're exempt from taxes really "lucky"? Are the poor the only ones who can end up paying no taxes?

This complicated system of progressivity and targeted rewards is creating a nation of two different tax-paying classes: those who pay a lot and those who pay very little. And as fewer and fewer people are responsible for paying more and more of all taxes, the constituency for tax cutting, much less for tax reform, is eroding. Workers who pay little or no taxes can hardly be expected to care about tax relief for everybody else. They are also that much more detached from recognizing the costs of government.

All of which suggests that the last thing the White House should do now is come up with more exemptions, deductions and credits that will shrink the tax-paying population even further.

Consider the source and the audience.

- The *Wall Street Journal* is a highly respected business newspaper. Its editorial writers are known for their conservative viewpoints. What does that fact tell us about the kind of argument this is, and the audience it is likely to be directed to?

Lay out the argument, the values, and the assumptions.

- Does this writer think that taxes are a good thing or a bad thing?
- What reasons would lie behind the writer's evident dislike for progressive taxation?
- Why does the writer think that poor people should pay a larger share of taxes? Is it simply because that outcome would be more just, or is there another reason?

Uncover the evidence.

- The writer cites many figures to support the contention that the rich are overtaxed and the poor undertaxed. Would any additional figures help us evaluate his or her claim?
- Does the writer offer an objective treatment of the evidence provided in this editorial? In the writer's discussion of the 26 percent of Americans with no tax liability at all, why does he or she mention the poor but not other groups who might claim exempt status by offsetting their often considerable income with losses from certain kinds of business activities?

Evaluate the conclusion.

- Would the constituency for tax-cutting grow if the poor were taxed more? Would it encourage poor people to protest high taxes if they paid more taxes themselves? Would it make any difference politically if poorer Americans joined in the demand for lower taxes?

Sort out the political implications.

- Many people who make the argument presented here add that if poor people paid more in taxes, they wouldn't be so likely to demand government services (knowing that they would be responsible for paying for them). Does this variation of the argument make sense to you? Why do people demand services for government? Would they be more or less likely to do so if they had less disposable incomes because they paid higher taxes?
- If the *Wall Street Journal* had its way here, what would the tax code look like? How might government services such as highway maintenance, national defense, and domestic security be affected?

15.5 Fireside Chat

The Works Relief Program

Franklin Delano Roosevelt, 28 April 1935

When President Franklin Roosevelt was inaugurated in the winter of 1933, roughly a third of Americans were unemployed. When he told the nation, in his inaugural address, that the only thing we have to fear is fear itself, he was referring in part to the devastating effects that economic panic had had on the system. Many Americans were very fearful that good times had permanently come to an end.

By the spring of 1935, FDR was halfway through his first term. He had already set in progress new legislation, including reforms designed to help heal the American banking system, but he had much more planned in his New Deal for America. In this "fireside chat" he outlines his ideas for a works relief policy—a temporary program to get people back to work at the public's expense—as well as for social security, the program for worker compensation and old-age pensions that is still with us, albeit in somewhat rocky financial shape today. In what ways does this speech show how FDR was redefining the way Americans thought about the purpose of government and the role of the presidency?

Since my annual message to the Congress on January fourth, last, I have not addressed the general public over the air. In the many weeks since that time the Congress has devoted itself to the arduous task of formulating legislation necessary to the country's welfare. It has made and is making distinct progress.

Before I come to any of the specific measures, however, I want to leave in your minds one clear fact. The Administration and the Congress are not proceeding in any haphazard fashion in this task of government. Each of our steps has a definite relationship to every other step. The job of creating a program for the Nation's welfare is, in some respects, like the building of a ship. At different points on the coast where I often visit they build great seagoing ships. When one of these ships is under construction and the steel frames have been set in the keel, it is difficult for a person who does not know ships to tell how it will finally look when it is sailing the high seas.

It may seem confused to some, but out of the multitude of detailed parts that go into the making of the structure the creation of a useful instrument for man ultimately comes. It is that way with the making of a national policy. The objective of the Nation has greatly changed in three years. Before that time individual self-interest and group selfishness were paramount in public thinking. The general good was at a discount.

Three years of hard thinking have changed the picture. More and more people, because of clearer thinking and a better understanding, are considering the whole rather than a mere part relating to one section or to one crop, or to one industry, or to an individual private occupation. That is a tremendous gain for the principles of democracy. The overwhelming majority of people in this country know how to sift the wheat from the chaff in what they hear and what they read. They know that the process of the constructive rebuilding of America cannot be done in a day or a year, but that it is being done in spite of the few who seek to confuse them and to profit by their confusion. Americans as a whole are feeling a lot better—a lot more cheerful than for many, many years.

The most difficult place in the world to get a clear open perspective of the country as a whole is Washington. I am reminded sometimes of what President Wilson once said: "So many people come to Washington who know things that are not so, and so few people who know anything about what the people of the United States are thinking about." That is why I occasionally leave this scene of action for a few days to go fishing or back home to Hyde Park, so that I can have a chance to think quietly about the country as a whole. "To get away from the trees", as they say, "and to look at the whole forest." This duty of seeing the country in a long-range perspective is one which, in a very special manner, attaches to this office to which you have chosen me. Did you ever stop to think that there are, after all, only two positions in the Nation that are filled by the vote of all of the voters—the President and the Vice-President? That makes it particularly necessary for the Vice-President and for me to conceive of our duty toward the entire country. I speak, therefore, tonight, to and of the American people as a whole.

My most immediate concern is in carrying out the purposes of the great work program just enacted by the Congress. Its first objective is to put men and women now on the relief rolls to work and, incidentally, to assist materially in our already unmistakable march toward recovery. I shall not confuse my discussion by a multitude of figures. So many figures are quoted to prove so many things. Sometimes it depends upon what paper you read and what broadcast you hear. Therefore, let us keep our minds on two or three simple, essential facts in connection with this problem of unemployment. It is true that while business and industry are definitely better our relief rolls are still too large. However, for the first time in five years the relief rolls have declined instead of increased during the winter months. They are still declining. The simple fact is that many million more people have private work today than two years ago today or one year ago today, and every day that passes offers more chances to work for those who want to work. In spite of the fact that unemployment remains a serious problem here as in every other nation, we have come to recognize the possibility and the necessity of certain helpful remedial measures. These measures are of two kinds. The first is to make provisions intended to relieve, to minimize, and to prevent future unemployment; the second is to establish the practical means to help those who are unemployed in this present emergency. Our social security legislation is an attempt to answer the first of these questions. Our work relief program the second. The program for social security now pending before the Congress is a necessary part of the future unemployment policy of the government. While our present and projected expenditures for work relief are wholly within the reasonable limits of our national credit resources, it is obvious that we cannot continue to create governmental deficits for that purpose year after year. We must begin now to make provision for the future. That is why our social security program is an important part of the complete picture. It proposes, by means of old age pensions, to help those who have reached the age of retirement to give up their jobs and thus give to the younger generation greater opportunities for work and to give to all a feeling of security as they look toward old age.

> Interesting rationale for social security—to move older people out of the workplace and make room for younger ones who need jobs. Why don't politicians use that argument today to make social security reform relevant to young people?

The unemployment insurance part of the legislation will not only help to guard the individual in future periods of lay-off against dependence upon relief, but it will, by sustaining purchasing power, cushion the shock of economic distress. Another helpful feature of unemployment insurance is the incentive it will give to employers to plan more carefully in order that unemployment may be prevented by the stabilizing of employment itself.

Provisions for social security, however, are protections for the future. Our responsibility for the immediate necessities of the unemployed has been met by the Congress through the most comprehensive work plan in the history of the Nation. Our problem is to put to work three and one-half million employable persons now on the relief rolls. It is a problem quite as much for private industry as for the government.

We are losing no time getting the government's vast work relief program underway, and we have every reason to believe that it should be in full swing by autumn. In directing it, I shall recognize six fundamental principles:

(1) The projects should be useful.

(2) Projects shall be of a nature that a considerable proportion of the money spent will go into wages for labor.

(3) Projects which promise ultimate return to the Federal Treasury of a considerable proportion of the costs will be sought.

(4) Funds allotted for each project should be actually and promptly spent and not held over until later years.

(5) In all cases projects must be of a character to give employment to those on the relief rolls.

(6) Projects will be allocated to localities or relief areas in relation to the number of workers on relief rolls in those areas.

. . . For many months preparations have been under way. The allotment of funds for desirable projects has already begun. The key men for the major responsibilities of this great task already have been selected. I well realize that the country is expecting before this year is out to see the "dirt fly," as they say, in carrying on the work, and I assure my fellow citizens that no energy will be spared in using these funds effectively to make a major attack upon the problem of unemployment.

Our responsibility is to all of the people in this country. This is a great national crusade to destroy enforced idleness which is an enemy of the human spirit generated by this depression. Our attack upon these enemies must be without stint and without discrimination. No sectorial, no political distinctions can be permitted. It must, however, be recognized that when an enterprise of this character is extended over more than three thousand counties throughout the Nation, there may be occasional instances of inefficiency, bad management, or misuse of funds. When cases of this kind occur, there will be those, of course, who will try to tell you that the exceptional failure is characteristic of the entire endeavor. It should be remembered that in every big job there are some imperfections. There are chiselers in every walk of life; there are those in every industry who are guilty of unfair practices, every profession has its black sheep, but long experience in government has taught me that the exceptional instances of wrong-doing in government are probably less numerous than in almost every other line of endeavor. The most effective means of preventing such evils in this work relief program will be the eternal vigilance of the American people themselves. I call upon my fellow citizens everywhere to cooperate with me in making this the most efficient and the cleanest example of public enterprise the world has ever seen. It is time to provide a smashing answer for those cynical men who say that a democracy cannot be honest and efficient. If you will help, this can be done. I, therefore, hope you will watch the work in every corner of this Nation. Feel free to criticize. Tell me of instances where work can be done better, or where improper practices prevail. Neither you nor I want criticism conceived in a purely fault-finding or partisan

Why is FDR emphasizing that his program isn't perfect? What is he trying to inoculate his administration against?

spirit, but I am jealous of the right of every citizen to call to the attention of his or her government examples of how the public money can be more effectively spent for the benefit of the American people.

I now come, my friends, to a part of the remaining business before the Congress. It has under consideration many measures which provide for the rounding out of the program of economic and social reconstruction with which we have been concerned for two years. I can mention only a few of them tonight, but I do not want my mention of specific measures to be interpreted as lack of interest in or disapproval of many other important proposals that are pending.

The National Industrial Recovery Act expires on the sixteenth of June. After careful consideration, I have asked the Congress to extend the life of this useful agency of government. As we have proceeded with the administration of this Act, we have found from time to time more and more useful ways of promoting its purposes. No reasonable person wants to abandon our present gains—we must continue to protect children, to enforce minimum wages, to prevent excessive hours, to safeguard, define and enforce collective bargaining, and, while retaining fair competition, to eliminate, so far as humanly possible, the kinds of unfair practices by selfish minorities which unfortunately did more than anything else to bring about the recent collapse of industries. There is likewise pending before the Congress legislation to provide for the elimination of unnecessary holding companies in the public utility field. . . .

Not only business recovery, but the general economic recovery of the Nation will be greatly stimulated by the enactment of legislation designed to improve the status of our transportation agencies. There is need for legislation providing for the regulation of interstate transportation by buses and trucks, to regulate transportation by water, new provisions for strengthening our Merchant Marine and air transport, measures for the strengthening of the Interstate Commerce Commission to enable it to carry out a rounded conception of the national transportation system in which the benefits of private ownership are retained, while the public stake in these important services is protected by the public's government.

Finally, the reestablishment of public confidence in the banks of the Nation is one of the most hopeful results of our efforts as a Nation to reestablish public confidence in private banking. We all know that private banking actually exists by virtue of the permission of and regulation by the people as a whole, speaking through their government. Wise public policy, however, requires not only that banking be safe but that its resources be most fully utilized, in the economic life of the country. To this end it was decided more than twenty years ago that the government should assume the responsibility of providing a means by which the credit of the Nation might be controlled, not by a few private banking institutions, but by a body with public prestige and authority. The answer to this demand was the Federal Reserve System. Twenty years of experience with this system have justified the efforts made to create it, but these twenty years have shown by experience definite possibilities for improvement. Certain proposals made to amend the Federal Reserve Act deserve prompt and favorable action by the Congress. They are a minimum of wise readjustment of our Federal Reserve system in the light of past experience and present needs.

These measures I have mentioned are, in large part, the program which under my constitutional duty I have recommended to the Congress. They are essential factors in a rounded program for national recovery. They contemplate the enrichment of our national life by a sound and rational ordering of its various elements and wise provisions for the protection of the weak against the strong. Never since my inauguration in March, 1933, have I felt so unmistakably the atmosphere of recovery. But it is more than the recovery of the material basis of our individual lives. It is the recovery of confidence in our democratic processes and institutions. We have survived all of the arduous burdens and the threatening dangers of a great economic calamity. We have in the darkest moments of our national trials retained our faith in our own ability to master our destiny. Fear is vanishing and confidence is growing on every side, renewed faith in the vast possibilities of human beings to improve their material and spiritual status through the instrumentality of the democratic form of government. That faith is receiving its just reward. For that we can be thankful to the God who watches over America.

> What does this paragraph reveal about FDR's goals and promises to the American people? Why does he frame the New Deal as having spiritual and constitutional import as well as being a plan of economic recovery?

Consider the source and the audience.

- FDR gave this speech to the American public over the radio—the first president to regularly sidestep the critical voice of the media to speak directly with his constituency en masse. Why did FDR choose to "go public"?

Lay out the argument, the values, and the assumptions.

- What does FDR see as the basic purpose of government in a time of crisis? How does this differ from the view of government as basically an administrative apparatus?
- What does FDR see as the fundamental difference between his social security proposals and the works relief program?
- In spite of the fact that FDR's audience wants him to fix their broken system, the solutions he proposes are unorthodox and even threatening to many Americans. How does he try to diffuse that fear?

Uncover the evidence.

- To make the point that the public should support his policies, FDR needs to argue that what he has done so far has been effective, but that more needs to be done. What evidence does he offer to support this claim? Is it enough?

Evaluate the conclusion.

- Is FDR right in saying that it is government's job to restore economic security, the enrichment of national life, confidence in democracy, and faith in human beings?

Sort out the political implications.

- It is now more than sixty years since FDR's New Deal changed our expectations of government and altered the way we perceive the office of the presidency. What would life today be like if we still believed that government should have a narrowly prescribed role and that the president's job is just to be chief among the bureaucrats running the administrative apparatus of government?

CHAPTER 16

Foreign Policy

t is clear from the last chapter that Americans are quite split over the role of the national government on domestic issues. Liberals generally want more government involvement, conservatives less. Americans are often just as divided over foreign policy. In fact, some of the most heated political debates deal with this issue. In what world affairs should we involve ourselves? Who are our allies? When do we use diplomacy as a tool, and when do international affairs require the use of force?

How do the parties divide on foreign policy issues? Keeping in mind that there are always exceptions, we can say that liberals are more likely to support aid to other countries and efforts to build democratic regimes abroad. They are more willing to support the United Nations and to engage in multilateral foreign policy—building support among several nations. In matters of war, they tend to be doves; that is, they hesitate to use force.

Conservatives, on the other hand, are generally nationalistic. They are more likely to be hawks (they tend to support military action) and are skeptical of the UN. As a consequence, they are more likely to endorse unilateral action, where the United States goes it alone without the support of allies or international organizations. They question aid to foreign governments or for building up new regimes because of the cost, and they believe that the money is better spent on programs at home—or not spent at all.

The United States is the only remaining superpower; no other country in the world has as complex a foreign policy or plays as large a global role. And yet, that hasn't always been the case. It was not until our belated, reluctant involvement in World War II that the United States emerged as a superpower. In some respects, the world then has remained similar to today's; in others, it is drastically different. After World War II, the fascist governments of Germany and Italy were defeated, but a new enemy emerged: the totalitarian and Communist Soviet Union. The development of hydrogen and nuclear weapons changed diplomacy as well, adding a weapon of mass destruction that the world had never seen before.

In the 1960s and 1970s, controversy surrounding U.S. involvement in Vietnam forced many to question the goals of American foreign policy. During the 1980s, the arms race heated up as President Reagan convinced Congress to put millions of dollars into military buildup and the development of missile defense technology. The collapse of the Soviet Union in the late 1980s brought the cold war to an end, but raised a number of new questions regarding U.S. foreign policy. The United States emerged as the world's only superpower, but that did not mean it was without enemies.

As a result of September 11, foreign policy issues have once again emerged at the top of a president's issue agenda. The Soviet Union is no longer the enemy—now it is a group of rogue nations and terrorist organizations, such as Al Qaeda, that many believe present the biggest threat to the United States. While the enemy may have changed, the foreign policy questions posed earlier haven't. In fact, they remain as important and controversial as ever.

In this chapter, we tackle many of those questions. We begin with an article about a person whose job it is to advise the president on controversial foreign policy issues, National Security Advisor Condoleezza Rice. Next, Peter Ford assesses the world's view of the United States and asks why so many countries are hostile toward it. Then, we examine an article by Steve Bonta, from the conservative *The New American,* who argues that the events of September 11 have forced us to focus on a new threat—terrorism—and made us forget about what he still considers the real threat to the country—a nuclear attack. Fourth, we look at a *New York Times* article comparing the decisions that President Bush has made regarding Iraq with those that President Kennedy had to make more than forty years ago during the Cuban Missile Crisis. Finally, for this chapter's "classic" we turn to President Ronald Reagan's address to the National Association of Evangelicals, in which he warned that we need to maintain national strength and defense capabilities against "evil empires" like the former Soviet Union—a foreshadowing of the arguments made by Bush for attacking Iraq (part of what he calls the "Axis of Evil") as one aspect of the war on terror.

16.1 The Quiet Power of Condi Rice

Born in "Bombingham," the Enigmatic Advisor Has Become the "Warrior Princess"—Bush's Secret White House Weapon

Evan Thomas (et al.), *Newsweek,* 16 December 2002

When it comes to understanding, smoothing, and navigating the complicated and often unpredictable relationships that can exist between the United States and other nations, the president has a team of advisors ready to assist him. Particularly in the days after September 11, 2001, and as he sought international support for waging war on Iraq, President Bush looked to Vice-President Dick Cheney, Secretary of State Colin Powell, Secretary of Defense Donald Rumsfeld, and the Joint Chiefs of Staff of the military for foreign policy advice. One of Bush's closest advisors and a crucial influence on his foreign policy strategy is National Security Advisor Condoleezza Rice. In this *Newsweek* feature Evan Thomas explores Rice's personality and background as a means to understanding how she plays her complex role. Is the personal background of political actors helpful in understanding how they behave today?

The vice president had gone too far. In a speech to the VFW on Aug. 26, Dick Cheney declared that a return of U.N. inspectors to Iraq could bring only "false comfort." The obvious implication, at least to reporters covering the speech, was that the United States would have to go it alone to knock off Saddam Hussein and eliminate his weapons of mass destruction. The speech drew big headlines and stirred talk of war; within the Bush administration, it was a source of some consternation. At the State Department, Secretary Colin Powell was more than a little vexed. He thought the administration had decided, in a private meeting of Bush's war cabinet, to give diplomacy another chance and work through the United Nations before plunging into war in Iraq. Were the war hawks, Powell wondered, trying to pull a fast one and force the president's hand? Down at his ranch in Texas, President George W. Bush did not question the vice president's motives, but he, too, was perturbed by the potential fallout. Had the vice president's speech, however inadvertently, boxed him in?

It was time for someone to have a quiet word with Cheney. The president's emissary was his national-security adviser, a trim 48-year-old woman with a wide, warm smile, a polite manner and an unmistakable steeliness. Meeting with the vice president at the White House, Condoleezza Rice was friendly and low key. Cheney's speech, she blandly suggested, had been "interpreted" by the press in a way that might "limit the president's options." Rice waited for Cheney himself to suggest a solution. The veep said he was giving another speech in a couple of days. He would tone down the derisive language about inspectors and leave the door open for the United States to work through the United Nations. The newspapers duly noted the shift in the vice president's tone, but Rice's intercession did not leak.

Quiet, respectful, anonymous—but firm, just the way the president wanted it. Rice's aides call her the "anti-Kissinger," meaning that she does not need to show off her influence or present herself as a master global strategist like Henry Kissinger. That may be in part because Rice is not a strategic genius, but no one doubts her power. Rice's aides also refer to her (affectionately) as the "Warrior Princess." She is proud, elegant, fastidious about her appearance (she keeps two mirrors in her office, so she can see her back as well as her front) and utterly unflappable. Rice has Bush's complete confidence; she speaks for the president, and everyone knows it. The harder question is how much she influences his thinking and his decisions.

Rice's role bears watching as the president faces a critical turning point in his long-running face-off with Saddam. According to knowledgeable sources, Rice played an important behind-the-scenes part in convincing Bush that he had to try to disarm Iraq with U.N. inspectors before sending in the military to do the job by force. Now her task is to try to make sure the inspection regime is real and not a sham. Last week Rice met with chief U.N. inspector Hans Blix to press him to take a hard line: to remove Iraqi officials (and their families) to a safe place where they can tell the truth about Saddam's WMD program. And over the weekend, Rice's team began poring over the 12,000-page Iraqi report on its arsenal—and building the case that Saddam was already in breach of the U.N. resolution.

In Washington, the job of national-security adviser to the president can mean nothing or everything. The post has been held by worldbeaters and virtual nonentities, by honest brokers and Machiavellian schemers. By law, the secretary of State is the president's chief foreign-policy adviser; the national-security adviser runs no department and commands no troops. But he or she (Rice was the first-ever woman to get the job) is usually the first to see the president in the morning and the last at night. Depending on the chemistry and level of trust between them, the president and the national-security adviser can work about as well together as FDR and Harry Hopkins—or Reagan and many of his five national-security advisers.

Rice has a certain demeanor, assertive yet deferential, eager yet calm, that reminds Washington insiders of Strobe Talbott, the former Clinton administration deputy secretary of State once described as "the kind of young man who reassures older men." Over the years, Rice has won the attention and support of a series of powerful men. Told by aides that *Newsweek* was pursuing this angle ("Oh, no," one adviser groaned, "they're going to say that she's good with old guys"), Rice joked that the magazine was trying to turn her into Madame de Sevigne, a 17th-century courtier and mistress of Louis XIV. "You're not really going to put me on the cover, are you?" she asked a *Newsweek* reporter. Her distress actually seemed sincere.

Madame de Sevigne was a famous gossip. Rice is anything but. In Washington, Where's Condi? is a favorite game, a Beltway version of Where's Waldo? Everyone thinks he knows the views of Cheney, Powell and Defense Secretary Donald Rumsfeld. But Rice wants people to think of her as an enigma. She has often said that she is "determined to leave this town" without anyone outside Bush's tight inner circle ever figuring out where she stands on major issues. She claims that she "rarely" tells the president her private opinions, and if she does, she never shares her advice to the president, not even with her closest aides.

In fact Rice is engaged in a very delicate juggling act. She does interject herself in some ways, but she has to be very careful to appear evenhanded. While privately she sometimes shows her hand to another cabinet officer, publicly, and in almost every meeting that includes anyone besides herself and Bush, Rice rarely takes an open stand. She wants the president's other advisers to believe that she doesn't play favorites or whisper into the president's ear. By seeming above the fray she preserves her ability to influence decisions, however subtly.

Why is Rice determined to keep her opinions private? How does appearing to be above the fray increase her influence?

Hers is a complicated game to play. Officials at both the State and the Defense departments complain that under Rice's management, the national-security "process," designed to bring together different government agencies to hammer out policy, has become close to dysfunctional. Decisions go unmade at the deadlocked "deputies" meetings or get kicked back or ignored by the president's "principals," his top advisers. The principals themselves tend to revisit unresolved issues or reopen decisions already made by the president, forcing him to decide all over again. Rice, who chairs meetings of the principals, does not bear all the blame. She is dealing with some huge egos who have known each other for years, respect and by and large trust each other, but aren't afraid to fight. A former senior national-security staffer who often attended meetings of Bush's war cabinet described a typical meeting: Powell gets "exasperated"; CIA Director George Tenet "yells 'Jesus Christ, what are we doing here?'"; Rumsfeld "will try to trample anybody."

Rice lets the battles rage. The departing Secretary of the Treasury Paul O'Neill told *Newsweek,* "I can't think of a time when I felt she [Rice] imposed herself. She never says, 'You're going to do it, whether you like it or not.'" At most, says the former NSC official, Rice will put an end to occasional outbursts of "locker-room joking" by saying, "All right, boys, knock it off." In private conversation, she often shares her views with the other principals. "Individually, none of us is ever at a loss as to what Condi thinks about all this stuff," Powell told *Newsweek.* But at meetings, especially when the president is in the room, she rarely does more than ask pointed questions.

Rice's light reins are perplexing and troubling to some who know her. After all, they say, Rice can be decisive, impatient and tough when she wants to be. When she's angry or wants to enforce discipline, she never yells, but her voice grows cold, her speech slows, her jaw clamps, her eyes narrow. Throughout her career, faced with clashing forces and loud dissenters, she has appeared unfazed and absolutely determined to get her way. To keep the president from becoming "overloaded" and the NSC from becoming "constipated," the national-security adviser needs to set limits and force decisions, says an old government hand close to Rice. Why then, he wonders, "does she seem to want to let a thousand flowers bloom?"

The answer may be because that's the way the president wants it. Bush is suspicious of bureaucracy and does not want to be fed decisions that have been precooked, watered down or papered over by his advisers. True, the president is by nature restless, with a short attention span, and he is said to disdain the kind of endless, circular seminars that Bill Clinton gloried in. Still, Bush's advisers say, the president welcomes debate on the big issues of war and peace. He wants clear choices and original thinking, and he's willing to put up with a certain amount of tumult to get it. Rice has repeatedly told *Newsweek* that her job as national-security adviser is to sharpen arguments, not squelch them or flatten them out. "She doesn't drive to consensus," O'Neill told *Newsweek.* "Rather, she drives towards clarity. Then he [the president] decides what the consensus is."

But Rice without question plays a critical, if largely hidden, role in the overall direction of the president's foreign policy. Bush is "instinctive," Rice often tells interviewers; her job is to translate his "good strategic instincts" into an "intellectual framework," usually in the form of major presidential speeches, particularly those on Iraq. This is probably a subtle, at times almost unspoken process, a matter of a nudge here and there, a phrase inserted into a speech that may seem minor at the time but that can nonetheless have deep long-term consequences.

Superficially, Bush and Rice are opposites: the rich white boy from Texas who goofed off in school; the middle-class black girl who was a grind. But in fact they are well matched, and not just by a well-publicized mutual fondness for working out and watching sports on TV. The two are possessed of a certain defiant independence, almost an orneriness. They know what it's like to be underestimated, and they take obvious pleasure in going their own way. Deeply religious, the Presbyterian Rice and the Methodist Bush share a messianic streak. Rice's real job is to help steer Bush's black-and-white moral impulses in the murky, morally ambiguous real world. It is a tricky course, but in a sense, her whole life has prepared her for it.

Rice once had hopes of becoming a concert pianist. She is still accomplished enough to have performed with cellist Yo-Yo Ma before 2,000 people at Constitution Hall earlier this year. Afterward, Ma asked her to name her favorite composer. "Brahms," she answered. "Why?" he inquired. Because Brahms's music was "passionate without being sentimental," said Rice. Ma asked, "Do you also think it's this irresolution in Brahms, the tension that is never resolved?"

Rice told that story to an aide without offering any larger meaning ("I'm not a very reflective person," she insists). But the fact is that she had to deal with "irresolution," with moral conflict and uncertainty, as a little girl, in ways most white people cannot begin to imagine. Rice is seen as living proof of the triumph of the civil-rights movement—and she is—but her story is more complicated and more interesting than simply discrimination overcome.

Rice was born into a secure, proud little world, a cocoon of civility carved from bigoted surroundings. In Titusville, a black middle-class enclave in Birmingham, Ala., children of black professionals—teachers, preachers, school administrators—were taught they would have to work twice as hard and do twice as well as whites, but never to think of themselves as victims. Condoleezza (named after an Italian musical term meaning "with sweetness") was a protected only child who adored her father, a high-school guidance counselor. "I never saw her as a little girl," says Julia Emma Smith, who worked with Rice's father in a church youth group. "She was around adults most of the time." A childhood acquaintance, Harold Jackson, says, "When we were running around, she was prim and proper, playing for the adult choir." There were music, dance and skating lessons. Rice felt ennobled and safe.

Then, in 1963, when Rice was 8, the Movement arrived. Civil-rights activists urged schoolchildren to march; when the kids were in the streets, they were firehosed by the Birmingham Police Department and chased by dogs (as the TV cameras rolled). Rice's father urged the local schoolchildren not to participate in the demonstrations, though he did take Condi downtown to watch. ("If we'd waited for the middle class to lead us, we'd still be waiting," the Rev. Fred Shuttlesworth, a leading activist of the time, told a reporter a few years ago.) Then bombs, set off by racists, began exploding in and around Rice's neighborhood and blew up the 16th Street Baptist Church, killing four schoolgirls, one of them Rice's schoolmate. Rice's father joined the other neighborhood men, armed with shotguns, to patrol the streets at night and protect the neighborhood. Today Rice says she cannot remember being afraid, though she remembers exactly how many days of school (31) she missed that year.

The Birmingham demonstrations raised the consciousness of the federal government and the liberal establishment. Civil-rights bills became law, and affirmative action followed. Rice was a beneficiary. Realizing that she would never make it as a concert pianist, she became fascinated by the study of power; her mentor was Soviet specialist Josef Korbel, the father of future secretary of State Madeleine Albright. An able student, Rice was vaulted ahead into various prestigious fellowships in academe and government: after graduating from the University of Denver at 19 and getting a master's at Notre Dame, she taught at Stanford and worked at the Pentagon for the then chairman of the Joint Chiefs, Colin Powell. One of the men who "discovered" her, Brent Scowcroft, the elder Bush's national-security adviser, recalls how "this slip of a girl" could stand up and ask sharp (but respectful) questions of her elders. Scowcroft gave her a job on the national-security staff, handling Russian affairs. By the time she was 40, Rice was on the board of Chevron and had an oil tanker named after her. In 1993, Rice was snapped up as the first black woman and youngest-ever provost of Stanford University.

> How has Rice been a beneficiary of affirmative action policies? Does Thomas offer evidence of this?

The politically correct faculty hailed the appointment—but many soon regretted it. "She set a tone of open season on minorities and women," recalls Linda Mabry, former associate professor at Stanford Law School. During the Rice years (1993–1999), the tenure rate for women professors declined, [as did the number of African-Americans on the faculty].* At a faculty meeting, a political scientist tried to introduce a resolution to make affirmative action an explicit criterion in granting tenure. Rice strongly opposed it—"as long as I am at Stanford," she vowed. As they left the room, a professor remarked to Rice on the tension. "After you've talked the Ukrainians out of their nuclear missiles, this stuff is just child's play," she responded. After she fired a Chicana dean, students taunted her for being a traitor. "You can't pull that on me," she told them. "I've been black all my life."

Editors' note: Newsweek printed a correction to this statement on January 27, noting that "[a]ccording to Stanford, the number of African Americans on the faculty increased from 36 to 44" during Rice's tenure as provost.

In April 1998, Rice was asked by her Stanford colleague, former secretary of State George Shultz, to attend a foreign-policy seminar for Texas Gov. George W. Bush. "You could see then that they clicked," Shultz recalls. Rice was soon flying to Austin to tutor the GOP presidential candidate. During the campaign, Bush would sometimes blurt out a foreign-policy "instinct," and it would be up to Rice to make sense of it. This could take some doing. During the presidential debates, Bush said he wanted to pull U.S. soldiers from the Balkans, saying it was Europe's time to "put troops on the ground." In fact, most peacekeeping troops were already European. Rice valiantly tried to spin the press about "a new division of labor" with the allies, but it took about a year to soothe their feelings.

Bush's moral impulses were easier to channel after 9-11. Rice was one of Bush's advisers who instantly saw that the war on terror was global. "The initial knee-jerk reaction after 9-11 was to go after Al Qaeda," Powell told *Newsweek*. He credits her with focusing as well on states that sponsor terrorism. Bush's description of an "Axis of Evil" caused a sensation in the press when Bush uttered the phrase in the State of the Union address this January, but in fact Rice had been privately talking to Bush about going after all rogue nations harboring WMD within a week of 9-11.

She appreciates—and tries to promote—creative chaos, but sometimes there is just chaos. Notes of national-security meetings about the assault on the Taliban leaked to *The Washington Post*'s Bob Woodward reveal a process so freewheeling that it verges on the unmanageable. An official who participated in those meetings told *Newsweek* that Defense Secretary Rumsfeld was particularly rambunctious. Every time the State Department came up with a scheme for using U.S. troops to keep peace in Afghanistan after the war, Rumsfeld would find a way to undercut the plan. Rice didn't appear able to control the headstrong Defense secretary (though she may not have tried very hard; Rice is no fan of using the military for peacekeeping, either).

When the Middle East blew up last winter, the hawks, Cheney and Rumsfeld, wanted to exile Palestinian leader Yasir Arafat. Powell argued that Arafat, though deeply distasteful, could not be simply banished without wrecking diplomacy. It fell to Rice to bridge the gap by suggesting that the United States call for "new leadership" in the Palestinian Authority, without mentioning Arafat's name. The fix was awkward and not altogether successful (Arafat is still there).

Rice has had more luck in the delicate business of balancing hawks and doves on Iraq. While she has embraced President Bush's hard line and rattled the saber as loudly as anyone on talk shows, she has tilted ever so slightly to the more dovish Colin Powell behind the scenes. Rice sometimes finds Rumsfeld's 1950s macho a little wearying. When she had a coughing fit at one meeting, Rumsfeld kept joking, asking her if she wanted him to show her the Heimlich maneuver ("He does that with everyone," said a Rumsfeld aide). On the other hand, she has a natural kinship with Powell (whose wife, Alma, also came from Birmingham's black middle class). The two tease easily. Last week Powell entered the White House Situation Room, deep in the West Wing basement, to find Rice cleaning up coffee cups left over from a principals meeting. "Well, pick stuff up," she admonished the secretary of State. "Real men don't clear tables," he replied. "Yes, they do," she said, and they laughed.

Powell and Rice worked closely together to produce a U.N. resolution on weapons inspections in Iraq that would have teeth, keep the hawks onboard—and still unanimously pass the Security Council. At the United Nations in September, U.S. Ambassador John Negroponte crafted with the British some language that got French and Russian support. Then he sent the document to Washington. When the hawks around Rumsfeld and Cheney were finished, the document was littered with traps designed to bring the inspection process to a quick end and trigger a war. As one Security Council diplomat described the document to *Newsweek*, "We had been shown the outlines of a beautiful young girl. Now she had turned into this hag."

Slowly, without directly confronting the hawks, Powell and Rice maneuvered to find language acceptable to everyone. It took eight weeks, but the final product passed the Security Council 15–0. That doesn't mean Rice believes that war can be avoided. But she wants to make sure America has international support if war comes. She knows Bush is betting his presidency on Iraq and, characteristically, wants to protect him.

> What does it mean to say that Bush "is betting his presidency on Iraq"?

It can be equally assumed that Rice was doing exactly what Bush wanted her to do. Rice could hardly be closer to Bush. Bush has joked about Rice's "motherhenning" him, but he seems to enjoy it, or at least depend on it; all his life, Bush has had an affinity for strong women, starting with his mother. The fact is that her job is Rice's life. She doesn't socialize much, if at all. Rice told an avuncular friend that she preferred to go out with black men. On his own initiative, the friend, a prominent Washingtonian, says that he asked another well-known Washingtonian, who is black, to arrange some suitable dates. They were not a success, reports this source.

Rice begins her day at 5 A.M. to exercise. Her chief recreations are going to concerts at the Kennedy Center, watching football on TV, playing her grand piano and shopping. "She may have more shoes than Imelda Marcos," jokes her closest friend, Stanford professor Coit Blacker. In Washington, Rice has a personal shopper, and Saks Fifth Avenue has been known to open up for her after hours. She dresses beautifully and agreed to pose for *Vogue*, she told an aide, because she thought it might help the Republican Party with the women's vote.

Posing for a women's magazine is about as close to elective politics as she wants to get. Although she is routinely rumored to be a potential U.S. Senate or vice presidential candidate, she scoffs at the idea. Her career aim, she often says, is to become NFL commissioner. That actually represents a step down from her childhood ambition. In 1965, when Rice was 11, her father took her to Washington, where she stood in front of the White House. Her father had encouraged her to believe that she could be president one day, even though at the time most blacks were not allowed to vote. "One day I'll be in that house," she told her father. It may have seemed a preposterous wish then, but Condi Rice made it come true.

Consider the source and the audience.
- *Newsweek* is a national newsmagazine that depends on a large national circulation. How might that fact influence the details they chose to emphasize in their study of Rice? Would a more policy-oriented or a more ideological magazine take the same human-interest approach?

Lay out the argument, the values, and the assumptions.
- Thomas and his co-authors draw a clear portrait of Rice. How do they characterize her personality? How do they imply that her personality leads her to interpret her role in a particular way? What is that interpretation?
- In the second part of the article, Thomas et al. describe Rice's role after September 11 as a leader in the formulation of a policy of preemptive strikes against rogue nations harboring weapons of mass destruction. Is her influence in the formulation of that global anti-terror policy what one would expect given the general description earlier in the article?
- What does it mean to say that part of her job is to "channel Bush's moral impulses"? Does Rice really just broker agreements between competing views, or does she have more of a creative policy role of her own than she (or Thomas) indicates?

Uncover the evidence.
- Thomas and his co-authors rely almost exclusively on interviews, many with sources who are not named. Who are these sources likely to be? What motives are they likely to have for agreeing to talk? How should we interpret what they have to say?
- Given the sensitive nature of national defense, are these anonymous interviews our only way to know what goes on behind the scenes? Are there other kinds of evidence that can be brought in?

Evaluate the conclusion.
- Most of the sources Thomas's team talks to indicate that Rice's role is just to clarify options for Bush, not to offer more substantive advice or to suggest what he should do. Is this role borne out by the examples they cite?

Sort out the political implications.
- Given the description here of Rice's role, how might Bush's foreign policy be different if she were not part of his administration?

16.2 Is America the "Good Guy"? Many Now Say, "No"

Peter Ford, *Christian Science Monitor,* 11 September 2002

The world's only remaining superpower, the top donor of foreign aid to less prosperous nations, the longest-lived constitutional democracy—the United States of America prides itself on being a world leader in military, economic, and moral terms. In global politics, we see ourselves as the "good guy," and we imagine the rest of the world follows our lead in that respect as in so much else. With increasing frequency and urgency, however, the voice of global public opinion is coming back with the opposite message. Immediately after the terror attacks on the World Trade Center in 2001 there was an outpouring of sympathy and support for the United States, but that support has been short-lived. In this *Christian Science Monitor* article, Peter Ford examines why the world no longer views America as the "good guy." Is it important that other nations like and respect us? What price might we pay for this newfound global unpopularity?

In a small, plain office over a downtown Seoul grocery, eight young men hunch over a bank of computers. They aren't writing software or playing video games. This is a command center for protest against American soldiers in Korea. Everyone wears a black ribbon that reads "US troops withdraw."

The group—one of dozens like it—sprang up after a US armored vehicle accidentally killed two Korean girls walking along a country road in June. The incident continues to galvanize anti-American feeling across the country. Members canvas neighborhoods, run e-mail campaigns detailing American soldiers' alleged crimes, and help organize a permanent silent vigil outside the presidential palace.

"We are like a military operation" says their leader, known only as Mr. Kim. "US troops here are a mistake of history and we won't be one country until they leave; 9/11 is not our problem."

Most Americans believe they are making a sacrifice—stationing 38,000 soldiers here—to defend South Koreans against possible Communist attack. Most ordinary Koreans, however, believe the US troops are actually here to promote American interests, opinion polls show. And "since 9/11, a strange but virulent anti-Americanism has gripped South Korea," notes one expatriate American who works at a US company in Seoul.

"The underlying reason that Uncle Sam is about as popular as the plague," he adds, "is because of a paradigm shift in the minds of a new generation of South Koreans" who regard the US troops as a colonial presence.

Along with Japan, South Korea is one of America's chief strategic partners in the Pacific. But you wouldn't think so to watch a recent music video by popular all-girl Korean band S.E.S. It features cowboy-booted Americans being beaten up, fed to dogs, and tossed off buildings.

Nor are American diplomats reassured by recent polls showing that nearly half of Koreans approved the February trashing of the US Chamber of Commerce in Seoul and that 60 percent of Koreans "don't like" America.

But if the US doesn't wear a white hat here, where then?

South Korea today offers one of the sharpest, and most surprising, examples of anger at the US role in the world since Sept. 11. The current campaign grew out of the girls' deaths—and a widespread sense that the US authorities handled the case clumsily. But there's more to it than that. It seems to feed on old grudges and a deep dismay at a newly unilateral America, touting a "with us or against us" approach.

A year ago, in the wake of Sept. 11, even some of Washington's fiercest critics proclaimed in sympathy, "We are all Americans." But those sentiments began to fade after the inadvertent US bombing of civilians in Afghanistan. Today, even some of the country's firmest friends are alarmed by America's apparent unwillingness to take into account the views of other nations on issues ranging from the environment to dealing with Iraq.

What does it mean to talk about a "newly unilateral America"? What does it mean to act unilaterally in foreign policy? Why does it inspire dismay on the part of other nations?

As the sole superpower for the past decade, America was already retooling its relationship with the rest of the planet before Sept. 11. It pulled out of the Kyoto treaty on climate change, a step that rankled many. But the attack on America accelerated the change. The United States feels threatened by Al Qaeda, and it's making its vast military and political superiority felt with unprecedented vigor—sending soldiers into Central Asia, Georgia, and the Philippines.

That is having an effect. Scores of interviews with government officials, political analysts, and ordinary citizens from one side of the globe to the other suggest that the US is now widely perceived as arrogant and—as war with Iraq looms—potentially reckless.

You can hear the misgivings in the voices of Russian steel workers burned by Washington's decision this year to ignore free-trade principles and raise import tariffs. You can see them in a McDonald's franchise in Jakarta that works to hide its American connection.

And in South Korea, for the first time, anti-Americanism is no longer a fringe emotion, fashionable on the political extremes. It has become a mainstream current of respectable opinion.

Fault-finding with America is becoming an instrument of national solidarity, especially among younger people like Yonsei University student Ham Chang, who thinks older generations that fought alongside US troops have been "brainwashed."

"My friends feel like the US acts as boss of the world," says Mr. Ham, who is studying literature. "Sept. 11 was terrible . . . but the US is using it as an excuse to do what it wants. The US government is in Korea to divide us. The US wants us weak and divided. They are not here for our security."

In an unusually candid acknowledgement of the problem, President Kim Dae Jung told reporters last Friday that he's worried by "a growing trend toward anti-American sentiment."

"It may be difficult for us to sustain the same mood we grew up with," says one older Korean diplomat who served in Washington. "We know the US helped us.

But those under 40 . . . aren't swayed by what we think. Their human nature is anti-US."

Respect for American values—freedom and democracy—persists, as does admiration of its free-enterprise prosperity. A visa for the US is still prized. But because of the way the US is wielding its military and political clout—more than its cultural hegemony—that admiration is increasingly overlaid by mistrust, misunderstanding, resentment, and even hostility across a broad spectrum of countries and citizens. There's a feeling that Washington doesn't care about them or their concerns.

"Foreign perceptions of the United States are far from monolithic," found a recent task force on public diplomacy set up by the Council on Foreign Relations (CFR) in New York. In Afghanistan and the Philippines, for example, US soldiers are generally well received. "But there is little doubt that stereotypes of the United States as arrogant, self-indulgent, hypocritical, inattentive, and unwilling or unable to engage in cross-cultural dialogue are pervasive and deeply rooted."

That is a far cry from the average American's perception. Sixty-six percent of Americans regard their country's actions as "usually or almost always" beneficial to the world according to a *Monitor*/TIPP poll taken in the past week.

"I'm amazed . . . that people would hate us," President Bush said last October. "Like most Americans I just can't believe it. Because I know how good we are."

Some say that is enough. "The rich hegemon will usually be unpopular, deservedly or not," says Lewis Manilow, a veteran public diplomacy specialist who dissented from the CFR report. "Americans want to be loved, but isn't it more important that we tell the world where we stand and follow up with appropriate action?"

Certainly, the US now holds greater economic, political, military, and cultural sway over the rest of the world than any power since the Roman Empire. It is the only military power with global reach, spending more on guns and soldiers than the next 11 countries combined. It has 27 percent of the world's economic output, equal to the next three biggest countries combined. And it is in a league of its own when it comes to film and TV exports.

> What does it take to be an effective global leader? What does leadership mean in an international context?

But brute strength does not always add up to leadership, and raw power rarely fosters the sense of international common purpose needed to address problems with the environment, disease, immigration, or global economic stability.

"Military power is necessary but not sufficient," argues Joseph Nye, dean of the Kennedy School of Government at Harvard University in Cambridge, Mass. "The US should pay more attention to its ability to attract others to work with it."

* * *

That is what Sgt. Larry Moore's job is all about. A soldier with the 489th Civil Affairs Battalion based in Knoxville, Tenn., he steps out of his pickup truck into the bright sunlight scorching the village of Karabagh, north of Kabul, and surveys the war-scarred desolation around him.

The few mud walls that are standing are pocked with bullet holes and the starburst signatures of rocket-propelled grenades. Shattered adobe buildings melt back into the dusty floor of the plain. But in the middle of the village rises a red-brick schoolhouse where 1,200 boys and girls will soon be studying, courtesy of the US Army.

"This school will be excellent," says Sergeant Moore with satisfaction, as he watches a turbaned tribesman use an adze to smooth ceiling beams while a dozen workmen in long shirts and billowing pantaloons slather on mortar and lay bricks. "It's going to do wonders for the village."

Karabagh's new school is one of hundreds of humanitarian-aid projects that the US military is funding in Afghanistan, and it has won over Dermont, a village elder. A few months ago, he says, American soldiers on patrol "saw our children studying under the shadows of trees and they decided to build a school. The school is a light in the darkness. I hope my children will be able to see."

Moore takes an idealistic view of his work. "We're doing this because these people need help," he says. "We are doing it for the same reason you would do it for your neighbor. Do it because that's what's in your heart. America has a kind heart."

The US Agency for International Development says it has sent $530 million in humanitarian aid in Afghanistan this year, making America the largest single donor to the war-torn country. But that does not impress Karabagh policeman Abdul Ghafur. "We have two targets," he says, "the reconstruction of Afghanistan and eradicating the terrorists. The US is more interested in the war against terrorists. We are more interested in reconstruction."

For Col. Nick Parker, a British officer who is director of operational planning at coalition headquarters in Kabul, those two goals go hand in hand. "The US is not doing this for purely altruistic reasons," he suggests. "If the US doesn't do it, in five years we'll all be back here fighting another terrorist organization."

When American goals match local aspirations, America has no difficulty presenting itself as the good guy. That is the logic behind the doctrine of "integration" outlined recently by Richard Haass, the State Department's director of policy planning, who described it as "persuading more and more governments, and at a deeper level, people to sign on to certain key ideas as to how the world should operate for our mutual benefit."

But getting the rest of the world to want what America wants is only one side of the coin, argues Professor Nye. America also has to offer other countries things they value if foreigners are to accept American moral leadership.

"Failure to pay proper respect to the opinion of others and to incorporate a broad conception of justice into our national interest will eventually come to hurt us," Nye argues in his recent book, *The Paradox of American Power.*

In the eyes of many global activists, Washington is ignoring that warning. In Johannesburg, for example, Korean environmental activists protested against Mr. Bush's absence from the recent World Summit on Sustainable Development. "He only cares about his personal war against terror," said Kim Yeon Ji of the Korean Federation for the Environment. "They want us all to join in with their war, but in the battle for the environment, we are all here and he says, 'Sorry, I'm on vacation.' We are very angry."

America's reluctance to join other countries in tackling issues they think are important—its current efforts to undermine the new International Criminal Court, for example; its rejection of an international treaty limiting biological weapons; or its refusal to strengthen a convention against torture—are squandering global goodwill, say critics.

In France, warns Dominique Moisi, a prominent foreign-affairs analyst, "there is a growing tendency in public opinion to view the US as a rogue state."

Not that this makes Americans personally unpopular, as Jacqui Resley's employees will attest.

Ms. Resley, a Kansan, strides around her crafts factory in Nairobi, constantly taking charge. "David," she admonishes one shy potter. "Stop painting those lines so squiggly. They look ugly."

Encouraging, correcting, yelling, insisting on it all being done the way she thinks best, the tall and angular Resley pushes her 70 Kenyan workers to their limits. "There is this attitude here of 'We can't do it,' and I say 'For God's sake why not?' she says, grimacing as she watches a weaver fumbling a ball of thread.

"She is bossy," acknowledges Fidel Namisi, the company's computer technician. "Bossy and hyper and good-hearted . . . very American."

Thirty years ago, inspired by a John Wayne movie filmed in the Serengeti plains, Resley picked up and set off to hitchhike across Africa. The Vietnam War was raging, and long before she reached Nairobi, she discovered that not everybody loved America.

"A lot of people just didn't like you because of the war," she remembers. "But no matter what Godforsaken place you found yourself in there was always someone with a Coke, complaining about Vietnam but also asking if you could help them to get a visa to the US."

Today, she still runs into people like that, but Resley no longer carries a backpack. Now she runs Weaverbird, the company she founded that supplies many of the high-quality carpets, wall hangings, and pots that decorate Kenya's best hotels. She has also become one of Nairobi's best-known community activists, agitating against corruption and litter and in favor of government accountability. As the only human face her workers can put on a distant superpower, Jacqui Resley hears a lot from them—good and bad—about America. On Sept. 11, Jane Mukonyo was on the factory floor, ball-winding wool, when she heard about the attacks on the radio. "Everyone looks around for Jacqui" she recalls. "We wanted to tell her we felt so bad."

"I don't know too many Americans, just Jacqui and those I see on TV," says Joyce Njeri, a dyer who has worked at Weaverbird for 15 years. "But what I know I like."

Americans, she explains, "know what they want, and others can't teach them too much. They want the bottom line. They take action. They are capable and have big, good ideas. America as a country, Njeri believes, is much the same. "But I have a question," she adds. "Why, if they have such good ideas, are they now bombing others just like they themselves are bombed?"

Mr. Namisi, the computer expert, is less enthusiastic. "I definitely think the US is a bully," he says. "They look down at the rest of us. They think their way is the only way."

Lunch break is over, and Resley charges onto the factory floor, her hands flying this way and that. "One, two, let's get moving here," she nags.

"Jacqui is an American and, yes, she is bossy too," says Namisi. "But we signed up to work for her, so we accept that. But neither Kenya nor any other country signed up to work for the US, so that is different."

Elsewhere in the world too, people are ambivalent about America: "Yankee Go Home, But Take Me With You," as an Indian politician, Jairam Ramesh, titled a talk he gave three years ago at the Asia Society in New York.

Chinese students are not shy about protesting US policies, but a demonstration outside the US Embassy in Beijing last month had an ironic twist in its tail: the college grads were demanding American visas.

"The international role of the US is rude, it is a very negative role," said Feng Ma, a young woman demonstrator who has won a full scholarship to the University of Maryland after preparing for five years. "But I view individuals separately. My friends live a comfortable life in Michigan. They work hard and they make in a year what it would take three years here to make.

How can someone view individual Americans separately from America? Can one like and admire the people but hate the country?

"We may hate the US when it is rude to China," she added. "But we long to go there."

Nor is it hard to find people anywhere in the world ready to express their admiration for the values and ideals that have inspired America's growth—especially in countries where such values are not officially shared.

"Yes, America wants to do good things in the world and spread democracy," says Yang Chu, a software salesman reading a raft of Saturday papers over a cup of coffee at a downtown Beijing Starbucks. "I wish China had more American-style democracy."

In Eastern Europe, too, plenty of middle aged people who knew life under Communism are grateful to the US for its role in bringing down the Soviet empire. (Warm feelings live on in the parlance of Czech hikers: When they find an especially beautiful site to pitch their tents, they call it "Amerika.") But that gratitude is ebbing away.

"I used to hold America in awe," says Vlastislav Vecerilek, a former air-traffic controller who has had a hard time making ends meet since he lost his job soon after Czechoslovakia's "Velvet Revolution." "But recently I have become annoyed with American policies."

"They promised us heaven and instead we got scraps," he complains. "We thought America was different from the Soviet Union, but in essence all superpowers are the same."

As gray flood waters crept toward the door of his Prague restaurant last month, waiter Jiri Kolar blamed America. "The floods [the worst in the city's history] are clearly caused by global warming, everybody knows that," he argued, as he took a break from carrying out food and electrical appliances.

"If the Americans don't stop their bad habits of pollution, we'll have more disasters," he predicted. "I am very angry at George Bush for rejecting the Kyoto Protocol. The Americans think only of themselves."

That sort of comment cuts no ice with Jan Urban, a commentator with the Czech service of US-funded Radio Free Europe. "There are now those in this country who believe anything the US does must be evil, but when those same people need help they will ask the US," he scoffs.

"Anti-Americanism here isn't so much hatred as it is envy," he adds. "It's a parent-child relationship. The child wants to be listened to and Dad is always busy."

If the world sometimes feels a need for American leadership, as Mr. Urban suggests, it is also hooked on American products.

Just ask Tayiba Abdul Rahman, a young Saudi mother who took her family holidays this summer in Turkey, rather than in America, where she has often been before. "I wouldn't go to America now. I don't want to be treated like a criminal," she says as she eats lunch at the Akmerkez, a new shopping mall in Istanbul that attracts the monied classes from around the Islamic world.

Frustrated by US policy in the Middle East, and upset by what they see as the way America has demonized Muslims since last September, Tayiba and her husband, Mohammed, are part of a grass-roots campaign at home to boycott US-made goods.

But Tayiba sheepishly admits that she couldn't pass up the lovely leather DKNY bag that sits on the table as the couple lunches with their two small boys. And although they have skipped the five American chain restaurants in the vast Akmerkez food court—preferring Middle Eastern food—they say they regret not having succeeded in weaning themselves off Coca-Cola and Pepsi, which the boys slug down with their rice and stewed eggplant.

(Ironically, Americans are most dubious about the aspects of their country that foreigners like best—its movies, its consumer goods and its culture. The *Monitor*/TIPP poll found that Americans overwhelmingly feel the US has a positive impact on fighting terrorism, or boosting the world economy, but are divided about its global cultural impact: 47 per cent consider it positive, against 44 per cent who think it is negative.)

Mr. Abdul Rahman is one of the astonishingly numerous people in the Middle East who do not believe Osama bin Laden was responsible for the Twin Towers attack. He thinks that Israel and the American government organized the atrocity so as to justify a war on the Islamic world.

Despite that sort of criticism aimed against it, many more governments are friendly to the US than was the case during the cold war, and many more have adopted the liberal democratic capitalist credo that America has been energetically exporting.

Not that it always gets them where they had expected to go, especially when Washington itself betrays the principles it seeks to impose on others, such as free trade.

Over the roar of the blast furnace in the Severstal steel mill at Cheropovets, 250 miles north of Moscow, Gennady Borisov will give you an earful on that subject. The tariffs on foreign steel imports of up to 30 percent that Bush announced last March to shield domestic producers from competition have hit everything in Cheropovets from Mr. Borisov's paycheck to local kindergartens.

As fire and smoke belch from the belly of one of the largest steel mills in the world, Mr. Borisov wipes the sweat from his brow with the grimy sleeve of his work shirt. "America wants to dictate its terms to the whole world," he complains. "They think they are superior. Their economy allows them to do it."

Accustomed to sermons from Washington about the value of open markets and free trade, Russians attribute the protectionist US stance on steel to an American disregard for international norms that they feel has grown since Sept. 11.

Severstal must now seek new markets for the steel it had planned to sell in America—and those markets are following Washington's protectionist suit. Severstal has pledged not to lay off any workers, but it has abandoned planned wage increases in view of the projected loss of profits.

The ripple effects—amplified by a cyclical downturn in the steel industry—are felt all over town, where the steel mill's 45,000 employees make up 15 per cent of the population.

Normally, for example, Severstal's tax payments constitute 80 percent of the city budget. But because of the drop in profits, the company's tax payments for the first half of 2002 are only half what they were last year.

That means that a city program to slowly wean people off Soviet-era perks such as free water and electricity has been dramatically sped up. Thirty kindergartens once funded by Severstal are now run by the cash-strapped city authorities.

"As a consequence, all citizens feel that they are paying more money for their apartments and to live," says Olga Ezhova, a Severstal spokeswoman. "This is the pain inflicted by the American decision."

The pain is only made harder to bear by the fact that Russia has been an enthusiastic partner in Washington's "war on terror." "We were spellbound" on Sept. 11, says Ms. Ezhova. "It was a shock. We hoped that after such a tragedy and our reaction to it, when [President Vladimir] Putin gave his hand to America, we had a common cause, and thought that this called for an appropriate reaction.

What reasons account for the Russian feelings of betrayal on steel tariffs? Are such feelings avoidable or inevitable?

"Of course [the tariffs] are such a small thing by comparison," she adds. "But what we heard in March did not correspond to our attitude to America."

And even in countries where capitalism is well established, some of the shine has rubbed off the American way of doing business in the wake of the Enron and WorldCom scandals.

In Japan, for example, "They've been having to listen to 'We know how to do things right and you don't'" from America for the past 10 years, says Ronald Bevacqua, a financial-markets expert from New York who has lived in Tokyo for a decade. "Now, when the stock market burst and these scandals came out, we found out that America was no better than Japan was 10 years ago," he adds. "The whole moralistic thing that America has been preaching was bogus."

From his plush office high above the traffic that clogs the streets of Bogota, an American oil company executive watches through his plate-glass window as a detachment of Colombian army soldiers patrols a wealthy residential district nearby.

This has been a tense year for him—tense enough that he doesn't feel safe giving his name. He knows that he is a juicy target for leftist guerrillas, especially since Sept. 11 landed him on the front lines of America's "war on terror."

Colombia has been enmeshed in political violence for more than half a century, and leftist rebels have long viewed US oil companies as thieves of the nation's resources. But Sept. 11 raised the stakes, as Washington folded Colombia into its global war.

The attacks on New York and Washington a year ago "changed the rules of the game," says one of the oil executive's Colombian colleagues, also unwilling to identify himself. No longer does the US government feel any hesitation in helping the Colombian government fight insurgents.

The State Department put Colombia's two largest rebel groups—and a right-wing paramilitary force that often cooperates with the army—on its list of terrorist groups. Earlier this summer, Congress approved the use of aid to fight the insurgents, not just the drugs trade they profit from.

That has jacked up the pressure, and the security risks for foreign oil workers.

The US executive is now required to use a bulletproof car driven by a chauffeur trained in evasive tactics, and he scarcely ever leaves the capital.

"I have the feeling that I'm appreciated [by Colombians] for what I do," he says. "And I think there's even greater appreciation because people look at you and say 'You're here even though you are more vulnerable than you were before.'"

"I think that in most Colombians' minds, America is the good guy," he adds. "It's the big brother that can help you when you've had your nose bloodied by the bully."

On the other side of the world, in another country battered by violence, America's "war on terror" is also welcome. In the Philippines, where US troops spent six months this year training local troops to fight Abu Sayyaf, an Islamic guerrilla group, polls have found overwhelming public support for their assistance.

"There has been no negativism at all, zero," says Richard Upton, a longtime American resident of Manila. "The Filipinos have been very mature about this: They needed some help so the US came in to help."

But in countries that have not suffered such direct exposure to terrorism, and where America is suspected of pursuing its own interests around the world at the expense of others, the erosion of support for the US is more evident.

In Europe, for example, Washington's almost single-handed prosecution of the war in Afghanistan, and its apparent readiness to stage a preemptive invasion of Iraq alone, has bred the uncomfortable feeling "that we don't matter any longer," says French analyst Dominique Moisi.

"America should at least give the impression that it needs its friends—show a sense of modesty," Moisi suggests, if it wants to cultivate support.

A Europe-wide poll last April by the Pew Research Center found that 85 percent of Germans, 80 percent of the French, 73 percent of Britons, and 63 percent of Italians felt that Washington was acting mainly on its own interests in the "war on terror," while less than 20 percent of Europeans thought it was taking allies' views into account.

"The view from the Old World seems to be that this is an American war on American enemies, not a universal struggle against evil," wrote Kenneth Pollack, director of National Security Studies at the Council on Foreign Relations, commenting on the poll results.

Behind that view, which is common outside Europe too, lies a sense that Bush has not offered the world a vision of what he wants everyone to fight for, beyond asking them to fight against "evil."

In its pursuit of terrorists worldwide, America has lost sight of its larger role as a global leader, complains Wilfrido Villacorta, a professor of international relations at De La Salle University in Manila. "As the only superpower with global responsibility [America] must use its leadership to address pressing problems like poverty, the deterioration of the environment, and the promotion of free trade," he argues.

* * *

In the Arab and Muslim world, there is one cause above all others to which people want America to commit its leadership: an end to the Palestinians' plight. But few there have any hopes for the current administration, and many see the "war on terror" as a war on Islam. Any invasion of Iraq would be bound to foster even deeper resentment. "It will have a negative impact," Pakistan President Pervez Musharraf told the *Monitor* this week.

From Morocco to Medina and beyond, the idea of America as the "good guy" is considered laughable, given Washington's sturdy support of the Arabs' traditional enemy, Israel. On the contrary, parts of Osama bin Laden's message resonate, even with people who deplore almost everything about Al Qaeda.

That's the case with Selcuk Yilmaz, who runs a cellphone shop in Istanbul's hectic Taksim Square. "Osama bin Laden says something: America will not be comfortable if the people of Palestine will not be comfortable. That's just right," he says, as Turks and tourists browse for phones and bring their vacation snapshots to his Kodak counter.

"If a Muslim is harmed, every Muslim has a problem," he adds. And current US policy, he believes, "is a war against the Muslim people."

That perception is especially dangerous, worries Mostafa al-Feqi, chairman of the Egyptian parliament's foreign-affairs committee. "The Americans should talk more to the world, should talk more to Arabs and Muslims," he urges. "We want the layman in the Muslim world to know that Americans are not against his religion."

David Welch has felt Muslim anger at firsthand.

In 1979 he was a junior diplomat at the US Embassy in Islamabad when false rumors of American involvement in an attack on the Grand Mosque at Mecca, Islam's holiest site, inspired a Pakistani mob to invade the embassy compound and set it alight, using gasoline from the motor pool.

For six hours, Mr. Welch and a hundred of his colleagues cowered in the embassy's metal-lined security vault as the heat ignited glue beneath the floor tiles. Eventually he was rescued.

"I carried a dead marine off the top of that embassy that night," recalls Welch, now the US ambassador to Egypt. "I was told they hated us back then, too."

Today, he finds himself dealing with another outburst of anti-American feeling, albeit less immediately life-threatening. But neither the assault on the Islamabad embassy nor Sept. 11 has prompted any outward sense of repentance about America's role in the world.

It is time for America to listen, he says, but also to be heard. Fighting terrorists does mean taking "a look at the swamp in which these guys operate," he accepts. But Arabs, he insists, must "look at themselves a little bit and say 'What is it that we do that might be putting more putrid water into this swamp?'"

Welch hears a lot of complaints about America's disdain for Palestinian aspirations and its support for Israel. He points out that Bush has outlined his vision of a Palestinian state, and adds that critics "should recognize . . . Americans do not like the murder of innocent people in the name of a political cause and they particularly cannot abide it after Sept. 11," he says. "So the association of the Palestinian cause with terrorism has come at great expense to their public support in the US. That is a fact. It doesn't take a diplomat to explain it to people. But they need to hear it."

The world can expect to hear more from America in the coming months, as the administration boosts its public diplomacy efforts in the wake of Sept. 11. Bush will soon announce the creation of a global communications office as a permanent White House fixture. Last year the State Department tapped J. Walter Thompson chairwoman Charlotte Beers to be the new undersecretary for public diplomacy, with the mission of rebranding America around the world.

"We learned that when you don't communicate, you are still communicating—a lack of interest, a lack of caring," says Tucker Eskew, deputy assistant to the president in the White House global communications unit.

Among the first fruits of the new policy is Radio Sawa, an Arabic-language station that replaced the Voice of America in the Middle East last April, offering Arabic and Western pop songs along with about 10 minutes of news each hour. It certainly reaches a wider audience—it seems as if every taxi driver in Amman, Jordan, tunes in—but critics wonder how good a job it does of explaining American policy, given its softer format.

And even the best public diplomacy efforts eventually run up against the reality of often unpopular policies. There was no disguising Bush's description of the Israeli prime minister as "a man of peace," even as his troops reoccupied the West Bank, points out Shibley Telhami, a Middle East expert at the University of Maryland.

"A single word from the president outweighs the millions we can spend on influencing hearts and minds," he says.

Christopher Ross, an American diplomat with long Middle East experience, was brought out of retirement to help Ms. Beers, and has been on two trips to the region to listen to ordinary people's gripes. "My impression is that the effort was very much appreciated," he recalls, "but then came their question: 'We are telling you all these things—what impact will it have?' I told them that I would report their views, but that policymaking is based on many things, not solely on what the foreign reaction is."

In the end, America may just have to resign itself to being unloved, conclude some officials at home and abroad. Its power, its wealth, its recurrent urges to make the world over in its image are bound to generate envy and resentment.

But the current administration's apparent readiness to come across as the "bad guy"—doing what it thinks is necessary now to defend America—is alienating the very friends and allies it needs to fight the war on terror, warns John Ikenberry, a professor at Georgetown University in Washington.

> Does the United States
> need friends and allies
> in the war on terror, or
> can we go it alone?

"If history is a guide, it will trigger antagonism and resistance that will leave America in a more hostile and divided world," he argues in the current issue of *Foreign Affairs*.

If the international debate over whether to invade Iraq is any measure, America is walking a lonely path. Twice in the 20th century, Americans decided that standing alone made the world a more dangerous place for them to live in. Will the new worldwide "war on terror" teach the same lesson?

Consider the source and the audience.

- The *Christian Science Monitor* is a U.S.-based independent daily (Monday through Friday) newspaper, particularly well respected for its international coverage. Does the fact that it has no ideological axe to grind give it more credibility in publishing a story of this sort?

Lay out the argument, the values, and the assumptions.

- Ford repeatedly refers to the concept of leadership, and so do critics who argue that America is failing to fulfill its role as a world leader in any but a military sense. What concepts of leadership are mentioned by the people Ford cites?

- In what ways do the people whom Ford talks to around the world believe that the United States has failed to live up to its leadership role? What are their specific criticisms of U.S. foreign policy? Whom do they blame? Why do some people have a more positive view of the United States?

- Most of the foreign policy experts cited by Ford think that it matters whether the United States is liked by other nations. Why? Why do some think that it doesn't matter? What impression does Ford leave his readers with?

Uncover the evidence.

- Ford relies largely on interviews. What types of people did he interview? Did he interview enough people? Can we know whether these people speak for the majority of their country?

- How does Ford use polling data to support his interviews? Are these data effective?

Evaluate the conclusion.

- The fact that Ford devotes so much attention to international complaints about America and scholarly beliefs that the United States needs to be more multilateral leaves his readers with the impression that he agrees that we need to be more conciliatory with other nations for their sake as well as for our own. Does he make that case?

- Is it his intention to persuade? Or just to wake Americans up to the fact that their positive self-image is not universally shared, and to prod them to consider the possible repercussions?

Sort out the political implications.

- Is it inevitable, as some claim, that a single superpower will be resented and disliked by all lesser powers?

- How is the war on terror likely to fare without international cooperation? Do we need anyone's help?

16.3 The Case for Missile Defense

The Fact That America Faces Novel Terrorist Threats Such as Hijacked Planes and Anthrax Spores Does Not Negate the Need for an Effective, Comprehensive Missile Defense

Steve Bonta, *The New American,* 3 December 2001

September 11 brought a new fear to the American public: terrorist attacks on our homeland. Until that point, while terrorism at home may have concerned some, most people believed that the biggest threat to the United States would come from a foreign missile attack. In the days of the cold war, the United States and its chief superpower rival, the Soviet Union, had contained the threat posed by each nation with a policy of mutually assured destruction (MAD), based on the idea that if each had the ability to destroy the other, each had an incentive not to guarantee its own destruction by launching the first attack. As part of the principle of MAD, the nations signed the Anti-Ballistic Missile (ABM) Treaty in 1972, promising not to build a missile defense system. Such a system, by protecting one side from nuclear attack, would render the policy of MAD ineffective, and the threat of nuclear war would no longer be contained.

The ABM Treaty did not end discussion of missile defense. In the 1980s, Ronald Reagan pushed Congress to authorize billions of dollars to create a missile defense system, nicknamed Star Wars, designed to protect the country from a nuclear strike by the Soviet Union. Although the United States has worked on developing missile defense technology since the early 1980s, it has yet to build a system that works in test situations.

We no longer live in a world defined by two nuclear superpowers. The cold war is over, the Soviet Union is gone, and its nuclear weapons are divided among its former republics, including Russia, now on more or less friendly terms with the United States. Today many other nations have nuclear weapons or are attempting to build them, and there is no guarantee that these nations can be "contained" in the same way the United States and the Soviet Union once were. The subject of missile defense continues to be controversial. When Bush came into office in 2001, he announced his intention of pulling out of the ABM Treaty, though he proceeded cautiously so as not to damage relations with our allies. Since September 11, some Americans have been divided between those who believe we should concentrate our resources on preventing threats like the terrorist attack on the World Trade Center and those, like the author here, who think the reasons for pursuing missile defense are stronger than ever. Why does he state his views with so much energy and vituperation? What underlying concerns are at stake for him in the issue of missile defense?

In an October 28th op-ed piece for the *New York Times,* ex-Soviet dictator Mikhail Gorbachev wrote that, in light of the shocking breaches of American security on September 11th, the United States might begin making a priority out of unilateral national defense. "It would be a cause of great concern," he fretted, "if major nuclear powers abandoned or neglected multilateral forums, or took steps that would endanger the entire structure of arms control treaties, many of which, such as the 1972 ABM Treaty, are of as much value today as they were during the decades of nuclear confrontation."

Gorbachev isn't a lone voice, either. In the aftermath of September 11th, with the Bush administration's intention to scrap the ABM Treaty attracting a lot of political support, a chorus of Establishment voices have been clamoring to keep the 1972 agreement and to nix any national missile defense. "Even in the wake of Sept. 11, Bush clings to the wasteful, improbable Son of *Star Wars*," complained the *Houston Chronicle* on October 23rd. On the same day, the *San Francisco Chronicle* warned, "[N]ow, more than ever, an anti-missile defense system mocks the actual dangers that threaten Americans—as well as the rest of the world. It won't defend against terrorist weapons that, so far, have included box-cutters, planes and anthrax spores. Nor will it protect us from plastic explosives, cyberterrorism, or chemical warfare."

Arguments like these are nothing new. For several decades, since the United States embarked on the suicidal policy of Mutually Assured Destruction (MAD) and underscored it with an ABM Treaty forbidding any substantive missile defense measures, foreign policy experts with more Ivy-League credentials than common sense have been promoting abstract goals like "containment," "stabilization," and "deterrence" rather than national defense per se. In the process, they have successfully convinced a large number of gullible Americans, including congressional leaders, that defense against a missile attack is technologically impossible, politically unwise, and strategically unnecessary—and they have kept the United States pitifully vulnerable to nuclear attack. Exploiting our supposed nuclear Achilles' heel, the fanatical adherents of appeasement and arms control have extracted dangerous concessions in national sovereignty—like the ABM and SALT treaties—that unilaterally limit our ability to defend ourselves.

> In what sense is the ABM Treaty a "dangerous concession in national sovereignty"? (Sovereignty is the principle that a nation recognizes no supreme power within its borders.) Why does Bonta later call it a "treasonous agreement"?

Changing Climate

With recent terrorist attacks, though, the political climate has changed. Suddenly national defense is a pressing urgency, and momentum is growing to scrap the ABM Treaty and other treasonous agreements with the former Soviet Union. But anti-American globalists, still eager to keep America weakened and vulnerable, have begun a campaign of withering propaganda to prevent this from happening.

The most common argument for continuing to neglect missile defense is that September 11th has shown us that, in the words of the *New York Times*, "the most immediate threat to the nation comes from terrorists, not nations with intercontinental ballistic missiles." Therefore, the critics argue, we should focus our resources on going after the men with the box cutters and the anthrax spores, rather than spend billions developing a system to shoot down Russian missiles.

That is, we should be *selective* in which threats to defend against. This is tantamount to choosing between a burglar alarm and a fire alarm, on the specious premise that we can't defend against both break-ins and fire hazards.

More importantly, a "threat" by its very nature is virtual, not actual. While no modern-day power has yet attempted a full-scale military assault, nuclear or otherwise, against the United States mainland, no one could credibly argue that any terrorist cell, however ingenious or well-equipped, could wreak as much havoc and loss of life as a Russian or Chinese nuclear missile attack. The most effective defense anticipates what might happen, rather than reacting too late to damage already done.

Are all potential threats equal, then? Or do we engage in a calculation of risk assessment? Does the likelihood of a threat being realized have a place in our calculations?

But, reply the critics, no country would dare launch a direct nuclear attack against the United States. As the *Houston Chronicle* put it, "such governments, even at their edge-of-reality looniest, would think twice about such an act because . . . U.S. retaliation would bring annihilation." This argument assumes that the only suicidal enemies of the United States are "non-state actors" like the terrorists who blew up the World Trade Center and the *USS Cole.*

But governments, even those of open societies, frequently act irrationally and against their best interests. The United States itself has done so consistently, under the influence of subversives hostile to American freedoms. And the verdict of history suggests that tyrannical regimes are even less rational. It is now well-known, for example, that some of imperial Japan's military and political leaders warned of the consequences of attacking Pearl Harbor. Saddam Hussein was deluded into believing that the West would not defend Kuwaiti oil fields. During the Gulf War, he even launched a barrage of SCUD missiles at Israel, undeterred by Israel's nuclear capability. The People's Republic of China has gone on record threatening to nuke Los Angeles if the United States comes to the defense of Taiwan in the event of a Chinese invasion. And a hypothetical nuclear regime like North Korea, facing military defeat in a future Korean conflict, might launch a desperation nuclear assault as a last-minute gesture of vengeful defiance. It is dangerously naive to assume that states and their leadership will behave rationally, especially in wartime.

Technological Capabilities

The next line of argument usually leveled against missile defense is the supposed technological limitations. "There is no indication that such a scheme would work and every sign it would cost billions even to find out," opined the *Los Angeles Times*. Wrong on both counts. Not only is a credible missile defense well within our technological capabilities, there is little question that such a system—if deployed—would work very effectively. As Sam Cohen, the inventor of the neutron bomb, wrote in these pages in October 1998, nuclear-tipped missile interceptors would be an extremely effective and easily achievable missile-defense system:

> Real strategic defense requires nuclear interceptors to overcome the huge economic and technical disadvantages of the non-nuclear defense systems that inherently favor attackers. . . . Nuclear explosives of the kind developed for Safeguard [a short-lived ABM system deployed in the '70s] included the six-kiloton Sprint, which could effectively take out attacking missiles within a radius of tens of yards, and the megaton Spartan, which could reach out to a radius of several miles to destroy missiles. These or similar systems could be launched from the ground, sea, air, or space, and a genuine ABM program would utilize a combination of these launch options to provide in-depth defense.

Even leaving aside nuclear ABM defenses, conventional anti-missile missiles like the Patriot have proven effective—especially against obsolescent models like the Iraqi SCUDs, the type of missile most likely to be used by a third-world rogue regime.

For those who insist on some kind of defense against enemy missiles, Establishment liberals have a pat concession: Limited ABM defenses are okay, as long as they don't pose a serious threat to a major nuclear-armed adversary like the Russians. This is, in fact, the position of Bush administration "conservatives" who insist, even as they loudly promote a limited missile defense against rogue regimes, that America will not consider building any significant countermeasures against an all-out nuclear assault by a superpower adversary like Russia or China. The Bush administration's tough-talking Donald Rumsfeld implied as much by announcing on October 25th that the Pentagon had postponed antimissile tracking tests to avoid the appearance of violating the ABM Treaty or provoking the Russians.

This poll was conducted shortly after September 11. If the same poll were conducted a year later, would the results have changed?

But there is evidence that, despite the propaganda smokescreen, many Americans are awakening to America's dangerous vulnerability not only to terrorism but to old-fashioned military assaults. A new poll on internationalist views conducted by the Pew Research Center in conjunction with the Council on Foreign Relations found "growing public support for a missile defense system" since September 11th. The study admitted uneasily that "nearly two thirds [surveyed] favor the development of a missile shield and a growing number say we need such a system now."

Americans must not be deluded by the false alternatives offered by the Establishment on missile defense. They must insist that the excuses and prevarications stop, and that our elected leaders take all steps to defend our country, as completely as possible, from nuclear attack. No government that has frittered away billions of dollars on risky Mars missions, many of which have failed abysmally, can cite lack of technology, risk of failure, or budget shortfalls as excuses for not developing missile defense. And since September 11th, no one with a shred of human decency can justify any but a comprehensive approach to national defense. National defense, after all, is the first responsibility of any moral government. It's time to stop holding Americans hostage by playing games with America's enemies.

Consider the source and the audience.

- *The New American* is a conservative magazine with the avowed purpose of protecting our freedom. What (or whom) does Bonta see as the threat to our freedom? Would a liberal publication define freedom in the same way?

Lay out the argument, the values, and the assumptions.

- What is Bonta's view of national power and sovereignty? What is the primary purpose of government, in his view? Bonta is worried about our leaders playing games with America's enemies. When it comes to protecting America, would he argue that we have any friends?
- According to Bonta, what was wrong with MAD, and why did it work against national defense? What arguments are frequently used by opponents of missile defense, and why, according to Bonta, are they wrong?

Uncover the evidence.

- Bonta cites many newspaper editorials and claims that they lack evidence to back up their arguments. Does he offer evidence to back up his own? What evidence does Bonta provide to counter the objection that the technology does not yet exist to create a successful missile defense system?

Evaluate the conclusion.

- Does Bonta successfully make the case that we should expand our missile defense spending? Why or why not?
- Does Bonta successfully refute the claims of opponents of a missile defense system? Does he deal with any of the positive aspects of treaty making? Would he agree there are any?

Sort out the political implications.

- If the U.S. government followed Bonta's suggestion, what tradeoffs, if any, would it have to make? Can we effectively deal with all threats facing the United States at the same time?
- How might the rest of the world view our increased spending on missile defense? Should the United States be concerned with the reaction of other countries?

16.4 At the Brink, Then and Now:

The Missiles of 1962 Haunt the Iraq Debate

Todd Purdum, *New York Times,* 13 October 2002

In the previous article, Steve Bonta criticizes those who want to cut missile defense funding. At no time in U.S. history did people wish we had an effective missile defense system more than in October 1962. The world stood on the brink of nuclear war as the Soviet Union moved nuclear warheads into Communist Cuba. President Kennedy faced an enormously difficult decision: how to force the Soviet Union to take back the missiles without launching a full-scale war. Forty years later, *New York Times* reporter Todd Purdum notes that President George W. Bush faced a similar dilemma with respect to getting Iraq to disarm. Were there lessons for Bush in JFK's actions during the Cuban Missile Crisis? How far can we use history to help us through the dilemmas of the present?

For 13 days starting Oct. 16, 1962, "the world stood like a playing card on edge," as Norman Mailer put it, while President Kennedy and his closest aides faced down the threat of Soviet missiles in Cuba. Forty years later, Washington and the world are again on the brink, and debates about the lessons of that long-ago October are as fresh as the morning headlines.

Then, as now, the threat was nuclear weapons and the risk was a wider war. Then, as now, the midterm elections were approaching and a president put in office by a razor-thin margin battled doubts about his reputation in the world. Then, as now, some of the president's aides urged a pre-emptive strike and invasion, while others counseled diplomatic isolation backed by the threat of force.

But much has also changed since the crisis that historians have called the most dangerous moment in recorded time. Then, it was uniformed commanders and some Congressional leaders who pushed hardest for military action, while a president all too familiar with World War II combat was skeptical. Now it is uniformed commanders scarred by Vietnam and politicians shaped by its legacy who most urge caution, while civilian Pentagon officials and a president who saw no combat as a home-front National Guard pilot seem more disposed toward force.

Even as a grizzled group of President Kennedy's New Frontiersmen met this weekend with Fidel Castro at a commemorative conference in Havana to review hundreds of newly released documents, current hawks and doves here summoned snippets from the already voluminous historical record to buttress their cases.

Campaigning for his first term 40 years ago this month, Senator Edward M. Kennedy of Massachusetts was warned by his brother's aides not to so much as mention Cuba, lest the Soviets read too much into his words. Last week, as the Senate's reigning liberal lion, he took to the floor to recall that "many military officers urged President Kennedy to approve a preventive attack" to destroy the Soviet missiles before they became operational. But, he said, their brother

Robert argued that would amount to "a Pearl Harbor in reverse," and he added: "That view prevailed. A middle ground was found and peace was preserved."

Hours later, Mr. Bush made a televised speech to the nation on the dangers posed by Iraq's efforts to acquire nuclear weapons, and cited President Kennedy's words to warn: "We no longer live in a world where only the actual firing of weapons represents a sufficient challenge to a nation's security to constitute maximum peril." Mr. Bush's aides say Mr. Kennedy wouldn't have succeeded if he hadn't been genuinely ready to start shooting, and by week's end Congress went along with the president, voting overwhelmingly to authorize him to use force.

> *Why did Bush quote Kennedy in his speech to the nation? Why did his aides insist that the two situations were parallel? Why did opponents of Bush's actions insist that they were different?*

"It's like fighting over biblical passages, and what the devil said," said Fred I. Greenstein, an expert on presidential leadership at Princeton. "On the one hand, there is the Kennedy who arrived at the judgment that we can't let those missiles stay in place. But Kennedy also did triple cartwheels to perform in as cautious and unprovocative a way as possible with the Soviet Union. He was not dealing with Saddam Hussein and a bizarre banana nonrepublic, but with Soviets who had proved throughout the cold war to be rational actors."

Some of Mr. Bush's advisers have pointed to the Kennedy decision to impose a naval blockade on Cuba—and to threaten drastic action if the missiles were not removed—as an example of pre-emptive military action. But Kennedy loyalists say the point was precisely the opposite. "The whole purpose of it was to avoid an American attack," a participant in the discussions recalled last week. "And the reason it was called a quarantine and not a blockade is because a blockade is an act of war. We were trying to find a way of communicating more forceful than the English language. It was communicating, not pre-emption."

In 1962, President Kennedy was taken with Barbara Tuchman's new book, *The Guns of August,* a history of the unintended chain of consequences that led to the devastation of World War I. He was obsessed with avoiding similar miscalculations.

This fall, White House aides have been reading another provocative work— by Ms. Tuchman's daughter, Jessica Tuchman Mathews, the president of the Carnegie Endowment for International Peace. The institution produced a report advocating a new regime of "coercive" weapons inspections in Iraq, backed up by force and aimed at disarming Mr. Hussein without resorting to war. Most military commanders faulted the idea as impractical, but Mr. Bush incorporated an echo of it in his proposal for a United Nations resolution that would force Iraq to submit to much more stringent inspections or face the consequences.

What does Mathews mean when she says that "there are never two choices in foreign policy"? Is she right?

"There are never two choices in foreign policy," Ms. Mathews said the other day, "and the right answer is not to choose an unacceptable one, but to look for a third. I think it's fair to say, in the missile crisis doing nothing was unacceptable, and so was going to war with the risk of nuclear holocaust." She added: "The other key lesson was, give your opponent some room to maneuver. Don't back him against the wall."

One problem with this argument: a version of it has already been tried for the decade since the Persian Gulf war. Kenneth M. Pollack, who as a C.I.A. analyst and national security official in the 1990's helped formulate the strategy of containing Iraq through economic sanctions and limited military actions, has reluctantly concluded in a new book, *The Threatening Storm* (Random House), that an invasion of Iraq is now the best approach.

"The fact that a war against Iraq could be potentially quite costly should make us think long and hard about whether or not we should embark upon such an endeavor, but it should never be an absolute impediment," he writes. "Often, the costliest wars are the ones that are the most important to fight."

Perhaps the biggest challenge of any conflict is the unknowns. A C.I.A. analysis released last week supported President Bush's portrait of Iraq's efforts to acquire nuclear weapons, but did not echo the White House's depiction of an immediate threat. In fact, it said, Mr. Hussein might be most inclined to unleash devastating weapons against the United States if he was convinced an American strike was inevitable.

In the missile crisis, the debate over invasion proceeded in ignorance of a threat that only came out 30 years later: the Soviets already had not only missiles but tactical nuclear warheads on the island before the quarantine began, and were ready to use them in the event of an attack.

"I now conclude that however astutely the crisis may have been managed," former Defense Secretary Robert S. McNamara said in Havana last week, "luck also played a significant role in the avoidance of nuclear war by a hair's breadth."

Graham T. Allison, the Harvard professor who wrote *Essence of Decision,* a seminal study of the crisis recently revised with Philip D. Zelikow (Addison Wesley, 1999), noted another element: President Kennedy's willingness to take a secret gamble on Sat. Oct. 27, the last full day of the crisis. The president's advisers worried that the blockade was failing; a U-2 surveillance pilot had been shot down over Cuba; the missiles were becoming operational.

"Everybody's been on overdrive for two weeks and is fraying, and there's a sense of 'Well, I guess we played out this hand and it didn't work,'" Professor Allison said. Then the president circled back to another possibility: A parallel American withdrawal of obsolete Jupiter missiles from Turkey. He sent Robert F. Kennedy to convey all this to the Soviet ambassador.

"Thus you had this rather bizarre package," Professor Allison added. "A public ultimatum to the Soviets, 'missiles out by next week,' and a pledge not to invade, then a private ultimatum that said, 'We really mean this,' and then, finally, a secret carrot, that if the missiles are withdrawn, then within six months, the missiles in Turkey will not be there, though Bobby insisted there could be no quid pro quo."

These details, too, were not confirmed conclusively until 20 years later. Is it just possible that the Bush administration could be working on some similar secret diplomacy now, say, exile for Saddam Hussein?

"I certainly hope so," said President Kennedy's special counsel, Theodore C. Sorenson.

What is the lesson in Kennedy's eleventh-hour offer to the Soviets to remove missiles from Turkey? Can that lesson be used in other foreign policy situations?

Consider the source and the audience.
- This *New York Times* story combines historical analysis with the analysis of a contemporary event. Why would Purdum be writing about something that happened in 1962? Who or what raised the issue?

Lay out the argument, the values, and the assumptions.
- What do the people Purdum talks to have at stake in claiming their conflicting interpretations of history? Can our understanding of history ever be entirely objective?
- What similarities does Purdum note between Kennedy's dilemma with respect to Cuba and Bush's with respect to Iraq? What differences? Do any of these matter?
- What course of action do Kennedy administration veterans and scholars want to see Bush pursue? Why?

Uncover the evidence.
- Purdum relies almost entirely on interviews to make his comparison. Are there any voices missing that might add a different perspective?

Evaluate the conclusion.
- By the time you read this, President Bush will likely have made a decision regarding Iraq. Does reading this historical comparison help you understand his actions? Would you modify Purdum's analysis in any way?

Sort out the political implications.
- During the missile crisis, many criticized Kennedy. More than forty years later, Kennedy's actions are recalled with relief as lucky but skillful. Forty years from now, how do you think the public will look back on Bush's Iraq decision?

16.5 Speech Before the National Association of Evangelicals

Ronald Reagan, Orlando, Florida, 8 March 1983

Along with tax cuts, less intrusive government, and increased defense spending, Ronald Reagan made winning the cold war a central part of his presidency. He believed that America needed to defend itself against a Communist threat, promote free governments, and limit Soviet power and aggression. In this speech before the National Association of Evangelicals, Reagan makes an impassioned plea to keep the "evil empire" in check and promote democracy throughout the world. Specifically, he is arguing that it would be foolhardy for the West to freeze its development of nuclear forces as it is only by being strong and armed that the United States can bring about peace.

Partly because of the audience, but also because of his own personal beliefs, Reagan casts the battle of democracy versus totalitarianism very much in terms of good versus evil, the godly versus the ungodly. How does his use of the word *evil* compare to President Bush's reference to the "axis of evil" in January 2002? Would his invocation of God work in the current war against terror, where our opponents are invoking the power of God against us?

[The beginning of this speech focuses on President Reagan's views on the place of faith in public life. Toward the end of his talk he turns his attention to the role of faith in foreign affairs. We pick up the speech at that point.]

And this brings me to my final point today. During my first press conference as president, in answer to a direct question, I point out that, as good Marxist-Leninists, the Soviet leaders have openly and publicly declared that the only morality they recognize is that which will further their cause, which is world revolution. I think I should point out I was only quoting Lenin, their guiding spirit, who said in 1920 that they repudiate all morality that proceeds from supernatural ideas—that's their name for religion—or ideas that are outside class conceptions. Morality is entirely subordinate to the interests of class war. And everything is moral that is necessary for the annihilation of the old, exploiting social order and for uniting the proletariat.

Central tenets of Marx's and Lenin's theories of communism held that religion merely served as the "opiate of the masses," to resign an exploited working class to its lot in life. Can you have a system of morality that is not tied to religion?

Well, I think the refusal of many influential people to accept this elementary fact of Soviet doctrine illustrates a historical reluctance to see totalitarian powers for what they are. We saw this phenomenon in the 1930s. We see it too often today.

This doesn't mean we should isolate ourselves and refuse to seek an understanding with them. I intend to do everything I can to persuade them of our peaceful intent, to remind them that it was the West that refused to use its nuclear monopoly in the forties and fifties for territorial gain and which now proposes a 50-percent cut in strategic ballistic missiles and the elimination of an entire class of land-based, intermediate-range nuclear missiles.

At the same time, however, they must be made to understand we will never compromise our principles and standards. We will never give away our freedom. We will never abandon our belief in God. And we will never stop searching for a genuine peace. But we can assure none of these things America stands for through the so-called nuclear freeze solutions proposed by some.

The truth is that a freeze now would be a very dangerous fraud, for that is merely the illusion of peace. The reality is that we must find peace through strength.

I would agree to freeze if only we could freeze the Soviets' global desires. A freeze at current levels of weapons would remove any incentive for the Soviets to negotiate seriously in Geneva and virtually end our chances to achieve the major arms reductions which we have proposed. Instead, they would achieve their objectives through the freeze.

A freeze would reward the Soviet Union for its enormous and unparalleled military buildup. It would prevent the essential and long overdue modernization of United States and allied defenses and would leave our aging forces increasingly vulnerable. And an honest freeze would require extensive prior negotiations on the systems and numbers to be limited and on the measures to ensure effective verification and compliance. And the kind of a freeze that has been suggested would be virtually impossible to verify. Such a major effort would divert us completely from our current negotiations on achieving substantial reductions.

A number of years ago, I heard a young father, a very prominent young man in the entertainment world, addressing a tremendous gathering in California. It was during the time of the cold war, and communism and our own way of life were very much on people's minds. And he was speaking to that subject. And suddenly, though, I heard him saying, "I love my little girls more than anything." And I said to myself, "Oh, no, don't. You can't—don't say that." But I had underestimated him. He went on: "I would rather see my little girls die now, still believing in God, than have them grow up under communism and one day die no longer believing in God."

> What does this story mean to Reagan? What are its political implications?

There were thousands of young people in that audience. They came to their feet with shouts of joy. They had instantly recognized the profound truth in what he had said, with regard to the physical and the soul and what was truly important.

Yes, let us pray for the salvation of all of those who live in that totalitarian darkness—pray they will discover the joy of knowing God. But until they do, let us be aware that while they preach the supremacy of the state, declare its omnipotence over individual man, and predict its eventual domination of all peoples on the earth, they are the focus of evil in the modern world.

It was C. S. Lewis who, in his unforgettable *Screwtape Letters,* wrote: "The greatest evil is not done now in those sordid 'dens of rime' that Dickens loved to paint. It is not even done in concentration camps and labor camps. In those we see its final result. But it is conceived and ordered (moved, seconded, carried and minuted) in clean, carpeted, warmed, and well-lighted offices, by quiet men with white collars and cut fingernails and smooth-shaven cheeks who do not need to raise their voice."

Well, because these "quiet men" do not "raise their voices," because they sometimes speak in soothing tones of brotherhood and peace, because, like other dictators before them, they're always making "their final territorial demand," some would have us accept them as their word and accommodate ourselves to their aggressive impulses. But if history teaches anything, it teaches that simpleminded appeasement or wishful thinking about our adversaries is folly. It means the betrayal of our past, the squandering of our freedom.

So, I urge you to speak out against those who would place the United States in a position of military and moral inferiority. You know, I've always believed that old Screwtape reserved his best efforts for those of you in the church. So, in your discussions of the nuclear freeze proposals, I urge you to beware the temptation of pride—the temptation of blithely declaring yourselves above it all and label both sides equally at fault, to ignore the facts of history and the aggressive impulses of an evil empire, to simply call the arms race a giant misunderstanding and thereby remove yourself from the struggle between right and wrong and good and evil.

I ask you to resist the attempts of those who would have you withhold your support for our efforts, this administration's efforts, to keep America strong and free, while we negotiate real and verifiable reductions in the world's nuclear arsenals and one day, with God's help, their total elimination.

While America's military strength is important, let me add here that I've always maintained that the struggle now going on for the world will never be decided by bombs or rockets, by armies or military might. The real crisis we face today is a spiritual one; at root, it is a test of moral will and faith.

Whittaker Chambers, the man whose own religious conversation made him a witness to one of the terrible traumas of our time, the Hiss-Chambers case, wrote that the crisis of the Western world exists to the degree in which the West is indifferent to God, the degree to which it collaborates in communism's attempt to make man stand alone without God. And then he said, for Marxism-Leninism is actually the second-oldest faith, first proclaimed in the Garden of Eden with the words of temptation, "Ye shall be as gods."

The Western world can answer this challenge, he wrote, "but only provided that its faith in God and the freedom He enjoins is as great as communism's faith in Man."

I believe we shall rise to the challenge. I believe that communism is another sad, bizarre chapter in human history whose last pages even now are being written. I believe this because the source of our strength in the quest for human freedom is not material, but spiritual. And because it knows no limitation, it must terrify and ultimately triumph over those who would enslave their fellow man. For in the words of Isaiah: "He giveth power to the faint; and to them that have no might He increased strength. . . . But they that wait upon the Lord shall renew their strength; they shall mount up with wings as eagles; they shall run, and not be weary. . . ."

Yes, change your world. One of our Founding Fathers, Thomas Paine, said, "We have it within our power to begin the world over again." We can do it, doing together what no one church could do by itself.

God bless you, and thank you very much.

What role might faith and spirituality have played in the ultimate defeat of the Soviet Union?

Consider the source and the audience.
- President Reagan gave this speech to the National Association of Evangelicals. Would he have emphasized the same factors in a speech to a political group?

Lay out the argument, the values, and the assumptions.
- What, for Reagan, is the relationship among freedom, democracy, peace, and a belief in God? What defines the difference between "good" and "evil"? Why is the Soviet Union the "evil empire"?
- What does Reagan think is the route to peace? What is the role of arms and national strength? What is the role of faith in God?
- Who is Reagan arguing against here? What do his opponents want the United States to do? How do they think our problems with the Soviets can best be handled?

Uncover the evidence.
- Reagan claims that the best way to bring about world peace is by increasing America's strength and refusing to take part in a nuclear freeze. What is his evidence or logic for this claim?
- Does Reagan offer any evidence for the link between freedom and faith in God? Is it a link that can be verified? What kind of evidence would support it?

Evaluate the conclusion.
- Can you accept Reagan's conclusions about the relationship of belief in God with freedom and democracy if you don't share his faith? What conclusions can nonbelievers take from his speech?

Sort out the political implications.
- President George W. Bush also uses the word *evil* to refer to the United States' enemies. Does it have the same meaning for him as it did for Reagan?
- What are the advantages of framing one's political struggles in terms of good and evil? What are the disadvantages?

Credits

Chapter 1

P. 4: From Nahal Toosi, "Election Season? Whatever: Most Twenty-Something Apathetic; Politicians Pay Little Attention to Group," *Milwaukee Journal Sentinel*, August 19, 2002, p. 1A. Reprinted with permission. **P. 8:** This article first appeared in *The Christian Science Monitor* on July 3, 2002 and is reproduced with permission. Copyright © 2002 The Christian Science Monitor (www.csmonitor.com). All rights reserved. **P. 13:** John F. Kennedy's Inaugural Address, delivered January 20, 1961.

Chapter 2

P. 18: From "Self-Made Texas: Energetic Trader Loya Personifies American Dream," by Dale Robertson, *The Houston Chronicle*, May 9, 2002. Copyright © 2002 Houston Chronicle Publishing Co. Reprinted with permission. All rights reserved. **P. 22:** From "One Nation, Slightly Divisible," by David Brooks, *The Atlantic Monthly*, December 2001. Reprinted with permission of David Brooks. **P. 43:** From "Life, Liberty, and the Pursuit of Division," by Anatole Kaletsky, *The Times* (London), July 4, 2002. Copyright © The Times, London, 2002. **P. 47:** From "America Is A Class Act: The US Regards Itself as the Ultimate Meritocracy, but Social Mobility is as Feeble as Europe's — and Declining," by Gary Younge, *The Guardian* (London), January 27, 2002. Reprinted with permission of Guardian News Service Limited. **P. 51:** Reprinted by arrangement with The Heirs to the Estate of Martin Luther King, Jr., c/o Writers House, Inc. as agent for the proprietor. Copyright 1963 by Martin Luther King, Jr., copyright renewed 1991 by Coretta Scott King.

Chapter 3

P. 56: From "Indiana, Split by Time, Struggles Anew," by Pam Belluck, *The New York Times*, January 31, 2001. Copyright © 2001 by The New York Times Co. Reprinted with permission. **P. 60:** From "A Federalism Worth Fighting For," by Michael S. Greve, *The Weekly Standard*, January 29, 2001. Reprinted with permission. **P. 65:** From "Will the Court Reassert National Authority?," by Linda Greenhouse, *The New York Times*, September 30, 2001. Copyright © 2001 by The New York Times Co. Reprinted with permission. **P. 68:** From "I Dissent! The Constitution Got Us Into This Mess," by Sanford Levinson, *The Washington Post*, December 17, 2000. Reprinted with permission of the author. **P. 73:** From "A Republic, If We Can Keep It," by Bruce Fein, *The Washington Times*, July 30, 2002. Copyright © 2002 News World Communications, Inc., The Washington Times. Reprinted with permission. **P. 76:** *Federalist* No. 51, by James Madison, 1788.

Chapter 4

P. 82: Scott Gold and Eric Bailey, "1 Plaintiff Against the Grain," *Los Angeles Times* January 29, 2002. Copyright © 2002, Los Angeles Times. Reprinted by permission of the Los Angeles Times Syndicate. **P. 86:** Wendy Kaminer, "Losing Our Religion." Reprinted with permission from *The American Prospect*, September 23, 2002. The American Prospect, 5 Broad Street, Boston, MA 02109. All rights reserved. **P. 89:** From "The Federal Eye," by Robert A. Levy, *National Review Online*, November 25, 2002. National Review Online reprinted by permission of United Feature Syndicate, Inc. **P. 93:** From "Measuring Lost Freedom vs. Security in Dollars," Edmund L. Andrews, *The New York Times*, March 11, 2003. Copyright © 2003 by The New York Times Co. Reprinted with permission. **P. 97:** *Federalist* No. 84, by Alexander Hamilton, The Federalist Papers.

Chapter 5

P. 102: From "People of Color Who Never Felt They Were Black," by Darryl Fears, *The Washington Post*, December 26, 2002. Copyright © 2002 The Washington Post. Reprinted with permission. **P. 108:** From Patrick Rogers, Don Sider, and Lori Rozsa, "Black and White Proms," *People Weekly*, May 19, 2003. Copyright © 2003 People Weekly Syndication. Reprinted with permission. **P. 111:** From "Tilt! Time's Up for Title IX Sports," by Jessica Gavora, *The American Spectator*, May/June 2002. Reprinted with permission. **P. 121:** E.J. Graff, "How the Culture War Was Won: Lesbians and gay Men Defeated the Right in the 1990s, But Tougher Battles Lie Ahead." Reprinted with permission from *The American Prospect*, October 21, 2002. The American Prospect, 5 Broad Street, Boston, MA 02109. All rights reserved. **P. 128:** Ain't I a Woman, by Sojourner Truth, delivered 1851.

Chapter 6

P. 131: From "Fade to White," by Jake Tapper, *The Washington Post,* January 2, 2003. Reprinted with permission of the author. **P. 143:** From "Another Record Year for Academic Pork," by Jeffrey Brainard, *The Chronicle of Higher Education,* September 27, 2002. Copyright © 2002 The Chronicle of Higher Education. Reprinted with permission. **P. 150:** From "Close House Races Go the Way of Rotary Phones, Newt Gingrich," by Ronald Brownstein, *Los Angeles Times, April 15, 2002.* Copyright © 2002, Los Angeles Times. Reprinted with permission. **P. 153:** From "In the House at Least, Moderation Is No Virtue," by Robin Toner, *The New York Times,* November 17, 2002. Copyright © 2002 by The New York Times Co. Reprinted with permission. **P. 157:** Margaret Chase Smith's Declaration of Conscience, Speech to the Senate, June 1, 1950.

Chapter 7

P. 163: From "Whitewater Lawyer Turns Proponent of Presidential Power," by Dana Milbank, *The Washington Post,* October 15, 2002. Copyright © 2002 The Washington Post. Reprinted with permission. **P. 166:** From "An Executive Order: Hiding Presidential Papers," *San Francisco Chronicle,* November 11, 2001. Copyright © 2001 by San Francisco Chronicle. Reproduced with permission of San Francisco Chronicle via Copyright Clearance Center. **P. 170:** From "Ask First, Shoot Later," by Gordon Silverstein, *The New Republic Online Daily Express,* September 5, 2002. Reprinted by permission of The New Republic, © 2002, The New Republic, LLC. **P. 174:** Ronald Brownstein, "Bush Moves by Refusing to Budge," *Los Angeles Times,* March 2, 2003. Copyright © 2003, Los Angeles Times. Reprinted by permission of the Los Angeles Times Syndicate. **P. 179:** Excerpt from Abraham Lincoln's Speech to Congress, 15 September 1863.

Chapter 8

P. 183: From "In Artist's Freeway Prank, Form Followed Function," by Hugo Martin, *Los Angeles Times,* May 9, 2002. Copyright © 2002, Los Angeles Times. Reprinted with permission. **P. 186:** From "AIDS Incorporated: How Federal AIDS Money Ended Up Funding Psychic Hotlines, Neiman Marcus, and Flirting Classes," by Wayne Turner, *The Washington Monthly,* April 2001. Reprinted with permission from The Washington Monthly. Copyright by Washington Monthly Publishing, LLC, 733 15th St., NW, Suite 520, Washington, DC 20005. (202) 393-5155. Web site:

www.washingtonmonthly.com. **P. 195:** From "FBI CYA: The Problem the Bureau Still Hasn't Fixed," by Scott Shuger, *Slate,* May 30, 2002. Copyright © SLATE/Distributed by United Feature Syndicate, Inc. **P. 198:** Copyright © NPR® 2002. The text of the news report by NPR's Pam Fessler was originally broadcast on National Public Radio's "All Things Considered®" on June 7, 2002, and is used with the permission of National Public Radio, Inc. Any unauthorized duplication is strictly prohibited. **P. 204:** Special Message to the Congress Recommending the Establishment of a Department of National Defense, Harry S. Truman, December 18, 1945.

Chapter 9

P. 213: Transcript from "Interview with David Williamson," Greta Van Susteren, *Fox on the Record with Greta Van Susteren,* September 4, 2002. Reprinted with permission of FOX News Channel. **P. 216:** Copyright © NPR® 2001. The text of the news report by NPR's Melinda Pankava was originally broadcast on National Public Radio's "Talk of the Nation®" on November 11, 2001, and is used with the permission of National Public Radio, Inc. Any unauthorized duplication is strictly prohibited. **P. 224:** From "Obstruction of Judges," by Jeffrey Rosen, *The New York Times,* August 11, 2002. Copyright © 2002 by The New York Times Co. Reprinted with permission. **P. 232:** From "The Truth Behind the Pillars," by Evan Thomas and Michael Isikoff, *Newsweek,* December 25, 2000. Copyright 2000 Newsweek, Inc. All rights reserved. Reprinted by permission. **P. 238:** *Federalist* No. 78, Alexander Hamilton.

Chapter 10

P. 247: From "Poll Says College Students Lean Left," by Rebecca Trounson, *Los Angeles Times,* January 28, 2002. Copyright © 2002, Los Angeles Times. Reprinted with permission. **P. 251:** From "Party On, Dudes! Ignorance is the Curse of the Information Age," by Matthew Robinson, *The American Spectator,* March/April 2002. Reprinted with permission. **P. 260:** From Andrew Kohut, "Simply Put, The Public's View Can't Be Put Simply," *The Washington Post,* September 29, 2002. Reprinted with permission of the author. **P. 264:** From "The Other War Room: President Bush Doesn't Believe in Polling—Just Ask His Pollsters," by Joshua Green, *The Washington Monthly,* April 2002. Reprinted with permission from The Washington Monthly. Copyright by Washington Monthly Publishing, LLC, 733 15th St., NW, Suite 520, Washington, DC 20005.

(202) 393-5155. Web site: *www.washingtonmonthly.com*. **P. 272:** Reprinted with permission of Simon & Schuster Adult Publishing Group, from *The Pulse of Democracy* by George H. Gallup and Saul F. Rae. Copyright © 1940 by George H. Gallup and Saul F. Rae. Copyright © renewed 1968 by George H. Gallup.

Chapter 11

P. 284: Reprinted with permission of Simon & Schuster Adult Publishing Group from *My Declaration of Independence* by Senator James M. Jeffords. Copyright © 2001 by James M. Jeffords. **P: 291:** From "The Party of Lincoln. But not of Hayes, Harrison, Hoover, Eisenhower, Nixon, Reagan, or Bush," by David Greenberg, *Slate,* August 10, 2002. Copyright © SLATE/Distributed by United Feature Syndicate, Inc. **P. 296:** From "To the Faithful, 'Nonpartisan' is a 4-Letter Word," by Jonathan P. Hicks, *The New York Times,* August 26, 2002. Copyright © 2002 by The New York Times Co. Reprinted with permission. **P. 300:** From "Why Voters Will Lose Out in Tuesday's Debate," by Ralph Nader, *The Boston Globe,* September 20, 2000. Copyright © 2000 by Globe Newspaper Co. (MA). Reproduced with permission of Globe Newspaper Co. (MA) via Copyright Clearance Center. **P. 302:** Washington's Farewell Address, George Washington, 1796.

Chapter 12

P. 310: From "My Life is Shaped by the Border," by Tanya Schevitz, *San Francisco Chronicle,* November 18, 2002. Copyright © 2002 by San Francisco Chronicle. Reproduced with permission of San Francisco Chronicle via Copyright Clearance Center. **P. 314:** From "Money Power Respect: The Black Woman's Vote Can Often Determine the Outcome of an Election," by Lonnae O'Neal Parker, *Essence Magazine,* February 2003. Reprinted with permission of the author. **P. 318:** From "Lobbyists on Both Sides Duel in the Medical Malpractice Debate," by Sheryl Gay Stolberg, *The New York Times,* March 12, 2003. Copyright © 2003 by The New York Times Co. Reprinted with permission. **P. 322:** From "Star-Spangled Lobbyists," by Bill Hogan, *Mother Jones,* March/April 2002. Copyright © 2002 Foundation for National Progress. **P. 329:** *Federalist* No. 10, James Madison, *The Federalist Papers.*

Chapter 13

P. 338: From "The Strategist: Republicans Say Rove Was Mastermind of Big Victory," by Elisabeth Bumweiller and

David E. Sanger, *The New York Times,* November 7, 2002. Copyright © 2002 by The New York Times Co. Reprinted with permission. **P. 342:** From "Memo to the Democrats: Quit Being Losers!", by Tucker Carlson, *The New York Times,* January 19, 2003. Copyright © 2003 by The New York Times Co. Reprinted with permission. **P. 350:** From "Sunshine Voters," by John H. Fund, *The American Spectator,* July/August 2002. Reprinted with permission. **P. 353:** From "Campaign Bill to Kids: Take a Hike," by Tony Mauro, *USA Today,* March 20, 2002. Copyright © 2002, USA Today. Reprinted with permission. **P. 356:** Al Gore's Concession Speech.

Chapter 14

P. 362: From "Huey Freeman: American Hero - Sure He's a Cartoon Character, But It Still Takes Courage to Speak Out," by John Nichols, *The Nation*. Reprinted with permission from the January 28, 2002 issue of The Nation. **P. 367:** Reprinted from "Framing the Flag," by Michael Scherer, *The Columbia Journalism Review,* March/April 2002. Copyright © 2002 by Columbia Journalism Review. **P. 370:** From "The Real Media Bias: Profits," by Margo Hammond, *St. Petersburg Times,* February 24, 2002. Copyright © 2002 St. Petersburg Times. Reprinted with permission. **P. 374:** From "The Weight of an Anchor," by Frank Rich, *The New York Times Magazine,* May 19, 2002. Copyright © 2002 by The New York Times Co. Reprinted with permission. **P. 386:** From "Mr. Hearst Answers High School Girl's Query," by William Randolph Hearst, *San Francisco Examiner,* October 8, 1935. Reprinted with permission.

Chapter 15

P. 391: From "Zero Tolerance Lets a Student's Future Hang on a Knife's Edge," by Barry Siegel, *Los Angeles Times,* August 11, 2002. Copyright © 2002, Los Angeles Times. Reprinted with permission. **P. 403:** From "Dead Wood: The Lousy Economics of Bush's New Forest Policy," by Douglas Gantenbein, *Slate,* December 4, 2002. Copyright © SLATE/Distributed by United Feature Syndicate, Inc. **P. 406:** From "Altared States: Bush Tries to Promote Marriage Through Welfare Reform," by Kate O'Beirne, *National Review,* May 6, 2002. Copyright © 2002 by National Review, Inc., 215 Lexington Avenue, New York, NY 10016. Reprinted by permission. **P. 410:** From *Wall Street Journal,* November 20, 2002. Copyright © 2002 by Dow Jones & Co., Inc. Reproduced with permission of Dow Jones & Co., Inc. via Copy-